LIVING THE TRUTH IN LOVE

*Living the truth in love we should grow in every way
into him who is the head, Christ, from whom the whole body,
joined and held together by every supporting ligament, with
the proper functioning of each part, brings about the
body's growth and builds itself up in love*
(Eph 4:15-16).

Living the Truth in Love

A BIBLICAL INTRODUCTION TO MORAL THEOLOGY

BENEDICT M. ASHLEY, OP

ALBA·HOUSE   NEW·YORK

SOCIETY OF ST. PAUL, 2187 VICTORY BLVD., STATEN ISLAND, NEW YORK 10314

Library of Congress Cataloging-in-Publication Data

Ashley, Benedict M.
    Living the truth in love: a biblical introduction to moral
theology / Benedict M. Ashley.
          p.   cm.
    Includes bibliographical references.
    ISBN 0-8189-0756-8
    1. Christian ethics — Catholic authors. 2. Christian ethics —
Biblical teaching.   I. Title.
BJ1249.A77   1996
241'.042 — dc20   96-10967
                                                      CIP

Produced and designed in the United States of America by the
Fathers and Brothers of the Society of St. Paul,
2187 Victory Boulevard, Staten Island, New York 10314,
as part of their communications apostolate.

ISBN: 0-8189-0756-8

Printing Information:

Current Printing - first digit   1   2   3   4   5   6   7   8   9   10

Year of Current Printing - first year shown

1996   1997   1998   1999   2000   2001

To
Albert Stephan Moraczewski,
Kevin David O'Rourke,
Ralph Austin Powell
brothers, critics, dialogue partners
in the Order of Preachers

Biblical Abbreviations

OLD TESTAMENT

Genesis	Gn	Nehemiah	Ne	Baruch	Ba
Exodus	Ex	Tobit	Tb	Ezekiel	Ezk
Leviticus	Lv	Judith	Jdt	Daniel	Dn
Numbers	Nb	Esther	Est	Hosea	Ho
Deuteronomy	Dt	1 Maccabees	1 M	Joel	Jl
Joshua	Jos	2 Maccabees	2 M	Amos	Am
Judges	Jg	Job	Jb	Obadiah	Ob
Ruth	Rt	Psalms	Ps	Jonah	Jon
1 Samuel	1 S	Proverbs	Pr	Micah	Mi
2 Samuel	2 S	Ecclesiastes	Ec	Nahum	Na
1 Kings	1 K	Song of Songs	Sg	Habakkuk	Hab
2 Kings	2 K	Wisdom	Ws	Zephaniah	Zp
1 Chronicles	1 Ch	Sirach	Si	Haggai	Hg
2 Chronicles	2 Ch	Isaiah	Is	Malachi	Ml
Ezra	Ezr	Jeremiah	Jr	Zechariah	Zc
		Lamentations	Lm		

NEW TESTAMENT

Matthew	Mt	Ephesians	Eph	Hebrews	Heb
Mark	Mk	Philippians	Ph	James	Jm
Luke	Lk	Colossians	Col	1 Peter	1 P
John	Jn	1 Thessalonians	1 Th	2 Peter	2 P
Acts	Ac	2 Thessalonians	2 Th	1 John	1 Jn
Romans	Rm	1 Timothy	1 Tm	2 John	2 Jn
1 Corinthians	1 Cor	2 Timothy	2 Tm	3 John	3 Jn
2 Corinthians	2 Cor	Titus	Tt	Jude	Jude
Galatians	Gal	Philemon	Phm	Revelation	Rv

CONTENTS

PART III: LOVE

FOREWORD

Any writer must agree with the inspired author of 2 Maccabees who confessed, "the task, far from being easy, is one of sweat and sleepless nights, just as the preparation of a festive banquet is no light matter for one who thus seeks to give enjoyment to others" (2 M 2:26-27). I could not have finished this book without the help of many to whom I am deeply grateful. It was drafted while I was teaching at the Pontifical John Paul II Institute for Studies in Marriage and Family, Washington, D.C. I want to thank Dean Carl Anderson and its faculty for their support and in particular, Rev. Francis Martin, Professor of Sacred Scripture, who read the draft and made helpful suggestions, and Fr. J. Raymond Vandegrift, O.P., librarian, who gave me constant and patient help, as did my graduate assistant Gloria Falcao Dodd. Very special thanks are due to Fr. Romanus Cessario, O.P., Professor of Moral Theology, St. John's Seminary, Brighton, MA, whose fraternal support and encouragement have been essential to the completion and publication of this book. Prof. Mark Johnson of Marquette University tested the draft in teaching. Sister Paul Jean Miller, Professor of Moral Theology, Mt. St. Mary's Seminary, Emmitsburg, MD, Mark Latkovic of Sacred Heart Seminary, Detroit, also read the draft and made valuable criticisms, as did Fr. Kevin D. O'Rourke, O.P., Director of the Center for Healthcare Ethics, St. Louis University. Fr. Victor LaMotte, O.P. was especially helpful with its final revision.

Quotations from the Scriptures are taken from the *New American Bible*, copyright 1991 by the Confraternity of Christian Doctrine, and used with permission. Full bibliographical information on the abbreviated citations in the notes will be found in the Bibliography. The defects of the book are, of course, my own, but my one intention has been to promote the teaching of moral theology as theology, that is, as firmly rooted in the Word of God, for

> Scarce do we know the things of earth, and what is within our grasp we find with difficulty, but when things are in heaven, who can search them out? Or who ever knew Your counsel, except you had given Wisdom and sent your Holy Spirit from on high? And thus were the paths of those on earth made straight, and men learned what was your pleasure and were saved by Wisdom (Ws 9:16-18).

Benedict M. Ashley, OP

LIVING THE TRUTH IN LOVE

CHAPTER 1

THE BIBLICAL FOUNDATION OF MORAL THEOLOGY

All Scripture is inspired by God and is useful for teaching,
for refutation, for correction, and for training in
righteousness, so that one who belongs to God may be
competent, equipped for every good work
(2 Tm 3:16-17).

Is Moral Theology Obsolete?

As "biology" is the scientific study of life (*bios*), "theology" is the scientific study of God (*theos*). Many today believe such study is impossible, either because they think there is no God, or if there is, God is unknowable, or if God is knowable it is only by some private experience that could never take on the systematic, critical, publicly debatable and verifiable character of a science. No wonder then that in many modern universities there is no department of theology, or at most there is a department of religious studies or of comparative religion devoted not to studying God but what various people have believed about God.

In the Catholic tradition of Christianity this possibility of a scientific theology is strongly defended.[1] Not indeed that we can subject God to the kind of controlled experiment that is typical of modern science, but in the broader sense of "science" according to which knowledge can be called scientific if it is critical, that is, if its assertions are testable by appropriate, publicly available evidence. This is so, first of

---

[1] See Yves Congar, O.P., *A History of Theology*, trans. by H. Guthrie, S.J., from "Théologie," DTC XV: 221-288. Congar shows (pp. 240-60) that theological pluralism is compatible with theology's scientific character.

all, because the existence of God and something of what God is can be known by the philosophical analysis of the broad features of the same human experience as that on which the other human sciences are founded. Such a merely "natural" theology, however, is unable to penetrate the mystery of the interior life of God or God's plan for human life.

A theology in the strong sense of a study of the mystery of God that shares in God's own self-understanding and purpose for creation can only be achieved if God chooses to reveal the divine life to us and to instruct us how to enter into that life. In the face of the vast injustices of poverty, war, genocide, and lying propaganda which deface our world today, it is no wonder that many cry out with Job, "Where is God? Why is God silent?"

Yet God is neither absent nor silent. God wants us to share the deathless life and joy which is totally shared by the Three Divine Persons in the unity of the Godhead. This is the reign of God for whose coming Jesus taught us to pray, "Your kingdom come, your will be done on earth as it is in heaven" (Mt 6:10). Since Jesus is Emmanuel, "God with us" (Mt 1:23) in his presence the kingdom has already begun.

Therefore, a theology in the strong sense (a "sacred theology" as contrasted to a merely natural or philosophical theology) based on the data of God's public self-revelation is possible, and Catholic tradition has attempted to provide such a critical theology. Any valid Christian theology must rest on faith in God's self-revelation in Jesus Christ, God's only Word, not *directly* on the data of our human experience.[2] But as I will show in Chapter 2, this faith in Christ is not a "leap in the dark" or mere wishful thinking. It is a reasonable, realistic faith, open to public dialogue with all other religions, and even with atheists and agnostics.

Where do we hear God's Word? The first Christians heard it from

---

[2] *The Catechism of the Catholic Church* (published in French, 1992; in English June 22, 1994), # 65-67, quoting Heb 1:1-2 and St. John of the Cross who said: "By giving us, as he did, his Son, his only Word, God has in that one Word said everything. There is no need for any further revelation." *The Ascent of Mt. Carmel*, II, 22.

the lips of Jesus and then from the Apostles who witnessed to what he had taught and done.[3] Their witness was kept true by the Holy Spirit whom the Risen Lord had sent them to guarantee the essential accuracy of their preaching. This handing on the Word by the power of the Spirit is called *Apostolic Tradition* (from *tradere*, to transmit) in distinction from mere human tradition which quickly becomes vague and even distorted.[4] In the apostolic age this Tradition was soon embodied in the New Testament writings along with the Jewish Scriptures which these writings presupposed and which they guaranteed as consistent with the New Testament.

Hence the Bible was recognized by the apostolic Church as a trustworthy formulation of this Tradition because written under the inspiration of the Holy Spirit. The Catholic Church recognizes Tradition and Scripture as the self-revelation of God which theology studies.[5] While the Eastern Orthodox churches also recognize both Scripture and Tradition as God's self-revelation, the Protestant churches stand on the principle of *sola Scriptura*, the Bible alone.

In many current writers we find the mention of "religious experience" along with Tradition and Scripture as the source of theological reflection.[6] In our age of pluralism we have become acutely aware that the meaning of any traditional formula is colored by the contemporary experience of anyone who tries to interpret such formulas. Although

---

[3] Vatican II, *Dei Verbum*, the most authoritative Catholic statement on the nature of revelation, biblical inspiration, and the relations of Bible and Tradition. See also CCC # 50-54.

[4] CCC # 75-79.

[5] CCC # 80-83. See also, on the interrelations of Scripture and Tradition, Edward Schillebeeckx, O.P., *Revelation and Theology*, vol. 1, pp. 3-86. On the strengths and limitations of current exegetical methods see Pontifical Biblical Commission, "The Interpretation of the Bible in the Church," *Origins*, 23, n. 29 (Jan. 6, 1994), 499-524; also Cardinal Joseph Ratzinger, "Biblical Interpretation in Crisis: On the Question of the Foundations and Approaches of Exegesis Today," in Richard J. Neuhaus, ed., *Biblical Interpretation in Crisis*, pp. 1-23.

[6] For an influential discussion see Edward Schillebeeckx, *Jesus: An Experiment in Christology*, pp. 44-62 with clarifications in *Interim Report on the Books Jesus and Christ*, pp. 50-63. For an example of how "experience" is used to de- and re-construct Scripture and Tradition through "the lens of women's flourishing" see Elizabeth A. Johnson, *She Who Is: The Mystery of God in Feminist Theological Discourse*, pp. 17-41.

we try to put ourselves into the historical context of those for whom the text was originally written, we can never wholly succeed. Ultimately we must interpret the Bible and other documents of the past in terms of the experiences of our own times.

Since, however, *authentic* religious experience is the work of the same Holy Spirit who has been at work in Tradition, Tradition is not merely the faithful transmission of the apostolic message but also includes its faithful reception today. Thus there is no need to add "religious experience" to the conciliar declarations that the source of divine revelation is "Scripture and Tradition." The Bible stands as the inspired witness of Jesus' teaching, but it must be understood in the light of the Church's Tradition as it has developed from the Apostles down to us in our Christian living here and now.[7]

Customarily we use the term "dogmatic theology" to refer to God's self-revelation to us, and the term "moral theology" for what God has told us of the response required of us if we are to enter and live in God's kingdom. Yet, in fact, moral theology cannot be separated from dogmatic theology, since God reveals the Trinitarian divine life to us in order that we may come to share in it. Hence moral and dogmatic theology are merely different perspectives on the same reality of God.

This unity of faith and morality is evident in the *Catechism of the Catholic Church*[8] and the papal encyclical *Veritatis Splendor*[9] in which the Holy See has recently formulated the moral teaching of the Church as it has been authoritatively proclaimed for our times by the Second

---

[7] In CCC, Book One, Chapter Two, "God's Initiative" is placed between Chapter One, "The Human Capacity for God" and Chapter Three, "Humanity's Response." Thus God's self-revelation speaks through human experience, yet transforms it.

[8] The plan of CCC is summed up in # 1692: "The Creed [Book One] confesses the greatness of God's gifts to us in the work of creation and even more in the work of redemption and sanctification. What faith confesses, the sacraments [Book Two] communicate: Christians have been reborn as children of God and made participants in the divine nature through the sacraments. When we recognize our new dignity in faith, that same faith calls us henceforth to lead a life worthy of Christ's Gospel [Book Three]. Through the sacraments and prayer, we receive both Christ's grace and his Spirit's gifts to make us capable of such a life [Book 4]." Book Three, "Life in Christ" covers the topics of moral theology.

[9] *Origins* 23, 18 (Oct 14, 1993), 298-236.

Vatican Council. Part III of the *Catechism*, "Life in Christ," is presented only in the context of the first two parts on the Creed and the Sacraments.

It is even less useful (though it is often tried) to separate "moral" from "spiritual" theology, as if the exterior and interior life of the Christian could be divorced from each other, or that there were two ways, a lower and a higher, of being a Christian.[10] A theology of the Christian life must deal with the whole of Christian living as a dialogue with God.[11] This means also that it studies not just the individual Christian in relation to God, but also the Christian community centered in God. The Christian lives in God's kingdom, God's community, as part of the very "body of Christ" (Rm 12:5). Hence morality is always a communal morality, a morality of liberation from the enslavement of sin in all its phases, individual and social. This, again, is evident in the *Catechism* where Part III on "Life in Christ" is completed by Part IV on prayer and spirituality.

Therefore, moral theology should be truly theology and not simply philosophy, sociology, or psychology. Theology is an effort to listen attentively to what God has to say to us, because God is wiser than we are and more concerned for us than we are for ourselves. In trying to understand and apply what God says to us we must use our God-given intelligence and with it all the information and scientific analysis which human intelligence has made available to us to date, but we must not allow this merely human wisdom to drown out the voice of God, even when that voice frightens us and exposes the specious folly of our human ways of thinking (1 Cor 1:26-31).

Thus if we ask: "Why study moral theology?" the answer is: (1) We humans are immersed in a world where injustice, war, poverty, loneliness, and death seem to have the upper hand. (2) Yet God has invited us into the divine kingdom of undying joy and mutual love. (3) Our human intelligence, however, is not powerful enough to enable us

---

[10] See Reginald Garrigou-Lagrange, O.P., *The Three Ages of the Interior Life*, vol 2, "The Axis of the Spiritual Life and Its Unity," pp. 628-651.

[11] Thus in CCC, Book Four on prayer *synthesizes* both the dogmatic parts (Books One and Two) and the moral part (Book Three).

to understand and follow out that invitation. (4) Therefore, to find our way, we need God's *Torah* or Instruction, and the careful study of this Instruction is that part of theology which is called "moral."

The Revision of Moral Theology

Since theology is a reflection on the Scriptures as understood in the light of the Spirit-guided Tradition, it seems obvious that *moral* theology is a reflection on the *moral* instruction contained in the Scriptures. When we open the Bible, however, we find a great variety of moral teachings, some of which even seem to contradict others and to lack a coherent unity. Hence Tradition has always turned to the moral teachings of Jesus in the Bible as the best interpretation and summary of this whole body of moral wisdom.

Modern critical scholarship supplies us with powerful tools for a better understanding of the Bible in its historical context and its literary expression.[12] If we are to base moral theology first of all on the authentic moral teaching of Jesus who said, "You have but one teacher, and you are all brothers... You have but one master, the Messiah" (Mt 23:8, 10), it is essential that this revised moral theology be freed from any fundamentalism that would read the Bible as if it were a "How to Do It" handbook published by one of our contemporaries.[13] Hence, we must be fully aware that critical scholarship raises certain difficulties about identifying the exact words of Jesus in New Testament documents written some years after his earthly life.[14] Other problems arise in relating Jesus' teaching to the different phases and theological strands

---

[12] For what can be known about the real Jesus by purely historical methods see John P. Meier, "Jesus," NJBC, pp. 1316-1328, and Meier's, *A Marginal Jew*, 2 vols. and Craig A. Evans, "Life-of-Jesus Research and the Eclipse of Mythology," TS 54 (March 1993), 3-36.

[13] See the warnings against a naively literal or "fundamentalist" interpretation of the Bible by the Pontifical Biblical Commission, note 5 above.

[14] The Jesus Seminar, "gospel specialists" who "teach at leading colleges, universities and seminaries in the U.S. and Canada" (p. xiii) has voted that of 111 Jesus' sayings in Mark, probably only 17 (15%) meet their historical criteria for authenticity! Robert W. Funk with Mahlon H. Smith, *The Gospel of Mark*; reviewed by C.C. Carlson, CBQ 52 (1990), 557-558 and Robert W. Funk, *The Five Gospels*.

in the Old Testament,[15] in the different Gospels, and in the apostolic writings. Due allowance must be made for progressive revelation and for the differences of religious perspective of the various biblical writers and the audiences they were addressing.

Nevertheless, for believers the essential continuity of New Testament teaching with that of Jesus is guaranteed by the doctrine of biblical inspiration, and this assurance is in no way inconsistent with the well-established results of historical research.[16] Our problem today rather is a hermeneutical (interpretative) one of seeing how Jesus' teaching, preached in times so different from ours, can still serve as a practical guide to living in a world very different from that in which the Bible was written.[17]

We no longer live in a uniform, traditional society where there is a general agreement on values, but in one that is constantly changing. Ours is a pluralistic culture where we are presented with all kinds of models and hear all kinds of opinions about right and wrong. No wonder we are puzzled! But this situation is not absolutely new. The early Church existed in the Roman Empire where Christians were in contact with pagan society and indeed with a number of cultures. In the Middle Ages Europe was invaded by northern pagans and influenced on the south by Islam. In the Renaissance the Church had to encounter a whole New World of non-European peoples and cultures. Since the eigh-

---

[15] To recognize that Judaism has its own unique history, which Christian history does not make obsolete, I considered using in this book "Hebrew Scriptures" or "First Testament," as some do, but the Catholic Old Testament is not coextensive with the Jewish canon, and "First" is no improvement over "Old."

[16] "Holy Mother Church has firmly and with absolute constancy held, and continues to hold, that the four Gospels just named, whose historical character the Church unhesitatingly asserts, faithfully hand on what Jesus Christ, while living among us, really did and taught for their eternal salvation until the day He was taken up into heaven (see Acts 1:1-2)." Vatican II, DV, n.19. For the reasons that the historical context of Jesus' teaching makes the authentic tradition of his sayings probable, see Rainer Riesner, "Jesus as Preacher and Teacher" in H. Wansbrough, ed., *Jesus and the Oral Gospel Tradition*. R.E. Brown, *The Gospel According to John*, pp. xliv-xlvii holds that even the highly elaborated and stylized Johannine discourses are rooted in an authentic tradition independent of the synoptics. Yet, this does not exclude valid questions about the origins of any particular dominical saying.

[17] See Raymond E. Brown, S.S. and Sandra Schneider, I.H.M., "Hermeneutics," NJBC, pp. 1146-1165.

teenth century it has been confronted by the rise of secularist cultures. Thus the Christian community again and again has had to meet in one form or another much the same moral confusion we today experience.

Some contemporary moral theologians think that our times are so different from the past that they must construct a "new morality" or a "revision of traditional morality."[18] They support this position by arguing that Jesus himself, and even more explicitly St. Paul, taught that the Gospel abolished the Old Law with its numerous concrete rules and replaced it by a freedom of decision unrestricted by fixed moral laws and guided only by the Holy Spirit to meet new and unique situations. They point out that in Jesus' own teaching there are few concrete norms of action, but rather simply *parenesis* or exhortations to act lovingly, and they interpret the detailed norms of the New Testament epistles as temporary guidelines, historically conditioned by local situations and therefore today obsolete; for example, the restrictions on women (1 Cor 11:3-6; Col 3:18, etc.) which today we would consider sexist.

Consequently, these "revisionists" turn to Scripture and Tradition only for Christian motivation, and mainly rely for today's concrete norms on a purely philosophical ethics. Concrete moral norms, they claim, are not specifically Christian but are accessible to believer and non-believer alike. They argue also that the Church's official moral teaching does not pertain to the realm of defined and infallible doctrine but merely represents the opinions of the "Roman schools" of theology which do not take into account the variety of current situations or the advance of the human sciences. When other moralists question these theses, revisionists often defend their views as the product of the new dynamic "historical consciousness" as opposed to the traditional static "classical consciousness."

These revisionists are certainly right in fearing an historical, fundamentalist literalism in the use of the Bible.[19] The advances in biblical

---

[18] For a collection of current opinions on the revision of moral theology, especially in relation to the Bible see the Bibliography at the end of this book.

[19] See the report of the Pontifical Biblical Commission, note 5 above, rejecting fundamentalism in exegesis.

scholarship and in the history of the development of doctrine in the Church have to be given full weight in any valid revision of theology. That a serious revision of moral theology is long overdue I enthusiastically grant and also that it should reflect the historicity of human existence. Such an appreciation for human historicity is indeed a characteristic of the theology of Vatican II. The "static vs. dynamic" dichotomy, however, is more rhetoric than analysis. Therefore, let us approach this issue historically, since any revision of theology must be based on a "return to sources," i.e. to Scripture and Tradition with attention to the hermeneutics by which these sources can be related to contemporary experience. This is the way pointed out by *Veritatis Splendor* and embodied in the *Catechism of the Catholic Church* which maintain the universality and permanence of the moral law, yet confirm that historical study of the ways in which our understanding of the moral law has developed is essential to its present application.[20]

The Unity of Biblical Torah

Historically, the moral tradition of the Hebrew Bible is primarily the written Torah, that is, the first five books of the Bible which all parties of the Jews in Jesus' time as in our own have regarded as the ultimate grounds of *orthopraxis* or right living. These consist of very concrete detailed codes of behavior placed in a narrative context of the Creation, the Fall, and the Exodus which serves to give authority and sense to these codes, illustrating the consequences of obedience or disobedi-

---

[20] "The truth of the moral law, like that of the 'deposit of faith,' unfolds down the centuries. The norms expressing that truth remain valid in their substance, but must be specified and determined *eodem sensu eademque sententia* [in the same sense and the same meaning] in the light of historical circumstances by the Church's Magisterium, whose decision is preceded and accompanied by the work of interpretation and formulation characteristic of the reason of individual believers and of theological reflection." VS, n. 53. Cf. also CCC # 1949-1984; especially # 1952 and 1960.

[21] On the Judaic concept of "Torah" see Jacob Neusner, *Torah Through the Ages* and R.E. Friedman "Torah (Pentateuch)," in ABD, 6:605-622. On Walther Eichrodt's view that "Covenant" is the unifying concept of Old Testament theology and other views see Robert B. Laurin, *Contemporary Old Testament Theologians*, especially the article of N.K. Gottwald, pp. 23-62.

ence to God's laws. The central concept of this Torah is that of the Covenant between God and Israel, initiated by God but demanding of Israel a free commitment of obedience to "the way of life" rather than "the way of death" (Dt 30:19).[21]

The rest of the Hebrew Bible consists of literature which received canonical status in relation to the Torah: (1) *historical narratives* (written in a manner quite different than that of modern history) which further illustrated the consequences of fidelity or infidelity to the Covenant, including the Babylonian Exile and Restoration; (2) *prophetic writings* that interpreted the Covenant by insisting not only on external obedience but on an obedience of the heart and warning of the consequences of infidelity; and (3) other writings which were *wisdom literature* praising "the way of life" and warning against "the way of folly" with much concrete traditional counsel drawn from daily experience, along with books like Jonah, Esther, Tobit, Judith, and others inculcating Torah obedience through morally instructive narratives not intended to be strictly historical. Thus from a Jewish point of view the Torah is the heart of the Bible encompassed by other literature that serves in a variety of ways as its largely homiletic commentary.

Modern historical scholarship has shown that the account of God's handing the Torah to Moses as a ready-made book must be understood as a dramatic way of declaring that it is the inspired Word of God having definitive moral authority. The codes of the Torah are historically the result of a very long process by which legal material common to many Near Eastern countries was gradually shaped and given its specific religious monotheistic character culminating in the Covenant theology represented by its final book, Deuteronomy.[22] There is evidence within the Pentateuch itself that the Jews recognized that God gave only a qualified approval to these laws, since they did not wholly correspond to God's intentions in the creation. Thus Genesis itself seems to say that the dietary law permitting the eating of meat given to Noah

---

[22] On current theories of the composition and dating of the Pentateuch see Moseh Weinfeld, *Deuteronomy 1-11*, Introduction, pp. 1-84, and J. Alberto Soggin, *Introduction to the Old Testament*, 3rd ed., pp. 91-186. Its final form and separation from the "Deuteronomic History" (Genesis through the books of Kings) probably dates from the time of Ezra in the middle of the 5th century.

(Gn 9:34) and included in the Mosaic law (Lv 17:10-16) was inferior to the vegetarian diet given to Adam (Gn 1:29).[23] The Torah, therefore, had a certain *provisional and eschatological character* looking forward to further revelation by a prophet like Moses (Dt 18:15).

In the other books of the Hebrew Bible this provisional character became *messianic*, looking to an age when the particularist law of Israel would somehow be universalized for all people. Thus it was prophesied (Is 56:1-8) that the eunuchs and foreigners excluded from the Temple by the Torah are someday to be admitted. The Torah, therefore, was not "static" but underwent a development both of content and of interpretation.[24]

This was reflected in the view taken by the ancient rabbis and still maintained in Judaism, that in addition to the written Torah there was also an oral Torah or tradition going back to Moses and maintained in its development by the chain of leading rabbis. This tradition, enshrined after the time of Jesus and the fall of Jerusalem in the *Mishnah* and the Babylonian and Palestinian *Talmuds*, has an authority in Judaism closely linked to that of the written Torah itself. It is this tradition and not the written Torah which is specifically that of Judaism,[25] while Christianity represents a different tradition of interpretation of this same Torah.

The Torah of Jesus

Jesus himself was not a rabbi in the technical sense, although his contemporaries perceived that he in fact functioned as such, that is, as an

---

[23] For the rabbinic views on the Noahian laws, of divine origin, yet accessible to reason and binding all nations see Gersion Appel, *A Philosophy of Mizvot*, pp. 124-127.

[24] On different forms of messianism before Jesus, see Gershom Scholem, *The Messianic Idea in Judaism*, pp. 19-33 (note the quote from Maimonides, *Code of Laws*, "Laws Concerning the Installation of Kings," paragraphs 11 and 12, pp. 28-29); Joachim Becker, *Messianic Expectations in the Old Testament*, pp. 25-36; and articles of B.M. Bokser, "Messianism, the Exodus Pattern, and Early Rabbinic Judaism," pp. 239-260 and J.M. Roberts, "The Old Testament's Contribution to Messianic Expectations," in James H. Charlesworth, et al., *The Messiah: Developments in Earliest Judaism and Christianity*, pp. 39-51.

[25] See Neusner, *Torah*, pp. 20-24, 38-87.

authoritative interpreter of the Torah (Mk 9:5, 11:21, 14:45; Mt 26:25, 49; Jn 1:38, 49; 3:2; 4:31; 6:25; 9:2; 11:8).[26] When we read the Gospel accounts of Jesus' controversies with the Pharisees, we may get the impression that he is defending those who break the detailed prescriptions of the law, but as scholars have recently shown, in these accounts Jesus, although his message is shockingly new, never violates or condones the violation of any rule of the written Torah.[27] Thus when Jesus is criticized for apparent violations of the law by healing on the Sabbath, etc., he defends his actions with rabbinical arguments based on biblical citations and analogies (cf. Mk 2:23-28; 3:1-6). At the same time he deepens the understanding of the Torah by returning to God's intentions in the creation, "The Sabbath was made for man, not man for the Sabbath" (Mk 2:27).

Jesus denounced *some* of the Pharisees because they did not practice what they preached (Mt 23:3, 25-27); because they proudly scorned the ignorant without helping them to know and observe the law (Mt 23:4-12); because they proselytized only to make sectarians of their converts (Mt 23:13); because they evaded the law by dubious casuistry (Mt 23:16-21); because they scrupled about minor details while ignoring the "weightier things of the law"; and because they persecuted their critics out of fanatical attachment to their own views (Mt 23:29-36). This is a catalogue of failings which religious people (including our-

---

[26] For the meaning of "rabbi" in Jesus' time cf. Riesner, "Jesus as Preacher and Teacher," pp. 186-188 and literature there cited. Was Jesus literate? Certainly he was living in a largely oral culture; see Paul J. Achtemeier, "*Omne Verbum Sonat*: The New Testament and the Oral Environment of Late Western Antiquity," JBL 109 (1990):3-27. A "carpenter" in a small village was not likely to have a scribal or rabbinical education. Luke 4:14-21, however, portrays Jesus as reading from the Torah scroll. History has many examples of talented persons of lowly background who taught themselves to read or got others to teach them. Or we can attribute Jesus' knowledge of the Scriptures to a good memory (not uncommon in oral cultures) which retained what he heard, read and discussed.

[27] Thus E.P. Sanders, *Jesus and Judaism* (1985) and *Jewish Law from Jesus to Mishnah* (1990). In the latter he concludes, pp. 95-96: "The synoptic Jesus lived as a law-abiding Jew... Even if each conflict narrative were literally true [which Sanders gives reasons for doubting], however, it would be seen that Jesus did not seriously challenge the law as it was practiced in his day, not even by the strict rules of observance of pietist groups — except on the issue of food" which exception was not due to Jesus but to a "subsequent debate in the early Church" (p. 96).

selves) often fall into, nor should it be generalized to all the Pharisees, nor to their tradition which has largely formed the Judaism of today.[28] Jesus himself supported the authority of these learned, zealous (and sometimes too human) teachers.

> The scribes and Pharisees have taken their seat on the chair of Moses. Therefore, do all things whatsoever they tell you, but do not follow their example (Mt 23:2).

In the Sermon on the Mount Jesus solemnly declared:

> Do not think that I have come to abolish the law or the prophets. I have not come to abolish but to fulfill. Amen, I say to you, until heaven and earth pass away, not the smallest letter or the smallest part of a letter will pass from the law, until all things have taken place. Therefore, whoever breaks one of the least of these commandments and teaches others to do so will be called least in the kingdom of heaven. But whosoever obeys and teaches these commandments will be called greatest in the kingdom of heaven. I tell you, unless your righteousness surpasses that of the scribes and Pharisees, you will not enter into the kingdom of heaven (Mt 5:17-20).

He then proceeded to give his own interpretation of several of the Ten Commandments, each time saying "You have heard that it was said..., but I say to you" referring not to what the Torah itself said, but to how some had misinterpreted the Torah, and then giving his own interpretation in view of the radical Good News he was sent by his Father to proclaim.[29]

What was the nature of this Christian interpretation of the Torah? It is most explicit in the discussion of the commandments of the Torah on divorce, which permitted husbands but not wives to divorce their

---

[28] Rabbi Michael Hilton with Fr. Gordian Marshall, O.P., *The Gospels and Rabbinic Judaism: A Study Guide* shows very well how different yet alike are the Jewish and Christian traditions.

[29] On the six antitheses or "hypertheses" of Mt 5:17-48 see Benedict T. Viviano, O.P., "The Gospel According to St. Matthew." NJBC, pp. 641-644.

mates because of "something indecent" (Dt 24:1-4).[30] The great Rabbi Hillel had interpreted this vague expression broadly; another rabbi Shammai had interpreted it narrowly. Jesus (no doubt recalling the words of the prophet Malachi — " 'I hate divorce,' says the Lord, the God of Israel" (Ml 2:16) — goes beyond even the strictness of Shammai and says:

> "Have you not read that from the beginning the Creator 'made them male and female' and said, 'For this reason a man shall leave his father and mother and be joined to his wife, and the two shall become one flesh'? So they are no longer two, but one flesh. Therefore, what God has joined together, no human being must separate." They said to him, "Then why did Moses command that the man give the woman a bill of divorce and dismiss her?" He said to them, "Because of the hardness of your hearts Moses allowed you to divorce your wives, but from the beginning it was not so. I say to you, whoever divorces his wife (unless the marriage is unlawful) [literally "because of something indecent"] and marries another commits adultery." His disciples said to him, "If that is the case of a man with his wife, it is better not to marry." He answered, "Not all can accept this word, but only those to whom that is granted" (Mt 19:4-11; Mk 10:5-12; cf. Mt 5:31-33).[31]

Thus Jesus took the view, which we have seen is already hinted at in the Torah itself and which was not unknown in the rabbinical schools, that the Torah of Moses falls short of that originally given by God in creation, a law that has tolerated certain aspects of human sinfulness until the "time of fulfillment," the Messianic age of the coming of the Reign of God in its perfection. Since the chief theme of Jesus' preaching is "*This* is the time of fulfillment. The kingdom of God is at

---

[30] For a thorough discussion of this question see J.A. Fitzmyer, S.J., "The Matthean Divorce Texts and Some New Palestinian Evidence," in *To Advance the Gospel: New Testament Studies*, pp. 79-111.

[31] The source of Mt 19:4-11 is usually attributed to Mk 10:5-12; while the doublet Mt 5:31-33 and its parallel Lk 16:18 are attributed to Q. 1 Cor 7:10-11 is an independent (and the oldest) attestation of this dominical saying.

hand. Repent and believe in the gospel" [i.e the good news of the coming of the kingdom] (Mk 1:15), he was indicating that Moses' Torah
was now "fulfilled" (Mt 5:17), that is, it has been restored to the original perfection of God's creation "in the beginning."

Hence in one sense Jesus as "the great prophet" (Dt 18:15) and
Messiah annuls the Mosaic law, but in another and deeper sense he
"fulfills" it by *perfecting* it. "Be perfect, just as your heavenly Father is
perfect" (Mt 5:48). Thus the "law of Christ" (Gal 6:2) transcends the
Mosaic law but does so not by abrogating it but by returning it to its
source, freed of the concessions that had resulted from the peculiar
historical situation of Israel in a sinful world. This Christian reinterpre-
tation and perfecting of the law may even involve *correction*, as in the
abolition of divorce and the transformation of the ancient "holy war"
into a purely spiritual warfare based on the love of enemies (Mt 5:43-
44). Thus Cardinal Joseph Ratzinger, speaking in Jerusalem to an international conference of Jews and Christians, has said:

> The law of the gospel fulfills the commandments of the law. The
> Lord's Sermon on the Mount, far from abolishing or devaluing
> the moral prescriptions of the old law, releases their hidden po-
> tential and has new demands arise from them: It reveals their
> entire divine and human truth. It does not add new external pre-
> cepts but proceeds to renew the heart, the root of human acts,
> where man chooses between the pure and impure, where faith,
> hope, and charity are found, and with them other virtues. The
> Gospel thus brings the law to its fullness through imitation of
> the perfection of the heavenly Father.[32]

This issue became acute for the early Church when it began to
attract Gentile converts, since the apostles were not at all clear whether
they ought to require them to observe the Jewish law. Acts (7:2-60)
tells us that Stephen provoked his own martyrdom before the Sanhedrin
by reminding his fellow Jews that the law was given to Moses by God
not directly but through an angel (Ac 7:38, 53), that a prophet succes-

---

[32] "Reconciling Gospel and Torah: The Catechism," *Origins* 23 (Feb. 24, 1994), 621,
623-628, n. 2, pp. 624-625 in which he also quotes CCC # 1968.

sor to Moses had been promised (Ac 7:37), and that the Temple with its rites was only of temporary value (Ac 7:48-50). Then later Peter received a vision which assured him that for Gentile converts the dietary rules of the law are no longer obligatory (Ac 10:1-11:18).

The Torah of Paul

Paul, a rabbi in the strict sense, a student of the famous Rabbi Gamaliel the Great, and a zealous Pharisee, was called in a vision to become an "apostle to the Gentiles" (Rm 11:13). It is not surprising, therefore, considering that Jesus and the Twelve had continued to observe the Mosaic law, that Paul was soon confronted in Galatia by a party of Jewish Christians who insisted that the Gentile converts be circumcised and observe all the prescriptions of the law. In fact, Christians who were Jews continued for a long time to keep the law, in some places as late as the fifth century!

The question of the obligation of the law, not only for Gentiles, but for *all* Christians could not, however, be long evaded. Paul's solution (stated vehemently and perhaps too one-sidedly in Galatians, yet evident throughout all his writings) was that while the law was divinely inspired and intended to prepare Israel for the coming of the Messiah, of itself it could not save anyone because as a mere set of external rules it did not have the power to change the human heart. Individuals might conform to it while remaining unconverted to God. They might even be made more rebellious against God by its constraints. Salvation could come only by *faith* in the Christ who had the power to send his Spirit into their hearts, converting them and enabling them to obey God out of love rather than fear.[33]

---

[33] Controversy has always surrounded the interpretation of St. Paul on law and gospel (cf. 2 P 3:15-16); however, Catholic and Protestant scholars are approaching a consensus. See James D.G. Dunn, *Jesus, Paul and the Law*, especially Chapters 7 and 8, "The New Perspective in Paul," pp. 183-214 and "Works of the Law and the Curse of the Law" pp. 215-241; and Joseph Fitzmyer, "Pauline Theology," NJBC, pp. 1382-1416, and "Paul and the Law" in *To Advance the Gospel*, pp. 186-201; also Hans Dieter Betz, "Paul," ABD, 5:186-201.

Hence, Paul taught that Jewish Christians could continue to live under the law (Paul himself sometimes conformed to it to avoid offending them; cf. Ac 16:3) as long as they did not put their trust in the law rather than in Christ. They were not obliged by the Old Law and could not bind Gentile converts to it. He even "opposed" St. Peter "to his face" when at Antioch Peter — in order to placate the Jewish Christians — stopped eating with the Gentile converts (Gal 2:11-14).

This first great moral controversy in the Church was arbitrated by the council at Jerusalem recounted in Acts 15:1-29, when after Peter's speech in favor of Paul's practice and the agreement of James of Jerusalem, leader of the Jewish Christians, the following decree was issued:

> The Holy Spirit and we have decided to lay no burdens on you beyond these necessary things: namely, to abstain from meat sacrificed to idols, from blood, from meats of strangled animals, and to refrain from unlawful marriages. If you avoid these things, you will be doing what is right. Farewell. (Ac 15:28-29).

Note that this decree is a compromise with the Jewish party in that the Gentiles, although not bound to the Mosaic law, were still bound to the "law of Noah" (Gn 9:1-17) which the rabbis usually required of proselytes. In seems, however, that Paul did not insist on even this from his converts. Does this mean that for Paul the Mosaic law had lost *all* validity? By no means. Paul in Galatians, after a vehement plea to the people not to allow themselves to be enslaved again under the Mosaic law (ending with the exasperated wish that the advocates of circumcision would castrate themselves! 5:12), goes on to say:

> For you were called for freedom, brothers. But do not use this freedom as an opportunity for the flesh; rather serve one another through love. For the whole law is fulfilled in one statement, namely, "You shall love your neighbor as yourself." ... I say then live by the Spirit and you will certainly not gratify the flesh. For the flesh has desires against the Spirit, and the Spirit against the flesh; these are opposed to each other, so that you may not do what you want. But if you are guided by the Spirit, you are not under the law (Gal 5:13-18).

Paul then lists the works of the flesh and of the spirit as already quoted above. This shows that for Paul the Mosaic law was transformed into the "law of Christ" (Gal 6:2) which is "faith working through love" (Gal 5:6; cf. Eph 4:15, "Living the truth in love"), and this "love" is the love of God and neighbor which the Lord himself had said sums up the whole law (Mt 22:40). Paul explicitly holds that this includes the Ten Commandments:

> Owe nothing to anyone, except to love one another; for the one who loves another has fulfilled the law. The commandments, "You shall not commit adultery; you shall not kill; you shall not steal; you shall not covet," and *whatever other commandment there may be*, are summed up in this saying, "You shall love your neighbor as yourself." Love does no evil to the neighbor; hence, love is the fulfillment of the law (Rm 13:8-10, italics added).

Since the Ten Commandments are the heart of the Torah,[34] and the Torah itself commands us to love our neighbor (Lv 19:18), it is evident that Paul never meant that the moral norms of the Old Law had ceased to bind. Indeed, by repeating Jesus' emphasis on the supremacy of "love" and founding this love on "faith" in Jesus, Paul proclaims that Jesus *perfected* these moral norms, as is evident in his support of Jesus' abolition of divorce (1 Cor 7:10-11). In light of this Paul is not inconsistent when in the pastoral sections of his epistles he glorifies Christian freedom and at the same time promulgates detailed norms commanding and forbidding certain actions. For him morality is above all to live "in Christ," in perfect unity with and by the power of the Risen Lord.[35]

What does this "freedom" consist in if it does not abolish the moral norms of the Torah, but in some cases makes them even more

---

[34] It would be a mistake, however, to restrict the moral instruction of the Bible simply to literal precepts, since much of this instruction is found in narrative, poetry, and wisdom sayings, cf. Richard N. Longenecker, *Galatians*, pp. xliii-lvii.

[35] On living *in Christo* see Robert F. O'Toole, S.J., *Who is a Christian? A Study in Pauline Ethics*, pp. 28-50.

restrictive? The "freedom" of which Paul speaks is twofold. (1) It is freedom from the law understood simply as an *external coercion* restraining human free choice: "For the kingdom of God is not a matter of food and drink, but of righteousness, peace and joy in the Holy Spirit" (Rm 14:17). (2) More profoundly, it is freedom from the *internal conflict* resulting from sin that hinders us in consistently pursuing what we know to be good: "For I do not do the good I want, but I do the evil I do not want" (Rm 7:19); "Freed from sin you have become slaves of righteousness" (Rm 6:18).

Without the grace of faith we find ourselves tempted to rebel against the law and indeed unable to keep it integrally, yet threatened by God's punishment for not doing so. But with faith we become free, because we now are able to love God, and therefore to obey not merely out of fear but out of love, confident that God's commands are only the expression of his love for us. Instead of being forced by the external law, we are moved from within by the Holy Spirit and discover that it is possible for us in Christ to obey the commands of God willingly and freely, although not without struggle and sacrifice. Thus even the hard moral precepts of the law are no longer impossible. As Jesus himself had said, "For my yoke [i.e., my commandments] is easy and my burden light" (Mt 11:30).

Christians, however, do not wish to be freed from the moral law summed up in the Ten Commandments and still more succinctly in the Great Commandment of love, because these commandments belong to the very order of God's creation and pertain to the very nature of humanity and its conscience, as Paul explicitly teaches when he shows that both Jews and Gentiles are sinners because they have broken the laws of God:

> All who sin outside the law [of Moses] will also perish without reference to the law, and all who sin under the law will be judged according to the law. For it is not those who *hear* the law [of God] who are just in the sight of God; rather, those who *observe* the law [of God] will be justified. For when the Gentiles who do not have the law [of Moses] by nature observe the prescriptions of the law [of God], they are a law for themselves even though they do not have the law [of Moses]. They show the demands of

the law [of God] are written in their hearts, while their conscience also bears witness and their conflicting thoughts accuse
or even defend them on the day when, according to my gospel,
God will judge people's hidden works through Christ Jesus (Rm
2:12-16; words in brackets mine).

Thus the Gentiles who are ignorant of the Mosaic law nevertheless know much of its content in a "natural" way and are obliged to it.
Sometimes it is said that the concept of "natural law" is Greek, derived
from Stoic philosophy, and hence is without theological standing. Paul,
however, links the Greek term for "nature" (*physis*) with that for "law"
(*nomos*) and thus speaks (Rm 1:18-32) of a law of God in creation
accessible to all humanity without the revealed Mosaic law.[36] The common content of the Mosaic and the natural law is clearly *moral*, and
does *not* include the *ceremonial* prescriptions (cultic, dietary, etc.) nor
the *judicial* ones (penalties, and civil provisions) peculiar to Jewish
history and culture. The ceremonial precepts of the law, such as circumcision —foreign to Gentile custom and therefore especially onerous to them —are what Paul refers to as the "yoke of slavery" (Gal 5:1)
from which Gentile Christians (and in principle the Jewish ones also)
are freed by the Gospel.

Why, if these ceremonial and judicial precepts are commanded
by God in the Torah, are all Christians, whether Gentiles or Jews, free
of them? Because the Mosaic law was only given to the Jews to equip
them for their special mission of witness, but the "law of Christ," the
Gospel, is *universal*. It is given to all humanity and hence extends the
moral provisions of the Torah — but only those — to all the world.
This Pauline distinction between the primary, universal and permanent
character of the moral precepts of the Torah and its secondary and
provisional precepts was rooted in the rabbinical thought in which Paul
was trained. It finds full expression in the work of the great medieval
Jewish rabbi Maimonides who influenced its exposition by St. Thomas
Aquinas, but it was already present in the Church Fathers.[37]

---

[36] See Appel's discussion of the Noahian laws, note 23 above.

[37] Maimonides, *The Guide for the Perplexed*, Part III, Chapter 32, p. 324 claims that the
Torah regulates animal sacrifices because they were already customary and hence:

The Judicial and Ceremonial Torah

Does the abrogation of the ceremonial and judicial precepts of the Torah mean that these portions of the Bible are of no significance for constructing a moral theology? By no means. The judicial laws of the Pentateuch are of course entirely relative to the political history of Israel in the Holy Land, and cannot be simply applied to other peoples, times, and places. Yet throughout the history of the Church, Christian statesmen have looked to these laws and the narratives which illustrate them and drawn lessons from them for their own times.

St. Thomas Aquinas, for example, derived from these laws support for the Aristotelian political thesis that in most circumstances the best form of government is a republic or "mixed" government with a monarchical element (a strong executive), an aristocratic element (a senatorial body), and a democratic element (election of officials from the people) not unlike that of the United States and many modern countries.[38] The political history of Israel as recorded in the Bible thus remains for us an ever interesting example of political wisdom and folly from which we can still learn. As St. Augustine showed in his *The City of God*,[39] this has special significance for Christian ethics because of the commentary on that history in the light of monotheism made by the biblical writers in the deuteronomic and prophetic traditions.

"God refrained from prescribing what the people by their natural disposition would be incapable of obeying, and gave the above-mentioned commandments as a means of securing his chief object, viz. to spread a knowledge of Him [among the people], and to cause them to reject idolatry," III, c. 32, p. 324. See Thomas Aquinas, *Summa Theologiae*, I-II, q. 98, a. 5, and for his use of Maimonides see Marvin Fox, *Interpreting Maimonides' Philosophy*, pp. 124-151; Isaac Franks, "Maimonides and Aquinas on Man's Knowledge of God: A Twentieth-Century Perspective" in Joseph A.Buijs, ed., *Maimonides: A Collection of Critical Essays* (1988), pp. 284-305; and Wolfgang Kluxen, "Maimonides and Latin Scholasticism" in Shlomo Pines and Yirmiyahu Yovel, *Maimonides and Philosophy*, pp. 224-232.

[38] *Summa Theologiae*, III. q. 105, a. 1, c.

[39] *De Civitate Dei*, Bks. XI-XXII on the "two cities," their origin (Bks XI-XIV), their progress (Bks XV-XVIII), and their final destiny (Bks XIX-XXII). E. Portalie, S.J., *A Guide to the Thought of St. Augustine*, p. 46 says, "The *Confessions* are theology as experienced in one soul and the history of God's actions in individuals; the *City of God* is theology as living in the historical framework of humanity and explains the action of God in the world."

The permanent significance of the ceremonial laws is more obscure. Yet not only do these cultic practices assist us in understanding the development of the Jewish religion, but, as the rabbis (notably Maimonides[40]) saw, they played a crucial role in the education of the moral sensitivities of the Jews. Thus the odd commandment, three times repeated in the Scriptures, "You shall not boil a kid in its mother's milk" (Ex 23:19; 34:26; Dt 14:21), is said both to forbid a cruel pagan superstition and to inculcate respect for life and the mother-child relationship.[41]

The division of objects into "clean" and "unclean," elaborately regulated in Leviticus 11-15, may sometimes have had health reasons or been intended to prevent idolatrous or superstitious practices, but anthropologists today believe the general purpose of such rules was to inculcate symbolically a sense of the order of God's creation and the unique identity of the Chosen People.[42] For the Bible, God above all is *holy*: "The Lord said to Moses, 'Speak to the whole Israelite community and tell them: "Be holy, for I, the Lord, your God, am holy" ' " (Lv 19:1-2). Hence Jesus said in the Sermon on the Mount, "Be perfect, just as your heavenly Father is perfect" (Mt 5:48).

The Hebrew root for this term "holy" means "separate" and thus indicates the fundamental tenet of monotheism, that God is "the wholly Other."[43] This, however, does not mean that God is distant, but that he is an absolutely mysterious Presence: "For I am God and not man, the Holy One present among you" (Ho 11:9), utterly different from all his creatures and in no way to be pantheistically or idolatrously confused with them. In this otherness God is purely "spiritual" in the sense of free from any of the limitations that obviously condition all visible,

---

[40] *The Guide for the Perplexed*, Part III, Chapters 26-50. He admits in many places, e.g., p. 312 that he was unable to find reasons for certain precepts.

[41] The precept "You shall not slaughter an ox or a sheep on one and the same day as its young" (Lv 22:28) had a similar purpose; cf. Maimonides, *The Commandments*, vol. 2, Negative Command 101, p. 98.

[42] Frank H. Gorman, Jr., *The Ideology of Ritual*, reviews the extensive recent literature.

[43] See Walter C. Kaiser Jr., *Toward Old Testament Ethics*, pp. 139-151 on the concept of "holiness" as central to Hebrew ethics; and David P. Wright, "Holiness (OT)," ABD, 3: 237-249 and "Unclean and Clean (OT)," ABD, 6:729-741.

perishable, material things. God is absolutely "pure," unadulterated by anything imperfect or alien; he is "clean." Therefore, the opposite of the "holy" is the "unclean," whatever is limited, imperfect, alien, disorderly, chaotic, or ambiguous.

Hence, since the Chosen People are called by God to an intimate Covenant with him, comparable to a marriage (Ho 1-3; Is 54:4-10; 62:1-5; Jr 2:2; 3:1-20; Ezk 16:1-63), the people must also be holy or clean to offer sacrifices to God (Hg 2:10-14), free of all that is alien or adulterating (the English words "adultery" and "adulterate" come from the Latin *ad-alter*, to add alien material to a commodity), of all that lacks the order and lawfulness established in creation as that is described in Genesis 1.

In that first narrative of the Torah, the cosmos is distinguished from God and is then divided spatially and temporally and each of its spaces and times furnished with its proper contents. This order in space, time, and status thus becomes the pattern to which human society and life ought to conform. Hence, the Chosen People are to be instructed in this order not only by the moral law, but also by rituals and regulations that inculcate this law symbolically.

When this cultic system was fully developed, the Chosen People had to be kept pure from intermarriage with other peoples who might corrupt their faithfulness to the Covenant (Dt 7:1-4; 23:4-9; Ezr 9:1-10; Ne 13:1-3; Ml 2:10-12). Their houses and clothing must be kept clean from mold ("leprosy," Lv 13:47-59; 14:33-57); their bodies from skin diseases (Lv 13:1-46; 14:1-32); and from seminal or menstrual uncleanness (Lv 15). Above all there must be no contact with the corpses of the dead: "Order the Israelites to expel from camp every leper, and everyone suffering from a discharge, and everyone who has become unclean by contact with a corpse" (Nb 5:2); and no consuming of blood: "for the life of a living body is in its blood" (Lv 17:11).

The dietary laws were part of this symbol system. For example, the eating of hoofed animals was permitted if they had cloven hooves and also chewed a cud; but the pig, because it had cloven hooves but no cud, was forbidden (Lv 11:1-8). Likewise, to be edible, fish had to have both fins and scales, etc. It seems the principle of this classification was that ambiguous, borderline creatures that did not clearly fit into customary categories such as those divided by the Creator in the creation account of Genesis 1, symbolized a lack of order, a return to chaos, and were thus unclean. The maintenance of this ritual purity, which was especially rigorous for the priests, required also all kinds of ritual baths and washing.

This concept of separating all of life into the sacred and the profane, alien to modern sensibility in which the very sense of "the sacred" has been attenuated,[44] underlies all liturgy in which there must be sacred times, places, things, and persons to signify the presence of God in human life. Thus the fundamental moral significance of this complicated system was the observance of the First Commandment, the honoring of the One God and the people's covenant with him. Therefore, the prophets complained frequently (1 S 15:22; Am 4:4; 5:21-25; Ho 6:4-6; Is 1:10-17; Mi 6:6-8; Jr 7:21-29; Ps 50) against excessive ritualism to the neglect of the moral commandments. Just before the exile under Josiah (2 Ch 34-35) and in the post-exilic period under the leadership of Ezra (Ezr 9-10), however, this system of cultic purity was completed and fixed as necessary to maintain the identity of the Chosen People in the face of threatened extinction by the Gentiles.[45] Its observance was again tightened in face of the Greek occupation in the time of the Maccabees, as when the holy scribe Eleazar endured martyrdom rather than taste pork (2 M 6:18-31).[46]

The Pharisees, who may have originated in this Maccabean struggle, and whose very name probably means "separate," especially occupied themselves with the scrupulous enforcement of these regulations of ritual purity, some of which they extended beyond the actual biblical precepts.[47] Jesus, although he was even more zealous than the Pharisees (Jn 2:17), like the ancient prophets (Is 29:13) insisted on the

---

[44] See Peter Berger, *The Sacred Canopy*, for a sociological discussion of our secularized culture.

[45] See Gersion Appel, *A Philosophy of Mizvot*, pp. 38-41.

[46] See J. Goldstein, *I Maccabees* (1976); *II Maccabees* (1983) (Garden City, NY: Doubleday Anchor Bible), introduction.

[47] E.P. Sanders, *Jewish Law from Jesus to the Mishnah* (summary, pp. 245-254) refutes the notions that the Pharisees observed the ritual purity required of priests or that they were mere "legalists."

supremacy of the moral precepts over the ritual ones (Mt 23:23-24). He especially condemned the way in which the Pharisees had themselves undermined these moral precepts by ritual niceties attributed to the oral Torah (Mk 7:1-17), saying to them, "You disregard God's command- ment but cling to human tradition" (Mt 7:8).

On the basis of this interpretation of the law by Jesus ("Thus he declared all foods clean," Mk 7:19), Gentile converts were received in the early Church without requiring them to observe the code of ritual purity.[48] Instead of this "food ritual" which had done so much to edu- cate the Jews in monotheism and its moral implications, the Christian Church developed its own liturgy based on Jesus' commands to bap- tize (Mt 28:19) and to perform the Eucharist (Lk 22:19), with the other sacraments (e.g., the Anointing of the Sick, see Jm 5:13-15). The rela- tive simplicity of this fundamental liturgy then left room for the further elaboration of religious ceremonies in each local church according to its own culture.

The Reformers, especially the Calvinists, in the sixteenth cen- tury attempted to reduce Christian worship to preaching and unaccom- panied hymn-singing, on the grounds of Jesus' and Paul's criticisms of the Pharisees.[49] Thus, they over-spiritualized worship and deprived their churches of that symbolic instruction which respects the bodily nature of humanity and which has important moral implications.

We can, however, conclude that the ancient Torah of the Old Testament in its *entirety* remains relevant to present day Christian morality, and should be a primary source of moral theology and the formation of the Christian conscience. Its Jewish particularity and his-

---

[48] Mark 7:1-4 probably rhetorically exaggerates Pharisaic practice in an effort to make the opposition of the Pharisees to Jesus intelligible to a Gentile audience. See D.E. Nineham, *The Gospel of St. Mark*, pp. 188-197 and E.P. Sanders, *Jewish Law*, pp. 39-41. But see the extensive review of opinions and discussion in Robert H. Gundry, *Mark: A Commentary on His Apology for the Cross*, pp. 357-371.

[49] John Calvin, *Institutes of the Christian Religion*, n. 435, p. 263, says "The Lord, who long ago declared that nothing so much offended him as being worshiped by humanly devised rites, has not become untrue to himself" and quotes Jesus' denunciation of the Pharisees' "human traditions"; hence Calvinists devised a form of strictly biblical worship. See William D. Maxwell, *The Liturgical Patterns of the Genevan Service Book*, pp. 20-40.

torical conditioning raises a problem of universalization but does not devalue its moral precepts.

The Structure of Biblical Moral Theology

The scholastic theologians of the Middle Ages in commenting on the biblical Old and New Law came to distinguish between different senses of the term "law."[50] The Old Testament "Wisdom" or New Testament "Word" (Jn 1:1) they called the *divine law*, that is, *God's wise plan for his creatures leading all created persons to share in the communion of his own happiness.* Thus no other law has any authority except from its conformity to the divine law, God's Wisdom or Word. "Peter and the apostles said in reply [to the command of the high priest not to proclaim the Gospel], 'We must obey God rather than men'" (Ac 5:29).

This divine law is known to us in two ways. First, since we are created in God's image and share his intelligence, we can read something of his plan for the world and for our own lives in the embodiment of this plan or wisdom in the order of the cosmos and in our own human nature and its needs. This is called the *natural law* as written in what St. Bonaventure called "the Book of Creation,"[51] but of course it is a "law" only in the analogical sense that the functions of a building or a machine or a living organism are "written" into its very structure. A knife, a fork, and a spoon obviously have different forms and our reason reflecting on these forms has insight into the purposes for which they were made. This natural law takes on the full character of law only as our reason grasps God's plan reflected in his creation and comes to cooperate with him in completing this plan, using and perfecting his creation according to God's purposes, and our own insofar as they conform to God's. Thus natural law can best be defined as *our human participation by our reason in God's wise care of the world.*

This does not mean that the natural law is obvious in all its details

---

[50] St. Thomas Aquinas, *S.T.*, I-II, q. 91; cf. CCC # 1952.

[51] E.g., *Journey of the Mind to God*, Chapter I, n. 14, p. 16.

to everyone, as some philosophers of the eighteenth century (who wanted to avoid the necessity of religious faith) contended.[52] God's creation is filled with mysteries, and in particular our own human nature and its needs are an unfathomable mystery, as Qoheleth says:

> I have considered the task which God has appointed for men to be busied about. He has made everything appropriate to its time, and has put the timeless into their hearts, without men's ever discovering, from beginning to end, the work which God has done (Ec 3:10-11).[53]

Moreover, sin with its passions, pride, and prejudices has darkened our insight into our own natures and destiny. Thus natural moral laws are discovered by humanity only through long historical experience and earnest thought to which philosophy and science have much to contribute. Our understanding of the laws of nature will never be total. While outlines of the natural moral law are clear to most people in all cultures, its details are obscured.[54] For example, it should be obvious from the fact that the human race is approximately 50% men and 50% women, that monogamy is part of God's order of creation, yet in many of the cultures of the world, including that of ancient Israel (2 S 3:2-5, 5:13-16), it was considered morally acceptable that men of power and prestige have many wives. Again, it seems obvious, as our Declaration of Independence says, that all human beings were created

---

[52] See Yves Simon, *The Tradition of Natural Law*; Johannes Messner, *Social Ethics: Natural Law in the Western World*; M.B. Crow, *The Changing Profile of the Natural Law*, on different concepts of natural law.

[53] NJB, p. 1017, n. 3, comments on verse 11b (NAB "put the timeless into their hearts"), "This phrase, however, is not to be taken in the Christian sense; it means simply: God has given the human heart (mind) awareness of 'duration,' he has endowed it with the power of reflecting on the sequence of events and thus of controlling the present. But, the author adds, the awareness is deceptive; it does not reveal the meaning of life." Qoheleth's skepticism is only one side of a dialectical theme running throughout the Bible: God has revealed himself and his purposes, yet he and his plans remain mysterious, because "My thoughts are not your thoughts, nor are your ways my ways, says the Lord. As high as the heavens are above the earth, so high are my ways above your ways and my thoughts above your thoughts" (Is 55:8-9).

[54] CCC # 1960.

"free and equal" yet slavery was still accepted by the founders of our Republic (as it still was in the New Testament, cf. the Epistle to Philemon).

Because of this sinful blindness of humanity, God in his mercy has revealed the divine plan to us in a second way, by revelation given through the prophets in the Scriptures. This *revealed law* contains both the outline of the natural law so that it will be clearly known to all (the Ten Commandments) and also some additional guidance for Israel in its special vocation and circumstances (the ceremonial and judicial prescriptions of the Torah) and for the Church (such as the sacraments and the general structure of the Christian community). These commands over and above the natural law are called the *divine positive law*, that is, freely "posited" (willed) by divine authority.[55]

Finally, because the natural law requires us human beings to live in civil society and the divine positive law requires us to live also in the Church, the civil and ecclesiastical authorities have authority from God to make whatever additional laws are necessary for the good order of state and church, provided these are in conformity with divine and natural law. Such laws are called *civil* or *ecclesiastical* (canon)[56] positive *law* because they are made by human beings to implement God's laws in particular situations and are always subject to change as these situations change.

Thus in constructing a Christian moral theology we must first begin with the following data: (1) The Torah of the Old Testament, without which the New Testament teaching cannot be understood, since the New Testament presumes the Old, comments on and completes it. (2) We must then look to the New Testament for the correct interpretation and perfecting of this Jewish heritage of moral teaching. (3) In order to discriminate between elements in both Testaments which are historically conditioned we must use the concept of "natural law" to free this teaching from particular situations and universalize it. For example the Torah contains the commandment, "You shall not kill"

---

[55] CCC # 1961-1974.
[56] On civil law, cf. CCC # 2234-2246; On church law cf. CCC # 894-896; 2041-2043.

(Ex 20:13), but does not raise the question of abortion. The New Testament presupposes this commandment and teaches respect even for children and unborn life (Lk 1:44; 18:16-17); while natural law considerations lead to the conclusion that all human beings have the right to life. Thus the reason the New Testament contains relatively few concrete moral norms is because it presupposes so much of the Old Testament Torah and also leaves the way open for a more universal formulation of its unchangeable moral norms in the light of the experience of all humanity.

Some Protestant thinkers have objected that it is a vicious circle to admit that our natural reason is obscured by sin and therefore we need to submit it to the judgment of the revealed Word, yet at the same time to make use of natural law reasoning to universalize the biblical precepts. But if the grace of God can heal our natural reason so that it becomes again a useful instrument of faith in correctly understanding God's Word, this apparent circularity is resolved.

This development of thought about Christian morality from its source in the Bible has always taken place in the context of the Tradition of the Church. For example two of Jesus' own commands in the Sermon on the Mount: "Swear not at all" (Mt 5:34; cf. Jm 5:12)[57] and

---

[57] For the history of exegesis of this fourth antithesis see Ulrich Luz, *Matthew 1-7*, pp. 310-322. Luz, who assumes that Jesus sometimes abrogated the Old Law, concludes that both the divorce and the oath pericopes are eschatological ideals which cannot always be observed. But if Jesus never abrogates the Old Law, but only corrects misinterpretations, then we can distinguish the two cases: (1) Divorce was not approved by the Law, but only *tolerated*; and Jesus (Mt 5:31-32; 19:1-12) absolutely rejected this toleration for his disciples, except for invalid marriages (Mt 19:9). (2) The Law actually commanded oaths (Ex 22:10; Nb 5:19-22,), portrayed God as swearing by himself (Dt 4:31; 7:8; Nb 14:21; cf. Am 4:2; 6:8; Ezk 20:3, 33:11), and condemned perjury (Ex 20:7; Dt 5:11, Lv 19:12; cf. Is 48:1; Ho 4:2; Jr 5:2, etc.). Therefore, the error of the ancestors (Mt 5:33) was not in approving oaths, but, in excusing false oaths when taken not in the name of God but of creatures (Mt 5:34-37). Hence, Jesus, in line with the cautions against vain swearing in the wisdom literature (Ec 5:1; Si 23:9-11), taught that any statement, whether made under oath or not, must be truthful and that all casuistic lying was of the devil (Mt 5:37). Evidently, this is because the Decalogue implies that oaths made in the name of a creature implicitly refer to the Creator and all lies show disrespect to God. Hence the phrase which has given so much trouble, "Do not swear at all" stands in antithesis not to the commands of God to swear truly, but to the erroneous notion of the ancestors that it is permitted to swear falsely if one swears only in the name of a creature, and means "Do not swear falsely no matter what your excuse."

"No divorce and remarriage" (Mt 5:31-32) were interpreted more precisely by St. Paul. In the former case, St. Paul took the command as a figure of speech meaning "Tell the truth, even when not under oath," not as a prohibition against all oath-taking, since he himself did not hesitate to take an oath (Rm 1:9; 2 Cor 1:23; Gal 1:20).[58] In the latter case, he took the command literally as absolutely forbidding divorce and remarriage (1 Cor 7:10-11), yet gave a new solution to the situation of converts deserted by their spouses because of their conversion (1 Cor 7:15-16).[59] The Church accepted this development and further refined it as we see today in the Code of Canon Law.[60]

In the early Church and throughout Christian history, the Sermon on the Mount in the version in Matthew 5-7 has been used as the best summary of the Savior's interpretation of the Torah.[61] St. Augustine and St. Thomas Aquinas say that it "contains the total formation of the Christian life."[62] Today the common view of biblicists is that the author of Matthew composed this Sermon out of separate sayings of Jesus and colored it with his own theology.[63] There is, however, an even more concise summary, that most scholars would recognize as Jesus' own,

---

[58] CCC # 2153-2155. Of course it is possible that St. Paul did not know of Jesus' teaching on oaths, but, as James 5:12 (cf. Jm 2:8-13) shows, there seems to have been a tradition of Jesus' interpretation of the decalogue on which Paul, James, and Matthew all depend.

[59] See Benedict Viviano, NJBC, p. 643; and J.A. Fitzmyer, *To Advance the Gospel*, pp. 79-111, who comments, "The Matthean Jesus' words appeal beyond the Mosaic legislation and any ideal to the divine institution of marriage itself," p. 101.

[60] CCL, Canons 1191-1204.

[61] According to Luz, *Matthew*, pp. 218-223, the Catholic interpretation has been predominantly "perfectionist," while the mainstream Reformation tradition with its two-level ethic generally has taken it as "unfulfillable" in the present *simul iustus et peccator* condition of humanity. The Radical Reformation, however, took it in the perfectionist sense and very literally.

[62] Augustine, *Sermon on the Mount*, PL 34, 1231, quoted by Aquinas, *S.T.*, III, q. 108, a. 3, *sed contra* and paraphrased in corpus.

[63] According to Luz, *Matthew*, pp. 213-214, the Sermon on the Mount is based on Q (the Sayings Source) as it appears in the Sermon on the Plain (Lk 6:20-49) to which Matthew has added other material, partly from Q and partly special to Matthew. See also, Jacques Dupont, *Les Béatitudes*, I, *Le problème littéraire*. For a review of opinions see Warren Carter, *What Are They Saying about Matthew's Sermon on the Mount?* (New York/Mahwah, NJ: Paulist Press, 1994), pp. 9-34.

namely, his reply to the scribe who asked him which was the first of all the commandments:

> "'Hear, O Israel! The Lord our God is Lord alone! You shall love the Lord your God with all your heart, and with all your soul, with all your mind, and with all your strength' [Dt 6:4-5]. The second is this: 'You shall love your neighbor as yourself' [Lv 19:18]. There is no other commandment greater than these" (Mk 12:29-31; par. Mt 22:34-40; Lk 10:25-28).

This saying of Jesus was already known to St. Paul before the Gospels were written (Rm 13:8-10; Gal 5:14; cf. Jm 2:8). Paul goes so far as to say, "For the whole law is fulfilled by one statement, namely 'You shall love your neighbor as yourself'" (Gal 5:14; cf. also 1 Jn 4:7-21; Tb 4:15a).

St. Paul further explicates this saying in the glorious Chapter 13 of 1 Corinthians where he shows that the "more excellent way" (more excellent even than the working of miracles and wonders) is the way of love, and concludes "faith, hope, and love remain, these three; but the greatest of these is love" (1 Cor 13:13; cf. 13:7; 1 Th 1:3; 5:8; Col 1:3-5).[64] Love is the greatest way of life, but the love of which Paul speaks is not just any "love" but the *agape* (charity) or love rooted in faith in God through Jesus by the power of the Holy Spirit and in the hope of his salvation, "Calling to mind your work of faith and labor of love and endurance in hope of our Lord Jesus Christ, before our God and Father" (1 Th 1:3). "Hope does not disappoint, because the love of God has been poured out into our hearts through the Holy Spirit that has been given to us" (Rm 5:5). Thus Paul correctly interprets Jesus' Love Commandment as meaning that the Christian life is summed up as a life of love based on faith and hope in Jesus.

Such a life is already a share in the divine life of Father, Son, and Holy Spirit because as 1 John (4:8b-16) teaches,

> God is Love. In this way the love of God was revealed to us: God sent his only Son into the world so that we might have life

---

[64] The most thorough exegetical treatment is Ceslas Spicq, O.P, *Agape in the New Testament*, vol. 2, pp. 120-121, 168-172, 218-222.

through him. In this is love: not that we have loved God, but that
he loved us and sent his Son as an expiation for our sins. Beloved, if God so loved us, we also must love one another. No one
has ever seen God, yet if we love one another, God remains in
us, and his love is brought to perfection in us. This is how we
know that we remain in him and he in us, that he has given us of
his Spirit. Moreover, we have seen and testify that the Father
sent his Son as savior of the world. Whoever acknowledges that
Jesus is the Son of God, God remains in him and he in God. We
have come to know and to believe in the love God has for us.

Are the Cardinal Virtues Biblical?

Thus a firm foundation for a Christian moral theology can only be a
study of Christian love, and the faith and hope such love presupposes.
Faith, hope, and love (1 Th 1:3; 5:8; 1 Cor 13:13) are technically called
the *theological virtues* (or more correctly as the Greek Fathers say,
theologal virtues[65]) because their object first of all is the Triune God.[66]
Yet, in the writings of Hellenistic Jews, such as Philo of Alexandria,
the Fathers of the Church, such as Clement of Alexandria, Origen, the
Cappadocians and Maximus the Confessor in the East, and Ambrose,
Jerome, Augustine, and Gregory the Great in the West, the scholastics
of the Middle Ages, the post-Tridentine moral theologians and now in

---

[65] The term "theological virtues" can be misunderstood to mean those virtues of which
theology treats, i.e., all virtues; while "theologal" signifies only those virtues which
have God as their direct object and thus applies exclusively to faith, hope, and love.

[66] CCC # 1812-1829. For biblical grounding see Ceslas Spicq, O.P., *Théologie Morale du
Nouveau Testament*, vol. 1, Chapters VVI, vol. 2, VII; also Hans Conzelmann, *1
Corinthians*, pp. 217-231.

[67] CCC # 1805-1809. In the East the tradition begins with Clement of Alexandria (who
was probably dependent on the Jewish writer Philo), *Stromata* VI, PG 9:316 (35).
Clement quotes Wisdom 8:7 and attributes the learning of the Greeks to Moses. In the
West St. Ambrose is the first to use the term "cardinal" (*In Lucam* 5, PL 15:1649)
where previous writers had spoken of "primary" or "principal" virtues. He treats them
extensively (*De Officiis* I, cc. 25-50, ANF, pp.20-43; PL 16:57-102) and accepts Philo's
four rivers of Eden allegory (*De paradiso*, 3. 14-18, PL 14:280-282, FC pp. 295-299),
but considers temperance the greatest of the four (*De Jacobo* 1.2.5, PL 14: 600-601; FC
pp. 122-123).

the *Catechism of the Catholic Church*,[67] there was and is also a recognition of the so-called *cardinal* ("hinge") *virtues: prudence, justice, fortitude* and *temperance*, terms which were borrowed from the Greek philosophy of Plato, Aristotle, and the Stoics.[68] Augustine sums it up:

> If God is man's chief good, which you cannot deny, it clearly follows, since to seek the chief good is to live well, that to live well is nothing else but to love God with all the heart, with all the soul, with all the mind; and, as arising from this, that this love must be preserved entire and uncorrupt, which is the part of temperance; that it give way before no troubles, which is the part of fortitude; that it serve no other, which is the part of justice; that it be watchful in inspection of things lest craft or fraud steal in, which is the part of prudence. This is the one perfection of man, by which alone he can succeed in attaining to the purity of truth. This, both Testaments enjoin in concert, is commended on both sides alike.[69]

In order to relate the patristic and medieval development of what today we call moral theology to a genuinely biblical foundation, it is necessary to ask whether this schema of the cardinal virtues has any real basis in the Bible. It would appear it does not, since this fourfold

---

[68] This fourfold division of virtue goes back to Plato (*Republic*, IV, c. 6) but was foreshadowed in the writings of some Greek poets and orators. Aristotle treats them in *Nicomachean Ethics* (Bk III, Chapter 6 to V, Chapter 11). The Stoics developed them (see Diogenes Laertius, *Lives of the Philosophers*, VII, "Zeno," 92), and they were taken up by Hellenistic Jews. Philo replaces *phronesis*, "prudence" with *eusebeia*, "piety" and compares them to the four rivers in Eden (*Legum Allegoriae* I, 19, 63-87); cf. also *Fourth Maccabees*. Cicero (*De finibus* V. c. 23, n. 67, pp. 469-470) defines them neatly: *Fortitudo in laboribus periculisque cernatur, temperantia in praetermittendis volumptatibus, prudentia in delectu bonorum et malorum, iustitia in suo cuique tribuendo* (Courage is displayed in toils and dangers, Temperance in foregoing pleasures, Prudence in the choice of goods and evils, Justice in giving each his due); but then reduced them to the single virtue of wisdom. See Helen F. North, "Canons and Hierarchies of the Cardinal Virtues in Greek and Latin Literature," *The Classical Tradition*, pp. 174-178 and Marcia L. Colish, *The Stoic Tradition*, II, pp. 59-66; 87-88; 212-220; 297-300.

[69] St. Augustine, *On the Morals of the Catholic Church*, Chapter 25, 46; PL 32:1309-1378, NPF, IV. p. 54. An especially clear presentation of these virtues (following Augustine) can be found in Julianus Pomerius, *The Contemplative Life*, Book III, Chapters 18-33, pp. 143-167.

list is only once explicitly mentioned in the Bible and then only in the late Old Testament deuterocanonical Book of Wisdom written not in Hebrew but in Greek: "For she [Wisdom] teaches temperance and prudence, justice and fortitude, and nothing in life is more useful for humans than these" (Ws 8:7).[70]

There is, however, an important text in the New Testament which implicitly confirms this fourfold list along with the threefold theologal virtues:

> He [God] has bestowed on us the precious and very great promises, so that through them you may come to share in the divine nature, and escape from the corruption that passion brought into the world. For this very reason, make every effort to supplement your faith (*pistis*) with virtue (*arete*), virtue with knowledge (*gnosis*), knowledge with self-control (*enkrateia*), self-control with endurance (*hypomene*), endurance with devotion (*eusebeia*), devotion with mutual affection (*philadelphia*), mutual affection with love (*agape*) (2 P 1:5-7).

Here we see faith (*pistis*) as the beginning of all virtue (*arete*), with love (*agape*) of God and of neighbor (*philadelphia*) as its consummation. Although the theologal virtue of hope is not named, the context shows that it is hope in God's promises and his power to fulfill them which motivates this whole search for virtue. Between faith and love the notion of *arete* is explicated as *gnosis, enkrateia, hypomene, eusebeia. Gnosis* and *enkrateia* are commonly used synonyms for *sophia* (wisdom; prudence as such is *phronesis*) and *sophrosyne* (temperance). *Hypomene* (endurance) is named rather than *arete* (fortitude) to avoid confusion with the use of *arete* as virtue in general in v. 5 and because the New Testament emphasizes the enduring, patient aspect of fortitude rather than its aggressive aspects. As for *eusebeia,* this is often translated "godliness" (RSV) and used even in pagan literature for righteousness or justice.

It is not necessary, however, to depend on these two unique texts from Wisdom and 2 Peter to ground the cardinal virtues biblically. As I will show in detail in subsequent chapters, they are each well attested

---

[70] See comments of C. Larcher, O.P., *Le Livre de La Sagesse*, vol. 2, pp. 528-529.

elsewhere in the Bible under various names, although not listed together as a group. We need to ask, however, "What is the relation of these four cardinal virtues, which are primarily directed to one's neighbor and one's self, to the three theological virtues, which are primarily directed to God?" As an answer to this question, I would suggest that these traditional cardinal virtues can be integrated with the three Christian theological virtues in the following way:

1. Prudence (Greek *phronesis*) in the Bible is often called "wisdom" (Hebrew *hokma*; Greek *sophia*) and true wisdom is identified with faith. "The wisdom that is from above is first of all pure, then peaceable, gentle, compliant, full of mercy and good fruits, without inconstancy or insincerity" (Jm 3:17; cf. 1 Cor 1:17-25). Thus Christian prudence is the practical aspect of faith, the understanding of what faith requires of us in response to God's self-revelation to us.[71]

2. Justice (Hebrew *sedaqa*; Greek *dikaiosyne*) in the Bible is often translated "righteousness" and is related to "covenant-love" (Hebrew *hesed* or *emet*; Greek *agape*). Thus Christian love always includes a respect for the rights of others. "Blessed are they who hunger and thirst for righteousness" (Mt 5:6); this is summed up in the Golden Rule, "Do to others whatever you would have them do to you. This is the law and the prophets" (Mt 7:12) while elsewhere (Mt 22:37-40) it is also said that "the whole law and the prophets depend on these two commandments," namely, the love of God and neighbor. It is this justice that makes possible the community of the Church in which our response to God's self-revelation is alone possible.

3. Temperance (moderation or discipline; in Greek *sophrosyne* or *enkrateia*) and fortitude (courage; in Greek *macrothymia* or *hypomone*, endurance, or *parresia*, boldness, confidence) relate to our own self-love. In our frailty as creatures and especially as bodily creatures we have to learn to love ourselves rightly if we are to "love our neighbors as ourselves," by controlling our desires for immediate bodily satisfactions or pleasures (temperance). "For the grace of God has ap-

---

[71] See EDNT, H. Hegermann, "*sophia*," 3:258-261; K. Kertelge, "*dikaiosyne*," 1:325-330; H. Goldstein, "*enkrateia*," 1:377-378; H.W. Hollander, "*makrothymia*," 2:380-381; H. Balz, "*paressia*," 3: 45-47; D. Zeller, "*sophrosyne*," 3: 329-330; W. Radl, "*hypomone*," 3:405-406.

peared, saving all and training us to reject godless ways and worldly desires and to live temperately (*sophronos*), justly, and devoutly in this age" (Tt 2:12). "The fruit of the Spirit is love, joy, peace, patience (*makrothymia*), kindness, generosity, faithfulness, gentleness, self-control (*enkrateia*)" (Gal 5:22-23; cf. 2 P 1:6). We must also learn to endure the sufferings, sacrifices, and spiritual warfare of life and yet courageously witness to the truth in word and deed (fortitude). "Pray... that speech may be given me... to make known with boldness (*parresia*) the mystery of the gospel... so that I may have the courage (*parresia*) to speak as I must" (Eph 6:18-20). Thus these virtues are integral to Christian hope, since hope of ultimate joy in God overcomes the immoderate search for earthly pleasure and the fear of suffering.

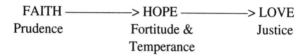

FAITH ————> HOPE ————> LOVE
Prudence   Fortitude &   Justice
                  Temperance

Therefore, the following introduction to moral theology will be organized around the three theological virtues and the four cardinal virtues integrated with them in the way just shown. The three supreme virtues will be further unified by the ordination of faith to hope and hope to love. It is love alone that attains to the everlasting life of the Trinity, but the One God is not only Love, he "is light and in him there is no darkness at all" (1 Jn 1:5). Hence, when the light of faith has become vision and all we hoped for fulfilled, love will rest in God's infinite Truth. This Truth even now shines forth to us in the glory of the life of the New Adam, Jesus and his saints, of whom the New Eve, Mary, is first of all.[72]

> You [the Messiah] are the most handsome of men; fair speech has graced your lips, for God has blessed you forever... All glorious is the king's daughter [the Bride, Israel, the Church, Mary] as she enters, her raiment threaded with spun gold. In embroidered apparel she is led to the king (Ps 45:3, 14-15).

---

[72] VS, nn. 1, 28-34, 116-117 on how morality must be grounded in the Truth, who is Christ. Hans Urs von Balthasar has especially developed the theology of *beauty* (glory) as the "splendor of truth" which begets love and thus draws us to live in harmony with God who is Truth. See John O'Donnell, S.J. *Hans Urs von Balthasar.*

PART I

FAITH

CHAPTER 2

LIVING BY FAITH

Are we then annulling the law by this faith [in Jesus Christ]?
Of course not! On the contrary, we are supporting the law (Rm 3:31)

A: THE VIRTUE OF FAITH

How Jesus Knew God

According to the faith of the apostolic Church recorded in the Gospels, John the Baptist, who was the last and greatest of the prophets of the Old Testament (Mt 11:11), testified that Jesus was far mightier than he, since Jesus would bring down the Holy Spirit on the baptized (Mk 1:7-8). The Gospels present Jesus in his human nature not only as the greatest of the prophets but also as a mystic, who in his own baptism heard the voice of the Father, and experienced the presence of the Spirit descending upon himself, as he again heard the divine voice in the transfiguration on the mountain (Mk 9:2-8), and also spoke with Moses and Elijah, the great prophets of old who had been taken up to God. The Gospels report that he foresaw his own destiny on the Cross and his resurrection (Mk 8:31-33; 9:30-32; 10:32-34; Mt 16:21-23; 17:22-23; 20:17-19; Lk 9:22-27; 9:44-45; 18:31-34; cf. Jn 2:19-22; 3:14-15, etc.).

In the Synoptics Jesus is portrayed as living in constant intimacy with his heavenly Father, "No one knows the Son except the Father, and no one knows the Father except the Son and anyone to whom the Son wishes to reveal him" (Mt 11:27; Lk 10:21-22).[1] The Fourth Gos-

---

[1] Most exegetes assign this text to the hypothetical early source Q, Klopenborg, *Q Parallels*, p. 79.

pel insists that Jesus was always conscious of the presence of the Father and of his own unity with the Father and knew the secret thoughts of human hearts (Jn 1:50-51; 2:24-25; 4:17; 6:64; 7:29; 8:14; 10:15; 10:30; 16:30, etc.).

Consequently, Aquinas and the scholastics generally held that in his human nature already during his earthly life Jesus always beheld God face-to-face in the "beatific vision" as we hope to do with the saints in heaven. Yet this has never been defined by the Church, although it was maintained by Pius XII in his encyclical, *Mystici Corporis* (1943).[2]

Post-Vatican II theology has raised serious questions about whether this scholastic teaching is compatible with the biblical doctrine that the historical Jesus was a man like us "who has been similarly tested in every way, yet without sin" (Heb 4:15) and with a few other texts that seem to indicate a lack of knowledge on his part (principally, Mk 13:32, par. Mt 24:36; Mk 5:30, par. Mt 9:22; Lk 2:52). But are these texts conclusive?[3]

---

[2] See Commissio Theologica Internationalis, "La conscience que Jesus avait de lui-meme et de sa mission. Quatre propositions avec commentaire," *Gregorianum* 67/3, 1986, pp. 413-427. For references to magisterial documents see William G. Most, *The Consciousness of Christ*, pp. 137-144. The present teaching of the Church on this question is summed up in CCC # 471-474: "# 472: This human soul that God's Son assumed is endowed with a true human intellect, which — precisely because it is human — could not be unlimited in itself, but was exercised in the historical conditions of his existence in time... This limitation corresponded to the reality of his voluntary emptying of himself into 'the condition of a slave' [Ph 2:7]." "# 473: But at the same time, this truly human knowledge of God's Son expressed the divine life of his person... Such is first of all the case with the intimate and immediate knowledge that the Son of God become human has of his Father [Mk 14:36; Mt 11:17; Jn 1:18; 8:55, etc.]. The Son in his human intellect also showed divine perception of the secret thoughts of the human heart [Mk 2:8; Jn 2:25; 6:61, etc.]." "# 474: By its union to the divine Wisdom in the person of the Word incarnate, Christ's human intellect enjoyed in all its fullness the knowledge of the eternal economy he had come to reveal [Mk 8:31; 9:31; 10:33-34; 14:18-20, 26-30] What he recognized himself as not knowing in this area, he declared himself not sent to reveal [Mk 13:32; Acts 1:7]." "# 478: Jesus knew and loved each and every one of us during his life, his agony and his passion, and gave himself up for each of us."

[3] See the bibliography in Most, *The Consciousness of Christ*, pp. 169-170. Widely known is the theory of Karl Rahner, "Dogmatic Reflections on the Knowledge and Self-Consciousness of Christ," *Theological Investigations*, V, pp. 193-215 who held for a "direct, but not beatific vision." Against Rahner, Most (pp. 148-153) argues that Christ's vision was superior to that of the blessed, since it was a direct consequence of the hypostatic union of his human soul with his Divine Person.

For our purposes here it is sufficient to say that since Jesus' human knowledge of the Father even in this life was the source of our faith, it transcended our faith, yet is the model for it, eminently exemplifying all that our faith should be, and tested by every trial that our faith must meet. This transcendent knowing of Jesus was not simply "trust" which relies on the goodness and power of God (that pertains rather to theologal hope), but was fidelity to the absolute truth of God who is Truth ("God is light," 1 Jn 1:5), to whom Jesus bears witness: "For this was I born and for this I came into the world, to testify to the truth. Everyone who belongs to the truth listens to my voice. Pilate said to him, 'What is truth?'" (Jn 18:37-38). The answer to Pilate's cynical question is to be found in the words the Fourth Gospel attributes to Jesus: "I am the truth, the way, and the life. If you know me you will also know my Father" (Jn 14:6-7). Christian faith, therefore, is absolute fidelity to the truth of God (the Word of God) as God reveals himself to us.

The total commitment of Jesus to God as Truth was the culmination of the history of faith recounted in the Old Testament and summed up in Mary of Nazareth's response to Gabriel's message from God of the Good News of the Savior's coming: "May it be done to me according to your word" (Lk 1:38). Mary did not speak for herself alone, but for all believing Israel throughout the ages. The often misunderstood doctrine of her Immaculate Conception expresses this long history by which God had prepared Mary to speak for her people the word of humble faith which alone could open the way for God's greatest act of grace, the Incarnation.[4]

In Hebrews 11-12:2 (cf. Si 44:1-50:21) we have the names of some of these great forerunners of Mary's faith: Abel, Enoch, Abraham, Isaac, Jacob, Joseph, Moses, Gideon, Barak, Samson, Jephtah, Samuel, David, and many others not named. The whole Old Testament turns on the narrative of how Abraham went out of his native land at the call of faith, even consenting to sacrifice his only son on whom all God's promises to him seemed to depend. Then it recounts how Moses led Israel out of slavery into the Promised Land and how the prophets

---

[4] CCC # 494, # 506. See André Feuillet, *Jesus and His Mother*, especially pp. 110-112.

foretold the coming of a righteous King anointed by the Spirit. Finally it tells how Ezra and Nehemiah led the people back from exile, and how the Maccabees revived the fidelity of the Chosen People to their vocation when they had lost their national freedom.

The Old Testament also gives unique praise to women of faith such as Sarah, Rachel, Deborah, Rahab, Ruth, Esther, Judith, and the mother of the Maccabees. Of all of these great women Mary is the spiritual daughter whose faith summed up and exceeded that of all her forebears, women and men. Of her Elizabeth, mother of the Baptist, said, "Blessed are you who believed that what was spoken to you by the Lord would be fulfilled" (Lk 1:45).

Faith and Life

The "Wisdom" which the Wisdom literature promotes is first of all this same faith in God the Truth: "The beginning of wisdom is the fear of the Lord, and knowledge of the Holy One is understanding" (Pr 9:10).[5] The prophetical books also are filled with the refrain, "Hear the Word of the Lord," which cannot be heard without faith. "An ox knows its owner, and an ass its master's manger; But Israel does not know, my people has not understood" (Is 1:3).[6]

To understand why all human history had to be a history of faith we must turn to the first chapters of Genesis where we have God's Word in narrative form showing us what God created us to be.[7] Superior to the rest of the visible creation, we were created in God's image

---

[5] William McKane, *Proverbs: A New Approach*, p. 368f. says this verse shows that earlier notions of "wisdom" as mere intellectual discipline developed into a realization that it must also be rooted in faith in God ("fear of the Lord").

[6] According to J. Jensen, NJBC, p. 231, this way of portraying the paternal complaint of God shows literary contact with the wisdom tradition.

[7] See CCC # 356-358 on the meaning of the phrase "the image of God." For exegetical discussion of its meaning see C. Westermann's commentary on Gn 1:26-27, *Genesis 1-11*. His own conclusion is that the "image of God" in v. 27 "means that the uniqueness of human beings consists in their being God's counterparts. The relation to God is not something which is added to human existence; humans are created in such a way that their very existence is intended to be their relationship to God" (p. 158).

(Gn 1:26, 27; 5:1), so that we are partners with him in the governance of the visible creation.

> "Let us make humans in our image, after our likeness. Let them have dominion over the fish of the sea, the birds of the air, and the cattle, and over all the wild animals and all the creatures that crawl on the ground" (Gn 1:26; cf. 5:3; 9:6; Si 17:1).

Adam and Eve are given the Garden to "cultivate and care for it" (Gn 2:15), that is, to conserve but also to perfect the world. This dominion over the world implies intelligence and free will, spiritual powers that make us like God, who is Spirit and hence not to be represented by any image (Ex 20:4) except the living, thinking, choosing human being.

Thus what makes us human and God-like is our intelligence, our capacity for *truth* and the freedom which flows from knowing the truth. "You will know the truth and the truth will set you free" (Jn 8:32). To be free is to be able to choose among real not merely apparent goods, and it is a true vision of reality that makes this possible for us. Adam and Eve,[8] if they had not sinned would have continued to see things as they really are, as when Adam named all other creatures and came to the self-awareness that none of the other creatures were his own kind (Gn 2:20), except Eve, "bone of my bones and flesh of my flesh" (Gn 2:23), whom he freely and joyfully took to be his covenant partner in life.

Our human capacity to know and rule our world, to conserve and cultivate it, however, has its limits. Although we are spiritual, God-like, yet we are also part of the material universe, made out of the mud of the earth (Gn 2:7) and by our bodily existence liable to death like the

---

[8] In the light of modern scholarship, it seems that the inspired and inerrant religious message of the Adam and Eve narrative is not concerned with who the first humans were, where they lived, or their anatomy or stage of cultural development, but with what God created all us humans to be and how we are intended to care and develop our environment, all of which would have been realized if our sins had never distorted the Creator's work. This message is conveyed in a picturesque and symbolic manner which needs to be interpreted in the light of ancient literature. Cf. CCC # 369-384. In # 375 CCC speaks of "the symbolism of biblical language" and # 390 of "figurative language" in these chapters of Genesis which requires authoritative interpretation by the Church.

other animals. Consequently, the author of Genesis understood very well that we need an *instruction* (*torah*, usually but somewhat misleadingly translated as "law"[9]) from God, a revelation of God's purposes for us beyond our own wisdom and our understanding of our own needs and destiny.

> The Lord God gave man this command: "You are free to eat from any of the trees of the garden except the tree of knowledge of good and bad. From that tree you shall not eat; the moment you eat from it you are surely doomed to die" (Gn 2:16-17).

The story has already told us that

> Out of the ground the Lord God made various trees grow that were delightful to look at and good for food, with the tree of life in the middle of the garden and the tree of the knowledge of good and evil (Gn 2:9).

We can surmise from this enigmatic text that God intended that someday Adam and Eve should eat of the Tree of Life at the center of their garden,[10] that the gift of immortal life was far beyond what their origin from the dust would have deserved, and that they could not eat of the Tree of Life without God's permission. Explicitly God warned them that if they chose instead the Tree of the Knowledge of Good and Evil the result would be a death like that of all the other animals. Why? They did not fully understand God's warning, but were asked to trust God's greater wisdom.

We learn why when the story goes on to tell us of how Eve was tempted by the serpent. The serpent began by implying that God's command is an arbitrary restriction on human freedom: "Did God really tell you not to eat from any of the trees in the garden?" Eve truth-

---

[9] For the wide sense which "torah" attained in Judaism see Jacob Neusner, *Torah Through the Ages*, pp. 89-91.

[10] This symbol is interpreted by the writer of Revelation as the gift of eternal life promised by God as a reward of obedience, "To the victor I will give the right to eat from the tree of life that is in the garden of God" (Rv 2:7b).

fully denies that God has forbidden any but the one tree, and the serpent then says:

> "You certainly will not die! No. God knows well that the moment you eat of it your eyes will be opened and you will be like gods who know what is good and what is bad." The woman saw that the tree was good for food, pleasing to the eyes, and desirable for gaining wisdom. So she took some of its fruit and ate it; and she also gave some to her husband, who was with her, and he ate it. Then the eyes of both of them were opened, and they realized that they were naked; so they sewed fig leaves together and made loincloths for themselves (Gn 3:1-7).[11]

From this text it is evident that the "knowledge of good and bad" is freedom to decide what is good and bad *independent* of God's judgment of what is good and bad. Merely to be God's co-workers in the governance of the world and human life can seem to us not to be enough. Hence, Adam and Eve demanded to be gods in their own right, rivals of God. The "eyes of both of them were opened" not because up to that time they were blind and ignorant (Adam must have seen the animals he so wisely named!), but in the sense that they now viewed the world no longer in the light of God's Wisdom, his instruction, but purely from their own point of view, which had become the serpent's point of view — and the serpent (the devil) "is a liar and the father of lies" (Jn 8:44). Henceforth humanity lives no longer in the truth of God but in a world of illusion.

---

[11] Feminists often criticize this account as blaming Eve rather than Adam, but in fact God demands an accounting from Adam, as head of this first family (Eph 5:23) and not from Eve. Adam's despicable excuse blaming both Eve and God, "The woman whom you put here with me — she gave me fruit from the tree, so I ate it," shows him in even a worse light than his wife. Probably Genesis intends to refute certain pagan myths (e.g., the Greek story of Pandora) which satirized woman as a trap created by the gods to keep man weak lest he become their rival. When 1 Tm 2:14 argues that women must obey their husbands because, "Further, Adam was not deceived, but the woman was deceived and transgressed," the logic of the argument requires the text to mean not that Eve alone sinned, but rather that she had no right to act independently of Adam, since he was head of the family. But Adam, since he "was not deceived" had the greater responsibility and the greater sin. Hence St. Paul blames original sin on Adam not on Eve (Rm 5:12-14; paradoxically the revised NAB in its care for inclusive language now reads "one person" instead of "one man"!).

Since Adam and Eve had lost their way to the Tree of Life, they were banished forever into the desert where death would eventually overtake them, and where they would live only in enslavement (the curse on Eve, Gn 3:16) and poverty (the curse on Adam, Gn 3:17-19). These punishments are not arbitrary actions of God, but the inevitable *consequences* of men and women trying to live only by their own truth rather than God's truth. Yet, as John Paul II says in *The Splendor of Truth*:

> No darkness of error or sin can totally take away from man the light of God the Creator. In the depths of his heart there always remains a yearning for absolute truth and a thirst to attain full knowledge of it. This is eloquently proved by man's tireless search for knowledge in all fields. It is proved even more by his search for *the meaning of life*. The development of science and technology, this splendid testimony of the human capacity for understanding and for perseverance, does not free humanity from the obligation to ask the ultimate religious questions.[12]

Hence, Genesis tells us that the merciful God did not abandon his wayward children but immediately began to ease their miseries (the gift of garments, Gn 3:21; the beginning of human crafts, Gn 4:2, 20-22) and to promise their eventual redemption (the defeat of the serpent, conversion from sin, Gn 3:14-15).

From this initial story of the Bible, expressed in symbolic and archetypal terms, but which is developed in various other ways throughout the Scriptures, we learn that the deepest need of our natures is for *truth*. Without a true understanding of who we are and what we were made for we cannot find the right way in life. Hence we desperately need God's instruction (*torah*) to guide our lives for two reasons: (1) God our Creator alone can fully know the purpose for which he created us, the goal toward which we must travel, which is nothing less than life with God, a mystery infinitely beyond our intelligence to imagine. "'What eye has not seen, and ear has not heard, and what has not entered the human heart, what God has prepared for those who love him,'

---

[12] N. 1.

this God has revealed to us through the Spirit" (1 Cor 2:9-10 quoting Is 64:3). (2) We no longer live in the luminous world which God designed to light us surely and safely to himself, but in a darkened world where God's plan has been obscured by human sin, a world of confusing lies and outrageous injustices.

Since God's instruction is a Wisdom that to our world seems foolishness (St. Paul says, "Now the natural person does not accept what pertains to the Spirit of God, for to him it is foolishness, and he cannot understand it, because it is judged spiritually" 1 Cor 3:14), we must walk by *faith* just as we are instructed by God. Thus faith is the foundation of the whole Christian life, "For in it [the Gospel] is revealed, the righteousness of God from faith to faith, as it is written, 'The one who is righteous by faith will live'" (Rm 1:17; cf. Heb 2:4, 10:38; Gal 3:11).[13]

As St. Augustine[14] and St. Thomas Aquinas[15] say, we believe God, by God, and in God, i.e., God is the object of our faith (*believe God*), the light (formal object) or authority on which we believe him (*by God*), and the One to whom we seek to be united by believing in him (*in God*). Faith is thus necessary to our salvation as the indispensable means of attaining to God.[16]

Faith and Doubt

Etymologically "faith" (*pistis*) in the New Testament corresponds to the Old Testament Hebrew root *'mn* signifying "stability," "solidity," and suggests the idea of "something that sustains, upholds, or is a durable support."[17] "The Lord your God is God indeed, the faithful God who keeps his merciful covenant down to the thousandth generation"

---

[13] On the translation of this verse, so important to the thought of Luther and the Reformers, see J.A. Fitzmyer, S.J., NJBC, p. 834.

[14] *Tractates to the Gospel of St. John*, FC, vol. 3, tract. 29, 14-21 (3) pp. 18-19; PL 35:1651.

[15] *S.T.*, II-II, q. 2, a. 2.

[16] CCC # 26-49, 144-184.

[17] Ceslas Spicq, O.P., *Théologie Morale du Nouveau Testament*, I. p. 230, note 2.

(Dt 7:9; cf. also Gn 15:6; Ex 14:3; Dt 32:4; Is 49:7; Jr 10:10; Ps 31:6; 145:13). Thus faith rests on God's fidelity to his promises, which is the same as God's fidelity to himself. He is the "Rock": "I love you, O Lord, my strength. O Lord, my rock, my fortress, my deliverer. My God; my rock of refuge, my shield, the horn of my salvation, my stronghold!" (Ps 18:3). As Balaam said in prophecy, "God is not man that he should speak falsely, nor human that he should change his mind. Is he one to speak and not act, to decree and not to fulfill?" (Nb 23:19), and St. Paul, "God must be true, though every human being is a liar" (Rm 3:4).

Therefore, we ought to put our faith in God alone. "It is better to take refuge in the Lord than to trust in man" (Ps 118:8), because he is Truth and human promises get their truth only from him: "He who takes an oath in the land shall swear by the God of truth" (Is 65:16).

This same complex of meaning is carried over into the New Testament. When St. Paul wants to assure the Corinthians of his fidelity to the promises he has made them, he writes:

> As God is faithful, our word to you is not "yes" and "no." For the Son of God, Jesus Christ, who was proclaimed to you by us, Silvanus and Timothy and me, was not "yes" and "no," but "yes" has been in him. For however many are the promises of God, their "yes" is in him; therefore, the Amen from us also goes through him to God for glory. But the one who gives us security with you in Christ and who anointed us is God; he has also put his seal upon us and given the Spirit in our hearts as a first installment (2 Cor 1:18-22).[18]

Thus Jesus is the fulfillment of all God's promises and our faith in him is faith in the Triune God. This text also indicates the liturgical use of "Amen" (a Hebrew word expressing trust, confirmation, agreement, and from the same root as the word for faith, 'mn) as an expres-

---

[18] Paul had sent word from Corinth that he was going to Macedonia and then would return to Jerusalem by way of Corinth, but had to change his plans. He does not want the Corinthians to think his Gospel message is as changeable as his travel plans. The same thought is found in Heb 13:8, "Jesus Christ is the same yesterday, today and forever." See also comment of Jerome Murphy-O'Connor, NJBC p. 818.

sion of confidence in and obedience to God's Word (see for example, the Twelve Curses, Dt 27:14-26 against those unfaithful to God's covenant).

In the New Testament the fullest statement on the nature of faith is in the texts of Hebrews 10:37-12:2 already referred to:

> "For, after just a brief moment, he who is to come shall come; he shall not delay. But my just one shall live by faith, and if he draws back I take no pleasure in him" [Hab 2:3-4; cf. Rm 1:17; Gal 3:11]. We are not among those who draw back and perish, but among those who have faith and possess life. Faith is the realization of what is hoped for and evidence of things not seen. Because of it the ancients were attested. By faith we understand the universe was ordered by the word of God, so that what is visible came into being through the invisible. By faith Abel, etc... [listing examples of faith: Heb 10:37-39; 11:1-4]... Yet all these, though approved because of their faith, did not receive what had been promised. God had foreseen something better for us, so that without us they should not be made perfect. Therefore, since we are surrounded by so great a cloud of witnesses, let us rid ourselves of every burden and sin that clings to us and persevere in running the race that lies before us, while keeping our eyes fixed on Jesus, the leader and perfecter of faith. For the sake of the joy that lay before him he endured the cross, despising its shame, and has taken his seat at the right of the throne of God.

The Fathers of the Church regarded Hebrews 11:1 in this text as the most succinct biblical definition of faith: "Faith is the substance (*hypostasis*) of what is hoped for, the proof (*elenchos*) of what is not evident (*blepomenon*)." Aquinas[19] says this is a good definition because it indicates that faith is a supernatural virtue since it attains the mystery of what is possessed now only in hope (since it "is not evident") but nevertheless is held with a firm conviction ("proof").[20]

---

[19] *S.T.*, II-II, q. 4, a. 1; *De Veritate*, q. 14, a. 2.

[20] While some modern exegetes question whether a definition is intended and disagree on the exact force to be given to *hypostasis* and *elenchos*, nevertheless this entire passage of Heb 10:35-12:2 is the richest exposition of the meaning of faith in the whole Bible.

Does Faith Assure Salvation?

As is evident from some of the texts already quoted, in the Bible "faith" is commonly not sharply distinguished from "hope" or "trust." Late medieval spiritual writers, in reaction to the dry nominalistic scholasticism that had come to dominate academic theology, exploited this wider biblical sense of "faith" to emphasize the subjective side of faith as a personal relation to God and not merely an intellectual assent to abstract propositions.

Luther and the other Protestant Reformers pushed this tendency to understand faith as *fiducia*, "trust" in God's forgiveness, to the limit. Thus Luther emphasized that the Gospel is the Word of God *pro me*, "for me," to assure *me* of *my* forgiveness and justification.[21] The danger of this exclusive stress on the subjective aspect of faith and on "personal assurance of salvation," is that it practically tends to reduce faith to wishful thinking, to a psychological consolation and feeling of security (which is what religion seems to mean to many people today). This trust belongs rather to divine hope, which I will discuss later. We cannot forget the objective character of faith as commitment to the *truth* of what God tells us about himself prior to and independent of what this means *for me*.

The Catholic Church has always stressed that "faith," as distinguished from "hope," has as its object *truth* and is a virtue of our intelligence in its grasp of realities independent of our human minds, while hope is in the will and has as its object the *goodness and power* of God which leads us to trust him unconditionally. The life problem with which faith deals, therefore, is how to listen to God's self-revelation which is the ultimate truth. Obviously, my trust in God cannot really be secure unless it is really true that God exists and is infinitely good and

---

[21] After remarking on the influence of Nominalism on Luther and comparing his theology to that of Aquinas, Marc Lienhard, *Luther's Witness to Jesus Christ*, p. 388, concludes: "Luther knew the thought of St. Thomas very little, but a comparison between [the] two systems of thought is interesting, for it shows that Luther is situated, more than St. Thomas, at the threshold of the modern world, which centers on the subjectivity of human beings."

powerful and therefore can truly be *my* God and Savior. The Reformers never questioned this reality of God, but our contemporaries do.

Today many people think that to act on faith is naive, even irresponsible. Have we not seen the disasters that follow when people trust such leaders as Hitler and Stalin? How often have the confident assertions of "experts" turned out to be wrong? Do we not see around us how often religious people seeking security and peace of mind place their trust in charlatans? And do not even the believers of the great religions seem to hold with equal faith beliefs contradictory to each other? This is why many since the eighteenth century Enlightenment have argued that it is irresponsible to base one's life on anything but the findings of science, subject to objective verification and constant revision. Today many post-modernists are arguing that even science is colored by subjective and political factors and requires "deconstruction." The result is that many laugh at "true-believers" and claim that only a hard-headed, critical, skeptical attitude is possible for the mature and sophisticated.[22]

Yet a little reflection will show us that human life without faith in the veracity of others is impossible. None of us has sufficient wisdom or information by our individual selves to be able to get through life. We are social animals who have to rely on the witness of others to complete and correct our necessary knowledge of the world and of ourselves. Therefore, we need not only the truth that is obtained by direct evidence of our own senses and reason, but also truth obtained by faith in what others tell us is true.

Of course, it is naive, foolish, and irresponsible to believe everybody or anything. Our faith must be *critical*. It must first establish that an expert or a witness is a person who might possibly be in possession of the truth and that this person is serious and trustworthy, before we believe him or her. But when we have *direct* evidence that a witness is trustworthy, then we can reasonably accept the *indirect* evidence they

---

[22] Skepticism is not a "modern" phenomenon. It was widespread in Hellenistic culture at the time of Christ, and again in the last half of the eighteenth century. See Richard H. Popkin, "Skepticism," EP, vol. 8, pp. 448-461.

mediate to us. We certainly live in a world of lies and misinformation, but at least some people tell the truth, and this fact makes life possible.

Skepticism, however, is easier than faith. We can always find some excuse, some fantasy of doubt or deceit, which will enable us to disbelieve, and thus not to accept the inconveniences or demands of a truth that we cannot see for ourselves. History shows us not only how credulous of false leaders people have often been, but also how often a mood of skepticism has promoted the decadence of a culture. People have become cynical and relativistic, doubting everything, "always trying to learn but never able to reach a knowledge of the truth" (2 Tm 3:7).

We need, in the phrase made popular by Paul Tillich, "the courage to believe," but this act of faith should not be as Kierkegaard exaggeratedly said, "a leap in the dark." Rather it should be the willingness to accept the truth which we do not see for ourselves but which we are obliged by our reason to accept on the trustworthy word of others. Thus, *faith is an act of our intelligence by which we adhere to the truth, even when our intelligence is not satisfied by its direct evidence, through the assistance of an act of the will which moves us to put away our hesitations and doubts and hold fast to the testimony of a trustworthy witness.* This act of the will involves the whole human person, including our memory, imagination, and emotions, even our bodies![23]

The foregoing philosophical analysis of the necessity of ordinary human faith in our lives applies to Christian faith, but only by an *analogy.* Human and Christian faith are similar to each other, but differ even more. Christian faith is not trust in human beings, who even when they tell the truth are also capable of lies or error. As the Psalmist sadly exclaimed, "I said in my alarm, no man is dependable" (Ps 116:11). But God is Truth and cannot lie. "If we are unfaithful, God remains faithful, for God cannot deny himself" (2 Tm 2:13; cf. Heb 6:18). Consequently, divine faith, because it rests on God the Rock (Ps 18:32) has an absolute *objective certainty* that exceeds all human certainty, even the best established conclusions of science or history or even personal experience.

---

[23] CCC # 154.

Of course that does not mean that *subjectively* the certitude of divine faith, although true certitude of the most profound sureness of which the human mind is capable, may not be very wavering because of the darkness of our understanding and the weakness of our will. Usually faith must grow and mature for it to achieve subjective stability. Moreover, we should not confuse *questions* about the faith with *doubts* about the faith. Because the truths of faith are not clearly evident to our minds, questions and difficulties will inevitably arise and stimulate us to study, reflection, and prayer — all of which will help us to a deeper understanding in faith. But deliberate doubt must be resisted by the will even to death and martyrdom to remain faithful to God who is ever faithful to us and who, in the Second Person of the Trinity, died for us.

Some matters, such as the existence of God, can be known both by reason and by faith, but not at the same time, because faith is of the unseen, and once our reason makes something evident we no longer simply believe it. The great mysteries of faith cannot be known by reason but only by faith. They are forever closed to those who are unwilling to believe God, just as love is closed to those who are unwilling to trust even a truthful friend.

Faith and Signs

While human faith is reasonable when we have evidence of the witnesses' trustworthiness, such evidence is impossible in the case of God's Word, since we do not have direct evidence that it is God who is speaking. In divine faith we must believe not only what God says but also that *it really is God who speaks.* How do we know that what Jesus taught is really God's Word, when Muhammad and many others have made the same claim? How do we know what the Bible says is God's Word?

A full answer to this question pertains to that part of Theology called Apologetics or Fundamental Theology.[24] Here I will only *out-*

---

[24] See Avery Dulles, S.J., *A History of Apologetics.*

line the Catholic answer which is especially derived from John Chapter 9 which narrates how Jesus healed the man born blind and how this event was diversely interpreted by different witnesses according to their good or bad will.[25] The Pharisees questioned the man three times and confirmed the fact of the healing, yet could not agree on what it meant. Some saw that this extraordinary healing must be the work of God. Others, who resented Jesus' teaching because it contradicted their own interpretation of the Law, denounced the man who had been healed as a sinner whose testimony was of no account.[26]

> When Jesus heard that they had thrown him out, he found him and said, "Do you believe in the Son of Man?" He answered him and said, "Who is he, sir, that I may believe in him?" Jesus said to him, "You have seen him and the one who is speaking with you is he." He said, "I do believe, Lord," and he worshiped him. Then Jesus said, "I came into this world for judgment, so that those who do not see might see, and those who do see might become blind" (Jn 9:35-39).

A very similar theme is expressed in the account of how the Apostle Thomas, when the other apostles told him they had seen the Risen Lord said, "Unless I see the mark of the nails in his hands and put my finger into the nail marks and put my hand into his side, I will not believe" (Jn 20:25). But when Jesus actually appeared to him and said,

> "Put your finger here and see my hands, and bring your hand and put it into my side, and do not be unbelieving but believe," Thomas answered and said to him, "My Lord, and my God!" Jesus said to him, "Have you come to believe because you have seen me? Blessed are those who have not seen and have believed" (Jn 20:27-29).

---

[25] For exegesis of Chapter 9 see Raymond E. Brown, S.S., *Gospel According to John*, vol. 1, pp. 369-382. Brown defends the essential historicity of the account but says, "A miracle story has been shaped into an ideal tool at the service of Christian apologetics and into an ideal instruction for those about to be baptized," p. 378.

[26] Note that Jn 9:38, "He said, 'I do believe, Lord,' and he worshiped him," is absent from some early manuscripts and may have been added to make the meaning of the pericope still more explicit when it was used in baptismal liturgies in the early Church.

On this text St. Gregory the Great comments, "Thomas saw one thing, but believed another. For by mortals the Godhead cannot be seen. Thomas saw a man, but confessed him to be God, exclaiming, 'My Lord and my God.'"[27]

But why should we accept the witness of the Bible? Protestant Christians faced with this question reply that the Bible is witness to itself, by its evident truth and its ability to convert the reader. The difficulty with this answer is that Muslims claim the same thing for the *Qur'an*. To this Protestants answer that the Holy Spirit who inspired the Bible moves the hearts of the readers to faith. But this begs the question: "How do we know that the Bible is inspired by the Holy Spirit?" And even if we grant that the Bible is inspired how do we know which books belong to the Bible (the Bible itself contains no such list of its own books), or whether our Christian Bible is essentially accurate rather than corrupted as the Muslims claim? And since so many interpretations are given to the Bible, how do we know which is correct? Therefore, today many Protestant scholars admit with the early Church, the Catholic, and Orthodox Churches that the Bible cannot be known as inspired or correctly interpreted apart from the Tradition of the believing community or Church.[28]

But why should we believe the witness of the Church? And which Church among the many Christian Churches? Certainly the history of all these Churches shows how very human they are, and how often they have failed to live up to Jesus' teachings! The Bible itself does, however, indicate how a church's claims can be tested. Jesus did not ask for people to believe in him and his teaching until he (1) fulfilled the predictions of the Old Testament prophets and his own prophecies, completing this demonstration by his death and resurrection of which the

---

[27] St. Gregory the Great, *XL Homiliarum in Evangelia*, Bk II, Hom. 26; PL 76, 1202.

[28] See the noted Protestant theologian Stanley Hauerwas, *Unleashing the Scripture: Freeing the Bible from Captivity in America*, 1993, pp. 19-28, who writes, "When *sola scriptura* is used to underwrite the distinction between text and interpretation, then it seems clear that *sola scriptura* is a heresy rather than a help in the Church. When this distinction persists, *sola scriptura* becomes the seedbed of fundamentalism, as well as biblical criticism. It assumes that the text of Scripture makes sense separate from a Church that gives it sense" (p. 27).

apostles were eyewitnesses; (2) worked many miracles of healing, freeing from demons, multiplying the loaves, etc.; (3) taught with a wisdom so profound as to provide a consistent answer to the greatest mysteries of human life; (4) perfectly exemplified these teachings in his
own life and sacrificial death.[29]

These *signs* worked by Jesus sufficiently manifested to those who
became his disciples that God spoke through him, and that it was against
reason and common sense for those who witnessed these signs to refuse
to believe him. Yet he made clear that what he was asking was not that
they believe simply because of the signs, but because these signs pointed
to God revealing himself to us, just as when we believe a trustworthy
human being we are believing that person as a person, not just the signs
by which her or his honesty has been made known to us. According to
the Fourth Gospel, Jesus said,

"If I do not perform my Father's works, do not believe me; but if
I perform them, even if you do not believe me, believe the works, so
that you may realize that the Father is in me and I am in the Father" (Jn
10:37-38).

Yet the signs related in the Bible are often questioned by scholars
today. They view many of them as purely natural events which today
we would regard as psychologically explicable. They also point out
that the biblical accounts are colored by the faith of those who wrote
the Bible and hence cannot be taken as objective history. How at a
distance of almost 2000 years can we be sure?

A Sign Accessible to All?

This question became acute in the last century when the theory of evolution and archaeological discoveries raised serious problems about
the inspiration of the Bible. In line with Catholic tradition Vatican I
gave an answer which was reaffirmed in our times at Vatican II. The
Councils declared that Jesus remains present to us today in his Church
and that this Church is a visible sign, a living "moral miracle." As the

---

[29] Vatican I, DS 3033-3034; Vatican II, *Dei Verbum* # 4; CCC # 547-550.

Catechism of the Catholic Church says of the clause of the Creed "I believe in one, holy, catholic, and apostolic Church":

> # 812. Only faith can recognize that the Church possesses these properties from her divine source. But their historical manifestations are signs that also speak clearly to human reason. As the first Vatican Council noted, "the Church herself, with her marvelous propagation, eminent holiness, and unexhaustible fruitfulness in everything good, her catholic unity and invincible stability, is a great and perpetual motive of credibility and irrefutable witness of her divine mission." [30]

Of course the visible Church is a "pilgrim church" which "will attain her full perfection only in the glory of heaven" but now "takes on the appearance of this passing world. She herself dwells among creatures who groan and travail in pain until now and await the revelation of the sons of God (cf. Rm 8:19-22)." Hence the Church requires unceasing purification and reform.[31]

Yet in spite of all its faults which come from the human sinfulness of its members, the Catholic Church manifests an essential *unity*, an inclusiveness (*catholicity*), a continuity (*apostolicity*), and a *holiness*, which transcend what is possible to a merely human community, especially one made up of sinful members as every human community is. These astonishing features mark the Church as a sign of the continuing presence of Jesus, true God yet truly human, in the world today.[32] This sign is manifest in the life of every community of baptized and faithful Christians, but most completely in the Church headed by the successor of St. Peter as Jesus had promised (Mt 16:17-20; Jn 21:15-17). Thus the Catholic faith although it transcends human experience is also justified by our experience of Jesus still present in his Church, transforming it by his Spirit.

The Catholic answer, therefore, to the question, "Why should I believe what the Bible and Tradition teach?" is that it should be be-

---

[30] The Vatican I quote is DS 3013-4; cf. also Vatican II, LG # 8; DV # 4.

[31] Vatican II, LG # 48; CCC # 825-827.

[32] These four "marks of the Church" are treated extensively in CCC # 811-870.

lieved as the Word of God because God speaks it to us and has given us signs accessible to our human senses and intelligence which are sufficient to manifest that really it is God who speaks. The great sign most accessible to all here and now is the Catholic Church itself in its life and teaching. This Church works throughout the world, and is striving to reach even those parts of the globe which are still closed to its missions. It is the living presence of Christ in today's world and what it says of Christ is to be believed for the very same reasons that he should have been believed in his own times.

But what of the counter-signs? What of the many sins of Catholics, even those most highly placed in the Church and the scandals of the past such as the Inquisition, anti-semitism, and religious wars? Do these not destroy the sign value of the Church? Certainly they dim its light. Jesus said,

> "Nor do they light a lamp, and then put it under a bushel basket; it is set on a lampstand where it gives light to all the house. Just so, your light must shine before others, that they may see your good works and glorify your heavenly Father" (Mt 5:15-16).

Nevertheless, the sins of Christians is not what makes them different from other people, it is that they form a Church, a community which is one, catholic, apostolic, and holy in ways that no other human organizations have ever succeeded in being. The presence and power of Jesus in the witness of Peter and Paul shone out all the more uniquely because we know of their personal failures (Mt 26:69-75; 1 Cor 15:9-11). We can experience all this in our lives in the love of the Church which brings us spiritual enlightenment, guidance in living, the sacraments and the beauty of the liturgy, care in time of need, mutual forgiveness, and abiding friendship in Christ.

Thus the essential *objective* motive of Christian faith is the authority of God in revealing himself to us. We do not believe because of the authority of the Church, which is only the *condition*, although a necessary one, of our faith, but only on God's authority through the Church he has given us as his witness. The essential *subjective* aspect of faith is the integrity and firmness with which Christians submit their minds and wills to God in their acceptance of his Word. Children, the mentally retarded or ill, persons poorly educated in their faith, who are ready to believe all that God says but who know little of the *objective* content of his Word or know it only in very naive and simple terms, may have a faith that is subjectively stronger than that of a learned theologian who knows much more about Scripture and Tradition.

Because Jesus' Church is a church for everybody, no doubt the majority of its members know only a little of what Jesus taught. Yet this was also the situation in Jesus' own day, since he was so concerned for the "little ones" whom the learned scribes and Pharisees despised because of their ignorance of the Torah.

B: THE CONTENT OF FAITH

What Does Faith See?

The object of our Christian faith is only those truths that lead us to God: "faith and morals," that is, what God has revealed to us about himself and our way to him. It only incidentally includes such historical facts as the wars of Judah and Israel, which, however, are important to help us understand this revelation, or other matters which can be learned by our human reason. Nevertheless, the content of faith does include not only what we find *explicitly* stated in the Bible or Tradition, but also what is stated *implicitly*. For example when the Scriptures tell us that Jesus was a man like us, it tells us implicitly that he was able to laugh, although this is never stated in the Bible.[33]

How can we know what this objective content of faith is? It is enshrined in the Bible, but as we have already seen, we cannot simply

---

[33] Theologians disagree as to whether truths which theologians *deduce* syllogistically by human reasoning from what is stated in the Bible (rather than simply *explicitate*) are or are not objects of faith. I favor the view that says theological conclusions precisely as such are not objects of faith, because in such cases, although the conclusion is certain, its certitude is grounded in human reason not in divine revelation. If, however, the consensus of theologians considered as a sign is confirmed by other signs, these signs can manifest that a certain truth is divinely revealed and is therefore definable. On the history of this controversy see, Jan H. Walgrave, *Unfolding Revelation*.

pick up the Bible and be sure we hear God rather than our own personal fantasies. Since the Wisdom of God utterly exceeds our human capacities to understand fully, we are very likely to misunderstand it, if we trust merely on our own powers. We must read the Bible in the light of Tradition and that means in the light of the living faith of the Christian community.

Jesus has promised to the Church the abiding presence of his Holy Spirit. Consequently, as Vatican II teaches,[34] because of the abiding presence of Jesus in the Church through the gift of his Holy Spirit, the Church can never fail (it is "infallible") both in its subjective fidelity to the Word of God and in its objective understanding of what that Word is.[35]

In the Old Testament God united his Chosen People to himself in a covenant of marriage; but except for a holy Remnant, Israel was unfaithful (Ho 2:6-7; Is 1:21; Rm 10:21). In contrast, in the New Testament the covenant of marriage between Christ and his Church is eternal because Christ has sent his Holy Spirit to the Church to keep her ever faithful. Hence St. Paul says to the Church in Corinth, "I am jealous of you with the jealousy of God, since I betrothed you to one husband to present you as a chaste virgin to Christ" (2 Cor 11:2). That Paul's prayer will be fulfilled for the Church as a whole is also prophesied: "I also saw the holy city, a new Jerusalem, coming down out of heaven from God, prepared as a bride adorned for her husband" (Rv 21:2).[36]

The Church's assurance that she will remain faithful to Christ and infallible in transmitting his Gospel without error is founded not on her own strength but on Jesus' promise to be with her invisibly until his return at the end of history.

> "All power in heaven and earth has been given me. Go, therefore, and make disciples of all nations... teaching them to ob-

---

[34] LG #25.

[35] On the infallibility of the Church, the successor of St. Peter, and Ecumenical Councils, see CCC # 888-892.

[36] See CCC # 796-801.

serve all that I have commanded you. And behold, I am with you always, until the end of the age" (Mt 28:18-20).

He is present through his Holy Spirit:

"I will ask the Father, and he will give you another Advocate to be with you always, the Spirit of Truth... The Advocate, the Holy Spirit that the Father will send in my name — he will teach you everything and remind you of all that I told you" (Jn 14:16, 26).

Hence, the Christian community is "the household of God... the church of the living God, the pillar and foundation of truth" (1 Tm 3:15).

Of course here or there, from to time, the Church in its individual members, or groups of them (perhaps even a majority), and even in her leaders may fail in their responsibilities or may personally accept ideas which greatly distort the Gospel. At times faith may weaken throughout the Church, or important truths of the Gospel be neglected. Jesus even asked of his disciples, "When the Son of Man comes, will he find faith on earth?" (Lk 18:8). Because of the human frailty of the members of the Church and the powerful forces of evil arrayed against it, we should not be surprised at terrible scandals in the Church's long history. Jesus foresaw them in anguish, "Woe to the world because of things that cause sin! Such things must come, but woe to the one through whom they come!" (Mt 18:7). The epistles of 2 Timothy, of St. Jude, and 2 Peter and the Seven Letters in Revelation show that such evils existed in the Church from its earliest days. Thus we read in the Epistle of St. Jude the following outraged denunciation of certain members of the early Church:

These people revile what they do not understand and are destroyed by what they know by nature like irrational animals. Woe to them! They followed the way of Cain, abandoned themselves to Balaam's error for the sake of gain, and perished in the rebellion of Korah. These are blemishes on your love feasts, as they carouse fearlessly and look after themselves. They are waterless clouds blown about by winds, fruitless trees in late

autumn, twice dead and uprooted. They are like wild waves of
the sea, foaming up their shameless deeds, wandering stars for
whom the gloom of darkness has been reserved forever (Jude
vv. 10-13).

Yet the writer concludes by urging the community to have mercy even
on these sinners (Jude vv. 22-23).

The Christian who deserts the Church because of such scandals
has failed to understand the mystery of the Cross, that God's "power is
made perfect in weakness" (2 Cor 12:9). Indeed these struggles and
back-slidings are used by God to promote a process of moral purification and *doctrinal development* by which, under the guidance of the
Spirit, the Church comes to a deeper and more perfect understanding
and practice of the Gospel whose riches are inexhaustible. This sense
of development as a mark of Tradition is characteristic of the Catholic
Church, whereas the Orthodox Churches have tended to understand
Tradition as the work of the first seven ecumenical councils before
their separation from the papacy, and the Protestants have tended to see
post-biblical development (or even the so-called "Early Catholicism"
of the later books of the New Testament) as a corruption of the pristine
Gospel. Such doctrinal development, however, cannot add anything to
God's self-revelation in Jesus Christ completed in the age of the
Apostles, but can only be a growth in the Church's understanding of
that completed revelation.[37]

Tradition

The invisible presence of Christ through the Holy Spirit in his Church
is made visible and effective through its members constituted as an
organic community.

---

[37] Some theologians speak of "continuing revelation" in the Church, but on closer
scrutiny this turns out to be "doctrinal development" not new divine truths which are
implicitly already contained in Scripture and Tradition.

> He [Jesus] gave some as apostles, others as prophets, others as
> evangelists, others as pastors and teachers, to equip the holy
> ones for the work of ministry, for building up the body of Christ,
> until all attain the unity of faith and knowledge of the Son of
> God, to mature adulthood, to the extent of the full stature of
> Christ (Eph 4:11-13).

Thus the Church is served by the bishops under the headship of the
successor of St. Peter, as Jesus provided.[38]

> "And so I say to you, you are Peter [the Rock], and upon this
> rock [Peter as the embodiment of faith in Jesus] I will build my
> church, and the gates of the netherworld shall not prevail against
> it. I will give you the keys of the kingdom of heaven. Whatever
> you bind on earth shall be bound in heaven, and whatever you
> loose on earth shall be loosed in heaven (Mt 16:18-19; cf. Mt
> 18:18; Lk 22:31-32; Jn 21:15-17; bracketed words are mine).

Thus the pope and the bishops with him (i.e., the *Magisterium* or teaching authority) in their definitive teaching "in defining a doctrine of faith
and morals" share that "infallibility which the divine Redeemer willed
His Church to be endowed."[39]

The Magisterium, however, can only define what the Church as
a whole has received from the apostles and already believes, the "deposit of the faith." "Take as your norm the sound words that you hear
from me, in the faith and love that are in Christ Jesus. Guard this rich
trust with the help of the Holy Spirit that dwells within us" (2 Tm 1:13-
14).[40] How, then, does it become evident in the Church that a certain
teaching really is a part of the revelation entrusted to the Church?

In the *ordinary* exercise of official teaching in the Church the
exact discrimination between the Word of God which can never be
reformed and human opinions and customs which are always open to

---

[38] LG # 18-29; CCC # 874-945.

[39] Vatican I, DS 1712 (3011); Vatican II, LG # 25; CCC # 889, 891, 2035, 2051.

[40] The word translated by NAB as "trust" is *paratheke* (Vulgate *depositum*) meaning
"property entrusted to another," e.g., a bank "deposit," from which is derived the
classical phrase *depositum fidei*, "deposit of the faith," i.e., the content of revelation.

reformation is not always clear. Gradually, through history, theological controversy, and deepening religious experience, under the guidance of the Holy Spirit, this discrimination of what truly pertains to the *depositum fidei* is gradually clarified. It can then take the form of definitive and *extraordinary* teaching by the pope speaking with his full authority *(ex cathedra),* or by the bishops in an ecumenical council which the pope confirms. It also becomes evident when the pope and bishops dispersed throughout the world affirm it definitively in their *ordinary and universal* teaching. All such definitive teaching is infallible and hence irreformable, and calls upon all Catholics to accept it on divine faith.[41]

It was also implied (but not defined) by both Vatican I and Vatican II that the Magisterium also teaches infallibly and irreformably a second class of truths which are not revealed and hence do not demand divine faith, but which are so closely connected with revealed truths that to deny the non-revealed would logically be to deny the revealed. If one were to deny, as some ultra-conservatives have done, that Vatican II was an ecumenical council (a truth certainly not mentioned in the Bible) one would logically also be denying the indefectibility of the Church, which, as we have seen, *is* revealed in the Bible. Hence the Magisterium can require Catholics to accept the Council as ecumenical with unqualified certainty, not indeed with the precise certainty of divine faith, but with a certainty guaranteed by the unfailing mission of the Church.[42] This second class of truths are said to pertain to the "secondary object" of infallibility, while the revealed truths are its "primary object." The exact scope of this secondary object of infallibility is still a matter of controversy and has not yet been defined by the Magisterium.

At any given time in the Church, the ordinary teaching of the Magisterium consists in the transmission and explanation of already defined truths of the first class (e.g., the Creeds and the Ten Command-

---

[41] A current treatment of this whole question is Francis Sullivan, S.J., *Magisterium.* See also Avery Dulles, "The Magisterium and Theological Dissent," pp. 105-118, in *The Craft of Theology.*

[42] Vatican I, DS 3074; Vatican II, LG # 25, DV # 10, 2; CCC # 891-892.

ments) and the second class just mentioned, along with a third, very extensive, class of teachings that the Magisterium has never defined, but which nevertheless it teaches authoritatively, such as a good deal that we find in the papal encyclicals, the bishops' pastorals, the *Catechism of the Catholic Church*, and the ordinary preaching on Sundays.

Some Catholics today think that on such matters they are free to have their own opinions, since these truths are not taught infallibly. Vatican II, however, cautioned against this mistake by saying that when the pope and bishops teach "in matters of faith and morals" even without using their full authority to define and to require the assent of divine faith, they nevertheless "speak in the name of Christ and the faithful are to accept their teaching and adhere to it with... a religious submission of will and mind."[43] For example, the Church has never yet solemnly *defined* that sexism or rape or racism or anti-semitism are sins, but this is part of its ordinary teaching and should be accepted by all Catholics, even if they are not convinced by the arguments for them or think such teaching goes against their personal experience.

> Remember your leaders who spoke the word of God to you. Consider the outcome of their way of life and imitate their faith. Jesus Christ is the same yesterday, today, and forever. Do not be carried away by all kinds of strange teaching (Heb 13:7-9).

Of course, since non-defined teachings are not taught with the ultimate sign of infallibility, namely solemn definition by the Magisterium, there remains a possibility that they may be proved wrong, but still here and now they are the best guides God has provided for us. Nor does the fact that some theologians, however learned, argue against a particular reformable teaching show that Catholics may dissent from it or are free to ignore it in their actions, because within the Church it is the Magisterium not theological scholars who have pastoral authority from God to be our guides in living by faith.

In Chapter 3 of 1 Corinthians St. Paul makes clear that this local

---

[43] Vatican II, LG #25; CCC # 892.

church ought to follow his preaching, rather than that of the learned teacher Apollos (whom he nevertheless calls "brother"), not because Paul claims to be more learned than Apollos, but because of Paul's apostolic authority from Christ. Even the theologian must ultimately submit his learned opinions to the discernment of the Holy Spirit vested ultimately in the successors of the apostles, who speak not in their own name but in the name of Christ who entrusted this task in the Church to them. They too must submit to the Word of God in Scripture and Tradition.

Since the third class of teachings are not known to be infallible they could possibly be in error, although not so regularly as to be inconsistent with the Holy Spirit's guidance of his Church. Some such "errors" as are commonly mentioned by historians turn out on critical examination to be debatable, but there are some clear examples of errors by the ordinary Magisterium, such as the medieval Church's acceptance of the requirement of the pagan Roman law that torture be used in certain trials and the condemnation in 1616 of Galileo's assertion that the earth moves around the sun as heretical because contrary to the Bible, etc.[44] The very rarity of such clear examples is a testimony to the Holy Spirit's guidance.

What should be the attitude of Catholics who think they recognize such an error in the non-infallible but authoritative teachings of the Magisterium? If they know with *objective certitude* that a teaching is wrong, they are not obliged to try to believe it. God never demands we try to believe what we really know to be false! Galileo, however, although he seems to have been subjectively convinced of the motion of the earth, did not at that time have *objective* certitude of his opinion since the "proofs" on which he relied were either defective or mere analogies. Today it is generally admitted that much of accepted science is merely probable, not certain.

If this be true of "hard" science, how much truer when it comes

---

[44] On the adoption of torture by the Inquisition see Edward Peters, *Torture*, pp. 52-73. As late as 1780, a distinguished French lawyer, Pierre Francois Muyart, was still defending the use of torture by the secular courts, pp. 72-73. For the Galileo case see G.V. Coyne, M. Heller, and J. Zycinski, *The Galileo Affair* and Richard Blackwell, *Galileo, Bellarmine, and the Bible.*

to questions of morality, which are often very complex and debatable? Catholics, therefore, who cannot prove the Church is mistaken on some point with objective and certain arguments, are obliged to accept its teaching. This obligation arises not from the arguments given by the Church — these may sometimes seem less probable to us than the contrary arguments — but from the authority the Church has from the Holy Spirit which is superior to that of any merely human expert.

> Let no one deceive himself. If anyone among you considers himself wise in this age, let him become a fool, so as to become wise. For the wisdom of this world is foolishness in the eyes of God... So let no one boast about human beings, for everything belongs to you. Paul or Apollos or Kephas, or the world or life or death, or the present or the future: all belong to you, and you to Christ, and Christ to God (1 Cor 3:18-19, 21-23).

Reforming Reformable Teaching

Yet when Catholics know for certain, or with high probability, that the Church is in error, they have a responsibility as members of the Church to assist the Magisterium to rectify this mistake, as St. Paul corrected St. Peter for his poor judgment in observing the *kosher* laws to the offense of the Gentile converts (Gal 2:11-14). Such corrections must be given, however, in a manner that does not injure the authority of the Church in a world where there are so many hostile forces attempting to weaken her authority. Theologians can properly discuss such a problem privately with the bishops or the Holy See, or even publicly in dialogue with other competent theologians, and even for the information of the general public, provided they make clear to their hearers or readers that they leave final judgment to the Magisterium.

Theologians must also make clear that they propose their views for discussion only and not to guide the belief or conscience of others, or to substitute for the guidance of the pastors of the Church *which alone have that authority from Christ*. If the Magisterium insists that theologians be silent on such topics in order to avoid controversies that undermine the faith and give time for calmer and more mature discussion, they ought to cooperate, confident that God in his providence will soon enable the truth to emerge.[45]

Since public revelation was complete with the apostolic age, and the Magisterium can only define what is known to have been revealed, how can it ever make a new definition? For example, how could Vatican I define papal infallibility as a revealed truth, if it was not already known, and how could it have been known already without being defined? We have already seen that truths of faith are not evident to us, but are reasonably believed because of the signs God gives that it is he who has spoken. As we have seen, the ultimate sign which removes any reasonable doubt by a Catholic is the solemn definition of a truth by the Magisterium. But previous to such a definition the Magisterium has to be itself certain that this truth is somehow included in the deposit of faith or so closely connected with it that to deny it would be to deny that deposit.

The Magisterium does not recognize a doctrine to be definable by some new revelation, but by the concurrence of other signs such as the witness of the Bible, the universality and continuity with which the doctrine has been taught in the Church, its long presence in Christian life and worship, its consistency with other revealed truths, the witness by the saints, its long acceptance by the practicing members of the Church (the *sensus fidelium* or *sensus fidei*[46]), etc. If such signs concur

---

[45] See Congregation for the Doctrine of the Faith, *The Ecclesial Role of Theologians*, n. 32-41.

[46] CCC # 889. The "supernatural sense of the faith" (*sensus fidei*) is not mere "public opinion" but the fidelity of the members of the Church guided by the Holy Spirit to adhere to the Word of God revealed in Scripture and Tradition. For example, the conviction of Christians prior to the definition of the Immaculate Conception in 1854 (DS 2800-2804) that the absolute sinlessness of the Mother of God was a truth at least implicitly contained in Scripture and Tradition. Thus theologians who dissent from the magisterial teaching on the sinfulness of contraception by appealing to public opinion polls as evidence of the *sensus fidelium* must ask themselves whether Catholics who favor contraception do so because they (a) believe that God has revealed in Scripture and/or Tradition that the Magisterium is mistaken on this point or (b) because they are influenced by our secular culture or (c) simply do not understand or accept the Church's authority in such matters. There are many historical examples of widespread public opinion among Catholics dissenting from Church teaching, which today are seen to be errors. For example, through several centuries dueling was widely considered a moral obligation of Christian gentlemen in spite of the Church's excommunication of

and pastoral considerations require or suggest it, the Magisterium strengthened in its judgment by the Holy Spirit defines that truth as contained in revelation at least implicitly, or as intimately connected with other certainly revealed truths. Thus papal infallibility is explicit in the Scriptures, as we have seen, and had been accepted in the practical life of the Church long before Vatican I defined it, as was the divinity of Christ long before the Council of Nicaea defined it.

Hence, before the definition of an infallible truth the Church as a whole already knows it to be true, but some members of the Church may still not be convinced because they have not yet seen the concurrence of the signs that would require their belief. In the Middle Ages the great Doctors of the Church, St. Bernard of Clairvaux and St. Thomas Aquinas were not convinced that Mary was conceived without sin, but Bl. Duns Scotus came to the realization that this doctrine was already implicit in what the Scripture tells us of her and therefore must be definable, as it was eventually defined by Pius IX in 1854.

While all theologians admit that the infallibility of the Magisterium extends not only to "faith" but also to "morals," i.e., to both dogmatic and moral truths, today some claim there have never been any definitions of concrete moral norms, and hence all present Church teaching on moral norms is reformable. Yet it is quite clear that the Church has always taught the basic principles of the Christian life as the Word of God — for example the Ten Commandments and the Sermon on the Mount — in its baptismal catechesis and required the acceptance of these moral truths by adult catechumens. In subsequent chapters I will try to show why certain of these moral norms are so clear in the Scriptures and Tradition of the Church that they must be acknowledged as *definable*, and hence infallibly true even if not yet defined.

It would be very wrong, however, to conclude that everything in the ordinary moral teaching of the Magisterium is certain and irreformable. Moral truth, by its very nature, is less clear, less easy to formulate accurately, and less certainly known by human reason than theoretical and dogmatic truth. A fact such as the sphericity of the earth

those who practiced it (cf. DS # 799, 1111, 1113, 1830, 2022, 2351, 2571-5, 3162, 3272; Code of Canon Law (1917): canon 1240.

is a fact, a universal theoretical truth such as that $2 + 2 = 4$ is timeless, but a moral truth has to be applied in a variety of complex and changing circumstances. Usually there is more than one right way to achieve our legitimate goals, and even right ways often have some bad consequences. While it is true, as I will try to show later, that certain kinds of actions are always and under any circumstances immoral (for example, *forced* sexual intercourse), it is not possible to say that a certain kind of action is always moral in all circumstances. Even prayer is immoral in some situations, for example when I should leave prayer to help my neighbor in need.

Because of this inherent tentativeness of moral truth, it should be no surprise that the moral teaching of the Church undergoes a marked development, more so, perhaps, than does its dogmatic teaching, although that too develops. In the Old Testament we see that the Jews, like other ancient peoples, at first had a very simple, crude, ethnocentric morality which was often violent, with little consideration of individual rights, or interior motives, e.g., for example, their practice of polygamy and of slavery (see the story of Abraham's wife Sarah and his slave concubine Hagar, Gn 16). Only little by little did this morality become refined, sensitive to individual needs, and concerned about motives as well as external acts. Even today the Jewish rabbis continue to refine it in their *responsa*.

In the New Testament we also see that Jesus' moral teaching was at first understood only in broad outline, and only through controversy within the Christian community was it refined. The same process of refinement and clarification has gone on in the history of the Church. Yet this development has included not only progress but regress, as we can see in the history of the wars of religion between Catholics and Protestants, or the persecution of the Jews. Thus we ought not be so influenced by our cultural bias in favor of progress in science and technology as to suppose that the Christian faith must change in its essential teachings "to keep up with the times" although it must be expressed in new ways in accordance with the "signs of the times" (Lk 12:54-56).[47] Rather, the faith provides a secure basis from which to judge true

---

[47] Vatican II, GS # 4.

from false progress. Yet faith *does* progress in the sense that it finds new developments, expressions, and applications in every age.

Today many find the Church's teachings on sexual morality and on social and business morality so contrary to what they see in the life around them and in the media, and are so often told that these teachings are unrealistic, that they simply ignore them as obsolete. This "morality gap" is not new. Throughout the history of the Church, there has been a sharp conflict between Christian moral teaching and the "way of the world." Sometimes, also Catholic life, even among its pastors, has been too much colored by the "way of the world," yet again and again the "world," whether of the Roman Empire, the Feudal Age, the Renaissance, or the Enlightenment has perished from its own folly, while the Gospel remains new and living.

Faith and/or Works?

To believe intellectually what the Magisterium teaches, however, is not enough. Jesus said, "Not everyone who says to me, 'Lord, Lord,' will enter the kingdom of heaven, but only the one who does the will of my father in heaven" (Mt 7:21; cf. Mt 25:31-46). St. Paul wrote, "For if you live according to the flesh, you will die, but if by the spirit you put to death the deeds of the body, you will live" (Rm 8:13). He warned the Philippians, "work out your salvation with fear and trembling" (Ph 2:12), and spoke to the Galatians of the "faith that works through love" (Gal 5:6). The Epistle of St. James asks, "What good is it, my brothers, if someone says he has faith, but does not have works?" (Jm 2:14). Christian faith demands certain actions on our part of which the first is to obey the negative command, *never* to deny the faith either directly or implicitly, in words, or in deeds (worshipping idols, trampling on the Crucifix, calling oneself a Muslim, etc.). As baptized and confirmed Christians we, like the martyrs, refuse to deny our faith even at the cost of our lives (see 2 M 6:18-31 and chapter 7; Ac 7:54-60). Our second responsibility as Christians is to obey the positive command to publicly proclaim ("confess") our faith when this is necessary for the honor of God and the salvation of our neighbor: "For one believes with the

heart and so is justified, and confesses with the mouth and so is saved"
(Rm 10:10).

Yet, although faith by its very nature should be publicly professed, there are circumstances which permit one, while not denying
one's faith, to conceal it at least for a time. For example, one is ordinarily not required to seek martyrdom, but may attempt to escape from
the persecutor.

The gift of faith, however, is not merely this or that act of faith
but is a stable capacity to make such acts, otherwise we could not speak
of the Christian life as a continuous "Way" to God (Jn 14:6; Ac 9:2). As
a divine gift it can be compared to a human capacity that Greek philosophy called a "virtue" (*arete*, a manly quality or ability, a word not
often used in the Bible, but see Ph 4:8; 2 P 1:5).

Such a virtue is a good "habit," but not just a habit in the common
English sense of a compulsion such as "the drug habit" or even of some
mechanical fixed pattern of behavior such as "a habit of early rising,"
but a special ability to act in an intelligent manner, as a skill or art. Thus
a trained pianist has acquired not only certain conditioned reflexes of a
mechanical sort, but also the ability to learn, adapt, and interpret music
in a creative and flexible way. A virtue does not enslave us like a compulsion or a routine, but *frees* us to achieve our purposes effectively
and gracefully.

"Faith of itself if it does not have works is dead" (Jm 2:17), while
a living faith is a "faith working through love" (Gal 5:6). Such biblical
expressions distinguish between a faith which is alive and one which is
dead, and indicate that it is love which gives birth to "works" that
inform and vivify faith. What then is "dead faith"? One who has been
given the gift of faith, may cease to live the Christian life, and yet not
give up the conviction that the Gospel is true, although he or she no
longer tries to live by it. Such a person is spiritually dead, but, as the
Council of Trent insisted,[48] this "dead faith" remains a precious gift of
God since it can lead sinners who retain it to repentance, and thus is for
them a great advantage over sinners without any faith at all. Faith can-

---

[48] DS # 1578; Vatican I, DS 3035.

not be entirely lost except by a deliberate act of denial not only of the faith as a whole but even of one defined doctrine of faith, since that is to deny the authority of God.

Faith as Gift

That Christian faith as a virtue is a pure gift of God is evident from the Council of Orange II against the Pelagians; from Trent against the accusations of the Reformers that the Roman Church had become Pelagian; and from Vatican I against nineteenth century Rationalism.[49] These Councils were only repeating many biblical affirmations (e.g., Jn 6:44, 45, 64; Eph 2:5, 8; 1 Cor 3:7; 2 Cor 3:5; Ph 1:29). This action of the Holy Spirit is even necessary to move the unbeliever to consider the decision of faith seriously, as was declared by Orange II against the Semipelagians.[50]

This gift of faith brings with it that "fear of the Lord" which "is the beginning of wisdom" (Ps 111:10; cf. Jb 28:28; Pr 1:7; 9:10; Si 1:16; 19:17), a fear that is loving (filial fear), or at least cautious (servile fear); and a purification (Ac 15:9) of the heart from the errors that render it blind, deaf, and hard as stone (Jn 13:36-43).

While faith is a gift which unites us *immediately* to God as Truth in a union of spirits, it is strengthened and deepened by certain "gifts of the Holy Spirit." These gifts, which Isaiah 11:2 prophesies will anoint the Messiah and hence be shared by all his faithful followers, are traditionally seven in number as perhaps indicated in the symbolic "seven horns of the Lamb" in Revelation 5:6.[51] Although the Hebrew of Isaiah 11:2 only lists six, and repeats "fear of the Lord," the Septuagint (LXX)

---

[49] Orange II, DS # 375-377; Trent, DS # 553;, Vatican I, DS # 3035; CCC # 154-155.

[50] Orange II, DS # 375.

[51] In Lk 1:69 *keras soterias* is used for the Messiah as power and strength; cf. Ps 88:18; 131:17 LXX, etc., EDNT, vol. 2, p. 283. Wilfrid J. Harrington, O.P., *Understanding the Apocalypse*, pp. 117-118 says that the seven horns stand for the plenitude of power and the seven eyes for the plenitude of knowledge of the Messiah. See also Austin Farrer, *A Rebirth of Images: The Making of St. John's Apocalypse*, pp. 99-101 on the seven eyes, seven candles, seven spirits, seven churches, seven horns, all indicating the Holy Spirit's work.

and Vulgate get seven by translating the second "fear of the Lord" as "piety" (Greek *eusebeia,* Latin *pietas*).[52] In any case, as we will see later, all seven are mentioned separately elsewhere in the Scriptures.

According to St.Thomas Aquinas[53] these gifts do not deal with problems other than those dealt with by the virtues, but enable us to use these virtues in a manner that transcends our ordinary human mode of acting. As humans we act in a somewhat mechanical, step-by-step manner, but to reach God we need to share in God's own divine way of acting, a way that is like that of the divine Wisdom who is "intelligent, holy, unique, manifold, subtle, agile, clear, unstained, and certain... firm, secure, tranquil, all-powerful, all-seeing" (Ws 7:22-23). We must be open to this guidance of the Spirit if we are to enter God's kingdom.

> I kneel before the Father... that he may grant you in accord with
> the riches of his glory to be strengthened though his Spirit in the
> inner self, and that Christ may dwell in your hearts through faith;
> that you, rooted and grounded in love, may have strength to
> comprehend with all the holy ones what is the breadth and length
> and height and depth, and to know the love of Christ that sur-
> passes knowledge, so that you may be filled with all the fullness
> of God (Eph 3:14-19).

These gifts render us flexible and docile to the Spirit's inspira-tion, as we see in the wonderful spontaneity of the goodness of the saints. In the case of faith this permits a growth which yields what St. Paul calls "fruits of the Spirit."[54]

---

[52] See Hans Wildberger, *Isaiah 1-12: A Commentary*, p. 461 on the textual question and for commentary pp. 471-74. He argues that Is 11:3a is a gloss.

[53] *S.T.*, I-II, q. 68, a. 1-3; cf. CCC # 1831, 1845. On the development of Aquinas' thought on the gifts see Odo Lottin, O.S.B., "Les dons du S. Esprit chez les theologians depuis Pierre Lombard usqu'à S. Thomas d'Aquin," in his *Psychologie et Moral au XIIe et XIIIe siècles*, vol. 4, Pt. 3, n. 2, 329-456, especially 411-433.

[54] CCC # 1832. There is no reason to suppose that Paul intends this catalogue of vices and virtues to be systematic, but Fitzmyer notes that Paul has many lists of virtues (Gal 5:18-23; 1 Cor 5:10-11; 6:9-10; 2 Cor 6:6-7; 12:10; Rm 1:29-31; 13:13 [Col 3:5-8, 12-14; Eph 5:3-5]). These often refer to "kingdom of God" mentioned elsewhere by Paul only in 1 Th 2:12; 1 Cor 4:20; 6:9-10; 15:24, 50; Rm 14:17. "The association of it ["kingdom of God"] with these catalogues seems to mark them as elements of pre-Pauline catechetical instruction, which he has inherited and made use of. These lists

If you are guided by the Spirit, you are not under the law. Now the works of the flesh are obvious: immorality, impurity, licentiousness, idolatry, sorcery, hatreds, rivalry, jealousy, outbursts of fury, acts of selfishness, dissensions, factions, occasions of envy, drinking bouts, orgies, and the like. I warn you, as I warned you before, that those who do such things will not inherit the kingdom of God. In contrast, the fruit of the Spirit is love, joy, peace, patience, kindness, generosity, faithfulness, gentleness, self-control. Against such there is no law (Gal 5:18-23).

This growth has three phases.

First, there is a deeper and deeper insight into the truths of the faith taken singly (the gift of understanding or insight, Latin *intellectus*). This is suggested in the sixth Beatitude, "Blessed are the clean of heart for they will see God" (Mt 5:8),[55] and has as its fruits "faith" in the sense of certitude in the mind and joy in the will.[56]

Second, comes an ability to see the relationship between these truths (knowledge, *scientia*) and their application in life. This is suggested by the third (or in some texts the second) Beatitude, "Blessed are they who mourn, for they will be comforted" (v. 4), because this knowledge centers on the mystery of suffering, on the Cross.

Third, faith is perfected by the gift of wisdom (*sapientia*) by which the whole of the Gospel is seen in its unity as the revelation of the one God. This mystical wisdom, as we shall see later, has a special relation to love, and can be related to the fourth Beatitude, "Blessed are they who hunger and thirst after righteousness," that is, to do the will of God.

Does faith depend on the natural intellectual virtues which we

---

have been compared with similar ones found in Hellenistic (esp. Stoic) philosophical writings and in Palestinian Jewish texts (e.g., of the Essenes; Cf 1QS 4:2-6, 9-11)." NJBC, p. 1413.

[55] For literature on the Beatitudes see Carter, *What Are They Saying About Matthew's Sermon on the Mount?* pp. 82-88, 97-102 and Matthew Luz, pp. 224-246. Jesus may have had in mind Is 61:1-4, one of the Servant Songs. According to Viviano, NJBC, p. 640: "In Matthew 'purity of heart' stands close to justice and includes covenant fidelity, loyalty to God's commands, sincere worship." A classic treatment is J. Dupont, *Les Beatitudes*, 3 vols. Paris, 1954-73.

[56] On the Beatitudes see St. Thomas Aquinas, *S.T.*, I-II, q. 69; Jacques Dupont, *Les Béatitudes*, and Simon Tugwell, O.P., *The Beatitudes*.

acquire by education and study? According to Aquinas[57] these natural virtues include the whole array of theoretical and practical insights, the various sciences, and philosophy. But one can have true faith and lack all intellectual education. Jesus, it is written, once exclaimed, "I give praise to you, Father, Lord of heaven and earth, for although you have hidden these things from the wise and the learned you have revealed them to the childlike" (Mt 11:25-26). Hence, God can give the virtue of faith even to the least intellectual and educated, even to small infants in Baptism. "There are those with little understanding who fear God, and those of great intelligence who violate the law" (Si 19:20).

Yet faith does not weaken human intelligence or learning but elevates it to a higher level of activity, and this purified human knowledge can be of great service to the Church, as the great Doctors of the Church have shown. Here the axiom "grace perfects nature" is verified and we could add also that "nature serves grace."

Faith and Baptism

The Risen Lord said (according to the canonical ending of Mark),[58] "Go into the whole world and proclaim the gospel to every creature. Whoever believes and is baptized will be saved; whoever does not believe will be condemned" (Mk 16:15-16; cf. Mt 28:19-20). Thus all who hear the Gospel and see the signs that it is the Word of God are commanded most solemnly by Jesus to profess their faith and be baptized. Baptism is an act of faith, but it is also an act of God through the ministry of the Church by which the Holy Spirit perfects our faith and confers the graces with which he anointed Jesus in *his* baptism when the Father said, "You are my beloved Son, with you I am well pleased" (Mk 1:11).[59]

---

[57] *S.T.*, I-II, q. 57.

[58] This is not found in many early Greek manuscripts, yet is found in others equally early and is *canonical*. Hence, its theological value is not lessened by the fact that it may have been added to the Second Gospel in the Apostolic Age. Most scholars think it is dependent on the other Gospels.

[59] On Baptism see CCC # 1213-1284. Note its unity with Confirmation and Eucharist as "the sacraments of Christian initiation" (CCC # 1285). Note also the historical

The Old Testament marked the reception of males as members of the Chosen People by the sacrament of circumcision (Gn 17:1-14; Ex 4:24-26; 12:44, 48) which Jesus himself received (Lk 2:21). But this rite did not of itself confer grace, as does the sacrament of Baptism in water and the Holy Spirit (Mk 1:8; Jn 1:33; 3:5) which has replaced circumcision in the New Testament and is conferred on females also.[60]

The Church's solemn liturgy of Baptism in the Easter Vigil recapitulates many of the events of salvation history, especially the creation (Gn 1), the purification of fallen creation by the flood (Gn 6:5-9:17), the exodus of the Hebrews from Egypt through the Red Sea (Ex 14), and their entrance to the Promised Land across the Jordan (Jos 3-4), the striking of the rock by Moses which brought forth a fountain (Nb 20:6-13), the many purification rites of the Old Law (e.g., Lv 8:6), the water flowing from the side of the temple to sweeten the Dead Sea (Ezk 47); as well as New Testament events such as the preaching of John the Baptist (Mk 1:1-11) and the flowing of water and blood from Jesus' heart on the Cross (Jn 19:31-37). Moreover, blessed water ("holy water") is used in many ways in Catholic devotional life as a reminder of the baptismal waters.

Another symbol of faith is the lighted candle or lamp. The *menorah* or seven-branched lampstand illumined the sanctuary of the Jewish temple (Ex 37:17-24). Candles are lit by the wife in Jewish homes on Friday evening to welcome the Sabbath. In the Church a special paschal candle is blessed and lighted at the Easter Vigil. Lighted candles are given to the newly baptized and to those renewing their baptismal vows, and candles are lit on the altars, before the reserved Eucharist, before the holy icons, and carried at the reading of the Gospel, etc. These lights stand for Christ, the Light of the World (Jn 1:3, 9), for our faith in Christ, and for our witness to others of our faith in the Gospel. "Your light must shine before others, that they may see your good deeds and glorify your heavenly Father" (Mt 5:16).[61] Thus in a very

---

explanation of the temporal separation of Baptism from Confirmation in the Latin Church, but not in the Eastern Church: CCC #1290-1292.

[60] CCC # 1150-1152.

[61] CCC # 1243.

rich and profound way Christian Baptism is a sacrament that sums up the teaching of the whole Bible on God's gift of true life.

By Baptism we are incorporated into Christ and made adopted sons and daughters as he is God's Son in the Trinity. We are reborn to a share in the divine life as a child is born from the womb of its mother (Jn 3:3-7), and as St. Paul says (Rm 6:3), we die to sin as Christ died that we might rise in him. Hence Baptism remits all sins committed before Baptism (Rm 6:7). Baptism and the faith it "seals" (2 Cor 1:22) is the foundation of the whole Christian life and Catholics renew their baptismal vows every Sunday in the Creed and every year in the Paschal Vigil. In the early Church and today in the Rites of Christian Initiation, instruction in the faith also includes basic instruction in Christian morality.

Since in Baptism not only are sins washed away, but the baptized becomes a temple of the Holy Spirit, in the early Church the Sacrament of Confirmation which symbolizes this anointing and indwelling of the Spirit was conferred immediately following Baptism, and this practice is continued in the Eastern Churches. In the Latin Church this is also done for adults, but Confirmation may be delayed for children until a suitable age determined by the bishops of the country.[62]

For adult converts Baptism, Confirmation, and the Eucharist are the completion of their preparation to be Christians and the beginning of their life as Christians through the Rites of Initiation. Christian parents also have a solemn obligation to have their children baptized soon after birth, because of Jesus' command quoted above and his saying to the apostles, "Let the children come to me, and do not prevent them; for the kingdom of heaven belongs to such as these" (Mt 19:14). Children are born into a sinful world and from the moment of their existence are touched by the effects of that world so different from what the Creator intended it to be. Hence from the beginning of their lives they should be received into the Church, the community which is the beginning of the redemption and transformation of the world, and thus be placed on the path to God by the faith of their parents and of the whole Church.

---

[62] CCC # 1212, 1285, 1289-1292. More will be said about Confirmation in Chapter 5.

Spiritual Blindness

The prophets of the Old Testament constantly called Israel back to faith and warned them of the consequences of turning away from the light of God into darkness. Jeremiah laments, "This is the nation that does not listen to the voice of the Lord, its God, or take correction. Faithfulness has disappeared; the word itself is banished from their speech" (Jr 7:28). But none of these prophets was more emphatic than Jesus who, for all his gentleness, the Fourth Gospel presents as declaring: "Whoever rejects me and does not accept my words has something to judge him: the word that I spoke, it will condemn him on the last day" (Jn 12:48).

To sin against faith is possible in several ways. The first and most serious is *infidelity* by which the faith is rejected knowingly and willingly, which on the part of a baptized Christian can be either (formal) *heresy* (stubborn denial of what is known to be a truth or truths revealed by God) or *apostasy* (total desertion of the Christian religion).[63] Such acts are sins "against the light of the Holy Spirit" and are more fatal than any other sin, except those against hope and love, because they close off the sinner from access to God as long as the sinner stubbornly persists in the refusal to believe. It is probably this kind of "deadly" sin of which John warns:

> If anyone sees his brother sinning, if the sin is not deadly, he should pray to God and he will give him life. This is only for those whose sin is not deadly. There is such a thing as deadly sin, about which I do not say that you should pray. All wrongdoing is sin, but there is sin that is not deadly (1 Jn 5:16-17; cf. Mk 3:29; Heb 6:4-6; 10:26-31).

Such texts were intended to impress on the early Church, so tempted to deny the faith under persecution, how serious such sins are. Since, however, we can never judge for sure that someone has actually committed such a sin interiorly, we can always pray for every sinner,

---

[63] CCC # 2087-2089.

no matter how wicked they seem, and God by his omnipotent power
can always convert them.

In the later books of the New Testament, after heresies and
apostasies had begun to be serious problems in the Christian community, there are many warnings against the influence of heretics. Thus
we read:

> Avoid profane, idle talk, for such people will become more and
> more godless, and their teaching will spread like gangrene.
> Among them are Hymenaeus and Philetus, who have deviated
> from the truth by saying that the resurrection has already taken
> place and are upsetting the faith of some (1 Tm 2:16-18).
> I now feel a need to write to encourage you to contend for the
> faith that was once for all handed down to the holy ones. For
> there have been some intruders, who long ago were designated
> for this condemnation, godless persons, who pervert the grace
> of our God into licentiousness and who deny our only Master
> and Lord, Jesus Christ (Jude vv. 3-4; cf. 2 P 2:1-22; 1 Tm 1:3-
> 20).

From the fifth century on it was traditionally held in the Church
that while force can never be used to coerce a person to accept the faith
and be baptized (or even the children of unwilling parents), once they
have been baptized they can justly be required even by force to live up
to their baptismal promises.[64] In this period it was universally assumed
that every state, Christian, Islamic, or whatever, in order to maintain its
civil unity required a state religion, so that those who did not adhere to
this religion were second-class citizens or aliens and those who undermine it were traitors to the state. Consequently, the governments of
Christian states held the Church responsible for maintaining religious
uniformity through its religious courts and by religious sanctions, while
the state itself enforced the Church's judgments by the usual criminal
sanctions of fines, imprisonment, or capital punishment.

---

[64] See Joseph Lecler, *Toleration and the Reformation*. Note especially his discussion of
how Augustine reluctantly came to accept the use of force against heresy as a result of
its use against the Church by the Donatists and the way his writing on the subject was
later distorted, pp. 56-59.

Hence at that time the Church accepted "religious liberty" in the modern sense only in the form of "toleration," that is, to avoid greater evils, and it strictly forbade any form of *communicatio in sacris*, that is, sharing worship of God with non-Catholics. This was the basis of the practice of the Inquisition when it not only excommunicated heretics but also called on the state to enforce the Church's decrees against heresy even by capital punishment.[65] In response to the rise of the modern secularized state such as the U.S.A. which is neutral both to religion and irreligion and because of a more perfect appreciation of the Gospel teaching on the dignity of the human person Vatican II declared that:

> A wrong is done when government imposes upon its people, by force or fear or other means, the profession or repudiation of any religion, or when it hinders men from joining or leaving a religious body.[66]

In the Middle Ages it was generally assumed that anyone who dissented from the teaching of the Catholic Church after warning was a *formal* heretic, and the Churches of the Reform took the same stance as regards the "reformed religion." Today, however, as a result of the pluralism of our society, and our better understanding of the *subjective* aspect of human thinking — the many factors of background and culture which hinder human communication — we generally assume that most people, even those raised as Catholics but who have left the Church, are so conditioned by their culture that their rejection of Christianity, and within Christianity of Catholicism, is not *formal* but *material*. That is to say, this rejection is due to lack of information, misunderstanding, or emotional compulsions, rather than of stubborn ill will. Vatican II made this assumption in its Decrees on *Religious Liberty*, on *Ecumenism* and on *Relations of the Church to non-Christian Religions*, and showed

---

[65] Recent studies are giving us a more objective view of this dread institution, e.g., see Gustav Hinningsen and John Tedeschi, eds. in association with Charles Amiel, *The Inquisition in Early Modern Europe*; William Monter, *Frontiers of Heresy* which deals mainly with Aragon 1530-1630 and John Tedeschi, *The Prosecution of Heresy* with Italy. For the much worse scandal of the Inquisition and witchcraft in Northern Europe see Richard Kieckhefer, *European Witch Trials*.

[66] DH # 6.

a sympathetic understanding even for the professed atheists of our day.[67]

Hence those of other religions are not merely to be tolerated by Catholics, but truly respected for the elements of truth these religions promote and the good will of their practitioners. A certain degree of shared worship with such non-Catholics is permitted, provided that no denial or appearance of denial of Catholic truths is entailed.[68] While such sharing with those who do not share the Catholic faith has risks of occasioning indifference to the unique truth of the Faith, it also opens the way to share the Gospel with others in its fullness. In particular Catholics have a serious responsibility to work for the unity of all Christians (ecumenism) according to the prayer of the Lord at the Last Supper, "Holy Father, keep them in your name that you have given me, so that they may be one as we are one" (Jn 17:11), a prayer that surely refers to all who acknowledge Christ as Lord.

Short of heresy is *error*, that is, a direct denial of a doctrine taught by the Magisterium as certain, but not solemnly defined. If this doctrine is closely related to defined doctrines, to deny it is said to be "near heresy." If on the other hand it is only against a teaching which is theologically certain, it is a *theological* error. To hold or teach such theological errors without good reasons or directly against *common and safe* teaching (generally admitted by theologians as conformed to revelation but not proposed as certain; for example, Augustine's and Aquinas' views on the analogy between the human soul and the Trinity), as well as to promote *improbable* opinions (e.g., that the Blessed Virgin was a priest) which lack solid reasons is *irresponsible* or "rash."

Responsible faith also requires that we express our opinions about matters of doctrine in a serious and reverent way, so that what we say does not "smack of heresy" or of error; for example, simply to declare without explanation "Jesus is just a man" suggests a wrong sense, as if He were not also God. Expressions can also "sound bad" (*male sonans*) which have a true sense but offend common usage, or are "offensive to pious ears" (*piis auribus offensivum*) although not false. Of course

---

[67] GS n. 19-21; CCC # 2123-2128.
[68] CCC # 820-821.

Catholics' familiarity with the sacred sometimes leads them to speak in a slangy and joking way about sacred matters without any intention of irreverence but rather with an attitude of affection, but here good taste and respect for what is sacred need to be observed.

Just as faith requires positively that we profess the faith publicly and bring it to others, so it forbids the sin of *blasphemy*, which is the opposite of the profession of faith and the praise of God. It consists in seriously defaming God and the things of God in our speech and actions, and is a very grave sin (Lv 24:15-16, Is 36:23; 2 K 19:6; Tb 1:18; 2 M 15; 1 Tm 1:20; Col 3:8) both because it shows our inner lack of love of God and because it can lead others to a wrong attitude toward our Creator. Blasphemy does not hurt God but it hides the holy, loving face of God from ourselves and others.[69]

In the Ten Commandments the first commandment against worshipping false gods implies negatively the positive obligation to believe in the True God; the second and third commandments oblige us to reverence his Holy Name and join in his worship by the community of faith. These first three commandments of the Decalogue are discussed at length in the *Catechism of the Catholic Church* (# 2083-2195) and its entire Part Two on the Sacraments and Part Four on Prayer are devoted to guidance on worship of God "in Spirit and in truth" (Jn 4:23). Since all the precepts of the Decalogue also involve obligations of justice, they will be further discussed below in Chapter 6. In the New Testament these obligations are often mentioned.[70] In prayer and especially in receiving the sacraments we should express our faith. That is why in the revision of the ritual of the sacraments after Vatican II, special care was taken to begin the celebration of each sacrament with a reading from Scripture to arouse the faith of the receiver and all attending, and why the renewal of baptismal vows with the Creed was made a central feature of the Easter Vigil as well as the recitation of the Creed on all Sundays and solemn feasts. In this way Christians constantly renew the faith that lights their way on their journey to God.[71]

---

[69] CCC # 2142-2167.

[70] DS 2116-2117; Vatican I, DS 3031; CCC # 2087-2140.

[71] CCC # 1153-1155, 1190.

Summary of Norms

Since the object of Christian faith is the Triune God as the Father has revealed himself through Jesus Christ and his Church animated by his Holy Spirit, we can formulate the following positive ethical norm pertaining to the theological virtue of faith and which is equivalent to the First Commandment of the Decalogue (Dt 5:1-10). Note that the biblical citations after each summary norm are intended not as "proof texts" but as illustrations of themes treated at greater length in this chapter.

1. Since union with God is the ultimate goal of human life which we can not attain by our own power but only by the grace of Christ, we must be baptized and must firmly believe all that God has revealed to us for our salvation in Scripture and Tradition as this may be defined for us by the bishops of the Church in union with the successor of St. Peter and must constantly follow it as the guide of our life to that goal (Mt 28:19-20; 16:18-19).

And consequently we can state the following negative norms which oblige always and under all circumstances:

2. Never give the worship due the one God to any creature (*idolatry*; this is forbidden by the First Commandment, Dt 5:7-9a).
3. Never deny the Word of God as definitively taught by the Catholic Church (*heresy*) or refuse obedience of mind and will to her ordinary teaching (*error*; cf. Mk 1:15; Jn 1:12-13; Lk 10:16).[72]
4. Never renounce one's baptismal vow (*infidelity*) or publicly deny one's faith (2 P 2:21).
5. Never speak or act in such a way as to show public contempt for God (*blasphemy, sacrilege*; this is forbidden by the Second Commandment, Dt 5:11).

---

[72] Some might object that, as already explained in the text, it is at least possible that there could be circumstances in which it would be a duty to dissent from the ordinary, non-infallible teaching of the Magisterium. In my opinion such dissent would not be contrary to this norm if (as also explained in the text) it was done in such a way as neither to undermine the authority of the Magisterium nor usurp this authority as a guide to faith and conscience, but prudently and loyally to assist the Magisterium in the better formulation or development of its doctrine.

6. Never cease to try to live in accordance with one's faith and to foster it by private prayer and communal worship (prescribed by the Third Commandment, Dt 5:12).

The breaching of any of these negative precepts is mortally sinful if fully deliberate (and, in the case of heresy and error, stubborn, or, as regards blasphemy really contemptuous, or, as regards communal worship, habitual). The negative precepts regarding sins against faith oblige only because their violation blocks the fulfillment of the positive precept of faith for ourselves and perhaps also for others, which is humbly to accept God's guidance as our teacher, the Light that guides us home.

> *From his [the Word's] fullness we have all received, grace in place of grace, because while the law was given through Moses, grace and truth came through Jesus Christ. No one has ever seen God. The only Son, God, who is at the Father's side, has revealed him (Jn 1:16-18).*

CHAPTER 3

LIVING WISELY

Solomon said: "Therefore I prayed, and prudence was given to me; I pleaded and the spirit of Wisdom came to me. I preferred her to scepter and throne" (Ws 7:7).

A: MORAL WISDOM

Is Faith Moral Wisdom?

In the Old Testament the term "Wisdom" (Hebrew *hokmah*, Greek *sophia*) is so common a theme that a whole class of biblical books are called "Wisdom literature" (the seven books of Job, Psalms, Proverbs, Qoheleth, Song of Songs, Wisdom, Sirach; but "Wisdom" influence is also found in other books such as Deuteronomy, Baruch, Chronicles, etc.). This type of literature was common in the ancient Near East, especially in Egypt.[1] Books like Proverbs are modeled on such literature, which was generally the work of a learned class, in the Bible called "scribes," and it is characterized by its praise of "the way of Wisdom" and its denunciation of "the way of Folly" (Pr 4:10-27).[2]

Wisdom literature reflects not the legal codification of the Torah, but the accumulated experience of the ages, usually in proverbial or poetic form, in a spirit that is worldly-wise, often earthy, and skeptical of human illusions. Such wisdom is one of the chief sources of the

---

[1] For texts and analyses of Egyptian and Mesopotamian wisdom literature see McKane, *Proverbs*, pp. 51-210.

[2] On the notion of "Wisdom" in the Old Testament see the article of Roland E. Murphy, ABD, VI, pp. 920-931 with bibliography, pp. 930-931; also Patrick Skehan and A. Di Lella, *The Wisdom of Ben Sira*, pp. 31-39, with bibliography, pp. 119-122.

moral teaching of the Bible, having its own special point of view complementary to that of the Torah.

In several of these books Wisdom is personified as feminine —
the Divine Wisdom by whom God created the world and by which he
instructs humankind in the right way of life:

> Does not Wisdom call,
> and Understanding raise her voice?...
> "The Lord begot me, the firstborn of his ways,
> The forerunner of his prodigies of long ago...
> When he established the heavens I was there...
> Then was I beside him as his craftsman,
> And I was his delight day by day,
> Playing before him all the while,
> Playing on the surface of his earth;
> And I found delight in the sons of men.
> So now, O children, listen to me;
> Instruction and wisdom do not reject!"
> (Pr 8:1, 22, 27, 30-33a).[3]

In the New Testament both the Second Person of the Trinity
("Christ the power of God and the wisdom of God," 1 Cor 1:24; the
Logos or Word of God, Jn 1:1) and the Third Person (the Holy Spirit,
"We speak... not with words taught by human wisdom, but with words
taught by the Spirit, describing spiritual realities in spiritual terms," 1
Cor 2:13), seemed to be identified with the Old Testament Wisdom. Or
perhaps it is better to say that Old Testament Wisdom is God's self-
revelation to us in Creation and the Law (Ps 19; Ba 3:9-4:4), while in
the New Testament this revelation is seen to be completed through the
Incarnation of the Word and the sending of the Paraclete.[4]

---

[3] McKane, p. 223 translates Pr 8:30-31 as follows: "I was beside him as his confidant,/ I
gave him pleasure daily,/ jesting before him continually;/ jesting about his created
world/ and the pleasure I got from human beings." See his commentary on pp. 336-358
according to which Wisdom rejoices with God over the marvels of his creation (cf.
"God looked at everything he had made and found it very good," Gn 1:31).

[4] See Roland E. Murphy, O. Carm., NJBC, 27: 15-17 on the personification of Wisdom.
He concludes: "Lady Wisdom, then, is a communication of God, through creation, to
human beings," i.e., the self-revelation of God as evident to us through the order of
creation. This is close to Thomas Aquinas' understanding of "natural law" (a term of
Stoic origin) as a manifestation of the divine law, or God's own wisdom.

This biblical Wisdom is both contemplative and practical, but the accent is on the practical or moral, because the contemplation of the wisdom of God in the works of creation is generally presented (e.g., Ba 3:9-38; 4:1-4) as an introduction to moral teaching with the implication that if God rules an orderly creation by wisdom, man should rule his life in the same way. Consequently, the opposite of biblical wisdom is usually not ignorance but foolishness, so that we find Dame Wisdom contrasted with a whore, Dame Folly (Pr 4-5).

Such moral wisdom is called in Greek *phronesis,* usually translated "prudence." For example we read, "In all wisdom and prudence [*sophia kai phronesei*, NAB, "wisdom and insight"] Christ has made known to us the mystery of his will" (Eph 1:8-9). Thus Jesus urged his disciples, "Be shrewd [*phronimoi*] as serpents and simple [*akeraioi*, unspoiled, pure] as doves" (Mt 10:16). He also illustrated this by the Parable of the Unjust Steward (Lk 16:1-9) whose moral is "For the children of this world are more prudent (*phronimoteroi*) than are the children of light" (v. 8b), and by the Parable of the Ten Virgins (Mt 25:1-13), five foolish and five prudent (*phronimoi*, NAB "wise"). In current English the term "prudent" tends to have connotations like "cautious" or "compromising" which give a one-sided impression, hence generally I will use the term "moral wisdom."

This practical wisdom as a gift of God is closely related to divine faith, but differs from it: the problem of faith, even its practical aspect, is how to listen to God's self-revelation, while the problem of practical wisdom is how to discern what the Christian should or should not do to live in God's Kingdom. Thus practical wisdom applies what God has revealed about our journey toward him to actual life decisions in their particular circumstances.

As the Parable of the Unjust Steward (Lk 16:1-9) indicates, to the divine gift of moral wisdom there corresponds a kind of practical wisdom acquired by human effort, which we see in people who effectively manage their own lives, or their families, businesses, or political subjects, by a purely rational kind of planning and decision. But as divine faith elevates the human sciences, so God-given moral wisdom elevates human practical wisdom in its own service.

Nevertheless, history tells us of saints (for example, Pope St.

Celestine V, who resigned the papacy) who lacked the naturally acquired moral wisdom they needed to fulfill a particular earthly office. Indeed it is not uncommon to meet truly pious people who do not manage their temporal lives very well. They are practical about the salvation of their own souls but not in dealing with their property or managing other people. Thus the divine gift of practical wisdom and human acquired moral practicality are complementary to each other. Since grace perfects nature and nature serves grace, and divine and human practical wisdom are *analogous* to each other, we can study them in parallel, while noting their differences.

Faith's Goal

In practical matters decisions are relative to the goal or goals to be achieved; we must decide where we want to go before we decide the best way to get there. Consequently, Greek ethical schools were divided primarily by what they took to be the *summum bonum* or supreme good of human life, its ultimate goal, true *happiness*. The Epicureans believed it to be pleasure, the Stoics self-control, the Platonists and Aristotelians the contemplation of truth to be realized in a just society. Thus these were *teleological* (*telos*, goal) systems of ethics, in contrast to the *deontological* (*deontos*, duty or obligation) systems of laws or rules resting on the authority of a lawgiver. (The Hebraic law, the Torah, is certainly deontological in form, but this legal form expresses a deeper teleology, as we will see in a moment.)

If these great Greek philosophers disagreed on the true goal of life, how can we know what it is?[5] The knowledge of this supreme goal, and of other subordinate goals necessarily related to it, is supplied by reason and by faith through a virtue of our intelligence that we call *conscience* in the broad sense of that term and to which the scholastics gave the special name of *synderesis*. This "voice of conscience" is the awareness we all have, from the common experiences of being human,

---

[5] CCC # 1716-1729. The term "beatitude" is commonly used in theology to mean the perfect happiness of eternal life with God promised us through the grace of Christ.

that we have certain fundamental needs, which as free beings we have the responsibility to try to meet.[6] No human being can be entirely ignorant of these fundamental needs which pertain to human nature, although some have a much clearer grasp of them than others, and in some persons the awareness of some needs may be dulled.

Germain Grisez has described the sum of these needs as they constitute the goal of human life as "integral human fulfillment" and has analyzed this goal into seven basic goods: (a) *reflexive* (existential): self-integration, reasonableness, justice and friendship, religion or holiness; (b) *non-reflexive* (substantive): life, knowledge and appreciation of beauty or excellence, activities of skillful work and play.[7] Aquinas' simple list of four basic goods, however, seems adequate: *life* (health), *reproduction*, *society*, and *truth*. These four needs are interrelated and form a hierarchy. Truth is the supreme value, since with wisdom comes all other goods and particularly the knowledge and worship of God. But the fullness of truth is attainable only as the common good of a human community (society) and such a community cannot exist and function without the reproduction of its membership and the health which makes this possible. Thus integral human fulfillment requires health, family, and society and culminates in wisdom.

These basic needs and the values which satisfy them, therefore, constitute the *first principles* of moral reasoning, i.e., of natural law and of ethics. Their application to the particular problems of life which constitute the *means* to this goal are the work of practical wisdom or prudence. The acts of judgment which tell us what to do in a given situation are *conscience* in the strict sense of the word.[8]

---

[6] Vatican II, GS # 16; CCC # 1777-1782, 1795-1797. The traditional metaphor "voice of conscience" should not be understood in a too literal way. It is simply our realization of our moral responsibility as rational and free human beings and of the primary precepts of the natural law as we know them from our experience of living.

[7] Grisez, *The Way of the Lord Jesus*, vol. 1, pp. 123-124. The difference between "reflexive" and "non-reflexive" goods is that the former "are both reasons for choosing and are in part defined in terms of choosing" (e.g., "Part of the meaning [of the reflexive good] of self-integration is choice which brings aspects of one's self into harmony"), while the latter "are not defined in terms of choosing" but "provide reasons for choosing which can stand by themselves."

[8] CCC # 1778.

Behind the deontological laws of the Old Testament is the teleology of God's *promises* made in his covenant with his chosen people. These promises set the goal of life for the Jews which had its concrete historical embodiment in their hope to live according to the Mosaic law as faithful members of the Chosen People of the Covenant settled in the Promised Land "flowing with milk and honey" (Dt 31:20). After the Exile this goal was pictured as the return to the Holy City with its rebuilt Temple (Ezk 39:25-40:1ff.) under King Messiah of the House of David (Jr 23:5-6) to which all nations would come to worship the One God (Is 66:7-24).

Jesus' goal in life is expressed in the words of the Psalm, "As it is written of me in the scroll, Behold I come to do your will, O God" (Ps 40:8-9; Heb 10:7). In the narrative of Jesus' temptation at the beginning of his ministry (Mt 4:1-11; Lk 4:1-13; cf. Mk 1:12-13) we find the same life goal stated more fully.[9] Jesus replies to Satan that his goal is not to satisfy his own hunger (by turning stones to bread), nor to achieve fame in the eyes of others (by working wonders in the Temple), nor to possess power (by gaining the whole world through submission to Satan, "god of this world": 2 Cor 4:4), but to fulfill the commandment, "The Lord your God shall you worship and him alone shall you serve" (Mt 4:10; Dt 6:13).

Thus Jesus pictured the Reign of God not as a nationalistic political kingdom but as conformity to the will of his Father, and hence perfect union with the Father.[10]

Jesus answered and said to them, "Amen, amen, I say to you, a son cannot do anything on his own, but only what he sees his

---

[9] CCC # 538-539. "Mark relates this event in a mere two verses (1:12-13). He tells the fact of the temptation but not its details. This is important because it probably accurately reflects the situation of the disciples regarding this event: they knew that Jesus had been tempted (the historicity of the event need not be doubted), but since temptation is essentially a personal, inner experience they did not know exactly what had gone on in Jesus' consciousness. The Q version in Matt and Luke thus probably represents a narrative midrash or interpretation of the event in such a way as to make it pastorally useful for believers. This is done by connecting the 40-day fast with Moses and Elijah in the desert and with the great temptation or trial of God's patience by the people in the exodus..." B. Viviano, NJBC, 42:19, p. 638.

[10] On the meaning of the term "Kingdom of God" see CCC # 436-448, 547-550.

father doing; for what he does, his son will do also. For the Father loves his Son and shows him everything that he himself does" (Jn 5:19-20).

This intimate knowledge of the Father is everlasting life in the Kingdom of God. "If what you heard from the beginning remains in you, then you will remain in the Son and in the Father. And this is the promise that he made us: eternal life" (1 Jn 2:25). This Kingdom he declared to be already inaugurated in his own incarnate presence (Lk 4:16-21; Jn 2:19-22) and he invited all humanity into his community (Mt 28:19-20).

The integral human fulfillment shared by all who enter the Kingdom of God is nothing less than the life of the Holy Trinity. "For our fellowship is with the Father and with his Son Jesus Christ" (1 Jn 1:3). We have entered this Kingdom of God through conversion and baptism. It will attain its eternal fullness in the Trinity's intimate revelation of Father, Son, and Holy Spirit in the "beatific vision" (the vision that brings blessedness, perfect happiness).[11]

Only by entering into the life of the ever-living Triune God, who is the source of all goodness, truth, and beauty can every desire of created persons such as we are be satisfied. If we possess anything less than God, no matter how good it may be, our intelligences can always conceive of something better and our wills desire that better thing. Only in God can we find that inexhaustible and infinite goodness which lacks nothing and thus can totally satisfy us as creatures endowed with intelligence and freedom. That cannot be said of any of the other things that humans desire, whether fame or fortune, health or pleasure, success or achievement, or the love of any creature.

> Beloved, we are God's children now; what we shall be has not yet been revealed. We do know that when it is revealed we shall be like him, for we shall see him as he is (1 Jn 3:2).

---

[11] CCC # 163, 2548-2550, 2557.

Nature and Supernature

The Church has defined against the heresy of Pelagianism that this goal of eternal life in God, promised by the Scriptures, is not possible to us through our own powers.[12] Some religions, such as those of India, claim that through a rigorous discipline of meditation we can arrive at a vision of the Absolute Spirit, because our own spiritual souls are in reality identical with the Absolute.[13] Jews, Christians, and Muslims, however, without denying the reality and profundity of the spiritual experiences of the great mystics of the Orient, are convinced that because God is the Creator and we are only creatures, we are absolutely distinct from God, and can never be identified with him. Our perfect happiness can only be to remain ourselves, yet to come to "see him as he is."[14]

In Genesis 1-2 the original state of humanity in the creation is pictured as one in which human nature, made in the image of God, existed in its integrity, as entirely good, though finite.[15] Yet, since by nature we are made of "the clay of the ground" (Gn 2:7) we are liable to death and all the other frailties of material things.

> The dust returns to the earth as it once was, and the life breath returns to God who gave it. Vanity of vanities, say Qoheleth, all things are vanity! (Ec 12:7-8).

Hence, when we read in Genesis 1-3 the symbolic account of

---

[12] Trent, DS # 1551; CCC # 1997-1999.

[13] In none of the major eastern religions of Hinduism, Buddhism, Confucianism, and Taoism is there an explicit doctrine of "creation" as there is in the religions of Judaism, Christianity, and Islam. In the Eastern religions the Absolute by the necessity of its nature *emanates* the universe and hence is never entirely distinct from it. It is true that some Hindu thinkers avoid the notion of "necessity" by speaking of creation as "playful" yet they do not admit that the Absolute could exist without playing, i.e., without a universe. Even in the insistently "dualistic" theology of the Hindu Ramanuja the universe is distinct from God only as the human body is from the soul (see John Braistead Carman, *The Theology of Ramanuja*). In the theistic religions, on the contrary, God produces the universe by an act of *free will*, so that God is absolutely "other" than the creation and could exist without it. See Frederick Copleston, S.J., *Religion and the One: Philosophies East and West.*

[14] CCC # 285.

[15] CCC # 374-379, 384.

how God placed Adam and Eve in a garden, a perfect environment where they were safe from every misery, and promised them immortality if they lived by his laws, we discover that in creating us God endowed us also with something beyond our nature, something supernatural.[16] Above all, we note that Adam and Eve lived in intimate communion with God, who walked in the garden with them and talked to them directly (Gn 2:16; 3:9). Only after sin did the angel with the flaming sword bar their access to the garden and to intimate conversation with God (Gn 3:23-24).

The early Church Fathers and the tradition of the Eastern Church were well aware of the sinful condition of humanity after the Fall and the need of Christ's grace for its restoration to its original integrity and intimacy with God, but they did not develop an explicit theology of the relation of grace to nature in humanity's original state, nor of the transmission of sin from Adam to all his descendants. In the Latin Church, however, in the fifth century the heresy of Pelagius led St. Augustine and others to develop a dynamic theology of the transmission of original sin, its effects on human nature made in God's image, and the restoration of this image by grace, a restoration which will not be fully realized until the end of history. Yet Augustine's dialectical resolution of this problem left many unanswered questions for the scholastic theologians to tackle.[17]

St. Thomas Aquinas[18] took the view that Adam and Eve were created in the state of grace, having an integral human nature imaging God but further transformed by grace so as to be united to the Trinity indwelling in them through faith, hope, and love, and called to the perfect vision of the Trinity as the reward of faithful obedience to God. Adam as head of the human race would have transmitted this heritage of grace to all his descendants, but he lost that treasure for himself and his heirs, thus leaving the whole human race stripped naked of its trans-

---

[16] Trent, DS 1510-1516; CCC # 374-379, 384-390.

[17] See Karl Rahner, "Original Sin," *Encyclopedia of Theology*, pp. 1148-1155, and my discussion in *Theologies of the Body*, pp. 377-385, p. 408 with selected bibliography p. 408, note 95.

[18] *S.T.*, I, q. 95-100; I-II, q. 81-83.

formation by grace and in a merely natural state, no longer able to obtain the intimate union with God for which he had destined humanity in creation.

This tragic divestment of grace has not corrupted the forces of our complex human nature, which continues to image its Creator, but it destroys that harmonization and unification of these forces which resulted from their orientation by grace toward union with God. Hence, we now experience in ourselves the effects of Adam's sin in the conflict between the different forces of our nature ("concupiscence"). As St. Paul says (speaking of his bodily "members" as typical of all the elements of human nature, the psychological as well as the physical):

> I see in my members another principle at war with the law of my mind, taking me captive to the law of sin that dwells in my members. Miserable one that I am! Who will deliver me from this mortal body? (Rm 7:23-25).[19]

According to Aquinas, the grace of conversion and baptism by restoring our orientation to perfect union with God (justification) begins the work of reordering our nature (sanctification), which must be completed before we can be united with God. Those who die in grace, but not yet completely sanctified must pass through Purgatory. Those who die without conversion to God will remain forever in Hell. Unbaptized children who have committed no personal sin but have not received the grace of Christ will remain in Limbo, a state of happiness proportionate to human nature, but still lacking the transformation through grace.[20]

The Reformers, suspicious of the scholastic theology and accepting only what was explicit in the Bible, yet still much influenced by

---

[19] Who is the "I" in this passage? See summary of positions by Fitzmyer, NJB, p. 850, who adopts, rightly I believe, the view of Ernst Käsemann, which he summarizes thus: "Paul is making use of a rhetorical figure, Ego, to dramatize in an intimate, personal way the experience common to all unregenerate human beings faced with the Mosaic law and relying on their own resources to meet its obligations." It is, therefore, not autobiographical except in the sense that Paul is included along with all of us.

[20] S.T., III, Suppl. q. 97-99; IV Sent., d. 21, q. 1; II Sent., d. 33, q. 2.

Augustine and the legalism of late medieval theology in their interpretation of the Bible, abandoned the distinction between integral human nature and its transformation by grace. For them grace was simply God's act of forgiving the legal penalties of sin. Consequently, they understood the Fall, not as the loss of transforming grace, but as the corruption of human nature itself and the disfigurement or even erasure of the image of God in us. Hence, original sin remains in us as the actual sins of rebellion of our corrupted nature against God. For Luther grace and faith appropriate for us the holiness of Christ as if it were our own, but leave us in this life still in our sinful condition. Hence until death a Christian, though justified by faith in Christ, still remains in him or herself a sinner (*simul justus et peccator*). Calvin and the more radical reformers put more emphasis on the power of grace to sanctify us and enable us to keep God's law, but they balanced this optimism by an even more pessimistic account of our fallen nature than Luther's.

A similar pessimism developed among Catholics with the Jansenists (followers of Baius and Jansenius of the University of Louvain). Against this tendency, eventually condemned by the Church, orthodox Catholic theologians speculated extensively about "the state of pure nature," i.e., about what humanity would have been like if it had not been created in grace. The unfortunate result was an anthropology in which human nature and supernature were portrayed as *parallel* possibilities, having only an *extrinsic* relation to each other — the so-called "two-story anthropology."[21]

The Natural Desire to See God

In our century some theologians have reacted strongly against this "extrinsicism." Led by the French Jesuit, Henri de Lubac,[22] they have

---

[21] The best introduction to this question is still Henri Rondet, S.J., *The Grace of Christ: A Brief History of the Theology of Grace* (1966).

[22] See the summary of his position, first proposed in *Le Surnaturel* (1946), in his *A Brief Catechesis on Nature and Grace* (1980).

revived the views of Augustine, or even those of the Eastern Church,[23] while interpreting them in terms of modern philosophy with its anthropology of the human subject defined by "self-transcendence." Arguments are brought forward to show that the human person by its very nature as a finite self-conscious subject *necessarily* tends to perfect union with the Infinite God.[24]

This line of thought, of course, raises the question as to why, if we have by nature an orientation to perfect union with God, should we require grace to be so oriented? De Lubac's answer is that although we have this orientation by nature, we are powerless to attain this goal, especially in our sinful condition. Hence we need grace to attain the goal to which by nature we tend.

Although de Lubac presents this as consistent with the teaching of St. Thomas if not that of Thomists, he neglects the point that in St. Thomas' philosophy, every nature must tend to a goal *proportionate* to itself and its own powers.[25] Human nature, therefore, to be a *nature*, must have its own appropriate *natural* end which it can achieve by its own natural acts, namely to know God by natural reason through his

---

[23] See Antoine Slomowski, *L'état primitive de l'homme dans la tradition de l'église avant saint Augustin.* It is a common error to claim that the Eastern Fathers did not teach the doctrine of original sin. Under the influence of the Platonic dualism of Origen they tended to identify the "Fall" with the material *embodiment* of the spiritual soul and the consequent need for sex to perpetuate the species beyond death. They speculated that if there had been no sin, there would have been no sex. Augustine was the first to clearly teach that there would have been sex in a sinless Paradise. On the development of Augustine's thought on this topic see Peter Brown, *Augustine's Sexuality.*

[24] Such arguments usually claim that human self-consciousness is immediately, although unthematically, aware of our intelligence as a real, existent being with an inherent dynamism to continue to question being until it attains Absolute Being. Since "no natural tendency can be in vain," the Absolute (God) must exist, and be known as the *a priori* horizon of all our thinking. It is claimed that because this argument takes its departure from the real existence of the intelligence as a dynamic entity, it escapes the criticism made of the "ontological arguments" refuted by Kant because they invalidly conclude from mental being to real being. On the history of this claim see Georges Van Riet, *Thomistic Epistemology,* 2 vols.

[25] See the discussion of de Lubac's position in J.-H. Nicolas, O.P., *Les profondeurs de la grace,* pp. 334-399 with the brief bibliography on the controversy, p. 332, n. 1.

creation and to live a life of virtue according to the natural law.[26] Not only did the Greek philosophers discuss such a naturally good life, but as we have already seen, the Jews of the Old Testament (with the exception of a few obscure texts that foreshadow something greater) did not conceive the good life as the enjoyment of the beatific vision, but in entirely human terms.

> There is nothing better for man than to eat and drink and provide himself with good things by his labors. Even this, I realized, is from the hand of God. For who can eat and drink apart from him? For to whatever man he sees fit he gives wisdom and knowledge and joy; but to the sinner he gives the task of gathering possessions to be given to whatever man God sees fit. This also is vanity and a chase after wind (Ec 2:24-26).

Nevertheless, the Gospel is the Good News that God has called us by grace not merely to this imperfect natural happiness but to an absolutely perfect happiness in intimate union with him.

If we can never attain God by our own powers, is it not (as Aristotle seems to have thought) *impossible* for us ever to cross the infinite gap between ourselves and God?[27] Indeed, we cannot prove by any philosophical reasoning that the beatific vision is even possible. What we

---

[26] A basic argument against the Thomistic position is that material natures are *determinatum ad unum*, determined to act in a uniform way, while the human person is essentially free and, therefore, it would seem cannot have a determinant natural end but must be "open" to grace. But Thomists have never used the term "human nature" as if it were univocally the same as a material nature. The natural end to which the nature of the human person is determined is first of all the *abstract* essential Universal Good which is existentially realized for the human person as "integral natural human fulfillment." This finality leaves us open and free with respect to the means to this natural goal, but also for elevation by grace to an infinitely higher supernatural goal, namely God, since God is, in fact, *concretely* the universal existential Good.

[27] "In friendship quantitative equality is primary and proportion to merit secondary. This becomes clear if there is a great interval in respect of virtue or vice or wealth or anything else between the parties; for then they are no longer friends, and do not even expect to be so. This is most manifest in the case of the gods; for they surpass us most decisively in all good things." *Nicomachean Ethics*, Bk VIII, Ch. 7, 1158b 33-36. St. Thomas Aquinas answers this, *S.T.*, II-II, q. 23, a. 1c, by pointing out that the Gospel tells us that "Since we have communion with God in this, that God communicates his own blessedness to us, on the basis of this communion a certain kind of friendship is established."

can show philosophically (as St.Thomas Aquinas argued[28]) is that since we are persons having intellects and wills open to all reality there is nothing in our nature which indicates it to be impossible for God, without destroying our natures, to grant us this gift of union with him. Old Testament Jews feared that to see God would mean death (Jg 6:22; 13:22, etc.). The New Testament tells us that to see God will be to enter into God's glory which will heal our nature and make it immortal.

Thus when Aquinas spoke of our "natural desire" for the beatific vision, he was only refuting the arguments of those who claimed that such a goal was impossible because it is *contradictory* to our natures. We have such a "natural desire" to see God face to face in the sense that our intelligence tends to seek all reality, and our will, following that intelligence, to approve all the goodness of all reality. Since, however, by reason we do not know whether this is even possible, as reasonable creatures we should be content with the imperfect happiness due to a creature. It is only when God himself invites us to union with him that this natural desire is transformed into the sublime love of charity which motivates the Christian life.

That God has indeed issued this invitation to all humanity becomes apparent when we find in all religions strong mystical tendencies and examples of sublime virtue,[29] and when in the Church we see the holiness of the saints, and above all of Jesus himself and his mother Mary.

> So then you are no longer strangers and sojourners, but you are fellow citizens with the holy ones and members of the household of God, built upon the foundation of the apostles and prophets, with Christ Jesus himself as the capstone. Through him the whole structure is held together and grows into a temple sacred in the Lord; in him you also are being built together into a dwelling place of God in the Spirit (Eph 2:19-22).[30]

Thus in the actual creation in which we live our natural goal to be fully human remains truly a goal for us, but it is in fact not our *ultimate*

---

[28] *S.T.*, I-II, q. 3, a. 8.

[29] On this see Vatican II, *Declaration on the Relationship of the Church to Non-Christian Religions* (NA); CCC # 839-849; also GS # 10.

[30] The "marks of the Church," see CCC # 813-870.

goal, which includes but far surpasses imperfect, natural happiness. As the shepherd boy David might well have been content to grow up a pastoral patriarch, a wise head of a household of fine sons and daughters and a rich owner of a great herd, but instead was called by God to lead his people as a great warrior and their anointed king, ancestor of the Messiah (1 S 16:1-13), so we are called to something much greater than might have been suspected merely from our human nature.

This higher calling by God, however, does not obliterate our nature or its needs, but widens and deepens them. Germain Grisez has accused Aristotle of reducing the needs of human nature to a single one, *contemplation* of the truths accessible to human reason; and has argued that this can be the goal only of an elite.[31] The fact, however, that Aristotle and Aquinas consider contemplation our deepest need and highest goal which unifies everything else we need, by no means shows that they failed to recognize that in the natural order the goal proportionate to our complex human nature is not one single good, but an ordered hierarchy of goods. Thus we have a *summum bonum* and also subordinated goals which too must be met.

The elevation of this integrated natural end by grace in no way contradicts or merely parallels these natural goods, but transforms them by replacing life and reproduction with immortal, eternal life and earthly society with the Kingdom of God centered no longer in the merely natural knowledge and worship of God but in the beatific vision. Thus in achieving our supernatural goal we also attain our natural goal of integral human fulfillment, and transcend it by becoming adopted children of God, participants in the divine life. This supernatural goal is not only inclusive of all natural goals, but *unifies* them completely, since in possessing God alone, we possess all that God has created. For natural happiness we need many essential goods, but for supernatural happiness "only one thing is necessary" (Lk 10:42),[32] God who is All.

---

[31] For my analysis of Germain Grisez's position with regard to the role of the ultimate end of human life in ethics and moral theology see my essay, "What is the End of the Human Person? The Vision of God and Integral Human Fulfillment."

[32] Literally "the one thing necessary" in the story of Martha and Mary is "listening to his word, (v. 39; see 8:21) and that is the best part" (cf. Robert J. Karris, O.F.M., NJBC, p. 702); but this surely implies that Jesus who speaks the word and is in fact the Word is "the one thing necessary." See St. Augustine, *De quest. evangel.* 2, 30.

The Fundamental Option

A person's commitment to this supreme goal, which for the Christian is nothing less than God in his inner triune life, requires an act of the will, and this act is the most profound act we can make since it motivates all our other choices and actions. Of course in making such choices we are not always fully aware of the fact that we are measuring them by our ultimate goal because it is so habitual with us. It is only in certain important decisions that we are awakened to the fact that some options are incompatible with the goal to which we have committed ourselves, so that if we were to choose them, we would also have to abandon all hope of reaching that goal.[33]

This means, obviously, that if we do in fact choose one of these options, we can do so only by *changing our ultimate goal*. Thus for a man who has committed himself to making money as the most important priority of his life, the decision to give a large sum to charity with no financial advantages in sight, means a *conversion* from one ultimate goal to another. Similarly for a Christian who has opted for God as his supreme goal, the decision to do serious harm (i.e., to sin mortally) to one's neighbor whom God loves, is possible only by a *conversion* from God to some other supreme goal, valuing some selfish interest in preference to God.

Recently, there has been discussion among moralists about whether it is psychologically possible for someone to undergo such a conversion from good to bad, or bad to good in a single act of choice. Some have argued, therefore, that there can be no such thing as a "mortal sin" in the sense of a single act, but only in a change of moral

---

[33] On "the fundamental option" see VS # 65-70. For different versions of the theory and its defense see Felix Poddimatam, O.F.M. Cap., *Fundamental Option and Mortal Sin*. Some (see Joseph A. Selling and Jan Jans, *The Splendor of Accuracy*) have complained that the encyclical does not do this theory full justice. But VS does not pass judgment on the type of phenomenological philosophy on which this theory is based. Rather, VS's concern is that some have used this theory, rightly or wrongly, to deny that acts which the Church has always taught to be mortal sins which separate us from God if we perform them knowingly and deliberately do so in fact. Those who defend the theory therefore have the responsibility to show that it does not logically lead to such errors.

orientation that develops over a long time. They think, therefore, that a Christian who commits adultery on a particular occasion may still remain in "the state of grace" (i.e., in union with God) as long as his fundamental orientation to live as a Christian has not changed.

The moralists who take this view have found support in a theory of Karl Rahner which distinguishes between "transcendental freedom" and "categorial freedom."[34] The latter is the freedom we experience in particular acts of choice, while the former is something much deeper, at the intuitive, non-verbalizable level of consciousness. This transcendental freedom becomes evident to us only when it is expressed in particular categoric acts that are perceived by us as turning points in our lives. Therefore, our commitment to a supreme goal in life, our conversion, is called by Rahner, our "fundamental option" to distinguish it from the particular categoric acts which may or may not express it.

This theory finds some support in St.Thomas Aquinas for whom the conversion and commitment to a "final end" (*summum bonum*) is the first principle of moral action.[35] This commitment, therefore, is an act of the will guided by intelligence operating as intelligence (*intellectus*, intuition) rather than as reason (*ratio*).[36] As such it is not easily put into words or made explicit in consciousness in an objective way, but is an act of the total person.

Nevertheless, Rahner's theory (which is related to his whole philosophical system of transcendentalism) must not be interpreted, as some moralists have done, to mean that mortal sin cannot be committed in single acts. In fact, for Rahner, our transcendental freedom cannot be exercised apart from single acts, and hence the act of conversion to mortal sin or to the state of grace in which that freedom expresses itself has to be a single act, although this crucial act is usually the culmination of a whole series of acts (venial sins of a more and more deliberate

---

[34] Karl Rahner, S.J., "On the Question of a Formal Existential Ethics," *Theological Investigations*, vol. 2, p. 217-234 and "Experience of the Spirit and Existential Commitment," *ibid.*, vol. 16, pp. 24-34.

[35] *S.T.*, I-II, q. 1-5.

[36] *S.T.*, I-II, q. 79, a. 8-11.

and serious character, or good acts moved by actual grace) which have prepared the way for the moment of conversion.

Hence, whether we accept Rahner's or Aquinas' epistemology, the "fundamental option" is changed by some *critical* act of conversion to God or to what is not God, but is usually the culminating act of a series of less significant acts. For example, the covenant of marriage between a couple is broken by a critical act of adultery or divorce, but this is unlikely to happen except after a long series of less serious offenses against the marriage have already weakened it.

No doubt, the phenomenon of the Christian who seems to be trying to live a Christian life, yet who repeatedly slips into objectively mortal sins, is puzzling to confessors. Yet it is best explained, not simply by denying that these failures may be objectively mortal sins, but by considering two facts: (1) Subjective guilt is often diminished by compulsive habits which cause actions that are objectively wrong but to which the actor does not consent with full deliberation or freedom. Hence they do not involve a change of final end. (2) Sins that involve strong emotions ("sins of weakness") and which are not committed with a clear head (as are "sins of malice"), may involve a temporary conversion to evil and hence are subjectively mortal, yet may be quickly repented because the person is habitually oriented by faith and by natural virtue to a Christian way of life.[37]

Thus a man seduced into adultery under strong temptation and in a moment of weakness, commits a mortal sin, yet may quickly repent. David, whose whole life had been directed toward God, in a time of idleness, at the sight of Bathsheba's beauty, changed the whole direction of his life not only by adultery but by the treacherous murder of his faithful soldier Uriah. Yet, when Nathan the prophet brought David to face the wickedness of what he had done, he repented and turned back to God (2 S 11-12). Thus David's faith in God, although a dead faith

---

[37] Those who sin mortally against any virtue except faith itself, retain the gift of faith, although it is a "dead faith." Trent (DS # 1544, 1577-1578) insisted, against those Protestants who held that mortal sin cannot exist in those with true faith, that those who sin mortally can still retain a true faith that calls them to repentance, although, if they refuse to repent, this dead faith, i.e., faith without love, cannot save them from hell.

that could not unite him with God, was still able to call him to repentance.

In practice, therefore, if we are struggling against falling into a mortal sin, yet fall, it should be confessed just as we see ourselves culpable, but we can console ourselves that if we keep praying sincerely God will not abandon us to our sins. On the other hand, we should remember that unrepented venial sins prepare the way for mortal sin.[38]

Choosing the Right Means

Moral wisdom (prudence), both as natural and as a gift of grace, builds on the first principles or goals which we have just discussed and applies them to form the judgment of conscience (in the strict sense) to particular decisions that must be made. Thus it is concerned with the *means* by which our goals can be effectively accomplished.[39] We must find means that lead to these goals and do not deviate either to the side of too much or too little. As a driver of an automobile steers straight down his lane, correcting any tendency of the car to swerve to left or right by slight turns of the wheel, so moral wisdom seeks to steer between *extremes* of action, an excess or a deficiency of response to a given situation. This principle of "the golden mean," so characteristic of Greek ethics, is not very explicitly stated in the Bible, which generally warns against that extreme of *excess* to which the average human is most liable, but frequently warning is also given against the other extreme of *defect*, e.g.:

> Let not wine-drinking be the proof of your strength
> for wine has been the ruin of many.
> As the furnace probes the work of the smith
> so does wine the hearts of the insolent.

---

[38] On the permanent validity and importance of the distinction between mortal and venial sin which after Vatican II was denied or minimized by some catechists, see VS # 69-70 and CCC # 1854-1864, 1874-1875.

[39] CCC # 1806.

> Wine is the very life to man
>   if taken in moderation,
> Does he really live who lacks the wine
>   which was created for his joy? (Si 31:25-27).

In reasoning from such practical principles to practical conclusions, we cannot expect the same certainty that we have about the first principles themselves. Some people see the first principles of moral reasoning which are accessible to human reason more clearly than others, yet all humans know them with certitude. These are said to be the *primary precepts* of the natural law, "Do good and avoid evil" (i.e., "Seek the true goal of life in all your actions").[40] This first precept, however, can be expressed more concretely as: "Seek bodily health, the preservation of the human species, the common good of society, and truth as the highest element of the common good, in ascending order of importance, and avoid whatever is contrary to these goods." Such a formula expresses the integration of the basic goods that form this true natural goal of life. The Old Testament states this in another, but equivalent way, since it teaches that God in creating us has established an order whose violation will lead to retribution:

> The last word, when all is heard: Fear God and keep his commandments, for this is man's all. Because God will bring to judgment every work, with all its hidden qualities, whether good or bad (Ec 12:13-14).

Those who in pursuit of truth have come to accept the Christian faith understand these principles of the order established by the Creator more profoundly than those who have not been granted faith. Although even among Christians some have deeper faith than others, all believers know the goals of the graced life with the certitude of faith. The application of such principles, however, requires many steps of reasoning and it is quite possible for many people to be ignorant of the secondary and tertiary norms of the natural law, and for many Christians to be poorly instructed in the Christian moral tradition.

---

[40] On the kinds of laws and in particular the natural law, see CCC # 1950-1986.

Moral wisdom enables us to do three things well: (1) to *deliberate* as to what are the best means to achieve the Christian goals of life, (2) to judge rightly which means to choose between possible extremes (this is *conscience in the strict sense*), and (3) to determine *to act* according to our conscience.

> I have examined my ways [*deliberation*]
>   and turned my steps to your decrees [*judgment*].
> I am prompt, I do not hesitate
>   in keeping your commands [*action*] (Ps 119:59-60).

The term "prudence" is not so common among the Church Fathers as such terms as "moderation" or "measure" to determine the middle way of virtue. In the monastic writers the term used instead is "discretion" and is constantly inculcated as the necessary balance between the extremes of the vices, because as the great authority on monastic life St. John Cassian said, "the extremes are equal."[41] St. Benedict, on whose rule all Western monasticism is still based, insisted on the great importance of this virtue.[42] One of the chief authors on the subject was Richard of St. Victor in the twelfth century who said:

> Virtues are turned into vices if they are not moderated by discretion... For fear often slips into desperation, immoderate hope into presumption, excessive love into infatuation. Do you not see how all the other virtues require discretion lest they lose the very name of virtue?[43]

Later, in the spirituality of St. Ignatius of Loyola, this concept of discretion became blended with that of "the discernment of spirits."[44] Experienced spiritual directors have always known that the fostering in their clients of a moral wisdom about what is fitting in the shifting

---

[41] He calls it an "old saying" (*akrotetes isotetes*); *Conferences* II, ch. 16.

[42] *Rule of St. Benedict*, Rule 64.

[43] *Benjamin Minor*, 66, PL 196, 47d-48a.

[44] See Piet Penning de Vries, *Discernment of Spirits According to the Life and Teachings of St. Ignatius Loyola*.

situations of Christian life in view of the particular temperament, development, and condition of that individual must be one of a spiritual
director's fundamental objectives in helping the one he or she guides to
form a sensitive and accurate moral conscience.

A Christian Ethics

What is the relation of such a determination of moral means to the
philosophy of morals which is usually called *ethics*?[45] Aristotle, the
first to formulate a systematic ethics,[46] showed that this discipline is
distinguished from metaphysics and natural philosophy because it deals
not with what is, but with what we as rational beings *ought* to do, i.e.,
it is not a theoretical but a practical discipline. Yet, although practical,
it has a more theoretical part which deals in a broad classificatory way
with the principles (i.e., the ends or goals) of reasonable human action
and the possible means of achieving these goals. Hence it also establishes the general norms or rules of reasonable action.

The concrete application of these norms to actual situations, however, cannot be reduced to theoretical statements, but requires experience and good moral dispositions and it is this that is rightly called
"prudence" or practical wisdom. Thus "ethics" in the narrower sense is
contrasted to prudence, since one may have studied this more theoretical ethics, and yet not achieved real moral practicality. But in a broader
sense, since the whole purpose of studying ethics is to live well, "ethics" includes "prudence" as its own ultimate *raison d'être*. Thus one
who studies the "theory of music" but who never listens to it or per-
forms it, studies in vain. Knowing the theory of music is of little value
unless it helps us to play or appreciate musical performances. So the

---

[45] Much that is today called "ethics" is in fact *meta*-ethics, that is, discussion of the
methodology of ethics, rather than of its substantive content.

[46] Aristotle wrote two (partly overlapping) treatises on ethics, the *Eudemian Ethics* and
the *Nicomachean Ethics*, named after the persons to whom they were dedicated. The
latter is the more famous work and with the *Politics* actually forms a single treatise.
Doubtfully attributed to him are also the *Magna Moralia* and the *De Virtutibus et
Vitiis*.

study of ethics apart from the development of the virtue of prudence is a waste of time.

Similarly moral theology compared to dogmatic theology is practical rather than theoretical, but it has a more theoretical aspect and a more practical aspect. Some treatises in moral theology (such as the Second Part of St. Thomas Aquinas' *Summa Theologiae*) stop short at this more theoretical aspect, while the more practical problems are left to what is today called "pastoral theology." This present work, because it is an introduction, is also devoted primarily to these broader principles, yet it studies them as simply an introduction to pastoral theology, to the truly practical aspects of Christian life.

The biblical writers and Jesus himself never attempted a systematic presentation of ethics or moral wisdom, but tended to keep to the practical level of rules that actually guide human action. Nevertheless, they also sought to stress certain crucial principles of action without which these rules would lack vitality. "The letter brings death, but the Spirit gives life" (2 Cor 3:6), says St. Paul, indicating that the letter of the rules of the Old Testament could not bring us spiritually to life, unless inspired by the Holy Spirit who gives true motivation, the very principle of authentic morality.[47]

Christian moral wisdom is to be found not merely in particular good acts, but in the *character* of a person who has the constant capacity to live as a Christian day in and day out in all kinds of circumstances. As Jesus says in the Sermon on the Mount, "A good tree cannot bear bad fruit, nor can a rotten tree bear good fruit" (Mt 7:18).[48]

Hence practical wisdom is truly a virtue and the source of the other virtues, since if we do not deliberate, judge, and act according to our consciences we cannot acquire or use our other virtues well. Prac-

---

[47] See VS # 1-27 in which the narrative of Jesus' encounter with the rich young man (Mt 19:16-30; Mk 10:17-31; Lk 18:18-30) is used to explain the nature of a Christian ethics. CCC # 1691-2051 deals with the general principles of such an ethics.

[48] This text should not be taken to deny that a bad person may occasionally perform good acts, or a good person perform bad acts. It only denies that a bad person can consistently do good, or a person be good who frequently acts wrongly. If this were not so, bad persons could never become virtuous through repeated good acts, or good persons become vicious by repeated bad acts, as in fact happens.

tical wisdom is a virtue that improves our *intellect* because it helps us
to think truly and realistically about moral matters, yet it also supposes
that we have a good will (otherwise we will not follow our conscience)
and also other moral virtues (because vices push us to extremes). Selfish
people who seek only their own narrow good, like alcoholics who think
only of drinking, cannot think straight or realistically about how to live
their lives. This means that moral wisdom as a divine gift cannot exist
in persons enslaved to sin, that is, who are not living for love of God
and neighbor.

The "Way of the Wise"

The process of acting in a morally wise way is not simple or easy.
Making and acting on good decisions is difficult, and that is why we
need God's guidance. No less than eight steps of moral prudence can
be distinguished, and all can be illustrated from the Book of Proverbs
and other wisdom literature (see especially Sirach 8 and 18:14-29 for
short essays on prudence).[49]

In order to judge well we must first understand the practical problem we face and to do this we must first evaluate the concrete problem
by (1) using our *memory* of our or others' experience of the results of
past actions ("Wise men store up knowledge, but the mouth of a fool is
imminent ruin," Pr 10:14); (2) using our *intelligence* to understand the
present situation ("The shrewd man's wisdom gives him knowledge of
his way, but the folly of fools is their deception," Pr 14:8). Then we
must gather information (3) by *learning from others* who may help us
to judge ("Plans fail when there is no counsel, but they succeed when
counselors are many," Pr 15:22); and (4) using our *ingenuity* to think of
all possible means to achieve our goals ("Many are the plans in a man's

---

[49] The following quotes from Proverbs are not to be understood as if the writers of that
book *systematically* dealt with the eight steps of prudence which Aquinas arrives at by
a philosophical analysis. What they illustrate is that experience had made the ancient
sages keenly aware of the need for all these acts in ethical decision-making. They well
understood that ethical decision is much more than the mechanical observance of rules.

heart, but it is the decision of the Lord that endures," Pr 19:21)[50]; and (5) *reasoning* about what should be done ("The senseless man seeks in vain for wisdom, but knowledge is easy to the man of intelligence," Pr 14:6). After judging, we then have to carry out our decisions by (6) *foresight* as to carrying out the steps to the goal ("A son who fills the granaries in the summer is a credit, the son who slumbers during harvest, a disgrace," Pr 10:5); (7) *circumspection* as to the surrounding situation in which we are acting ("The simpleton believes everything, but the wise man measures his steps," Pr 14:15; cf. Si 18:27, "A wise man is circumspect in all things; when sin is rife he keeps himself from wrongdoing"); (8) *caution* about obstacles which may frustrate our completion of the task ("The wise man is cautious and shuns evil; the fool is reckless and sure of himself," Pr 14:16). These steps integrate the whole moral action.

The moral wisdom necessary for individuals to manage their own lives well is not adequate to manage their families, because individuals know their own needs and abilities, but in families it is necessary to deal with others of a different sex and age. Similarly it takes much more experience and skill to manage a business or some other larger institution such as a school or the army. Finally the moral wisdom required to be a really good statesman or politician, or even that required to be a good citizen of a country is greatest of all. Hence acquired moral wisdom is *individual* (ethics), *domestic* (family ethics), *administrative* (military, business, etc., ethics[51]); *civil* (ethics of citizenship); and *political* (ethics of government).

Why then do so many Christians manage their own lives, their family lives, and the Church so badly? It is because they do not use

---

[50] The sense here (see McKane, *Proverbs*, p. 534) is that human ingenuity, although necessary to wise action, must be tested by divine guidance.

[51] Aquinas, *S.T.*, II-II, q. 49, a. 4, names only "military prudence," and in his reply to the second objection explains that "other affairs which exist in a city are ordered to particular benefits, but military affairs are ordered to the defense of the whole common good." But it might be argued that according to the principle of subsidiarity, the administration of recognized corporate bodies within the state also require certain types of prudence as well as technical skill. In any case there is an analogy between political prudence and lesser kinds of administrative ability.

their gifts well or grow in them, and one of the causes of this is that they fail also to develop the appropriate human moral wisdom which would be an instrument in the service of these gifts. King David, although "his heart was entirely with the Lord" (1 S 13:14), and though he was a ruler and military leader of great prudence, in his private life was not free of grave folly, as we see in his adultery (2 S 11) and in his failure to train his sons wisely (2 S 13ff.).

St. Thomas Aquinas noted that we can also distinguish three *auxiliary* virtues connected with moral wisdom, which facilitate its proper use, but do not themselves fully deserve the name of moral wisdom. These are (1) good *counsel* or skill in deliberating over possible ways of action, which aids in the first four steps listed above (see the story of the wise and foolish counselors of King Rehoboam, 1 K 12:1-25); (2) good *judgment* about how to apply the general norms to the situation (see the prudence of Abigail in dealing with David, 1 S 25); (3) good judgment about how to meet *exceptional* cases (for example, the "judgment of Solomon," 1 K 3:16-28). Not everyone has all three skills; some are good in counseling, but not in judgment, and some are good in judgment about the rules in the book, but not in how to meet unusual situations in a flexible, practical way.

In order to live the Christian life, however, we are all gifted with all these aspects of moral wisdom, if we only use them. And in addition we have the Gift of the Holy Spirit called counsel (Is 11:2) which enables us to yield to the guidance of the Spirit in our thinking about how to live as a Christian.

> I, Wisdom dwell with experience,
>> and judicious knowledge I attain...
> Mine are counsel and advice;
>> Mine is strength and understanding.
> By me kings reign,
>> and lawgivers establish justice;
> By me princes govern, and nobles,
>> all the rulers of the earth (Pr 8:12, 14-16).

Since the Christian is traveling to a farther and more mysterious goal than the unbeliever even dreams about, the Christian's judgment of right and wrong, the important and unimportant in life, is necessarily very different. A non-Christian reading the life of Thérèse of Lisieux would probably say that this woman was a fool to lock herself up in a convent where tuberculosis was rife and the superior a petty tyrant. Yet read in the light of the Gospel we see Thérèse, although not free of faults and neuroses, as an extraordinarily strong and wise woman who made very few false steps in life, but walked straight to God on her "little way of spiritual childhood" based on the words of Jesus, "Amen, I say to you, whoever does not accept the kingdom of God like a child will not enter it" (Lk 18:17). She understood profoundly the teachings of Jesus and knew how to apply them in her life circumstances.

Jesus' own prudence is shown in his choosing to preach in Jerusalem, knowing that it meant his death, because he knew that this was the best of all means to manifest the selfless love of the Father even for his enemies.

> "Behold, I cast out demons and I perform healings today and tomorrow, and on the third day I accomplish my purpose. Yet I must continue on my way today, tomorrow, and the following day, for it is impossible that a prophet should die outside of Jerusalem" (Lk 13:32-33).

This is what St. Paul calls the "folly of the Cross" (1 Cor 2:6-16).

> Now the natural person does not accept what pertains to the Spirit of God, for to him it is foolishness, and he cannot understand it, because it is judged spiritually. The spiritual person, however, can judge everything but is not subject to judgment by anyone (1 Cor 2:14-15).

Such spiritual wisdom is closely connected with the *fifth Beatitude*, "Blessed are the merciful, for they will be shown mercy" (Mt 5:7), because mercy to others is one of the best means to obtain mercy (i.e., salvation) for ourselves, and its fruits are the works of mercy. Therefore, living mercifully toward others, is living wisely.

The "Way of Fools"

All sin is foolish, but to sin directly against moral wisdom one has to fail to try to form one's conscience rightly before acting. One may act *rashly* by rushing ahead and acting without thinking (i.e., against the first four phases of prudence listed above), particularly by ignoring good advice. "The wise man is cautious and shuns evil; the fool is reckless and sure of himself" (Pr 14:16). Or one may *reason unreasonably* about what should be done by allowing one's pet prejudices or dislikes or favoritism to interfere with conscience, or by giving way to unreasonable fears or rationalizations that blind one to reality. "The way of the fool seems right in his own eyes, but he who listens to advice is wise" (Pr 12:15). Or one may be *inconstant*, wavering in one's judgment for foolish reasons instead of sticking to what one really knows is best. "A fool's mind is like a broken jar — no knowledge at all can it hold" (Si 21:14). Or finally one may simply be *negligent* by failing to carry out in practice what one had decided to do. "The sluggard loses his hand in the dish; he is too weary to lift it to his mouth" (Pr 26:15). If the matter is serious, or the negligence arises from contempt of God's guidance, such a sin is mortal because it turns us away from our road to God.

Lack of moral wisdom of this sort is often to be observed in adolescents (although through lack of experience they are not often culpable), as in the boy who drinks and drives wildly or the girl who gets pregnant, heedless of the consequences of their very unrealistic actions. Such imprudence comes from a lack of thoughtfulness often denounced in the Wisdom literature, but there is also a kind of imprudence at the other extreme, and this is denounced in the Gospel. Namely this is that "worldly wisdom" or "shrewdness" which we find in the actions of people who think little of God and the future life but a great deal about "getting ahead" in this world. "There is a shrewdness keen but dishonest, which by duplicity wins a judgment" (Si 19:21; cf. 19:17-21), and St. Paul speaks of what he calls the "concern of the flesh" (in some translations "carnal prudence") "which is hostility to God" (Rm 8:6). The Epistle of James speaks of a "false wisdom" which "does not come down from above but is earthly, unspiritual, demonic. For where jealousy and selfish ambition exist, there is disorder and every foul practice" (Jm 3:15-16).

Jesus, with ironic humor, told the Parable of the Dishonest Steward (Lk 16:1-8) who was commended by his kindly master for the cleverness he showed in avoiding the consequences of his fraud.[52] Jesus drew the moral of the story by saying,

> "For the children of this world are more prudent in dealing with their own generation than are the children of light. I tell you make friends with dishonest wealth, so that when it fails, you will be received into eternal dwellings" (Lk 16:8b-9).

He meant that as worldly people are so clever in managing their money, often dishonestly, we should also manage our earthly affairs intelligently but always in view of our true goal of love of God and neighbor.

> For those who live according to the flesh are concerned with the things of the flesh, but those who live according to the spirit are concerned with the things of the spirit. The concern of the flesh is death, but the concern of the spirit is life and peace (Rm 8:5-6).

This prudence of the flesh is not truly practical wisdom, in spite of the fact that such a person goes through all the processes of careful judgment, because in such cases intelligence is used to achieve a wrong and ultimately self-defeating end. Moreover, worldly prudence often takes great care to do what is harmful and destructive just as the prudence of the spirit always strives to be helpful and constructive. Thus false prudence has three species: (1) *cunning* in the use of intelligence to do wrong: "There is shrewdness keen but dishonest, which by duplicity wins a judgment" (Si 19:21); (2) *deception* in words: "Better a

---

[52] This story is open to different interpretations; see Robert J. Karris, O.F.M., NJBC, 43: 148-149. Is it an "example story," or a true parable of the Kingdom? It may in fact be both, and here I take it as an example story. The verse about "dishonest wealth" (literally: *"mammon* of iniquity" Lk 16:9) means that just as worldlings are very shrewd about dishonestly making and spending money in order to get rich, so Christians ought to use their material goods very prudently in charitable ways to attain the Kingdom of God.

thief than an inveterate liar, yet both will suffer disgrace" (Si 20:24); (3) *fraud* in deeds; "False scales are an abomination to the Lord, but a full weight is his delight" (Pr 11:1). We have only to read the newspapers to learn of the many talented "con-men" low and high who use their gifts carefully to plan and perhaps conspire with other crooks to exploit others, often the simple and unsuspecting. But such false prudence is also seen in those who, without criminal activity, nevertheless neglect the most important things in human life to obtain worldly success (see the Parable of the Rich Fool, Lk 12:16-21). Thus the capital sin of *avarice* is often the motivation of this "worldly wisdom."

B: CONSCIENCE

The "Voice of Conscience"

Conscience (in the strict sense) is not a special virtue. As the practical judgment of what is right and wrong it is the act of moral wisdom (prudence) through the instrumentality of its auxiliary virtues of good counsel and good judgment, both in common and in exceptional cases. It has always been a teaching of the Catholic Church that *conscience is the proximate subjective rule of all human acts*, that is, that we are always obliged to follow a prudent (well-formed) conscience, even when this happens to be mistaken. St. Paul teaches this very clearly in Romans 14:13-23 where he shows that although Christians are not bound by the food regulations of the Mosaic law, yet if they believe they are still bound by it they must follow their consciences: "But whoever has doubts is condemned if he eats, because this is not from faith ["good faith," conscience]; for whatever is not from faith is sin" (Rm 14:23; see all of Rm 14-15 and 1 Cor 8:1-3; 10:25-33; also Gal 5:3; Jn 9:41; 15:21-24).[53]

Therefore, a subjectively good but objectively mistaken conscience is said to be *invincible* (i.e., unable to be corrected).[54] On the

---

[53] CCC # 1178.

[54] CCC # 1790-1794, 1801.

other hand, to follow one's conscience which is mistaken because one has been imprudent (that is, because one has not taken the necessary steps to form one's conscience according to moral wisdom), is to act on a conscience whose mistake is *vincible* (correctable), and this is to sin against moral wisdom. "A wise son loves correction, but the senseless one heeds no rebuke" (Pr 13:1). The rule of conscience, therefore, is not, as some theologians teach, "Follow your own conscience," but *"Form your conscience as objectively as you can and then follow it."*

Thus it is fundamental in moral theology to clearly distinguish between *objective morality*, that is, whether in fact a certain action is a help or a hurt in achieving one's own true happiness and the common good of others, and *subjective morality*, that is, whether one honestly believes this action is a helpful or harmful means to these good goals.

Morality consists *formally* in whether one's actions are subjectively good or bad, and it is on this that a merciful God will judge us as saints or sinners. "Keep the faith that you have to yourself in the presence of God; blessed is the one who does not condemn himself for what he approves" (Rm 14:22).[55] Nevertheless, it is also true that when we act on an honestly mistaken conscience, although we do not sin,[56] we still do harm to ourselves or others. Therefore to have a good conscience we must always strive to have one that is not only subjectively but objectively good. If we do not make this effort, then our mistakes become sins through our foolishness.

Therefore, before performing any free act we are obliged to take serious care to inquire whether what we are about to do is morally right and to follow what our reason tells us is right. Consequently, Christians facing decisions give the amount of thought to them that is proportionate to the seriousness of the matter in hand and their own state and

---

[55] St. Paul is saying, "Follow your conscience in doing what you see before God to be good, and do not have false guilt because others disagree with your decision. God blesses you for doing so even if they do not." See J.A. Fitzmyer, S.J., NJBC, 51-125, p. 866 on this verse. Note the phrase "in the presence of God" which implies that the person has taken care to form their conscience by God's teaching known through the Church.

[56] Pope Alexander VIII in 1690 condemned the following Jansenist error: "Even when there is invincible ignorance of the natural law, this does not excuse from formal sin one who in the state of fallen nature acts from such ignorance" (DS 2302).

condition. They consult those who know better than themselves. They pray for the Holy Spirit's guidance. And they try to put away prejudices or emotions that might hamper an honest judgment.[57]

Hence, Christians today must form their consciences by looking for instruction (torah) from the Bible as that has been interpreted in the Church's Tradition. We have already seen that as this Tradition is presented in the *ordinary* teaching of the Church there are infallible and non-reformable elements and other elements which are not infallible and thus reformable, i.e., elements which are possibly but not likely erroneous, and therefore better guides than mere human opinion. The possible reform of Church teaching includes not only the correction of errors but also the better statement of moral norms and truths, and a more precise and detailed application of them to new problems.

Some make the mistake of thinking that since it is possible that the ordinary teaching of the Magisterium may be less than perfect at a given time and hence may be corrected in the future, these teachings are useless guides to present-day conscience and may be disregarded. Others read the opinions of theologians who propose such corrections and revisions and conclude that since these are the "morality of the future" such opinions can be followed today.

In the seventeenth century the development of moral theology had already led to the currency of many different opinions among theologians on a great variety of moral topics. Individual Christians on reading such a diversity of opinions were left in a quandary as to which they might follow. The result was a famous controversy which lasted into the eighteenth century, the "Controversy on Moral Systems," or on "Probabilism." If this controversy now seems alien to a Christian ethics based on love, we have only to remember that Jesus himself did not hesitate to enter into debates on their own terms with the rabbinic scribes and Pharisees whose method of argument followed much the same mode of legal precedents and application to difficult cases (Mt 9:9-13; 12:1-37; 15:1-20; 19:1-30; 22:15-23:26). Jesus did not reject this method of moral thinking, but only its abuse.

---

[57] CCC # 1779, 1783-1785.

The moral systems developed by the theologians after Trent can be arranged in the following spectrum:

1) *Absolute Rigorism* (Tutiorism): Always follow the more difficult (safer) opinion, unless the easier is certain, or (*Mitigated Rigorism*) at least very probable. This was defended by a number of theologians at the University of Louvain and by the Jansenists.

2) *Probabiliorism*: Always follow the more probable opinion. This was defended by most Dominicans (after 1656) and some Jesuits. *Compensationalism* added that in some special cases there could be proportionately grave reasons for taking the easier course.

3) *Aequiprobabilism*: One may follow the easier course if this is as equally probable as the more difficult. St. Alphonsus Liguori (d. 1787), the great proponent of this system, said this meant that if it was doubtful the law existed, one was free; but if the question was whether a known law had ceased to exist one was still bound by it.

4) *Probabilism*: It is generally licit to follow an easier opinion if it is solidly and certainly probable, even if the opposite is more probable, except when there is serious risk of very grave damage, spiritual or physical, etc., when only a safe course should be followed. This view, first put forward by a Dominican, Bartholomé de Medina in 1577, became the common view of the Jesuit theologians.

5) *Laxism* (extreme Probabilism): It is always licit to follow an easier opinion even if it is somewhat or doubtfully probable. This view was held by many Jesuits of the seventeenth century (Sanchez, Leander, St. Bauny, Escobar, Tamburini, M. Moya), as well as by the Theatine Diana, and the Cistercian Caramuel.

Alexander VII in 1665 and Innocent XI in 1679 and 1680 condemned Laxism, and Alexander VIII in 1690 condemned Rigorism.[58] The three middle positions are still permitted by the Church, although Probabilism has become the more common view.

---

[58] By condemning theses typical of these extreme positions: Alexander VII, DS # 2021; Innocent XI, DS # 2101; 1680, DS # 2175-2177; Alexander VIII, DS 2290-2291.

The Certitude of Conscience

What is certain is that in order to act prudently one must always *be certain* that what one is about to do is not wrong.[59] This moral certitude, however, is not a theoretical, but a practical one — "As far as I can determine here and now in my circumstances and with the information available to me this action is moral." To expect any greater certitude is itself contrary to moral wisdom which recognizes human limitations.

Such a practical certitude is compatible with *negative* doubts, that is, foolish or slight doubts without any solid reason behind them.[60] Hence, the rule, "When a merely negative doubt arises stick to the view of which you were practically certain beforehand." When this is a doubt about whether there is a law one can say, "In doubtful matters privileges are to be interpreted broadly, restrictions narrowly," but if the negative doubt is whether the law has ceased, it should be assumed that it has not. In negative doubts about facts one should say, "In negative doubt one can presume that what ordinarily happens has happened in this case." Or "A fact should not be presumed but must be proved," or "It should be presumed that what has already been done has been done rightly."

But when the doubt is *positive*, that is, serious, one should generally act on the rule: "When serious doubts cannot be resolved do what is safer." This is especially the case when the doubt is about some fact which concerns a means absolutely necessary to obtain the ends of human life such as the life — physical or spiritual — of oneself or another. For example, if there is a *positive* doubt (not a merely imaginary negative doubt) about the validity of the sacraments, or whether a medicine is a deadly poison, or about serious questions of justice (e.g., whether a person on trial for a felony is really guilty) one must follow the *safer* course. But in other matters after a reasonable attempt to determine the truth one may follow the rule, "A doubtful law is not binding." These are practical rules of decision which the theory of probabilism purported to defend.

---

[59] CCC # 1790.

The practical conclusion of this controversy for our times is that it is licit for anyone to follow any one of the three moderate prudential procedures, which in practice do not greatly differ provided that only *solidly* probable opinions are in question. In directing others, however (e.g. a confessor with his penitent), it is not permissible to impose a stricter opinion than a solidly probable one.

Now what is a "solidly probable" opinion? It may be probable for *intrinsic* reasons, in which case those who know this after prudent examination, may act on it, and may present these arguments to others, provided that they do not undermine the teaching authority of the Church by the way they do this. For example, one may refuse the military draft, because one sees that it is really probable it would result in one's fighting in an unjust war. But if the reasons are only *extrinsic*, i.e., the authority of some "expert," then they are probable only if such an expert is reliable. For example, one may follow the advice of one's confessor who has received at least a seminary education, provided one does not discover that he is dissenting from Church teaching. Moral theologians are not reliable, however, if they dissent from authoritative moral teachings of the universal Church. Hence such views are not even *extrinsically* probable no matter how many or how famed the theologians who support them.[61]

For example, there are some Catholic theologians today who argue that *in vitro* fertilization as a means for a sterile couple to have a child is morally justified. However, as long as this opinion continues to be rejected by the ordinary Magisterium,[62] it is not a solidly probable opinion, and it cannot be followed in conscience.

---

[60] These "reflex principles" of moral judgment which were developed as a result of the Moral Systems Controversy are those found in the standard manuals published before Vatican II, but are still reasonable. I have followed the formulations of Benedict Merkelbach, O.P., *Summa Theologiae Moralis*, vol. 2, pp. 78-113.

[61] "Instruction on the Ecclesial Vocation of the Theologian of the Congregation for the Doctrine of the Faith," May 24, 1990, *Origins* 20 (July 5, 1990): 117-26, nn. 32-41. For an analysis of this important document see Avery Dulles, *The Craft of Theology*, pp. 105-118.

[62] S. Congregation for the Doctrine of the Faith, "Instruction on Respect for Human Life in its Origin and on the Dignity of Procreation" (*Donum vitae*), *Origins* 16 (40, March 19, 1987): 697-709.

Views which are not clearly rejected by the Church are probable if they are the common teaching of theologians, or of some great authority such as Aquinas, Suarez, Liguori (whose reliability was confirmed by the Holy See in 1831) or of five or six reputable (but nondissenting) authors. Obviously a view is not probable merely because it is new or popular, even if not in dissent from the Church,[63] but only if it is consistent with magisterial teaching and has good objective arguments for it.

After the encyclical *Humanae Vitae* of Paul VI in 1968, a number of prominent moral theologians dissented from the encyclical on the immorality of contraception, and soon dissented on other magisterial teachings, especially on sexual questions. Since up to that time such dissent had been very rare, Catholics generally assumed that theologians "spoke in the name of the Church" and hence their opinions, especially an opinion supported by four or five "standard authors" was at least solidly probable and could be safely followed in practice. It was not generally recognized that a "paradigm shift" was taking place among academic theologians who no longer claim to "speak for the Church" but simply to enter into scholarly debates like their colleagues in other university fields.

Yet the laity, and even some confessors, continued to think that, as formerly, the views of reputable theologians were safe pastoral guides for their lives, at least as long as the Church tolerated their publication. This confusion has finally forced the Magisterium, which at the Council had hoped to increase the freedom of theologians for the sake of the development of doctrine, to deny explicitly that a few much publicized dissenters had the right to be regarded as "Catholic theologians," since they no longer "spoke for the Church" and could not be regarded as pastoral guides in the formation of conscience. This might have been avoided if the dissenters had made clear to the public that they were presenting their arguments for debate but not as substitutes or even supplements for the pastoral guidance of the members of the Church by the Magisterium, which alone has this pastoral authority. It must be admitted, however, that the public media of communication today, by

---

[63] Alexander VII, DS # 2047.

sensationalizing theological debate, make it very difficult for theologians to keep these distinctions clear before the public.

Is the Good What Authority Commands?

How do we form our consciences from the *intrinsic reasons* for saying something is morally good or bad? It is not easy to answer that question, as we can see from the diversity of answers historically proposed. We have seen that the Bible (at least at first sight) presents a Divine Command Ethics, that is, an ethics according to which something is morally right or wrong because God has willed to command it to be done or not done.

> Moses, with the levitical priests, then said to all Israel: "Be silent, O Israel, and listen! This day you have become the people of the Lord, your God. You shall therefore hearken to the voice of the Lord, your God, and keep his commandments and statutes which I enjoin on you today" (Dt 27:9-10).

According to such an ethics, it is not for creatures to question why the Creator has so commanded but simply to obey. Some of the Church Fathers speak in these terms, as do the Muslims with regard to the *Qur'an*.

In the late Middle Ages the Nominalist theologians, anxious to emphasize the sovereign freedom of God to do as he chooses and for philosophical reasons increasingly skeptical of the natural law arguments of earlier theologians, defended a Divine Command Ethics. The civil lawyers also extended Command Ethics to the justification of secular laws by the theory of the Divine Right of Kings, who like God could make whatever laws they wanted. From Trent to Vatican II this voluntaristic type of ethics strongly shaped the teaching of moral theology which thus became largely assimilated to Canon Law.[64]

---

[64] See Louis Vereecke, "Moral Theology, History of (700 to Vatican Council I)," NCE 9:1120-22. For the general theological background to this development see William C. Placher, *A History of Christian Theology: An Introduction*, pp. 162-180.

Today it seems obvious that a Divine Command Ethics is too *authoritarian*. If the ultimate criterion of justice is the will of the authorities, how can those they oppress claim any rights? Hitler was the highest legal authority in the Third Reich and Stalin in the Soviet Union! Such voluntaristic theories of ethics are said to be *deontological* (from Greek *deontos*, duty or obligation) since they only require obedience *without thought of the consequences*. According to such a theory it would seem that the terrible consequences for Germany of Hitler's or for Russia of Stalin's commands were entirely those leaders' responsibility, not of the officers who obeyed them.

Of course God never commands what he knows will ultimately have bad consequences for those who obey him, since he can always bring a greater good out of evil, yet an ethics based merely on divine commands leads to a false picture of God. Thus it is a mistake to take God's command to Abraham to sacrifice his son Isaac (Gn 22) as typical of the moral laws of the Old Testament. God put the founder of the Chosen People to a special test of faith in view of his special role in the history of salvation, but in the Old Law as a whole, as the great Jewish theologian Rabbi Maimonides showed,[65] God usually supplied understandable and practical reasons for what he commanded.

Unfortunately the Protestant Reformers were educated in this late medieval theology. John Calvin, whose theology has so much influenced American Protestantism and survives among the Fundamentalists, pictured God as an absolute sovereign who issues commands to assert his authority and test our blind obedience. This authoritarian image of God has turned many away from Christianity, and so has the presentation of Catholic morals as a set of unrealistic commands arbitrarily imposed by the Church.

In reaction against this authoritarianism, other systems of ethics were developed by the Enlightenment. These systems generally tried to retain the main values of Christianity, but to divorce them from their foundations in biblical revelation and defend them on purely philo-

---

[65] See Maimonides, *The Commandments*, vol. 2, Appendix II, "Maimonides' Doctrine of the Truths Underlying the Divine Commandments," pp. 337-347 by the translator and editor Rabbi C.B. Chavel.

sophical grounds. One such system is *emotivism*, which originated in the eighteenth century with Jean Jacques Rousseau and in a different version with the Scottish Common Sense School, of which David Hume was a principal member. This line of thought did not break cleanly with deontologism, but instead of founding morality in the will of the sovereign, founded it in the moral instincts, the *feelings*, or emotions of preference, the moral intuitions. Consequently, one might justifiably disobey the commands of authority if these violated one's moral instincts.[66]

Recently, analytic philosophers following Hume, such as G.E. Moore have argued that moral or "ought" (value) statements cannot logically be reduced to "is" (fact) statements.[67] Ought statements do not describe a state of affairs but simply express *feelings* (preferences) about certain states of affairs. To say that adultery is wrong is simply to say that one's wife's adultery makes one angry.

Emotivism tends to total individualism, since emotional preferences vary so widely. Rousseau and Hume tried to avoid this result by appealing to the "natural" feelings of the majority, what Rousseau called "the general will." Thomas Jefferson, who was familiar with the ideas of the Scottish School, incorporated this notion in our Declaration of Independence, and our politicians assure us often that "the people know best."[68] Ultimately this line of ethical thought has produced the legal positivism of our Supreme Court, according to which public consensus is the ultimate criterion of right or wrong. Not only does this threaten to become "the tyranny of the majority" but it degenerates into *moral relativism*, since different cultures and different times have different feelings about right and wrong, and none of these provide a solid basis for human rights.[69]

An important attempt to overcome this dilemma was the Utili-

---

[66] See Vernon J. Bourke, *History of Ethics*, vol. 1, pp. 241-242; vol. 2, pp. 13-18 for introduction and bibliography.

[67] *Ibid.*, vol. 2, pp. 167-189 and bibliography.

[68] Gary Wills, *Inventing America: Jefferson's Declaration of Independence* (Garden City, NY: Doubleday, 1981) emphasizes also the influence of other members of the "Scottish Common Sense School."

[69] VS # 51-53; 95-97.

tarianism of Jeremy Bentham. He accepted the idea that the feeling of pleasure, free of pain, is the ultimate motive of human action, but argued that this can be reconciled with the common good of society by the rule, "Seek the greatest good of the greatest number." He believed this "greatest good" could be determined objectively by reducing feelings of pleasure to quantitative units so that a calculation of benefits could be made.[70]

Adam Smith of the Scottish School in a similar way developed the notion, widely predominant today and typical of the United States, of the "free market."[71] In a free market the subjective preferences of individuals are balanced against available resources so as to stimulate the production of more resources as the options of consumers are enlarged. Smith claimed that this is an automatic way of achieving the "greatest good of the greatest number" through competition.

Another major attempt to meet this dilemma of ethical relativism was made by the humanist Immanuel Kant in reaction to the views of Rousseau and Hume.[72] Kant was a voluntarist and deontologist of the most extreme sort since for him the obligation of moral commands comes from the will, but he rejected mere obedience to any *external* authority as immoral. One must obey only one's own will (autonomism), but this will to be good must never be guided by feelings or preferences, but only by objective reason (rationalism). How then can social consensus be achieved? Kant thought he could avoid individualism, because he believed that the reason of all human beings, unhampered by self-serving passions, will legislate the same moral rules, just as in his day all scientists accepted Newton's law of gravitation. Kant's rationalism has now lost credibility (Einstein changed Newton's laws!), so that Kantians today settle for the idea that the best that can be hoped for is a rationally *consistent* ethics based on moral consensus, a consensus which they hope will be supported by a historical tradition. Thus ultimately they also accept *moral relativism*.

---

[70] Bourke, *History of Ethics*, vol. 2, pp. 22-25 and bibliography.

[71] See R.B. Fulton, *Adam Smith Speaks to Our Times: A Study of His Ethical Ideas.*

[72] See A.E. Teale, *Kantian Ethics.*

To reject these types of ethical theory, however, is not to accept (as Kant did) a rationalistic position which neglects the role of feeling and imagination in good ethical decisions, nor to deny the relevance of history and of induction from experience to ethical analysis. A sound foundation for moral theology in the Bible and Tradition makes very clear that moral thinking undergoes historical development to which serious attention must always be given. An epistemology of the Thomistic type which I have employed in this book, and which the Magisterium has favored as most consistent with biblical realism,[73] also insists that deductive thinking to be valid must always be based on induction from human experience. Finally, no one can read the Bible or the Church Fathers without seeing that these sources are not rationalistic, but give full credit to the role of the human "heart" (i.e., human feeling and the images which move it) in moral decision-making.[74]

Is the Good Natural to Us?

From the time of Socrates who protested against the moral relativism of the Sophists, other thinkers have proposed ethical systems based not simply on the will of authority, nor on the feelings of the individual or the crowd, but on two principles: (1) that there is only *one true goal* for all human life which is determined by the very nature of humanity; (2) that ethical problems are concerned with the realistic choice of the *means* to this goal. Such a system is said to be *teleological* (Greek *telos*, end or goal).[75] The Greek systems differed, however, in two ways.[76]

---

[73] Vatican II, OT # 15-16 with its references to previous Church documents approving Thomism as the basis of Catholic education; cf. also *Code of Canon Law*, c. 252, # 3.

[74] See Philip S. Keane, S.S., *Christian Ethics and Imagination*. Note the bibliographical note, p. 184, n. 51.

[75] A confusion was introduced by Henry Sidgwick in a famous book, *The Methods of Ethics* (1886), who distinguished "deontological" from "teleological" systems of ethics on the basis that the former held for absolute moral norms and the latter did not. To avoid this confusion of terms VS # 75 distinguishes between "teleology" and "teleologism" (i.e., teleology in Sidgwick's sense). The Catholic tradition has generally favored a teleological ethics (a means-ends ethics as contrasted to a legalistic, deontological ethics) but one which supports absolute moral norms.

[76] Bourke, *History of Ethics*, vol. 1, pp. 15-68.

On the one hand, there was disagreement about the priorities among these ultimate values or goals. The Epicureans argued that the most desirable value is pleasure and freedom from pain (thus anticipating emotivism). The Stoics argued that the greatest value is peace of mind (thus anticipating Kant). The Platonists and the Aristotelians argued that the highest value was the contemplation of truth, but the latter with the proviso that the pursuit of knowledge also presupposes other lesser values as its condition.

The Church rejected the Epicurean view because it was incompatible with the Cross. It praised the Stoic view but found it ultimately inhuman, empty, and self-righteous. Since the Aristotelian view was at first not well known, the Church favored Platonic ethics insofar as Plato taught that the vision of God is the highest good, but the Church emphasized that the attainment of this vision is not so much through thought as through love, made possible by grace.

When Aristotle's *Nicomachean Ethics* became known in the Middle Ages, the scholastic theologians recognized that it surpassed Plato in its realism, balance and method, and adopted it. Thus Aristotle's ethics has remained a basic tool of moral theology, although obscured after Trent by the trend toward voluntarism. With the rise of Enlightenment Humanism in the eighteenth century as a rival of Christianity, the Church began to feel a great pressure to revise her traditional moral theology in the light of the newer systems I have already mentioned.[77]

In Continental Europe the predominant influence on Christian thought was Kantianism. This was largely adopted by liberal Protestantism, especially in the idealistic forms it took in Germany, in which values were seen as constructs of the human mind inspired by the Absolute working through the "spirit" of various cultures and times. Thus values were given a more historical, relativistic character than in Kant's rationalism. This tradition ultimately ended in the extreme individualism of existentialism (Jean Paul Sartre) and in phenomenological ethics (Edmund Husserl, Max Scheler, Martin Heidegger). Scheler, the

---

[77] See the article of Vereecke, note 67 and "Preface à l'Histoire de la Theologie Morale Moderne," *Studia Moralia*, I, pp. 87-120 above and Bernard Häring, *The Law of Christ*, I, Chapter 1.

most influential of the European ethicists, accepted Kant's basic approach but attempted to give it more content by adopting Rousseau's notion that absolute ethical values (phenomenological essences) are known by intuitive feeling, while their concrete applications remain relative to particular historical and cultural circumstances.[78]

The dissent over the encyclical *Humanae Vitae*, to which I have already referred, has led to a remarkable attempt by some moralists to revise the traditional Catholic moral system, since the dissenters logically concluded that a moral system which condemned what they had approved (for what no doubt seemed to them very good reasons) must demand such revision. To understand this system of "Proportionate Reason"[79] it is necessary first to explain the traditional Thomistic view which it was intended to revise.[80]

According to St. Thomas Aquinas who followed the Aristotelian teleological system, moral decisions must begin from the true goal of human life. For the Christian this is union with God in the beatific vision rather than merely the knowledge of God possible by human reason in this life, as Aristotle had thought. This goal is not subject to ethical discourse because it is known from revelation with the certitude of faith. The ethical problem, therefore, is to determine the means necessary to attain this supernatural goal. Some of these means are necessary, as known either by revelation or by reason, but most of them present a range of options among which abstract reason cannot absolutely determine which ought to be preferred. Consequently conscience informed by moral wisdom must judge which means are preferable in

---

[78] Max Scheler, *Formalism in Ethics and Non-Formal Ethics of Value: A New Attempt Toward the Foundation of an Ethical Personalism*. For a good analysis see Alfons Deeken, *Process and Permanence in Ethics: Max Scheler's Moral Philosophy*.

[79] For a survey of the main authors of this school see Bernard Hoose, *Proportionalism: The American Debate and its European Roots* and John A. Gallagher, *Time Past, Time Future: A Historical Study of Catholic Moral Theology*. For my criticism, see Benedict M. Ashley, O.P. and Kevin D. O'Rourke, O.P., *Healthcare Ethics: A Theological Analysis*, (3rd ed. 1989), pp. 158-159, 165-169.

[80] The basic text is *S.T.*, I-II, q. 18. For critical analysis see Brian Thomas Mullady, O.P., *The Meaning of the Term "Moral" in St. Thomas Aquinas*; Servais Pinckaers, O.P., "La question des acts intrinsèquement mauvais et le 'proportionalisme.'"

particular situations, and morality formally consists in following this judgment of conscience.

The question, therefore, is how conscience is to make this judgment about what to do here and now as a means to union with God. Aquinas held that moral wisdom requires us *first* to determine whether the act we are about to intend to perform is itself — objectively in its own essential character — an act capable of leading us toward God, or one which will frustrate this movement toward God. If then the latter is *intrinsically immoral*, not simply because it is contrary to God's command — although in fact God forbids that kind of actions — but because it obstructs the relation to God which the Christian and God mutually seek to strengthen, then no circumstances or good intentions can make such an action morally good.[81]

Sometimes our consciences can perceive this intrinsic immorality of an act because we can see that it is incompatible with the love of God, but sometimes we have not yet attained that degree of moral wisdom and therefore must rely on the superior wisdom of God. Then we must obey his command with confidence that it was issued only because in fact the action is immoral and harmful to ourselves or others. We cannot make the intention to perform a harmful act moral by also intending to use that act as a means to some further good intention, e.g., to steal in order to give to charity. Nor can any circumstance in which it may be performed render it good, because of its intrinsic harmfulness. Thus rape, because it is intrinsically contradictory to the basic rights of another and hence of our love of neighbor and hence of our

---

[81] "Reason attests that there are objects of the human act which are by their nature 'incapable of being ordered' to God, because they radically contradict the good of the person made in his image. These are the acts which, in the Church's moral tradition, have been termed 'intrinsically evil' (*intrinsice malum*); they are such *always and per se*, in other words quite apart from the ulterior intentions of the one acting and the circumstances. Consequently, without in the least denying the influence on morality exercised by circumstances and especially by intentions, the Church teaches that 'there exist acts which *per se* and in themselves, independently of circumstances, are always seriously wrong by reason of their object.'" (VS # 80). See also CCC # 1749-1761. Since VS was issued some proponents of proportionalism have claimed that they never denied that some kinds of human acts are intrinsically evil, but were only concerned to refine the definition of such acts. Fine, if they accept the definitions formulated by the Magisterium!

love of God, cannot be made a good act simply because of some special circumstances which might make it seem less vile (e.g., if the woman is a prostitute or a prisoner of war) or because of some additional good intention of the rapist (such as the case where a man rapes his reluctant wife so as to avoid temptations to adultery!).

If, however, conscience perceives the act to be intrinsically an appropriate means to the true end of human life, this is still not sufficient to judge it good. Conscience must then take into account the circumstances in which the act is to be performed, since these circumstances may make the act less appropriate, or even entirely inappropriate and bad. Among these circumstances will be any additional intentions *extrinsic to the intention to perform the act*. For example, in the Sermon on the Mount Jesus rebukes those who give alms (an intrinsically good act), but do it in such circumstances that they call attention to their generosity (Mt 6:1-4). In this case the intention to perform the act (i.e., to give alms to the poor) is good; but the intention extrinsic to the act (i.e., to gain a reputation for generosity) is a circumstance of the act, since the same act could be performed without that intention.

Note that in such a teleological way of judging, the *consequences* of an act (insofar as they can prudently be determined) are important, but good consequences which are circumstantial (that is, which do not necessarily follow from the nature of the act) cannot make an intrinsically evil act good. What account must be taken of the bad consequences which are foreseen, in deciding to act, we will consider later in explaining the so-called "Principle of Double Effect."

Obviously, the consequences of our acts cannot be foreseen completely, but what we can foresee is that in performing an intrinsically bad act there will at least be damage *to ourselves*, because we will be acting contrary to moral wisdom. Our free acts make us the kind of persons we are, because they either develop or obscure the image of God in which we are created. Every intrinsically evil act dims that image, no matter what other good consequences seem to flow from it. The man who cheats in business may grow rich, but he also obscures the image of God in himself, for God never cheats.

Exceptionless Moral Norms

The system of "proportionate reason," whose chief author was Josef Fuchs, S.J., was influenced by the Kantian, phenomenological and intuitionist ethics of Max Scheler, already mentioned, especially through the theological system of Karl Rahner.[82] Fuchs himself was influential in writing the so-called "Majority Report" (never officially published) of the papal commission which recommended a modification of the Church's traditional position against contraception.[83] The fundamental thesis of the system of proportionate reason is that at least in the case of concrete moral norms it is never possible to judge that any human act is intrinsically immoral, without at the same time considering all the circumstances (including circumstantial intentions). Consequently, the basic principle of moral judgment is that to determine whether a concrete act is moral it is necessary to weigh the positive and negative values involved in this act, including its circumstances, and then to judge it good if there is a proportionate reason to perform the act, i.e., if the positive values outweigh the negative.

Although this principle of proportionate reason is nowhere mentioned in the documents of Vatican II, its proponents argue that it is consonant with the "historical consciousness" of that Council because it recognizes that all human acts take place in historical circumstances from which they receive their objective character, and cannot be fully defined merely in the timeless abstract. To the objection that this means one may "do evil that good may come of it," which St. Paul rejects (Rm 3:8), proportionalists answer that the weighing of values and disvalues is "pre-moral" (*ontic*), that is, *prior* to moral judgment.[84] Therefore

---

[82] See the work of Hoose, note 85 above and the dissertation of Timothy O'Connell, *Changing Catholic Moral Theology: A Study of Josef Fuchs*.

[83] The text is available in Robert Hoyt, ed. *The Birth Control Debate: Interim History from the Pages of the National Catholic Reporter*. The most complete history of this affair is Robert B. Kaiser, *The Politics of Sex and Religion* which, as the title indicates, sees the affair as a power struggle, and does not take adequate account of the theological issues involved.

[84] The distinction of "ontic" vs. "ontological" derived from phenomenology was introduced into the debate by Louis Janssens in an article, "Ontic Evil and Moral Evil," to replace the traditional distinction between *malum physicum* and *malum morale* because the contemporary meaning of "physical" corresponds more to the meaning of

only when the decision is made to choose an act which has *already* been judged to be of more positive than negative value (or vice versa) does the act take on moral character and become morally good or evil.

For example, in deciding on surgery, a physician balances the pre-moral disvalue of cutting the patient against the pre-moral value of the healing that will result and judges the latter outweighs the former. He then makes the good moral decision to operate, accepting the disvalue of cutting along with the greater value of healing. Thus, while he does something of negative value, namely cutting the patient, which in other circumstances might be morally evil, in these circumstances it is not morally evil but morally good, because justified by a "proportionate reason" for performing it. Hence he is not "doing evil for the sake of good."

Many serious criticisms of this system of proportionate reason have been raised, in spite of its acceptance by what is claimed to be the "mainstream" of prominent post-conciliar moral theologians and in confessional practice by many of the clergy. Josef Fuchs has frankly admitted that according to this system even such a *prima facie* valid moral norm as "It is evil to torture innocent children" might at least admit of exceptions in circumstances which are very hard to imagine but which are theoretically possible.[85] This admission, however guarded,

---

"material." Granted that the term "physical" is now misleading, it is difficult to see how "ontic vs. ontological" clarified the problem. Nor did "pre-moral vs. moral" help. A human act can be "evil" in *some* sense, without being *morally* evil, that is, a disordered means *in relation to the true end of human life*. For example, the acts of a surgeon in cutting the human body or of a preacher in rebuking a sinner are "evil" in some sense, since the first causes a physical wound, the second a spiritual one, but they are good considered *in relation* to physical or spiritual health. On the other hand, the act of an adulterer is "good" as an expression of passionate love, but is morally evil considered in relation to the true welfare of the parties concerned. It is the objective relation of the act to the true end of human life that is significant for ethical discussion.

[85] Thus in an article which is perhaps the most persuasive statement of proportionalism, "The absoluteness of moral terms," *Gregorianum*, 52 (1971): 415-458, Fuchs states: "Theoretically, no other answer seems possible. Probably there can be no universal norms of *behavior* in the strict sense of '*intrinsice malum.*' *Practically*, however, norms properly formulated as universals have their worth." He then cites as an example, "There can be norms stated as universals, including, that is, a precise delineation of the action, to which we cannot conceive of any kind of exception; e.g., cruel treatment of a child which is of no benefit to the child. Despite misgivings on the level of theory, we get along very well with norms of this kind."

is exceedingly dangerous since it opens the way to defending the most heinous acts by claiming that they are excused by exceptional circumstances, e.g., the nuclear annihilation of an enemy on the grounds that it will save more lives than would otherwise be lost. If Catholic moral theology were to adopt this method of ethical reasoning, surely it would degenerate into mere utilitarianism, as is sadly evident in some of the uses to which it is now being put by its less cautious proponents in sexual ethics.

Proportionalism has two basic philosophical errors:

(1) Proportionalism is self-contradictory because it demands that one weigh the values and disvalues of an act *before* judging it to be moral or immoral. The values relevant to moral decision, however, must be weighed as they are appropriate or inappropriate means to the true final end of life; a value is positive if it is an effective means, negative if it is an ineffective or harmful means. But as soon as one considers an act as a means *in relation* to the end of life, one is judging it morally. Proportionalists therefore contradict themselves by claiming first to weigh pre-moral values to determine their proportionate weight when in fact they are either already weighing them as moral values, or they are weighing them with respect to characteristics which are morally irrelevant.

(2) Proportionalism is mistaken in denying that some acts are intrinsically immoral.

Why are some concrete acts intrinsically immoral? Because by their very nature they are contradictory to the true goal of human life, and can never serve as a means to it. Proportionalists themselves admit that hatred of neighbor is intrinsically evil and always wrong. "If anyone says, 'I love God,' but hates his brother, he is a liar" (1 Jn 4:20). But they deny that this is a concrete norm, since it does not say exactly what "hate" amounts to in different circumstances. But if hatred of the neighbor is intrinsically wrong, then acts whose intrinsic nature is to do serious harm to our neighbor cannot be justified by using them as a means to our own or someone else's benefit.

To intend to bomb even one *innocent* person to save lives, no matter how many, is to treat that innocent person as if he were a hated enemy, and hence no longer to love God who loved him as a son. Thus we would be justifying ourselves as did the high priest Caiaphas to the Sanhedrin when they hesitated to kill Jesus:

> "You know nothing, nor do you consider that it is better for you that one man should die instead of the people, so that the whole nation may not perish" (Jn 11:49-50).

The fundamental reason that proportionalists do not admit that concrete acts can be wrong intrinsically, is their *historicism* (a modern version of the old Nominalism) which denies the possibility of knowing the universal natures of concrete things. Scheler, the phenomenologist, did admit the existence of moral *essences*, but for him these essences are known intuitively *a priori* by "feeling" and not by reason, and are existentially realized only *approximately*.[86] When proportionalists are criticized for relying in this way on "feeling" and thus coming close to Emotivism, they defend their system as embodying "historical consciousness" in contrast to the "classical consciousness" which they accuse of viewing the universe as static.[87] But, as I have already shown, this dichotomy is unnecessary and erroneous. The historicity of human life is no contradiction to the universality and continuity of human nature but confirms them, nor to our ability to come to know our nature by reasoning from experience.

The Bible, without entering into these philosophical niceties, teaches both in the Old and New Testaments that the human race throughout history and the globe is one single family in Adam and in Christ, that is, that there is such a reality as human nature and conse-

---

[86] See Max Scheler, *Formalism in Ethics and Non-Formal Ethics of Value*, pp. 491-404.

[87] This dichotomy was made popular by the insightful essay of Bernard J.F. Lonergan, S.J., "The Transition from a Classicist World-View to Historical Mindedness" in *A Second Collection*, pp. 1-9. Lonergan certainly is correct in emphasizing the importance of historical consciousness for modern thought, but it is a mistake to conclude from this that all "classical" thought was "static." Greek philosophy centered on the problem of *change*. While Parmenides and, to a degree, the Platonic tradition came to deny the reality of change, the Aristotelian tradition defended it. As for Thomist philosophy, I argue in my *Theologies of the Body*, pp. 251-412 that it is a philosophy of "radical process."

quently that some acts are intrinsically contradictory to human nature and its universal needs as God created it. Consequently the theory of proportionate reason was rejected definitively by John Paul II in the encyclical *The Splendor of Truth* (*Veritatis Splendor*, 1993) as incompatible with the Scriptures and Catholic Tradition.[88] What is to be retained from proportionalism is a more sensitive awareness of the ways in which circumstances affect the morality of acts, especially how subjective factors affect subjective morality in the course of history, and the role of feelings and imagination in moral decision.

Healing the Sick Conscience

The supreme goal of life in any teleological ethics measures the value of all lesser goals and also of all means to these goals. A means is good if it leads to this goal, bad if it stands in the way, but it is not always easy for us to discern this relationship of means to end realistically. The proportionalists emphasize the *ambiguity* of many moral decisions, and this has always been an important concern of the moral theologian whose task it is to help *resolve* these ambiguities, not compound them.[89] It is basic to this enterprise of moral discernment that we have confidence that even very difficult moral dilemmas can be objectively solved. "God does not demand the impossible," hence it must be possible, even in a confused and darkened world, with God's help to find the right way in life. While in the face of moral dilemmas we sometimes ask ourselves like the weary Solomon in the Book of Qoheleth, "For who knows what is good for man in life, the limited days of his vain life (which God has made like a shadow)?" (Ec 6:12a). Yet the Book of

---

[88] As an encyclical letter, VS was an act of the Pope's *ordinary* teaching authority and requires a "religious submission of mind and will" which is not "simply exterior or disciplinary but must be understood within the logic of faith and under the impulse of obedience to faith," according to the "Instruction on the Ecclesial Role of Theologians" which is based on Vatican II, LG # 25 which speaks of a "religious assent of soul" and declares: "This religious submission of will and of mind must be shown in a special way to the authentic teaching of the Roman Pontiff, even when he is not speaking *ex cathedra*."

[89] CCC # 1786-1788.

Wisdom (7:7) reassures us in other words that it puts in Solomon's mouth, "Therefore I prayed, and prudence was given me; I pleaded, and the spirit of Wisdom came to me." God knows what is good for us and has made it known to us in Jesus Christ.

To assist us in solving puzzling cases moralists have worked out a number of prudential principles. These are called "reflex principles" because they are not moral norms, but rules of prudent thinking by which moral norms can be applied. They have to do not with content but with the process of moral reasoning. We have already noted some such reflex principles in discussing moral systems.

How can we make a moral decision in situations where it seems to us that "I am damned if I do, and damned if I don't," i.e., where it seems that there are no good options, but all involve sin? We have seen that objectively such a situation is not possible, but subjectively it may *seem* so, and such a person is traditionally said to have a *perplexed conscience*. The answer is that in such a case the moral thing to do is *to do what seems the lesser evil* and if both evils seem equal, then *it is all right to do either*. Persons who act in this way do not sin, since their intention is not to do the lesser evil, but to do the only good that appears possible. Note that this reflex principle should be used only when we are truly perplexed. To use it as an ordinary principle of moral solution is to fall into utilitarianism or proportionalism.

Someone who has decided to perform an evil action, but is persuaded by someone to do a less evil action instead, still commits a sin, but a lesser sin. Consequently, in some situations it is permissible for a counselor who has failed to persuade a person not to commit a sin, to suggest that it would be better (but still wrong) for him instead to commit the lesser sin (do less harm), provided that the counselor does not give the impression that he or she is approving this lesser evil as no sin at all.

What are persons to do who become aware that they are imprudent in the way they think about moral decisions because they go to extremes of *laxity* on the one hand, or *scrupulosity* on the other? Jesus perceived these two types of imprudence in the scribes and Pharisees (one person can fail both ways) when he said to the lax:

> "Beware of the scribes, who like to go around in long robes and accept greetings in the marketplaces, seats of honor in synagogues, and places of honor at banquets. They devour the houses of widows and, as a pretext, recite lengthy prayers. They will receive a very severe condemnation" (Mk 12:38-40).

and to the scrupulous:

> "Woe to you, scribes and Pharisees, hypocrites. You pay tithes of mint and dill and cumin, and have neglected the weightier things of the law: judgment and mercy and fidelity. But these you should have done, without neglecting the others. Blind guides, who strain out the gnat and swallow the camel" (Mt 23:23-24).

The lax person is sometimes simply someone who always takes the easier way if there is any excuse, however thin, even a mere rationalization. The author of Proverbs counts as one of the four greatest of wonders, "the way of an adulterous woman, who eats, wipes her mouth and says, 'I have done no wrong'" (Pr 30:20). Such a conscience can become *callous*; it sins without any feeling of guilt, or it can be "pharisaic" when it makes a great fuss over minor points while ignoring really important ones. Persons who have lax consciences often have a faulty religious education and ignore the advice of others, live an easy, indulgent life, with no control of their passions, think only of worldly success, and have the idea that "God will understand!" without remembering that God is not only merciful but just.

1 Timothy 4:2 speaks of "the hypocrisy of liars with seared consciences" and 2 Peter 2:12 (cf. Jude vv. 5-19) of men who are like "irrational animals" who "revile things that they do not understand" who "in their destruction... will also be destroyed." They need to be awakened to a healthy fear of God's justice and to a realization of how destructive of others and themselves they are. Their conversion can be assisted by a good retreat, confession, regular spiritual reading, getting out of bad company, and charitable works that bring them into contact with the sufferings caused by sin.

Sometimes the lax conscience becomes a genuine neurosis as in the "sociopathic personality" who commits acts that have very serious consequences for others and even for the offender, without showing any sense of how foolish such acts are or exhibiting any feelings of guilt or remorse. The irrationality of such behavior shows that the person has diminished freedom and is less responsible for this irresponsible behavior. The causes of such a neurosis are not very well understood, and it requires careful professional diagnosis and treatment. Such persons are often very plausible and likeable, easy liars and "con-men"; for example, the man without medical training who passed himself off with false credentials as a physician and actually performed surgical operations in several hospitals.

The scrupulous person is one who becomes excessively anxious about making decisions for fear of committing sin, or of not having confessed sins properly; for example, the great moral theologian St. Alphonsus Liguori who suffered this affliction all his life. Decision is not easy for most of us in difficult matters, but for the scrupulous person every decision (or decisions about particular kinds of matters) becomes very painful — especially about matters that are inherently ambiguous, e.g., sexual feelings or feelings of hate or of lack of trust in God. This scrupulosity can reach the point of a severe neurosis that is classified as a form of obsessive-compulsive behavior or anxiety neurosis that requires professional psychological help. It seems to have both physical and psychological causes. In milder cases it yields to a counselor's assurances and guidance to a less anxious way of living. As Jesus advised the scribes, it is also helped by counseling the person to become more occupied in really important services to God and neighbor, so that small worries slip into the background.

Moral Dilemmas

Moral decisions, however, truly do involve some difficult situations which require reflex rules to help us sort out the various points to be prudently considered. Of these, the two famous principles that have been developed in the history of moral theology are the *Principle of Double Effect* (or of Two Effects) and the *Principle of Material Coop-*

eration. The purpose of these two reflex rules of prudence is that we often find ourselves in situations where we foresee that in doing a good action certain bad consequences ("side-effects") will also be entailed. The question therefore arises, "Can I do this good without also being morally responsible for the harmful side-effects?"

The first of these principles says that one may perform the action if:

1. It is in itself not an intrinsically evil action.[90]
2. If one intends only this good act, and does not intend (although one may foresee) the harmful side-effects. (In this case one is said to intend the good *directly*, the evil *indirectly*, but in fact one does not really intend evil at all; one would prevent it if one could without neglecting to perform the good act).
3. If the evil consequences are not the *means* by which good consequences are to be obtained.
4. If the harmful consequences do not exceed the good consequences.

Proportionalists reject the first three of these conditions and accept only the last, which becomes their *Principle of Proportionate Reason* which is the fundamental prudential principle of their whole moral system.[91] The first two of these conditions, however, are the essential ones. The last two are simply signs that the agent intends only the good, and accepts the evil consequences only as an unavoidable side-effect. When Jesus preached in the Temple in Jerusalem he undoubtedly foresaw that this might lead the religious authorities to put him to death (Jn 2:13-25). What he intended, however, was to preach the Gospel for the salvation of the people. His death was a side-effect, not directly intended by him, although foreseen. Nor was his execution the means of the people's salvation, since we are not saved by Jesus'

---

[90] "One may never do evil so that good may result from it" (CCC #1789).

[91] Very influential in the development of the proportionalist theory was the article of Peter Knauer, S.J., "The Hermeneutic Function of the Principle of Double Effect," *Natural Law Forum*, 12 (1967):140-162, which argued for the reduction of all moral decision to this single principle. It was then only a short step to eliminate three of its conditions, especially the primary condition that the act not be *intrinsically* evil, and to argue that proportionality was the sole principle of moral decision.

death simply as such, but by the sacrificial love with which he endured that death. Christian martyrs do not commit suicide, because they intend not their own death but to be faithful witnesses to the Gospel.

Similarly the *Principle of Material Cooperation* is necessary because we can do few things without cooperating with other human beings, yet in this social action we often become unavoidably implicated in actions by others which are evil. Jesus prayed for his disciples, "I do not ask that you take them out of the world but that you keep them from the evil one. They do not belong to the world any more than I belong to the world" (Jn 17:15-16). This principle says that one may act in cooperation with other people, even when one sees that this may be of some assistance in their performing morally evil actions, but only under the following conditions:

1. One intends and does only what is morally good in the cooperative action, and disapproves and even attempts, if possible, to prevent what is evil.
2. One does not *formally* cooperate with the evil action of another by directly assisting it, advising it, or approving it.
3. One's *material* cooperation with this evil action is proportionately more remote the greater the evil of the other's action in relation to the good one hopes to achieve by the cooperation or harm that would result from non-cooperation, taking also into account possible scandal, i.e., the *appearance* of formal cooperation which might be a cause of temptation to others.[92]

For example, Jesus, by eating with tax-collectors (Mk 2:14-17) — who were agents of the oppressive Roman government who exploited the poor — seemed to the Pharisees to give approval to the tax-

---

[92] When the material cooperation is *proximate* to the evil act it is said to be "immediate" and is always immoral. When it is remote from the evil act it is said to be "mediate." Only mediate material cooperation can be moral, and then only if the other conditions mentioned in the text are also satisfied. For example, the nurse who cares for a patient after an abortion cooperates with the evil act of abortion only remotely (mediate material cooperation) and might be justified if the other conditions mentioned are satisfied; but a nurse who assists the doctor at an abortion, although she disapproves of abortion and only carries out her ordinary duties in the surgery thus perhaps rendering her cooperation material rather than formal, nevertheless, cooperates materially and *immediately* and hence her action is immoral.

collectors' actions and thus cooperate formally with them. But Jesus answered, "Those who are well do not need a physician, but the sick do. I did not come to call the righteous but sinners" (v. 17). Thus his association with these sinners was only material, since he was only eating with them, not helping them collect unjust taxes. Moreover, it was justified by the fact that only by making friends with them could he bring the Gospel to them — an act remote from tax-collection and justified by the great good of their conversion. Moreover, to have withdrawn from them as the Pharisees did would have left them in sin, a very great evil. Finally, the "scandal" which he risked giving to help the tax-collectors was not real scandal, because Jesus' whole life of care of the poor was sufficient proof that he did not approve injustice to the poor.

Summary of Norms

What then are the concrete norms of the virtue of prudence? The positive norm of prudence can be formulated as follows (again note that the biblical citations after these norms are intended as illustrative, not "proof-texts"):

1. Since one cannot attain union with God unless one uses the intelligence and the faith God has given the Christian to choose the right means to that ultimate goal, the baptized should inform their consciences as objectively as possible, in the light of reason and of faith with the guidance of the Church, and then act in accordance with this judgment (cf. Mt 19:16-22).

Hence, the negative norms of prudence are:

2. Never act without informing one's conscience according to reason and the Gospel as interpreted by the Magisterium of the Church, and never act in practical doubt (cf. 1 Cor 8).
3. Never neglect as far as practically possible to use one's experience, intelligence, foresight, and creativity and when needed, the counsel of trustworthy others, in forming one's conscience (cf. Mt 10:16; Lk 16:8b-9).

4. Never act on laxist or rigorist moral opinions; nor on less than safe opinions at the risk of one's own or another's union with God (cf. Mt 23:23; 19:1-12).

These concrete norms and those at the end of Chapter 2 on Faith are specified as Christian by the fact that they are derived not only from reason but from Scripture and Tradition and that they are intended to guide us not to our natural end of integral human fulfillment but to the supernatural end of life in the Trinity.

They are concrete, since they do not merely label actions but describe them succinctly (they are more fully described in the texts of the chapters). The negative norms are *exceptionless* because they forbid acts which by their very nature are contradictory to the Christians' goal of life, e.g., to publicly deny the faith is contradictory to the Christians' obligation to witness to the faith even at the risk of death as Jesus did.

The Sacrament of Pastoral Prudence

The *pastoral* prudence needed by bishops, priests, and deacons resembles both domestic and political prudence; a bishop is both a father and a shepherd.[93] The various levels of moral wisdom can be acquired naturally by experience and training, but the moral wisdom necessary to live the Christian life is a divine gift given at Baptism. A paternal and maternal wisdom to govern the Christian family is conferred in the Sacrament of Matrimony. But the pastoral wisdom needed to govern the Church is also a special gift of the Holy Spirit given in the Sacrament of Holy Orders.[94] Because this priestly prudence is given for the service of the whole Church, it seems appropriate to associate the Sacrament of Holy Orders in a special way with the cardinal virtue of

---

[93] Ancient kings were called "shepherds," but in the Old Testament, although this term was applied to various kinds of rulers of the people (e.g., Jr 2:8), it was not directly given as a kingly title, since it belonged properly only to Yahweh (Psalm 23). See John L. McKenzie, *Dictionary of the Bible*, article "Shepherd," 902-904.

[94] CCC # 1536-1600.

prudence, as Baptism is associated with the theological virtue of faith for every member of the Church.

The model of this pastoral prudence is, of course, Christ the Good Shepherd (Jn 10:1-18; cf. Mk 6:34, 14:27; Nb 27:17; Gn 48:15; 49:24; Mi 7:14; Ps 23:1-4; 80:1). "I am the good shepherd. A good shepherd lays down his life for the sheep" (Jn 10:11). "They will hear my voice, and there will be one flock, one shepherd" (Jn 10:16).

In the early Church the clergy, although they were generally celibate after ordination,[95] were commonly chosen from married men who had proved themselves good fathers of families. A bishop "must manage his own household well, keeping his children under control with perfect dignity; for if a man does not know how to manage his own household, how can he take care of the church of God?" (1 Tm 3:4-5). The study of the Bible and of theology is encouraged for the laity as well as the clergy, but those in Holy Orders have a special obligation to continue its study throughout their lives.[96]

Conclusion to Part I

The norms which we have summarized at the ends of Chapters 2 and 3 are abstract, but they are derived from a real model, Jesus, who is the

---

[95] See the evidence as presented by Christian Cochini, S.J., *Origines apostoliques du celibat sacerdotal* and Roman Cholij, *Clerical Celibacy in East and West*. For critiques of this position see H. Crouzel, S.J., *Nouvelle Revue Theologigue*, 1971: pp. 649-653 and "Dix ans de recherches sur les origines du célibat ecclésiastique: Reflexion sur les publications des années 1970-1979," *Revue Theologique Louvain*, 1980: pp. 157-185; also Charles Martin, S.J., *Nouvelle Revue Theologique*, 105 (1983): pp. 437-438. For a different interpretation of the data see Roger Gryson, *Les origines du célibat ecclésiastiques du premier au septieme siècle*. It should be noted that Jerome D. Quinn, *Letter to Titus*, Anchor Bible (1990) holds that the requirement (Tt 1:6) for a "bishop" to be a man "of one wife" (rev. NAB, "married only once"), often quoted to show that in the early Church the clergy were married, probably means that although married a priest must become sexually continent, pp. 85-87. What is certain is that Pope Siricius in 385 (DS 185) insisted that the practice then existing (cf. DS 118) of requiring all priests and deacons to refrain from marital relations should be maintained. It does not appear that the Eastern Church departed from this same practice until the seventh century and it still requires it of bishops.

[96] *Code of Canon Law*, c. 279 #1; cf. 276 # 2, 2

perfect exemplification of obedience to the Father's guidance and its application to life through moral wisdom. Our faith is only a sharing in Jesus' intimate knowledge of the Father.

> No one knows the Son except the Father, and no one knows the Father except the Son and anyone to whom the Son wishes to reveal him" (Mt 11:27; Lk 10:21-22).

Our moral wisdom or prudence is also Jesus' gift by which we are guided in our free life decisions by his teaching, because we have "only one master [referring to the title "rabbi"], the Messiah" (Mt 23:8). Only through faith can we share the very wisdom of God showing us the goal which is our destiny, union with the Father, the road we must travel by a life of discipleship, and the power of the Spirit by which only are we able to walk that road.

In the teaching of Jesus we find an interpretation and perfecting of the Mosaic law so that, freed from the compromises resulting from original sin, it again conforms to the order of the universe given in the beginning by the Creator for all humanity, the establishment of the Reign of God on earth and beyond this in immortal life in the community of the Trinity (Mt 23:10). Moral theology, therefore, is the use of our God-given human reason, illumined by the infinitely greater gifts of Christian faith and moral wisdom, seeking an understanding of this divine teaching and its application to our daily lives as a Christian community.

> *Who among you is wise and understanding? Let him show his works by a good life in the humility that comes from wisdom... Wisdom from above is first of all pure, then peaceable, gentle, compliant, full of mercy and good fruits, without inconstancy or insincerity. And the fruit of righteousness is sown in peace for those who cultivate peace* (Jm 3:13-18).

PART II
HOPE

CHAPTER 4

LIVING IN HOPE

[Christ] was known before the foundation of the world but revealed in the final time for you, who through him believe in God who raised him from the dead and gave him glory, so that your faith and hope are in God (1 P 1:20-21).

A: THE VIRTUE

Hope Rooted in Faith

Since the eighteenth century, modern life has been powered by the idea of progress to be achieved by the rapid advance of a scientific understanding of the world and the technological control over natural forces which science makes possible. Yet since the Second World War a deep shadow of disillusionment, even of despair has lengthened across the modern world. The possibility of nuclear destruction, the threat to the environment, the seeming irradicability of poverty for most of the world's peoples, the babel of irreconcilable ideologies have made it an "Age of Anxiety," of existence on the "edge of the abyss."[1] Existential despair is not a new experience for humanity. The Bible again and again expresses this anguish — magnificently in the Book of Job, in weary disgust in Qoheleth, in piercing cries in the Psalms such as Psalm 88 which ends:

> Your furies have swept over me;
> your terrors have cut me off.

---

[1] See GS on "The Situation of Men in the Modern World," # 4-8. Different aspects of the problem of hope today are treated in the following: A.M. Carré, O.P., *Hope or Despair,* Jean Galot, *The Mystery of Christian Hope,* Monika Hellwig, *What Are They Saying About Death and Christian Hope?,* Jürgen Moltmann, *Theology of Hope,* Josef Pieper, *On Hope,* Josef Ratzinger, *Death and Eternal Life,* and Edward Wojcicki, *A Crisis of Hope in the Modern World.*

> They encompass me like water all the day;
> on all sides they close in upon me.
> Companion and neighbor you have taken away from me;
> my only friend is darkness.

Or Psalm 22 which Jesus recited on the cross when he wailed, "My God, my God, why have you forsaken me?" (Mt 27:46).

Every age appears to be the End Time to those who live in it. The disaster of the Flood (Gn 6-9) is the type of the catastrophes of every age, when it looks as if the very existence of humanity is threatened by its own folly. Yet the narrator of Genesis hastens to conclude the story of the Flood with the rainbow of hope. God promises:

> "Never again will I doom the earth because of humankind, since the desires of the human heart are evil from the start; nor will I ever again strike down all living beings" (Gn 8:21; cf. Is 54:9-10).

In fact this note of hope is sounded in Genesis immediately after the Fall, when God does not at once execute the sentence of death on Adam and Eve but settles them to live in exile from Eden, clothing them with skins, but not withdrawing from them the blessing of fertility by which they were to become the parents of all the living (Gn 3:20-24).[2]

Messianic Hope

This promise and this hope are sounded throughout the Scriptures, but the *material object* of this hope is gradually seen in a new light. From the very origins of Yahwist faith in Israel the true Hebrew believer hoped from God not mere physical benefits but some true friendship with God. This was to be a restoration of that intimacy between God and the first humans pictured in Genesis 1 and 2, when they stood before God "naked and unashamed" (Gn 2:25) and spoke to him directly in all innocence. This longing to meet God face to face emerges again and again in the Old Testament, although inhibited by a great fear that "to see God is to die" (Jg 6:22-23; 13:22). Thus the Psalmist sings

---

[2] CCC # 402-421; see especially # 410-411.

that, unlike those "Whose portion in life is in this world," "I in justice shall behold your face;/ on waking I shall be content in your presence" (Ps 17:14-15).[3]

The Jews still lacked any clear revelation of the future life. As Sirach says (41:4), "Whether one has lived a thousand years, a hundred, or ten, in the nether world he has no claim on life."[4] They could not accept the myths of the Egyptians and Babylonians because these myths pictured the after-life in images which were irreconcilable with Israel's faith in the One God. Hence the Jews' spiritual longing for union with this One God came to center in the experience of worshipping him present in the Tabernacle and the Temple.

> Send forth your light and your fidelity;
>   they shall lead me on
> And bring me to your holy mountain,
>   to your dwelling place.
> Then will I go in to the altar of God,
>   the God of my gladness and joy;
> Then will I give thanks upon the harp.
> O God, my God! (Ps 43:3-4).

We should not be surprised, therefore, nor accuse the Jews of materialism, when we see that the writers of the Old Testament put their stress on hope for the goods of this earthly life, rather than on those of a future concerning which they had as yet no clear and trustworthy revelation. We have the liberation theologians to thank for reminding us of the fact, supported by historical-criticism, that it was the Exodus experience and its renewal in the return from the Babylonian exile, especially as expressed by the unknown author we call Deutero-Isaiah (Is 40-55), which was the major source of Jewish monotheism.[5]

---

[3] On the longings of the human heart for perfect happiness see GS # 9-10.

[4] See Nicholas J. Tromp, *Primitive Conceptions of Death and the Nether World in the Old Testament*. See my discussion in *Theologies of the Body*, pp. 579-585, with notes 27-35, pp. 622-624.

[5] See the use made of the Creation and Exodus themes in Gustavo Gutiérrez, *A Theology of Liberation: History, Politics and Salvation*, pp. 155-160. John L McKenzie, S.J., NJBC, p. 1287, says, "As for [the] unicity [of God], in Israel there is no clear and

God revealed himself as Creator not just of the heavens and the earth, but most clearly of all in the wonderful Liberation, the birth and rebirth of his chosen people: "Thus says the Lord, who created you, O Jacob, and formed you, O Israel: Fear not, for I have redeemed you; I have called you by name: you are mine" (Is 43:1). Yahweh was the Creator of the world and of a people especially chosen to witness him to the whole fallen world. "I formed you, and set you as a covenant of the people, a light for the nations" (Is 42:6). "My house shall be called a house of prayer for all peoples" (Is 56:7).

The Jews, therefore, hoped for the coming of the Reign ("Kingdom") of God (Ws 10:10). "Who is this king of glory? The Lord, strong and mighty, the Lord mighty in battle" (Ps 24:8). "Indeed the Lord will be there with us, majestic; yes, the Lord our judge, the Lord our lawgiver, the Lord our king, he it is who will save us" (Is 33:22). "They [the just] shall judge nations and rule over peoples, and the Lord shall be their King forever" (Ws 3:8). The Jews were sure that when God would reign once more as he did at the beginning of creation before sin, the Covenant and its promises would be perfectly fulfilled.

As the Jews in the Babylonian Exile reflected on their former glory in the reigns of King David and Solomon and mourned over the decline of their kingdom through the division and religious corruption recounted in 2 Kings, their hope began to center on a more concrete presence of God through an earthly king, a Messiah (the Anointed, the Christ), of the house of David, who would bring about God's Reign.[6] He would establish universal justice, prosperity, and peace (see the prophecy of Nathan, 2 S 7:5-16; cf. Ps 89; 1 Ch 18:1-15). This hope inspired the return from Exile, but was sadly disappointed when the restoration was so meager. "Who is left among us who saw this house

---

unambiguous denial of the existence of gods other than Yahweh before Dt-Is in the 6th cent. B.C. However Deut 32:39 has the same emphasis as Dt-Is, and some scholars would date this Song of Moses to a considerably earlier period. . . The absence of such a denial does not mean that the Israelites share in some mitigated way the polytheistic beliefs of other ancient peoples; rather, they rejected these beliefs, but couched their rejection in other than philosophical terms." Cf. L. Labuschagne, *The Incomparability of Yahweh in the Old Testament.*

[6] See Raymond E. Brown, S.S., "God's Future Plan for His People: (I) Messiah," NJBC, 1310-1312.

[the Temple] in its former glory? And how do you see it now? Does it seem like nothing in your eyes?" (Hg 2:3).

Any real fulfillment of these hopes was shattered by Alexander the Great's conquests (1 and 2 Maccabees) and the Roman domination which followed. Yet, in the period of the Maccabees, the martyrdom of those who resisted the Greek rulers in their attempts to enforce idolatry on the Jews, led to a firm conviction of the resurrection of the just.[7] As the mother of seven martyred sons said to encourage her youngest in accepting martyrdom:

> "Therefore, since it is the Creator who shapes each man's beginning, as he brings about the origin of everything, he, in his mercy, will give you back both breath and life, because you now disregard yourself for the sake of the law" (2 M 7:23).

Moreover, these disasters aroused an apocalyptic expectation (Dn 7-9) of a Messiah from heaven:

> As the visions of the night continued I saw
> One like a son of man coming,
>   on the clouds of heaven;
> When he reached the Ancient One
>   and was presented before him,
> He received dominion, glory, and kingship;
>   nations and peoples of every language serve him.
> His dominion is an everlasting dominion
>   that shall not be taken away,
> His kingship shall not be destroyed (Dn 7:13-14).[8]

---

[7] See Jonathan A. Goldstein's commentary, *II Maccabees*, Anchor Bible 41A, pp. 291-317, 448-457, who argues that Jason of Cyrene, whose history was the chief source of 2 Maccabees, was a pietist who believed in the resurrection as prophesied in the Book of Daniel and who attributes the same view to the Maccabees who were in fact of the Sadducean party which rejected resurrection.

[8] There have been protracted discussions without consensus on whether this "like a son of man" was taken up by Jesus in the phrase "Son of Man" frequent in the Gospels, whether he or the early Church originated this title, and what its significance is. See John Meier, NJBC, pp. 1324-1325 for a good discussion and Mary Margaret Pazdan, O.P., *The Son of Man: A Metaphor for Jesus in the Fourth Gospel*, pp. 13-29 for recent literature.

Yet other prophecies spoke of the Messiah as coming in meekness (Zc 9:9ff.) and rejection as the Suffering Servant (Is 42:1-4; 49:1-7; 50:4-11; 52:13-53:12), and as the greatest of prophets (Ml 3:23; Mt 16:14) and also as a priest (Ps 110:4). He was to sum up in his person the whole vocation of the Chosen People in all its paradoxical aspects.[9]

The New Testament, in turn, proclaims that this Messiah is the Son of God, Jesus Christ, who confirmed his identity by his miracles, his perfecting and fulfillment of the Torah, his sacrificial death and his victorious rising from the dead and return to the Father. By these deeds he initiated the Reign of God on earth, of which his Church remains a permanent witness through the ages, and he will come again at the end of history to bring it to perfect fulfillment.[10]

> Then comes the end, when he [Christ] hands over the kingdom to his God and Father, when he has destroyed every sovereignty and every authority and power. For he must reign until he has put all his enemies under his feet. The last enemy to be destroyed is death (1 Cor 15:24-26; cf. Ps 110:4 and 8:7).

In the Synoptics' account of Jesus' preaching the coming Kingdom of God[11] it is clear that his Kingdom like that promised by the Old Testament prophets includes *earthly* justice and peace, since he teaches his disciples to pray, "Your kingdom come, your will be done, on earth as in heaven" (Mt 6:10). Moreover (if, as some exegetes argue,[12] the Lukan form, 6:20-22, is the more original) the Beatitudes as actually preached by Jesus declared that the poor, the hungry, the suffering in the Kingdom already at hand are to share in all those good things of life which until then only the rich had possessed — a theme anticipated in the prophets (1 S 2:8; Ps 107:9) and Mary's *Magnificat* (Lk 1:53).

---

[9] CCC # 572. See C.R. North, *The Suffering Servant* in Deutero-Isaiah, 2nd ed. and Pierre Grelot, *Les Poèmes du Serviteur.*

[10] CCC # 436-440, 528-529, 540, 590, 711-716, 674, 840.

[11] Matthew, writing in a Jewish Christian milieu, says "Kingdom of Heaven" because of the reverent reluctance of the Jews to use the Divine Name.

[12] See Ulrich Luz, *Matthew, 1-11,* pp. 226-228, for reasons for this view which to me do not seem to be conclusive since Luke's theological insistence on the dignity of the poor might have influenced his version.

Hope of Christ's Return

In the Johannine literature, however, the spiritual implications of the great fact of Jesus' Resurrection become more profoundly developed. Through baptism the Christian already lives in Christ a divine life that will never end, which death cannot touch.

> "Just as the living Father sent me and I have life because of the Father, so also the one who feeds on me will have life because of me. This is the bread that came down from heaven. Unlike your ancestors who ate and still died, whoever eats this bread will live forever" (Jn 6:57-58). "Beloved, we are God's children now; what we shall be has not yet been revealed. We do know that when it is revealed we shall be like him, for we shall see him as he is. Everyone who has this hope based on him makes himself pure, as he is pure" (1 Jn 3:2-3).

Thus, what the Christian hopes for at the deepest level of hope is the "beatific vision," the face to face union with God.

Yet this hoped for union is not merely for oneself, since it is a union of generous love (*agape*) that must extend to all God's creation; hence it is a hope for the union of the Church and of the whole cosmos with the Creator, pictured in the Book of Revelation as the "marriage feast of the Lamb," of Christ and his bride the Church, a universe transformed and descending from heaven to earth (Rv 21-22). It is this scene which closes the Bible as the panorama of creation opened it (Gn 1-2).[13]

Before this glorious promise, however, we sinful human beings feel utterly powerless. Not only in our times has the hope of human progress through science and technology failed because, while they give us control over nature, they do not give us control over ourselves and our societies. All human history makes evident that humanity cannot of itself attain even earthly justice and peace, and certainly not eternal life with God. St. Paul in the Epistle to the Romans (1:16-2:16) vividly depicted humanity's universal "falling short" of the goal for

---

[13] CCC # 1042-1060.

which it was created and the internal conflict within every human between conscience and desire, between the true "inner" person, the real I, and the false "outer" person enslaved to sin:

> We know that the law is spiritual; but I am carnal, sold in slavery to sin. What I do, I do not understand. For I do not do what I want, but what I hate. Now if I do what I do not want, I concur that the law is good. So it is no longer I who do it, but sin that dwells in me. For I know that good does not dwell in me, that is, in my flesh. The willing is ready at hand, but doing the good is not. For I do not do the good I want, but the evil I do not want. Now if I do what I do not want, it is no longer I who do it, but sin that dwells in me. So, then, I discover the principle that when I want to do right, evil is at hand. For I take delight in the law of God, in my inner self, but I see in my members another principle at war with the law of my mind, taking me captive to the law of sin that dwells in my members. Miserable one that I am! Who will deliver me from this mortal body? (Rm 7:14-24)[14]

We all experience this utter powerlessness to overcome our own weaknesses or to solve the tragic problems of a world of war, delusion, and injustice, and it seems to make a mockery of hope. It is this existential despair that drives people to deny the very existence of a good God. "In their insolence the wicked boast, 'God doesn't care, doesn't even exist'" (Ps 10:4). "I will punish the men... who say in their hearts, 'Neither good nor evil can the Lord do'" (Zp 1:12). But St. Paul answers his own temptation to despair with a cry of hope, "Thanks be to God through Jesus Christ our Lord!" (Rm 7:25). Christian faith provides this answer in Jesus Christ, risen from death, Savior of all who believe in him. "In the world you will have trouble, but take courage, I have conquered the world" (Jn 17:33).[15]

---

[14] In this passage Paul's statement, "So it is no longer I who do it, but sin that dwells in me" should not be taken too literally as if he was denying personal responsibility for his actions, and blaming it on a personified "Sin," like the comedian who kept saying, "The devil made me do it!" Paul means that it is not his true self as God created him to be and as his conscience says he ought to be, but his false sinful self who sins. Paul dramatizes this inner self-contradiction as two persons struggling within himself, Dr. Jekyll and Mr. Hyde. See Chapter 3, note 19.

[15] CCC # 638-658.

Of course this victory of Christ and of all who are in Christ is now known only in faith. It is not experienced, except obscurely, in a world that today remains so very troubled. Jesus constantly urged his disciples to be vigilant for his Second Coming, as in the great Eschatological Discourse of Mark 13 (Mt 24) and the Parable of the Ten Virgins (Mt 25:1-13). Some exegetes have claimed that Jesus expected this to take place soon after his death. Hence they argue that his moral instructions were only an "interim ethic" and no longer apply 2000 years after. They also maintain that the early Church at first shared this expectation and, only after it had failed to be fulfilled, accepted the idea of the continuation of history.[16]

Other exegetes, however, have pointed out that Jesus made no recorded prediction of a date, but rather is reported to have replied to the question, "But of that day or hour, no one knows, neither the angels in heaven, nor the Son, but only the Father. Be watchful! Be alert! You do not know when the time will come" (Mk 13:32-33).[17] What the Twelve could be sure of was that the Kingdom would begin to be manifest "in power" even in the time of those who heard him. This was fulfilled by the ending of the old order with the inauguration of the new covenant by the founding of the Church at Pentecost (Ac 2:1-47) and the destruction of the Temple in 70 A.D. (Mt 24:1-2; Mk 13:1-2; Lk 21:5-6).

What We Hope For

Thus what we hope for (with a hope born of faith) as supremely good, but still in the future and impossible to obtain by any human effort, yet possible with God, is first of all God himself — not just *our* happiness but the coming of the Reign of God in which we and all who love God

---

[16] The thesis of a merely "interim ethics" in the New Testament is argued by Jack T. Sanders, *Ethics in the New Testament.* Such views seem now to have little support among scholars. By the time of the last books of the New Testament (cf. Rv 20:3, 7, and 2 P 3:8), though the expectation of a sudden Second Advent of Christ was still very lively, the "interim" was being spoken of in terms of a "thousand" years.

[17] CCC # 1048, 672-674.

will share. God has freely invited us to share eternal life with him (see the Parable of the Wedding Feast, Mt 22:1-14). Secondarily we hope for the means, supplied both by nature and by grace, to reach God. "God is able to make every grace abundant for you, so that in all things, always having all you need, you may have an abundance for every good work" (2 Cor 9:8).

This note of hope sounds throughout the Bible. The Psalmist of the Old Testament sings, "Whom else have I in heaven? And when I am with you, the earth delights me not" (Ps 73:25). St. Paul says, "We boast in the hope of the glory of God" (Rm 5:2), which Titus (1:2) describes as "the hope of eternal life that God, who does not lie, promised before time began" and Hebrews (7:19) as "a better hope... through which we draw near to God."

Strangely, our need for God's gift of the virtue of hope has sometimes become obscured in the Church. In the late Middle Ages the legalism fostered by the Nominalists in the universities often led to a kind of Pelagianism that emphasized human effort at the expense of confidence in God's grace.[18] The result was that some Christians like the young Luther felt they could not live with the seemingly impossible demands of God's holy law.[19] Consequently he and others of the Reforming party sought *assurance* of their personal salvation in a one-sided interpretation of St. Paul's teaching on salvation by faith.[20] The Council of Trent replied to this question not only by its teaching on faith and works, but also by teaching that it is hope, rather than the Reformers' subjective "assurance" of election and forgiveness, which

---

[18] Francis Clark, S.J., "A New Appraisal of Late Medieval Theology" answers the charge of Heiko Oberman, *The Harvest of Medieval Theology* that these Nominalist theologians were Pelagians, by showing that they never denied our total dependence on God's grace to do good. On the contrary, out of pastoral concern, they sought to exalt God's mercy in accepting such of our better dispositions which he might use to prepare the way for the grace he alone can bestow. Unfortunately the Nominalist formulations were easily misunderstood in a Pelagian or Semi-Pelagian sense.

[19] For a sympathetic account of Luther's theology of Law and Gospel, see Paul Althaus, *The Theology of Martin Luther*, note especially pp. 53-63, 157-158, 169-178.

[20] Paul Hacker, *The Ego in Faith: Martin Luther and the Origin of Anthropocentric Religion.*

is the grounds for true Christian trust in God's saving power. Trent said that faith without hope cannot give us a share in God's life.[21]

In the seventeenth century, Catholic Jansenists and Quietists (no friends of each other) proposed the absurd theory that Christian perfection ("perfect love") implies a resignation to one's own damnation if that be the will of God. In other words, perfect Christians no longer hope for their own salvation! Pope Innocent X, 1687, rejected this error taught by the pseudo-mystic Michael Molinos; Alexander VIII, 1690, rejected it in its Jansenist version, and Innocent XII, 1699, in its Moderate Quietist version by Fenelon. These popes insisted on the intimate link between faith and hope.[22]

What we hope for is nothing less than God himself. Thus, at the end of each of the letters to the seven churches in the Book of Revelation a reward for fidelity to Christ is given which symbolizes eternal life with God; for example, "To the victor I will give the right to eat from the tree of life that is in the garden of God" (Rv 2:7). Yet it is entirely consistent with such hope to seek other, secondary rewards for our effort. Not only does the Old Testament promise material and spiritual rewards to those who trust in God's promises, but Jesus in the Beatitudes (Mt 5:3-11) promises both kinds of rewards (the meek will "inherit the land," v. 5, while the clean of heart "will see God," v. 8).

Faith requires an effort of the will, a determination to walk the hard path to heaven even in darkness. Who would long endure this effort without hope? But hope seems difficult in dark times, and it therefore requires from God a virtue by which we are able to hope as Abraham did, "hoping against hope" (Rm 4:18) without ever giving up. For "... in hope we were saved. Now hope that sees for itself is not hope. For who hopes for what one sees? But if we hope for what we do not see, we wait with endurance" (Rm 8:24-25).

The Council of Trent in insisting on the necessity of hope in

---

[21] Trent, DS # 1528-1531, 1536-1540, 1545-1550, 1581, 1704.

[22] Alexander VIII, against Jansenists, DS # 2310, 2313; Innocent XI against the quietism of Michael Molinos, DS # 2207, 2212; and Innocent XII against Fenelon's notion of "totally disinterested love," DS # 2351-2352, 2361.

addition to faith[23] was only affirming the many Scriptural exhortations to hope in God or affirmations of its necessity, such as:

> You shall return by the help of your God, if you remain loyal and do right and always *hope* in your God (Ho 12:7). Cursed is the man who trusts in human beings... Blessed is the man who trusts in the Lord, whose *hope* is in the Lord (Jr 17:5a-7). Only in God be at rest, my soul, for from him comes my *hope* (Ps 62:6). For you are my *hope*, O Lord; my trust, O God, from my youth (Ps 71:5). Trust God and he will help you; make straight your ways and *hope* in him (Si 2:6). But since we are of the day, let us be sober, putting on the breastplate of faith and love and the helmet that is *hope* for salvation (1 Th 5:8). If for this life only we have *hoped* in Christ, we are the most pitiable people of all (1 Cor 15:19). Rejoice in *hope*, endure in affliction, persevere in prayer (Rm 12:12). So when God wanted to give the heirs of his promise an even clearer demonstration of the immutability of his purpose, he intervened with an oath, so that by two immutable things, in which it is impossible for God to lie, we who have taken refuge might be strongly encouraged to hold fast to the *hope* that lies before us. This we have as an anchor of the soul, sure and firm (Heb 6:18b-19a).[24]

The Motive of Hope

Thus what we hope for (the material object of hope) is God himself and all the means required for us, along with the whole Church and all humanity, to complete our journey to God. But what precisely is the reason or motive (the formal object) for which we can hope without fear of disappointment? The scholastic doctors discussed this question extensively. St. Bonaventure seems to have thought it to be God's faithfulness.[25] Many others thought it to be God's mercy, or God as our

---

[23] DS # 1531; CCC # 2090, 2134.

[24] In the New Testament "hope" is *elpis*. On its word group see B. Mayer, EDNT, I, pp. 437-440.

[25] *II Sent.*, d. 26, q. 1, a. 2.

highest good, or some combination of these motives. St. Thomas Aquinas with more precision held that the motive or formal object of hope is God's omnipotence, his infinite power.[26] It is because "for God all things are possible" (Mt 19:26; except, of course, to contradict himself!) that our hope in him can be absolute. Nothing can prevent the salvation of those who hope in God, except their own rejection of his grace, and even such hardness of heart can be overcome if we ask God for his help. "A clean heart create for me, O God; renew in me a steadfast spirit" (Ps 51:12).

Of course this proper and principal reason for hope presupposes as more remote motives God's goodness and mercy (Ps 13:6; 51:3; 98:3) and his promises (Heb 10:23; Tt 1:2), along with such mediating motives as the merits of Christ, the merits and prayers of the saints especially Our Lady, and even our own merits, but only as these merits are God's work in us by grace through Christ's merits.[27] Nevertheless God's mercy and promises would not be grounds for hope if God were powerless to fulfill his promises, nor for absolute hope unless God's power were without limits. Thus the recent attempts of Alfred North Whitehead, Charles Hartshorne and the "process theologians" to solve the problem of evil by positing a God who is not omnipotent can succeed only at the expense of undermining the fundamental Christian doctrine of hope.[28]

In nature religions God's *power* is his chief attribute; he is the Almighty. Often God is understood not so much as a person but as a Force (as in the *Star Wars* science-fiction films).[29] This is the predominant theme of many passages of the Old Testament: God is manifested in the voice of the thunder (Ps 29:3), the storm wind (Ps 29:9), the volcano (Ps 97:5), the earthquake (Ps 99:1); or in the bedrock (Ps 18:3), the mountains (Ps 121:1), the vastness of the ocean and the sky (Ps 104;

---

[26] *S.T.*, II-II, q. 17, a. 1.

[27] Trent, DS # 1553, 1556-1557, 1576; CCC # 956, 1370, 1820-1821, 2683.

[28] For the philosophical basis of process theology see Charles Hartshorne, *The Divine Relativity*.

[29] On the view that a transcendent "force" which empowers persons and things is the basis of all religion see Emile Durkheim, *The Elementary Forms of Religious Life*, pp. 216-234.

Jb 38). He is also Yahweh Sabaoth, the Lord of Hosts (armies), a warrior God (Ex 15:1-18; Is 1:9, quoted by St. Paul in Rm 9:29; Ps 24:10, etc.).

Today, we tend to downplay this terrific, awesome side of God, yet only the Almighty can be our assurance that the great forces of evil in the world and within us can be conquered. Because God is the "Strong One, the Holy One," as the Eastern Church loves to praise him in the liturgy, and because Christ is "the power of God" (1 Cor 1:24), the Son of Man who will "come in the clouds with great power and glory" (Mk 13:26) as he himself predicted, our hope is not wishful-thinking but absolutely realistic.

B: ITS CERTAINTY

Is Hope Assured?

Hope is a virtue which strengthens the will as faith strengthens the intellect, and to hope is an act of free choice, since we hope for what we do not see except by faith. Since throughout his life Jesus was already in perfect union with his Father as the saints in heaven are now, he did not in the strict sense hope for what he already possessed, but he did hope for the completion of his mission from the Father, for the salvation of the whole world, and for the glorification of his own body.[30] Hence, the Fourth Gospel gives us his prayer at the Last Supper:

> "Holy Father, keep them [the Twelve] in your name that you have given me, so that they may be one just as we are... I pray not only for them, but also for those who will believe in me through their word, so that they may all be one, as you, Father, are in me and I in you" (Jn 17:11b; 20-21a).

All Christians in this world must live in hope of final fidelity to God at death, while the souls in purgatory hope for the completion of their purification and face-to-face union with God.

---

[30] S.T., III, q. 7, a. 4.

Hope is given with faith and charity to all in baptism and can be lost only by sinning directly against it, or indirectly by sinning against faith, since hope is rooted in faith. Some Catholics have a very inadequate conception of hope. They think that it means, "I hope, because I know that God will save me if I do my part." But of course that leaves the awful thought, "Yes, but probably I won't do my part!" It is true that Christian hope is absolutely certain and infallible only as far as God is concerned, while from our side it is only conditionally certain, since we are always free to sin. As St. Paul says, "Whoever thinks he is standing secure should take care not to fall" (1 Cor 10:12). "Work out your salvation with fear and trembling" (Ph 2:12b).

Yet *simply speaking* hope is certain and participates in the certitude of faith, as is often affirmed in the New Testament.[31]

> Take courage and be stouthearted, all you who hope in the Lord (Ps 31:25). Hope does not disappoint, because the love of God has been poured out in our hearts through the Holy Spirit that has been given to us (Rm 5:5). Be strongly encouraged to hold fast to the hope that lies before us. This we have as the anchor of the soul, sure and firm (Heb 6:18, 19). I am suffering these things; but I am not ashamed, for I know him in whom I have believed and am confident that he is able to guard what has been entrusted to me until that day (2 Tm 1:12).

The Council of Trent[32] in answer to the Reformers' insistence that true faith gives the believer an absolute assurance of being saved, defined that faith does not itself reveal who is and who is not saved, but that hope, born of true faith, assures us that no matter how weak we are, the power of God can overcome all our defects. Consequently, hope tells us not merely, "God will save you, *if* you do your part" but much more: "God can and will give you the power to do your part, and even the actual doing of your part, if you ask him in hope."

Christian hope is a *filial hope*, the hope of a child in its loving parents, because God has assured us, "Can a mother forget her infant, be without tenderness for the child of her womb? Even should she

---

[31] *S.T.*, II-II, q. 18, a. 4.

[32] DS # 1559, 1563, 1566, 1568; CCC # 2091-2092.

forget, I will never forget you" (Is 49:15). Yet for that very reason it also includes an element of *filial fear*, the kind of fear that is "the beginning of wisdom" (Ps 111:10; Pr 9:10; Si 1:16, 24), the fear of losing God by our own sin, from which we must pray to be freed.

What of those who fear God with only a *servile* fear, that is, only because they fear punishment if they offend him (Si 1:25-29)? Some Jansenists condemned such fear as sinful, but the Council of Trent[33] and Alexander VIII and Clement XI[34] rejected this opinion and taught that such fear is of itself not sinful but a real deterrent to sin, which John the Baptist (Mt 3:7-10) and Jesus himself (Mt 10:28; Lk 12:5) did not hesitate to preach. Yet it can never have the justifying effect of the filial fear that accompanies the virtue of Christian hope. In heaven when hope is fulfilled, even filial fear will cease, because sin is no longer a possibility for the blessed.

In the Old Testament the great example of hope is Abraham who at God's command was willing to offer Isaac, his only son, on whom all his hopes seemed to depend (Gn 22:1-14); but all the prophets sound this same note. Thus Jeremiah, who at one time came close to despair: "You duped me, O Lord, and I let myself be duped... All the day I am the object of laughter; everyone mocks me" (Jr 20:7), still proclaimed, "Hear the word of the Lord, O nations, proclaim it on distant coasts and say: He who scattered Israel, now gathers them together, he guards them as a shepherd his flock" (Jr 31:10).

The gift of the Holy Spirit which relates to hope and perfects it by the immediate strengthening and guidance of the Spirit is the Gift of Fear, while the First Beatitude, "Blessed are the poor in spirit, for theirs is the kingdom of heaven" (Mt 5:3) indicates the acts of hope by which we acknowledge our spiritual poverty, our powerlessness, and place our trust solely in God's almighty power.

Jesus furnished us with a perfect example of hope with its poverty of spirit when he rejected Satan's offer of "all the kingdoms of the world" (Mt 4:8-10), when to save the world he chose poor simple men

---

[33] DS # 1558, 1676.

[34] Alexander VIII, 1690, against the Jansenists, DS # 2313-2314; Clement XI, 1713, against the Jansenist Quesnell, DS # 2460-2464.

as his apostles (Mk 1:16-20), and when he refused to save himself from
the Cross, saying to Peter:

> "Put your sword back into its sheath... Do you think that I can-
> not call upon my Father and he will provide me at this moment
> with more than twelve legions of angels? But then how would
> the scriptures be fulfilled... ?" (Mt 26:52-54a).

In her *Magnificat* Mary expresses the same absolute confidence:
"He has helped Israel his servant, remembering his mercy, according
to his promise to our fathers, to Abraham and to his descendants forever" (Lk 1:54-55). This confidence is also manifest in the lives of all
the saints, many of whom passed through times when all hope seemed
vain. Yet the Bible never minimizes how hopeless the human condition is when it is not illumined by the light of faith, as we can see from
the Book of Job, Lamentations, or Qoheleth which contain some of the
darkest portrayals of the human lot in all literature.

Despair

Hope can be destroyed either by giving up — the sin of *despair*, or by
relying on it without warrant — the sin of *presumption*.[35] Despair in the
strict sense of the term is deliberate acceptance of the thought that,
"Even God cannot save me from ultimate disaster." This is not the
same as a sin against faith, because those who have no faith have no
reason to hope, and because those who despair may still believe in
God's promises of salvation in general, but doubt it applies to them in
particular.

Obviously, such an act of despair *directly* against hope is for the
Christian intrinsically wrong and, when fully deliberate (which is probably rare), mortally sinful, since it cuts off the one who despairs from
asking God for the help without which salvation can never be attained.
Such sins against hope are much worse than sins against prudence, temperance, and fortitude, but they are less serious than sins against faith or

---

[35] CCC # 2091-2092.

love which deny God's truth and goodness. This is because God's truth and goodness are more basic attributes of his divinity than his power. Yet sins against hope are a greater obstacle to salvation than these other sins.

Thus Jesus was probably speaking about sins against hope when he said, "Therefore, I say to you, every sin and blasphemy will be forgiven people but blasphemy against the Spirit will not be forgiven" (Mt 12:31).[36] That is, a sin against hope cannot be forgiven, because until one is willing to hope for forgiveness, forgiveness is blocked.

It would be a great mistake, however, to judge that every person who *seems* without hope has committed this grievous sin of despair. A very common pathological mental condition is what is called *depression*, which can have many causes, genetic, hormonal, or the result of severe shocks such as the death of loved ones or the traumas of wartime combat. Depressed persons often perceive the world and themselves as exaggeratedly dark. They are filled with groundless anxiety and guilt, and feel themselves utterly worthless and powerless to carry on their lives. Probably most suicides result from such pathological conditions. Since these states are usually not the fault of the victim, any more than other diseases, and the victim's ability to deliberate and make free decisions is severely limited, there is no question here of grave sin.[37] Jesus in the passage quoted above was speaking of some Pharisees who were not depressed, but coldly malicious in their accusations that Jesus was working miracles by the power of the devil Beelzebul.

Even when a person is not suffering from mental pathology, but is simply grieving over tragic losses, or suffering under the heavy burdens of life and sickness, as Job was, their temptations to despair are spiritual trials not sins. One has only to read the Psalms to see how those who truly love God and hope in him, nevertheless complain to him, and find hope very hard.

---

[36] According to Benedict Viviano, NJBC, p. 654, the dominical saying of Mt 12:31 has been transmitted in both Q and Marcan forms, which Mt tries to combine. The Q form implied that sins against the Son of Man were forgivable, but not those against the Holy Spirit. The likeliest meaning is that the unforgivable sin is obstinate resistance to the Holy Spirit, i.e., to God's grace and mercy.

[37] CCC # 2282-2283.

> How long, O Lord? Will you utterly forget me?
> How long will you hide your face from me?
> How long shall I harbor sorrow in my soul,
>   grief in my heart day after day?
> How long will my enemy triumph over me?
> Look, answer me, O Lord, my God! (Ps 13:2-4a).

Such prayer is in fact an expression of the virtue of hope, since in these trials hope becomes purified of every other motive except confidence in God's almighty power. St. Francis de Sales as an adolescent, troubled by the gloomy theological discussions about predestination initiated by Calvinism, and feeling no "assurance" of his election, suffered for a long time from a terrible feeling that he was predestined to hell. St. Paul of the Cross, the founder of the Passionists, for forty years suffered a similar darkness. St.Thérèse of Lisieux tells us in her autobiography that after having lived a childhood and adolescence when heaven was always a vivid picture for her, she entered into eight years during which she was tempted by atheistic thoughts and seemed to be in "a dark tunnel with no light at the end."[38] Such Christian men and women, however, continued to pray and through the darkness of their faith and the secret power of their hope became great saints.

Spiritual Boredom

The direct cause of sinful despair is the cardinal sin of *acedia*, often translated "sloth," but better "boredom," that is disgust with spiritual values. St. John Cassian calls this "the vice of monks"[39] because the experience of the Desert Fathers showed that those living the contem-

---

[38] On these purifying experiences see John G. Arintero, O.P., *The Mystical Evolution*, vol. 2, pp. 63-117; 184-204.

[39] "Our sixth combat is with what the Greeks call *acedia*, which we may term weariness or distress of heart. This is akin to dejection, and is especially trying to solitaries, and a dangerous and frequent foe to dwellers in the desert; and especially disturbing to a monk about the sixth hour, like some fever which seizes him at stated times, bringing the burning heat of its attacks on the sick man at usual and regular hours. Lastly, there are some of the elders who declare that this is the 'midday demon' spoken of in Psalm 91:6." *Institutes*, Bk X, chapter 1.

plative life often become weary with constant prayer and meditation on spiritual realities which are invisible and intangible to the bodily senses and imagination. The temptation then is to turn back from contemplation to a life of sensual indulgence or excessive busy-ness. On the other hand, the same distaste for the spiritual realm arises in those who give themselves up to the avid pursuit of sex, drugs, and other sensual experiences. Because such pleasures leave the human soul empty and disgusted with life, despair and suicide often follow, as we have seen in the lives of so many "rock stars."

What are the remedies for spiritual boredom and despair? Obviously the wrong remedy for the weary contemplative is to abandon prayer and seek diversion in the world, or in feverish activity. St. Benedict (d.c. 543), the great guide of western monasticism, taught that the remedy was a good balance in life, a rhythm of work and prayer, good companionship, and moderate recreation,[40] and this advice goes for all Christians in their own situations. For the bored sensualist, the answer is to return to a sane way of life, taking pleasure in the simple good things it provides, and to begin to pray again. Generous efforts to help others will turn one's thoughts outward, away from self-pity and depression. St. Paul says, "Do not grow slack in zeal, be fervent in spirit, serve the Lord. Rejoice in hope, endure in affliction, persevere in prayer" (Rm 12:11-12).

When, on the other hand, this gloom arises from feelings of guilt, genuine or neurotic, from grief, or from a sense of failure in life, of disappointment with efforts to overcome sin, the remedy is to consider the passion of Jesus, his love for us symbolized by his Sacred Heart, the great mercy of God and his promises to help the worst of sinners, typified in the motherliness of the Blessed Virgin Mary, and in the lives of the saints who were once great sinners, like St. Mary Magdalene or St. Augustine.[41]

---

[40] See *The Rule of St. Benedict*, with its introduction and notes by A.C. Mersel and N.L. de Mastro.

[41] Cassian, *Institutes*, X, chapters 7-20, comments on 1 Th 4 and 2 Th 3 which he regards as St. Paul's pastoral remedy for *acedia* and lack of charity. The fundamental remedy, he argues, is steady work, since it is laziness that breeds this depression. Hence it was that in the Benedictine tradition *acedia* was called "sloth." In the *Life of the Servant* of

If *acedia* arises from bottled-up anger, frustration, and feelings of revenge, the remedy is the forgiveness of enemies, made possible by the realization that Jesus has forgiven us. "As the Lord has forgiven you, so must you also so do" (Col 3:13). Finally, the despairing should not hesitate to seek the help of other Christians whom they may find much more willing to help than they suppose.

Presumption

While despair is too little hope, *presumption* is too much; or rather it is a false hope, because it produces a confidence not based on trust in God but on our own powers to gain this happiness while neglecting the means God offers. The Bible often warns against this false hope in our own powers to attain happiness, as the Psalmist says: "Some are strong in chariots; some in horses [we might say today "in our nuclear weapons"]; but we are strong in the name of the Lord, our God" (Ps 20:8). Presumption is directly against the virtue of *magnanimity* which encourages to great actions, rather than against theological hope. But it is directly against theological hope to mock the mercy of God by delaying repentance, the Sacrament of Reconciliation, and good works, in the "hope" (i.e., the presumption) that after a bad life, we can have a death-bed conversion.

Presumption is often expressed by such statements as "God is good. He will understand why I am doing what the Church tells me is sin, and he will forgive." The prophets confronted this presumption among the people of their times who worshipped idols and oppressed the poor in the confidence that because they were members of the Chosen People they would be saved. John the Baptist denounced the same folly: "Do not presume to say to yourselves, 'We have Abraham as our father.' For I tell you, God can raise up children to Abraham from these stones" (Mt 3:9; Lk 3:8). And Jesus uttered the even more terrible words:

---

the great medieval mystic Henry Suso, O.P., Henry describes a deep depression into which he fell and then a voice that said to him, "Get up and sweep your cell." This began his recovery.

"If you were Abraham's children, you would be doing the works
of Abraham. But now you are trying to kill me, a man who has
told you the truth that I heard from God; Abraham did not do
this. You are doing the works of your father!... You belong to
your father the devil and you willingly carry out your father's
desires" (Jn 8:39b-40a, 44).

Such presumption is fostered by certain heresies. For example,
Pelagius' one-sided emphasis on good works can lead to presuming
that we can save ourselves, while Luther's one-sided emphasis on faith
in opposition to Pelagianism can lead to presuming that God will save
us no matter how we live — although, no doubt, both Pelagius and
Luther intended to reform Christian life not to encourage such foolish
exaggerations. Presumption also is caused by vanity or pride which
make us deaf to the words of our Lord in the Fourth Gospel, "I am the
vine, you are the branches. Whoever remains in me and I in him will
bear much fruit, because without me you can do nothing" (Jn 15:5).

Presumption, unlike despair, is only *indirectly* against hope, since
it does not deny God's power, but rather is against God's providence in
that it does not respect his plan to save us through our conformity to the
due order of means to ends which God has provided. Hence it does not,
like despair, utterly block God's grace, and is not always a mortal sin.
For example, to hope for miracles to solve problems that one could
solve by ordinary means, or to expect from God graces for which one
has not done what one could to prepare, or for which one has not prayed,
can be only a venial sin if it does lead to the neglect of the essential
means to salvation. To commit a mortal sin with the knowledge that it
can be forgiven if repented or to hope that one will repent and confess
does not add to that sin (and may even diminish it), but to commit a
mortal sin because we presume we can repent and go to confession
adds to the first sin another mortal sin of presumption.

When we sin mortally, we do not know we will ever repent, since
repentance requires the grace of God to which we have no right. The
remedy for the vice of presumption is humility before God and meditation on the mystery of God's free bestowal of grace. An Old Testament story that instructs us in this matter, is how Esau thought so little

of his father Isaac's blessing that one day when hungry he sold it to his younger brother Jacob for a pot of stew (Gn 25:29-34), because he "cared little for his birthright" (v. 34). The sin of presumption shows that same lack of appreciation for the gift of God's mercy which becomes our "birthright" through baptism. A New Testament story that shows how disastrous is the sin of despair is that of Judas' suicide (Mt 27:3-10; Ac 1:16-20) in contrast to the repentance of Peter (Mt 26:69-75; Mk 14:66-72; Lk 22:56-62; Jn 21:15-17). A Church Father, Julianus Pomerius (d.c. 500) said:

> Let faintheartedness not be present lest we despair of being able to do what we can do; let there be no vicious presumption lest we ascribes to ourselves what we are to do only by the grace of God.[42]

Aquinas says[43] that in the Ten Commandments there is no explicit command to hope, because it is implied in the promises on which the Covenant was founded: "Choose life then, that you and your descendants may live" (Dt 30:19b). By the natural law we are bound to hope in God, since even reason tells us that ultimately God alone can move all things to the goal for which he created them, and therefore our ultimate trust ought to be in him alone. The Bible confirms this also as regards the supernatural end to which God has called us by his grace. If we meditate on the Scriptures we will find them full of God's promises and words of hope.

> You shall return by the help of your God, if you remain loyal and do right and always hope in your God (Ho 12:7). Who among you fears the Lord hears his servant's voice and walks in darkness without any light, trusting in the name of the Lord and relying on his God (Is 50:10). Hope in God! For I shall again be thanking him in the presence of my savior and my God (Ps 42:6). Trust in him at all times, my people! Pour out your hearts before him; God is our refuge! (Ps 62:9). O Israel hope in the Lord,

---

[42] Julianus Pomerius, *The Contemplative Life*, III, c. 20, p. 148.

[43] *S.T.*, II-II, q. 22, a. 1.

both now and forever (Ps 131:3). You who fear the Lord, hope
for good things, for lasting joy and mercy (Si 2:9). Everyone
who has this hope based on him [God] makes himself pure, as he
is pure (1 Jn 3:3). Therefore, gird up the loins of your mind and
live soberly, and set your hopes completely on the grace to be
brought to you at the revelation of Jesus Christ (1 P 1:13).

The Sacrament of Hope

Alexander VII in 1665 rejected the opinion that it is not necessary for
Christians often throughout their lives to express at least interiorly this
hope of attaining God.[44] It is necessary to arouse our hope in times of
temptation and discouragement by a positive effort, and also when we
sincerely receive the sacraments since these are signs of hope.

Of all the sacraments, the Anointing of the Sick seems to have a
special relation to hope.[45] Among the Psalms there are many that cry
out for God's help in sickness (e.g., 6, 30, 32, 38, 41, etc.) which the
ancients associated closely with sin. It is in sickness and the fear of
death that we experience our utter powerlessness and are confronted
with the mystery of the judgment and future life. Modern medicine is
a marvelous proof of what human intelligence can do to overcome our
powerlessness, but in the end death or at least the liability to death
inherent in our bodily nature can never be overcome. Consequently, in
serious sickness the Sacrament of Anointing still provides hope for life
now and forever.

> Is anyone among you sick? He should summon the presbyters of
> the church, and they should pray over him and anoint him with
> oil in the name of the Lord, and the prayer of faith will save the
> sick person, and the Lord will raise him up. If he has committed
> any sins, he will be forgiven (Jm 5:13-15; cf. Mk 6:13; 16:18).

The Sacrament recalls how Jesus healed the sick physically, but
it also brings spiritual healing, especially by arousing the spirit of hope

---

[44] DS # 2021.
[45] CCC # 1499-1532.

in the sick who are discouraged and fearful, and makes them confident that even if death comes they will rise with Christ. Everyone who is in serious illness, or about to undergo major surgery can and should receive this sacrament, and the pastor, family and friends of the sick have a responsibility to make this possible. Since Vatican II, people less and less see this as a frightening sign that death is imminent, but as hopeful and helpful; not a substitute for medical care, but a celebration of God's healing power with which medical care cooperates. The reception of the Eucharist as Viaticum[46] (food for the journey), when possible, is the most fitting way to celebrate the actual passage of the Christian from this troubled life to the peace of the everlasting wedding feast.

Summary of Norms

The positive norm for the theologal virtue of hope, whose formal object is God as the Almighty Savior and which is included in the First Commandment,[47] can be formulated as follows:

1. Since union with God is the ultimate goal of human life which cannot be reached unless we hope to attain it and strive for it by the aid of grace, we the baptized must continue firmly to hope for eternal life in God through Christ by the power of the Holy Spirit in spite of our sins and trials in this life even to death.

The exceptionless negative norms can be stated as follows:[48]

1. Never despair of the mercy of God no matter what our sins may be.
2. Never presume that we will attain eternal life without sincerely striving to keep God's commandments or that because of God's mercy we can sin with impunity.
3. Never lose trust that God hears and answers according to his wisdom and merciful will our prayers for ourselves and others, especially for the coming of God's Kingdom.

---

[46] CCC # 1517.
[47] CCC # 2086.
[48] CCC # 2090-2092.

CHAPTER 5

LIVING MODERATELY

*Do not love the world or the things of the world. If anyone
loves the world, the love of the Father is not in him. For all that is in the
world, sensual lust, enticement for the eyes, and a pretentious life is
not from the Father but is from the world. Yet the world and
its enticements are passing away. Whoever does the will of God,
however, remains forever* (1 Jn 2:15-17).

A: SELF-DISCIPLINE

Christian Asceticism

The meaning of the above famous text and the classical medieval theme
De Contemptu Mundi is not that we should have contempt for the world
which God created, which we ought to love for the sake of its Creator
and its own goodness. Our contempt is for its present sinful state which
makes it an obstacle to reaching God, rather than the gracious road to
God which God intended.[1]

The need for self-discipline is a lesson which the first pages of
Genesis sought to teach. To get her to eat the fruit of the Tree of the
Knowledge of Good and Evil the serpent tempted Mother Eve with a
"pretentious life" (1 Jn 2:16), namely, the illusion that she could live as
the gods do if she would only cut herself loose from her dependence on
the Creator: "Your eyes will be opened and you will be like gods who
know what is good and what is bad" (Gn 3:5). "The woman saw that the
tree was good for food" (the lust of the flesh), "pleasing to the eyes"
(the lust of the eyes), and "desirable for gaining wisdom" (a pretentious

---

[1] A famous example of the *De Contemptu Mundi* genre is the work of Pope Innocent III,
On the misery of the human condition (De miseria humanae conditionis). He intended
to write a companion "Praise of the World" but never got to it!

life) (Gn 3:6). "Then the eyes of both of them were opened, and they realized that they were naked; so they sewed fig leaves together and made loincloths for themselves" (Gn 3:7).[2]

Thus, "the lust of the flesh," which St. Paul calls "the law of my members" (Rm 7:23) or "the outer man" as distinguished from the "law of my mind" or "inner man" (Rm 7:22-23)[3] is the first hurdle that we must leap to reach God, although no doubt the lust of the eyes and a pretentious life are still higher hurdles, as we shall see later.

It is essential in considering the meaning of the texts from 1 John and Romans not to misread them in terms of Greek philosophical ideas which may have influenced their manner of expression but which are not consistent with the main perspective of the Bible. The philosophy of Plato was based on a *dualism* between the visible, material world, and an ideal, spiritual world of which the former was only a shadowy copy. For Platonism the real human person is not the material body which is only the garment of the real human self, namely, the spiritual mind or soul. The body will perish, but the soul has always existed and will always exist. Salvation, therefore, consists in the mind's liberation from the body. The ethical consequence is the notion that virtue consists in quieting the impulses of the body so that the mind can be free of the body's noise and become completely attentive to the spiritual reality which is innate within it.[4]

This Platonic dualistic conception of the human being, although it was very useful to the early Church Fathers in trying to explain the Gospel to peoples of Hellenistic culture because of the points of contact it had with biblical teaching, cannot be entirely squared with that

---

[2] See John Paul II, *Original Unity of Man and Woman: Catechesis on the Book of Genesis*, pp. 123-140 on the meaning of "nakedness" in Gn 2:25 and "shame" in 3:7.

[3] "The 'inner person' (in Rm 7:22) is what the individual should be, in distinction from what he actually is. According to a person's essential determination by God he should find his joy in the law (according to Psalm 119). In fact he is dominated by the strivings of *sarx* [flesh] and is hostile to God's will," N. Walter, EDNT, p. 65. Walter says also that in 2 Cor 4:16 (and analogously in Eph 3:16) "the contrast is between the visible and the invisible in the existence of the Christian... not between the unreal and the real." It is between Paul's visible suffering and his invisible confidence in Christ.

[4] On the influence of Platonic anthropology on Christian theology see my *Theologies of the Body: Humanist and Christian*, pp. 103-147.

teaching, since the Bible does not teach the pre-existence of the human soul. Hence, the central Christian teaching on the resurrection of the body is quite contrary to the Platonic idea of escape from the body.

Therefore, St. Paul — whose perspective is thoroughly Jewish and for whom, because of his own experience of the risen Christ (1 Cor 9:1, 15:8; Gal 1:16; Ac 9:3-9) the doctrine of Resurrection is fundamental — when he contrasts "the spirit" and "the flesh" (e.g., in 1 Cor 15:12-19) ought not to be understood in terms of Platonic matter-spirit dualism. As the writer of 1 John likes to contrast "darkness" vs. "light" (1:5-7), "world" vs. "God" (4:4-5) and "death" vs. "life" (3:14), so for Paul the duality is that of "the flesh" vs. "the spirit," or "the law of the members" vs. "the law of God" (Rm 7:23), or "the outer" vs. the "inner man" (Rm 7:22), that is, the human person in the state of sin, powerless to attain salvation, and the person redeemed by grace and empowered to reach God.

Yet the New Testament writers also recognized the psychological truth in the Greek anthropology: namely, that we most vividly experience sin as the struggle between our minds which show us what is worthy of our human nature and the unruly sensual desires of our bodies. We are driven by the lust for physical pleasure and the desire for immediate gratification to do all sorts of things that our realistic reason tells us are foolish and self-destructive.

Our current culture, even more worldly than the Greeks, while it readily denounces social injustices and violence, hates to admit the fact that sins of the flesh are really sins at all, and complains that the Church talks too much about such private sins rather than much more serious public, social abuses. Yet it is obvious enough that alcoholism, drug addiction, incest, sado-masochism, and the disruption of families by adultery are major sources of injustice and violence in our society.

The reaction to this widespread moral laxity in Greek society was not only the spiritualistic philosophy of Plato, but more popularly the philosophy of Stoicism.[5] The Stoics were materialists, but they sought, within the perspective of materialism, to raise moral standards.

---

[5] See Michael Spanneut, *Permanence du Stoïcisme de Zenon à Malraux*, especially pp. 130-178.

What they proposed was a system of *self-control*. They hoped that at least philosophers by right-thinking and rigorous self-discipline could so strengthen the control of their wills over their bodily passions and feelings that they would achieve a state of perfect serenity of mind and a resignation to the inevitable which could not be troubled either by the hunger for pleasure or the fear of pain. The early Christians saw much in common between the Gospel and Stoicism.[6] Many of the Church Fathers used the terminology of this philosophy to make the Gospel understandable to the people of their times, especially to the practical-minded Romans for whom Stoicism often had more appeal than Platonism.

Yet the Gospel could not be perfectly squared with Stoicism. The Stoics as materialists did not believe in the survival of the individual soul after death (in this respect Platonism was closer to Christian faith); and they could not accept the central Christian doctrine of the Passion and compassion of Christ. For them a man like Jesus, who wept at the death of a friend ("And Jesus wept," Jn 11:35, the shortest verse of the Bible!), who shuddered with fear in Gethsemane (Lk 22:39-46), and cried out in agony on the Cross (Mk 15:34), was a weak person, not a true philosopher, not a man of virtue.

The Fathers of the Church were somewhat embarrassed at these philosophical objections, and did not find it to easy to explain why the Bible did not teach so lofty a spirituality as Plato, or so rigorous a system of self-control as the Stoics. Sometimes the Fathers were overly influenced in their apologetics and moral teaching by the attitudes they strove to counter. Yet, gradually the Church was able to develop its own system of personal discipline which we call Christian *asceticism* (from Greek *askesis*, training, exercise, practice).

This notion of the disciplined control of the bodily drives and feelings was not, as is sometimes said, alien to the Jews. The Wisdom literature is full of instructions about self-discipline, and the Mosaic law institutionalized the complicated system of ritual purity (Lv 11-16) which required great self-control, especially for priests (Lv 21) and for

---

[6] On this subject see Marcia L. Colish, *The Stoic Tradition from Antiquity to the Early Middle Ages*, vol. 2, *Stoicism in Christian Latin Thought through the Sixth Century*.

the persons consecrated by the Nazarite vow (Nb 6:1-21).[7] But these strict regulations did not imply that the human body, its sexuality or other biological needs, human emotions, or the world of material things were in themselves evil. On the contrary, since they were created by God, they are all good in themselves, when *used in accordance with the purposes intended by the Creator*. As Julianus Pomerius wrote:

> Not by having emotions, then, but by using them badly, do we transgress. For the nature of human emotions indicates the Creator of man; their quality shows man's good or bad will. And so, these same impulses which are emotions in men become virtues in those who use them well and passions or agitations or, as some like to say, disorders in those who lead evil lives.[8]

The Need for Discipline

Discipline of the passions was necessary because, after the world has fallen into sin, human beings are very much inclined to abuse the good things of the Creator, to make idols of them, and thus to overthrow the whole moral order — as witness the history of Solomon, wisest of men, who was trapped by lust into idolatry (1 K 11:1-13), and of whom Sirach laments:

---

[7] See J. Milgrom, *Numbers*, Excursus 11, pp. 355-359 for commentary. He says that "Israelites who crave the austere life of the priesthood can achieve it by taking the Nazarite vow (6:1-21), although this in practice, it seems, is transitory and discouraged" (p. xli). The Nazarite vowed for a time (or was vowed by his parents for life) not to drink wine, or fresh grapes, or dried grapes, or even their kernels or husks (Nb 6:3-4) and not to shave or cut his hair (Nb 6:5), nor render himself unclean by contact with the dead (Nb 6:7-8). If accidentally he was defiled by the dead, he had to shave his head and begin the period of his vow anew (Nb 6:9-12). Unless he was dedicated for a lifetime, on the completion of his vow he must offer his hair and other sacrifices (Nb 6:13-21). A woman could be a Nazarite. See Jg 13:14 concerning the wife of Manoah who apparently also dedicated her son Samson to be a Nazarite for life; cf. Dr. Chavel, the editor of Maimonides, *The Commandments*, vol. 1, p. 105, who also quotes another work of Maimonides in which, to explain this vow, he says, "The chief object of the Law is to [teach man to] diminish his desires, and to cleanse his outer appearance after he has purified his heart."

[8] *The Contemplative Life*, Bk. III, c. 31, p. 162.

You abandoned yourself to women and gave them dominion
over your body. You brought dishonor upon your reputation,
shame upon your marriage, wrath upon your descendants, and
groaning upon your domain (Si 47:19-20).

That there were ascetics in Israel in the time of Jesus is evident
from what we know of the desert-dwelling Jews of the Qumran sect,
who were scrupulously observant of the law and at least some of whom
were celibate.[9] We see this also in the account in Luke (2:22-38) of
Simeon, a "man righteous and devout, waiting the consolation of Israel, and the Holy Spirit was upon him" and of Anna, a widow and "a
prophetess" who "never left the temple, but worshipped night and day
with fasting and prayer" and of John the Baptist, "clothed in camel's
hair, with a leather belt around his waist... fed on locusts and wild
honey" (Mk 1:6).[10]

Jesus accepted the discipline of the Old Law. As he said when
John the Baptist hesitated to baptize him in the baptism of repentance,
"Allow it now, for thus it is fitting for us to fulfill all righteousness
[dikaiosyne, justice]" (Mt 3:15). Jesus also fasted for forty days in the
desert before beginning his mission (Mt 4:1-11), kept vigils for prayer
(Mk 1:35; 14:32-42), regularly made the pilgrimages to the Temple in
Jerusalem for the great feasts (Jn 2:13; 5:1; 7:2-10, 37; 10:23-24; 11:55;
12:12) and, like the Qumran ascetics, observed celibacy.[11] Nevertheless, in face of the criticisms of the Pharisees, he did not allow these
austerities to prevent him and his disciples from eating and drinking
with the sinners whom he had been sent to call to repentance, with the

---

[9] See Raymond E. Brown, NJBC, p. 1075, n. 108, for summary on the celibacy at
Qumran. He concludes: "Probably one group (the elite, or the priests, or the fully
initiated) did practice celibacy, at least for periods of their life — the priestly line had
to be continued — but the rest were married. This agrees with Josephus' evidence
about non-marrying and marrying Essenes (*Jewish War*, 2.82 and 13 # 120, 160)."

[10] See also the description of the asceticism of St. James, the second bishop of Jerusalem,
whose "knees, from praying, were like those of a camel," in Eusebius, *Church History*,
II, c. 23.

[11] William E. Phipps, *Was Jesus Married?* (New York: Harper and Row, 1970) and
response by another Protestant theologian, George Wesley Buchanan, "Jesus and Other
Monks of New Testament Times," *Religion in Life* 48 (1979): 136-142.

result that he was accused of being "a glutton and a drunkard" (Mt 9:10-13; 11:16-19).

After Jesus' crucifixion, Christians discovered a new motive for asceticism in addition to the old ones: namely, to identify with Jesus in his expiatory sufferings for the sins of the world and to offer an effective sacrificial prayer for sinners. St. Paul had practiced the discipline of the law with pharisaic rigor (Ph 3:5-6), and he felt the need to continue some such asceticism after he no longer felt himself bound by the law: "I drive my body and train it, for fear that, after having preached to others, I myself shall be disqualified" (1 Cor 9:27). Yet the Pauline tradition always urged moderation in asceticism itself, and relativized its value, warning against exaggerations:

> For while physical training (*somatike gymnasia*) is of limited value, devotion (*eusebeia*) is valuable in every respect, since it holds a promise of life both for the present and for the future. This saying is trustworthy and deserves full acceptance (1 Tm 4:8-9; cf. 4:1-7).

Paul found the best discipline to be the immense sufferings entailed by his ministry (2 Cor 11:23-29; 12:7b-10) and his identification with the Crucified:

> For his sake I have accepted the loss of all things and I consider them so much rubbish, that I may gain Christ and be found in him, not having any righteousness of my own based on the law but that which comes through faith in Christ, the righteousness from God, depending on faith to know him and the power of his resurrection and the sharing of his sufferings by being conformed to his death, if somehow I may attain the resurrection from the dead (Ph 3:8-11)... Now I rejoice in my sufferings for your sake, and in my flesh I am filling up what is lacking in the afflictions of Christ on behalf of his body, which is the church... (Col 1:24).

Similarly St. Peter advises, "Rejoice to the extent that you share in the sufferings of Christ, so that when his glory is revealed you may also rejoice exultantly" (1 P 4:13).

Institutional Asceticism

From the beginning the Christian communities included some members who lived an ascetical, celibate life. When Paul, while approving marriage, recommended celibacy, he added, "Only, everyone should live as the Lord has assigned, just as God called each one. I give this order in all the churches" (1 Cor 7:17).[12] Yet Paul also cautioned against an excessive asceticism (as regards marriage: 1 Cor 7:5; cf. 1 Tm 4:1-5; Heb 13:4, and as regards wine-drinking: 1 Tm 5:23).[13] It was not, however, until the fourth century, after the end of the persecutions and the Constantinian establishment of the Church, when the original Christian severity of life had become compromised by superficial conversions, that monasticism (the solitary, ascetical life) arose in Egypt and spread through the Church. This hermitic life received its classical description in *The Life of St. Antony* attributed to St. Athanasius and *The Lives of the Desert Fathers*.[14]

These hermits (the term "monk" is from the Greek, *monos*, a solitary; the word "nun" is ultimately from the Sanskrit for "mother"), men and women, sought to live lives of prayer accompanied by very severe physical penance, but some did so without the necessary prudence or "discretion." Consequently, they soon found it necessary to gather into communities under the direction of a spiritually prudent abbot ("father") with a definite "rule." This *cenobitic* (from "common table") asceticism, attributed to St. Pachomius (d.c. 346), has taken various forms but remains a permanent feature of the Church, fruitful of many saints. In the West among the Celtic monks, monasticism at first emphasized a very severe asceticism which afterwards under the *Rule of St. Benedict* was considerably moderated.[15] Monasticism's role in the Church is not to divide Christians into the ascetic and the non-

---

[12] Hans Conzelmann, *1 Corinthians*, pp. 125-126, says, against certain other exegetes, that it matters little whether the first word of this verse is translated "But (or: Only; or: Nevertheless)"; nor whether it concludes or begins a section since as a linking verse it does both.

[13] Simon Tugwell, O.P., *Ways of Imperfection*, pp. 1-12, emphasizes that the earliest Church Fathers are suspicious of "perfectionism," i.e., the pursuit of an extraordinary asceticism apart from participation in the common life of the Christian community.

[14] St. Athanasius, *The Life of St. Antony*; Palladius, *Lausiac History*; Helen Waddell, *The Desert Fathers*.

ascetic, but to keep the ascetic ideal alive, thus encouraging *all* the baptized to live soberly in their current situations, according to the Pauline advice:

> For the grace of God has appeared, saving all and training us to reject godless ways and worldly desires and to live temperately [*sophronos*, prudently], justly, and devoutly in this way, as we await the blessed hope, the appearance of the glory of the great God and our savior Jesus Christ... (Tt 2:11-13).

In the Sermon on the Mount (Mt 5-7) Jesus made clear that fasting, poverty, almsgiving, chastity of mind and body are required of all. While, no doubt, there is a "spirituality for the laity,"[16] fitted to life in the world, this spirituality is based on the same fundamental principles as that of institutionalized asceticism. Thus the whole Church shares in the discipline of Lent and days of fast, abstinence, and vigil.

Pleasure

As these experiences of the Christian community showed, the first moral problem for every human being is control of our love of bodily pleasure and our fear of bodily pain. We are not simple spirits, but complex bodily beings, with a variety of needs and biological drives. Wherever there is multiplicity, if there is to be a unified, consistent, cooperative activity this multiplicity must be harmonized and focused; otherwise the organism destroys itself by internal conflict. In the human being this unity is produced by the will guided by reason which strives to take all factors into account, like the conductor of an orchestra.[17]

---

[15] *The Rule of St. Benedict*, in Latin and English with notes, Timothy Fry et al., eds. The introductory history on monasticism and the Rule is very helpful, pp. 3-155; also cf. M.D. Knowles, O.S.B, *Christian Monasticism* on varieties of monastic life.

[16] On the "Types of Spirituality" see Geoffrey Wainwright in Cheslyn Jones et al., *The Study of Spirituality*, pp. 592-605.

[17] Aristotle, *Politics*, Bk I, c. 5, 1254b 2, says, "We may firstly observe in living creatures both a despotical and a constitutional rule; for the soul rules the body with a despotical rule, whereas the intellect rules the appetites with a constitutional and royal rule." Aquinas frequently quotes this, e.g., *S.T.*, I, q. 81, a. 3, ad 2; I-II, q. 9, a. 2, ad 3; q. 17, a. 7 c., q. 56, a. 4, ad 3.

For the Christian, reason is enlightened by faith in the Word of God, and the will conforms to this faith through love. This control of faith, therefore, is not despotic, seeking only the good of reason itself, but is concerned for the total good of the person in all its dimensions.[18] Such is the *true* self-love that should be the model for our treatment of our neighbor.[19]

> "Do to others whatever you would have them do to you. This is the law and the prophets" (Mt 7:12). "You shall love the Lord your God... You shall love your neighbor as yourself. The whole law and the prophets depend on these two commandments" (Mt 22:37a, 39-40).

But there is also a *false* self-love which first of all begins with the aggrandizement of *sensual pleasure* or *hedonism* (from Greek for "honey") as if true happiness consisted in such pleasure, as the Epicureans and Jeremy Bentham (d. 1832), author of the ethical theory called "utilitarianism," maintained. Such a view is plausible only if under the term "pleasure" we include satisfactions which are not merely sensual. Certainly, the pleasure of the bodily senses is not of itself something bad. Nothing is more obvious or natural than that every human being, even the baby at the breast, seeks sensual pleasure, and as St. Thomas Aquinas said, "No one can live without some bodily, sense pleasure."[20]

---

[18] Control of reason over feelings is not despotic. On the morality of the "passions" see CCC # 1762-1774.

[19] "A man is said to love himself when he loves himself as he is by nature spiritual... And in this way a man ought to love himself, after God, more than any other, as is evident from the very essence of loving... For God is loved as the source of good on which is grounded the love of charity; and from charity a man loves himself because of what he shares of this good, while the neighbor is loved because of what he also shares of this good. To share jointly, however, is a reason for love according to a certain communion in relation to God. Whence, as '*unitas potior est quam unio*' ['identity' is greater than 'communion' — a man is identical with himself but only in communion with his neighbor, cf. q. 25, a. 4], the fact that a man himself shares in the divine good is a greater reason for loving than the fact that another shares with him in this same sharing. Therefore a man ought to love himself more from charity than he does his neighbor. A sign of this is that a man ought not to sin, which is contrary to sharing in blessedness, in order that he might free his neighbor from sin." St. Thomas Aquinas, *S.T.*, II-II, q. 26, a. 4.

[20] *S.T.*, I-II, q. 34, a. 1 c.

It is also obvious, however, that pleasure is not always good for us. Sometimes it is deadly, as witness the victims of alcohol and drugs, or those who get AIDS from sexual promiscuity. Experiments show that if given the chance to stimulate the pleasure centers in the brain animals will kill themselves by repeating this stimulus until they die of exhaustion. Pleasure, therefore, is good for an organism only when under control.

What principle guides this necessary control of pleasure so that it enhances our human lives rather than corrupts and destroys them? It is evident from animal life that pleasure has a biological function; it serves as an inducement to perform acts necessary for the survival and well-being of the animal and its species.[21]

There is a natural pleasure in the sheer comfort of the body in activity and in rest. How delightful the feeling of healthy, vigorous activity when dancing, working, playing in a stimulating environment, in sunlight and good weather! Or resting in a comfortable chair, or taking a good night's sleep! There is great satisfaction simply in traveling, seeing new sights, gazing on the beauty of flowers and smelling their perfumes, listening to music, feeling a textured fabric or a gentle breeze on the skin.

Jewish culture as reflected in the Bible does not dwell on such pleasant sensations as much as Greek literature did, but neither does it ignore or reject them, since much of the Bible is poetry, and poetry works through sensuous images, pleasant or unpleasant. Jesus uses such images in his parables and in the Sermon on the Mount as when he said, "Learn from the way the wild flowers grow. They do not work or spin. But I tell you that not even Solomon in all his splendor was clothed like one of them" (Mt 6:28-29). These few words show us Jesus was no Stoic, indifferent to the pleasure of the senses. His way of healing through touch and his establishment of the sacraments which always involve a sensible element also show his appreciation of the senses.[22]

These pleasures of the senses arise simply from the normal exer-

---

[21] For modern research see Thomas A. Szasz, *Pain and Pleasure: A Study of Bodily Feelings* and Richard A. Steinbock, ed., *The Psychology of Pain.*

[22] CCC # 1146-49, 1189.

cise of our bodily functions. They facilitate such functions, and when we feel discomfort or pain in these functions it is an important signal to us to withdraw from the situation lest the body suffer injury, and to seek rest or healing for the body. Persons who lack this capacity for pain are very liable to severe accidents, as the paralyzed man who lets his cigarette badly burn his hand. Thus pleasure is beneficial when it promotes proper functioning and harmful when it promotes injurious functioning of the body.

But what is good and bad functioning of the body? It is not difficult to decide this question if we simply consider the effects of an action on bodily health (e.g., to decide whether smoking causes lung cancer and circulatory disease), but bodily health is not all there is to being a human being. There is also psychological health, and supremely the good of the person as a whole which we call "moral health" or *virtue*. A person can be physically healthy and yet neurotic, or psychologically normal and yet an evil human being. We cannot reduce the viciousness of a Stalin or a Hitler merely to physiological or psychological causes, as some psycho-historicists and medico-historians have attempted.

The Pleasure-Pain Drive

Therefore, pleasure has to be morally regulated in view of the movement of the whole human person to its ultimate goal, which the Christian knows by faith to be union with God in the community of those who love God and neighbor. When pleasure-seeking becomes an obstacle, an idol, substituting for joy in God and neighbor in their spiritual personhood, it is morally evil. When, on the contrary, it facilitates that journey to God and his community of persons, as God intended it to do, it is morally good, a precious gift of God, for which we must be greatly thankful.[23]

Now for the most part the pleasures of human life do in fact facilitate our living as Christians and help us bear the pains and bur-

---

[23] CCC # 1767.

dens that sin has brought into the world. Catholic Christianity has not favored the grim asceticism of the Puritan or Jansenist who thinks that the Fall has totally corrupted the work of the Creator. The Bible itself approves the simple pleasures of life, while warning that they are fleeting.

> Therefore, I commend mirth, because there is nothing good for man under the sun except eating and drinking and mirth: for this is the accompaniment of his toil during the limited days of his life which God gives him under the sun... Go eat your bread with joy and drink your wine with a merry heart, because it is now that God favors your works. At all times let your garments be white, and spare not the perfume for your head. Enjoy life with the wife whom you love, all the days of the fleeting life that is granted you under the sun. This is your lot in life, for the toil of your labors under the sun. Anything you can turn your hand to, do with what power you have; for there will be no work, nor reason, nor knowledge, nor wisdom in the nether world where you are going (Ec 8:15; 9:7-10).[24]

Cultures fostered by Catholic Christianity have produced great art, music, and literature, and a way of worship that is aesthetically appealing. The Church has especially encouraged the folk cultures of every nation with their simple pleasures.

One genuine human need is *play* or recreation. The Bible recognizes play as the natural activity of childhood (Zc 8:5; Jesus' own parable in Mt 11:16-19), but it also recognized the need of feasting for adults, in the many exhortations in the Torah to "make merry" (e.g., Lv 23:40; Dt 12:7, 14:26, 16:14) and the Third Commandment (Dt 5:14) obliged the Jews to the Sabbath day of rest.[25]

We rest not only by doing nothing, but also by activities different from the necessary labors of life, which have no purpose except their recreative benefit. When, however, play, or the pleasure that is its over-

---

[24] Compare with Qoheleth's appreciation of the good things of this life the ten "better than's" of Si 40:17-27, which acknowledges these same goods but which ends "better than these is fear of God." Yet Qoheleth also ends his whole book, "The last word, when all is heard: Fear God and keep his commandments, for this is all" (Ec 12:13).

[25] CCC # 2168-2195.

flow, becomes an end in itself, it becomes *serious*, and then it ceases to
be true play. Professional football may be recreation for the spectators,
but is very hard work for the players. Thus, even in play pleasure should
not be sought for its own sake, but for the rest and re-creation of our
energies for more valuable activities, and it must be moderated by what
it contributes to these activities. "All work and no play makes Jack a
dull boy" — but so does too much play. As the prophet Amos warned
the Samaritans who made merry as the disaster of the Assyrian inva-
sion approached threatening their land, the inheritance of the tribe of
Joseph:

> Lying upon beds of ivory,
>   stretched comfortably on their couches,
> They eat lambs taken from the flock,
>   and calves from the stall!
> Improvising to the music of the harp,
>   like David, they devise their own accompaniment.
> They drink wine from bowls
>   and anoint themselves with the best oils;
>   yet they are not made ill by the collapse of Joseph!
> Therefore, now they shall be first to go into exile
>   and their wanton revelry shall be done away with (Am 6:4-7).

There are two areas of human life which are so important to survival and health that they are biologically supplied with intense pleasures, the proper management of which, as experience shows, requires
considerable discipline to bring under due control by virtue. These are
the pleasures of food and drink necessary for the survival of every
individual (the "lambs," "calves" and "wine from bowls"), and the
pleasures of sex necessary for the survival of the species (the "beds of
ivory"). The other pleasures of the senses ("the music of the harp" and
anointment "with the best oils") are naturally closely ordered to these
two functions; and the pleasure connected with them is the most intense and urgent.

Of these needs, however, that for food and drink is more necessary and, if too long unsatisfied, the human being perishes; whereas the
individual can remain healthy without sexual pleasure, though not eas-

ily. Yet sexual pleasure is more intense, no doubt because biologically the existence of the species is more important than that of the individual, and because the task of achieving it is more complex, involving as it does the responsible collaboration of human parents in the maintenance of the offspring that may result from intercourse.

We can understand then why the problem of physical health in human life turns largely around the question of the proper use of food and drink and why the abuse of alcohol and drugs (which are a kind of pseudo-food) are so destructive. And again, why the problem of human relations turns so much about sexual love and family conflicts. Christian asceticism, therefore, aims first of all to moderate these pleasures and bring them under the control of reason for the good of the whole person and the community.

The search for immediate sensual gratification tends to be *addictive*. The glutton, the drunkard, the "junky," the Don Juan, the nymphomaniac, are enslaved in a vicious cycle of a seemingly irresistible need for a "fix" with a high and a consequent low that again demands a fix. Such addiction reduces human freedom to a minimum, and blocks the way to anything in life but the all-consuming pursuit of a pleasant physical relief and the avoidance of the pain that follows from its deprivation. Such a condition is far different than the flexible normal rhythm of hunger and satisfaction of a healthy and free life.

But the two fundamental biological drives for nourishment and reproduction are not the only ones. Besides the drives connected with pleasure and the avoidance of pain, which the scholastics called "the concupiscible appetites" ("concupiscence" means "desire" of any kind), we also have a drive that the scholastics called the "irascible appetite" (from *ira*, anger).[26] These two basic drives respond to images which we have learned to regard as pleasant or painful. They produce changes in our bodies experienced as "feelings" or "emotions" — pleasurable or painful, aggressive or resistant reactions which our reason judges appropriate or inappropriate to the reality of the situation.

---

[26] CCC # 1765 does not use these terms but instead speaks of "love" (concupiscible appetite) and "anger" (irascible appetite). It uses (in quotes) the term "passions" which I have avoided by speaking of "drives."

The Effort Drive

Sigmund Freud, who at first attempted to reduce all biological drives to the pleasure principle or satisfaction of the *libido* (desire), was led by his clinical experience to add a second and contrary principle, which he misleadingly called "the death wish," but which today is recognized as *aggression*. Even this term is somewhat misleading, because it tends to have a negative connotation. What this drive really is, is the urge to make an *effort* to overcome obstacles or difficulties that stand in the way of achieving satisfying pleasures.

If animals had only the pleasure-pain drive, then, when in their search for pleasure they ran into an obstacle, they would simply run away from it or succumb to it passively, without attempting to overcome it at the risk of pain. But often to survive an animal cannot just escape its enemies, or give up when it confronts an obstacle in its search for food or a mate, or simply allow itself to be injured or killed. It must fight to overcome that obstacle, even at the cost of painful effort and great risk or at least endure the attack until it can escape or fight back. Hence, animals need a *fighting* drive that moves them to struggle against difficulties in order to be free of pain and achieve pleasurable satisfaction.

Various names have been given in modern psychology to this drive, but I will call it the *effort drive*, since what characterizes it is the overcoming of a difficulty, sometimes by conquering it, sometimes by enduring it until it passes, usually accompanied by a feeling of effort or strain.

> This God who girded me with might,
>   kept my way unerring,
> Who made my feet swift as a deer's
>   set me safe on the heights,
> Who trained my hands for war,
>   my arms to bend even a bow of bronze (Ps 18:33-35).

Thus the search for nourishment and procreation entails not only the maximization of pleasure and the minimization of pain, but also the struggle to survive the many enemies and natural obstacles that prevent these pleasures and comforts. Hence *security* is as important to the animal as food and sex.

Today, there is much concern about human "feelings" and "emotions," and many systems of therapy to cure people of neurotic emotions and restore healthy ones are current. Yet surprisingly, there is no generally accepted *classification* of emotions or feelings.[27] One of the reasons for this, no doubt, is that the term "emotion" is ambiguous. Sometimes it is taken as identical with "feeling," that is, a complex of conscious bodily sensations and mental images. Thus the feeling of fear includes sensations of tensing muscles, accelerated heartbeat and breathing, chill, and a strange sensation in the pit of the stomach, etc.

On the other hand "emotion" also refers to the drives, or appetites, which we have just discussed and which are not directly conscious phenomena except through the feelings to which they may give rise. Thus it is possible to be hungry (the drive for food) without feeling hungry, or to feel hungry without really being hungry. It is best, therefore, to use "feeling" for the sensation, "drive" for the appetite, and "emotion" to include both, since they are normally associated as cause and effect.

Aristotle, basing himself on the very developed study of the emotions by the Greek rhetoricians interested in "moving" their audiences, proposed a very simple classification of the basic emotions which has become traditional in moral theology, although in English it is not easy to find unambiguous terms for them.[28] The two basic emotions are *attraction* (love) and *repulsion* (hate) which arise when we sense or imagine something that appears pleasant or painful respectively.

Often these emotions remain as mere tones of feeling without stimulating us any further. For example, in the Song of Songs when Solomon says, "Ah, you are beautiful, my beloved, ah, you are beautiful! Your eyes are doves behind your veil" (Sg 4:1a), he feels the *attraction* of the Shulamite. When he says, "Come from Lebanon, my

---

[27] For modern research see B.L. Schemes, *The Psychology of the Emotions.*

[28] Aquinas classifies the passions (*S.T.*, I-II, q. 23, a. 1) based on Aristotle, *Nicomachean Ethics*, Bk. II, c. 5, 1105:19-28; *De Veritate*, q. 26, a. 4. Much of what he has to say about them in detail is derived from Aristotle's *Rhetoric*, Bk. II, 10-11.

bride! come from Lebanon, come!" (Sg 4:8), his *desire* for her is en-kindled. Finally, when he says, "How beautiful is your love, my sister, my bride, how much more delightful is your love than wine" (Sg 4:10), he is filled with *joy* in union with her.

On the contrary, in the Book of Jonah we read that the prophet is dismayed by the call of the Lord to preach repentance in the city of Nineveh and feels the emotion of *repugnance*, since he has only hatred for the Ninevites, his people's enemy (Jon 1:1-2). Then he seeks to run away, feeling the emotion of *flight* (Jon 1:3), and finally as he was caught in the storm at sea he is filled with *sorrow*, since he knows he can not escape the Lord and he asks the sailors to throw him overboard (Jon 1:12). As these texts illustrate, the pleasure-pain drive develops in the positive sequence: *attraction, desire, joy*; or the negative sequence: *repugnance, flight*, and *sorrow*; while the effort drive runs through the sequence: *hope, aggression, joy*; or the negative sequence: *fear, discouragement, anger, sorrow* (anger is the emotion felt when one is failing but is still resistant to the evil). Notice that all drives begin in *love* (attraction) or *hate* (repugnance) and end either in *joy* or *sorrow*.

The Gospels relate incidents in which Jesus, as perfectly human, seems to have experienced the whole gamut of these emotions. Thus he is *attracted* by goodness in others, as in the incident with the rich young man: "Jesus, looking at him, loved him" (Mk 10:21); and again when "Jesus saw Nathanael coming toward him and said of him, 'Here is a true Israelite: There is no duplicity in him'" (Jn 1:47). Jesus also felt *desire*, yearning for the accomplishment of his mission, "There is a baptism with which I must be baptized, and how great is my anguish until it is accomplished" (Lk 12:50) and when he said at the Last Supper, "I have eagerly desired to eat this Passover with you before I suffer" (Lk 22:15). Finally, when he saw that his work was beginning to take effect, he was filled with joy at the Supper where he instituted the Eucharist: "I have told you this so that my joy might be in you and your joy might be complete. This is my commandment: love one another as I love you" (Jn 15:11-12).

But Jesus also suffered and felt *repugnance* at the dishonesty of some of his opponents, "Woe to you, scribes and Pharisees, you hypocrites. You are like whitewashed tombs, which appear beautiful on the outside, but are full of dead men's bones and every kind of filth" (Mt 23:27) and sometimes he had to take *flight* from those who sought to kill him (Lk 4:30) and to avoid arousing the opposition of the authorities as long his mission permitted: "After this, Jesus moved about within Galilee; but he did not wish to travel in Judea, because the Jews[29] were trying to kill him" (Jn 7:1).

Jesus is often pictured as a passive figure, but in fact he was a fighter for the truth and for the defeat of the Devil. The Book of Revelation symbolizes him as a Lamb who is a Lion (Rv 5:1-8). Hence, he also experienced the *effort-drives* both in their negative and positive sequence. He felt overpowering *fear* in the Garden of Gethsemane as his death approached: "He was in such agony and he prayed so fervently that his sweat became like drops of blood falling on the ground" Lk 22:44.[30] When Judas came up to him and it was apparent he was doomed, this fear turned into profound *discouragement* as he saw his sleeping disciples and then confronted Judas with the bitter words, "Judas, are you betraying the Son of Man with a kiss?" (Lk 22:48). Finally as he hung on the Cross, he recited the great Psalm 22 which expresses one's temptation to the hopeless *sorrow* of despair, "My God, my God, why have you abandoned me?" (Ps 22:1; cf. Mt 27:46; Mk 15:34), just as he had mourned over Jerusalem just before his own death,

> "If this day you only knew what makes for peace — but now it is hidden from your eyes. For the days are coming upon you when your enemies... will smash you to the ground and your children within you... because you did not recognize the time of your visitation" (Lk 19:42, 44).

---

[29] Note that often in the Fourth Gospel the word "Jews" does not mean the whole people of Israel (after all Jesus was one of them himself) but the party of persons in Judea who were Jesus' opponents. See NA 4 and CCC # 595-598 which explain the grave error of blaming the great majority of the Jewish people of Jesus' own time for his death, let alone subsequent generations of Jews. In fact all of us human beings, inasmuch as we are all sinners, share in the guilt of his death since he had to die to save us from the consequences of sin.

[30] The textual authenticity of Lk 22:43-44 is disputed; see Robert J. Karris, O.F.M., NJBC, 43:184, p. 717; but with somewhat less vivid detail, the Agony in the Garden is also related in Mt 26:39-46; Mk 14:32-42.

Yet Jesus was also firm in the positive emotion of *hope*, because as he three times predicted his death, each time he concluded by promising the disciples his Resurrection three days after his death (Mk 8:38; 9:31; 10:34). Consequently, when the time came to go to Jerusalem for a definitive confrontation with the Temple priests, he did not hesitate. "When the days for his being taken up were fulfilled, he resolutely determined to journey to Jerusalem" (Lk 9:51) and he steeled himself to endure his death without resort to violence lest it distort the meaning of his mission. "Father, if you are willing, take this cup away from me; still, not my will but yours be done" (Lk 22:42; Jn 10:11). And the writer of the Fourth Gospel implies the profound joy that filled the heart of Jesus in his dying words on the Cross, "It is finished" (Jn 19:30), meaning not only that his suffering was over, but that his mission to save all humankind was completed.

But did the "gentle and humble" Jesus (Mt 11:29) ever feel *anger*? Indeed he did, and often. He is recorded to have gotten angry at the commercialization of religion, when he scourged the money-changers in the Temple and overturned their tables (Mk 11:15), at the indifference of the scribes and Pharisees to the sufferings of the people (Mt 23:1-36), at the hard-heartedness of the crowd toward the disabled man (Mk 3:5), at the lack of faith of his apostles, "O faithless generation, how long will I be with you? How long must I endure you?" (Mk 9:19), and surprisingly even at the behavior of mourners who seemed to lack faith in the resurrection (Mk 5:38-39; Jn 11:33).[31] One cannot "hunger and thirst for righteousness" (the Beatitude, Mt 5:6) without hating injustice and all evil, and therefore one should feel anger when confronted with it. As Jesus said, "No one can serve two masters. He will either hate one and love the other, or be devoted to one and despise the

---

[31] Jesus, for example, in Mark 5:38-39, seems disturbed especially by the noisiness of the mourners. In Mk 8:33, he severely rebukes Peter, "Get behind me Satan!" and in Mk 9:19, in evident exasperation at the ineptitude of the Twelve, Jesus exclaims, "O faithless generation, how long will I be with you? How long will I endure you?" In Jn 11:33 the phrase describing Jesus, rendered by NAB as "perturbed and deeply troubled," in the Greek is literally "groaned [or snorted] in the [his] spirit" or as "troubled himself." NAB in a note suggests that this was "perhaps in anger at the presence of evil" (death).

other" (Mt 6:24b). To love God is to hate all that is evil in the world, without, however, hating our enemies, whom we are to love and pray for (Mt 5:43-48) because God loves them for the good he created them to be and wants to re-create them to be again.

Of course most of our feeling states are not pure examples of any of these eleven simple states, but very complex combinations of them whose subtlety it takes a sensitive poet, novelist, or playwright to untangle, and which are perhaps better expressed in music which imitates the tensions and resolutions of our feelings more subtly than words can. Any psychotherapist knows how difficult it is for clients to explain how they feel, and how ambiguous these feelings often are.

The biblical writers, of course, were not concerned with the analysis or classification of the emotions, but many of them, especially the poets, were highly gifted in their portrayal of human feelings. Who has better expressed the emotions of erotic desire and joy than the writer of the Song of Songs or the grief of loss than the writers of Job or Lamentations? The Psalms are almost an encyclopedia of the emotions and, as St. Augustine understood, the Church by singing the Psalms in its liturgy has taught its members how to *feel* in a truly human way.[32] Did not God promise through Ezekiel that he would give us "a new heart... taking from your bodies your stony hearts, and giving you natural hearts" (Ezk 36:26)?

The parables of Jesus perhaps give us the best insight into his own experience of and sympathy with human feelings, as we see in the Parable of the Two Sons (the Prodigal, Lk 15:11-32) or of the Rich Man and Lazarus (Lk 16:19-31). Some are touched with a wry humor, as are the Parable of the Dishonest Steward (Lk 16:1-8) and the Parable of the Persistent Widow (Lk 18:1-8). As for St. Paul, his epistles are passionate almost to the extreme, eloquent with indignation, anger, sorrow, tenderness, and sarcasm. The Johannine writings overflow with love and exaltation. St. Paul says that one of the effects of sin is to deaden the healthy human emotions; hardened sinners become "senseless, faithless, heartless, ruthless" (Rm 1:31).

---

[32] See *Confessions*, Bk 9, iv, 8; vi, 14 (Chadwick, p. 160, 164).

The Virtue of Moderation

How then are we to redeem human emotions, especially the fundamental appetites for the pleasures of food, drink and sex and the drives to fight or flee, by a proper self-control under the guidance of faith and prudence? One has only to glance at world literature, of which the Bible is a major classic, to see how food and drink, love and war, provide much of the comedy and tragedy of human life. No wonder the Greeks worshipped Demeter and Dionysius (Roman Ceres and Liber), the goddess of wheat and the god of wine; and Aphrodite and Ares (Roman Venus and Mars), the goddess of love and the god of war!

When we read two of the most artful biblical stories, that of Joseph (Gn 37-50) and of David (1 S 16-2 S 24; 1 K 1:1-2:11), we see they pivot on struggles that arise from hunger for food and for love. Joseph rose to power in Egypt because he refused to be seduced by his master's wife who was passionately attracted to the young man. He used this power to save his father and his treacherous brothers from famine. David fought many battles to secure the welfare of his people, but, when idled by peace, then yielded to lust and through his many wives got embroiled in disastrous dynastic struggles. In Greek literature, the epics of the Trojan War and the tragedies and comedies, or in English the plays or novels of writers such as Shakespeare or George Eliot turn on the same great themes. What virtues bring these rebellious appetites and emotions under control of reason?

The Greeks spoke of *sophrosyne* (sanity, prudence), the Latins of *temperantia*, the New Testament of *moderation* under various terms. "But we will not boast beyond measure [*métron*] but will keep to the limits [*kanón*, rule] God has apportioned us" (2 Cor 10:13a). A bishop should be a model Christian, "a man of one wife, temperate [*nephálion*, no alcoholic], self-controlled [*sóphrona*]," etc. (1 Tm 3:2). Women in their dress should have "modesty [*aidoûs*, respectability] and self-control [*sophrosyne*]" (1 Tm 2:9).

The basic idea of this virtue of moderation is an ability to stick to the middle between the extremes of too much and too little in matters of pleasure in relation to the true goal of life, which faith tells us is ultimately union with God, but is immediately the preservation of the bodily life of the individual and of the species. The *mean* (middle) in such matters, of course, differs somewhat with individuals and their circumstances.

The virtue of moderation consists *formally* in the ability to achieve the mean as regards physical pleasures and *materially* in the pleasure itself. The chief problems of moderation have to do with the two intense pleasures of food and drink (which are not so much those of taste and smell as of feeling full) and sex, both of which are especially connected with the sense of touch, itself the most basic of all the bodily senses. Hence three kinds of moderation are needed to discipline the pleasures of touch: *abstinence* as regards food, *sobriety* as regards drink, and *chastity* as regards sex. The opposite vices are gluttony, drunkenness, and sexual impurity or "luxury." In all these matters what is needed is the self-control that limits and often defers the satisfactions of the body for the sake of health and puts the body in service of the more specifically human activities of life.

For the Christian this means that life is not primarily for the body which will someday die, but for the soul which will live forever and share its eternal life with the risen body, which then will no longer be a natural body subject to suffering and decay, but a "spiritual" and "heavenly" body (1 Cor 15:36-48) always experiencing pure joy. Jesus exclaimed:

> "O you of little faith! So do not worry and say, 'What are we to eat?' or, 'What are we to drink?'. . . All these things the pagans seek. Your heavenly Father knows that you need them all. But seek first the kingdom of God and his righteousness, and all these things will be given you besides" (Mt 6:30b-33).

And Paul said:

> "Everything is lawful for me," but I will not let myself be dominated by anything. "Food for the stomach and the stomach for food," but God will do away with both the one and the other (1 Cor 6:12b-13a).

For many... conduct themselves as enemies of the cross of Christ.
Their end is destruction. Their god is their stomach; their glory
is in their "shame." Their minds are occupied with earthly things
(Ph 3:18-19).

Paul is also presented as telling Titus to be strict with the Cretans,
one of whose poets had said of them, "Cretans have always been liars,
vicious beasts, and lazy gluttons" (Tt 1:12).

The Greeks felt that while all human virtue adds beauty to the
person and to life, moderation is especially "the beautiful virtue," since
excess or defect in taking one's bodily pleasures distorts human nature
and is disgusting. The Old Testament supports this idea by praising the
chastity of women even more than their appearance, and thus condemning the modern "cult of beauty" so constantly preached by our
consumerist advertising:

Charm is deceptive and beauty fleeting; the woman who fears
the Lord is to be praised (Pr 31:30).

Choicest of blessings is a modest wife,
    priceless her chaste person.
Like the sun rising in the Lord's heavens,
    the beauty of a virtuous wife is the radiance of
        her home.
Like the light which shines above the holy lampstand,
    are her beauty of face and graceful figure.
Golden columns on silver bases are her shapely limbs
    and steady feet (Si 26:15-18).

The New Testament expresses similar advice (1 Tm 2:9-10; 1 P
3:3-5), and it also uses terms such as *kosmios* (modest, decent) and
semnos (dignified) as proper marks of the bishop and deacon. The
Church Fathers frequently praise moderation. Thus Julianus Pomerius
says:

Temperance makes a man temperate, abstemious, frugal, sober,
moderate, chaste, silent, serious, modest. Residing in the soul,
this virtue bridles lust, tempers the affections, multiplies holy
desires and represses corrupt ones, sets in order all that is disor-

dered within us, strengthens all that is well-ordered, removes wicked thoughts and implants holy ones, quenches the fire of lustful passion, kindles the tepidity of our soul by a desire of future reward, soothes our mind with peaceful tranquillity, and ever preserves it intact from every storm of vices.[33]

Shame

We can sin against moderation by apathy and emotional coldness to pleasure, but generally such sins do little damage and therefore are venial; so strong are the biological drives toward the pleasurable that excess is far more likely. Nevertheless, if emotional coldness or neurotic inhibitions cause someone to fail in fulfilling serious responsibilities to health or to others they can become mortal, as when a married person is cold to his or her partner. The excessive pursuit of pleasure can also be venial, but it is very likely, as we have already seen, to result in addictive habits that degrade and depersonalize the self-indulgent, lowering them to the level of the brutes, and destroying that dignity and beauty of personality which results from the moderation that comes from intelligent self-control. As Proverbs (7:21-23) says of the fool who becomes an adulterer:

> He follows her [Lady Folly] stupidly,
>   like an ox that is led to slaughter;
> Like a stag that minces toward the net,
>   till an arrow pierces its liver;
> Like a bird that rushes into a snare,
>   unaware that its life is at stake.

Moderation includes among its integrating aspects first, negatively, the sense of *shame*, illustrated so well by the experience of Adam and Eve after the Fall: "Then the eyes of both were opened, and they realized they were naked" (Gn 3:7). Pope John Paul II has discoursed sensitively on the phenomenology of this fundamental human experi-

---

[33] *The Contemplative Life*, III, c. 19, pp. 144-45.

ence of our own "nakedness" or vulnerability.[34] Shame is a fear of the
loss of personal dignity in one's own eyes and those of others because
of immoderate behavior. The Bible further illustrates this by its story (a
diatribe against Egypt) of how Ham, son of Noah, scornfully exposed
his father as he lay in a drunken slumber, but his brothers Shem and
Japheth reverently with averted eyes covered their father's shame (Gn
9:20-27).

A second more positive aspect of moderation is the sense of *de-
cency*, which is the appreciation of the beauty and reasonableness of
moderation. The language of the Bible is frank and direct about our
bodily nature and its functions and sometimes shocks the prudish, but
it is also free of the vulgarity, obscenity, and pornography which have
become a part of modern Western culture. Thus, when Isaiah went
walking "naked and barefoot" to shock the public into believing his
prophecy of the conquest and degradation of Egypt and Ethiopia by the
Assyrians (Is 20), it was because such conduct was so utterly contrary
to Jewish custom, which unlike that of the pagans insisted on very
modest garments for its priests (Ex 20:26; 42-43). Thus in 1 M 1:14-15
we find the indignation of the orthodox Jews at the adoption under
Greek domination of the hellenistic gymnasium in which the athletes
competed naked. For Christians, freed from the ritual prescriptions of
the Old Law, the ways of observing modesty may somewhat differ
from one culture to another, but nevertheless modesty of person is still
a responsibility.

B: INTEGRITY

Fasting

As the Jews feasted, so they also fasted. The Scriptures describe the
obligatory religious feasts in detail, beginning first of all with the weekly
Sabbath required by the Third Commandment (Ex 23:12-17; 34:18-26;

---

[34] See reference in note 2 above.

Lv 23; Dt 16:3-12; 2 Ch 8:13), while fasting was a sign of mourning and of petition to God. Thus Moses fasted before receiving the tablets of the law (Ex 34:28). The Israelites fasted before battle (Jg 20:26; 1 S 7:6), and at the funeral of Saul (1 S 31:13; 2 S 1:12). David fasted in petition for his son's life (2 S 12:16). Jezebel proclaimed a public fast before an unjust trial and Ahab in repentance for it (1 K 21:9, 27; 1 Ch 10:12), as did Jehoshaphat in time of siege (2 Ch 20:3). Elijah fasted in flight until fed by an angel (1 K 19:3-8). Isaiah instructed the people on true fasting (Is 58:1-12). Jeremiah declared that God ignores the fasts of the unrepentant (Jr 14:12), as does Zechariah (Zc 7), and had his prophecies read to the people by Baruch on a fast day (Jr 36:9). The exiles in Babylon fasted (Ba 1:5). Ezra fasted in preparation for leading the exiles back to Jerusalem (Ezr 8:21-23). Joel fasted at the time of the locust plague (Jl 1:14; 2:15). Mordecai and Esther fasted severely to prepare to plead with the Persian king for their people (Est 4:16). Judith (Jdt 8:6) and the prophetess Anna (Lk 2:37) in their widowhood fasted. Daniel and his companions adhered rigidly to the dietary laws (Dn 1) and he fasted for three weeks in preparation for his great visions (Dn 10:3). The Maccabees fasted in preparation for battle (1 M 3:47) and the repentant pagan Ninevites even made their animals fast (Jon 3:7)! Zechariah prophesied that only in the days of the Messiah will the need for fasting cease (Zc 8:19), hence John the Baptist and his followers continued the practice (Mt 9:14).

The principal acts of worship were sacrifices at which (except at the whole burnt-offerings) the offerers and the priests ate part of the victim in a kind of communion. Moreover, daily meals were ritualized with blessings and by an elaborate system of dietary rules based on the distinction between the "clean" and the "unclean." How important ritual purity was for the Jews is seen from the fact that in the Maccabean period the holy scribe Eleazar accepted martyrdom rather than eat pork (2 M 6:18-31).

For example, the eating of hooved animals was permitted if their hooves were cloven and they also chewed a cud, but the pig, because it had cloven hooves but no cud, was forbidden (Lv 11:1-8). Likewise, fish had to have both fins and scales, etc. The principle, it seems, was

that ambiguous border-line creatures that did not clearly fit into customary categories such as those divided by the Creator in the creation
account of Genesis 1, symbolized a lack of order, a return to chaos, and
were thus unclean.[35] Later I will discuss the social and liturgical significance of this symbol system at greater length, but here the point is that
these rituals provided a continual discipline of the appetite for food and
drink.

Christian Fasting

In the New Testament the concept of dietary uncleanness was abolished (Mk 7:19). "Now food will not bring us closer to God. We are no
worse off if we do not eat, nor are we better off if we do" (1 Cor 8:8).
Yet Jesus in the Sermon on the Mount had given instructions on the
proper motivation for fasting (Mt 6:16-18) and had answered the disciples of John the Baptist about why his disciples were not fasting as
frequently as John's followers and the Pharisees did, "Can the wedding
guests fast while the bridegroom is with them? ... But the days will
come when the bridegroom is taken away from them, and then they
will fast on that day" (Mk 2:19-20; cf. Mt 6:16-18). Therefore, the
Church continued to fast, for example in exorcisms (Mt 17:21),[36] in
preparation for laying hands on Barnabas and Paul (Ac 13:3), and when
they in turn established presbyters in the churches they had founded
(Ac 14:23).[37]

---

[35] See Mary Douglas, *Purity and Danger: An Analysis of the Concepts of Pollution and
Taboo*; Victor Turner, *The Ritual Process: Structure and Anti-Structure*; and Frank H.
Gorman, Jr., *The Ideology of Ritual* for current anthropological theories. Jacob
Milgrom, *Numbers [Ba-midbar]*: The traditional Hebrew Text with the New JPS
Translation/Commentary by Jacob Milgrom is extremely helpful in applying such
anthropological insights to the biblical text and E.P. Sanders, *Law from Jesus to
Mishnah*, especially pp. 131-308, to the Pharisaic understanding of these laws.

[36] Mt 17:21 is omitted by NAB on the basis of the best manuscripts, and seems to be a
variant of Mk 9:29 which omits "and fasting." The textual variant perhaps reflects the
actual early Church practice of priests fasting before performing the sacraments or
exorcisms.

[37] See also Lk 2:37; 2 Cor 6:5; 11:27.

The *Didache*, Clement of Alexandria, and Tertullian[38] all mention the Friday fasts to mourn the Crucifixion, and Friday fasting was often extended to Saturday in preparation for Sunday. The Lenten fast in preparation for Easter was established by the Council of Nicaea in 325, and other fasts on vigils of great feasts. The Ember (Old English for "anniversary") Days that marked the four seasons, and the Rogation (Latin for "petition") Days that preceded the feast of the Ascension were added later.

Fasting often included abstinence from flesh meat and from wine. The Eastern Church in its fasts abstains from all food except bread, salt, water, fruits and vegetables[39]; and the Western Church from flesh meat on Fridays and some other days. The very changed living circumstances of modern life and great variation in local customs led Vatican II to simplify the traditional fasting rules to require a strict fast only on Ash Wednesday and Good Friday, but encouraged fasting throughout Lent and at certain other times.

A biblical basis for abstinence from meat is implied in the creation narrative which says that only the plants were given to Adam and Eve for food (Gn 1:29). Only after the Fall and the Flood was flesh (and even then only without the life blood) permitted and wine invented (Gn 9:20-21). These narratives seem to mean that the original creation was harmonious and therefore excluded bloodshed and intoxication. The ascetics also believed their experience had showed that meat and wine encourage an excess of sexual desire. Certainly meat and wine add to the immediate satisfactions of eating which require moderation.

Gluttony

As John Cassian's *Conferences* make very clear, fasting in imitation of Jesus' own desert fast (Mt 4:2) was basic to the asceticism of the Desert

---

[38] See *Didache* (Audet) 8; Clement of Alexandria, *Stromata*, Bk VI, 75, PG 8:685-1382; 9:9-602; Tertullian, *De Jejuniis*, PL 2, 953-978. On the history of fasting see F. Cabrol, "*Jeunes*," DACL 7 (2): 2481-2501.

[39] St. Epiphanius, *Expositio Fidei*, 22, PG 42:828; *Apostolic Constitutions* V, 8, PG 1:889-896.

Fathers and thence was taken up by all the subsequent religious orders. Cassian tells us that experience taught the Desert Fathers that the capital sin of gluttony was the first of all the appetites for a monk to learn to control, and was especially difficult because food and drink are indispensable for survival. But Cassian also urges moderation in the practice of fasting.[40] The Fathers of the Church and later spiritual writers produced a considerable literature on the value of fasting; for example St. Augustine, *Seven Sermons on Fasting* and Jerome, *Against Jovinian.*[41] On the other hand, the Church did not forget the biblical warning (1 Tm 4:1-3) against those

> ... who forbid marriage and require abstinence from foods that God created to be received with thanksgiving by those who believe and know the truth. For nothing created is to be rejected when received with thanksgiving, for it is made holy by the invocation of God in prayer [note the commendation for "grace" at meals].

Therefore, the Church has condemned such sects as the Encratites, the Manichees, and the Montanists who absolutely forbade meat and wine as evil in themselves. St. Paul even advises Timothy, "Keep yourself pure. Stop drinking only water, but have a little wine for the sake of your stomach and your frequent illnesses" (1 Tm 5:23). Sirach in an excellent essay (31:12-31) on the etiquette of moderate eating and drinking as they contribute to the true humanity of life writes:

> When wine is present, do not pour out discourse,
>   and flaunt not your wisdom at the wrong time.
> Like a seal of carnelian in a setting of gold
>   is a concert when wine is served.
> Like a gold mounting with an emerald seal
>   is string music with delicious wine (Si 32:4-6).

---

[40] Cassian, *Institutes*, Bk V is "Of the Spirit of Gluttony."

[41] Augustine, *De Utilitate Jejunii*, PL 40:70-714.

Gluttony and Chemical Dependency

It is possible to sin against moderation negatively by deliberate neglect to eat the food and take the drink necessary for health. This, of course, is a relatively rare sin, but today it is recognized that not a few persons diet excessively to keep their figures. Sometimes excessive dieting (or even overdone ascetic fasting) becomes a neurotic compulsion (*anorexia nervosa*) which is not easy to treat and which is often aggravated by overeating followed by vomiting (*bulimia*).[42]

Much more common is the positive vice of gluttony or the excessive pursuit of the pleasure of eating, either because one eats too much for health (the gourmand), or is over concerned about the quality of one's food, or spends too much of one's income on food, or eats in too piggish a manner, or too often, or to the point of vomiting, or indulges in food which is harmful to health (the gourmet). Individual acts of gluttony are not ordinarily seriously harmful and therefore are venial, but habits that seriously harm health (at least in the short range), if not corrected, are mortal. Such overeating, however, can also be the result of neurotic compulsions that greatly diminish culpability, and may also have a physiological and even genetic basis, and require professional help to overcome.[43]

Much the same can be said about the abuse of alcohol and of all forms of *chemical dependency* on such substances as nicotine, caffeine, and the still more serious consciousness-altering or narcotic drugs which have become a major problem in our society. Smoking in excess does serious and even fatal harm to the lungs and circulatory system. Alcohol and narcotics in excess damage the nervous system and liver, and are characterized by their psychoactivity, diminishing the use of

---

[42] Today it is recognized that even some of the saints may have unknowingly subjected themselves by excessive fasting to the morbid physiological cycle of *anorexia nervosa*. Their motivation, of course, was to achieve self-control and do penance for their sins and those of others, not to be thin as with modern victims of the disorder. See Rudolph M. Bell, epilogue by W.N. Davis, *Holy Anorexia* and Julius H. Rubin, *Religious Melancholy and Protestant Experience in America*. For a different point of view see Caroline Walker Bynum, *Holy Feast and Holy Fast*.

[43] See Jim Orford, *Excessive Appetites*.

reason and causing permanent brain damage. In pregnancy they can cause birth-defects in the child.[44]

The Old Testament provides many examples of the evil consequences of drunkenness, from the disgrace of Noah (Gn 9:20-27) and the incest of Lot (Gn 19:30-38), to the decadence of the pagan Persians (Est 1:6-10), and of the Jewish religious leaders lamented by Isaiah:

> These also stagger from wine and stumble from strong drink. Priest and prophet stagger from strong drink, overpowered by wine; led astray by strong drink, staggering in their visions, tottering when giving judgment. Yes, all the tables are covered with filthy vomit, with no place left clean (Is 28:7-8).

No wonder old Tobit in his parting counsels to his adolescent son for the first great journey of young Tobias' life says, "Do not drink wine till you become drunk, nor let drunkenness accompany you on the way" (Tb 4:15).

Things had not much improved in the time of Jesus. St. Paul lists drunkenness among "the works of the flesh" (Gal 5:21) and of "darkness" (Rm 13:13). These had been common among the Gentiles before their conversion (1 P 4:3) and continued to be a problem among the baptized (Eph 5:18) even at the Eucharistic assemblies (1 Cor 11:21), so that Paul had to urge the Christians not to associate with drunkards (1 Cor 5:11), and to caution the churches not to elect heavy drinkers as bishops, deacons, and deaconesses (1 Tm 3:8, 11; Tt 1:7).

Excess in drinking for the non-alcoholic is venial unless the person knows in advance that it will make them liable to other mortal sins. Thus a doctor or judge, a driver, someone given to violence or to sexual indulgence when drunk may cause serious harm. Serious scandal can also be given by a priest celebrating the sacraments or preaching when drunk, a judge on the bench, parents before their children, etc. Moralists have traditionally held that it is also a mortal sin if drinking merely

---

[44] For current research see Claudia Bialke Debner, ed., *Chemical Dependency: Opposing Viewpoints*; Jim Orford, *Excessive Appetites: A Psychological View of Addictions*; Roger E. Meyer, *Psychopathology and Addictive Disorders*; Gerald Bennett, Christine Vourakis and Donna S. Woolf, eds., *Substance Abuse*; Gerald G. May, *Addiction and Grace*.

for pleasure goes to the point of total loss of reason because this is brutish and contrary to human dignity. Knowingly to become addicted to alcohol is, of course, a mortal sin because of the enslavement of one's freedom and the very grave consequences to oneself and others. The fact that such actions are often regarded as comic simply show the incongruity between the dignity of the human person and the subhuman state of inebriation.

The same norms apply to other forms of chemical dependency. Some forms, such as nicotine and caffeine addiction, are probably only venial for most people, because the consequences are long-range and not strictly predictable; and the same probably goes for addiction to mild tranquilizers, etc. But generally speaking, psychoactive substances such as opium, heroin, cocaine, etc. are so addictive that even experimental use of such drugs can create a grave risk for some persons.[45] To take such a risk (and who knows in advance their own vulnerability?) is generally a mortal sin because it opens the way to self-destruction. The gravity of the use of marijuana, which seems not physiologically addictive, is less clear, but it is probable that its habitual use often leads to more serious addictions.[46] For pregnant women who take drugs, the risk of birth-defects for the child is a very serious consideration requiring the advice of a physician.

The Measure of Moderation

Once aware that one has become addicted to alcohol or the more dangerous drugs, one has a grave responsibility to seek professional help to overcome the addiction. Only in this century has it become clear medically that moral exhortations and "temperance pledges" are not sufficient to help those whose drinking has become a vicious cycle of addiction with a physiological basis. In such cases freedom to reform or even to recognize one's problem is greatly reduced and requires

---

[45] See Lawrence J. Hatterer, M.D., *The Pleasure Addicts.*

[46] See Helen C. Jones and Paul W. Lovinger: with a Foreword by C. Everett Koop, *The Marijuana Question.*

outside intervention and support, which must be provided by family, friends, employers, groups like Alcoholics Anonymous, and the Christian community.

Moderate use of alcoholic beverages as a mild relaxant is not (for non-alcoholics) harmful to health, but excess is extremely destructive. The Psalmist (104:15) thanks God for the rains "producing bread from the earth, and wine to gladden men's hearts" and the sages advise, "Go, eat your bread with joy and drink your wine with a merry heart, because it is now that God favors your works" (Ec 9:7), but they also warn, "Wine is arrogant, strong drink is riotous; none who goes astray for it is wise" (Pr 20:1).

> Who scream? Who shriek?
>   Who have strife? Who have anxiety?
> Who have wounds for nothing?
>   Who have black eyes?
> Those who linger long over wine,
>   those who engage in trials of blended wine.
> Look not on the wine when it is red,
>   when it sparkles in the glass.
> It goes down smoothly;
>   but in the end it bites like a serpent
>   or like a poisonous adder.
> Your eyes behold strange sights,
>   and your heart utters disordered thought;
> You are like one now lying in the depths of the sea,
>   now sprawled at the top of the mast.
> They struck me, but it pained me not;
>   they beat me, but I felt it not;
> When shall I awake to seek wine once again? (Pr 23:29-35).

> It is not for kings, O Lemuel,
>   not for kings to drink wine;
>   strong drink is not for princes!
> Lest in drinking they forget what the law decrees,
>   and violate the rights of all who are in need.
> Give strong drink to one who is perishing,
>   and wine to the sorely depressed;
> When they drink, they will forget their misery,
>   and think no more of their burdens (Pr 31:4-7).

Thus the measure of moderation for eating and drinking is the purpose which these basic human functions serve, namely the preservation of the individual by nutrition. We eat or drink too much or too little when we eat more or less than health requires. Is it, then, sinful to eat or drink more than health requires simply for pleasure? Obviously it is if this injures health, but what if it does not injure health and is done for a good purpose, namely, pleasurable recreation? We have already indicated that such recreation is justified if in turn it is limited by a real need to prepare for other good activities (the same is true when the purpose is a humane sociability, as will be shown later).

Nevertheless, it remains true that if the pleasure sought becomes separated from the fundamental purpose of eating and drinking, or is contradictory to that purpose, then the action becomes sinful, because when pleasure becomes an end in itself, rather than the facilitation of a morally good activity, it is injurious to the person, who then becomes addicted to its immoderate pursuit. Thus the glutton or drunkard who makes the pleasure of food or drink his end, will exhaust himself in seeking more and more.

For the same reason, behavior that deliberately renders acts of eating or drinking *totally* void of any nutritive value, as vomiting after eating for pleasure (*bulimia*), or eating substances that are not food, are unreasonable and contrary to human dignity. Ordinarily such acts, however, are only venially sinful unless in fact they seriously encourage addiction.

> Wine is very life to man
> if taken in moderation.
> Does he really live who lacks the wine
> which was created for his joy?
> Joy of heart, good cheer and merriment
> are wine drunk freely at the proper time.
> Headache, bitterness and disgrace
> is wine drunk amid anger and strife.
> More and more wine is a snare for the fool;
> it lessens his strength and multiplies his wounds.
> Rebuke not your neighbor when wine is served,
> nor put him to shame while he is merry;

Use no harsh words with him and distress him not
in the presence of others (Si 31:27-31).

Chastity

Since the sexual drive relates to the need to preserve the species and is
directed to a partner and to offspring, it raises not only the problem of
moderating desires for pleasure by reason in view of the good of the
individual but also questions of justice and love toward the partner and
offspring. Therefore, in this chapter we are concerned with sexuality
only as it is a pleasurable activity which contributes to the physical and
mental health of the individual. Its deeper interpersonal and social aspects will be considered in later chapters. Since, as we have seen, pleasure takes its moral character from the morality of the activity which it
facilitates, the question that needs to be asked here is, "How can individuals discipline themselves so that their pursuit of sexual pleasure is
in keeping with the purpose for which God made us sexual beings?"

What is primarily in question is sexual activity in the full sense of
genital activity, that is, the pleasure of touch that arises from use of the
sexual organs so as to produce that sensation called *orgasm* which
gives full satisfaction to the sexual drive. In the male, orgasm is produced by the ejaculation of semen and cannot be repeated immediately.
In the female it results primarily from the stimulation of the clitoris at
the entrance of the vagina and can be quickly repeated. Preparatory to
full intercourse there can be much sex play in embraces, kisses, and
touches especially of the erotic zones of the body.

The Bible speaks frankly of sexual pleasure as a gift of God.
Adam exclaims in delight when God presents him with Eve,

> "This one, at last, is bone of my bones and flesh of my flesh. This
> one shall be called 'woman,' [*ishsha*] for out of 'her man' [*ishah*]
> this one has been taken." That is why a man leaves his father and
> mother and clings to his wife, and the two of them become one
> body. The man and his wife were both naked, yet they felt no
> shame (Gn 2:23-24).
>
> Have joy of the wife of your youth, your lovely hind, your graceful

doe. Her love will invigorate you always, through her love you will flourish continually (Pr 5:18-19). Enjoy life with the wife whom you love, all the days of fleeting life that is granted you under the sun. This is your lot in life, for the toil of your labors under the sun (Ec 9:9). "Let him kiss me with kisses of his mouth! More delightful is your love than wine... Bring me, O king, to your chambers" (Sg 1:2, 4b).

Although these texts (except Sg 1:2, 4b) are written from the male view, they apply also to the woman's need for sexual pleasure which is just as real.

Since, as shown earlier, recreation through pleasure is a legitimate human activity necessary for physical and mental health in preparation for the serious activities of life, sexual play can be morally good, simply because it relaxes tension and restores physical and mental freshness, but it must remain within the limits of moderation. What sets these limits? The reasonable limits of pleasure, both as too much and too little, are to be determined in view of the nature of the pleasurable activity and its relation to the basic goals of life. The question, therefore, is "What is the intrinsic purpose of sexuality?" Or, to put the question more theologically, "Why did God create human beings sexual?"

It is obvious enough from common sense and biology that the most fundamental and intrinsic reason that human persons are sexual is the need of the human race for procreation. Modern biology has added further understanding of why the sexual mode of reproduction is preferable to the asexual mode found in some lower forms of life. It guarantees both the continuity of the species and at the same time the individual variety which enables the species to adapt to varied circumstances. Theologically, the Bible confirms this biological emphasis on procreation in its account of the creation:

> Then God said: "Let us make man [humankind] in our image, after our likeness..." God created man [humankind] in his image; in the divine image he created him [humankind]; male and female he created them. God blessed them, saying: "Be fertile and multiply; fill the earth and subdue it" (Gn 1:26a, 27-28a).

Many exegetes have contrasted this account in Genesis 1 (perhaps based on the priestly tradition P), with the account in Genesis 2 (perhaps based on the Yahwist tradition J, generally thought to be the older),[47] in which, they claim, the purpose of the creation of Eve is not in view of procreation, but for companionship.

> The Lord God said: "It is not good for the man to be alone. I will make a suitable partner [more literally, "a helper"] for him" (Gn 2:18).

Yet theologically both accounts form part of a document which, whatever the age or origin of the components, must be taken as authoritative and inspired in its finally edited form and interpreted as such. The second account, therefore, must not be read in opposition to the first, but as its fuller elaboration. In fact the second account says much the same as the first but in more vivid and concrete terms. In the second account Adam (i.e., archetypical humanity) names the animals and discovers that every human person is alone in the world and needs companionship, that is, we humans are by nature social. We can live only in community. God therefore makes a "helper" for him whom Adam immediately recognizes as of the same nature as himself (Gn 2:23).

Thus Adam and Eve are partners in life, but this still does not say why they are of different sexes, or why they are sexual at all. The answer to this is immediately supplied by the Yahwist's comment, "That is why a man leaves his father and mother and clings to his wife, and the two of them become one body" (Gn 2:24). Thus, as we come to

---

[47] Thus Anthony Kosnick, et al., *Human Sexuality: New Directions in American Catholic Theology*, pp. 24-25, claims that "The older Yahwist tradition sets the sexual nature of men and women within the framework of our nature as social and relational beings" and contrasts this with "Some four hundred years later, the Priestly tradition came to relate sexuality with procreation, regarding the power to propagate as the direct result of God's blessing." This neglects to note that the Yahwist narrative is an etiological story of the origin of the human race by procreation. As for the "four hundred years later" one must distinguish between the time of the editing of the material of the narratives and their origin. On the antiquity of the Priestly tradition see J. Milgrom, *Numbers*, pp. xxxii-xxxv.

be from a father and a mother, so we grow up to be father or mother in our turn, and hence the human community in which no one is alone continues. Thus God's blessing of fertility announced in Genesis 1 is repeated here in a more concrete way.

These chapters of Genesis are first of all etiological. That is, they are intended not so much to relate the past for its own sake, as to *explain* the human condition in which we find ourselves, and therefore to explain how the human community came to be, as is apparent from the constant insertion of genealogies.[48] Nothing is said in them about how Eve helped Adam (her persuasion of Adam to join her in eating the forbidden fruit was certainly no help!), except to continue the human race in spite of their being doomed to die, "The man called his wife Eve ["Living"], because she became mother of all the living" (Gn 3:20). It is our modern individualism which has forgotten *community* that has led some exegetes to miss the fact that the biblical writers are first of all interested in understanding the origin and destiny of the human community within which alone can individuals exist.

We should not conclude, however, that the Bible sees sex *only* as the procreative source of the human community. I have already indicated the recreative role of sex and will consider its interpersonal and social aspects later, but the Bible does see the survival of the species as the *fundamental* purpose without which the very existence of the sexual differentiation of humanity into male and female would be unintelligible. The very difficulty modern science has met in trying to develop a "safe contraceptive" is evidence how God and nature have intimately related sex with procreation.

In the tradition of the Church there has always been unanimity on this fundamental purpose of sexuality (until new theories have been proposed in this century), but among the Fathers of the Church there were two different understandings of these texts of Genesis. The Eastern Fathers and even the Latins before St. Augustine, generally, interpreted the creation narratives as meaning that if there had been no sin, the human community would have been multiplied by further creative

---

[48] On the function of genealogies in the Bible see R.R. Wilson, *Genealogy and History in the Biblical World.*

acts by God, and that sex would never have been exercised. Consequently, they thought that humanity was created sexed only in anticipation of the Fall, when human mortality would make procreation necessary.[49]

These ancient exegetes based this interpretation on the fact that human intercourse is only mentioned in the Bible *after* the Fall (Gn 4:1). St. Augustine (often mistakenly labeled today as anti-sexual), followed by St. Thomas Aquinas, rejected this Platonizing and dualistic view and rightly taught that if there had been no sin there would still have been sexual intercourse in Eden. The rabbis also interpreted Adam's exclamation of delight at first seeing Eve as implying the intention of such intercourse (Gn 2:23-25).

Impurity

Thus *chastity* (from root meaning "clean," "pure") is a virtue moderating the sexual appetite or genital pleasure according to a true understanding of the God-given purpose of sexuality. Since moderation orders our emotions and saves them from chaos, in the metaphorical language of the Bible "cleanness" or "purity" means what is healthy, normal, and life-affirming, in harmony with the order of the world established by the Creator. Sexual moderation first of all tempers sexual desire, of which Jesus taught in the Sermon on the Mount, "I say to you, everyone who looks at a woman with lust has already committed adultery with her in his heart" (Mt 5:28). Note that Jesus is speaking of *deliberate consent* to impure pleasure, not of unwilled, transient images which are only temptations to sin, not sin itself. *Modesty* is the aspect of chastity which avoids external actions that might unreason-

---

[49] See Gary Anderson,"Celibacy or Consummation in the Garden? Reflections on Early Jewish and Christian Interpretations of the Garden of Eden," *Harvard Theological Review* 82, 2 (1989): 121-148, who shows that the inter-testamental Book of Jubilees excluded sex from Eden because Eden was a Temple, but rabbinic tradition included it because Eden was a place of joy like the Messianic age; and the lengthy study of both Jewish and Christian commentators by Jeremy Cohen, *"Be Fertile and Increase, Fill the Earth and Master It"*.

ably stimulate sexual desires and thus occasion impurity, such as voyeurism or exposing or touching one's body or another's inappropriately.

The principal object of the virtue of chastity, however, is the moderation of sexual activity. *Masturbation* (self-abuse) is a manipulation of the genitals so as to produce orgasm without copulation. It usually refers to solitary acts, but in a wider sense to such acts performed between partners. Today the lax opinion has arisen among some moralists, although repudiated by the Holy See, that masturbation is not objectively a sin, or at least not a mortal sin.[50] The arguments for this are (1) that it does no harm to another; (2) that masturbation does no harm to the masturbator either physically or psychologically; (3) that it may even do good, because it is said to be a normal phase of adolescence. Statistics seem to show that 90% of males and many females indulge in it at some time. Moreover, it seems that male adolescents who have never masturbated are often physiologically or psychologically abnormal. Some also argue that masturbation helps adults learn to have successful orgasm, and that it relieves sexual tension for those who have no other sexual outlet.

The Bible certainly says little directly about masturbation. Formerly such self-abuse was often joined with contraception under the label "onanism" because of the biblical story of Onan who was struck dead by God for trying by *coitus interruptus* (withdrawal from copulation before ejaculation) to evade the Levirate law (Dt 25:5) that required him to beget a son by his brother's widow (Gn 38:6-10). Today exegetes commonly say that what was condemned was Onan's inten-

---

[50] "The traditional teaching of the Catholic Church that masturbation is gravely sinful is frequently doubted nowadays if not expressly denied... The opinion, however is contrary to both the teaching and pastoral practice of the Church. Whatever force there may be in certain biological and philosophical arguments put forward from time to time by theologians, the fact remains that both the Magisterium of the Church, in the course of a constant tradition, and the moral sense of the faithful have been in no doubt and have firmly maintained that masturbation is an intrinsically and gravely disordered action. The principal argument in support of this truth is that the deliberate use of the sexual faculty, for whatever reason, outside of marriage is contrary to its purpose." Congregation for the Doctrine of the Faith, "Declaration on Certain Problems of Sexual Ethics" (*Personae Humanae*), Dec. 29, 1975; cf. CCC # 2352. Of course in judging the gravity of acts, subjective factors must be considered.

tion to evade the Levirate law, not the means he used. Moreover, *coitus interruptus* is not strictly masturbation.

Some exegetes, however, point out that the story occurs as part of a longer narrative (Gn 38:1-30) in which Onan "greatly offended the Lord" (v. 10) by "wasting his seed on the ground."[51] The text also links it with some nameless crime of his elder brother Er which also "greatly offended the Lord" (v. 7) and with the prostitution and incest of Tamar which was ordinarily liable to the penalty of burning (v. 24). Since God struck Er and Onan dead, although breaches of the Levirate law were ordinarily punished merely by a money or nominal penalty (cf. Dt 25:5; Rt 4:5-12), it is hard to deny that the "wasting of seed" in this story is regarded as shameful not only in its purpose but as a means. Nor can moralists who denounce Greek dualism in favor of a non-dualistic biblical anthropology consistently argue that this Old Testament condemnation of onanism is obsolete because it appeals to the "physicalistic" notion of the evil of "wasting seed."

Certainly Jesus seems to be speaking of masturbation in the Sermon on the Mount, when after speaking about committing adultery in the heart in the text already quoted, he then says:

> "If your right eye causes you to sin, tear it out and throw it away. It is better for you to lose one of your members than to have your whole body thrown into Gehenna. And if your right hand causes you to sin, cut it off and throw it away. It is better for you to lose one of your members than to have your whole body go into Gehenna" (Mt 5:29-30).[52]

---

[51] Although most current commentators claim that Onan's sin was only his violation of the Levirate, under the law this was not a capital offense (Dt 25:5-10; Rt 4). More plausible is the comment of the Jewish scholar Robert D. Sacks, *A Commentary on the Book of Genesis* who says, "Onan's action was displeasing to God for two reasons. It was an attack on his fundamental political duty. Personal immortality through procreation of his own name replaced communal immortality which was to have been ensured by the Jubilee Year (see... Gn 34:11). In addition, his act was a conversion of seed into chaos" (p. 416). Sacks sees this last sin as a grave violation of the God-given order of creation, i.e., an attack on monotheism.

[52] On Mt 5:29-30 (cf. Mk 9:43-47; Luke omits this, probably as a hyperbole open to misinterpretation), Luz, *Matthew*, p. 297, notes that certain rabbinical texts prescribe cutting off the hand as judicial punishment for sexual offenses. J.D.M. Derrett, *Law in the New Testament*, although he holds that for Jews in Jesus' time any deliberate

The obvious sense of this text is that Jesus condemns the external act of adultery, then deliberate impure desires, then immodest voyeurism, and finally, impure manipulation; which last could include masturbation as the most obvious case. But again not all exegetes agree to this. Nevertheless, the Church has always understood the many texts of Scripture about personal purity as applying *a fortiori* to masturbation. The laws of holiness in Leviticus 15 insist on purification after seminal or menstrual flow. This is no mere superstitious taboo but was a discipline intended to emphasize the sacred power of sexuality and the respect due to it. While this form of discipline was time-conditioned and is no longer obligatory for Christians, its purpose still requires to be fulfilled in ways appropriate to our times.

The fundamental reason that masturbation is intrinsically and always wrong is that it violates chastity by using sex for the sake of pleasure alone, without any relation to the procreative purpose for which God gave it, and thus opens the way to an addiction to this abuse. Nor can self-abuse be justified as a kind of recreation relieving sexual tensions, for the same reason that the use of food or drink for recreation but totally unrelated to their nutritive purpose was said earlier to be sinful.

Moreover, sexual self-abuse is essentially more serious than the misuse of food and ordinary drink and more like the use of alcohol and drugs in that the pleasure sought is much more intense and therefore more addictive. Habitual masturbators are probably not harmed physically by their habit as are alcoholics, nor do they become psychotic (as some nineteenth century physicians mistakenly thought from observing psychotics with this habit), but they are addicted to a narcissistic and selfish pleasure which raises an obstacle to their learning to use sex for its real purposes of forming the family community. Thus to argue

---

orgasm outside the marital act was included as "adultery" under the commandment (p. 380), argues (pp. 363-388) that Eastern peoples never use the right hand for unseemly purposes and therefore this saying cannot refer to masturbation. In my opinion Jesus is using speech which is both metaphorical and exemplary. He is saying, "What is more precious than your right (best) eye and your right (best) hand? Yet it would be better for you to be blind than to sin by lustful looks and to be crippled rather than to sin by lustful touches; so avoid all occasions of the sin of lust." Thus it refers to all lustful touches, including masturbation.

that masturbation may help someone learn to have better orgasms in intercourse misses the point that it also teaches them to treat intercourse as a mere search for self-satisfaction.

Again, the fact that most adolescent boys and many girls masturbate at some time, no more proves that it is a "normal" or a necessary stage of maturation, than the many other dangerous and foolish acts adolescents perform experimentally. While in some sense we learn by making mistakes, the mistakes are still mistakes and sometimes very damaging ones. Moreover, it is truer to say that we learn not by making mistakes, but by repeatedly doing what is right.

Why has the Church taught that even a single act of deliberate masturbation freely consented to is not only a sin but a mortal one, while the misuse of food and drink is ordinarily only venial? Sexual pleasure is much more intense than pleasure in eating, because it is associated with a function more vital to the common good, and less necessary to the individual; consequently it is more addictive, more important, and less excusable. One sexual act can initiate a virgin into a life-long misuse of sex. In the case of someone struggling to overcome the habit of self-abuse each new act keeps them locked in the habit, like each new bout with the bottle locks in the alcoholic.[53]

Depersonalized Sex

As for the assertion that adolescents, particularly males, so frequently pass through a masturbatory phase that it must be regarded as a part of "normal development," it is truer to say that given original sin, most adolescents have to learn self-control by rather painful discipline if they are ever to become mature. For the average male, the learning of sexual self-control in preparation for marriage is one of the major crises of his life. A personal victory over masturbation thus is an impor-

---

[53] On the psychological similarity of sexual sin to other forms of addiction see Ralph Earle and Gregory Crow, with Kevin Osborn, *Lonely All the Time: Recognizing, Understanding, and Overcoming Sex Addictions: For Addicts and Co-Dependents.*

tant step in the formation of a mature masculine personality and readiness for the responsibilities of fatherhood.

It should also be obvious from these principles that certain other practices, formerly listed as "sexual perversions" and "deviations" — now called by psychologists "paraphilias" and often excused as "sexual variations" — are intrinsically wrong because they seek sexual pleasure by a use of sex contrary to its fundamental procreative function, and thus, like masturbation, can be called "unnatural." Most people will admit that sado-masochism in which sexual pleasure is sought through performing or submitting to acts of cruelty is perverse. Rape or intercourse against the will of the partner is an even more cruel act, as are pedophilia and child-incest which are forms of child abuse. Similarly sexual relations with an animal or by pseudo-intercourse with inanimate objects is obviously perverse. The same must be said of homosexual intercourse, and even heterosexual intercourse when performed anally or orally to orgasm, and finally of contraceptive acts, that is, fertile acts which have been deliberately made sterile by mechanical, surgical, or chemical means in order to obtain sexual pleasure unrelated to procreation.[54]

Today many find it hard to understand how the Church has been consistent in its teaching on contraception when it approves and even promotes "natural methods" of avoiding conception by abstention in the fertile periods of the woman's menstrual cycle which we now know is only about five days.[55] Since, however, I have shown that sex for recreation, like eating for recreation, is not intrinsically wrong if within the limits of moderation, married couples may have sex even at times when they know conception is impossible (or when in fact one or both are permanently sterile), provided that it is not deliberately separated from its intrinsic tendency to procreation.

---

[54] See CCC # 2351-2356 on the sinfulness of these sexual practices; homosexuality is treated separately in # 2357-2359.

[55] On the contraception question see Janet E. Smith, *Humanae Vitae: A Generation Later* and Germain Grisez, *The Way of the Lord Jesus*, vol. 2, *Living a Christian Life*, pp. 504-519. On Natural Family Planning see Mary Shivanandan, *Natural Sex*; John and Sheila Kippley, *The Art of Family Planning*; and John J. McCarthy, M.D., et al., *The Ovulation Method*.

While the married are normally required also to have intercourse in known fertile periods in order to conceive and beget a family, this obligation is limited, and does not require them to have more children than their circumstances in life or that of the society in which they live enable them to care for properly, or when the health of the woman might be injured. Hence, while the limitation of their family by contraception, that is, by deliberately rendering fertile acts sterile is a wrong means, deliberate abstention from the fertile period and intercourse in the sterile period is not a wrong means to this legitimate end, since the sterile period has a God-designed natural relation to fertility.

The parallel to sexual abstinence within marriage for a legitimate purpose is that it is licit to reduce the amount of nutrition in one's diet in order to continue the recreative aspect of eating without gaining weight, provided one does not take to vomiting after meals or using food of no nutritional value. As I will show later, the intrinsic evil of contraception results even more profoundly from its disruption of the interpersonal and social meaning of sexuality, but even at this level of the virtue of moderation it is manifest as a perversion.

Since the scriptural precepts with regard to these sins take into account their dimensions of justice and charity along with those of moderation, I will defer further citation until later. Here it is sufficient to conclude by repeating what has already been said above, that Christian asceticism means a freeing of the individual from an excessive pursuit of pleasure, but not of a legitimate use of it as a facilitator of good activities and as a recreative preparation for them. Such asceticism is motivated by the hope of a greater and more permanent life than this sinful and passing world can provide.

Self-Control

The Bible does not take for granted that the Christian by the very fact of baptism is "perfect." In the Sermon on the Mount Jesus says, "Be perfect (*téleioi*, completely formed) just as your heavenly Father is perfect," implying that we are not yet perfect images of God, but must strive to become such. In Ephesians 4:15-16 we are told:

Living the truth in love, we should grow in every way into him who is the head, Christ, from whom the whole body [of Christ, i.e., the Church], joined and held together by every supporting ligament, with the proper functioning of each part, brings about the body's growth and builds itself up in love.

Hence, before we can acquire the perfect virtue of moderation which will enable us to live the Christian life spontaneously and easily in perfect purity of heart, as in the Beatitude, "Blessed are the clean of heart, for they will see God" (Mt 5:8),[56] we will experience an inner struggle in which we must use our *will* to control our rebellious drives for pleasure and aggression. This condition of struggle is that of *self-control* (*continentia* in Latin) which is a firm resistance of the will to excessive physical desires. While the virtues of moderation are in the sense appetites themselves, self-control is in the will controlling the sense appetites when they have not themselves become sufficiently refined by virtue.

St. Paul often (Rm 7:7-8:17; 2 Cor 3:17; Gal 4:1-7) contrasts the person who lives under the outward constraint of the Mosaic law but has not yet internalized it as the law of the Spirit, to one who lives by "the perfect law of freedom" (Jm 1:25), which is the perfect virtue given by the Holy Spirit. Thus, until one has become a truly moderate person disinclined by perfect virtue to gluttony, drunkenness, or impurity, with a positive distaste for these vices, a sincere but imperfect Christian may still be strongly inclined to them but be firmly determined to keep such rebellious appetites under strict control.

Lack of self-control, on the other hand, is a vice to which certain temperaments are liable. Melancholics (who react slowly but stubbornly to situations) like Saul (see 1 S 18:6-13; 19:9-24), or cholerics (who react quickly and decisively) like David (2 S 11:1-12:25) are inclined to lose control of their strong passions. St. Paul was certainly a choleric, as his letters often manifest (cf. Galatians). Nevertheless, he was self-controlled and generally truly moderate (e.g., 1 Cor; 2 Cor 2:1-

---

[56] In this Beatitude, "clean" or "pure" (*kathoroi*) is broader than sexuality, but includes it, i.e., in "the clean of heart" the tension between conscience and desire, whether sexual or other desires, has been mastered by the virtues.

11). Indeed, to lose control through lust, like David did (2 S 11), is more shameful than to do so through anger, as did Saul (1 S 18:10-11), because it betrays weakness not strength.

On the other hand, mercurial personalities (who react quickly but change quickly) like St. Peter (cf. Mk 14:27-31; Jn 18:10-12; Mk 14:66-72, and perhaps Judas? Jn 12:6; 13:27) and phlegmatic ones (who react slowly and change quickly) like the Galatians against whom St. Paul complains, "I am amazed that you are so quickly forsaking... the gospel of Christ" (Gal 1:6), or the Laodiceans (Rv 3:14-22) similarly rebuked by John, suffer more from *inconstancy*, that is, they lose control by letting trivial events weaken their resolutions.

C: SIMPLICITY

Humility

Aquinas identified five moderating virtues which are needed to deal with less urgent drives than those for food and sex, all of which are given considerable attention in the biblical Torah.[57] Four of these relate more to the pleasure-pain drive, namely: moderation in (1) self-esteem; (2) in curiosity; (3) in external manners; and (4) in external clothing and possessions, and one relates more to the effort-drive, namely (5) moderation of anger. Of the pleasure-pain group the most fundamental one, of special concern to Christians, is the virtue of *humility*[58] which moderates our human tendency to take pleasure in self-esteem, in fantasizing that we are more excellent than we really are, and our pain at being humiliated.[59]

---

[57] See St. Thomas Aquinas, *S.T.*, II-II, q. 143 and q. 155-169.

[58] On the Greek *tapeinos* which means simply "lowly" (Lk 1:48) — Old Testament "poor" or "afflicted" but which takes on the sense of "humble" (e.g., Pr 3:34 LXX), see the article of Walter Grundmann, "*Tapeinos*" in TDNT, vol. 8, p. 16, and G.E. Mendenhall, *The Interpreters' Dictionary of the Bible*, vol. 2, pp. 659-660; also H. Giesen, EDNT, vol. 3, pp. 334-335.

[59] CCC # 1866 names "pride" as a capital sin. CCC # 2559, 2628, 2631, 2706, 2713 shows the importance of humility for prayer.

To desire excellence, to be "like gods" and escape death as the serpent said to Eve (Gn 3:5) is not itself wrong, since Jesus commanded us to "be perfect, as your heavenly Father is perfect" (Mt 5:48) and God has invited us to share in his divine life (cf. Jn 10:34-36; 2 P 1:4). But it is the sin of *pride* to claim for ourselves by our own power to be anything but what we are, or to forget that even what we are is God's gift.

> For pride is a reservoir of sin, a source which runs over with vice. Because of it God sends unheard-of afflictions and brings men to utter ruin. The thrones of the arrogant God overturns and establishes the lowly in their stead (Si 11:13-14).

The Virgin Mary herself takes up this theme in her *Magnificat*, "God has shown might with his arm, dispersed the arrogant of mind and heart. He has thrown down the rulers from their thrones, but lifted up the lowly" (Lk 1:51-52; cf. 1 S 2:7; 2 S 22:28).[60] Because it implies contempt of the Creator, pride, if deliberate, is always a mortal sin, unless it is merely implicit and about light matters.

Pride should be distinguished from *vainglory*, i.e., too much concern for what other people think of oneself. Vainglory is a much less serious sin than pride in the strict sense, yet it is nevertheless one of the seven capital sins. But pride in the strict sense of an excessive claim to superiority is the root of all sin, and it was the original sin of Adam and Eve. St. Gregory the Great says pride breeds presumption, ambition, and vainglory and from them all other sins spring.

Today we hear so much from the psychologists about how important it is to have "a good self-image" and we are so urged by our democratic and competitive culture to be ambitious and to reject as

---

[60] On the authenticity of the *Magnificat* see Joseph A. Fitzmyer, S.J., *The Gospel According to Luke I-IX*, pp. 357-362, who agrees with the conclusion of Raymond E. Brown, S.S., whom he quotes as saying in *The Birth of the Messiah*, p. 355, "Thus, it is not impossible that, in the last third of the century when he was composing Luke/Acts, Luke came upon these canticles [*Benedictus* and *Magnificat*] in a Greek-speaking Jewish Christian community in an area influenced by Jerusalem Christianity," i.e., it is not a Lucan composition, but based on a pre-Lucan tradition which Luke may have encountered in Jerusalem where traditions about Mary may have been preserved.

shameful and weak any admission of failure or inferiority that we tend to be blind to the importance of a *realistic* self-understanding and of a willingness to accept our actual limitations. In truth *every* human person has from God a great dignity and many gifts, and especially the gift of being a unique individual created by God for himself. Therefore, we *should* have a good self-image as Sirach (10:27-28) says, "My son, with humility have self-esteem, pride yourself as you deserve. Who will acquit him who condemns himself? Who will honor him who discredits himself?"

Thus proper self-esteem is not incompatible with admitting that other human beings, perhaps even *all* human beings are somehow superior to ourselves. The false democracy that tries to pretend that everyone is equal in all respects (egalitarianism) is an illusion which the Bible exposes as sheer folly.

The moderation of this tendency to over-rate ourselves is the virtue of *humility* in opposition to the vice of *pride*. In the Old Testament humility is commonly connected with repentance as, for example, when God says:

> When their uncircumcised hearts are humbled and they make amends for their guilt, I will remember my covenant with Isaac, and my covenant with Abraham (Lv 26:41-42; cf. 1 S 2:7; 2 S 22:28; 1 K 21:29; Ps 69:11, etc.).[61]

God is ready to show mercy to the humble:

> For he brings down the pride of the haughty, but the man of humble mien he saves (Job 22:29). The Lord is exalted, yet the lowly he sees, and the proud he knows from afar (Ps 138:6). He guides the humble to justice, he teaches the humble his ways (Ps 25:19). When he is dealing with the arrogant he is stern, but to the humble he shows kindness (Pr 3:34). Humble yourself the more, the greater you are, and you will find favor with God; For great is the power of God, by the humble he is glorified (Si 3:18-19).

---

[61] See note 58 above.

Pride ends in degradation:

> Man's pride causes his humiliation, but he who is humble of spirit obtains honor (Pr 29:23, cf. 18:12). When pride comes, disgrace comes, but with the humble is wisdom (Pr 11:2). Pride goes before disaster, and a haughty spirit before a fall. It is better to be humble with the meek, than to share plunder with the proud (Pr 16:18-19; cf. Ob 1:2-4).

Sirach 10:6 to 11:6 provides us with a little essay on humility and how it brings true rather than illusory honor, summed up in the verse: "The roots of the proud God plucks up, to plant the humble in their place" (Si 10:15). In the New Testament we find the same admonition, "Humble yourself before the Lord and he will exalt you" (Jm 4:10).

Humility is a recognition of our true condition: "Do not esteem yourself better than your fellows... More and more humble your pride; what awaits man is worms" (Si 7:16-17). Or as St. Paul, echoing several passages of the Old Testament asks:

> Who indeed are you, a human being, to talk back to God? Will what is made say to its maker, "Why have you created me so?" Or does not the potter have a right over the clay, to make out of the same lump one vessel for a noble purpose and another for an ignoble one? (Rm 9:20-21; cf. Ws 15:7; Is 29:16; 45:9-12; Jr 18:6).

It is to the humble that the messianic blessings are promised by the prophet Zephaniah:

> Seek the Lord, all you humble of the earth, who have observed his law. Seek justice, seek humility; perhaps you may be sheltered on the day of the Lord's anger (Zp 2:3). For then will I remove from your midst the proud braggarts, and you shall no longer exalt yourself on my holy mountain. I will leave as a remnant in your midst a people humble and lowly, who shall take refuge in the name of the Lord, the remnant of Israel (Zp 3:11-12).

It is this remnant that will remain to praise the Lord, "Holy men of humble heart, bless the Lord" (Dn 3:87).

Christ's Humility

Humility has a very special place in Christian morality, because Jesus said of himself, "Learn from me, for I am meek and humble of heart; and you will find rest for yourselves. For my yoke is easy, and my burden light" (Mt 11:29-30). An early Christian hymn compares the humility of the New Adam to the pride of the Old Adam, saying of Jesus:

> Though he was in the form of God,
> > he did not regard equality with God something to be
> > > grasped.
> Rather, he emptied himself,
> > taking the form of a slave,
> > coming in human likeness,
> > and found human in appearance,
> > he humbled himself,
> > becoming obedient on a cross (Ph 2:6-8).[62]

Therefore, the Son of God in his humanity accepted the human condition. He was born poor (Lk 2:7; cf. Lv 12:8), worked with his hands as a carpenter like his father Joseph (Mk 6:3; Mt 13:55), chose as some of his apostles fishermen (Mk 1:16-20), preached as a homeless wanderer (Mt 8:20), refused to accept any earthly honor or power (Mt 4:8-10; Jn 6:15), washed the feet of his own apostles (Jn 13:1-17; cf. Lk 12:37-39), died naked on the cross (Jn 19:23-24), and was buried in another's tomb (Mt 27:59-60).

---

[62] Because of the poetic structure of Ph 2:6-11 it is generally believed to be a pre-Pauline hymn, perhaps even originally in Aramaic. The view that the first line merely contrasts Jesus to Adam, although supported by some noted exegetes such as Oscar Cullmann and J. Murphy-O'Connor, O.P., according to Brendan Byrne, S.J., NJBC, pp. 794-795, "is difficult to prove" as shown in the article of T.F. Glasson, "Philippians 2:6-11," *New Testament Studies* 21 (1974-75): 133-39.

Moreover, Jesus first of all directed his mission to the poor and lowly. "Blessed are you who are poor, for the kingdom of God is yours" (Lk 6:20), which Matthew spiritualizes as "Blessed are the poor in spirit" (Mt 5:3). Jesus rebuked his disciples for not permitting little children to approach him, saying, "The kingdom of heaven belongs to such as these" (Mt 19:14b), and:

> "Amen, I say to you, unless you turn and become like children, you will not enter the kingdom of heaven. Whoever humbles himself like this child is the greatest in the kingdom of heaven. And whoever receives a child such as this in my name receives me" (Mt 18:3-5).

It is not that children or the poor are especially virtuous, but that they are less likely to fall into the pride which is so great an obstacle to accepting the Gospel. Jesus exclaimed to the proud and self-righteous Pharisees that the "tax collectors and prostitutes are entering the kingdom of God before you" (Mt 21:31).

In several Lucan parables Jesus stresses the folly of pride in one's good works (the Pharisee and the Tax-Collector, 18:10-14) or one's wealth (the Rich Fool, 12:16-21 and Lazarus and the Rich Man, 16:19-31). But his most forceful words on the subject are in the Parable of the Places at Table (Lk 14:7-11):

> "When you are invited, go and take the lowest place so that when the host comes to you he may say, 'My friend, move up to a higher position.' Then you will enjoy the esteem of your companions at table. For everyone who exalts himself will be humbled, but the one who humbles himself will be exalted" (Lk 14:10-11).

James stresses the same theme:

> The brother in lowly circumstances should take pride in his high standing, and the rich one in his lowliness, for he will pass away "like the flower of the field" (Jm 1:9-10).

1 Peter also urges humility:

Be of one mind, sympathetic, loving toward one another, compassionate, humble (1 P 3:8)... You younger members, be subject to the presbyters. And all of you, clothe yourselves with
humility in your dealings with one another, for "God opposes
the proud but bestows favor on the humble" [Pr 3:34]. So humble
yourselves under the mighty hand of God, that he may exalt you
in due time (1 P 5:5).

The great spiritual writers of the Church call humility "the foundation of the spiritual edifice" because it opens us up to God's grace
("God resists the proud, but gives grace to the humble," Jm 4:6) and is
necessary to conversion. As such it excels the other virtues of moderation, but is inferior to prudence, justice, and the theological virtues.

The practice of humility as the foundation of sanctity formed an
important part of the monastic tradition, and the *Rule of St. Benedict*
lists twelve steps of growth in humility.[63] St. Bernard of Clairvaux, the
founder of the Cistercians, simplified these to three: (1) to have *sufficient* humility is to submit to superiors without striving to rival them;
(2) to have *full* humility is to count oneself as in the bottom rank and be
content with it; and (3) to have *overflowing* humility is serenely to
count oneself least of all.[64] The *Rule of St. Augustine*, followed by the
canons and friars, says of those in high places (cf. Mt 20:20-28):

Superiors are not bound to ask pardon of their subjects even
though they may feel conscious of having used harsher words in
correcting them than the necessities of discipline required, lest
by an indiscreet exercise of humility the authority of the superior should be weakened. Still, he should ask pardon of the Lord
of all who knows how tenderly you love those whom you have
rebuked, perhaps too severely... Your superior should not take
pleasure in ruling you but rather in serving you with all charity.
While the honor you pay him exalts him in your eyes, let fear
prostrate him at your feet before God.[65]

---

[63] Chapter 7, Mersel-Mastro, ed., pp. 191-203.

[64] St.Bernard of Clairvaux, *The Steps of Humility.*

[65] St. Augustine of Hippo, *The Rule of St Augustine*, c. 7. Translation quoted is from a
private edition of the *Dominican Constitutions*, 1968; but see Van Bavel edition, pp.
23-24.

Thus, Christian humility is only caricatured by the hypocritical posing of Moliere's Tartuffe or Dickens' Uriah Heep and by those who pretend to it in order to manipulate the feelings of others and thus to control them covertly. Two marvelous examples of true Christian humility are St. Francis of Assisi, "the little poor man," and St. Thérèse of Lisieux, teacher of "the little way of love."[66]

If we are to grow in humility we should (a) meditate on the unearned gifts we have received from God; (b) honestly attribute these gifts to God, and our neglect or misuse of these gifts to ourselves; and (c) recognize without envy that our neighbors *may* have received even greater gifts from God than we have, so that we may well be their inferior. But is it really possible to think or say honestly that we are "the least" as Jesus and Bernard tell us we should do? St. Thomas Aquinas' solution of this strange Gospel paradox[67] is that humility does *not* require us always to believe that the gifts we have received from God are inferior to what our neighbors have received, nor that what we have accomplished by our natural gifts is inferior to what they have accomplished. Yet we can *always* consider, says Aquinas, that if our neighbors had received the gifts God has given us they might very well have used them better than we have, considering how little use we have made of them. Hence we can honestly suppose that we may be in fact in the lowest place in God's eyes, even lower than Judas!

Docility

Another basic human trait which requires moderation is our pleasure in learning new things, and our pain in acknowledging our own ignorance, of which Aristotle said, "Every man desires to know." We have all been amused by the curiosity of the monkey, but the human being is infinitely more inquisitive. More than any other it is this trait that makes us human, made in the divine image, *homo sapiens*. Yet if "curiosity

---

[66] See *St. Francis of Assisi: Writings and Early Biographies* and St. Thérèse of Lisieux, *Autobiography of a Saint*.

[67] *S.T.*, II-II, q. 161, a. 3 and a. 6, 1.

killed a cat," it can also be self-destructive of human beings, as we are told by the myth of Pandora, the Greek Eve, who was tempted by curiosity to release from a sealed box all the evils that beset humankind.

The virtue which moderates the vice of curiosity is *docility* ("teachability") or *studiousness*, the desire to know what we ought to know and the willingness to be taught it.[68] We see this openness to truth and the disciplined search for it in the great and saintly Doctors of the Church, such as Gregory of Nyssa, Augustine of Hippo, Bonaventure, Thomas Aquinas, Alphonsus Liguori, Catherine of Siena, and Teresa of Avila, but also in the great Christian philosophers and scientists such as Descartes, Pascal, Galileo, and Pasteur, and scholars such as Origen, Baronius, Battifol, and Lagrange.

The Bible praises studiousness primarily in regard to the study of the Torah, as in the longest of the psalms:

> How I love your law, O Lord!
>   It is my meditation all the day.
> Your command has made me wiser than my enemies,
>   for it is ever with me.
> I have more understanding than all my teachers,
>   when your decrees are my meditation (Ps 119:97-99).[69]

The rabbis cultivated this constant study of the Torah and inculcated it in their pupils, so that to this day in Orthodox households after supper the men stay at table and study the Bible. Jesus broke the precedent of excluding women from this discussion when he praised Mary for listening to his instructions more than Martha for serving the meal. "Mary has chosen the better part and it will not be taken from her" (Lk 10:42).[70] It is this tradition of constant study which has enabled Jews today, although a tiny minority, to be leaders in the intellectual world. But the rabbis saw it as more than intellectual prowess, it was *worship*

---

[68] *S.T.*, II-II, q. 161.

[69] On this topic see Benedict T. Viviano, O.P., *Study as Worship.*

[70] Luke's point, characteristic of his Gospel, may simply be that Jesus admitted women to discipleship and that they in turn received the Church into their houses. See Ben Witherington, *Women in the Ministry of Jesus*, pp. 100-103.

of God as Truth. They even made the point with a little puzzle: Question: "What does God do all the while in eternity?" Answer: "One third of his time is given to creating the world, one third to governing it, and one third to studying Torah!"[71]

The Bible also praises more secular kinds of learning, as typified in the Wisdom literature by the figure of Solomon, who asked God for wisdom to govern his people. God's answer was:

> "Because you asked for this — not for a long life for yourself, nor for riches, nor for the life of your enemies, but for understanding so that you may know what is right — ... I give you a heart so wise and understanding that there has never been anyone like you... In addition, I give you what you have not asked for, riches and glory" (1 K 3:10-13).

Solomon's wisdom was not only that of statecraft; he declares of God that:

> "He gave me sound knowledge of existing things, that I might know the organization of the universe, and the force of the elements. Cycles of years, positions of the stars, natures of animals, tempers of beasts, powers of the winds, and thoughts of men, uses of plants and virtues of roots. Such things as are hidden I learned and such as are plain" (Ws 7:17, 19-21).

Yet a lack of moderation in the desire to know on the part of the scholar can be self-destructive, and Qoheleth expresses the weary puzzlement of the researcher:

> "When I applied my heart to know wisdom and to observe what is done on earth, I recognized that man is unable to find out all God's work that is done under the sun, even though neither by day nor by night do his eyes find rest in sleep. However much

---

[71] This story was related to me by a rabbinical scholar without mentioning its source. It should be noted that while the Reformation's emphasis on Bible study made such study suspect for many Catholics after Trent, Vatican II strongly encouraged it: DV #21-22; CCC # 131-133, 141.

man toils in searching, he does not find it out; and even if the
wise man says he knows, he is unable to find it out" (Ec 8:16-
17).

Thus curiosity becomes a vice of too much desire for knowledge
when one wants to know something for a bad purpose (e.g., the search
for nuclear weapons or abortifacients); or when it is a waste of energy
on trivial matters (research on the biographies of movie stars); or when
it is an effort to learn from illicit sources (from the devil by divination,
or by reading other peoples' letters to which one has no right), or a
study of creatures without reference to the Creator (as the atheistic
scientist); or simply beyond one's capacity with the danger of falling
into error (as those who predict the future by astrology).

> What is too sublime for you, seek not,
> > into things beyond your strength search not.
> What is committed to you, attend to;
> > for what is hidden is not your concern.
> With what is too much for you meddle not,
> > when shown things beyond human understanding.
> Their own opinion has misled many,
> > and false reasoning unbalanced their judgment.
> Where the pupil of the eye is missing, there is no light,
> > and where there is no knowledge, there is no
> > > wisdom (Si 3:20-24).

Like undue intellectual curiosity, so also curiosity of the senses
can be sinful if it is a waste of time, or has an evil purpose, or unnecessarily occasions temptations. Monastic asceticism therefore taught a
strict discipline of the senses, but this should not exclude their use for
careful observation and aesthetic appreciation when this has a good
purpose. Since truth of itself is good, curiosity is of itself only a venial
sin because of its lack of reasonable moderation and waste of time and
energy, but it can be mortal if it leads us to the neglect of serious duties,
or when wrongly motivated as mentioned above.

Humane Manners

Moderation in our emotions needs also to be reflected in our external behavior since we take pleasure in the expression of our feelings in gesture, speech, and manners and this pleasure of sociability and conviviality can become coarse and offensive. Certainly etiquette is not morals, yet it expresses our moral attitudes, and as social beings this human communication is not a trivial matter. Moderation in such matters consists in a middle course between an exaggerated civility that betrays vanity and affectation on the one hand, and a boorishness that is offensive and embarrassing on the other. Such failings if deliberate are venial sins, unless they express serious contempt or give serious scandal.

We can distinguish between the etiquette of serious affairs (*eutaxia*, e.g., in the liturgy and public ceremonies) and in recreation (*eutrapelia*, e.g., in social conversation or sports). Lack of decorum destroys the beauty and dignity of serious affairs, and the enjoyment of recreation. Traditionally moralists, treating of decorum, discussed the morality for Christians of two types of recreation. First, many Church Fathers and Councils declared the gladiatorial games, then so popular, to be mortally sinful because of their cruelty and destruction of human life.[72] In the Middle Ages the Church also condemned the popular knightly jousts, except when really necessary for military training.[73] Today, serious questions can be raised about such sports as bull-fighting, professional boxing, and dangerous car races. Second, many Church Fathers denounced the theater, on the grounds of its obscenity.[74] Thus

---

[72] For example the work of Tertullian, *De Spectaculis* (PL 1:627-662) written about 200 AD and (probably, although attributed to St. Cyprian) Novatian, *De Spectaculis* (c. 250) (PL 4:779-788). The gladiatorial games were abolished by Constantine I soon after he granted freedom to the Church; this was later codified in the *Theodosian Code*, 15, 12. 1 (438).

[73] DS # 799, 1111, 1113, 1830, 2022, 2571-2575, 3162, 3672. The last of these condemnations by the Holy See was in 1925 against German student dueling even when there was no risk of death, but only of wounding. See the article of V. Cathrein, "Duel," CE, 5: 184-187.

[74] See the dissertation of Ignatius W. Butler, *The Moral Problems of the Theater*; Mendel Kohansky, *The Disreputable Profession: The Actor in Society*; Jonas A. Barish, *The Antitheatrical Prejudice*; Mortimer J. Adler, *Art and Prudence*, for various aspects of the debate on the morality of the theater as an institution.

in the seventeenth century in France, actors (including the great play-wright Moliere) were automatically excommunicated. The theater, films, and television in our own day exhibit many of these same excesses of sex and violence. Nevertheless, the theater, movies, and television are certainly legitimate forms of recreation, but they cannot be considered true recreation if they provide an occasion of sin to the audience or promote wrong moral attitudes, such as racism, sexism, or other forms of hatred and contempt for human dignity.

Simplicity of Life-Style

We also need to moderate the pleasure we take in being well-dressed and in our houses, furniture, automobiles, and other external posses-sions.[75] The way we use such goods also expresses moral attitudes and no doubt influences them. The Bible pictures Adam and Eve in para-dise as "naked, yet they felt no shame" (Gn 2:25). Living in a perfect environment they had no need of protection, and the beauty of their bodies was no obstacle to living rightly but added to its pleasure. With the Fall, they "realized they were naked; so they sewed fig leaves to-gether and made loincloths for themselves" (Gn 3:7). Out of Eden they needed protection from a hostile environment; so "for the man and his wife, the Lord God made leather garments, with which he clothed them" (Gn 3:21). The Fathers of the Church say that because humans had fallen to the level of animals, it was fitting they should be clothed in animals' skins![76]

---

[75] CCC # 2407 (quoted in VS, n. 100) says, "In economic matters, respect for human dignity requires the practice of the virtue of *temperance*, so as to moderate attachment to this world's goods." CCC # 2415 says, "Man's dominion over inanimate and other living beings granted by the Creator is not absolute; it is limited by concern for the quality of life of his neighbor, including generations to come; it requires a religious respect for the integrity of creation." On care for the environment also see CA, nn. 37-38.

[76] See Westermann, *Genesis 1-11*, pp. 269-270, on this passage; also Stephen N. Lambden, "From Fig Leaves to Fingernails: Some Notes on the Garments of Adam and Eve in the Hebrew Bible and Select Early Post-Biblical Jewish Writers," in P. Morris and D. Sawyer, *A Walk in the Garden*, pp. 74-90, for rabbinical speculations on this text. For a patristic view see St. Gregory of Nyssa, *The Great Catechism*, c. 8, pp. 482-484.

Thus with a touch of dry humor the Bible indicates the three purposes of clothes: protection of the body, moderation of sexual attraction by modesty, personal beauty and dignity. The most common moral failings in the use of clothing regard the second two purposes when people dress immodestly, or when they dress ostentatiously and extravagantly. What is true of our clothing is true of our homes: we need shelter, privacy, and a pleasant environment worthy of human dignity.

When the Bible speaks of immodesty and extravagance in dress, because its writers were males, these complaints usually are aimed at vain women, but they apply equally to vain men.[77] Jesus contrasts those who live "in royal palaces" and "wear fine clothing" (Mt 11:8) with John the Baptist who wore a hair shirt and leather belt (Mt 3:4), marks of a prophet. The former prophets also denounced the extravagance and luxury in housing and clothing of the rich who neglect the poor. Thus Amos (4:1-3) denounced the elaborate dress of the Samaritan women as Isaiah did that of the "daughters of Zion," predicting they would someday be reduced to rags (Is 3:16-24; 32:9-14).

In the New Testament after an admonition especially to men about quarreling and neglecting prayer, we read the following admonition especially to women:

> Women should adorn themselves with proper conduct, with modesty and self-control, not with braided hairstyles and gold ornaments, or pearls, or expensive clothes, but rather, as befits women who profess reverence for God, with good deeds (1 Tm 2:9-10).

> Your adornment should not be an external one: braiding the hair, wearing gold jewelry, or dressing in fine clothes, but rather the hidden character of the heart (1 P 3:3-4a).

---

[77] See Marcia L. Colish, "Cosmetic Theology: The Transformation of a Stoic theme" and *The Stoic Tradition*, pp. 27-29, 34-36, 51, 86-87, 93, 99-107, 211-212, 243-248, 257-259. The Fathers did not complain only of women's styles, but spent more time on denouncing their vanity than that of men. I would note that the complaints about women both in the Bible and in the Fathers of the Church reflect the androcentricity of the writers, but theologically they apply to men *mutatis mutandis*. Thus texts condemning feminine vanity in dress apply equally to the vanity of men in machismo.

Similarly, Amos denounces the luxurious houses of Israel:

> "Then will I strike the winter house and the summer house. The ivory apartments shall be ruined and their many rooms shall be no more, says the Lord" (Am 3:15).

> "You hasten the day of violence! Lying upon beds of ivory, stretched comfortably on their couches" (Am 6:4).

And Jesus began the Parable of the Rich Man and Lazarus:

> "There was a rich man who dressed in purple garments and fine linen and dined sumptuously each day. And lying at his door was a poor man named Lazarus covered with sores" (Lk 16:19-20a).

These admonitions warn us today against our consumerism and the cult of youth and beauty at the expense of more important values. Yet it is also against moderation to neglect one's appearance or one's home out of laziness, insensitivity, or lack of respect for others, or simply, as with some adolescents, to "show off" or annoy their parents. Lack of moderation in all such matters, however, usually does only a little harm and is a venial sin, but it can lead to serious harm and mortal sin if the extravagance or immodesty is grave. Moderation in such matters depends, however, a good deal on the custom and the times, rather than on any absolute standard.

Meekness

Finally, we need to moderate the anger that arises in us when our effort-drives seem to be frustrated and we desire to strike back at an offender. The virtue which helps us to control this anger is called *meekness*.[78] "Insolence is not allotted to a man, nor stubborn anger to one born of

---

[78] In Nb 12:3 Moses is said to be "by far the meekest man on the face of the earth." C. Rogers, "Moses: Meek or Miserable," *Journal of the Evangelical Theological Society* (1986): 257-63, says that "meek" (*anaw*) may mean "miserable"; others would translate it "forbearing" or "patient" or "humble." In the New Testament Greek *prautes* means

woman" (Si 10:18); "Wrath and anger are hateful things, yet the sinner hugs them tight" (Si 27:30). In fact strong personalities are especially liable to this:

> The more wood, the greater the fire, the more underlying it, the fiercer the fight;
> The greater a man's strength, the sterner his anger, the greater his power, the greater his wrath. (Si 28:10).

One of the remarkable features of the patriarchal narratives in Genesis is that these Fathers — far from being pictured as heroic men of violence as in Homer's *Iliad* and *Odyssey* and other ancient stories — are generally portrayed as very mild and patient men, as we will see later. Thus Moses, who in youth impetuously killed an Egyptian who was striking a Hebrew (Ex 2:11-15a), became a mature man who, in spite of all his exasperation with the refractory Hebrews he was trying to lead to freedom, earned the traditional tag, "as meek as Moses." "Moses was the meekest man on the face of the earth" (Nb 12:3). "For his [Moses'] trustworthiness and meekness God selected him from all mankind" (Si 45:4).

Jesus said, "Blessed are the meek, for they shall inherit the land" (Mt 5:5; cf. Ps 37:11) and of himself, "Learn from me, for I am meek and humble of heart" (Mt 11:29). The special excellence of meekness among all forms of moderation is that it is closely connected to love, which prefers to be hurt by the beloved than to hurt the beloved.

Related to meekness is *clemency*, a virtue important for parents and those who have the public responsibility of inflicting punishments on offenders. While meekness moderates our feelings of revenge, clemency moderates the execution of punishment when justice requires this. Thus, Moses pleaded with God for the people after they worshipped the golden calf (Ex 32:7-14) and for his sister Miriam after she was struck by God with leprosy for her sedition (Nb 12:1-15). David also

---

gentleness, kindness, mildness. On the various shades of meaning of this term in the New Testament see H. Frankemölle, EDNT, III, pp. 146-147. He sums it up thus: "*Prautes* is the courage necessary for service — renouncing violence and in faithful trust in Yahweh." On Moses' meekness see Gordon J. Wenham, *Numbers*, pp. 111-112.

displayed clemency to Shimei, who had cursed him and his descendants (2 S 19:20-24).[79]

While *cruelty* is the opposite of clemency, so is *excessive leniency* on the part of those who have the duty to punish. Thus, we read how the priest Eli brought doom on his house by his neglect to correct his priest sons severely enough when he found they were abusing their office by exploiting the people who brought sacrifices to the Temple (1 S 2:12-17, 22-36). Yet throughout the Old and New Testament God himself exhibits a wonderful clemency in withholding richly deserved punishment until people have time to repent. "But you, O Lord, are a merciful and gracious God, slow to anger, most loving and true" (Ps 86:15).

In the Old Testament God is, however, often represented as angry. In fact 375 times in the Old Testament nouns meaning "anger," "wrath," refer to God, while only 80 times to humans.[80] In Nahum, a prophecy against Nineveh, we find this view of God typical of the Old Testament:

> A jealous and avenging God is the Lord,
>   an avenger is the Lord, and angry;
> The Lord brings vengeance on his adversaries,
>   and lays up wrath for his enemies;
> The Lord is slow to anger, yet great in power,
>   and the Lord never leaves the guilty unpunished (Na 1:2-3).

This divine wrath was not just against God's enemies. The Psalmist felt it keenly in his own life:

> Truly we are consumed by your anger,
>   and by your wrath we are put to rout.
> You have kept our iniquities before you,
>   our hidden sins in the light of your scrutiny.

---

[79] Cursing a ruler was a capital offense (Ex 22:28). John Gray, *I and II Kings*, pp. 103-104, points out that the effects of a curse were thought to extend to the family and descendants of the accursed. Hence, while David accepted the curse on himself as a punishment, he ordered Shimei to be killed after his own death to prevent that curse affecting Solomon or his royal line.

[80] J. Fichtner, article "*Orge*," TDNT 5:392-409, especially p. 395, n. 92.

> All our days have passed away in your indignation;
>   we have spent our years like a sigh...
> Who knows the fury of your anger
>   or your indignation toward those who should fear
>   you (Ps 90:7-9, 11).

The New Testament continues to speak of God's anger. "The wrath of God is indeed being revealed from heaven against every impiety and wickedness" (Rm 1:18). "The wrath of God is coming upon the disobedient" (Eph 5:6; cf. Col 3:6). "Vengeance is mine; I will repay" (Heb 10:30; cf. Dt 32:35-36). In Revelation (15-16) we read of the "seven bowls of God's fury" to be poured forth upon the earth and of the "cup filled with the wine of his [God's] fury and wrath" which "great Babylon" must drink (Rv 16:19).

We must understand these expressions about God's wrath, like all terms applied to God, analogically. God has no bodily emotions such as human anger, but like truly moral humans (and far more vigorously than they) he condemns all injustice and oppression and is determined to bring justice to the world (Is 10:1-4). The divine wrath is God's judgment on the evil of unrepentance (Is 9:12-16; Jr 4:4); idolatry (Ezk 5:11-15); unjust war (Ho 5:10); pride (Is 9:8-11); cruelty (Is 9:18); the arrogance and violence against the Chosen People (Is 10:5-15; 59:15b-19; Ezk 25:15-17).[81] Such anger is virtuous, not evil, because moderated by the divine wisdom.

As the prophet Nahum insisted, "God is slow to anger" (Na 1:3; cf. Ex 34:6; Nb 14:18; Ps 103:8); and he is "rich in clemency, loathe to punish" (Jon 4:2). Sirach says, "Mercy and anger alike are with him [God] who remits and forgives, though on the wicked alights his wrath" (Si 16:11b).

Jesus, in his humanity, when faced by injustice felt such anger keenly and expressed it in words and actions, as we have already seen. When his critics complained because he healed a man with a withered hand on the Sabbath, "Looking around at them with anger and grieved at heart, he said to the man, 'Stretch out your hand.' So he stretched it

---

[81] On God's judgment, a topic too often neglected in catechesis and preaching today, see CCC # 1020-1060.

out and the man's hand was restored" (Mk 3:5). Referring to the religious leaders of Jerusalem, he cursed the fig tree that bore no fruit, as a parable in action (Mk 11:12-14) which warned them of what would happen to them if they did not repent.

Jesus also declared himself to be the final judge who will pass sentence on sinners in terrible anger: "Depart from me, you evildoers!" (Mt 7:23) or "Amen, I say to you, I do not know where you are from. Depart from me, all you evildoers" (Lk 13:27; Mt 24:51). It is thus that Michelangelo represented the victorious Christ in the Sistine Chapel with his upraised arm of condemnation. St. Paul too regularly speaks of God's "wrath" (1 Th 5:9; Rm 1:18; 5:9; 9:22; Eph 2:3; Col 3:6) and of the judgment as "the day of wrath" (1 Th 1:10; Rm 2:5) and his own epistles exhibit moments of real anger:

> But even if we or an angel from heaven should preach to you a gospel other than the one that I preached to you, let him be accursed! As we have said before, and now I say it again, if anyone preaches to you a gospel other than the one that you received, let him be accursed! (Gal 1:8-9; cf. Rm 5:1-5; 2 Cor 13:1-4).

Capital Sin of Anger

The human failure to moderate feelings of anger and revenge by the control of reason, is the *capital sin* of *unrighteous anger* that often leads to violence.[82] The Epistle of St. James cautions:

> Know this, my dear brothers; everyone should be quick to hear, slow to speak, slow to wrath, for the wrath of a man does not accomplish the righteousness of God (Jm 1:19).

And a Pauline epistle exhorts, "Be angry but do not sin; do not let the sun set on your anger, and do not leave room for the devil" (Eph 4:26). Such anger is wrong either because one has no authority to punish an

---

[82] CCC # 1866, 2259, 2262, 2302.

offender, or because the motive is not justice but the satisfaction of one's own feelings, or because in fact the person does not deserve punishment, or because these feelings are not moderated by meekness, or the punishment by clemency.

Anger, if it leads to serious injustice or to internal consent to such injustice, or blasphemy, scandal, etc., can be a mortal sin, but if not, it is venial. When scandal occurs it is usually because such angry behavior often provokes similar anger from others, so that the evil escalates into quarrels, feuds, and wars.

Anger can be unreasonable and thus immoderate either because it is sudden and violent anger for a slight offense, or because it is persistent, stubborn anger which cannot be appeased. Of itself it is less sinful than hatred because the angry person may not really intend any harm. It is also less sinful than lust because it aims not at selfish pleasure but at overcoming (although mistakenly or in a wrong way) an injustice. Hence of itself excessive anger is a venial sin, but as a capital sin it easily gives rise to many much more serious and even mortal sins, including murder. God cautioned Cain when Cain grew angry because God loved Abel more than himself:

> Why are you so resentful and crestfallen? If you do well, you can hold up your head, but if not, sin is a demon lurking at the door: his urge is toward you, yet you can master him (Gn 4:6-7).[83]

But Cain, instead of heeding God's advice, nourished his anger and finally murdered Abel. "When the unjust man [Cain] withdrew from her [Wisdom], he perished through his fratricidal wrath" (Ws 10:3). This is portrayed as the beginning of all the bloody feuds and wars which are narrated at such length throughout the Old Testament and which came to their climax in the fury of the religious leaders who put Jesus to death.

---

[83] Westermann, *Genesis 1-11*, argues that attempts to explain why Cain's sacrifice was less acceptable to God than Abel's are mistaken. Cain's envy, although understandable was not justified, because God's elections (as in the case of Jacob and Esau, etc.) are free and transcend our scrutiny. Westermann also says that the verses Gn 4:6-7 have never been satisfactorily explained, but probably temptation to sin is personified as a demon like a wild beast waiting at the door and which must be tamed.

The Wisdom literature has much to say about controlling anger:

> Rejoice not when your enemy falls, and when he stumbles, let not your heart exalt, lest the Lord see it, be displeased with you, and withdraw his wrath from your enemy (Pr 24:18). One cannot justify unjust anger; anger plunges a man to his downfall (Si 1:19). Should a man nourish anger against his fellows, and expect healing from the Lord?... If he who is but flesh cherishes wrath, who will forgive his sins? Remember your last days, set enmity aside; remember death and decay, and cease from sin (Si 28:3-6).

These writings also say much of the harm caused by angry words and the importance of calming angry feelings:

> The fool immediately shows his anger, but the shrewd man passes over an insult (Pr 12:16; cf. 19:11-12). A mild answer calms wrath, but a harsh word stirs up anger (Pr 15:1). The fool gives vent to all his anger; but by biding his time, the wise man calms it (Pr 29:11).

Proverbs even suggests that a bribe may be necessary to placate an enemy: "A secret gift allays anger, and a concealed present, violent wrath" (Pr 21:14); and yet points out that frank expression of justified anger may be a kindness: "Better is an open rebuke, than a love that remains hidden" (Pr 27:5) and warns that anger can end in murder: "For the stirring of milk brings forth curds, and the stirring of anger brings forth blood" (Pr 30:33); "Pitch and resin make fires flare up and insistent quarrels provoke bloodshed" (Si 28:11); and can even be self-destructive: "Envy and anger shorten one's life; worry brings on premature old age" (Si 30:24).

In our efforts to be disciplined, to practice a Christian asceticism of moderation in order to achieve peace within ourselves and to free our energies to serve God and neighbor, we should remember the vigorous words of St. Paul. He was writing to the Corinthians who were so familiar with the races and boxing matches at the great Greek games held in their city:

> Do you not know that the runners in the stadium all run in the race, but only one wins the prize? Run so as to win. Every athlete exercises discipline in every way. They do it to win a perishable crown, but we an imperishable one. Thus I do not run aimlessly; I do not fight as if I were shadowboxing. No, I drive my body and train it, for fear that, after having preached to others, I myself should be disqualified (1 Cor 9:24-27).

The Sacrament of Chastity

Although I have not yet discussed marriage in its full meaning as a sacrament of love, yet it is obvious that the virtue of chastity has a special relation to the Sacrament of Matrimony.[84] St. Augustine named the "control of concupiscence" (i.e., disordered sexual desires) as one of the goods of marriage. This must be understood not merely in a negative sense, that the married need not seek sexual satisfaction outside of marriage, but in the positive sense that the Sacrament enables the married to acquire the virtue of chastity as the holy and humanly fulfilling use of God's gift of sexuality.

Moreover, this right use of sexuality in our fallen human condition requires a genuine asceticism. The couple must not treat each other as mere sexual objects, but according to the dignity of their human personhood. This demands tenderness, sensitivity, thoughtfulness, unselfishness, and cooperation in the regulation of births; and hence a certain practice of abstinence within marriage.

This asceticism of marriage, aided by the Sacrament, thus participates in the mystery to which the Sacrament of Matrimony points: the eternal wedding of the Church to Christ, and of each human person to God in faith, hope, and love.

Summary of Norms

The positive norm of the cardinal virtue of moderation (temperance) by which the pleasure-pain drives (passions) participate in reason and

---

[84] CCC # 1601-1679.

thus serve as means to union with the Trinity is contained in the Decalogue in the Sixth Commandment against adultery considered as a typical case of the violation of moderation. In its full scope, however, it can be formulated as follows:[85]

1. Moderate the drives for pleasure and avoidance of pain in such a way that they submit to the guidance of reason and faith by avoiding extremes and thus facilitate and not substitute for the free moral acts necessary as means to our goal of life in the Trinity.

And the negative norms can be stated as follows (first in general for all such acts, then in particular for those that are most difficult):

2. Never make physical pleasure an end in itself, but seek it only as it facilitates free moral acts.

3. Never eat or drink or assimilate other chemical substances which do not contribute to health or healthful recreation.

4. Never engage in genital sexual acts unless within marriage and in a manner consistent with the true ends of marriage.

We have shown in this chapter that the relation to the procreation of children is essential to the true ends of marriage, but have not yet discussed the God-given purpose of marriage in full.

> *The end of all things is at hand. Therefore, be serious and sober for prayers... Be sober and vigilant. Your opponent the devil is prowling around like a roaring lion looking for someone to devour. Resist him, steadfast in faith* (1 P 4:7, 5:8)

---

[85] CCC # 1809, 1838, 1762-1775

CHAPTER 6

LIVING COURAGEOUSLY

"In the world you will have trouble, but take courage.
I have conquered the world" (Jn 16:33).

A: THE VIRTUE

The Need for Courage

The problem of self-control with regard to our *effort* appetites follows on the problem of moderating our *pleasure-pain* appetites. The proximate problem to be dealt with is how to overcome our fears in the face of danger and to check our too violent impulses to attack, so as to continue on the path to our true end as our reason dictates. This, of course, presupposes the perils and labors themselves, especially the danger of death, which must be met.

> Lively is the courage of those who fear the Lord, for they put their hope in their savior;
> He who fears the Lord is never alarmed, never afraid; for the Lord is his hope (Si 34:13-14).

The motive (formal object) of our facing these dangers is to act reasonably for the *common good*, which is the same as doing God's will ("fear of the Lord") even when our emotions of fear or impulses to attack tempt us to panic. The Fathers of the Church emphasize this virtue of fortitude as a "principal" virtue.[1]

---

[1] See Julianus Pomerius, *The Contemplative Life*, Bk. III, Chapter 20.

Thus we need both to be able to attack when reason shows us we can win, but also to endure this *stress*, or *pressure*, without capitulating when we see that for now attack is useless. Of these two kinds of acts, the second is certainly the more difficult, and requires the greater courage. Veterans of war often say that life in the trenches or a fox-hole is harder to take than "going over the top" in active combat, and many of us have experienced that waiting in the doctor's office in anticipation of news that we must have surgery is worse than the surgery itself.

Courage is especially needed to stand firm in our good resolutions in the midst of a storm of conflicting thoughts and impulses. As Ben Sirach says:

> Masonry bonded with wooden beams
>   is not loosened by an earthquake;
> Neither is a resolve constructed with careful deliberation
>   shaken in a moment of fear.
> A resolve that is backed by prudent understanding
>   is like a polished surface of a smooth wall.
> Small stones lying on an open height
>   will not remain when the wind blows;
> Neither can a timid resolve based on foolish plans
>   withstand fear of any kind (Si 22:16-18).[2]

The virtue of courage (fortitude) uses the emotion of anger as its instrument to get our bodies prepared to sustain or attack. It is known that the hormone *adrenalin* is excreted to produce the bodily changes required for anger, and most of us recognize these bodily sensations as we "get our dander up," our "fighting spirit." Psychologists have studied anger extensively, and today we are all familiar with ways of "dealing with stress" on the one hand, and "assertiveness training" on the other.[3]

---

[2] Skehan-Di Lella, *Wisdom of Ben Sira*, p. 314, explain that the small stones in v. 18b were placed on top of walls of vineyards in Palestine to alert the watchers by their rattling if a fox tried to climb over the wall.

[3] See Robert J. Blanchard and D. Caroline Blanchard, eds., *Advances in the Study of Aggression*, for a review of the main findings of current psychology on the aggressive drive.

Courage is needed to be faithful to the dictates of all the other virtues. A coward will yield to temptation against any virtue, if sticking to it becomes difficult. Hence courage is a cardinal virtue and is superior to the cardinal virtue of moderation to which it adds this note of strength. Yet it is less important than justice, prudence, or the theological virtues,[4] because a courageous person can also be an oppressor, a fool, and an atheist, and thus ultimately self-destructive.

Courage in the strictest sense is concerned with the greatest evil, namely death, when the highest good, the common good, is at stake, especially when a crisis comes on one suddenly with no opportunity to prepare for it. Thus when a decree went out for the slaughter of all the Jews in the Persian Empire, Queen Esther prayed: "My Lord, our King, you alone are God. Help me, who am alone and have no help but you, for I am taking my life in my hand" (Est C:14-15). As Judith made ready to meet Holofernes, general of the Assyrians, she prayed:

> "Lord, God of my forefather, Simeon!... Give me, a widow, the strong hand to execute my plan. With the guile of my lips, smite the slave together with the ruler, the ruler together with his servant; crush their pride by the hand of a woman" (Jdt 9:2a, 9b-10).

In less dangerous situations courage is also necessary, but is not exhibited in its full force. It should be noted that the aggressive appetite is involved not only in such destructive actions as annihilating an enemy, but also in constructive activities that require the overcoming of difficulties. Thus the builder, the engineer, the inventor, the artist, the organizer, the athlete, the explorer, the parent all have to attack a thousand difficult problems and overcome them *constructively*, creatively.

Although courage concerns the dangerous and therefore the painful, we experience a certain kind of pleasure in exercising it, because it makes us feel powerful. That is why sports and recreations that involve a certain element of risk and fear and even pain are "exciting" and give us pleasure. If this becomes exaggerated and even confused with our

---

[4] St. Thomas Aquinas, *S.T.*, II-II, q. 123, a. 12.

sexual appetites, it ends in *sadism* or cruelty in inflicting pain. On the other hand, it can express itself in *masochism*, the erotic pleasure in being hurt. Sadism or masochism can even go the point that orgasm is produced by such actions.[5]

The reason for these pathological responses probably has something to do with the fact that even normal love-making involves a certain element of aggression (particularly but not exclusively on the part of the male) and submission (particularly on the part of the female). If this love play becomes exaggerated, it can turn into an act of violence. The act of rape reflects an essentially sadistic conception of sex inherent in stereotypes of *macho*, violent masculinity and helpless, passive femininity.[6]

Not all indifference to danger is real courage. "Greenhorns" often seem very daring and take great risks, because their inexperience hides from them the possible consequences of their acts. Veterans of war or other dangerous occupations may also seem very cool in danger, simply because they have become so used to it and so fatalistic about its risks that they do not feel normal fear. But such pseudo-courage fails when the greenhorn begins to realize what he has got into, or when the veteran is faced with a danger that is unfamiliar to him.[7]

Courage is often thought of as a masculine virtue because of its relationship to the male's stronger aggressive tendencies that can be traced back to the hormonal differences with which evolution has supplied him to fulfill his role as husband and father, while chastity is generally considered a feminine virtue. But if we remember that to endure is harder than to attack, we realize that women's roles in life have often required an even greater power of endurance than men's, so that women's courage, although less evident in aggression, may very

---

[5] See Margarete Mitcherlich, M.D., *The Peaceable Sex: On Aggression in Women and Men*, pp. 171-191, for a discussion of sadism and masochism.

[6] The book of Susan Brownmiller, *Against Our Will: Men, Women and Rape* — which argues that rape is primarily motivated by aggression not by sexual desire as such — has been widely influential. For the complexity of this and similar issues involving the relation between the aggressive and the sexual drives see Mary Roth Walsh, ed., *The Psychology of Women: Ongoing Debates*, pp. 62-98.

[7] Aristotle, *Nicomachean Ethics*, Bk. III, c. 6, 1115a 7.

well be on the whole the greater. The courage of Mary and the holy women who stood at the foot of the Cross with the dying Jesus put to shame that of the apostles who had fled (Mt 27:56; Mk 15:40; Lk 23:49; Jn 19:25).[8]

In most cultures the model of courage is the warrior who risks his life for his country. Certainly, the Old Testament speaks of many such warrior heroes. Moses was not primarily a warrior, but a leader, and yet he waged war on the Egyptians and those who opposed the Hebrews' entrance into the promise land. Moses' successor Joshua was also a warrior, and after him came the "judges" or saviors of Israel, including women like Deborah (Jg 5:15-31) and Jael (Jg 4:17-24), and later Judith. The judges were called to lead the people in emergencies, but they were succeeded by Saul and David and the whole line of kings who were permanent captains-in-chief, although they sometimes turned this duty over to subordinates, as in later life David did to the ruthless Joab (2 S 18:11-12).[9] After the exile, for a long time the Jews lacked military leaders, until about a century and a half before Jesus' time when they were again led to war by the Maccabees.

These Jewish fighters were certainly models of aggressive courage. Hebrews in its great praise of men and women of faith (Chapter 11) includes:

> Gideon, Barak, Samson, Jephtah, David…, who by faith conquered kingdoms, did what was righteous, obtained the promises, they closed the mouths of lions, put out raging fires, escaped the devouring sword; out of weakness they were made powerful, became strong in battle, and turned back foreign invaders (Heb 11:32-34).

Thus the Jews were commanded by God not to give in to fear during the "wars of the Lord." God says to Joshua:

---

[8] The Synoptics say that the women stood watching "at a distance" (Mk 15:40; Mt 27:55; Lk 23:49) but John 19:25 says they came to the foot of the Cross.

[9] On Joab, a loyal friend of David and yet indeed a "man of blood," see McKenzie, *Dictionary of the Bible*, pp. 438-439.

"Do not be afraid or dismayed. Take all the army with you and prepare to attack Ai. I have delivered the king of Ai into your power, with his people, city, and land" (Jos 8:1).

And to Isaiah:

"Go out to meet Ahaz... and say to him: Take care you remain tranquil and do not fear; let not your courage fail before [the invaders]" (Is 7:3-4).

Yet Proverbs says, "A patient man is better than a warrior, and he who rules his temper, than he who takes a city" (Pr 16:32), and Jeremiah unceasingly declared to the Jews that they could not save themselves by military alliances or warfare, but only by patient endurance and internal reform.[10] In the New Testament this latter conception of courage is more fully developed. Jesus deliberately refuses to take up the sword to enforce his mission, because, as he says to Peter who tries to defend him:

"Put back your sword into its sheath, for all who take the sword will perish by the sword. Do you think that I cannot call upon my Father and he will not provide me at this moment with more than twelve legions of angels? But then how will the scriptures be fulfilled which say it must come to pass in this way?" (Mt 26:52-54).

In the Sermon on the Mount he had already taught:

"You have heard that it was said, 'An eye for an eye, a tooth for a tooth.' But I say to you, offer no resistance to one who is evil. When someone strikes you on your right cheek, turn the other one to him as well" (Mt 5:38-39).

---

[10] On Jeremiah's pacificism see the introduction of John Bright to his commentary on *Jeremiah*, pp. ciii-ccxviii.

Martyrdom

The social implications of this non-violence of Jesus I will discuss in a later chapter, but what is clear here is that the mission of Jesus ("how will the scriptures be fulfilled") was too difficult to be accomplished by the easier means of force. It had to be accomplished through the much harder way of courageous suffering and dying in witness of the truth. Hence the New Testament model is not the warrior but the *martyr*, of which Jesus on the Cross is the supreme example, accompanied by his mother Mary, her heart pierced spiritually by the same lance that pierced the heart of her son "that the scriptures might be fulfilled" (cf. Lk 2:34-35).

Today the term "martyr" is applied very freely to all sorts of people; for example, the Japanese kamikaze pilots, the Buddhists who burnt themselves as a protest to communism, and the Shiite soldiers in the Iran-Iraq war are all called "martyrs." But this most honorable title, which means "witness" has a specifically Jewish and Christian meaning.[11] True martyrdom requires three conditions: (1) that the victim actually die, (2) that he or she dies in witness of faith in Christ which is directly expressed in words, or implicitly in acts done or sins refused because of faith, and (3) that the victim accepts death voluntarily. They are not martyrs who do not actually die, or die from disease, for the sake of merely natural truths, or heresy, or for their country in war, or through suicide, etc.

Thus the Blessed Virgin Mary, although she surpassed the martyrs in her sorrows (the liturgy applies to her the words, "Come, all you who pass by the way: Look and see whether there is any suffering like my suffering!" Lm 1:12) was not strictly speaking a martyr, since she

---

[11] "Martyr" is often used loosely of anyone who dies for the sake of any cause. But the Christian cause is (a) in fact *objectively true*, and not a subjective illusion, as are many of the causes for which persons die sincerely but deludedly; and furthermore (b) the truth in question is a truth of *reasonable faith* exceeding all human experience. Thus those who die for the sake of fanatical religious cults, or as terrorists, or for their own glory, however sincere, are not genuine martyrs, but are objectively suicides. Nor are those who die for a noble but merely human motive, as the parent who dies to save a child, or a soldier for his country, since such virtuous acts can pertain simply to the order of natural virtue.

did not die from her sorrows. Nor was Judas Maccabeus a martyr, although he died fighting for the law ("The other acts of Judas, his battles, the brave deeds he performed have not been recorded, but they were many," 1 M 9:22), because he died fighting, not as one submitting to being killed.

Since the Church has always held that martyrdom is equivalent to baptism for those not yet baptized ("There are three that testify, the Spirit, the water, and the blood," 1 Jn 5:7-8), the Holy Innocents, although they are not strictly martyrs since they did not die voluntarily, are nevertheless honored as martyrs in the liturgy because they died in the place of the infant Christ and received the baptism of blood.

The strict concept of martyrdom is first clearly stated in the Bible in the story of the seven Maccabean brothers and their mother (2 M 7) who died rather than eat pork which the Greek oppressors tried to force upon them to indicate their renunciation of the law and the covenant with God. This story is also important because it clearly expresses for the first time the doctrine of the Resurrection in the words of the mother to her youngest son:

> "Since it is the Creator of the universe who shapes each man's beginning, as he brings about the origin of everything, he, in his mercy, will give you back both breath and life, because you now disregard yourselves for the sake of his law" (2 M 7:23).

The first Christian martyr after Jesus himself, was St. Stephen, stoned to death in Jerusalem for preaching the Gospel.

> As they were stoning Stephen, he called out, "Lord Jesus, receive my spirit." Then he fell to his knees and cried out in a loud voice, "Lord, do not hold this sin against them"; and when he said this, he fell asleep (Ac 7:59-60).

Thus the Christian martyr does not die out of hatred of the enemy as a soldier might, but out of love for his killers, as Jesus taught and lived (Mt 5:43-48). "No one has greater love than this, to lay down one's life for one's friends" (Jn 15:13), but for the Christian our enemies are also our friends as long as their conversion is possible. After

Stephen, St. Peter, St. Paul (before his conversion an accomplice in St. Stephen's death, Ac 7:58b), and St. James the Apostle (Ac 12:2) were all martyrs, and following them a "great cloud of witnesses" (Heb 12:1). In the liturgy of the Church special honor is given to the Virgin Martyrs (women and men, Rv 14:4) who are models of both the virtues of chastity and of courage.

Christians who do not die for the faith, may yet share in martyrdom, as the Virgin Mary did, by being ready to die for it.

> In your struggle against sin you have not yet resisted to the point of shedding blood... Endure your trials as discipline; God treats you as sons... They [our earthly fathers] disciplined us for a short time as seemed right to them, but he [our heavenly Father] does so for our benefit, in order that we may share his holiness. At the time, all discipline seems a cause not for joy but for pain, yet later it brings the peaceful fruit of righteousness to those who are trained for it (Heb 12:4, 7, 10-11).

Christians are engaged in a *spiritual* warfare[12] against a greater than any human power:

> Put on the armor of God so that you may be able to stand firm against the tactics of the devil. For our struggle is not with flesh and blood but with the principalities, with the powers, with the world rulers of this present darkness, with the evil spirits in the heavens. Therefore, put on the armor of God, that you may be able to resist on the evil day, and having done everything, hold to your ground (Eph 6:11-13; cf. Is 11:5; 59:16-17; Ws 5:17-23). Be sober and vigilant. Your opponent the devil is prowling around like a roaring lion looking for someone to devour. Resist him, steadfast in faith, knowing that your fellow believers

---

[12] A. Yusuf Ali commenting on Sura 9, 20 of the *Qur'an* says, "Here is a good description of *Jihad*. It *may* require fighting in God's cause, as a form of self-sacrifice. But its essence consists in (1) a true and sincere Faith, which so fixes its gaze on God, that all selfish or worldly motives seem paltry and fade away, and (2) earnest and ceaseless activity, involving the sacrifice (if need be) of life, person, or property, in the service of God. Mere brutal fighting is opposed to the whole spirit of *Jihad*, while the sincere scholar's pen or preacher's voice or wealthy man's contribution may be the most valuable forms of *Jihad*." *The Holy Qur'an*, p. 444, note 1270.

throughout the world undergo the same sufferings (1 P 5:8-9).
So submit yourselves to God. Resist the devil, and he will flee
from you (Jm 4:7).

Had not Jesus said, "Do not be afraid of those who kill the body but
cannot kill the soul; rather, be afraid of the one who can destroy both
soul and body in Gehenna" (Mt 10:28)?

The virtue of courage like the virtue of moderation is a middle
way between two extremes. We can yield too much to our appetite for
fighting and then we have the vice of *rashness,* or we can be too weak
in our fighting spirit and then we have *cowardice.* Of these, the second
sin against the virtue of courage is the more common; while for the
virtue of moderation the opposite is true, namely that an excessive
search for pleasure is the more common extreme. Hence most people
have to learn to restrain their love of pleasure and to reinforce their
courage. That is why the contrary motto of the "hippies" of the '60's,
"Make love, not war," was so seductive. But there are temperaments
which care little for pleasure and are eager for a fight (they can be very
dangerous) and there are others who are excessive in both respects, or
weak in both respects.

Cowardice is a despicable vice, and the early Church did not
hesitate to excommunicate Christians who showed cowardice in the
face of persecution by denying the faith, or even by handing over the
Sacred Books to the Roman persecutors.[13] Yet fear is natural to us all.
Even Jesus in the garden sweated blood from fear (Lk 22:44), but with
courage he resolutely accepted the Cross. On the other hand an excessive aggressivity, a combativeness and rashness in the face of danger,
although sometimes mistaken for courage and therefore praised, is
suicidal and often the source of great misery for others. We have only
to think of the great conquerors of the past, Alexander, Caesar, Genghis
Khan, Napoleon, Stalin, Hitler for whom war became the very purpose

---

[13] In Africa the name of *traditor* (from which we get the word "traitor") was given to
those who surrendered the Bible to the government in the Diocletian persecution. The
Donatist schism resulted from their rejection of Caecilian (said to have been consecrated [311] by a *traditor*) as Bishop of Carthage, and their adherence to a new bishop,
Donatus; see article "Donatism," *Oxford Dictionary of the Church,* p. 419.

of life, to realize how evil such a vice can become. The Bible, especially the Prophets (e.g. Nahum on the fall of Nineveh, Na 2:2-3, 14) and Revelation on the fall of Rome ("Babylon," Rv 18:1-19:4) are filled with denunciation of these bloody oppressors. According to the Chronicler, God even said to David, although David seemed to have fought in God's own cause, "You have shed much blood, and you have waged great wars. You may not build a house [the Temple] in my honor, because you have shed too much blood in my sight" (1 Ch 22:8).

Cowardice and aggression can be mortal sins; cowardice when it withholds us from serious duties out of fear, aggression when it leads us to accept seriously unreasonable risks to ourselves or others. If the harm entailed in either case is not serious, such sins are only venial. It must be remembered, however, that habitual cowardliness in trivial matters so weakens one's character that one may very well become liable to mortal sin when the situation demands courage about serious matters. Habitual rashness in trivial ways can also easily lead to serious risks, e.g., the careless driver can become the really reckless driver. "The man of violent temper pays the penalty; even if you rescue him, you will have it to do again" (Pr 19:19).[14]

The integrating elements of courage are four: with regard to its aggressive aspect, (1) *confidence* that important goals can be achieved; (2) *effort* or work in developing the means to reach these goals and in sustaining the difficulties; (3) *patience* and endurance; and (4) *perseverance* and constancy in persisting until victory. Thus Jesus and Paul were motivated by great confidence in God as they undertook their missions, tirelessly carried them out, in sweat and tears, patiently enduring the sufferings incurred, and holding out to the end.

> In everything we commend ourselves as ministers of God, through much endurance, in afflictions, hardships, constraints, beatings, imprisonment, riots, labors, vigils, fasts; by purity, knowledge, patience, kindness, in a holy spirit, in unfeigned

---

[14] According to McKane, *Proverbs*, p. 529, the phrase "pays the penalty" should be translated "should pay his fine," i.e., should be punished, because otherwise he will commit the same offense again and again.

love, in truthful speech, in the power of God, with weapons of
righteousness at the right and at the left; through glory and dishonor, insult and praise. . . as sorrowful yet always rejoicing, as
poor yet enriching many, as having nothing and possessing all
(2 Cor 6:4-8, 10).

B: RELATED VIRTUES

Nobility

Corresponding to the four elements of courage there are four virtues
related to it, but not identical with it. First, there is *magnanimity* (Greek
megalopsychia, "great-souledness") or perhaps a better name would
be *nobility* of which Aristotle says much,[15] and which is the partner of
the virtue of humility, of which the Bible says so much, and Aristotle
little or nothing. Magnanimity is sometimes translated "ambition" (in
the good sense of the term), since it is a development of that integrating
element of courage which gives one confidence that important goals
can be achieved in spite of serious obstacles in the way.

Magnanimity is also recognized in the Bible although in different terms and is obviously closely related to Christian hope. Who could
be greater-souled than Jesus who came to save the whole world ("For
God did not send his Son into the world to condemn the world, but that
the world might be saved through him," Jn 3:17), or Paul who boldly
claimed, "For so the Lord has commanded us, 'I have made you a light
to the Gentiles, that you may be an instrument of salvation to the ends
of the earth'" (Ac 13:47). Magnanimity and hope differ only in that the
goal of hope is God himself, while magnanimity has less ultimate objectives. Christians should be humble, content with even the lowest
place in view of their real defects; but on the other hand, they should
aspire, in view of God's great gifts to them, to great deeds in his ser-

---

[15] *Nicomachean Ethics* Bk. IV, c. 3, 1124b 28 - 1125a 34. Ross translates *megalopsychia*
as the virtue of the "proud man" which in the context is very misleading. On this virtue
see Aquinas, *S.T.*, II-II, q. 129.

vice. The Parable of the Talents (Mt 25:14-30; cf. Lk 19:11-27) clearly says that God, like a hard master, will require a profit on his investment in us.

Although magnanimity strengthens the aggressive appetites, it is primarily in the will where it is needed to maintain commitment to the goals to be accomplished. Humility restrains magnanimity, keeping it to the realistic mean between foolish extremes, by a wisely realistic self-knowledge of one's own gifts and limitations. "For great is the power of God; by the humble he is glorified" (Si 3:19). The lack of magnanimity is *non-commitment* (pusillanimity, small-souledness) which leaves a person without any important goals to live for, because of the fear of commitment to anything through timid rationalizations. "The sluggard says, 'A lion is outside; in the streets I might be slain'" (Pr 22:13; cf. 26:13). Such a person drifts through life aimlessly, a rather common vice in our times when young people are often confused about values and goals. The excess of magnanimity takes three forms: *foolhardiness, ambition, vainglory.*

We have already defined the term *presumption* as a kind of sin against hope in respect to attaining to God; *foolhardiness* refers to an excess of hope with regard to lesser goals. It is foolhardiness to commit oneself to goals that prudence tells us are beyond our powers to attain, and is of itself a foolish but venial sin. Yet, when foolhardiness is motivated by serious pride or leads one to do seriously harmful things or to neglect important duties, it is a mortal sin. Thus when the young King Rehoboam, son of Solomon, full of pride in his new power, listened not to the elders but to other young men and imposed heavy taxes on the people, he caused the revolt that divided the kingdom (1 K 12:1-25).

Ambition is the unreasonable desire to attain honors beyond one's real deserts (as when one claims to have a Ph.D. without having earned it, or gains a Ph.D. by plagiary or sexual sin, or achieves a Ph.D. for the prestige with no intention to use it in the service of others), or finally when ambition undermines one's Christian humility so one no longer recognizes that ultimately only God deserves honor. Thus when Jesus said:

> "Do not be called 'Rabbi'. You have but one teacher, and you
> are all brothers. Call no one on earth your father; you have but
> one Father in heaven. Do not be called 'Master'; you have but
> one master, the Messiah" (Mt 23:8-10),

he should not be understood literally to have forbidden all use of hon-
orific titles, since elsewhere in the same Gospel Jesus uses the titles
"father" and "mother" (Mt 10:21, 35, 37; 15:4-6; 19:29, etc.), and St.
Paul calls himself the "father" of the Corinthians (1 Cor 4:15, 2 Cor
6:13, etc.). Instead, Jesus was denouncing the ambition of those who
seek the honor of such titles forgetful of humility before God.

Vainglory or vanity should be distinguished from pride in the
strict sense of the word. Pride, as we have seen, is the immoderate
desire of superiority, but vainglory is a desire for the mere *appearance*
of superiority (today we speak of "image"), and thus also to be distinguished from true "glory," "fame," "honor," or "reputation."

> Let us not be conceited, provoking one another, envious of one
> another (Gal 5:26). Do nothing out of selfishness or out of vain-
> glory; rather, humbly regard others as more important than your-
> selves, each looking out not for his own interests, but also every-
> one for those of others (Ph 2:3-4).

This immoderate desire to be thought more handsome, strong,
intelligent, rich, or holy than we really know ourselves to be is of itself
a venial sin, since it only harms ourselves by making us appear ridicu-
lous. Yet vainglory is also a *capital sin* because it easily leads to other
sins, and sometimes to mortal ones as when a man to appear *macho* in
the eyes of others burglarizes, drives recklessly, takes drugs, or forni-
cates; or a woman to appear beautiful seriously injures her health or to
appear sophisticated ruins the reputation of others.

> King Nebuchadnezzar... as he was walking on the roof of the
> royal palace in Babylon... said, "Babylon the great! Was it not
> I, with my great strength, who built it as a royal residence for my
> splendor and majesty?" While these words were still on the king's
> lips, a voice spoke from heaven, "It has been decreed for you,
> King Nebuchadnezzar, that your kingdom is taken from you!"
> (Dn 4:25-28).

Generosity

Related to the integrating element of courage which I have called *effort* is what the scholastics called "magnificence." Perhaps it could better be called *generosity*. Courage itself requires personal effort, but in striving for a goal we must also be ready to expend our external resources, money, materials, etc., in a generous way that makes possible a complete and perfect work. Our possessiveness and fears about risking our property makes this difficult and requires a virtue to overcome. In the Scriptures a splendid example of this generosity is the description of Solomon's expenditures on the building of the Temple in honor of God and to fulfill David's will (1 K 6; 1 Ch 3-4).

The difficulty involved in magnificent expenditures is relative to the affluence of the giver. Hence the New Testament examples are especially taken from poor people. Thus Jesus praises the poor widow's gift of "two coins worth a few cents" to the Temple (some have suggested she might be none other than Jesus' own mother).

> "Amen, I say to you, this poor widow put in more than all the other contributors to the treasury. For they have all contributed from their surplus wealth, but she, from her poverty, has contributed all she had, her whole livelihood" (Mk 12:43-44).

The early community in Jerusalem was also very generous, "No one claimed any of his possessions as his own, but they had everything in common" (Ac 4:32b). That this generosity was not easy is seen from the story of Ananias and Sapphira who deceitfully retained some of the money from the sale of their property (Ac 5:1-11). When persecution reduced the Jerusalem community to penury, Paul praised the Greek churches for helping them out by a great collection (Ac 11:27-30; Gal 2:6-10; 1 Cor 16:14; Rm 15:25-28; 2 Cor 8-9) as well as for their generosity to himself (Ph 4:10-20). Nor should we forget the generous women who greatly facilitated Jesus' ministry and the growth of the early Church by their financial support and warm hospitality (e.g. Rm 16:1-2).[16]

---

[16] See Ben Witherington, *Women and the Genesis of Christianity*.

Generosity is also exhibited in the effort we put into our daily work to support ourselves and in the service of society. Some in the early Church thought that the expected Second Coming of the Lord excused them from work, so that St. Paul had to say:

> We urge you, brothers, to progress even more, and to aspire to live a tranquil life, to mind your own affairs, and to work with your own hands, as we instructed you, that you may conduct yourselves properly toward outsiders and not depend on anyone (1 Th 4:10b-12; cf. 2 Th 3:6-16; Eph 4:28).

While a "work ethic" is often attributed to the Calvinist Reformation, Vatican II and John Paul II have also pointed out that Jesus by his own life as a carpenter redeemed human work, which had fallen under the curse of original sin ("By the sweat of your face shall you get bread to eat," Gn 3:19), and that in imitation of Jesus St. Paul worked with his hands (1 Cor 4:12; 9:1-18). *Ora et labora*, "pray and work," was also the motto of monastic life. Work requires an effort that can become wearisome and even painful, and for which that kind of courage which is generosity is required. "From the fruit of his words a man has his fill of good things, and the work of his hands comes back to reward him" (Pr 12:14).

Patience

To develop the integrating element of courage called *patience* a related virtue of the same name is necessary. This secondary kind of *patience* is not in the effort-drives but in the pleasure-pain drives, because what it regulates is the emotions of sadness and discouragement (*acedia*) which result from the pain and weariness of life so that they do not deflect us from the courageous pursuit of our goals. Christian patience is not stoic apathy or lack of feeling, but a strong endurance in the confidence of God's love and power, closely related to Christian hope. The whole Old Testament can be read as a praise of patience, since God's promises seemed so long delayed, and without faith the future seemed so hopeless.

Job, of course, is the great poem on the subject of patience, so that the expression "patient as Job" sums up the whole topic. But Qoheleth in a different way also portrays the believer struggling with the temptation to *acedia* and despair, yet remaining unshaken in faith in God, since after lamenting bitterly that in earthly life, "Emptiness of emptiness! All things are empty!" (Ec 1:2), Qoheleth concludes:

> The last word, when all is heard: Fear God and keep his commandments, for this is for human creatures all; because God will bring to judgment every work, with all its hidden qualities, whether good or bad (Ec 12:13-14).[17]

The Wisdom books emphasize that patience brings peace of mind.

> The patient man shows much good sense, but the quick tempered man displays folly at its height (Pr 14:29). An ill-tempered man stirs up strife, but a patient man allays discord (Pr 15:18). A patient man need stand firm but for a time, and then contentment comes back to him (Si 1:20). Accept whatever befalls you, in crushing misfortune be patient; For in fire gold is tested, and worthy men in the crucible of humiliation (Si 2:4-5). Better is the end of speech than its beginning, better is the patient spirit than the lofty spirit (Ec 7:8).

Endurance

We may now add to patience the virtue related to the integrating element of courage we have called "perseverance," namely *endurance* (longanimity), which enables patience to hold up through what seems endless waiting for relief. Note how Moses kept the Hebrews on the march for forty years, Jeremiah and Ezekiel kept up the people's spirits through the seventy years of Exile, and then Ezra and the Book of Daniel renewed that spirit again and again during the 400 years until the coming of the Messiah.

---

[17] Some exegetes of course think that this is a pious corrective added to this otherwise cynical work, but it must be remembered that it is the *canonical* form of the work which is the Word of God, not necessarily earlier versions.

> Blessed is the man who has patience and perseveres until the one thousand three hundred and thirty-five days. Go, take your rest, you shall rise for your reward at the end of days (Dn 12:12-13).

Psalm 13 is the cry of these years, "How long, O Lord? How long?" and it is still echoing in the prayer of the martyrs at the end of the Bible, "How long will it be, holy and true master, before you sit in judgment and avenge our blood on the inhabitants of the earth?" (Rv 6:10).

Although the people of the New Testament had a lively hope of the Lord's return soon, they too had to be patient and endure, and there are many New Testament texts on patience:

> We even boast of our afflictions, knowing that affliction produces endurance, and endurance proven character, and proven character hope, and hope does not disappoint, because the love of God has been poured out into our hearts through the Holy Spirit that has been given to us (Rm 5:3-5). Rejoice in hope, endure in affliction, persevere in prayer (Rm 12:12). May the God of endurance and encouragement grant you to think in harmony with one another, in keeping with Christ Jesus, that with one accord you may with one voice glorify the God and Father of our Lord Jesus Christ (Rm 15:5-6). Remember the days past when after you had been enlightened, you endured a great contest of suffering... Therefore, do not throw away your confidence; it will have great recompense. You need endurance to do the will of God and receive what he has promised. "For, after just a brief moment, he who is to come shall come; he shall not delay [Is 26:20]." "But my just one shall live by faith, and if he draws back I take no pleasure in him [Hab 2:4]." We are not among those who draw back and perish, but among those who have faith and will possess life (Heb 10:32, 35-39). Consider it all gain, my brothers, when you encounter various trials, for you know that the test of your faith produces perseverance. And let perseverance be perfect, so that you may be perfect and complete, lacking in nothing (Jm 1:2-4). (See also 2 Cor 6:4; Gal 5:22, 1 Th 5:14; Eph 4:2; Col 3:12; 1 Tm 1:16; 2 Tm 3:10, 4:2; Jm 5:10; Heb 6:15, 5:7-8; Rv 2:2, 19; 16:11, etc.).

It has been said that patience has three grades: patience without self-pity, patience without complaining to others, patience with joy. The Bible relates of the apostles after they were flogged in the presence of the Sanhedrin for preaching the Gospel: "So they left the presence of the Sanhedrin, rejoicing that they had been found worthy to suffer dishonor for the sake of the Name" (Ac 5:41). Jesus promised that patience will be rewarded with eternal life: "You will be hated by all because of my name, but not a hair on your head will be destroyed. By your perseverance you will secure your lives" (Lk 21:17-19).

The vices opposed to patience are *callousness* or cynicism ("They did not listen or give ear. Each one followed the hardness of his evil heart," Jr 11:8), which makes one indifferent to evil and unable to be outraged by injustice, and *impatience* which renders one unable to bear the slightest evil ("The patient man is better than a warrior, and he who rules his temper, than he who takes a city," Pr 16:32). Of themselves these are venial sins, but could occasion mortal sins of failure to right serious wrongs when we have the responsibility to do so, or resist seriously unjust attacks on others. The sin against endurance is *weakness* that gives in to every threat, like that of the elders of Bethuliah before the threat of Assyria whom Judith rebuked (Jdt 8:9-36), and *stubbornness* that refuses to retreat from a fight even when it is hopeless. "Thus, although Moses and Aaron performed these various wonders in Pharaoh's presence, the Lord made Pharaoh obstinate, and he would not let the Israelites leave his land" (Ex 11:10).[18]

Holy Spirit's Gift

The Gift of the Holy Spirit that facilitates the virtue of courage is called by the same name (or "fortitude") and to it relates the Beatitude "Blessed they who hunger and thirst for righteousness" (Mt 5:6), since "hunger

---

[18] The phrase "God made Pharaoh obstinate" should not be understood as if God made Pharaoh sin, since elsewhere the Bible teaches that we are each responsible for our own sins (Ezk 15:12-23; 18:1-32) but in the sense that God in his providence permitted the king to sin that it might be an opportunity to manifest the divine saving power to Israel.

and thirst" here implies a persevering desire in the face of difficulties that stand in the way of its satisfaction. The fruits it bears are "patience and long-suffering" (Gal 5:22).[19]

The Ten Commandments do not contain a precept directly concerning courage since they deal with justice. There are, however, as we have seen, many commands scattered throughout Scripture demanding that we fight against evil and endure suffering for the sake of the good.[20] For example:

> "Hear, O Israel! Today you are going into battle against your enemies. Be not faint-hearted or afraid; be neither alarmed nor frightened by them. For it is the Lord, your God, who goes with you to fight for you against your enemies and give you victory" (Dt 20:3-4),

and "Resist the devil, and he will flee from you (Jm 4:7b).

The civil obligation to defend one's country will be discussed in the next chapter under the topic of just war, but it suffices to say here that conscientious objection to war cannot be defended simply on the grounds of fear of suffering and death. If justified, it must be as courageous as is military service, a way of fighting the evils of unjust war.

To become courageous we need to meditate frequently on the fact that to fear temporal evils, even death, is foolish in view of the fact that faith tells us these are passing things that cannot harm our eternal happiness. Also we need to look at death and the other evils of life with a realistic vision and to prepare ourselves for them. If we learn every day to live our lives energetically and to enjoy vigorous effort to solve life's problems, instead of shrinking before these problems and indulging in self-pity, we gain in strength. Above all we need to be motivated by a great love of God, inspired by Jesus' own courage, and energized by prayer.

---

[19] The Vulgate distinguishes between "patience" and "long-suffering" but the Greek only gives *makrothymia*, long-suffering.

[20] See St. Thomas Aquinas, *S.T.*, II-II, q. 140, a. 1, on how the precepts of courage are contained in the Bible.

The Sacrament of Spiritual Warfare

In Chapter 2 the Sacraments of Initiation were discussed as the foundation of all Christian life, and it was noted that Baptism and Confirmation, for adults at least, form a single celebration expressing the washing away of sins through a sanctifying rebirth in Christ by the action of the Holy Spirit. Yet Confirmation is, in a special way, the sacrament associated with the cardinal virtue of courage.[21]

St. Paul, as we have seen, speaks frequently of spiritual warfare which demands the strength that can only come from the Holy Spirit to overcome the world, the flesh, and the devil. Speaking of his own struggle to preach the Gospel, Paul writes, "For, although we are in the flesh, we do not battle according to the flesh, for the weapons of our battle are not of flesh but are enormously powerful, capable of destroying fortresses" (2 Cor 10:3-4). Formerly, in the Latin Roman Rite the confirming bishop struck the candidate lightly on the cheek to signify this aspect of the sacrament. In the post-Vatican II revision of the rites this has been omitted to emphasize the anointing, but, as the *Catechism* notes, the anointing with oil (the anointing of athletes and wrestlers) "limbers" and hence is a sign of "strengthening."[22]

Summary of Norms

The Decalogue does not include a specific positive norm about courage, but it is implied in the Fifth Commandment, "You shall not kill," that is, kill unjustly since this requires the control of the effort-drive by reason. The positive norm of courage can be formulated as follows:

1. Moderate the effort-drives so that they facilitate free moral acts necessary to attain eternal life in the Trinity even when this involves unavoidable pain or even death.

---

[21] See Chapter 2, pp. 78 ff.
[22] CCC # 1293-1294.

And the negative norms can be formulated as follows:

2. Never perform out of fear of pain or death free moral acts contradictory to the goal of eternal life in the Trinity.
3. Never fail out of fear of pain or death to perform free moral acts necessary to attain the goal of eternal life in the Trinity.
4. Never perform acts which entail a risk of pain or death more harmful than the good which they achieve.

Conclusion to Part II

We share our biological drives and emotions with our fellow animals with whom Genesis 1:24-31 groups us by assigning us to the sixth day of Creation. Yet, in us, because we are superior to the other animals because we have been created in God's image and likeness (Gn 1:27), these drives and emotions are transformed by reason and freedom. Furthermore, our human reason and freedom are transformed by the virtues of faith and hope, so that through discipline and the virtues of moderation and courage our affectivity is placed in the service of a life that far transcends that of our fellow animals.

Yet this discipline is not easily achieved. Indeed it cannot be achieved unless we take up our Cross daily and follow Jesus (Mt 10:38-39) in his poverty, humility, chastity, and martyrdom. These are possible for us as Christians whatever our vocation in life. As St. Paul exultantly proclaimed, we must find all the magnificent courage this requires in Christ's love for us and ours for Christ:

> *No, in all these things we conquer overwhelmingly through him who loved us. For I am convinced that neither death, nor life, nor angels, nor principalities, nor present things, nor future things, nor powers, nor height, nor depth, nor any other creature will be able to separate us from the love of God in Christ Jesus our Lord* (Rm 8:37-39).

PART III
LOVE

CHAPTER 7

LIVING JUSTLY

In the path of justice there is life,
but the abominable way leads to death (Pr 12:28).

A: JUSTICE AND RIGHTS

The Virtue of Justice

We have considered the faith and practical wisdom which are the light
that guides Christians on their way to God. We have also considered
the self-discipline of our desires and fears motivated by the hope of
reaching God. We have now to consider our relations to our *neighbors*,
our fellow pilgrims. We must respect their rights. But to be Christ-like
we must be more than just, we must be loving according to the "Golden
Rule" which Jesus gave in the Sermon on the Mount, "Do to others
whatever you would have them do to you. This is the law and the
prophets" (Mt 7:12).

Because Christian love of God and neighbor unites all the other
virtues, and because in the Bible the Old Testament reveals God's justice, but the New Testament more clearly reveals God's love,[1] I will
discuss justice in this Chapter 7 and then, because its scope is so extensive, complete that discussion in Chapter 8, leaving love in the final,
most excellent place, the summation of all virtues, in Chapter 9.

---

[1] Note that I say "more clearly reveals." It is false to say that the Old Testament speaks
only of justice and the New Testament only of love, as is sometimes claimed. When
Jesus proclaimed the Great Commandment of Love (Mk 12:28-34; Mt 22:34-40; Lk
10:25-28) he was quoting the Old Testament (Dt 6:4-5; Lv 19:18). On the other hand,
St. Paul (Rm 1:17) says that in the Gospel "is revealed the righteousness [justice] of
God from faith [of the Old Testament] to faith [of the New Testament]" and then
quotes the Old Testament prophet Habakkuk 2:4.

Biblical "justice" in the widest sense is "righteousness" (Hebrew *sedaqa*, Greek *dikaiosyne*) and means conformity to the Divine wisdom and will, that is, "sanctity," "holiness."[2] "Blessed are they who hunger and thirst for righteousness" (Mt 5:6). "For in it [the Gospel] is revealed the righteousness of God from faith to faith; as it is written 'The one who is righteous by faith will live [Hab 2:4]'" (Rm 1:17). It also applies to good works, "righteous deeds" (Mt 6:1; cf. Mt 5:20). "Justification" is God's action freeing us from sin to live in the "state of grace" by which we are transformed by the Holy Spirit into adopted sons and daughters of God in Christ.[3]

> For if, by the transgression of one person, death came to reign through that one [Adam], how much more will those who receive the abundance of grace and of the gift of justification (*dikaiosyne*) come to reign in life through the one person Jesus Christ (Rm 5:17).

Yet "justice" is also sometimes used in the strict sense of a special virtue: God "has established a day on which he will 'judge the world with justice' [Ps 9:9] through a man he [Christ] has appointed" (Ac 17:31). In this strict sense *justice is the virtue by which we have a constant and permanent will to give each person what is that person's right*. As St. Paul teaches:

> Pay to all their dues, taxes to whom taxes are due, toll to whom toll is due, respect to whom respect is due, honor to whom honor is due. Owe nothing to anyone, except to love one another (Rm 13:7-8).

Hence, while moderation and courage deal with objects in relation to oneself, justice has to do with a *relation* to another or others.[4] It concerns a *right*, that is, what is due some person, and this implies a

---

[2] For a useful discussion of biblical ethics from the perspective of "holiness" see Walter C. Kaiser, Jr., *Toward Old Testament Ethics*, Part III, pp. 139-246.

[3] On justification see CCC # 1987-1995, 2018-2020.

[4] See St. Thomas Aquinas on why justice is a special virtue, *S.T.*, II-II, q. 58, aa. 1, 7, 8.

certain *equality* between what the agent does and what is due to the recipient. Strictly speaking, we cannot be just to ourselves or even to our families because they are not entirely "other," nor to God because we owe him too much (although we can love him with "all our heart, with all our understanding, with all our strength" [cf. Dt 6:4; Mk 12:30]). Justice implies *distinction* of persons; love implies *union* of persons so the other is one's other self.

Need for Justice

Justice is the most evident kind of morality. I have already shown that we can sin against ourselves by failing in moderation or courage, yet many do not perceive such self-injuries as immoral. But even small children recognize unfairness in games, or in the distribution of gifts. Hence, the Ten Commandments are all concerned with justice; the Fourth to Tenth with strict justice.[5] In our times the "social doctrine of the Church" has formulated the principles of justice in many important documents beginning with the encyclical *Rerum Novarum* of Leo XIII in 1891 and continuing to *Gaudium et Spes* of Vatican II. Recently, in the perspective of the present world situation after the collapse of Marxism in Eastern Europe, this body of doctrine on social justice has been summed up in John Paul II's encyclical *Centesimus Annus,* promulgated on the hundredth anniversary of *Rerum Novarum.*[6]

The biblical concept of justice is very rich and in the course of history the canon lawyers and theologians have elaborated its manifold aspects, but the simplest example is the repayment of a loan or the payment of wages. Sirach says, "Pay back your neighbor when a loan falls due" (Si 29:2), and Jesus in a parable has the generous farmer say to a harvest-hand who asked for more money, "My friend, I am not

---

[5] The writers of CCC decided to follow the traditional catechesis on the Decalogue as the framework for presenting the moral teaching of the Church, rather than the more theological framework of the virtues as this book does.

[6] CCC # 1929-1948; 2197-2257. For syntheses of this Social Doctrine see Joseph Gremillion, ed., *The Gospel of Peace and Justice*; Thomas M. Gannon, S.J., ed., *The Catholic Challenge to the American Economy*; and Thomas O. Nitzch, et al., *On the Condition of Labor and the Social Question One Hundred Years Later.*

cheating you. Did you not agree with me for the usual daily wage? Take what is yours and go" (Mt 20:13-14). The Bible repeatedly reminds us, "The worker deserves his wages" (1 Tm 5:18; cf. Lv 19:13; Dt 24:15, 25:4; Ml 3:5; Si 34:22; Mt 10:10, Lk 10:7; 1 Cor 9:10; Jm 5:4).

Thus the material object of justice is proximately some action (the payment), more remotely some thing (the loan or the wage) to which a person has a right. What is done or given must be *equal* to what is due the person (the exact amount of the loan, the wage agreed upon). Therefore, the motive or *formal object* of justice, is *to render what is due a person.* Sirach urges the debtor to decide to repay in full and Jesus shows us that God in his mercy, like the generous farmer, is also just.

This determination to be fair in which justice formally consists is not only in our minds or feelings but in the *will.* It takes a real effort of will to go beyond ourselves and our own interests to respect the rights of another. Love, on the other hand, stretches itself even further than justice, since it is the will not only to respect the rights of another, but the total good of others even when they have no just claims.

Yet the moral obligations of justice are sometimes more strict than those of love, because they imply equality, that is a *precise* fulfillment of an obligation. The farmer in the parable just quoted was obliged in justice to pay those who had worked longest the full wage agreed upon; but he also, out of generosity, paid the harvest-hands who were hired last as much as the others.

Justice is a cardinal virtue[7] because it deals with one of the four basic needs of human nature, our need for *society*, since society is impossible without a mutual respect among the members of that society for each other's rights. Since justice is in the will, a spiritual faculty, it is a nobler virtue than moderation and courage which are in the bodily emotions, and thus is much more emphasized in the Scriptures — for example in the Decalogue. Aristotle also says, "Justice is often thought to be the greatest of virtues and 'neither evening nor morning star' is so

---

[7] Cf. p. 34 ff.

wonderful."[8] Yet justice is inferior to prudence which is in the spiritual intellect because the intellect guides the will in which justice is seated. Justice is also inferior to the virtue of religion and the theologal virtues which are directed not merely to human society as justice is, but to the divine community of the Trinity.

Foundations of Human Rights

Today when we speak of justice we generally have in mind our "rights," although the Bible tends to emphasize the correlative notion of "obligations" or "duties" or "responsibilities" more than that of "rights." The term "justice" is used both in an *active* (or subjective) sense and a *passive* (or objective) sense. Active justice is the right, the dominion or moral power to possess, do, or demand something as exclusively one's own for one's own use. Thus in the Old Law we read, "Cursed be he who violates the rights of the alien, the orphan, or the widow" (Dt 27:19; cf. 24:17).

Jesus recounted the Parable of the Persistent Widow (Lk 18:1-8) who kept demanding of an unjust judge, "Give me my rights (*ekdíkesón*) against my opponent (*antidíkou*)." Note the root *dike*, "right" to which the judge finally had to give in. Jesus concludes, "Will not God then secure the rights of his chosen ones who call out to him day and night?" (Lk 18:7).

Passive (objective) justice, on the other hand, is the object or action to which one has a right — for example, the property which the widow was demanding as rightly belonging to her. Because rights and obligations are mutually correlative, my right places on others an obligation to respect it, and my moral obligations in justice (not *all* moral obligations) arise from someone else's rights. Thus the unjust judge was finally forced to act justly by fulfilling his obligation to the persistent widow.

Commonly we also metaphorically refer to the law or code which

---

[8] *Nicomachean Ethics*, Bk. V, c. 1, 1129b 26; cf. St. Thomas Aquinas, *S.T.*, II-II, q. 58, a. 12.

requires such a payment, the science of law (jurisprudence), the courts, the judges, all as "justice," which the Romans personified as a blindfolded woman with a balance to indicate that justice is impartial. For the New Testament the supreme symbol of justice is Jesus himself, the all-merciful Lord, sitting as judge in the final judgment of history.

> Jesus said to them [the Twelve], "Amen, I say to you that you who have followed me, in the new age, when the Son of Man is seated on his throne of glory, will yourselves sit on twelve thrones judging the twelve tribes of Israel" (Mt 19:28).

> "When the Son of Man comes in his glory, and all the angels with him, he will sit upon his glorious throne, and all the nations will be assembled before him. And he will separate them one from another, as a shepherd separates the sheep from the goats" (Mt 25:31-32).

The proximate but secondary foundation of right is the dignity of the human person, but the primary and ultimate foundation is God:

> You are just, O Lord, and your ordinance is right;
> You have pronounced your decrees in justice
>   and in perfect faithfulness...
> Your justice is everlasting justice,
>   and your law is permanent...
> Your decrees are forever just;
>   give me discernment that I may live (Ps 119:137, 142, 144).

This is because it is God who fixes our ultimate goals and therefore prescribes the necessary means to them. Or, to put it a different way, our basic needs are goals fixed in our nature by our Creator, and we are morally obliged to fulfill them because rights and obligations are correlative. "Your hands have made me and fashioned me; give me discernment that I may learn your commands" (Ps 119:73; cf. the essay on Divine Wisdom in Si 16:22-17:18).

False Foundations for Rights

Numerous are the philosophical errors concerning the nature of justice and human rights which require to be corrected in the light of God's Word. For example, the materialists deny the difference between human beings and brute animals, and hence either deny both any rights, or (more recently) claim that animals have the same rights as humans.[9] The legal positivists, stemming from Spinoza, Hobbes, and Rousseau, hold that the foundation of human rights is a social contract often expressed by a written constitution, but admit no higher law.[10] The transcendental rationalists such as Thomasius and Kant separate morality based on internal liberty from law based on external liberty. Hegel and the idealists defend the omnipotent State as the expression of transcendental Reason.[11] Finally, the historical school of legalists such as Lévy-Brühl and Durkheim content themselves with simply describing what various cultures and legal systems regard as just.

In the last analysis all these modern systems, which pass over the foundation of justice in a natural law expressive of the wisdom and will of the Creator, have contributed to the *moral relativism* which dominates the scene today.[12] According to this relativism, justice is conformity to purely man-made norms, whether these are due to conscious legal enactments and contracts or to subconsciously developed customs, and they are subject to change either by individual or social will. Philosophers who accept relativism attempt to show how positivistic morality can be rendered sufficiently stable to permit society to survive. However, they are always faced by the objection that a sufficiently powerful tyrant like Hitler or a sufficiently cohesive cultural system or tradition can decree an order of "justice" which in fact will prove utterly destructive of parts or the whole of that society. To this objection moral relativism has never found an answer.[13]

---

[9] See Peter Singer, *Animal Liberation* for this tendency.

[10] The contract theory is basic to the U.S. Constitution.

[11] See Georgio del Vecchio, *Philosophy of Law,* pp. 60-134 for a history of these theories of law.

[12] VS # 35-53 on freedom and law.

[13] Alasdair MacIntyre, *After Virtue* is a penetrating analysis of modern moral relativism.

Since relativists have to admit that in our historical experience all the great cultures of the past have destroyed themselves and the survival of the human species itself has no guarantee, they are forced simply to accept the lack of a firm foundation for morality as the tragedy of the human condition. The Christian seeks a firmer foundation, "the Rock" (Ps 31:3) on which our house of life can be built in justice (Mt 7:24-29). God, who does not fail, in creating us has built into our nature, for all its fragility, certain basic needs and goals that ground a natural moral law and the human rights which flow from it.

> When at the first God created his works
> > and, as he made them, assigned their tasks
> He ordered for all times what they were to do
> > and their domains from generation to generation...
> He [the Lord] puts the fear of humankind in all flesh
> > and gives them rule over beasts and birds.
> He forms humans' tongues and eyes and ears,
> > and imparts to them an understanding heart.
> With wisdom and knowledge he fills them;
> > good and evil he shows them...
> He has set before them knowledge,
> > a law of life as their inheritance (Si 16:24-25; 17:4-6, 9).

To attack this conviction that morality must rest on secure and certain foundations as "foundationalism" or "a neurotic need for security in an ambiguous world" as some have done,[14] is mere rhetoric. Even if one doubts that such a sure foundation exists, it is still most reasonable to seek it. One should give up the search for a sure foundation of human rights, only if one is really certain that it does not exist, and these lovers of ambiguity cannot consistently claim to be certain about anything. The arguments they bring forward for their position are well-known and often soundly refuted.[15]

---

[14] Some deconstructionists treat the "ambiguity" of language as a virtue and so exaggerate "intertextuality" as to claim that language refers only to other language, not to non-linguistic realities. This however is only a form of epistemological idealism. In fact, we learn to speak a language by reference to real objects and events and we clear up ambiguities in usage in the same way. If I ask for "bread" and you hand me a "stone," you either do not know my language or you are being perverse.

[15] For a succinct refutation of relativism see Germain Grisez, *The Way of the Lord Jesus*, vol. 1, pp. 102-103.

Kinds of Human Rights

There are various kinds of rights. By origin rights are established either as *natural*, based on those needs with which we are endowed by nature and the Creator and which are expressed in the Decalogue, grounded as it is in age-old human experience, or *positive* because posited by the will of a legislator, whether *divine* (as the Old Law), or by human authority whether *ecclesiastical* (canon law) or *civil*.

The canonical tradition, which reflects the property provisions of the Old Law, also distinguishes the right *in* a thing (*jus in re*) or actual possession, from the right *to* a thing (*jus ad rem*) or claim on a debtor.[16] To have full ownership or *dominion* (domain) over a thing, is to have the right to *use* it as one's own or to completely *dispose* of it in any way not forbidden by law. This ownership or dominion establishes four principles evident in Near Eastern law and the Old Testament, but now known by their Latin tags: (1) *Res clamat domino*, a thing should be returned to its owner ("When you come upon your enemy's ox or ass going astray, see to it that it is returned to him," Ex 23:4); (2) *Res fructificat domino*, the products of a thing belong to its owner:

> For six years you may sow your land and gather in its produce. But the seventh you shall let the land lie untilled and unharvested that the poor among you may eat of it and the beasts of the field may eat what the poor leave (Ex 23:10-11).

(3) *Res perit domino (nisi alterius culpa pereat)*, when something is destroyed it is the owner's loss, unless it was someone else's fault:

> When a man borrows an animal from his neighbor, if it is maimed or dies while the owner is not present, the man must make restitution. But if the owner is present, he need not make restitution (Ex 22:13-14).

(4) *Nemo ex re aliena, tamquam a causa, locupletari debet cum alterius injuria vel jactura*, no one ought to profit from what belongs to another so as to cause the other injury or expense:

---

[16] This also echoes Roman law.

> When a man steals an ox or a sheep and slaughters or sells it, he shall restore five oxen for the one ox, and four sheep for the one sheep (Ex 21:37).

Use is the real right of employing something belonging to another for one's own utility as if one owned it, but without consuming or destroying it. *Usufruct* is the real right to own a thing and its product, or, if one only uses it also to own its product. *Service* is the right to require or perform an action involving another person and that person's possessions.

God alone as Creator has universal, absolute, independent and principal dominion over all his creatures, and his dominion is not arbitrary or self-serving but a wise and loving care of his creatures for their sakes:

> The Lord's are the earth and its fullness; the world and those who dwell in it. For he founded it upon the seas and established it upon the rivers (Ps 24:1).

> But as you [God] are just, you govern all things justly... For your [God's] might is the source of justice; your mastery over all things makes you lenient to all (Ws 12:15a, 16).

Only angels and humans among God's creatures share in his ownership of the world.

> God blessed them, saying: "Be fertile and multiply; fill the earth and subdue it. Have dominion over the fish of the sea, the birds of the air, and all the living things that move on the earth" (Gn 1:28).

"The Lord God then took the man [and woman, Gn 3:2] and settled them in the garden of Eden, to cultivate and care for it" (Gn 2:15). That this dominion, however, is limited by God's superior rights, is indicated in Gn 1:29 when God gives Adam and Eve the right to eat only plants, and in Gn 2:17 when he forbids them to eat of the Tree of the Knowledge of Good and Evil.

Because these rights belong to humans as such — not as man or woman or white or black or adult or child — children (born and un-born) and those with disabilities (mentally defective, psychotic, senile, comatose) all have the same basic rights. This definition of the subject of human rights is rejected today by the legal positivists who hold that rights are given not by God, but by society. Hence, for positivists the line between persons and non-persons is arbitrary. In our Western culture it is usually drawn at those who can feel pain, thereby excluding the irreversibly comatose and children at the embryonic and early fetal stage.[17]

Primary and Secondary Rights

Thus there are *primary* or basic rights which are founded in the fundamental needs of the human person for four kinds of necessary goods as we mentioned before: (1) life; (2) reproduction; (3) society; and (4) truth. These are recognized in Genesis 2 when God gives *life* to Adam (v. 7), then creates Eve as his partner with the promise of children (*reproduction* and *society*, v. 18), and instructs them by his commandments while also allowing Adam to name the animals (*truth*, v. 16-17; 19-20).

These primary rights belong to every human person, since without their satisfaction the human community cannot be preserved or its members achieve fulfillment. These should be distinguished from *secondary* rights which are relative to social roles and which may differ among humans, provided they do not detract from their basic rights and are appropriate to legitimate social roles.[18] Thus, the secondary rights of parents are not identical with those of their children, nor of teachers and students, bosses and employees, public officials and citizens, clergy and faithful, although all have the same primary rights in the natural, civil and ecclesiastical orders.

---

[17] For this position see Joseph Fletcher, "Four Indicators of Humanhood: The Enquiry Matures," *Hastings Center Report* 4, pp. 4-7, with replies in *Correspondence* 5 (4), pp. 43-45.

[18] The *United Nations Universal Declaration of Human Rights*, 1948, is an important attempt to state such rights in the formulation of which the Vatican played an important role.

St. Paul makes use of this distinction between rights that are primary and those that are secondary when he instructs the Corinthians (1 Cor 12) on right order in their Christian community by appealing to the analogy of the human body in which all members share in one and the same life (and hence all the baptized have the same primary rights), but the organs have different functions (and hence the baptized have different secondary rights based on their roles of service within the Church: clergy and laity, married and single, adults and children, etc.).

> God placed the parts, each one of them, in the body he intended. If they were all one part, where would the body be? But as it is, there are many parts, but one body... If one part suffers, all the parts suffer with it; if one part is honored, all the parts share its joy (1 Cor 12:18-19, 26).

Error of Egalitarianism

The confusion of these two kinds of rights leads, on the one hand, to forgetting that primary rights are not subject to change by any human legislator, and on the other, to an exaggerated egalitarianism which treats all differentiation in rights as a violation of human equality. Repeatedly in the history of the Church and even today some have wrongly concluded from Jesus' teaching on the equality of all before God and the dignity of even "the little ones" that Christians ought to be *anarchists* (*an-arche*, no authority). That is, that they ought to reject all authority of one human being over another both in the Church and in the State.[19]

But Jesus always commanded respect for both religious and civil authority:

> The scribes and Pharisees have taken their seat on the chair of Moses. Therefore, do and observe all things whatsoever they tell you, but do not follow their example (Mt 23:2-3).

---

[19] See George Woodcock, *Anarchism: A History of Libertarian Ideas and Movements.*

> Repay to Caesar what belongs to Caesar and to God what belongs to God (Mt 22:21).

St. Paul enjoined this in very strong terms:

> Let every person be subordinate to the higher authorities, for there is no authority except from God, and those that exist have been established by God. Therefore, whoever resists authority opposes what God has appointed and those who oppose it will bring judgment upon themselves. For rulers are not a cause of fear to good conduct, but to evil. Do you wish to have no fear of authority? Then do what is good and you will receive approval from it, for it is a servant of God for your good. But if you do evil, be afraid, for it does not bear the sword without purpose; it is the servant of God to inflict wrath on the evildoer. Therefore, it is necessary to be subject not only because of the wrath but also because of conscience. This is why you also pay taxes, for the authorities are ministers of God, devoting themselves to this very thing. Pay to all their dues, taxes to whom taxes are due, toll to whom toll is due, respect to whom respect is due, honor to whom honor is due (Rm 13:1-7).

As did the First Epistle of Peter:

> Be subject to every human institution for the Lord's sake, whether it be the king as supreme, or governors as sent by him for the punishment of evildoers and the approval of those who do good (1 P 2:13-14).

These texts must be understood, of course, along with the other qualifying text, "But Peter and the apostles said, 'We must obey God rather than men'" (Ac 5:29), i.e., earthly authorities are themselves subordinated to the authority of God. No doubt Peter had learned this lesson from the example of Jesus' own life of witness to God in the face of the abuse of authority by the civil and religious leaders of his time.

Secondary rights pertaining to social roles should themselves be distinguished into those which have a natural basis, such as the difference of rights of parent and child both of which are included with basic rights as *natural rights*, and those which lack any such basis and depend purely on human social construction, such as the difference in the rights of members of a business corporation. Thus the Old Testament acknowledges both the right of a worker to his wages based on the inherent (natural) value of the work of his own hands (Lv 19:13; Dt 24:14-15), and the right to property based on a human agreement, as when Abraham and Lot divide the land between them so as to avoid disputes (Gn 13:5-12; cf. CA n. 6, nn. 30-43).

Such special secondary rights belong to many different roles in society and are determined by custom and by law. For example, the clergy or their equivalents, teachers and scientists, authors, inventors, and artists play important social roles related to what they contribute to the worship of God and to the discovery and dissemination of truth; while business men, manual workers, etc., have rights related to what they contribute to our economy.

B: PROPERTY

Property Rights

How is ownership or dominion over external goods acquired? As we have seen, the earth and indeed all of material nature within our occupancy was given by the Creator to Adam and Eve (i.e., to the human race) in common to use according to our true needs (Gn 1:28-30; 2:15-17; CA n. 6, nn. 30-43). Yet the human community has found it useful by the *jus gentium* ("law of nations," i.e., customary, cross-cultural law[20]) to divide these common resources among its members and thus

---

[20] For the concept of *jus gentium* see Aquinas, *S.T.*, I-II, q. 95, a. 2 and a. 4; II-II, q. 57, a. 3, who says that all human laws to be valid must be derived from natural law, either as conclusions from natural law principles (e.g., fairness in buying and selling and other such laws as are necessary for the existence of any human community) and these laws are called *jus gentium*; or as further determinations of such laws and such laws are *civil laws*. Aquinas also recognizes that some of the *jus gentium*, like the right of private property (II-II, q. 66, a. 2) and the institution of slavery (II-II, q. 57, a. 3 ad 2), are not derived from human nature as such but from the *fallen* condition of humanity.

establish a secondary right of *private property* based on two primitive
or original titles.

The first title to ownership is the *need* each person has for a certain *limited* supply of material things for sustenance and use:

> Give me neither poverty nor riches; provide me only with the
> food I need; Lest being full I deny you, saying "Who is the
> Lord?" Or, being in want, I steal and profane the name of my
> God (Pr 30:8-9).

The second title to ownership is the *labor* expended by a person to
discover, care for, and develop this material. "For every man... to eat
and drink and enjoy the fruit of all his labor is a gift of God" (Ec 3:13;
cf. 5:15-19). A third, derived title is that of *gift* by which a person
shares what he owns with others or passes it on to his heirs to assist
them in satisfying their limited needs. "If a prince makes a gift of part
of his inheritance to any of his sons, it shall belong to his sons; that
property is their inheritance," but he "shall not seize any part of the
inheritance of the people by evicting them from their property" (Ezk
46:16, 18).

The human agreements by which the rights to private property
are established in a given society are illustrated by numerous examples
in the Old Testament: e.g., the agreement between Lot and Abraham
(Gn 13:5-12), Abraham's purchase of a burial place for Sarah (Gn
23:1-20), and Jacob's purchase of land at Shechem (Gn 33:19). In the
New Testament a special emphasis is placed on the duty of alms (Mt
6:1-4; Ac 11:28-30; 1 Tm 6:17-19) which presupposes such a right of
the giver, and on the duty to work to support oneself, rather than to
await the judgment in idleness (1 Th 4:11; 2 Th 4:11; 3:10).

Limits to Property Rights

Communist and socialist theorists, observing the many abuses of private property, have argued against the right to private property on the
grounds that it is contrary to the basic equality of all humans. Nevertheless, it is admitted even by them that all have a right to private *use* of

goods, since we cannot all eat the same slice of bread, wear the same clothes, or live in one room. Material goods, by their very nature as objects extended in space, exclude common occupancy. Consequently, even the classical communist denial of private property was limited to *productive* goods and the share in their increase. Moreover, Marxists generally admit the two original titles of need and labor. What socialists really deny, therefore, is that individuals may accumulate "capital" goods beyond the limit of their own needs, because, socialists argue, such excess goods should be used for the common goals of the society.[21]

These socialist theories can appeal to certain elements of the Christian tradition: in the Old Law in the regulations in all three codes concerning the cancellation of debts in the sabbatical year (Ex 23:10-11; Dt 15:1-3; Lv 25:2-8), and in the communism practiced by the early Jewish Christian community of Jerusalem (Ac 5:32-37; 5:1-11). Biblical scholars are inclined to believe that this form of Christian communism was prescribed and pictured only as an ideal rather than a historical actuality, but in any case this ideal has been successfully put into practice by religious communities from the time of the early Church until today.[22]

Yet St. Augustine defended private property, as did Innocent III against the Waldenses. Some Spiritual Franciscans were condemned by the Church for holding that Christian perfection consists in poverty, as were Wycliff and Hus for denying the right of the Church to own property.[23] Since the rise of modern capitalism the papal social encyc-

---

[21] CA # 10, 13, 34, 44; CCC # 2424-2425. For a comparison of the Marxist philosophy view of man and ethics see Tom Rockmore, William J. Gavin, James G. Colbert, Jr., and Thomas J. Blakeley, *Marxism and Alternative* and for a broader view of "socialism" see John Joseph Marsden, *Marxian and Christian Utopianism.*

[22] See Philip F. Mulhern, *Dedicated Poverty: Its History and Theology.*

[23] Innocent III condemned this error of the Waldenses (DS # 797). Some "Spirituals" were condemned by the Church for holding that Christian perfection consists in poverty (DS # 930, 1087-1097), as were Wycliff (DS # 1160, 1166, 1182, 1186, 1189, 1194) and Hus for denying the right of the Church to own property (DS # 1274, 1275). The right of private property has been defended in the major social encyclicals of the popes since Leo XIII (e.g., DS # 3133, 3265, 3271, 3949-3951, 3965) but the extremes of individualism and collectivism have been condemned (DS # 3726, 3741). See GS # 69-71.

licals have repeatedly explained the limitations of the right of private property but defended it against extreme socialist theories which wish to vest all rights to productive property in the State or community as a whole.[24]

Note that legitimate titles to private property do not license anyone to waste or destroy the natural environment which God has given us,[25] nor to amass unlimited wealth that is useless or that excludes others from satisfying their needs by extravagant consumption and waste (consumerism). All such titles are limited by the moderate, virtuous use of external things discussed in Chapter 3 and by the needs of others. God gave Adam and Eve the earth "to fill and to subdue" (Gn 1:28) but also "to cultivate and care for it" (Gn 2:15).[26]

Two considerations show that these limitations on property rights which the Church has consistently recognized do not cancel the right to private ownership of productive property.[27] The first is that some necessary *uses* of material goods also require ownership. A farmer for example, like a tenant farmer, who has the use of land to make a living, is insecure, because the owner can end the lease or sell or give the land to another less just owner, with the loss of the improvements made by the tenant's labor. "The poor man toils for a meager substance, and if ever he rests, he finds himself in want" (Si 31:4).

Again, an artisan who invents some new object which he wishes to make with materials and tools that are only rented, is not free to experiment with what he does not own. Consequently, under communism there is a hindrance to initiative, invention, and experiment, since

---

[24] CA # 6-7.

[25] CA # 37; CCC # 2415-2418, 2456-2457.

[26] NAB translates the two Hebrew verbs "cultivate and care"; J.B. Westermann, *Genesis 1-11*, p. 181, cf. pp. 220-222, translates them "to till and watch over" and Cassuto, *Genesis*, vol. 1, pp. 122-123, "to dress it and keep it." Yet Cassuto seems to favor the rabbinic view that the first verb can mean "serve" in the sense of "worship," since this is paralleled in Near Eastern texts. Westermann, p. 220 argues that for the Bible work as such is not a punishment for sin, but intrinsic to human nature. "The 'blissful enjoyment' in paradise [without work, which some exegetes assume was the condition of Adam and Eve before the Fall] comes from an understanding of humanity which undervalues manual work over against the activities of spirit and mind, because it is too clearly bound to material objects. But this is completely foreign to Gen 2:3."

[27] CA # 30; CCC # 2402-2406, 2452.

permission must always be sought from public authority to do anything new with resources. "While breath of life is still in you, let no man have dominion over you. Give not to another your wealth, lest then you have to beg from him... Keep control over your own affairs" (Si 33:21, 22).[28]

Thus the original title of labor implies that for human beings fully to exercise their personal creativity, they must not only be able to use but also to own some productive property of their own. Aristotle pointed out that Plato, the first great advocate of communism, due to his excessive spiritualism, neglected the reality of matter and the pluralism of which it is the principle, and attempted to over-unify and centralize society.[29] The existence of many bodily members of a society means that the unity of society must be loose enough to permit individual initiative and independent action especially in relation to material goods.

To this basic philosophical reason for private property the Bible adds the doctrine of original sin, which says that as a result of the fall, human beings struggle with selfishness and self-centeredness, so that it is unrealistic to expect that in most cases they will be able to achieve sufficient unity and harmony to work in close cooperation in the use of goods. Such harmony is to be found only in highly motivated religious communities.

Hence in the Old Law a balance is achieved between the acquisition of private property on the one hand by the hard-work and prudence so often praised in the Wisdom literature (e.g., the praise of the industrious ant in Pr 6:6-11; cf. 24:30-34) and on the other hand its limitation by the sabbatical year (Lv 25) when all debts were to be canceled. In the New Testament we have the simple Pauline rules:

> We instructed you that if anyone was unwilling to work, neither should that one eat (2 Th 3:10; cf. 1 Th 4:11-12). The thief must

---

[28] For the text and commentary on these verses see Skehan-Di Lella, *Wisdom of Ben Sira*, pp. 403, 405; the general sense is, however, clear enough. These verses, of course, must be understood as expressing the principle of subsidiarity, not as denying all authority. On the right of initiative in economic matters see CCC # 2429.

[29] *Politics*, II, 5-6, 1262b 38 - 1264a 11.

no longer steal, but rather labor, doing honest work with his own
hands, so that he may have something to share with one in need
(Eph 4:28).

Thus, the right of private property does not imply that there is a
right to accumulate hoards of private property, or to retain a control
over its use that excludes others from using it to meet their needs. Only
in a situation of unlimited abundance of material goods could one grow
vastly rich without depriving others of what they really need, and this
cannot be achieved even by modern "miracles" of technology, since
we have discovered that there is always a price to pay for technological
advance and have not been able to eliminate all poverty.[30]

Material and Immaterial Property

What can we own? Goods are material or immaterial. Material goods
are mobile or immobile and mobile goods are consumable or not, and
"fungible" (i.e. one unit able to substitute for another, as one bushel of
wheat for any other bushel of wheat) or not. We do not own our own
persons, neither our material body nor our immaterial soul, since only
the Creator gave these and only he has full dominion over them. "Think!
The heavens, even the highest heavens, belong to the Lord, your God,
as well as the earth and everything on it" (Dt 10:14), but from God we
have rightful use of our faculties in accordance with the purposes for
which God made them: "The Lord from the earth created man and in
his own image he made him... He endows man with a strength of his
own, and with power over all things else on earth" (Si 17:1, 3; cf. Gn
1:26, 28; Ps 8). Properly speaking our ownership is of external, material goods. As human persons, we have full, permanent dominion of
the goods we own and the results of our work as these are necessary to
attain our true goals in life and care for our families.

We do not, however, have any dominion over or claim to the
goods of eternal life which we can only receive as gifts from God. "For

---

[30] CA # 31.

by grace you have been saved through faith, and this is not from you; it is the gift of God; it is not from works, so that no one may boast" (Eph 2:9). Yet there is also a strict property right in certain goods that are *intermediate* between material and spiritual goods, namely the intangible goods of fame, honor, and reputation. As Sirach says of the damage done by the slanderer:

> A blow from a whip raises a welt,
>> but a blow from the tongue smashes bones;
> Many have fallen by the edge of the sword,
>> but not as many as by the tongue.
> Happy he who is sheltered from it
>> and has not endured its wrath (Si 28:17-19a).

While Christians should forgive those who defame them, yet when this causes scandal or injures the rights of others, they should refute these false accusations. Thus a priest, when innocent, should defend his character in order that the Church not suffer (see the example of St. Paul, 2 Cor 10:13), and a business man his reputation for honesty to prevent injury to his corporation or his family. "My son, with humility have self-esteem; prize yourself as you deserve. Who will acquit him who condemns himself? Who will honor him who discredits himself?" (Si 10:27-28).

There are also certain property rights in such immaterial goods as *ideas* when these are expressed in writing, works of art, inventions, etc. These are recognized in law by patent and copyright laws and other laws that protect creativity. This is justified in order to protect the livelihood of writers, artists, and inventors since it is for the common good that such creative persons should be able to live and work in a society. The "brain-drain" of such talent and genius from countries that do not have such protective laws can do serious damage.

Property in Persons?

If we have only a qualified ownership of spiritual goods, can we have dominion over other human persons? We cannot have ownership of them in the sense of using them simply as means to our own good, because all persons are ends in themselves.[31] Social authority or dominion is always for the sake of the common good and of the person as a member of the common good, never for the sake of the authority, who is always in a position of service. For social officials to use their positions for their own aggrandizement is *tyranny*. "Like a roaring lion or a ravenous bear is a wicked ruler over a poor people" (Pr 28:15).

What then of slavery? The Old Law accepted the institution of slavery common to all ancient societies (in democratic Athens half the population were slaves) and permitted the enslavement of non-Hebrews taken in war and of Hebrew bondsmen who put themselves in slavery in payment of a debt (indenture), but the sabbatical year ended indenture and the Law limited the institution in other humane ways (Ex 20:17; 21:2-11; Lv 25:39-55; Dt 15:12-18).[32]

The early Church, living in the Roman Empire where slavery was an essential part of the economic system, did not condemn slavery as a social institution.[33] However, it insisted that the master treat the slave as "a most dear brother," as St. Paul says in the Epistle to Philemon, which obviously means to consider the slave as a member of the household who shares in the common good (cf. 1 Cor 7:21-24; Eph 6:5-9; Col 3:22-4:1; 1 Tm 6:1-2; 1 P 2:18). Jesus had himself come to the world "taking the form of a slave" (Ph 2:7) and taught his disciples that:

> "Whoever wishes to be first among you will be the slave of all.
> For the Son of Man did not come to be served but to serve and to
> give his life as a ransom for many" (Mk 10:44).

Hence, early Christians saw no shame in being a slave.

Aristotle had argued[34] that, since in the societies of the economic

---

[31] CCC # 2414.

[32] For the pervasive effects of slavery on culture in the period of the early Church see, Philippe Ariès and Georges Dubay, *A History of Private Life*, Paul Veyne, ed., vol. 1. Index, "slavery," p. 669.

[33] See my Notre Dame Ph.D. dissertation, Winston Ashley, *The Theory of Natural Slavery According to Aristotle and St.Thomas.*

[34] *Politics*, I, c. 3-7, 1253a 1 - 1256a 1 on slavery.

level which he knew it was not possible to give all members an education that would fit them to be free citizens, it was better for the uneducated to be slaves sharing in the well-ordered life of the household, than free artisans who did not have that opportunity. We can better understand these arguments if today we consider the under-class of our cities which lives in misery and neglect because it has no recognized role in society.

Aquinas modified this argument and argued[35] that slavery is in accordance with the natural law in the same way as private property; that is, it is natural not in the original order of creation but by the *jus gentium* for fallen man. Therefore, he thought it was justified only on two titles: (1) as a punishment for engaging in an unjust war, since it was more merciful to enslave rather than to kill the defeated aggressors; (2) as a hereditary status in which the children of slaves followed the social condition of their parents.[36] This view assumed the medieval situation where social mobility from class to class was economically difficult.

While the Church always insisted that slaves of whatever race are persons with primary human rights, only in the nineteenth century did it come to realize fully that the age-old legalization of slavery by secular governments was so radically inconsistent with its own teachings on natural law and human dignity that it could no longer be tolerated, just as today it is pondering whether capital punishment is ever right. Hence, the Church's moral teaching has sometimes to change to remain true to the Gospel's unchanging principles. "Every scribe who has been instructed in the kingdom of heaven is like the head of a household who brings from his storeroom both the new and the old" (Mt 13:52; cf. Mt 9:16-17).[37]

The principle involved in this doctrinal development is that no human being can have full dominion over another human being because of their equality in basic rights, but that in appropriate circum-

---

[35] *S.T.*, II-II, q. 57, a. 3 ad 2; cf. I-II, q. 2, a. 4 ad 3; q. 94, a. 5 ad 3.

[36] *IV Sent.*, d. 36, q. 1, a. 4.

[37] CA # 54-55.

stances there can be dominion as regards secondary rights, provided these do not infringe primary rights. The Church never condoned killing slaves, forbidding them to marry, or sexually exploiting them, because that is contrary to a primary right; but it did permit the restriction of their residence and employment, because freedom in this regard is a secondary right.

C: COMMUTATIVE JUSTICE

Kinds of Justice

Because in human society there are three basic relationships — of the members to the community, of the community to the members, and of the members to each other — there are only three species of justice.[38] First, *legal* justice or the debt of the individual to the community paid by observing its laws. Second, *distributive* justice or the debt of the community to share the common good among its individual members. Third, *commutative* (exchange) justice or the debts of the individual members to each other: "When you sell any land to your neighbor or buy any from him, do not deal unfairly" (Lv 25:14). Legal and distributive justice are today commonly grouped together as *social* justice.[39]

I will first consider commutative justice because it demands absolute (arithmetic) equality between the debt and the repayment; while social and distributive justice demand only a relative (geometric) equality, as we shall see. This is why commutative justice, but not the other two species, demands *restitution*, i.e., full repayment. Commutative justice is required in two kinds of cases: fair recompense for wrongful *injuries* (called in law *torts*) and the fulfillment of *contracts*.

---

[38] CCC # 2411.
[39] CCC # 1928-1472.

Injuries

A formal sin of injustice is a voluntary and effective violation of the rights of another, either as regards their person or property. Thus the prophet Jeremiah denounced the leaders of his time:

> They grow powerful and rich,
> fat and sleek.
> They go their wicked way;
> justice they do not defend
> By advancing the claim of the fatherless
> or judging the cause of the poor (Jr 6:27b-28).

And Jesus denounced the self-righteous Pharisees of his time: "They devour the houses of widows and, as a pretext, recite lengthy prayers" (Mk 12:40).

An injury that is not voluntary is said to be *material* and is not sinful, but in some cases may require compensation. We cannot do an injustice to someone who knows and consents to what we do (although we may sin against them in other ways), nor by making use of another's property which the owner is *unreasonably* unwilling for us to use (e.g., to cross his property in a emergency), nor does the mere intention to injure constitute an injustice. Yet we can injure another's rights not only in actions and in words, but even in thought (e.g., rash judgment). We may infringe someone's rights without doing any actual damage, as for example, opening another's mail that contains nothing secret.

The gravity of the sin of injustice is to be judged from the gravity of the injury or damage done. Thus to steal someone's pencil does only a slight damage and is a venial sin, to steal his car is a mortal sin. That injustice can be a mortal sin, contradictory to love of God and neighbor, cutting us off from them and condemning us to hell, is clear in the Bible, since Jesus says in answer to the young man who asks him:

> "Teacher, what good must I do to gain eternal life?"
> "If you wish to enter into life, keep the commandments."

When the young man asks him "Which ones?" Jesus replies, "You shall not kill, etc." referring to the Ten Commandments of the Torah

(Ex 20:13-17; Mt 19:17-18) which lists the principal kinds of injustice. Also St. Paul, when warning against certain kinds of acts, many of which violate human rights, says, "Do you not know that the unjust will not inherit the kingdom of God?" (1 Cor 6:8-10).

Justice requires us both to do good, and avoid evil so that we do not commit injustice either by commission or omission. Thus Jesus in the great concluding Sermon on the Judgment (Mt 25:31-46) speaks both of caring for the poor and of their neglect:

> " 'Amen, I say to you, whatever you did for one of these least brothers of mine, you did it for me... [and] what you did not do for one of the least ones, you did not do it for me.' And these will go off to eternal punishment, the righteous to eternal life" (Mt 25:40b, 45).

We have already seen many biblical passages relating to commutative justice, such as wages and the repayment of loans. I will next treat of injury to the lives of persons, and then of injury to their property.

Injuries to Persons

The Scriptures again and again praise and thank the Creator for the gift of life:

> How precious is your kindness, O God!
> The children of men take refuge in the shadow of your wings.
> They have their fill of the prime gifts of your house;
> from your delightful stream you give them to drink.
> For with you is the fountain of life,
> and in your light we see light (Ps 36:8-10).

Since life, spiritual and bodily, is one of the four basic human needs, it is intrinsically and therefore *always* unjust directly (that is, intentionally) to do injury to the life of human persons except as a punishment necessary for their spiritual good or the common good of society.

Spiritual injury can be still more serious than injury to bodily life. This is why the Church has always regarded propagating heresy or schism as very serious injustices to the innocent persons led into these errors. "There will be false teachers among you, who will introduce destructive heresies and even deny the Master who ransomed them, bringing swift destruction on themselves" (2 P 2:1). But even in secular courts today damages are assessed for psychological trauma caused by unjust acts, for libel, and even the spread of false information.

Murder

Any killing of a human being raises a grave moral problem and the Fifth Commandment simply says, "You shall not kill" (Dt 5:17). The respect for human dignity created in God's image is already reflected in Genesis: when the first murder, that of Abel by Cain, occurred (Gn 4:1-16), God did not kill him, but placed a mark on his head as a warning, and said, "If anyone kills Cain, Cain shall be avenged sevenfold," indicating that God wished to check at once the human tendency for one killing to lead to others out of revenge. But after the flood, God says to Noah, "If anyone sheds the blood of man, by man shall his blood be shed; For in the image of God has man been made" (Gn 9:6), indicating that in a world become very evil, retribution is necessary.

Hence, it is clear that it is always wrong to kill a human being who is doing or has done no serious harm to others, as Abel had not harmed his brother Cain, but simply occasioned his envy. To do so is the very grave sin of *murder* which the Church considers one of the "sins that cry to heaven for punishment."[40] "Then the Lord asked Cain, 'Where is your bother Abel? ... What have you done! Listen: Your brother's blood cries out to me from the soil!'" (Gn 4:9a-10).

Yet, when we read in the Book of Exodus how God through Moses commanded his people, "You shall not kill" (Ex 20:13), we find that in the very next chapter the same God also commanded his people, "Whoever strikes a man must be put to death" (Ex 21: 12)! No wonder there is much disagreement in society today about how this commandment not to kill applies. Therefore, it is necessary to analyze different

---

[40] CCC # 1867.

types of homicide in some detail and then other kinds of injuries to persons less than death. I will first discuss two kinds of cases in which there is current disagreement as to whether or not the victim is a subject of human rights: (a) a human fetus; (b) a non-human animal.

Abortion

An old opinion, supported by the Jewish rabbinical tradition,[41] held that abortion to save the life of the mother was a case of self-defense from an aggressor. The Bible contains no specific statement concerning abortion. Exodus 21:22 only concerns damages for a miscarriage resulting accidentally during a fight (*pharmakeia* listed in Gal 5:20 among the sins of the flesh may refer to use of abortifacient drugs).[42] From the *Didache* written at the end of the first century or the beginning of the second, early Christian literature condemned abortion and infanticide, and this has been the constant tradition of the Church; the only disagreements being about how to classify the sin or how to apply the principle of double-effect in certain difficult cases.[43]

In Jesus' time not only abortion but infanticide was common. The Lord's incarnate existence in Mary's womb (Lk 1:39-45), his blessing of little children (Mt 10:13), and the practice of infant baptism[44] was understood by the Church as showing the dignity of the child and its rights. If the child once born has these rights, why not before it is

---

[41] On rabbinic views on abortion see Sir Immanuel Jakobvits, *Jewish Medical Ethics*, pp. 170-191.

[42] See John T. Noonan, Jr., "An Almost Absolute Value in History" in *The Morality of Abortion: Legal and Historical Perspectives*, pp. 1-59, who in a note on page 8 quotes Clyde Phare, "The Interdiction of Magic in Roman Law," *Transactions and Proceedings of the American Philological Association* 63 (1932): 272-73 as showing that to translate *pharmakeia* as "sorceries" (as does the revised NAB) is an error. On the prevalence of abortion and infanticide in Greco-Roman culture see Philippe Ariès and Georges Dubay, *A History of Private Life*, Paul Veyne, ed., vol. 1, pp. 9-32.

[43] CCC # 2270-75. For the history of Church teaching on abortion see the essay of Noonan cited in the previous note.

[44] CCC # 1252, 1282. On the debate about this topic see Joachim Jeremias, *Infant Baptism in the First Four Centuries*, and criticism by Kurt Aland, *Did the Early Church Baptize Infants?*

born? It already actually exists as an organism distinct from its mother, though dependent on her, even as it remains still very much dependent for long after birth. The "pro-choice" arguments for abortion generally are based on the assumption, refuted above, which says that human rights are not inherent in the person but are assigned to the person by society. Thus the child has a natural right to develop within the mother and cannot be called an aggressor, but is an innocent human being which has a right to its natural and necessary sustenance from the mother. Hence its life cannot be directly destroyed for the sake of the mother, since mother and child have *equal* rights to life.

The Church's condemnation of abortion does *not* depend, be it noted, on the question as to whether life begins at conception (i.e., completed fertilization of the ovum, not implantation as some physicians define "conception"), although *this is now the only view that is scientifically probable.*[45] Even in the Middle Ages when science held that human life begins only a month or so after conception, the Church still condemned direct abortion as mortally sinful and equivalent to murder for two reasons: (1) The doubt as to when human life begins entails a serious *risk* of murder; (2) To destroy the embryo, which even if it were not human, yet is certainly developing into a human being, is a mortal sin against God's dominion over human life. While this would not be murder technically, it is akin to murder, and is reducible to the Fifth Commandment.

---

[45] The efforts of some today to revive the old notion of "delayed hominization" — i.e., that the human "pre-embryo," embryo, or fetus is not a human person endowed with the same rights as a child after delivery or an adult — is contradicted by all presently known biological evidence that the human individual comes into existence at conception and continues to exist until total brain death. See Benedict M. Ashley, O.P., and Albert S. Moraczewski, O.P., "Is the Biological Subject of Human Rights Present from Conception." See also S. Congregation for the Doctrine of the Faith, "Instruction on Respect for Human Life in its Origin and on the Dignity of Procreation," *Donum Vitae* (Rome: Vatican Polyglot Press, 1987), I, n. 1.

Animal Rights

It is odd indeed that today when so many doubt that the unborn child has rights, or at least rights equal to the already born, that there should be others who believe we should grant an equal right to life to non-human animals as to human ones. Christian respect for God-given human dignity extends proportionately to all God's creatures including sub-human animals and plants as wonderful works of the Divine Wisdom which like any work of art deserve care.[46] One has only to read Psalm 104 or the magnificent poetry of Job 38-40 to see how the Bible praises the wonders of animal life and God's providential care for his creatures. If we are stewards of God's creation can we give them any less love?

Cruelty to non-human animals tends also to brutalize us and leads to cruelty to humans. Hence, we read in Genesis the symbolic story of how God until after the Flood did not permit the killing and eating of animals, but only of plants, to teach us respect for life, "which is in the blood" (Gn 9:3-4). Jesus also in the Sermon on the Mount marvels at the order and beauty of animals and plants (Mt 6:26-30) as had the scribes of the Wisdom literature (e.g., Si 39:12-35; 43:1-35).

Nevertheless, "moral rights" in the sense I have defined them are grounded in the fact that human beings are *persons*, i.e., beings with spiritual intelligence and free will. Animals can experience pain and pleasure and have feelings. They can act by instinct and learn certain new patterns of behavior. They can communicate with each other by certain signs. These facts do not prove that they have intelligence and free will comparable to that of human beings, since they never invent a culture or a true syntactical language as do human beings and hence give no evidence of the kind of abstract thought which is proper to spiritual persons.[47]

Thus it is perhaps not so paradoxical after all that those who

---

[46] CCC # 2417-2418.

[47] The widely disseminated notion that apes can be taught to communicate is analyzed in Thomas A. Sebeok and Jean Umiker-Sebeok, eds., *Speaking Apes: A Critical Anthology of Two-Way Communication with Man* and the difficulty shown of eliminating unconscious cues given by the human partner.

defend abortion on the grounds that an early embryo feels no pain often defend the "right" of animals not to suffer pain. Their erroneous assumption is that the basis of rights is the capacity for pain and pleasure. In fact, as we have shown, it rests on a much more profound principle, namely, spiritual personhood. If the ability to feel pain were the basis of human rights, it would not be murder for a doctor to kill a patient once the patient was anesthetized! Hence, as Gn 1:26 teaches, humankind created in God's image, has dominion over all other living things and can use them to meet human needs provided they do so in cooperation with God's plan for creation.

Suicide

I will next treat of cases which certainly involve human persons, but ones whose condition in life is such that some hold it were better that they be killed than live — and first those who think it is best to kill themselves. It might seem that suicide, i.e., killing oneself or helping another to kill him or herself, involves no injustice since it is not an injury to another. But this is not the case, since in fact it has serious consequences for those closely related to the suicide and to society.

Suicide must be evaluated as intrinsically wrong and therefore always mortally sinful if done freely and deliberately, as would seem to be the case in such instances related in the Bible like that of Saul (1 S:31:3-6; 2 S 1:6-10) and Judas (Mt 27:3-10; Ac 1:18-19).[48] Probably, however, in most cases suicides are persons whose mental condition is such that they are not free and hence their responsibility is removed or greatly reduced. The Church in the past often refused Christian burial to suicides on the assumption they were responsible for their act and with hope to deter others from self-destruction. Today, with better psychological information, suicides are usually permitted a regular funeral Mass and Christian burial and the *Catechism of the Catholic Church* urges us not to despair of their salvation.[49]

---

[48] Perhaps even Saul, since he was often depressed (1 S 17:14-15), was not wholly responsible for his own death! Also note the catastrophic conditions in which this suicide took place. On suicide see CCC # 2280-2283.

[49] CCC # 2282-2283.

Objectively, however, suicide is a grave injury first of all to God, who as author of our life alone has full dominion over it.

> Learn then that I, I alone, am God, and there is no god besides me. It is I who bring both death and life, I who inflict wounds and heal them, and from my hand there is no rescue (Dt 32:39).

> O Lord, for you have dominion over life and death; you lead down to the gates of the nether world, and lead back. Man, however, slays in his malice, but when the spirit has come away, it does not return, nor can he bring back the soul once it is confined. But your hand none can escape (Ws 16:13-15).

Second, suicide is an injury to oneself since all things naturally seek to preserve themselves. Third, it is an injury to society and to one's family and friends from whose service suicides remove themselves without their family and community's consent and without fulfilling all the suicide's obligations to them.

Even in ancient times it was argued by the Stoics, and now again by such organizations as the Hemlock Society that a person should have the right to decide when he or she is to die (*euthanasia* or "good death"). Examples given include persons facing great suffering or prolonged incapacity to function well, or disgrace or loneliness, or a spy who might reveal important secrets under torture, or protesters against injustice like the Buddhists who set themselves on fire, or soldiers who commit suicide to defeat their country's enemies like the Japanese *kamikaze* pilots. The examples of the martyrs, some of whom seem to have sought martyrdom, even the example of Jesus who refused to defend himself, have been used to support euthanasia. This argument from martyrdom is invalid because Jesus and all true martyrs have not sought their death nor caused it, but have only refused to give up witnessing to the truth of the Gospel in spite of the fact that they knew others would kill them.

But what of the biblical examples of two men in the Maccabean wars, Eleazar, called Avaran, who stabbed an attacking elephant in the belly and was crushed in its fall (1 M 6:42-46) and Razis who "caught on all sides, turned his sword against himself, preferring to die nobly rather than fall into the hands of vile men and suffer outrages unworthy

of his noble birth" (2 M 14:37-46)? The first of these examples, like
that of the Japanese *kamikaze* pilots is open to debate since it is not
clear that these soldiers really intended to kill themselves, but rather to
attack the enemy although the risk to their lives was almost certainly
fatal. As for the second, the Bible explicitly states Razis' motivation
and relates it as an evidence of the desperate courage and faith of the
Maccabees. However, such examples of the Old Testament in general,
as we have often pointed out, are not to be taken as perfect moral norms,
unless confirmed by the teaching of the New Testament or at least in
harmony with it, which the act of Razis is not.

Euthanasia

The claim to a "right to die" is a claim to have full dominion over one's
own life, which, as we have seen, is contrary to the Christian conviction that only the God who gave life has such a dominion. It also shows
a lack of faith in God who will help us live the life he gave us to its very
end in such a way that even our suffering will contribute to our spiritual
welfare or that of others.[50]

> But rejoice that you share in the sufferings of Christ, so that
> when his glory is revealed, you may also rejoice exultantly...
> Let those who suffer in accord with God's will do right and
> entrust their souls to a faithful Creator (1 P 4:13, 19).

Moreover, medical treatments are now available to us which can
prevent severe pain without killing, although not always with the re-
tention of mental functioning or without some risk to life. For others to
cooperate with suicide on the plea that this is "mercy killing" or "assisted suicide" is equally wrong. It is also sometimes more motivated
by a desire not to suffer oneself from watching another suffer than from
a concern for the other's real welfare.

Euthanasia should not be confused with a decision made either
by a person or, when they are incompetent, by their guardians not to

---

[50] CCC # 2276-2279, 2324.

employ "extraordinary" means to maintain life, but rather to allow some pathology from which the person suffers to take its natural course to death. An extraordinary means is one which in the concrete circumstances of the person is of so little benefit in enabling the person to recover or to perform conscious human functions that it does not justify the burdens it places on the patient and on those who must care for the patient. Finally, it should be pointed out that to desire and pray for death, provided it is with a good motive and with resignation to God's will, is not sinful.[51] Sirach says, "Preferable is death to a bitter life, unending sleep to constant illness" (Si 30:17), and St. Paul says:

> If I go on living in the flesh, that is fruitful labor for me. And I do not know which to choose. I am caught between the two. I long to depart this life and be with Christ, for that is far better. Yet that I remain in the flesh is more necessary for your benefit (Ph 1:22-24).

Eugenic Killing and Genocide

In Nazi Germany there was widespread acceptance even among the medical profession of the claim that it was justifiable to put to death persons who were mentally ill or defective or suffering from other severe disabilities or incurable debilitating diseases, especially if these had a genetic origin, in order to relieve the burden of such persons on the nation and to improve the genetic quality of the population (*eugenics*). Thus not only did the government attempt to eliminate Jews, but also Gypsies, persons of Slavic origin, etc., and exterminated many senile and otherwise "useless" people in hospitals.[52]

More recently, we have seen horrible examples of "ethnic cleansing" in Bosnia and Rwanda, and other similar tragedies can be found throughout human history and in the Bible itself. In fact it would seem from the texts in the Torah concerning "holy war" and the "ban" (*herem*,

---

[51] S. Congregation for the Doctrine of the Faith, *Declaration on Euthanasia*, May 5, 1980. See CCC # 2278.

[52] See Robert Jay Lifton, *The Nazi Doctors*.

Dt 7:1-11, etc.) that the God of the Old Testament himself commanded the Hebrews to subject the pagan people occupying the Holy Land to genocide! Because this is an issue of "holy war" I will discuss it later when I take up the question of the "just war theory." Suffice it here to say that this command belongs to a stage of moral development which is completely overcome in the New Testament by Jesus' command, "Love your enemies; and pray for those who persecute you" (Mt 5:44), and cannot be used today to justify any form of eugenic or genocidal killing.

The argument for getting rid of "useless" people is based on the false assumption, which I have exposed several times already, that human worth (dignity) and human rights rest on special gifts or qualities of individuals other than the simple fact that they were created in the image of God as members of the human species. As for the notion that it is practical to improve the genetic heritage of a population by killing persons with undesirable genes, this has been thoroughly disproved by modern biology, which has shown that any such program would eliminate any given genetic defect from a population very slowly, would not prevent it from soon returning, and would at the same time eliminate many desirable traits.[53]

Similarly, the attempts to justify "ethnic cleansing" depend on false racialist theories or an exaggerated nationalism supported by unjust war. Again, human rights are not based on issues of racial superiority or inferiority nor on nationality, but on the equal personhood of all human beings.

Self-defense

I will next consider cases in which homicide is justified on the grounds of defending oneself or others from aggression. First it must be asked: May a private person kill someone in self-defense or to defend another?[54] The words of Jesus already quoted (Mt 6:38-48) indicate that

---

[53] On the illusion of "eugenics" see Albert Jacquard, *In Praise of Difference: Genetics and Human Affairs.*

[54] CCC # 2263-2266.

it is of counsel to let oneself be injured, rather than to injure an aggressor, the reason being that we must love even our enemies as ourselves. Nevertheless, this is a counsel, not a precept, and therefore does not remove the natural right of self-preservation provided that the means used in defending one's life or some good equivalent to life are not more harmful than is absolutely necessary (*moderamine inculpatae tutelae*) to insure one's safety. Thus only the prevention of the aggression not the death of the aggressor must be intended. Therefore, the frustration of the aggressive act not the killing of the agent is the means to self-defense, and the killing of the aggressor is, when unavoidable, *indirect.*

The phrase "one's life or some good equivalent to life" is not easy to define and Alexander VII and Innocent XI had to reject lax opinions on the matter.[55] Probably it is justifiable to kill someone to save an organ of one's body or one's mental sanity, but it is disputed by moralists whether this is ever permitted merely to save one's material possessions or one's reputation.[56]

To kill in defense of another is permitted only in an emergency when police protection is unavailable. In such a case a citizen acts not as a private person but as a delegate of public authority.

Dueling and Exhibitions of Skill

Sometimes homicide is justified not so much as a defense of one's life as of one's honor or simply as an exhibition of skill. Thus in the not distant past *dueling* was widely accepted in polite society because the aristocracy was originally a military class which believed it had an obligation to defend its "honor" when insulted. Even in our American democracy it was still common until after the Civil War. A gentleman was bound by this custom to defend his honor or that of his family (or

---

[55] DS # 2038, 2131-2132.

[56] It would seem that killing a robber can be justified if there is grave risk that he will also do serious bodily harm to his victims, but not merely to avoid the loss of material possessions.

even his mistress!) against any insults from another gentleman by the use of sword or pistol. While this was often a mere formality, it did involve at least the risk of death, and as such was condemned by the Church, because private individuals have no authority to inflict capital punishment.

Also homicide has often been risked in the exhibition of the martial arts or other dangerous competitions. The Church in its early days fought against the pagan gladiatorial combats, in the Middle Ages against the chivalric tournaments and civic feuds, and from the Council of Trent against duels, excommunicating all who participated in them, even the "seconds."[57] Moralists generally have doubted the morality of professional boxing, of the bull-fighting popular in Hispanic culture, of speed-car racing, and of various kinds of stunting in which there is serious risk of death or grave bodily injury.

Specific evaluation of such dangerous activities is beyond the scope of this book, but it is sufficient to say here that their morality depends on whether human skill is able to reduce the danger to a minimum. It is clearly immoral for people to seek entertainment in sports where the pleasure is not in the skill but in the injury or death of human beings. What has to be balanced is the admiration for courage and skill consonant with human dignity against the cheapening of human life.

There has often been a great deal of support for dueling and similar homicidal activities which the Church has condemned or at least sought to discourage. This is a good example of the fact that popular opinion, which approved such duels as noble and honorable, is not of itself the *sensus fidelium*, or the *vox Dei*, but requires to be instructed by the pastors of the Church witnessing authoritatively to the Gospel.

Police Action and Just War

Granted the right of self-defense, few would question that the State has the right and a duty to deter crime by the use of force through a disciplined police. The early Church, although it suffered much from the

---

[57] DS # 799, 1111, 1113, 1240, 1830, 2022, 2351, 2571-2575, 3162, 3272-3273.

Roman police, nevertheless supported the right of the State to enforce its laws and the duty of Christians to obey them. In passages that I have quoted before, St. Paul says that the State "does not bear the sword without a purpose, it is the servant of God to inflict wrath on the evildoer" (Rm 13:4b), and 1 Peter (2:14) says that the State is "sent by him [God] for the punishment of evildoers and the approval of those who do good."[58] That police power is often abused, however, is also notorious. The police are morally obliged to act within the law, to act impartially, to use no more force than is necessary to defend themselves, prevent crime, or retain a prisoner, and they must refrain from torture, cruelty, and other similar abuses.

Far more serious is the question of the employment of force between nations. Can *war*, which is usually justified on the grounds of the self-defense, not of individuals, but of nations, ever be just?[59] Today some Christians are *pacifists*, claiming that in teaching us to "turn the other cheek," Jesus forbade all use of force. Others accept the use of moderate force by the police, but reject war.

The early Church, before Christians had secular public responsibilities, although it accepted police force, often discouraged Christians from entering the army.[60] The medieval Manichees, and later Wycliff, Erasmus, many of the "peace churches" of the Radical Reformation, and the Quakers of a later period, claimed military service to be forbidden to Christians. Some French Catholics in the Second World War opposed the Resistance by arguing that the nation's sins required submission to the Nazis as a punishment.[61]

Nevertheless, such great Doctors of the Church as St. Ambrose, St. Augustine, and St. Gregory the Great taught that in extreme neces-

---

[58] See William Klassen, "War in the New Testament," ABD, VI:867-875 with its bibliography, pp. 874-875. On p. 869 he points out that the Septuagint translated the title "a man of war" applied to God in Ex 15:3, Is 42:13, and Jdt 9:7, 16:3 as "he who destroys war," thus indicating a doctrinal development among the Jews in the Hellenistic period toward non-violence.

[59] CCC # 2302-2317, 2327-2330.

[60] See J. T. Johnson, *Just War Tradition and the Restraint of War: A Moral and Historical Inquiry* and William O'Brien, *The Conduct of Just and Limited War*.

[61] On the various attitudes in France to submission to the Nazi regime see Robert Aron, *The Vichy Regime, 1940-44*, "The National Revolution: Doctrine," pp. 145-148.

sity the State has the responsibility to wage a just war.[62] This position is not necessarily inconsistent with the advocacy of non-violence such as that of Gandhi and Martin Luther King, Jr., nor with "conscientious objection" to military service by Christians, since modern war is commonly conducted with the use of unjust means.[63]

Oddly today many who advocate pacifism, at the same time seem sympathetic to the Marxist notion of the class-struggle or anti-colonial uprisings which use violent means. Anarchists, such as Kropotkin and Tolstoy, have urged that the State be abolished because it inevitably uses force and thus becomes oppressive and unjust. Therefore they advocated a non-violent social order based solely on voluntary cooperation.[64] In fact Marx, although he believed revolutionary force to be necessary to overthrow capitalism, agreed with the anarchists in hoping for a non-violent, stateless, classless, cooperative democracy. Gandhi and Martin Luther King, Jr., without adopting the whole program of anarchism, believed that revolutionary reforms in society were best accomplished by non-violent means. These advocates of non-violence were only repeating Jesus' teaching, but failed to take into account Christian realism about the fallen human condition. Until the coming of God's Reign on earth there will always remain at least the possibility of unjust aggression and the need to oppose it by force.

Jesus counseled that it is better for one not to resist attack out of love for one's enemies (Mt 5:38-48), and practiced this counsel himself when he forbade Peter to defend him, saying, "Put your sword back into its sheath, for all who take the sword will perish by the sword" (Mt 26:52). Yet, as we have seen, St. Paul (Rm 13:4b) and the First Epistle of St. Peter (2:14) prove that the early Church acknowledged not only the right but the obligation of the State to use force to maintain law and order. This also implies that individuals in an emergency when

---

[62] St. Ambrose (*De Officiis*, I, c. 40); St. Augustine (*De Civitate Dei*, XXII, c. 74); and St. Gregory the Great (*Epistles*, 72; PL 77:441-1328).

[63] See Mahatma Gandhi, *Non-violence in Peace and War, 1942-1949*, 2 vols., and James P. Hanigan, *Martin Luther King, Jr. and the Foundations of Nonviolence*.

[64] See pp. 282 ff.

the State cannot protect them have the right to defend themselves and others by force.

Hence, the words of Jesus just quoted must be understood not as a universal *precept*, but as a *counsel* to be followed as a way of perfection by individuals when the protection of third parties is not in question. That is, when only one's own safety is at stake, it is a Christ-like act of love for one's enemy to let oneself be injured by that enemy than to injure him. Old Testament sayings about "holy war" were then interpreted in a spiritual sense:

> For, although we are in the flesh, we do not battle according to the flesh, for the weapons of our battle are not flesh but are enormously powerful, capable of destroying fortresses (2 Cor 10:3-4).

In the Book of Revelation (5:1-7) the Messiah is at once "the Lion of Judah" and the "Lamb," symbol of non-violence.[65]

Moreover, as the philosopher Jacques Maritain has shown,[66] we can learn from Jesus' non-violence that in the long run non-violence is a more effective means of witnessing to the truth and establishing social justice than are violent means, however necessary they may be in an emergency to stop a particular act of aggression. Jesus said to Peter when he attempted to defend him from his captors, "All who take the sword will perish by the sword" (Mt 26:52), meaning that the use of violence even in a good cause inevitably leads to secondary effects of further hatred, revenge, disorder, and violence, while non-violent, constructive acts lead to conditions of peace and order in which forceful defense becomes unnecessary. The use of force, therefore, can be justified only as a means to stop aggression temporarily so that more constructive means can then be employed.

This right and obligation of defensive war, however, is limited and to be just must fulfill the following conditions.[67]

---

[65] See G.B. Caird, *The Revelation of St. John the Divine* on these verses for discussion on the Lamb and non-violence.

[66] Jacques Maritain, "The Purification of Means," and "The Doctrine of Satyagraha as Set Forth by M.K. Gandhi," *Freedom in the Modern World*, pp. 139-192 and 215-223.

[67] CA # 17-19.

1. It must be declared by the authority of the supreme civil power of a nation;
2. It must be waged only to restore justice and establish peace;
3. It must use only moral means;
4. It must be necessary, the last resort to achieve this just purpose.

This fourth condition assumes that both natural law and international law (written and unwritten *jus gentium*) are observed. It should be noted that soldiers in a just war, or police acting lawfully, unlike private persons acting in self-defense, may, at least in some cases, *directly* intend the death of the enemy, since they act as agents of public authority which has the right and duty not only to prevent but also to *punish* unjust aggression (as will be shown later). This does not mean, however, that the military can act out of hatred of the enemy, nor do injury to the enemy combatants that exceeds what is necessary to stop the aggression.

The natural and divine law requires, as the foregoing conditions indicate, that public authority itself can never justly wage war against non-aggressors, that is, the civil population, even if indirectly their work contributes to the war effort by maintaining normal national life. Since in modern warfare, obliteration and nuclear bombing, as well as the use of other uncontrollable weapons such as lethal gases and contagious diseases, are becoming more and more accepted means, it is difficult to see how war can be justified in our times. It can be argued that it is legitimate to possess such weapons as a deterrence to their use by others, but unless this is accompanied by the most serious efforts to obtain international disarmament agreements, it seems impossible to produce and store such weapons without the real intention to use them if attacked, which is intrinsically and always wrong.[68]

In concluding this section it is necessary to return to the question, often raised as a fundamental accusation against the inspiration of the Old Testament, as to the "holy wars" of the Jews which were not only defensive, but were offensive wars of conquest to drive out the occu-

---

[68] Vatican II condemned "total war" and the use of "weapons of indiscriminate destruction," GS # 80-81. CCC # 2312-2316, 2328-2329.

pants of Palestine in an "ethnic cleansing" which often involved genocide. Through Moses God commands the Israelites:

> "When the Lord, your God, brings you into the land which you
> are to enter and occupy, and dislodges great nations before you
> — the Hittites, Girgashites, Amorites, Canaanites, Perizzites,
> Hivites and Jebusites, seven nations more numerous and power
> ful than you — and when the Lord your God delivers them up to
> you and you defeat them, you shall doom them. Make no cov
> enant with them and show them no mercy. You shall not inter
> marry with them, neither giving your daughters to their sons nor
> taking their daughters for your sons. For they would turn your
> sons from following me to serving other gods, and then the wrath
> of the Lord would flare up and quickly destroy you" (Dt 7:1-4).

What this "doom" (*herem*, ban) meant is clear from the words, "At that time we seized all his [Sihon, King of Hesbon] cities and doomed them all, with their men, women, and children; we left no survivor" (Dt 2:34; cf. Ex 23:23, 35:11-12; Nb 21:3; Dt 3:6, 7:16, 13:16, 20:16; Jos 2:10, 6:16-17, 8:25-26, 10:28, 10:40, 11:11, 21; Jg 1:17; 1 S 15:9-22; 1 K 9:20-21).

These passages need to be read in the light of the doctrine of biblical inspiration, of canonical criticism, and of the relation of the Old to the New Testament explained in Chapter 1.[69] According to current scholarship, the Deuteronomic Torah was edited in the Exilic period long after the actual historical events. Thus, it could not have been intended to direct the Jews in wars of conquest which for them, a conquered people, were no longer a practical possibility. This was recognized by the rabbinical tradition which argued that these commands held only for the unique situation of the entrance into the Promised Land and therefore could never be taken as general moral norms.[70]

The real purpose of these texts was to interpret Israel's history so

---

[69] See pp. 11 ff.

[70] See Haim H. Cohn, "The Penology of the Talmud," in the book which he edited, *Jewish Law in Ancient and Modern Israel*, pp. 61-82 for the ways in which the rabbinical tradition came to interpret the punishment required by the Torah in ever more humane ways.

as to show the disheartened Jews in Exilic times: (1) that Israel's conquest of the Holy Land had not been obtained by their own power and so could not be regained by that power, but only by fidelity to the Covenant; (2) that fidelity to the Covenant would be endangered if they allowed themselves to be assimilated to the pagan culture for the sake of marriage or material benefits. Therefore, the "holy war" of the Torah, freed of its inevitable historical and rhetorical conditioning, must be understood as the inspired Word of God still morally binding today in the light of Jesus' own understanding. The Old Testament, in spite of its teaching on holy war, recognized that even a just war is the occasion of many sins. Thus God told David that although he had fought in God's cause, "You may not build a house in my honor, because you have shed too much blood upon the earth in my sight" (1 Ch 22:8b). As a good Jew, Jesus certainly believed in the inspiration of the Torah, yet in his teaching its command to exterminate the pagans men, women, and children is transformed into the ironic words:

> "Do not think that I have come to bring peace upon the earth. I have not come to bring peace but the sword. For I have come to set a man against his father, a daughter against her mother, and a daughter-in-law against her mother-in-law; and one's enemies will be those of his own household" (Mt 10:34).

In other words, the Christian community today along with its efforts to inculturate itself in our times in order to bring the Gospel to others, must also remain counter-cultural in its fidelity to the New Covenant, even at the cost of sacrificing both material benefits and desirable personal relationships.

One may still ask, of course: Why would God inspire authors in a particular historical epoch to write texts that in future times, taken out of context, could so easily be misunderstood and misused to justify terrible crimes against the natural law and to portray himself as commanding such crimes? The answer to this question, I believe, is that, as the Catholic Church has always held, the Bible is indeed a dangerous book if it is left to "personal interpretation" (2 P 1:20; cf. 15-16) rather than to the tradition of the Church. God inspired the Bible to be read within the Church, not apart from it, so that only when we read it with the "mind of Christ" (1 Cor 2:16) are we listening to the Word of God.

Before going on to the topic of the use of force in punishment, I note that as there are injustices against life by murder, abortion, suicide, euthanasia, and unjust war, so there are also injustices against the basic human right of the transmission of life through procreation. Yet because procreation involves not only commutative justice but also the social relations between members of the family, it is best treated later under social justice.

Capital Punishment?

So far we have been primarily concerned with the use of force, even to homicide, as a means to stop aggression; what of its use as a punishment for injustices already committed? The Torah prescribes many such punishments ranging from fines to capital punishment according to the principle called the *lex talionis*, "You shall give life for life, eye for eye, tooth for tooth, hand for hand, foot for foot, burn for burn, wound for wound, stripe for stripe" (Ex 21:23-25; cf. Lv 24:18-21; Dt 19:21). I have known modern Catholics who were shocked at the idea that God punishes sin. "Oh no!" they said, "God is a God of love. Why would he hurt anyone?" Yet, needless to say, not only does the Old Testament have a great deal to say about God's punishments, but so does Jesus who says of himself:

> "When the Son of Man comes in his glory, and all the angels with him, he will sit upon his glorious throne, and all the nations will be assembled before him. And he will separate them one from another, as a shepherd the sheep from the goats. He will place the sheep on his right and the goats on his left... Then he will say to those on his left, 'Depart from me, you accursed, into the eternal fire prepared for the devil and his angels! For I was hungry and you gave me no food, I was thirsty and you gave me no drink'" (Mt 23:31-33, 41-42).

A loving God punishes not out of revenge as if human injustice injured him (which it can in no way do), but because it injures his creatures whom he loves. For the same reason he has given the authorities in the human community the right and duty to punish injustice in his name for the good of its members. As St. Thomas Aquinas says,[71] there are three purposes for lawful punishment: (1) to reform the criminal; (2) to deter the criminal and others from committing future crimes; (3) to maintain the standard of justice.

Most people admit the necessity of punishments for the first two purposes; but there has been much debate about the third, because to some it seems that this is either the same as deterrence or it is a euphemism for revenge, i.e., the satisfaction of the hatred of the victim or his friends for the criminal. I believe, however, that Aquinas is right in listing this as a third and distinct purpose, because it is essential to a society that its members not only know that there is a difference between what is just and unjust, but that they know this to be *publicly* recognized and enforced. If a heinous crime is committed and the criminal goes free, the public is outraged and loses confidence in the security of law and order.

For the same reason God must punish sin, not for his own satisfaction, but for our sense of security. It is true, as the Psalmist so often complains (Ps 10, etc.) that God's justice is not always evident in this life. That is because God's mercy delays punishment to give us time for repentance (cf. the Parable of the Weeds and the Wheat, Mt 13:24-30 and the Parable of the Good and Bad Fishes, Mt 13:47-50).

Yet the Old Testament is not mistaken in its confidence that *ordinarily* even in this life "crime does not pay" (Ps 37, etc.). God usually punishes our sins not by a special act on his part, but simply by permitting us to suffer their natural consequences (e.g., lying is punished by the loss of trust by others). Even in the next life the essential punishment of hell is not some torture added above the agony of eternal separation from God which God has not inflicted but we have ourselves freely chosen in the very act of mortal sin.[72]

---

[71] *S.T.*, II-II, q. 108, aa. 1 and 4.

[72] CCC # 1033-1037. This is not to deny that God may in his providence or by a miracle sometimes inflict special punishments (e.g., the death of Ananias and Sapphira, Ac 5:1-11) as signs to awaken and warn us when we refuse to recognize the natural conse-

Granted then, that the use of force as punishment can be just, necessary, and consistent with the Great Commandment of love of God and neighbor, what kinds of punishment are just? We have already said that torture and other cruel punishments cannot be defended today. On the other hand, few would deny that the restriction of a criminal's freedom by prison or parole under humane conditions is a legitimate form of punishment. The debated question is the morality of the death penalty.

Some would argue that the threat of death is no way to lead a human being to *true* repentance. They question whether it really deters the crimes of violence and passion for which it is most often prescribed. They argue that rather than maintaining the standards of justice in a society, killing criminals is more likely to brutalize society and cheapen the regard for the dignity of human life. Finally, if it is true, as I have argued in rejecting suicide and euthanasia, that dominion over human life belongs to God only, what right does the state have to take human life, even the life of a criminal?

In the Bible, however, God seems to delegate that right to human society, since the Fifth Commandment is contained in the Covenant Code which, on the basis of the *lex talionis*, also provides the death penalty for numerous crimes (e.g. for murder, Ex 20:21; for kidnapping, v. 16; for cursing parents, v. 17; sorcery, 22:17; bestiality, v. 18; idolatry, v. 19, etc.).

On the other hand, in the Sermon on the Mount, Jesus seems to abrogate the *lex talionis*:

> "But I say to you, offer no resistance to one who is evil. When someone strikes you on your right cheek, turn the other one to him as well" (Mt 5:38-42).

This saying, however, can be read not so much as a norm or precept, as a counsel to private persons urging them to be peacemakers (Mt 5:9)

---

quences of our acts. It would be arbitrary to dismiss *a priori*, as some exegetes have done, such "miracles of punishment" as mere legends simply because they seem strange to "the modern mind."

rather than to perpetuate the vicious cycle of hatred and revenge. I have already quoted the teaching of Jesus, Peter, and Paul (Mt 22:21; 1 P 2:13-14; Rm 13:1-7) in approval of the state's use of what Paul calls the "sword" to punish crime. As for the principle of *lex talionis*, Jesus approves it powerfully in his indignant warning:

> "Whoever causes one of these little ones who believe in me to sin, it would be better for him if a great millstone were put around his neck and he were thrown into the sea" (Mk 9:42).

Yet Jesus' counsel *does* apply even to public authority by calling on such authorities to resort to force only when necessary. Rather they should put their energies into the rehabilitation of criminals and build up a society free of the conditions that breed crime.

Although its martyrs suffered the death penalty simply for being Christians, the Church has never denied the right of the state to use the death penalty for true and grave crimes. In the Middle Ages when the Waldensian heretics preached against this right, Innocent III in 1208 defended it, with the proviso that the state exercise this right "not out of hate, but by judgment; not hastily, but with due process."[73] Much later the Waldensian position was revived by the Quakers, and supported on other than religious grounds by Cesare Beccaria (d. 1794) and Jeremy Bentham (d. 1832).[74]

Against Beccaria and Bentham the right of capital punishment can be argued from considerations of purely natural law. Experience shows that if individuals are forced to defend themselves because the State permits homicide to go unpunished by some proportionate pen-

---

[73] DS # 795.

[74] The great moralist St. Alphonsus Liguori still took torture for granted as a part of legal due process in the eighteenth century, although as early as the sixteenth century Luis Vives had argued powerfully against it; see Franz Böckle and Jacques Pohier, *The Death Penalty and Torture*. On Beccaria see Marcello T. Maestro, *Cesare Beccaria and the Origins of Penal Reform*, who points out that although Diderot (p. 43) and Voltaire (p. 45) supported Beccaria's ideas, they still thought torture might be necessary in cases of conspiracy. Bentham introduced Beccaria's ideas to England; see his "Principles of Penal Law," part 2, c. xi, pp. 441-450 and Appendix "On Death Punishment," pp. 525-532, *Works of Jeremy Bentham* (Bowring edition), vol. 1.

alty, the result is lawless feuding. Therefore, it is precisely respect for the dignity of human life that requires the state to deter the taking of many lives by taking the lives of a few who have had no respect for life.

The question today, however, is not the abstract question of the *right* of the state to take human life as a punishment when necessary for the common good, but whether in the circumstances of our modern societies capital punishment is either necessary or effective justice. We have the capacity to imprison people and to use various methods of rehabilitation which did not exist in former times and in other places. Moreover, given the complexity of modern life and the judicial system which it requires to protect human rights, it is difficult to administer capital punishment quickly, and it often appears to be unfair, directed more against the poor criminal than the rich one. For these reasons the Church today seeks to discourage recourse to capital punishment, without denying the authority of the state to use it if really necessary.[75]

It would seem to follow that by the natural law the state may in extreme cases inflict corporal punishment short of death and even mutilation, as well as imprisonment (which is a kind of corporal punishment), but human dignity demands that the greatest moderation be used in employing all such punishments, both in view of the rehabilitation of the criminal and the avoidance of the brutalization of those who administer the punishments and of the public that is morbidly fascinated by them.[76]

What then are we to say of such Old Testament texts relating to the duties of parents as follows?

> Blessings are for the head of the just,
>> but a rod for the back of the fool (Pr 10:6).
> Withhold not chastisement from a boy;
>> if you beat him with the rod, he will not die.
> Beat him with the rod,
>> and you will save him from the nether world (Pr 23:13-14).

---

[75] CCC # 2263-2267.

[76] CCC # 2298.

Jesus taught us to respect children as persons (Mk 10:13-16; Mt 19:13-15; Lk 18:15-17). Hence the passages just quoted from the Old Testament, like the punishments it prescribes for adults, should be understood to mean that parents should correct their children but in ways more appropriate to their true dignity.

Mutilation and Neglect of Health

After discussing the injury to persons that lead to death, it is necessary to consider lesser bodily injuries by *mutilation*.[77] Granted that mutilation motivated by hatred or cruelty or even for well-intentioned punishment is contrary to human dignity, what of therapeutic mutilation or the donation of organs for transplantation? The right to life permits one by a "principle of totality" to destroy or to consent to the destruction of one *function* of the body if this is necessary to save the whole body, whether because of internal disease, or some external cause, as when a leg needed for the function of walking is trapped under a fallen building. Hence, for a good reason one may remove a functionless part of the body (hair, wisdom tooth, appendix) or a paired organ (kidney, lungs) or donate it to another in grave need if the donor's own functions are not notably impaired. The transplantation of other organs, however, is ethical only after the donor is certainly dead.

Contrary to some recent opinions, however, the "principle of totality" cannot be invoked to permit the sacrifice of some basic bodily function in order to solve problems which can be rightly solved by a change of behavior, e.g., to mutilate the stomach of an obese person so that they need not change their diet. Such a mutilation cannot honestly be said to be "for the good of the whole person" since in fact it sacrifices the integrity of the person without true necessity (or in charity for the true necessity of another). When this need can be met by a change of behavior without loss of integrity, such a true necessity is not verified. This is true even when the necessary change of behavior is not an

---

[77] CCC # 2297. On sterilization see S. Congregation for the Doctrine of the Faith, "Sterilization in Catholic Hospitals," 12 March, 1975, pp. 454-455.

easy one. The example of the famous Church Father and ascetic Origen of Alexandria who castrated himself so as not to be tempted against chastity has always been rejected by Catholic moralists.[78]

This is why the Church opposes *sterilization* of either the man or the woman when its purpose is contraceptive, i.e., the prevention of pregnancy. This is true even in cases where the avoidance of pregnancy is justified for very serious reasons of physical or mental health; for example, when a woman is subject to grave post-natal depression or to serious diabetes. Since in these cases the pregnancy can be prevented by the practice of periodic abstinence (Natural Family Planning), although this may be difficult, the loss of personal integrity by mutilation is not justified by the principle of totality. On the other hand, mutilation would be justified if, for example, it was necessary to remove a cancerous uterus or kidney to prevent death.

The principle of totality also implies that it is a sin of omission to neglect the health of the body, i.e., its functional integrity, by failing to use the ordinary means to health. More will be said about this in discussing the healthcare profession in Chapter 9.

Injuries to Property

Since human life is not possible without a material environment and private persons have a limited right to own portions of the environment as their own property, it is possible to commit an injustice to persons by injuring their property. Hence the Seventh Commandment, "You shall not steal" (Ex 20:15).[79] Some exegetes think this originally referred specifically to man-stealing, i.e., kidnapping,[80] but certainly in the Covenant Code there are numerous provisions to protect private property rights (Ex 21:33-22:15; cf. Dt 23:20-24:7).

---

[78] See Henri Crouzel, *Origen*, pp. 9-10 and note 32.

[79] CCC # 2401-2463.

[80] Ex 21:16 and Dt 24:7 are explicitly about kidnapping. Rabbinical opinion held that this Seventh Commandment covered all kinds of stealing including kidnapping; cf. Maimonides, *The Commandments*, vol. 2, pp. 232-233.

Theft can be a mortal sin (St. Paul, 1 Cor 6:10, lists thieves and robbers among those will not "inherit the kingdom of God") when it deprives another of goods of serious importance to that person's virtuous life or when it is so large as to constitute a serious breach of the social order without which its citizens cannot live in peace.

Moralists are accustomed to speak of the *relative* and the *absolute* amount required to constitute a mortal sin of theft.[81] Relatively a theft is grave if it does serious harm to the owner, and the traditional standard is that to steal a day's wage of a worker is a serious harm to him or her. Absolutely the amount may not do serious harm to a rich man, but if in a given culture it is generally considered sufficient to give the appearance that, if it be not punished, law and order is breaking down, it must be considered serious. Thus looting stores may be more serious than the value of the property taken by a single person, because it initiates extensive disorders. If one steals small amounts but with the intention of eventually taking a large amount, or if one sees that the damage to the other is becoming serious, or if one retains the whole large amount, the theft becomes serious.

Yet it is not theft to use the property of another in *urgent* necessity, e.g., to take food when starving, or to borrow a car to take a very sick person to the hospital.[82] Nor is it theft secretly to recover property (occult compensation) certainly due one in strict justice which one cannot recover in any other way, provided one take only one's due and there is no proportionate risk to oneself or scandal given.[83] Such a method of obtaining justice requires great prudence and is obviously open to serious abuses and could lead to a breakdown of social order and trust. The Bible urges caution in such matters:

---

[81] Moralists have disagreed a great deal on this topic. I follow the standard manualist Benedict H. Merkelbach, *Theologia Moralis*, 3rd ed., vol. 2, pp. 418-427.

[82] Innocent XI, DS # 2126, condemned laxist opinions which tried to argue that common or ordinary necessity justifies theft, e.g., that anyone can steal their daily food needed for life, rather than make an effort to obtain it by work or other lawful means.

[83] Yet Innocent XI, DS # 2137, condemned as too lax the opinion that a domestic servant could secretly take more than the agreed salary because he believed his work was worth more. Later magisterial pronouncements, however, have made it clear that an employer cannot require an employee to accept an unjust wage; cf. GS # 67.

Men despise not the thief if he steals
to satisfy his appetite when he is hungry;
Yet if he be caught he will have to pay back sevenfold;
all the wealth of his house he may yield up (Pr 7:30-31).

Defamation

Persons' reputation and honor are external to their personal value, and yet are very important for their social relationships and thus can be considered property.[84] Each of us wishes both to be thought well of by others, and to be spoken and treated as persons of good character. The Bible has an astonishing number of texts about "sins of the tongue," most of which consist in injuries to the reputation of others (e.g., Jm 3:2b-12; Pr 10:19; 18:21; Ps 52; 58:5-6; 140:4, 12; Si 28:22).

The New Testament especially condemns "rash judgments" (e.g., Mt 7:1-5). It is rash judgment to conclude that another is guilty of wrongdoing on the basis of insufficient evidence. When it is the deliberate, definitive imputation of serious sin, it is itself a mortal sin. We can never have sufficient evidence, except when persons themselves confess such sins, that another person's acts are subjectively sinful, since we cannot read their conscience. We can, however, have sufficient evidence of objectively serious sin and can condemn it, and if in official position, punish it.

It is with regard to subjective guilt that Jesus said:

"Stop judging that you may not be judged. For as you judge, so will you be judged, and the measure with which you measure will be measured out to you" (Mt 7:1; cf. Rm 2:1; Jm 4:11).

This is evident, since Jesus refers to God's judgment of our *formal* guilt which, we have explained,[85] is based not on objective but subjective conscience, known to God alone. But Jesus also in many of his sermons explicitly passes judgment on certain kinds of objective

---

[84] CCC # 2477-2479, 2507.
[85] See p. 119.

behavior, as does St. Paul, e.g., in excommunicating the incestuous man (1 Cor 5:1-5). To be a mortal sin, rash judgment must be a definitive conclusion, not a mere suspicion, which is only venial.

Unjust injury to someone's reputation by speech without the victim's knowledge and therefore irrefutable by him or her is *detraction*. If it is also lying it is *calumny* or libel. Detraction can be a mortal sin (less grave than homicide, but more grave than theft). "A good name is more desirable than great riches, and high esteem, than gold and silver" (Pr 22:1). It is a mortal sin if it does serious harm to the person's reputation, unless there is a proportionate reason to make public the private sins of another, even if the detractor does not intend to do harm but merely to gossip. "Cursed be gossips and the double-tongued, for they destroy the peace of many" (Si 28:13; see the whole essay 28:12-26). One should not spread even publicly known facts in another region where they are not public.

One may publicly confess to one's own sins and thus injure one's own reputation, but this should not be done without good reason (see Si 41:14-24 on true and false shame). The recent practice of making money out of autobiographies that "tell all," even about one's parents, is dishonorable and scandalous. One can also sin by cooperating in detraction by spreading it more widely. Especially detestable is detraction aimed at destroying friendships and trust between people, particularly in families (Pr 6:16-19; Si 6:14-16; 21:31; 22:19-26; 28:12-26; Rm 1:29-32).

But we can also injure others when we humiliate them by making public their faults or defects in their presence (*contumely*) when there is no proportionate reason for doing so. "Mock not the worn cloak and jibe at no man's bitter day" (Si 11:4). Jesus said of those who humiliate others by contemptuous words, "Whoever says to his brother, 'Raqa' ['imbecile'] will be answerable to the Sanhedrin, and whoever says, 'You fool,' will be liable to fiery Gehenna" (Mt 5:22).[86]

---

[86] See Luz, *Matthew*, pp. 279-288 on Mt 5:22. Luz is puzzled because the rabbis gave similar admonitions and therefore tries to find something new in Jesus' saying to make it an antithesis to all rabbinic teaching. In my opinion this is unnecessary since Jesus was correcting only the teaching of *some* rabbis, not all. Luz shows that although it is

We can humiliate others by practical jokes and mockery, as Jesus was mocked in his passion (Mt 27:41-44; Lk 23:36), or by gestures of scorn (Mt 26:68; 27:27-30; Lk 22:63-65). Such contempt is even more grave when it is mockery of good people (2 K 2:23-24; Job 12:4); one's parents, "The eye that mocks a father, or scorns an aged mother, will be plucked out by the ravens in the valley; the young eagles will devour it" (Pr 30:17); or God, "Whom have you insulted and blasphemed? ... The Holy One of Israel" (Is 37:23).

Heaping scorn or curses on others, except when this is a punishment by one who has authority to punish, makes contumely even worse, as when Shimei cursed the exiled David (2 S 16:5-14). Christians who are thus humiliated ought to suffer patiently and forgive the calumniator, but sometimes they ought to denounce the abuser lest he or she should be encouraged to attack others, or lest there would be scandal to others. Those who commit calumny are bound immediately insofar as possible to repair the damage they have caused and foreseen, even confusedly.

Covenants and Contracts

After this long discussion of commutative justice involving the compensation of injuries done by one party to another, I now take up a second major kind of commutative justice — that involved in covenants or contracts, i.e., the just recompense of benefits received by one party from another.

In the Old Testament one of the chief concepts (some have thought it the central concept) is that of the Covenant between God and Israel. The Covenant was initiated by God, but it was bilateral, not indeed between equals, but between a God who deigned to enter into a mutual relationship with his creatures. Certainly "covenant" is a richer, more personal notion than the legal term "contract," yet a contract is a less

---

traditional to seek a graduated intensification in the three expressions of anger and the three punishments due them, it is not clear that this is really the case. More likely they are a threefold repetition of the same admonition in different words simply for emphasis. Against dishonoring others in speech see also Rm 12:10 and Ph 2:3.

personal form of covenant. Both are founded on an agreement between parties and involve promises and obligations. But God's Covenant with Israel was both conditional and unconditional. He promised them blessings if they obeyed his commandments:

> "If you continue to heed the voice of the Lord, your God, and are careful to observe all his commandments which I enjoin on you today, the Lord, your God, will raise you high above all the nations of the earth" (Dt 28:1).

Yet God went beyond this to promise that whether the Jews all fulfilled their part of the bargain or not, God would irrevocably insure that at least a remnant would do so and hence that the promises would inevitably be fulfilled in the end:

> I will leave as a remnant in your midst,
>   a people humble and lowly,
> Who shall take refuge in the name of the Lord,
>   the remnant of Israel...
> The King of Israel, the Lord, is in your midst,
>   you have no further misfortune to fear (Zp 3:12, 15; cf. Rm 11:1-12).

The Covenant was between a personal God and Israel as a corporate person. Such relations of one person to another are governed by commutative justice and imply an exchange of promises and obligations.[87] Doubtless, this is the most common and easiest understood form of justice, and in Israel all justice ultimately flowed from the Covenant.

Commutative justice applies not only to injuries inflicted on persons directly and through their property, but also to matters that involve a mutual agreement or contract, a voluntary exchange between parties. Such agreements are frequently mentioned in the Bible, notably in the Parable of Workers in the Vineyard already quoted in which

---

[87] Of course the two parties to the Covenant, God and Israel, are utterly unequal, and it is God who graciously takes the initiative. Nevertheless, by doing so God raises Israel to a marvelous kind of "equality" with himself as a father with an adopted child.

Jesus teaches that God's mercy exceeds his justice. The employer says to the harvest-hands who grumbled because he paid all of them the same no matter how long they had worked:

> "My friend, I am not cheating you. Did you not agree with me for the usual daily wage? Take what is yours and go. What if I wish to give this last one the same as you? Or am I not free to do as I wish with my own money? Are you envious because I am generous?" (Mt 20:13-15).

The chief principle of commutative justice governing contracts is the equality between what is agreed upon and what is carried out by each party. The positive civil law is especially concerned with the regulation and enforcement of contracts, and its provisions (when reasonable) must be obeyed impartially.

> You shall appoint judges and officials throughout your tribes to administer true justice to the people in all the communities which the Lord, your God, is giving you. You shall not distort justice, you must be impartial... Justice and justice alone should be your aim that you may have life and may possess the land which the Lord, your God, is giving you (Dt 16:18-20).

To make a binding contract there must be free and deliberate consent by both parties. The canonists and casuists have developed many particular rules that can be used to determine the validity of contracts,[88] such as the following:

1. Substantial error as to the terms of the contract makes it invalid, while accidental error if antecedent to the agreement invalidates gratuitous contracts (such as gifts) but not onerous contracts (such as ones that require something from each party).
2. Substantial deceit invalidates a contract, while accidental deceit invalidates gratuitous contracts, but only renders onerous ones rescindable. Accidental deceit by a third party does not invalidate a contract.

---

[88] These rules are excerpted from the very detailed treatment of contracts by Merkelbach, *Theologia Moralis*, vol. 2, pp. 464-645.

3. When a contract is made under the pressure of fear, it may or may not be binding according to the degree of fear and the type of contract. Thus a marriage contract or religious vow can be invalidated by grave fear of parental anger, because it ought to be entirely free, but not by a light fear of such anger. But a business contract made under grave fear that if it is not made one will suffer serious financial harm is still valid.
4. Contracts to do illicit things are not antecedently binding, but *post factum* the price agreed upon (for example to a prostitute for her services) must be paid and can be retained by the creditor.
5. By natural law anyone who has the use of reason can make a contract, but civil law forbids or makes rescindable contracts by minors, etc., and ecclesiastical law forbids religious to make contracts without the consent of their superiors.
6. The obligations of contracts can cease under a variety of conditions too complicated to mention here but which are discussed at length in the standard manuals.

The chief unilateral or gratuitous contracts are *promises*, *gifts*, and *wills* (testaments). Promises must be kept (see the section on validity and annulment of oaths, Nb 30:1-17 and the words of Jesus in the Sermon on the Mount, Mt 5:33-37), unless the beneficiary consents to their non-fulfillment, or unless this fulfillment would be harmful to the supposed beneficiary (see the story of Herod's foolish promise to the daughter of Herodias, Mk 6:17-29).

Gifts are irrevocable, except when the recipient is gravely ungrateful (since the giver reasonably expects at least minimal gratitude), or if a childless donor has a child with a right to what is given, but can be rescinded if the gift was conditional and the conditions are not fulfilled.

> A gift from a rogue will do you no good,
> > for in his eyes one gift is equal to seven.
> He gives little and criticizes often,
> > and like a crier he shouts aloud.
> He lends today, he asks back tomorrow.
> Hateful indeed is such a man (Si 20:13-14).

Galatians 3:15-29 explains the biblical concept of covenant in terms of a testament or will, and the Epistle to the Hebrews uses this notion to explain the death of Christ, "Now where there is a will, the death of the testator must be established. For a will takes effect only at death; it has no force while the testator is alive" (Heb 9:16-17). The civil law usually provides laws of inheritance where there is no will, and the conditions of previous wills may limit the terms in which a present possessor can pass on inherited property to the next heirs. But ordinarily one has the right to determine who will or will not receive one's property at death and the conditions under which it will be used or disposed of. When these conditions appear immoral or at least unreasonable, recourse must be made to the courts, who should seek to protect the true rights of all concerned, but also the common good.

Whoever injures the spiritual life of others by an unjust means, or by neglect of an official duty, has an obligation in justice to do what is possible to repair that spiritual damage; but if the means were not unjust they are held to do so only from charity. Thus priests or physicians, etc., who knowingly mislead clients to sin by erroneous advice are bound in justice to do what they can to correct this; but if those who are not professional counselors unknowingly give bad advice, they are bound to correct it only out of charity. We should, however, heed the advice of Ben Sirach, "Be swift to hear, but slow to answer. If you have knowledge, answer your neighbor; if not, put your hand over your mouth" (Si 5:13-14).

Honesty in Business

Bilateral onerous contracts require specified performances by each of the parties. The most common of these are contracts of *buying and selling*. In such contracts the chief ethical question is the determination of a *just price*. Thus the Old Law was very concerned about just prices (see Lv 25 on prices in relation to the sabbatical years and 27:14-25 on the valuation of Temple offerings). Proverbs (28:8) warns "He who increases his wealth by interest and overcharge, gathers it for him who is kind to the poor," i.e., he will be deprived of his fortune by God in favor of the charitable.

The just price is not determined simply by the intrinsic value of a thing. What is more valuable to us than air? Yet air is ordinarily free. The medieval writers said a just price was determined by the "common estimation" of a thing's marketable value. But in modern so-called "free market" economies this common estimation in the market is itself determined by the balance of supply and demand. The state, however, can when necessary justly regulate prices so as to keep the prices of scarce necessities sufficiently low to meet the needs of all, or raise prices to stimulate production or assist the producers. It can also tax products that are harmful or merely luxurious to decrease the demand for them.[89]

Sellers can also justly raise the prices somewhat above the cost of production plus a reasonable profit in payment for their own work in producing and marketing them (entrepreneurship), when they can show that this "markup" is necessary to offset their risks or losses that will arise from actual conditions in the market,[90] but "better a little with virtue, than a large income with injustice" (Pr 16:11; cf. 28:6). Sellers must manifest substantial defects in what they sell, must supply what was purchased, and must protect it until delivered. Buyers must pay the price agreed on, take the purchased object away unless delivery was promised, and make sure the payment reaches the seller. Agents acting as proxies in a sale must fulfill their obligations honestly.

The possibilities of dishonesty and exploitation on the part of *sellers* in advertising for sale and creating spurious or harmful "needs," of manipulating prices through monopoly, and of failing to deliver the goods promised; and, on the part of *buyers*, of failing to pay or incurring debts that can never be paid, are as countless as human ingenuity. The law and the prophets often denounce dishonest business practices:

> You shall not keep two differing weights in your bag, one large and the other small; nor shall you keep two different measures in your house, one large, and the other small. But use a true and just weight, and a true and just measure, that you may have a long life on the land which the Lord, your God, is giving you.

---

[89] Cf. CA # 34-35; CCC # 2423-2425, 2429.
[90] Cf. CA # 35.

Everyone who is dishonest in any of these matters is an abomination to the Lord, your God (Dt 25:13-16; cf. Lv 19:35; Pr 11:1, 20:10; Ezk 45:10-12; Am 8:5; Mi 6:10-11, etc.).

So frequent are the temptations in business that Sirach says:

A merchant can hardly remain upright, nor a shopkeeper
    free from sin.
For the sake of profit many sin, and struggle for wealth
    blinds the eyes.
Like a peg driven between fitted stones, between buying
    and selling sin is wedged in (Si 26:20-27:2).

In the Middle Ages businessmen were often regarded as notorious sinners, as in New Testament times were the tax collectors (publicans), as we gather from Jesus' words to the Pharisees, "Amen, I say to you, tax collectors and prostitutes are entering the kingdom of God before you" (Mt 21:31b; cf. Lk 18:9-14). Because of the frequency of such frauds, the Church still severely limits by canon law any kind of participation in business for profit by the clergy to avoid bringing the clerical office into disrepute.[91]

Jesus, however, did not hesitate to associate with businessmen in spite of the "scandal" it gave the Pharisees (Mt 9:9-13; Lk 19:1-10). Although undoubtedly his purpose was to convert these money-makers from their sins of greed and fraud, we do not find that he ever demanded that they give up business as such. In fact the activity of business is necessary for the economic well-being of any but the simplest societies. Today when business is honestly conducted it makes possible a level of productivity and economic welfare impossible in the past. Interestingly, one of the most explicit biblical commendations of economic productivity is in the Praise of the Ideal Wife: "She makes garments and sells them, and stocks the merchants with belts" (Pr 31:26). I am reminded too of another businesswoman whom St. Paul and St. Luke met in the city of Philippi. Luke tells the story:

---

[91] Canons # 286, 1392.

On the Sabbath we went outside the city gate along the river where we thought there would be a place of prayer. We sat and spoke with the women who had gathered there. One of them, a woman named Lydia, a dealer in purple cloth, from the city of Thyatira, a worshiper of God, listened and the Lord opened her heart to pay attention to what Paul was saying. After she and her household had been baptized, she offered us an invitation, "If you consider me a believer in the Lord, come and stay at my home," and she prevailed on us (Ac 16:14-15).

Wages

Not only things, but services can be sold, but the sale of human labor cannot be reduced to that of a commodity, as the papal social encyclicals constantly insist.[92] In the Old Testament slaves were still bought and sold; e.g., in the Covenant Code we read, "When you purchase a Hebrew slave, he is to serve you for six years, but in the seventh year he shall be given his freedom without cost" (Ex 21:2). But, as we have already seen, the New Testament established the principle that all human beings are ends in themselves and cannot be the property of others, for among Christians a slave is to be received "no longer as a slave but more than a slave, a brother, beloved... as a man and in the Lord" (Phm v. 16).

Although in any free market system the price of labor is subject to the law of supply and demand, yet this price must at least equal a *living wage*.[93] Sirach compares the failure to pay a workman a living wage to murder (and this in biblical times certainly included the support of the breadwinner's family): "He slays his neighbor who deprives him of his living; he sheds blood who denies the laborer his wages" (Si 34:22; cf. Jr 22:13). Hence, the Church traditionally classes this injustice among the "sins that cry to heaven" (Dt 24:14-15; Jm 5:4).[94]

This means that in justice a full time worker (male or female) on

---

[92] CA # 34.

[93] Cf. CA # 39.

[94] CCC # 1867.

whom the life of a family depends must receive not just a living wage for themselves but a *family wage*. That is, a wage sufficient for them to support themselves and family in a manner consistent with human dignity, and if they are unmarried to marry in a reasonable time and begin a family. Women who work outside the family should receive equal pay for equal work by men, and if their husbands are not paid a living wage for the family, they should be paid enough for their work at home to compensate.[95]

Actually in our society the family wage as a norm of justice is not being met. Women, who are needed by small children in a special way for which the father can substitute only in part, are not free to take care of their children and home. In increasing numbers they are forced to work outside, while commonly continuing to have heavy duties at home. Moreover, modern wages often pressure spouses to practice contraception to limit their families severely to meet their income. Besides paying them a just wage and paying it on time, employers must also respect the human dignity of workers, be concerned for their welfare, safety, health and other working conditions, and refrain from sexual harassment, racial discrimination, etc.[96]

Sirach gives some rather harsh advice about the discipline of servants: "Force him to work that he be not idle, for idleness is an apt teacher of mischief" (Si 33:28; cf. 33:25-33), but he makes the point that employers have a right to demand fair work from their employees.[97] They must do the work and at the time agreed, without unjustified absenteeism. They must not injure or steal property, must abide by reasonable regulations, and not engage in quarreling, drinking or taking of drugs, or immoral conduct at work. In the Parable of the Faithful and Unfaithful Servants (Lk 12:42-48) Jesus tells a satiric story of servants who become disorderly when the master is away.

The Church defends the right of workers to form associations

---

[95] CCC # 2434; GS # 67.

[96] CCC # 2407, 2414, 2424-2427, 2433, 2455.

[97] CCC # 2427-2428. Vatican II, GS, n. 67, spoke of "everyone's duty to labor faithfully and also everyone's right to work." John Paul II developed this theme in one of his most important encyclicals, *On Human Work* (*Laborem Exercens*) of Sept. 14, 1981.

(unions) for the protection of their rights and for mutual social and educational benefits, and encourages the formation and just administration of such unions.[98] "A brother is a better defense than a strong city, and a friend is like the bars of a castle" (Pr 18:19). Workers also have the right to strike, i.e., to refuse as a group to work, when this is necessary to obtain a just contract or its execution, but not to use violence against the employer, his property, or non-strikers. Nor can employers hinder the formation of unions, nor use violence to end strikes. Lockouts of workers by employers can rarely be justified, since workers are then left without subsistence for their families. Nor can employers simply eliminate large numbers of jobs or move factories away from unions in order to evade paying just wages or without a sincere effort to cooperate with workers in finding new employment.

It should be noted that in modern economies most business is not a question of a relation between an individual employer and his workers, but is conducted through corporations, many of them of immense size and in control of a great variety of enterprises. These have now expanded on an international scale, thus escaping government regulation by a single state.[99] The administrators of a corporation are not its primary owners, but are themselves employed (often at very high salaries and with large blocks of shares in the corporation) by the board of the corporation. The board in turn is responsible to the stockholders who are the real owners, but who often take no part in the actual productive work of the enterprise. To speak of their stock in the company as "private property" is therefore somewhat misleading, since their relation to this property is very indirect. What they really possess is the right to a share in its profits, as a dividend on their stock.

A common kind of business contract which is not buying and selling, but is gratuitous yet bilateral, is an agreement *to rent or lease* property to another for use for an agreed upon time and payment, without any sale. Rents are also determined today largely by the free market, but in some places (New York City is a prime example) rent con-

---

[98] Cf. CA # 16, 43; CCC # 1882-1893, 2435.

[99] See Robert B. Dickie and Leroy S. Rouner, eds., *Corporations and the Common Good* for discussion.

trols have been enacted in a largely unsuccessful attempt to supply all with affordable housing.

Loans

Of great interest from the moralist's point of view is the *loan* of money, for which debtors pay a fee (interest) depending on how long they have the use of the money before they repay it. This is explicitly forbidden by the Covenant Code:

> If you lend money to one of your poor neighbors among my people, you shall not act like an extortioner toward him by demanding interest from him (Ex 22:24; Lv 25:35-37; Dt 23:20; 15:7-10; Ps 15:5; Ezk 18:5-20; Ne 5:7, 9).

The Bible regards a loan as an act of charity not of investment, as is evident from the essay on lending in Sirach (29:1-20), whose theme is "Lend to your neighbor in his hour of need, and pay back your neighbor when a loan falls due" (Si 29:2; cf. Ex 22:24; Lk 6:35-35). Such texts, however, were qualified by the explicit command in the Law:

> "You shall not demand interest from your countrymen on a loan of money or of food or of anything else on which interest is usually demanded. You may demand interest from a foreigner, but not from your countryman, so that the Lord, your God, may bless you in all your undertakings on the land you are to enter and occupy" (Dt 23:20-21).

Thus in the Middle Ages when everywhere religious uniformity within a state was taken for granted, Jews were excluded from most trades but were often tolerated in Christian states so that they might lend money to Christians, who were forbidden to take interest, and then were hated and persecuted by them because of this!

New Testament texts (Lk 6:35; Mt 5:42) urge those who can to make loans to the poor without interest, although they do not explicitly say interest-taking is sinful. The Parable of the Talents (Mt 25:14-30) compares God himself to a capitalistic master who says:

"You wicked, lazy servant! So you knew that I harvest where I
did not plant and gather where I did not scatter? Should you not
then have put my money in the bank so that I could have got it
back with interest on my return?" (Mt 25:26-27).

This parable obviously gets its *ironic* force from the fact that Jesus'
hearers were poor people very familiar with loan-sharks.

The teaching of the Church Fathers against usury is strong and
consistent: Clement of Alexandria, Cyprian, and Tertullian urge charitable loans; Basil denounces interest-taking as unjust, as do John
Chrysostom and Leo the Great. The "sterility" of money compared
with agriculture and other productive arts is taught by Gregory of Nyssa,
Ambrose, and Augustine.[100] The Church first prohibited only clerics to
take interest, but in the twelfth century Gratian's *Decretals* extended
this prohibition to the laity.

To explain this biblical teaching, the scholastic moralists established the principle that all payment above the return of a loan is *per se*
prohibited by the natural law as unjust *usury* (the Latin *usus* also has
the sense of "gain," and usury is an unjust "gain" on a loan). They
considered that the repayment of the loan should be precisely equal to
what was loaned, and that if the creditor demanded any more simply
because the debtor needed the money, he would be taking an unjust
advantage of the debtor's hardship to demand something to which he
had no justifiable claim.

It was admitted, however, that in the case of the rental of productive property, such as a piece of land, the owner had a right not only to
the return of the land but to a part of what the renter had produced from
it minus what was due to his labor. But since, reasoned the medievals,
money is not productive property, this cannot be the title by which the
lender can claim interest. They did, however, recognize that the lender
could charge a fee for hardship suffered by not having his property
available for use (*damnum emergens*), or the loss he suffered by not
having it on hand to sell opportunely (*lucrum cessans*), or as insurance
against loss (*periculum sortis*), or as a penalty for late payment (*poena*

---

[100] See John T. Noonan, Jr., *The Scholastic Analysis of Usury.*

conventialis). The always realistic Ben Sirach had already recognized how much risk a lender undergoes of not being repaid:

> If the lender is able to recover barely half,
>   he considers this an achievement;
> If not, he is cheated of his wealth
>   and acquires an enemy at no extra charge;
> With curses and insults the borrower pays him back,
>   with abuse instead of honor.
> Many refuse to lend, not out of meanness,
>   but from fear of being cheated (Si 29:6-7).

Investment

In the late Middle Ages, the economy changed from a barter basis to a money basis, and banking and investment became common. Therefore, the moralists gradually came to recognize that in a money economy, money itself can be productive, since the accumulation of capital and its investment in capital goods makes possible commercial and technological advances which permit the mass production of goods at relatively low prices. Thus interest on loans today compensates the lenders for the profits they might have made if they had invested the same money in a corporation or other profitable business.

In the sixteenth century the Fifth Lateran Council had permitted the *montes pietatis* (loan companies founded by religious orders to provide loans to the poor) to charge a small rate of interest. Yet even in the seventeenth and eighteenth centuries Popes Alexander VII, Innocent XI, and Benedict XIV were still condemning laxist opinions on the subject, although the last of these popes had already begun to make some concessions to the changing situation.[101] With the nineteenth century, however, and the rise of modern industrial productivity, it finally became clear that interest on loans had a different function than for-

---

[101] Alexander VII (DS # 2062), Innocent XI (DS #2141-42), and Benedict XIV (DS # 2546-2550).

merly. Hence, the Holy Office (18 August, 1830 and 17 January, 1838); and the Sacred Penitentiary (16 September, 1830 and 11 November, 1831) gradually began to permit moderate interest. Finally the Code of Canon Law not only permitted it but required ecclesiastical moneys to be invested at interest.

This apparent contradiction by the Church of its own long-standing interpretation of natural law is today often cited as clear evidence that even apparently definitive positions of the Church's ordinary Magisterium on morals have in fact been changed, and therefore the Magisterium can also reverse its position on contraception and other issues of sexual morality. Nevertheless, it will be seen that this argument is of little weight. What changed in the teaching on usury was not the moral norm, namely, that it is intrinsically wrong to demand that the debtor return more than the principle of the loan plus (a) recompense for any losses (or risk of losses) to the creditor in making the loan; (b) a share in any fruits of the productive use of the principle. What has changed is not this norm but its prudential application to a changed economic system. Thus if one advocates change in the current teaching of the Church on sexual questions, it must be argued in terms of application to new facts or a new knowledge of the facts, not on the grounds so often given that "the Church is always behind the times; it will catch up."

The many other questions concerning justice in financial transactions (some of which are touched on in the Old Law), such as deposits, insurance, betting, lotteries, the stock market, insurance, etc., form the whole field of *business ethics.* This was first treated systematically in the fifteenth century by St. Antoninus, O.P., Archbishop of Florence (then the very center of rising capitalism) in his great *Theologia Moralis.*[102] Today it forms an important field of research for moral theologians.[103]

---

[102] See Bede Jarrett, O.P., *S. Antonino and Medieval Economics* for an introduction.

[103] See R. Edward Freeman, ed. *Business Ethics: The State of the Art,* for essays describing this discipline.

Restitution

In both kinds of commutative justice, compensation of injuries and fulfillment of contracts, there is a strict obligation of precise repayment of the debt incurred. Consequently, it is characteristic of this kind of justice that *restitution* is obligatory if such justice is violated. If the damage or debt is serious relative to the creditor's welfare, then to fail to make restitution to the creditor when this is possible is a mortal sin. The Covenant Code of Exodus (21:33-22:5, etc.) has many provisions for restitution (sometimes double or greater), and the penalties are often grave, for example, enslavement (22:2). The stories of how the destitute Tobit insisted on his wife's returning the goat he suspected she had stolen (Tb 2:11-14) and how Zacchaeus, after he was converted by Jesus, made restitution four-fold from his tax-collection extortions (Lk 19:1-10) make the same point (cf. also Ezk 33:14-16). The Epistle of James warns:

> Come now, you rich, weep and wail over your impending miseries... Behold, the wages you withheld from the workers who harvested your fields are crying aloud, and the cries of the harvesters have reached the Lord of hosts (Jm 5:1, 4).

This precept of restitution implies the negative prohibition of retaining ill-gotten goods and thus is an absolute or exceptionless norm. Seeming exceptions (such as not giving back a stolen gun to a criminal or a would-be suicide) are not in fact exceptions to the norm, because the one who withholds does not acquire ownership or the right of use, but only temporary guardianship of the weapon.

The casuists of the post-Tridentine period worked out many rules for just restitution. The most important of these rules[104] are:

1. If one actually has unjust possession of goods one must restore them to the owner immediately.
2. If one *voluntarily* does something that may cause damage to these goods one must try to prevent this if the effort is proportionate to the

---

[104] Merkelbach, *Theologia Moralis*, vol. 2, pp. 282-341.

injury, and if one cannot prevent the damages one must compensate for them.

3. If it is only by an error that one is in unjust possession of another's goods still one must try to prevent any damage to them.

4. If, while in unjust possession of another's goods, one by an unavoidable error does damage to them, one is only bound to compensate for such damage as one foresaw, unless one also realized the risk of damage.

5. If one injures someone thinking that person is another, one is still bound to restore to the injured party.

6. If one destroys something borrowed thinking it to be something else, one is at least required to restore the thing of lesser value.

7. If one is in doubt whether an action will cause injury before the fact, one may not take the risk of injuring another. If after the fact one is doubtful about whether one unjustly caused the damage, one is not strictly held to restore; but if one is not sure whether one actually caused the damage, but is sure that one did what would ordinarily cause damage, then one must restore.

8. If one has possessed something in good faith and then discovers it is really someone else's, one must return the thing and its products (unless civil law says otherwise), or at least what remains if any; but one can retain what one has added by one's labor, compensating oneself for whatever value one may have added to the property.

9. If one cooperates with others in an injustice, one must restore in proportion to one's degree of cooperation.

10. One must make restoration to the injured party if this is possible, but one need not reveal one's guilt, unless this does a further injustice to the creditor or a third party.

11. If one does not know or is in doubt who was injured or how to restore to them, one may give the equivalent value to charity.

12. If one is unable to restore, one must restore in part, or over a period of time, unless the civil law limits the obligation by bankruptcy laws, etc., but it is unjust to incur bankruptcy deliberately in order to escape debts.

These casuistic rules reflect a keen sense of fairness, and many can be paralleled in the rabbinic literature of the Jewish tradition which strove to apply the Old Testament laws to a great variety of practical cases.

Summary of Norms

The positive norm of commutative justice can be formulated as follows:

1. If we are to live with God in his community here on earth and in eternal life, we must respect the rights of others destined to that same goal by exactly fulfilling our contracts with them as regards their personal integrity, their reputation, and their property which are their means to that common goal, and if we injure these rights we must make exact restitution to them as far as within our power.

The negative positive norms can be stated thus:

2. Never usurp God's dominion over human life from conception to death by depriving someone of that life who is not in a serious act of aggression against ourselves or another, or liable to punishment for such an act.
3. Never deprive ourselves or another of bodily functional integrity unless this is necessary to save our own or the other's life.
4. Never deprive another of their rights to own and use their own property and maintain a good reputation in subordination to the common good.[105]

These norms of commutative justice must be interpreted in the light of social justice, that is, of legal and distributive justice and their auxiliary virtues, which I will discuss in the next chapter.

May my tongue sing of your promise,
for all your commands are just (Ps 119:172).

---

[105] The phrase "in subordination to the common good" means that all rights to own and use private property exist only in relation to the true common good of the society; cf. CCC # 2401-2402

CHAPTER 8

LIVING JUSTLY, CONTINUED

Love justice, you who judge the earth; think of the Lord in goodness, and seek him in integrity of heart (Ws 1:1).

A: LEGAL JUSTICE

Legal and Social Justice

The Old Testament with its fundamental notion of the covenant between God and the People of God, Israel, always presents human life in a social context. The moral life is that demanded by citizenship in the Kingdom (Reign) of God. Righteousness (justice) is to live as a good citizen of that Kingdom, obedient to God's rule.

> The God of heaven will set up a kingdom that shall never be destroyed or delivered up to another people; rather, it shall break in pieces all these [other] kingdoms and put an end to them, and it shall stand forever (Dn 2:44).

> I saw one like a son of man coming on the clouds of heaven; when he reached the Ancient One and was presented before him, he received dominion, glory, and kingship; nations and people of every language serve him. His dominion is an everlasting dominion that shall not be taken away, his kingship shall not be destroyed (Dn 7:13-14).

Jesus' preaching centered on the coming of this "Kingdom (Reign) of God" (Mk 1:15) and his disciples came to recognize in him the Messiah (Mk 8:29), the anointed king to whom God would commit this everlasting kingdom. Theologically, therefore, earthly governments have to be measured by the way they reflect this ultimate kingdom, and biblical righteousness (justice) is above all a *social justice*.[1]

"Social justice" as the term is used today, especially in the documents of the Church's Magisterium comprises both what the scholastics called "legal justice" and "distributive justice." It is called "social" because it concerns both the obligations of the members of society to the society as a whole, and of the society as a whole to its members. In an ideal way it is ascribed to the earliest Christian community in Jerusalem:

> The community of believers was of one heart and mind, and no one claimed that any of his possessions was his own, but they had everything in common... There was no needy person among them, for those who owned property or houses would sell them, bring the proceeds of the sale, and put them at the feet of the apostles, and they were distributed to each according to need (Ac 4:32, 34-35).

The first part of this quotation describes legal justice; the last clause, "they were distributed to each according to need" describes distributive justice.

Legal justice regulates what is due the common good of a society from its members. It is a virtue of the citizens who obey the laws necessary for the common good (good citizenship), but it is also an "architectonic" (regulative) virtue for those in government positions who make and execute these laws in the service of the common good. "If a king is zealous for the rights of the poor, his throne stands firm forever" (Pr 29:14; cf. 20:28).

By *common good* we mean an order of real and mental relations which constitute the welfare or happiness of a society as an organic whole. Society is bound together both by real relations, such as familial and racial origins and common humanity, and also by mental relations such as legal citizenship. Thus the common good consists primarily in the spiritual good of the achievement of true understanding and moral living by all members of the society, but also secondarily and instru-

---

[1] CCC # 1877-1948.

mentally in the material prosperity and security that are the conditions of this achievement. The Scriptures often speak of this true welfare of God's people, both spiritual and material, as "peace."

> Pray for the peace of Jerusalem!
>   May those who love you prosper!
> May peace be within your walls,
>   prosperity in your buildings.
> Because of my relatives and friends
>   I will say, "Peace be within you!"
> Because of the house of the Lord our God,
>   I will pray for your good (Ps 122:6-9).

Principle of Subsidiarity

The only secular society which is "perfect" in the sense that it includes all the means for human worldly fulfillment is the national state, although even it is becoming more and more dependent on international society. But the Church is also a perfect society in respect to its transcendent spiritual purpose, which is to witness on earth to the coming of the Reign of God under Christ the King.[2] According to the social encyclicals of the popes from Leo XIII to the present, the state must seek the prosperity of the community and its members, and peace, morality, family life, justice, public works, and the increase of the arts and business, and agriculture.[3] It should not, however, intervene in local affairs except when local authority cannot or will not make its own provisions for the welfare of its members (the *principle of subsidiarity*).[4]

Biblically this principle of subsidiarity is proposed in the narrative in which wise Jethro, Moses' father-in-law, sees how Moses is over-burdened in his task of leading Israel and counsels him:

"You will surely wear yourself out, and not only yourself but

---

[2] CCC # 758-780, 2244-2246.

[3] CCC # 459, 1877-1927, 2234-2257.

[4] CA # 16, 48; CCC # 1883-5, 2209.

also these people with you. The task is too heavy for you; you cannot do it alone. Now, listen to me, and I will give you some advice, that God may be with you. Act as the people's representative before God, bringing to him whatever they have to say. Enlighten them in regard to the decisions and regulations, showing them how they are to live and what they are to do. But you should also look among all the people for able and God-fearing men, trustworthy men who hate dishonest gain, and set them as officers over groups of thousands, of hundreds, of fifties, and of tens. Let these men render decisions for the people in all ordinary cases. More important cases they should refer to you, but all lesser cases they can settle for themselves. Thus your burden will be lightened, since they will bear it with you. If you do this, when God gives you orders you will be able to stand the strain, and all these people will go home satisfied." Moses followed the advice of his father-in-law and did all that he suggested (Ex 18:18-24).

Just Forms of Government

When the people of Israel requested their judge, the prophet Samuel to establish a king for them "as other nations have" (1 S 8:5), God warned them through Samuel that they would live to regret their request. A king:

> ... will take your sons and assign them to his chariots and horses, and they will run before his chariot. He will also appoint for them his commanders of groups of a thousand and a hundred soldiers. He will set them to do his plowing and his harvesting, and to make his implements of war and the equipment of his chariots. He will use your daughters as ointment-makers, as cooks, and as bakers, etc.... . He will tithe your crops and your vineyards and you yourselves will become his slaves (1 S 8:11-17).

Thus the Bible distinguishes between an unjust government or tyranny which rules for the advantage of those who rule, and a just government which rules for the welfare of the people as a whole. Aristotle made the same distinction and described three fundamental models of just government:(1) rule by a single executive (monarchy) which has the advantages of unity of action but the disadvantages of the limited prudence of a single man; (2) rule by a select group (aristocracy) which has the advantage of the greater prudence of a group of experts but the disadvantage of less unity of action; and (3) rule by all the citizens (democracy) which has the advantage of greater freedom of action for individuals but the disadvantage of the lack of prudence of the masses and lack of unity of action.[5]

To maximize the advantages and balance the disadvantages of these pure forms, many States have tried to combine all three forms in various ways under the title of a "republic" (*res publica*, "people's business"). Aquinas argues[6] that the law provided Israel with such a mixed government, since they had a supreme leader in Moses, assisted by seventy-two elders (Dt 1:9-18) who were chosen from among the people (Dt 1:13) and that, prior to the institution of Saul as an absolute monarch, this aristocracy of leaders chosen from among the people prevented the leader from becoming a tyrant.

The governments of England and the United States have proved remarkably stable in modern times. They also combine the monarchical principle of a strong executive (a Prime Minister acting for a hereditary monarch in England, a President elected from the people in the United States) with an aristocratic principle (Parliament in England, Congress in the United States), and a democratic principle (election of a majority party in England, election of a majority party and, independently of Congress, of a President in the United States).[7]

Today it is often thought that only a "democracy" is a just form of government, but this is to confuse two different things: the ends of government and the means of government. Any of the three pure forms and the various modes of the mixed forms can be just or unjust depending on whether it acts for the common good or for the good of the governors. It can be argued, however, that governmental action will probably be just the more the principle of subsidiarity is followed, i.e.,

---

[5] *Politics*, Bk. III, c. 6-13, 1278b 7 seq.

[6] *S. T.*, II-II, q. 105, a. 1.

[7] See Mattei Dogan and Dominique Pellasy, *How to Compare Nations*.

the greater the participation in decision-making by all the citizens (Lincoln's "government of the people, by the people, for the people"). No one knows the actual needs of the people better than the people themselves, and the combined prudence of all the people exceeds that of any single group.[8]

Yet, how is this maximum participation to be achieved? In large modern "democratic" states (and most modern states claim to be democracies or at least "republics") the actual participation of the citizens is often quite low, as is evidenced in the United States by the meager turn-out for many elections.[9] A state with a monarchical constitution may actually have a higher level of participation than one with a democratic constitution, if it observes the principle of subsidiarity and if the monarch before making major decisions carefully consults the citizens at every level. On the contrary, a state with a democratic constitution may in fact be ruled by a small group at the head of the major party while the great majority of citizens are passive. The justice of a government, therefore, should be judged by considering whether it serves the common good through a unity of action achieved by the maximum possible consultation of its citizens.[10]

Duties of Citizenship

Besides the duty to observe the just laws of the community and participate in its life by voting and consultation, all citizens have a responsibility to contribute to the support of necessary government and hence to pay taxes.[11] Members of the Church have a similar responsibility to contribute to its financial support.[12] The Jews of Jesus' time were required by the law to pay taxes for the support of the Temple and of the monarchy. When they lost their monarchy they had to pay taxes to the

---

[8] CA # 46.

[9] On the causes of this low participation by the electorate, one of which paradoxically was the efforts at electoral reform early in this century, see Walter Dean Burnham, *The Current Crisis in American Politics*, Chapters 1, 2, and 4.

[10] This is argued in my book, *Justice in the Church: Gender and Participation*, Chapters 1-2.

[11] CCC # 2436.

[12] CCC # 2043.

Roman government, and the tax-collectors (publicans) for this oppressive government were hated and despised. Jesus sought to convert these tax-collectors from their exploitative abuse of their office, but he required his followers to pay both the Temple tax and the tax to the Romans (Mt 17:23-26; Mt 22:21; Rm 13:5-7). Thus everyone has a duty in justice to pay their fair share to the administration of government and its services, a share proportionate to the ability of each to pay.

Some have claimed that a graduated income tax is contrary to the right of private property. This is not true since the wealth of the rich cannot be attributed simply to their own efforts, but is a function of the society which has protected them and their property and made it possible for them to operate their business. Hence they deserve to pay more than those who have received less from society. This obligation is not merely penal (i.e., to avoid the penalty) but a moral obligation in social justice.[13] In general citizens are obliged to pay whatever is assessed them by law, but in circumstances in which assessments are commonly understood as not to be taken to the letter of the law, it is permissible to pay the customary percentage, since it is the responsibility of the government to interpret the law by the way it enforces it.

Military service (including police service) is also an obligation on all citizens. It would seem that even women today have some responsibility in the defense of the country, and certainly do all men physically and mentally qualified. The government must administer the draft impartially. It can, however, take into consideration other services a person renders to society and defer draftees for that reason.[14]

Because modern wars commonly fail to meet the requirements of just war, it is morally required of those who believe that a given war or a probable war to come is radically unjust, to refuse to serve in that war. This "conscientious objection" must, however, not be simply a refusal to assume the burdens and risks of military service. Those who are sincerely convinced that a war is just or who are unable to judge the justice of a war are obliged to serve (since they need to trust their government unless they know to the contrary). In modern conditions,

---

[13] CCC # 2240, 2436.
[14] CCC # 2310-2311.

however, it is easier to know if radically unjust means such as nuclear warfare are likely to be used. It is wise of a state in modern conditions to permit conscientious refusal of military service out of respect for conscience and for army morale, and instead to require some equivalent social service. The Old Testament permitted those recently married to stay home for a year so that they might at least beget a child for the people (Dt 24:5). To escape the draft by unjust means such as bribery or self-mutilation is of course wrong.

Those who act as criminal judges and executioners of punishment also bear a special burden. A judge must execute the law according to the information he has as judge and not as a private person. Citizens have a duty to serve as jurors and to decide on the evidence.

Witnesses have an obligation to testify even at some risk to themselves (but probably not if they cannot obtain police protection) and must be truthful. Modern law permits the accused not to confess, or incriminate himself, and to plead innocent even if he is not, in order to gain a fair hearing; but he must answer honestly to questions if he answers at all. The accused may not bribe or threaten the judge, witnesses, or prosecutor.

The Ethics of the Learned Professions

Since the French Revolution many think of the State as the locus of all social power at one end and the citizens with their rights guaranteed by the state at the other, with nothing in between.[15] Catholic social doctrine, on the contrary, has always insisted that the principle of subsidiarity[16] requires the distribution of civil power among a variety

---

[15] See Simon Schama, *Citizens: A Chronicle of the French Revolution,* pp. 859-861.

[16] "Authorities must beware of hindering family, social, or cultural groups, as well as intermediate bodies and institutions. They must not deprive them of their own lawful and effective activity, but should rather strive to promote them willingly and in orderly fashion. For their part, citizens both as individuals and in association should be on guard against granting government too much authority and inappropriately seeking from it excessive conveniences and advantages, with a consequent weakening of the sense of responsibility on the part of individuals, families, and groups." Vatican II, GS, n. 75. GS uses the term "participation" (*actuosa participatio*) both of economic (n. 68) and political participation (n. 75). See CA # 48 for a more concrete discussion of subsidiarity.

of social institutions which the state does, indeed, have the responsibility of coordinating and, when necessary, correcting and even supplementing. In this book it is not possible to discuss all these institutions of which business, the military, the arts, communications, and the learned professions are the chief. I have said something of business ethics in discussing commutative justice. I will say something of the military in discussing just war. Here I will only treat briefly of the responsibilities of the learned professions, and include the arts and communications under the educational function.[17]

It is difficult to exaggerate the importance of the four traditional "learned professions," i.e., physicians, lawyers, teachers, clergy, in forming the values of a society, although they are not, as such, officials of the state. Their services involve in a very direct way the basic rights of human beings. For that reason the relation of trust between client and professional is essential.

Moreover, the conduct of these professions is vital to maintaining a high level of morality and spiritual well-being in any community. This is obvious in the case of the *clergy*, but it is also true for *teachers* — since on them depends the access of their students to truth, a fundamental spiritual good, and for *lawyers* — since they assist their clients to avoid crime and to defend their basic rights, which again are spiritual concerns, and for *physicians* — since on their skill depends the great life events of birth and death.

The Bible[18] acknowledges the honor due the physician as an instrument of God for our healing in Sirach 38:1-15:

> Hold the physician in honor, for he is essential to you,
>   and God it was who established his profession.

---

[17] See Alan H. Goldman, *The Moral Foundations of Professional Ethics*; Dennis M. Campbell, *Doctors, Lawyers, Ministers*; Paul F. Camenisch, *Grounding Professional Ethics in a Pluralistic Society*; Francis A. Eige, ed., *The Professions in Ethical Context*; John Callahan, ed., *Ethical Issues in Professional Life*; Banks McDowell, *Ethical Conduct and the Professional's Dilemma*; Steven Brint, *In an Age of Experts*.

[18] In 2 Ch 16:12b, King Asa was condemned by God because "Even in his sickness he did not seek the Lord, but only the physicians" as in war he had "'relied on the king of Aram and did not rely on the Lord, your God'" (16:7); but in both cases his sin was not reliance on his army or his doctor but his failure to base this trust on a superior trust in God.

From God the doctor has his wisdom,
    and the king provides for his sustenance...
Thus God's creative work continues without cease
    in its efficacy on the earth...
He who is a sinner toward his Maker,
    will be defiant toward the doctor (Si 38:1-2, 8, 15).

Not only physicians are honored in the Bible, but also lawyers, since the rabbis were interpreters of the law and Jesus said of them, "The scribes and the Pharisees have taken their seat on the chair of Moses. Therefore, do and observe all things whatsoever they tell you" (although he added, "but do not follow their example," Mt 23:2-3a). Teachers are honored also, for "The teaching of the wise is a fountain of life, that a man may avoid the snares of death" (Pr 13:14). Sirach also praises the teacher (scribe) and says of the scholar, "Many will praise his understanding; his fame can never be effaced; Unfading will be his memory, through all generations his name will live" (Si 39:9), though Jesus cautions the scribes against pride, "Do not be called 'Master,' you have but one master [teacher], the Messiah" (Mt 23:8).

Along with teachers we can include those professionals in the fine arts and the media of social communications who in today's society are actually the most influential of our instructors. Sirach[19] praises the artists too:

So with every engraver and designer who,
    laboring night and day,
Fashions carved seals,
    and whose concern is to vary the pattern.
His care is to produce a vivid impression,
    and he keeps watch till he finishes his design (Si 38:27).

---

[19] Sirach (38:24-39:11), however, groups these fine artists along with other manual workers, the farmer, the smith, the potter. It is a feature of modern culture to separate sharply the "fine arts" from other kinds of skilled craft. On the Egyptian "Satire on the Trades" written in the Twelfth Dynasty (c. 1991-1786 B.C.) see the commentary of Skehan-Di Lella, *The Wisdom of Ben Sira*, pp. 449-453. The Egyptian writer, probably named Kety, exalts his own vocation of scribe by demeaning the tasks of manual workers. Sirach, on the contrary, although he also exalts the work of the scribe, does not ridicule but praises the other vocations.

But the author of Wisdom warns that such art can be used to make idols:

> But the handmade idol is accursed,
>> and its maker as well;
> he for having produced it,
>> and it, because though corruptible,
> it was termed a "god" (Ws 14:8).

Our journalists and media pundits are not unlike the self-professed prophets of the Bible who claimed to read "the signs of the times" (Mt 16:3), and for such I join the lament of the ancient poet:

> Your prophets had for you
>> false and specious visions;
> They did not lay bare your guilt,
>> to avert your fate;
> They beheld for you in vision
>> false and misleading portents (Lm 2:14).

Yet undoubtedly journalists and TV newspersons can perform for the public a necessary service, like the two swift runners Ahimaz and the Cushite who brought David both the good news of victory and the bad news of the death of his son Absalom (2 S 18:19-32).

The role of the clergy is varied, whether, among Jews and Muslims, it is that of a religious lawyer who interprets the law of Moses or of the *Qur'an*, or the Protestant pastor who is principally a religious teacher and preacher, or the Catholic and Orthodox priest who is above all a celebrant of the sacraments and an offerer of the sacrifice of the Eucharist. Sirach describes the venerable high priest offering sacrifice in the Temple:

> Vested in his magnificent robes,
>> and wearing his garments of splendor
> As he ascended the glorious altar
>> and lent his majesty to the court of the sanctuary (Si 50:11).

Unfortunately today, as the frequency of malpractice litigation evidences, the learned professions are not in good repute. One of the fundamental reasons for this decline (besides quack doctors, crooked lawyers, negligent teachers, mercenary TV evangelists and the like) in respect is the tendency in modern society to reduce even these professions to businesses for profit, when in fact they deal with the spiritual destiny of persons.

Since the services of these professions deal with basic goods, salvation, truth, justice, life and death which are *priceless* and necessary, there is a fundamental obligation for the professional to supply these services to whoever needs them whether they can pay or not. If they can pay it is not to buy the service or make a profit but to offer a *stipend*, that is, a fee based on the expenses involved and the living expenses of the professional and his or her family so that the service can be continued for the client and for others.

Clearly the clergy cannot *sell* the Gospel nor the sacraments because these are sacred and beyond price. To do so is the very serious sin of *simony*, so named after Simon the Magician who tried to buy the gift of the Holy Spirit from St. Peter who said, "May your money perish with you, because you thought that you could buy the gift of God with money" (Ac 8:20).[20] The rule given by Jesus to his disciples as to the Gospel, "Without cost you have received; without cost you are to give" (Mt 10:8b), holds for other kinds of teaching and counseling and for all the learned professions that counsel their clients about their very lives.

All these professionals also have the obligation to be competent in the services which they provide, which means they must constantly study, deepen, and update their knowledge. Moreover, they must be genuinely concerned for the interests of their clients, not merely their own advantage. Thus a lawyer should strive to see that his client obtains a fair trial. All these professionals must also observe an appropriate confidentiality to protect the interests and reputation of their clients.

Although in all these professional relationships the interests of the individual client are a primary concern, these interests must always be considered in the perspective of the common good. Thus a teacher should not incite students to rebellion, nor a lawyer cooperate in crime,

---

[20] CCC # 2121.

nor a priest promote heresy or schism, nor a physician perform abortions or sterilizations. As Sirach says:

> Seek not to become a judge
>> if you have not strength to root out crime,
> Or you will show favor to the ruler
>> and mar your integrity (Si 7:6).

Church Government

After considering the forms of civil government as they are ordered by justice and the learned professions as they contribute to maintaining and promoting ethical values in subsidarity to the state, I will treat briefly the order of justice in the Catholic Church as a paradigm of problems which are found in various degrees also in other religious communities.[21] The government of the "Catholic and Roman Church" is often said to be monarchical, because it claims that Jesus established St. Peter and his successors as its head (Mt 16:18-19; cf. Lk 22:32; Jn 21:15-17). Yet it also teaches that according to the Bible the head of the Church is Christ himself (Eph 5:23), of whom the Bishop of Rome is only a vicar bound to govern the Church according to a "constitution" established by Christ.[22]

Moreover, Jesus chose Peter from among the apostles to govern *with* them, so that the Pope must govern with the college of bishops of which he is the head (an aristocratic principle). Finally, the bishops are not hereditary, but chosen from among the people and (at least in principle) with their consent, and by Vatican II are required to seek extensive consultation with the laity. Thus the Catholic Church, although it has a strong executive, might be considered in principle a republic.

Yet the Catholic Church is also unique in its form of government,[23] since unlike any earthly government its bishops are obliged to govern only in the name of Christ and by his mission received in their

---

[21] For a more complete exposition see my *Justice in the Church*, note 10 above.

[22] LG on the constitution of the Church; CCC # 871-945.

[23] CCC # 748-870.

consecration, not by their own will or wisdom, nor by the will or wisdom of the laity. As St. Paul says:

> Thus should one regard us: as servants of Christ and stewards of the mysteries of God. Now it is of course required of stewards that they be found trustworthy. It does not concern me in the least that I be judged by you or any human tribunal... the one who judges me is the Lord (1 Cor 4:1-3a, 4).

Justice in the Church, therefore, must not be judged by secular standards, but by faith in Christ's presence and guidance of the Church through the Gospel and the pastors whom he has called in the Spirit. Yet the principle of subsidiarity, i.e., the maximum possible participation of all members of the Church in the mission of the Church, holds for the Church even more than for secular communities.[24]

The Family

In Chapter 3, I showed that all Christians must practice an asceticism with regard to the sexual appetites in order to be able to use their sexuality in a manner conformed to the procreative purposes for which God created humanity sexual, as well as with regard to other purposes consistent with that procreative purpose, including its recreative use.[25] But there is a further aspect of sexual morality now to be discussed, namely the obligations in justice to others which its use may entail. In the Torah, Genesis pictures human culture largely at the level of patriarchal family life, and only in the subsequent books is a truly civil society created.

While it is true that justice, strictly speaking regards what is due to the *other*, and members of a family are so close as not to be clearly "other,"[26] yet as persons they have primary rights which can be un-

---

[24] See *Justice in the Church* (note 10 above).

[25] See Chapter 5 and Chapter 6 above.

[26] According to Aquinas, *S.T.*, II-II, q. 30, a. 1, ad 2, our parents or children are, as it were, parts of ourselves, so that our relation to them is not, properly speaking, one of justice, but of love.

justly violated. Although some moralists treat justice between the sexes under commutative justice because sexual relations are between individuals, I believe this question is more adequately treated as a matter of social justice for three reasons: (1) Human persons were created sexual in view of procreation, and procreation respects not just the individual but the social good, the preservation of the community through time; (2) The family, although not a perfect society, is a true society and the natural foundation and basic unit of the perfect societies of state and church; (3) The sexual roles, as well as the age roles, which get their moral significance from the family, are the primary social relations within state and church. Hence, injustices involving sex cannot be fully weighed except in relation to social justice.[27]

Children certainly have the same primary or basic rights as their parents. When the disciples treated children as of little importance, Jesus "became indignant and said to them, 'Let the children come to me; do not prevent them, for the kingdom of God belongs to such as these'" (Mk 10:14). Such biblical phrases as "fruit of my womb" (Dt 7:13; Ps 127:3; Is 13:18; Lk 1:42) and "son of thy loins" (Gn 35:11; 1 K 8:19; 2 Ch 6:9; Ac 2:30; Heb 7:5, 10) show a keen sense of the physical bonding of the child to mother and father, as do the genealogies that are so prominent in the biblical narrative. The intimacy of the sexual union is described as the man "knowing" his wife, out of which "knowing" the child is generated (Gn 4:1, 17, 25; Lk 1:34) in a mysterious process in which the Creator is the chief agent:

> I too am a mortal man, the same as all the rest,
> a descendant of the first man formed of earth.
> And in my mother's womb I was molded into flesh
> in ten-month's period — body and blood,
> From the seed of man, and the pleasure that accompanies
> marriage (Ws 7:1-2).

But human generation is not possible without the mysterious immedi-

---

[27] Note that much of CCC's treatment of family is not under the Sixth but the Fourth Commandment, along with the state. CA # 39; CCC # 1882, 2201-2233, 2248-2253.

ate creative action of God raising us to existence in the divine image
(Gn 4:1; Jb 31:15; Ps 139:13-15).[28]

Child Rights

Thus, God has provided in marriage and the creation of the child through
intercourse a marvelous way to insure its bonding to the parents by an
intimate bodily and psychological linkage which is an important guarantee of its care, of the protection of its rights, and of its own sense of
identity. Adoption or other forms of child care, although of great importance when necessary, cannot perfectly substitute for this natural
bonding.[29] Nor can the new efforts of medical technology which seek,
laudably enough, to find a remedy for sterility by various forms of
artificial reproduction supply this bonding.

Therefore, although of course a child has no rights before it exists, yet from the first moment of its existence at conception it has first
of all the right to live, and second the right to an environment which
makes a good life for it possible, and this environment is both biological and familial. Thus a child has a right to come into this world as the
offspring of parents who are permanently committed to each other in
the covenant of marriage and through the natural sacrament of intercourse which seals that covenant. This right of the child to have parents
in the fullest sense of the term is violated by those who beget children
out of wedlock, or even within wedlock by artificial insemination by
the husband (*a fortiori* from a donor other than the husband) or by *in
vitro* fertilization.[30] At the same time adoption of a child who otherwise
would lack proper care is a true work of Christian charity, as the many
biblical passages about orphans attest, and this love of the adopting
parents can go a long way to compensate for the orphan's deprivation.

---

[28] Pius XII, DS # 3896 declared that the teaching that the human soul is "immediately
created by God" is a truth of the Catholic faith.

[29] See Miriam Reitz, *Adoption and the Family System.*

[30] *Donum Vitae* discusses the morality of artificial reproduction at length; see also CCC #
2366-2379.

> Religion that is pure and undefiled before God and the Father is this: to care for orphans and widows in their affliction and to keep oneself unstained by the world (Jm 1:27; cf. Dt 14:29, 27:19; Is 1:17; Jr 5:28; Zc 7:10; Jb 29:12, etc.).

No doubt adoption of a child by a single parent, especially a member of its extended family, may be best for the child when adoption by a married couple is unavailable. Homosexual couples cannot provide the child with a true family since their union is not a true marriage[31] and does not provide the child with a proper model for its own future married life.

This argument about the child's right to be born normally in a normal family, I believe, also applies to parents who know certainly that if they beget a child it will have a radical genetic defect. Since, however, this is usually only a matter of probabilities, the issue is essentially prudential, a balance between a couple's right to attempt to beget a child in the normal manner and the probability of the child being radically defective. This applies also to couples who, for one reason or another, do not believe they can furnish the child with the fundamental necessities of life or proper care. It does not follow that the poor should not have children, because even the poor may be able to supply the child's essential needs, and often do, as the Holy Family exemplifies. "Better a little with fear of the Lord than a great fortune with anxiety" (Si 15:16).

Precisely because children are immature, they have needs and secondary rights to protection from abuse and for health care, education, and guidance, that adults do not have. Children also can own property, but its use by them is under the administration of the parents, and the rights that others may have in their labor is limited by their natural right to grow and be educated in normal circumstances. The neglect or abuse of children and adolescents, including their seduction and sexual abuse, especially incest, are very grave sins. Jesus said:

> "Things that cause sin will inevitably occur, but woe to the person through whom they occur. It would be better for him if a

---

[31] See pp. 427 ff. below.

millstone were put around his neck and he be thrown into the sea than for him to cause one of these little ones to sin" (Lk 17:1-2).[32]

Sexism

The primary rights of women and men do not differ, since both are equally human persons created in God's image (Gn 1:27); but *in relation to the family* husband and wife and children have different secondary rights grounded in the God-given nature of human sexuality and reproduction.[33] These secondary rights, however, must be regulated in such a way as not to derogate from the primary equality of all members of the family. In other than familial roles the secondary rights of men and women differ only insofar as they are more or less qualified for these roles by their sexual differences, and hence designated by the laws or customs of the society to fulfill these roles.

For example, it does not seem unjust that men have rights and obligations to combat duty in war, while women are denied these rights and are free of these obligations, both because they often have special obligations of child care and because they are in general physically less powerful and psychologically less aggressive than males. It is no derogation of a woman's basic rights that she does not have to fight, but, in a situation where this would be necessary to preserve her life or another's, these primary rights would take precedence over the secondary, as in the biblical example of Judith. Nor is it a derogation of a man's basic rights to admit that in some tasks that women alone can do (bear and nurse a child) or that they can do better (care for small children) that he can be only an auxiliary or a substitute.

---

[32] In this text "little ones" probably means "uninstructed persons," but it certainly includes minors and children. Most authors attribute this text to Q. It is also found in *I Clement* (46:7b-8) where instead of "little ones" we read "my elect." See Kloppenborg, *Parallels*, p. 183.

[33] CCC # 2202-2203, 2214. The *Catechism* largely avoids the controversial question about the difference between the role of father and mother in the family, but FC # 22-27 is devoted to the various different roles in the family.

This does not mean that the rights of women have not been grossly violated in the past. Feminists may very well be right in saying that the oppression of women is the origin of all oppressions. Certainly Genesis (4:19) places the polygyny of Lamech immediately after the murder of Abel by Cain and just before Lamech's even greater violence (4:23-24) as evidences of human sinfulness. The basic cause of this oppression is that men, because of their physical strength and their freedom from the problems of pregnancy, have been able to exploit women and treat them as sexual slaves.

The Old Testament, while still very much a part of the ancient world of male oppression, teaches the original equality of men and women as to basic rights, and as regards secondary rights provides for many protections of women against male abuse (e.g. Ex 21:7-11, 22; 22:15, 21; Dt 21:13-14; 22:13-29; 24:5). Jesus by abolishing the double standard of divorce reasserted the original sexual equality intended by the Creator (Mk 10:1-11). The early Church tried to apply this principle in the social condition of its times, as it did that of human equality to the institution of slavery (Phm v. 16).

The Christian answer to the sin of sexism is not to deny the differences of the sexes in social roles or natural basis, but to strike at the *abuse* of the hierarchical structures necessary for social organization by insisting that those having authority must use it in the service of the common good.[34]

> "You know that the rulers of the Gentiles lord it over them, and the great ones make their authority over them felt. But it shall not be so among you. Rather, whoever wishes to be great among you shall be your servant; whoever wishes to be first among you shall be your slave. Just so, the Son of Man did not come to be served but to serve and to give his life as a ransom for many" (Mt 20:25-28).

> "You call me 'teacher' and 'master' and rightly so, for indeed I am. If I, therefore, the master and teacher, have washed your feet, you ought to wash one another's feet. I have given you a

---

[34] See Ben Witherington, *Women in the Ministry of Jesus.*

model to follow, so that as I have done for you, you should also do" (Jn 13:13-15).

Thus oppression of women in the family can be remedied only by the conversion of men to follow the Pauline advice to love their wives as Christ does the Church (Eph 5:25). All this does not lead to the conclusion that the roles of women in society are only domestic, while roles other than the domestic are open only to men. It is true that the woman's care of the children and the home gives her fewer opportunities to enter into other social roles than the man, but in principle they are open to her whenever qualified, just as for men.[35]

Parental Responsibility

If men and women marry, then they must limit their careers to what is truly compatible with their domestic responsibilities. When men neglect their children for their career, they are committing a fundamental injustice. If they want to be entirely free for other social roles, then they must remain celibate, and the same is true of women. Nor does the celibacy of men or women mean that they must enter religious life, but only that they must remain chaste in the single life.

Thus women, just as men, may enter any profession, work, or political role they may choose, provided that this role is not incompatible with their choice of married or single life, and that they are qualified for it by talents and education. This does not mean, however, that it is necessary for all social roles to be 50% male and 50% female, since sexual differences may make a job more suitable for one than the other.

---

[35] "There is no doubt that the equal dignity and responsibility of men and women fully justifies women's access to public functions... While it must be recognized that women have the same right as men to perform various public functions, society must be structured in such a way that wives and mothers are not in practice *compelled* to work outside the home, and their families can live and prosper in a dignified way even when they themselves devote their full time to their own family. Furthermore, the mentality which honors women more for their work outside the home than for their work with the family must be overcome." John Paul II, *Familaris Consortio*, n. 23, ASS 74 (1982): Flannery, *Vatican Council II: More Documents*, pp. 832-834.

Right of Privacy

The sexual injustices other than the unjust discrimination based on mistaken stereotypes of sexual differences arise from the search for sexual pleasure in ways inconsistent with its basic purpose of procreation. Such perverse abuses of sex, as well as normal heterosexual intercourse by unmarried adults (fornication) although seriously wrong, are not directly acts of injustice to the partner (unless because of the risk of pregnancy or venereal disease such as AIDS) since they are either solitary or are with a consenting partner; yet they are harmful to the partner and to oneself.

Since public order is primarily an order of justice, can the state punish such behavior? Today, many argue that a right of privacy prohibits this and propose that there should be no laws against sexual actions between consenting adults.[36] On the contrary, societies in the past, including Israel under the Mosaic law did enact severe punishments, even the death penalty, against such actions (e.g., Ex 22:18; Lv 20:10-17; Dt 22:22, etc.). The reason seems to have been that it was believed that because such actions are an offense against human dignity and its Creator, to tolerate them would bring down a divine curse on the community, which, therefore, had to be cleansed of them by punishment.

In the Middle Ages such sins were often left to the Inquisition of the Church to judge (physical punishment was left to the state) on the grounds that they were commonly linked with demon worship and heresy.[37] In modern pluralistic society where there is no common agreement on the nature of sexuality, it seems logical enough that the legislature and the courts cannot arrive at a consistent and fair regulation of such acts, which therefore should be treated as belonging to the private sphere.

Yet such private acts do have public effects, first of all because prostitution, pornography, sexually enticing advertising, etc., are very profitable business enterprises; and second, because the practitioners

---

[36] See Richard F. Hixson, *Privacy in Public Policy.*

[37] John Tedeschi, *The Prosecution of Heresy*, pp. 105-108 gives some interesting statistical tables of actual trials; see also E. William Monter, *Frontiers of Heresy.*

of these acts seek recruits to their lifestyle and procure its public acceptance by various kinds of propaganda. Thus persons innocent of these vices, especially the inexperienced young (and those in middle-life crisis) can be recruited to them, with a consequent decadence of the social order, an increase of violence associated with sadistic sex, and especially a corruption of family life.

Therefore, it is commonly admitted that even in our pluralistic society, the state must protect the young from at least some of these sexual attractions, and furthermore that there must be some limits on the public advocacy and commercial exploitation of sexual vice. Quite naturally the Church feels that it has the responsibility of discouraging such social decadence. It is not an easy task in a society where individual "freedom" is almost the only value on which there is consensus. Yet it remains true that the great majority of American citizens draw the line at child pornography and pedophilia and support laws to criminalize such practices.

Sexual Abuses

Sexual actions which are manifestly unjust include seduction of the innocent (Ex 22:15-16) such as incest with father or mother, brother or sister (Lv 18:6-18), *rape* or sexual commerce against the will of the partner (Gn 34:1-31) and *adultery* (2 S 11:1-27; Jn 8:1-11), where one or both parties are married to other partners.

Seduction, especially in the form of incest, is a heinous injustice to children or inexperienced persons, because it leads them into objectively sinful behavior for the pleasure of the seducer.[38] It is thus intrinsically wrong since it is contradictory to the God-given purpose of sexuality which must be a truly *free* expression of marital love. Incest (Gn 19:30-38), in particular, often leaves deep psychic scars on the child, and may, of course, lead to pregnancy and a further injustice to the illegitimate offspring. Yet this is no justification of abortion, which only makes the innocent child a party to a further injustice even more grave than incest.

---

[38] CCC # 2356, 2388.

The seducer has the obligation to break off this behavior and, if it is compulsive, seek psychological help. While the compulsive character of this behavior may lessen the subjective guilt of the pedophile, it does not lessen the objective damage to the child. Since it is a disorder difficult to cure, pedophiliacs must not accept, nor be allowed by their employers to accept, positions of trust in which they might exploit children.

Rape is commonly not so much a matter of sexual desire as an expression of aggression with the intention to humiliate the victim, sometimes going as far as murder.[39] It is intrinsically wrong, since it violates the victim's right to her (or his) own body. The rapist should pay as far as possible for the physical and psychological damages and for the support of any offspring (although pregnancy from rape is not common). Rape can also occur in marriage, since although the husband has a right to the use of his wife's body, he has no right to use violence against her, even psychological violence by threats, to obtain the payment of this debt.[40] Associated with this is wife-abuse, much more common than often suspected. The husband's proper role as head of the family does not give him the right to use corporal punishment over his wife, let alone to use her as a punching-bag to work off his anger and frustration at life.[41]

The Decalogue in its Sixth Commandment takes adultery as typifying other sexual sins also forbidden by the law.[42] It is an injustice to the innocent partner or partners, who by the marriage covenant has exclusive right to the sexual use of the spouse's body. The depth of this injustice can be explored only after we have considered the nature of the personal relation between committed spouses. The offended party can *in justice* refuse permanently to continue to cohabit with the adulterous one, and this gives no justification for the adulterer to seek a divorce or to avoid fulfilling any other marriage obligation.

Adulterers have the responsibility to support and educate any

---

[39] CCC # 2356.

[40] See Edward J. Bayer, *Rape Within Marriage*.

[41] See Leonora E. Walker, *The Battered Woman*.

[42] CCC # 2380-2386.

illegitimate children who are born, and to repair the damage they have done to their own marriage and to that of a married accomplice. If the offended husband condoned the situation, he still has responsibility for his wife's child even if he is uncertain whether it is his, but if he is certain it is not his he does not have this responsibility in justice. As regards the rights of legitimate or illegitimate children to inheritance, the civil law should be followed.

B: DISTRIBUTIVE JUSTICE

Distributive Justice

Distributive justice is the distribution of the benefits or sanctions at the disposal of the officials of a community to its members according to their needs and merits. In the passage from Acts (4:35) already quoted, we are told that the goods put in the hands of the apostles by the members of the Jerusalem community "were distributed to each according to need." Not everyone in a community has the same needs, nor has everyone in the community deserved from the community equal benefits or incurred the same just penalties. The officials who have the responsibility of this distribution exercise just judgment in carrying out this responsibility when they do not favor or disfavor persons for any other motive than justice and act according to prudence.

> You shall not distort justice; you must be impartial. You shall not take a bribe; for a bribe blinds the eyes even of the wise and twists the words even of the just. Justice alone shall be your aim, that you may have life and may possess the land which the Lord, your God is giving you (Dt 16:19; cf. Ps 82; Jm 2:1-13).

"Justice is blind." Hence judges who punish crimes or adjudicate disputes over rights must exercise their power impartially, for Jesus asked, "Why do you notice the splinter in your brother's eye, but do not perceive the wooden beam in your own eye?" (Mt 7:3) and St. Paul stated, "By the standard by which you judge another you condemn yourself, since you, the judge, do the very same things" (Rm 2:1). Nor should human authorities pass judgment on anyone's ultimate worth, but only on their external merits which are publicly known.

> Who are you to pass judgment on someone else's servant? Before his own master he stands or falls (Rm 14:3).
>
> There is one lawgiver and judge who is able to save or to destroy. Who then are you to judge your neighbor? (Jm 4:11-13).

Yet because judges are sometimes themselves criminals does not render their judgments invalid. Hence the Council of Constance[43] condemned Wycliff's and John Hus' claims that the acts of authorities in mortal sin are invalid. Note how David after murdering Uriah unwittingly passed a valid judgment on himself (2 S 12:1-12). Yet when it is known that a judge is himself a criminal, this is certainly a cause of great scandal, as shown by the case of the two wicked judges who used their power for sexual harassment and condemned Susanna (Dn 13) and by Jesus' words against the sexist crowd of men who sought to kill the woman caught in adultery, "Let the one among you who is without sin be the first to throw a stone at her" (Jn 8:2-11).

To be impartial, judgment should presume innocence and should ordinarily be by law. "In rendering judgment, do not consider who a person is; give ear to the lowly and to great alike, fearing no man, for judgment is God's" (Dt 1:17). Yet to insure this impartiality special care must be given to the rights of the powerless.

> You shall not wrong any widow or orphan (Ex 22:21).
>
> You shall not deny one of your needy fellow men his rights in his lawsuit. You shall keep away from anything dishonest. The innocent and the just you shall not put to death, nor shall you acquit the guilty. Never take a bribe, for a bribe blinds even the most clear-sighted and twists the words even of the just. You shall not oppress an alien; you well know how it feels to be an alien, since you were once aliens yourselves in the land of Egypt (Ex 23:6-9; cf. 22:20; Dt 16:19).

---

[43] DS # 1165 and 1230.

> If you take your neighbor's cloak as a pledge, you shall return it to him before sunset, for this cloak of his is the only covering he has for his body. What else has he to sleep in? (Ex 22:25-26a, cf. Dt 24:12-13).

> When one of your fellow countrymen is reduced to poverty and is unable to hold out beside you, extend to him the privileges of an alien or tenant, so he may continue to live with you (Lv 25:35-37).

In the New Testament, the Epistle of St. James is especially concerned about this matter of impartiality:

> My brothers, show no partiality as you adhere to the faith in our glorious Lord Jesus Christ. For if a man with gold rings on his fingers and in fine clothes comes into your assembly, and a poor person in shabby clothes also comes in, and you pay attention to the one wearing the fine clothes and say, "Sit here, please," while you say to the poor one, "Stand there," or "Sit at my feet," have you not made distinctions among yourselves and becomes judges with evil designs?... Did not God choose those who are poor to be rich in faith and heirs of the kingdom that he promised to those who love him? But you dishonored the poor person... If you fulfill the royal law according to the scripture, "You shall love your neighbor as yourself," you are doing well. But if you show partiality, you commit sin, and are convicted by the law as transgressors (Jm 2:1-4, 5b-6a, 8-9; cf. also Eph 6:9).

Children's Needs

Besides impartiality in the administration of justice in the courts, there must be impartiality and distributive justice in the allotment of the benefits supplied by the common good. Children obviously have different needs than their parents, and therefore the parents have the responsibility to supply these needs without playing favorites.[44] The story of the envy of Joseph's brothers when they thought Jacob had favored

---

[44] CCC # 2221-2231, 2252-2253.

Joseph over them (Gn 37) and the succession of conflicts in David's family (2 S 13-18) illustrate the damage of this sibling rivalry. Childhood and adolescence is primarily a time of education and play not of work, and young people have a right to this period of growth.

Yet the history of childhood reveals that the human race is often very cruel to its children or neglectful of them.[45] The Old Law forbade the sacrifice of children practiced by the pagans (Lv 18:21; 20:2-5). I have already mentioned the historic prevalence of abortion and infanticide and the Church's struggle against it, especially by the practice of infant baptism. Upper class families have often turned over their children to wet-nurses and tutors or sent them away to boarding schools or simply left the servants to care for them.[46]

Lower class families have often been forced to put their children to work at an early age. In our society economic conditions are pressuring families to send their small children to day-care centers or leave them with baby-sitters. Moreover, the injustices of inequality in education, including neglect of children needing special education, and of miseducation are major failings of distributive justice. Again, Jesus' teaching on the dignity of the child has to be our guide and motivation.

Gender Needs

Do women have special needs which society is obliged in distributive justice to fill? Traditionally, it was believed that women because of physical and psychological differences and liability to pregnancy had need of various protections not supplied to men, and the Christian Church and early feminists worked for these protections. There is only one text in the New Testament in which the term "weaker sex" occurs:

---

[45] On the treatment of children in history see Philippe Ariès, *Centuries of Childhood* and Shulamith Sahar, *Childhood in the Middle Ages.*

[46] The education of the "Sun King" Louis XIV of France was utterly neglected by the Queen Mother so that in later life, in spite of the great pomp of his court which he assiduously cultivated, he felt more at home in the kitchen with the servants who had raised him! See W.H. Lewis, *The Splendid Century*, pp. 5-7.

> You husbands should live with your wives in understanding,
> showing honor to the weaker female sex, since we are joint heirs
> of the gift of life, so that your prayers may not be hindered (1 P
> 3:7).

The true sense of this text is not that women are intellectually or morally inferior to men, as some have quoted it to prove, but that Christian husbands have an obligation to appreciate the special problems of their wives (who in a pagan society were powerless), so that they can live in harmony and thus be able to pray together in good conscience.

Many of the features of other cultures and of our own in the past which are regarded as evidence of patriarchal oppression, in fact originated in the effort to supply this protection for women very much demanded in a violent society. Even now feminists generally admit that women have a special need for affirmative action to right inequalities, especially economic ones, and most admit that women now need special protection against sexual harassment at work and against rape and wife-abuse.

Some feminists, however, strongly resist the idea that women will always need to be protected by men, and believe that this protection will come from organized efforts by women to enact anti-discrimination laws and to re-educate future generations. I would suggest that secular history gives scant grounds for such optimism. Christian hope does give us a conviction that males can be transformed by conversion to Christian principles which, however, maintain that men and women do have some distinct and special needs within their basic equality.[47]

Social Differentiation

What of the distribution of the common good based on distinctions of birth, class, education, talent, virtue, and effort? The Christian tradition has not considered such distinctions as intrinsically unjust, pro-

---

[47] Accusations, not infrequent in feminist literature, that "the Church has been women's worst enemy" generally fail to compare the treatment of women by the Church with other truly comparable institutions. Obviously it will not do to compare the medieval Church's attitudes to women to that of twentieth century Europe or the U.S., rather than to those of medieval Islam, Hinduism, or Confucianism.

vided that primary human equality is respected. A developed social organism requires a diversity of gifts in the service of the common good.

St. Paul explicitly makes this point (very familiar to Greek philosophy) in 1 Corinthians 12 and applies it to the organism of the Church. So does the author of *1 Clement* (by tradition the fourth Bishop of Rome) writing only a few years after Paul to this same Corinthian church, who also compares the organization of the Church to that of an army.[48] Modern political science, public administration, economics, and sociology all affirm the same, and even anarchist and Marxist theorists admit it. Only the most extreme egalitarians could dream otherwise.[49]

The real issue of distributive justice is whether the present modes of secondary inequality are actually of service to the common good. Thus even an aristocracy based on birth would have social justification if it supplied a real "aristocracy" (rule of the best) to a society by reason of the ability of certain families to maintain a tradition of experience and spirit of *noblesse oblige* which would serve the whole community.

In society today, however, this social differentiation is based chiefly on three factors: wealth, competitive energy, and education. The inequality which has resulted is probably even more extreme than that found in older non-democratic societies, but it does differ from them in greater social *mobility*, the possibility of changing one's social rank. Nevertheless, it must be admitted that the vast majority of humankind will live and die in the socio-economic rank of their parents.[50]

Consequently, distributive justice in this area consists principally in seeking to defend primary rights and in opening greater opportunities for individuals to exercise their talents to the full. It does not consist in attempting to level all members of society to equality in all

---

[48] *1 Clement*, n. 7-38. Thomas J. Herron, *The Dating of the First Epistle of Clement to the Corinthians* has argued persuasively that the accepted date of A.D. 96 is based on biased evidence; c. 70 A.D. is more probable.

[49] See Ricky W. Griffin, *Management*, pp. 306-343 on organizational structure, especially pp. 309-312.

[50] For the recognition, even by rather conservative authors, of the existence of a persistent "under-class" in the United States, see William Julius Wilson, *The Truly Disadvantaged* and Kevin Phillips, *The Politics of Rich and Poor*.

things, since this can only eliminate from society the specialization of functions required to operate the social system for the good of all. Thus socialist states have not found it possible to go beyond a certain degree of leveling of education, income, and political influence.[51]

These considerations apply also to the Church where some hierarchical differentiation is necessary, as St. Paul showed (1 Cor 12) but where there has always been greater social mobility than in secular society.[52] While in former times the clergy often fared much better than the laity in education and even in lifestyle, this is hardly the case any longer. The main complaints of injustice here have to do not with the distribution of benefits (since all members of the Church have access to the Church's principal benefits, namely, the sacraments, preaching, counseling, and community encouragement) but with the distribution of offices (election of bishops, admission of women to Church office, lay participation in decisions, etc.).[53]

Option for the Poor

In modern society, as in the past, the most glaring inequality in the distribution of the common good has to do with economic goods, on which most other kinds of inequality rest. The struggle of the rich and the poor continues today in every society, and is more and more marked in the form of the struggle of the poor countries vis-a-vis the richer

---

[51] For what is the most successful of semi-socialist States, see Henry Milner, *Sweden: Social Democracy in Practice*, "Social Equality: Pro and Con," pp. 200-205. It should be noted that Sweden has a high degree of the sense of social solidarity, surviving even from medieval times, which is lacking in many modern societies where individualism has been stressed.

[52] It is true that under the "old regime" in Europe the upper clergy were commonly from the aristocracy, due in part to various forms of royal patronage, but the lower clergy has usually been drawn from the lower and lower-middle classes, since the middle class generally has not regarded this as a road to social advancement. Moreover, talented and energetic lower clergy were often able to rise into the upper clergy. Today in the United States the bishops are very largely of "humble" origin.

[53] A good picture of the actual working of the U.S. Catholic Church from an organizational point of view can be found in the works of Thomas J. Reese, S.J., *Archbishop: Inside the Power Structure* and *A Flock of Shepherds: The National Conference of Catholic Bishops.*

nations. The prophets of old never ceased to denounce this inequality, not because they advocated communism, but because this inequality denied to the poor their primary rights to a decent living conformed to human dignity.

Aristotle observed[54] that in the actual world (which our faith tells us is a fallen world) most states have two fundamental parties, one representing the rich, the other the poor, and both are more motivated by their own interests than by the common good. "Can there be peace between the hyena and the dog? Or between the rich and the poor can there be peace?" (Si 13:17). Marx developed this idea in his theory of the "class struggle." Vatican II, recognizing the truth contained in this theory, pointed out that although the Church has often been co-opted by the party of the rich, its essential mission from Christ demands that it make "a preferential option for the poor."[55] "For he is a God of justice, who knows no favorites. Though not unduly partial to the weak, yet he hears the cry of the oppressed" (Si 35:13).

Thus the Church must announce the coming of the Reign of God to all humanity without exception. This is of special significance to the poor, the powerless, and the marginalized, because they have been excluded by the domination of the rich from a full share in the common good.[56] "The rich man speaks and all are silent, his wisdom they extol to the clouds. A poor man speaks and they say, 'Who is that?' If he slips they cast him down" (Si 13:22). The great sign which Jesus gave John the Baptist to prove he was the Messiah was that "the poor have the good news preached to them" (Mt 11:5).

Jesus, in the Lucan account, declares the Beatitudes in these stark terms:

> Blessed are you who are poor,
> for the kingdom of God is yours.
> Blessed are you who are now hungry,
> for you will be satisfied.

---

[54] *Politics*, Bk. IV, c. 11, 1295a 25 sq.

[55] CCC # 2448, cf. also 2443-2449, 2462-2463.

[56] CA # 33.

> Blessed are you who are now weeping,
> for you will laugh...
> Woe to you who are rich,
> for you have received your consolation.
> Woe to you who are filled now,
> for you will be hungry.
> Woe to you who laugh now,
> for you will grieve and weep (Lk 6:20-21, 24-25).

Liberation theology has developed this point and (when freed from Marxist materialism and promotion of violence) is biblically founded.[57] The mission of the Church requires it to preach justice for the poor and to be their advocate in the face of governmental and social injustice,[58] and even to approve revolution by force when this conforms to the standards of a just war. At the same time it cannot support hatred of the rich, but must seek peace and reconciliation based on justice to all (the principle of solidarity).[59] "The rich and the poor have a common bond: the Lord is maker of them all" (Si 22:2; cf. 29:13). A principal obligation of the state is to defend the rights of its citizens, even by the use of force when necessary, both internally by police power and externally by war. I have already discussed the conditions under which such use of force is justified.

Today the term "socialism" is used by many to mean a political organization which seeks to redistribute wealth more equitably at the expense of the property "rights" of the rich. As we have seen, the term "socialism" properly refers to a particular theory of how the economic system should be regulated by centralized planning to produce the maximum efficiency and is contrasted to "capitalism" in which this regulation is left to the free market.

Since in actual practice it has been found that neither the theoretical model of socialism nor of capitalism can actually be realized in practice, but that a combination of both forms of regulation must be

---

[57] See Congregation for the Doctrine of the Faith, *Instruction on Certain Aspects of "The Theology of Liberation"* and *Instruction on Christian Freedom and Liberation.*

[58] CA # 43.

[59] CCC # 1939-1942, 1948.

used to make a society efficiently productive, the ideological struggle between socialism and capitalism is of little real interest.[60] The real interest of societies is to find an appropriate mix of these two forms of regulation which have a common objective, namely to produce and distribute an abundance of economic goods to all members of the society in such a way that at least the basic needs of all are met and an effective division of labor is maintained.

Because of its "preferential option for the poor," the Church today has a special role to play in promoting economic justice as an advocate for the basic rights of the most neglected members of society, just as Jesus did in his time and as the Church has tried to do, more or less successfully, throughout its history.[61] This theme has been developed by the liberation theologians of Latin America, partly through the use of Marxist social analysis. Unfortunately, this commendable effort to assimilate what is valid in Marxism has often been marred by utopian illusions about how economic justice can be obtained in undeveloped countries where the economic systems are still insufficiently productive to supply the needs of all.[62]

Duty to Work

Distributive justice concerns not only the distribution of the benefits of the common good, but also its *burdens*. This distribution of burdens places on each person and group certain obligations in social justice, since rights and obligations are reciprocal. Of these the first is the obligation to work for the common good. Contrary to the ancient and aristocratic attitude that despised manual work as servile, Jesus was known as "the carpenter's son" (Mt 13:55) and himself worked as a

---

[60] CCC # 2425. On individual economic initiative see # 2429. CA # 30-43 deals with the relation of private property, economic initiative, productivity, and social justice and shows that a medium between socialism and the unregulated free market must be sought.

[61] CCC # 2419-2449.

[62] See references in note 57 above.

carpenter (Mk 6:3).[63] St. Paul also said, "We toil, working with our own hands" (1 Cor 4:12) to support himself as a tentmaker (Ac 18:3). Because some of his converts misunderstood his teaching on the Second Coming of Christ to imply that they need work no longer and could live off the Christian community he also said:

> For you know how one must imitate us. For we did not act in a disorderly way among you, nor did we eat food received free from anyone. On the contrary, in toil and drudgery, night and day we worked, so as not to burden any of you. Not that we do not have the right. Rather, we wanted to present ourselves as a model for you, so that you might imitate us. When we were with you, we instructed you that if anyone was unwilling to work, neither should that one eat. We hear that some are conducting themselves among you in a disorderly way, by not keeping busy but minding the business of others. Such people we instruct and urge in the Lord Jesus Christ to work quietly and eat their own food (2 Th 3:7-12; cf. Eph 4:28).

Contemplatives

Vatican II teaches that all members of society have a duty to work for society, to employ their talents not only for their individual or family good, but for the common good.[64] The notion of a "leisure class" in the sense of a group of people who because of their wealth can simply enjoy life without contributing to society is therefore untenable, since, as we have shown, pleasure is not an end in itself and recreation is justified as a preparation for work.[65] Work and appropriate leisure are for all. This does not mean, however, that society can do without a "contemplative class," that is, a group of people freed from economic burdens to devote themselves to the pursuit of truth and the worship of

---

[63] The movement for the celebration in the liturgy of a feast of Jesus the Worker was very active during the papacy of Pius XII, but then faded; see "*Jésus-Ouvrier*" in J. Jacquemet, *Catholicisme*, 6:810-811. With the Vatican II reform of the liturgy, May 1 was designated the Feast of St. Joseph the Worker.

[64] See Vatican II, GS # 67; the encyclical of John Paul II, *Laborem Exercens*, Sept. 14, 1981 (AAS 73, 1981), pp. 577-647[2]; and CCC # 2427-2428 on the dignity of work.

[65] See pp. 189 ff. above.

God, a class that includes intellectuals, artists, writers, scientists, scholars, philosophers, and religious contemplatives. This "contemplative class" makes an extremely important social contribution, although what they do is not directly productive of material goods.[66]

Neither is the military (police, soldiers) engaged in work in the narrow sense, yet they are necessary for the protection of the society. Yet all these groups "work" in the broader sense of employing their energies in a manner which serves the whole society. Thus it is contrary to distributive justice for people of talent to waste their talents, or to refuse to assume the burdens of a special vocation, including the vocations to social service, political office, and the religious and priestly life.

Gender Roles?

Feminists today in their commendable campaign to defend the equal basic rights of men and women have too often confused this issue of distributive justice by the indiscriminate use of the term "patriarchy," which they define as "oppressive male domination."[67] This seems unfortunately to imply that the term "father" means a "tyrant," when in fact it signifies a man in a very positive role as one who tenderly cares for his children. It was in this sense that Jesus called God "Abba" (Mk 14:36) and taught us to pray the "Our Father" (Mt 6:9; Lk 11:2-4). The fact that for so many women today the term has negative connotations probably reflects the prevalence in our culture of incestuous child abuse and wife abuse. Incestuous and abusive fathers do not deserve the name.[68]

---

[66] CA # 49-50. See also Congregation for Religious and Secular Institutes, *"Instructio de vita contemplativa et de monialium clausura,"* Nov. 10, 1969 and "The Contemplative Dimension of Religious Life," Feb. 12, 1981 for the Church's high evaluation of the contemplative life.

[67] See Elizabeth Wendel Moltmann, *A Land Flowing with Milk and Honey*, Chapter 2, "What is Patriarchy?" pp. 29-41.

[68] See Chapter 3 of my *Justice in the Church*. There is extensive sociological and psychological research on the role of the father in the family: see Clayton Barbeau, *The Head of the Family*; Leonard G. Benson, *Fatherhood: A Sociological Perspective*; David B. Lynn, *The Father: His Role in Child Development*; L. McKee, and M. O'Brien, eds., *The Father Figure*; Michael E. Lamb, ed., *The Father's Role: Cross-cultural Perspectives*; Phyllis Bronstein and Carolyn Pape Cowan, eds., *Fatherhood Today*; Stanley M. Cath, et al., eds., *Fathers and Their Families*.

The biblical notion of true fatherhood can be found in the portrait of Tobit, "a noble and good father,... righteous and charitable" (Tb 7:7), who urges his son:

> "Honor your mother, and do not abandon her as long as she lives. Do whatever pleases her, and do not grieve her spirit in any way. Remember, my son, that she went through many trials for your sake while you were in her womb" (Tb 4:3b-4),

or Jesus' description of the wise and forgiving father in the Parable of the Two Sons (Lk 15:11-32).

Some Christian feminists think that although Jesus treated women as equals to men, and St. Paul formulated this teaching in the famous dictum, "There is neither Jew nor Greek, there is neither slave nor free person, there is not male and female; for you are all one in Christ Jesus" (Gal 3:28), yet the same Paul and the early Church soon compromised with the "patriarchal" society of their times. They believe this oppressive patriarchalism is reflected in certain passages of the New Testament (1 Cor 11:1-16; 14:33b-36), especially in later writings (Eph 5:21-6:9; Col 3:19-25; 1 Tm 2:1-6:2; Tt 2:2-3:2; 1 P 2:13; 3:7), which speak of the husband as "head" of the family, and urge the wife (as also children and slaves) to "submit to their husbands in everything" (Eph 5:4).[69]

While it is certainly true that these pastoral passages of the New Testament relating to family life, the so-called "domestic codes," reflect the social conditions of the Roman Empire in the first century and require critical-historical interpretation, it is also true that they are applications of certain principles that flow from the whole Judaeo-Christian ethic.

Philip Towner has shown[70] that contrary to some exegetes these codes are not simply borrowed from the Stoics (although they have borrowed Greek literary forms). Nor do they reflect the development of

---

[69] For a review and analysis of feminist exegesis see Francis Martin, *The Feminist Question* (Grand Rapids, MI: Eerdmans, 1994).

[70] *The Goal of Our Instruction*, pp. 201-199, and Salvatore M. Ballacchino, *The Household Order Texts*.

an "early Catholic" or "Christian bourgeois" morality of conformity to Hellenistic society which is supposed to have developed when the Church lost hope in the Second Coming of Christ. Instead, they are based on the need to keep that faith alive in the face of false teaching and to witness the Gospel to pagans quick to seize on every evidence that Christians were a source of the moral decadence of Roman society.

According to natural law the family is a natural institution designed by God as the source of new life and of human society.[71] The child cannot come into existence without a mother and requires her as its nurse and the first person to whom it is bonded. Thus in the family the woman has a vital role which requires that at least during the childhood of her children she be first of all occupied physically and psychologically with pregnancy and child-care. Given our fallen condition, just as work which God intends to be a joyful share in his own creativity is now a sentence to hard labor, so child-bearing which God gave woman as a great gift, can become a heavy burden. God declared that the consequence of humanity's going its own way would be that men would be forced to struggle to make a living, and to women he said:

> "I will intensify the pangs of your childbearing; in pain shall you bring forth children. Yet your urge shall be for your husband and he shall be your master" (Gn 3:16).[72]

Consequently, mothers and their children require the care of a husband, who beyond his biological role as an impregnator is also equipped by his greater physical size and strength and psychological aggressiveness to protect his family and to seek food and other material needs for it. In our fallen condition this task of the male is also a heavy and dangerous one (Gn 3:17-20), but the man is compensated for its labor and risks by the fact that in the human species (unlike other mammals) his mate is always physically prepared for intercourse with him. They are thus bonded both by sexual pleasure and by human compan-

---

[71] CCC # 2201-2203.

[72] For exegesis of this text see Claus Westermann, *Genesis 1-11*, pp. 261-267.

ionship.[73] Furthermore, the male discovers that in his children, with whom he shares his experience and wisdom (as does the mother too, but in her own way), he relives his youth and finds consolation against death, inevitable in our fallen state.

Domestic and Public Roles

Moreover, in a social unit of two adult persons and minor children, decisions must be made by agreement of the adults, but agreement is not always achieved even with good will. Since decisions cannot be made by majority vote with only two voters, and since an absolute right of veto by either would make action impossible, it is necessary that the responsibility for final decision be assigned to one or the other partner. This assignment cannot be based on virtue or wisdom, because which of the partners is to evaluate such qualifications? Hence this headship ought ordinarily to be decided by some obvious natural difference. This designation is furnished by the male's physical strength and aggressiveness, and by his role of dealing with the wider world outside the domestic circle during the child-bearing period of his wife.

The wife, on the other hand, ought to be consulted in all important decisions, especially if they directly concern her own interests. Since sometimes she is in fact more intelligent and virtuous than her husband he often ought to follow her lead, though she continues to respect his proper role. Thus the biblical position that the man is by nature the head of the family is consistent with the natural law and with the complementarity of the sexes and the mutuality of their dignity and love. It may be true that the biblical statements of this teaching are somewhat conditioned by the "patriarchalism" of the culture in which they were written. However, this conditioning does not extend to their essential intention, which is to defend the equal personal dignity of husband and wife, while at the same time recognizing their difference of roles in marriage in mutual service.

---

[73] For reviews of research on sexual differences in primates and humans see Robert Pool, *Eve's Rib* and Robert Wright, *The Moral Animal.*

> Be subordinate to one another out of reverence for Christ. Wives be subordinate to your husbands as to the Lord. For the husband is head of his wife just as Christ is head of the Church, he himself the savior of the body. As the Church is subordinate to Christ, so wives should be subordinate to their husbands in everything. Husbands, love your wives, even as Christ loved the Church and handed himself over for her... So also husbands should love their wives as their own bodies. He who loves his wife loves himself. For no one hates his own flesh but rather nourishes and cherishes it, even as Christ does the Church, because we are members of his body. "For this reason a man shall leave his father and his mother and be joined to his wife and the two shall become one flesh" [Gn 2:24]. In any case, each one of you should love his wife as himself, and the wife should respect her husband (Eph 5:21-33; cf. 1 Cor 11:3-16; Col 3:18, 4:1; 1 Tm 2:11-15; Tt 2:5; 1 P 3:1-7).

The historical fact that this male dominance in the family has been the situation, although in various degrees and forms and often abusively, in all known human cultures supports this conclusion.[74] The feminist idea that somehow in the future some other arrangement will be achieved by legislation and education seems utopian, and stands in the way of realistic efforts to work against the constant danger of the sin of sexism, i.e., of real exploitation of the vulnerability of women.

Although these structural relations in the family are determined by the very nature of human sexuality, it does not follow, as was often supposed in the past, that the domestic roles of either woman or man ought to determine their roles in the wider social order whose structures are a matter not of nature but of human invention. Therefore, it is a form of the sin of sexism to pass over women for promotion in business, the professions, the academy, the Church, etc., simply on the grounds of sexual *stereotypes*, i.e., preconceived views of the different talents or performance of women and men. The qualifications of individuals for tasks must be judged on individual merit.

---

[74] Stephen Goldberg, *The Inevitability of Patriarchy*, gives the evidence for the cross-cultural universality of male dominance. Peggy Reeves Sunday, *Female Power and Male Dominance*, marshals some of the difficulties about this thesis. Robert Pool, *Eve's Rib*, pp. 194-236 discusses the nature/culture debate.

This principle obviously raises a question about the long tradition in both the Eastern and Western Churches of considering only men as qualified for ordination to priesthood (and in the Latin Church only celibate men for priesthood and in the East for the episcopacy). This tradition has been recently again affirmed by both Catholic and Orthodox Church authorities. However, this is too complex a biblical, historical, theological, and pastoral problem to be discussed here.[75]

The principle of appointment to office in view of the common good of the community also condemns nepotism, cronyism, and other forms of favoritism in organizations, including the Church. Some allowance, though, must be made for the fact that an executive needs assistants whom he knows well and who are loyal to him. The question of political *patronage* is especially difficult, since in a two-party system political unity of action of a party finds its support in the power to fill offices with persons of the dominant party. When public service does not suffer significantly from this patronage, it seems it is not unjust, since the opposition party will also have its opportunity to appoint in due time; but the abuses are legion and public service often does suffer. In all such matters if appointment to office is by means of election, the electors have the duty in justice to vote for the person they regard as best qualified for the office.

C: RELATED VIRTUES

Related Kinds of Justice

The cardinal virtue of justice perfects our will to give to others what is strictly due them, but the Bible includes under the notion of justice or

---

[75] For my views and bibliography on the ordination of women see my article "Gender and the Priesthood of Christ: A Theological Reflection," *The Thomist*, 57, 3 (July, 1993):343-379, an excerpt from my *Justice in the Church* where the question is further argued. The official declarations on the topic are: Congregation for the Doctrine of the Faith, "Declaration on the Question of the Admission of Women to the Ministerial Priesthood," *Inter Insigniores*, Oct. 15, 1976, AAS 69 (1977); *Origins* 6, 33 (Feb. 3, 1977):518-531 and John Paul II, "Apostolic Letter on Ordination and Women," *Ordinatio Pastoralis*, May 22, 1994, *Origins* 24, 4 (9 June, 1994):50-52.

"righteousness" proper behavior in many other situations. St. Thomas Aquinas identified and classified these secondary forms of virtue as follows:

- A. Our debt may be strictly obligatory but too great to repay in full.
    1. Our debt to God by *religion*.
    2. Our debt to our parents by *obedience*.
    3. Our debt to our country by *patriotism*.
- B. Our debt is real but not strictly obligatory.
    1. Our debt to tell the truth, but not about all we know in *truthfulness*.
    2. Our debt to thank benefactors sufficiently in *gratitude*.
    3. Our debt to get moderate compensation for injustices in *leniency*.
- C. Without a real debt, still it is appropriate that we
    1. Show *liberality* to others.
    2. Show *affability* to others.
    3. Show *fairness* to others.

Virtue of Religion

Religion (*eusébeia*, Ac 3:12 or *threskeía*, Jm 1:27, better translated in English as "piety" or "devotion") is the virtue which helps us to show due worship to God as the source and goal of all things, an obligation which is strictly binding, but cannot be paid in full.[76] The virtue of religion as a distinct and specific virtue regulates various acts of worship such as prayer and sacrifice (its material object) according to a kind of justice or appropriateness or equality (its formal object), so that this worship does not err either by excess or defect. Therefore, it is a moral not a theological virtue since its object is not God himself but acts of worship. Yet, it falls short of being a species of the cardinal virtue of justice, because, although we certainly owe God worship, we can never pay God a worship that is equal to his worth, except as we

---

[76] CCC # 2105; cf. the whole treatment of the first three commandments, CCC # 2083-2195. CCC Part II on the sacraments and Part IV on prayer also deal largely with the practice of this virtue.

join Jesus in his worship of the Father. As Son of God Jesus alone can offer that full measure.

> So be imitators of God, as beloved children, and live in love, as Christ loved us and handed himself over for us as a sacrificial offering to God for a fragrant aroma (Eph 5:1).

> We have such a high priest, who has taken his seat at the right hand of the throne of the Majesty in heaven, a minister of the sanctuary and of the true tabernacle that the Lord, not man, set up.... For if the blood of goats and bulls and the sprinkling of a heifer's ashes can sanctify those who are defiled so that their flesh is cleansed [Lv 16:6-16], how much more will the blood of Christ, who through the eternal Spirit offered himself unblemished to God, cleanse our consciences from dead works to worship the living God (Heb 8:1-2, 9:13-14).

True religion is, therefore, one of the greatest virtues, but it is less than the theological virtues whose object is not merely the worship of God, but God himself.

The natural law as well as the first three of the Ten Commandments (Ex 20:2-11; Dt 5:6-15) requires that we worship God, since as intelligent creatures we must in truth recognize him as our Creator and need to express this by word and gesture in the human community, as we express every other important truth. To be silent about the greatness of God is completely unnatural. Of old the wife of David, Michal mocked him for dancing, half-clad, before the ark when it was brought into Jerusalem, and was punished by being sterile (2 S 6:20-23). As Jesus said when the Pharisees demanded he silence his disciples as they came singing into Jerusalem, "I tell you, if they keep silent, the stones will cry out!" (Lk 19:40).

The first three Commandments demand that first we worship God alone and not idols; second, that we honor his Name; third, that we keep the Sabbath.[77] The universal natural law which this Third Commandment implements is that we set aside proper time for worship.

---

[77] CCC First Commandment # 2083-2141, Second Commandment # 2142-2167, Third Commandment # 2168-2195.

Hence the early Church used its freedom from the ceremonial precepts of the law (Col 2:16) to choose Sunday, the day of the Resurrection, in place of the Sabbath to indicate the new creation of the New Covenant, contrary to certain modern "sabbatarian" Protestant sects such as the Seventh Day Adventists.[78]

As we have seen, the prophets of the Old Testament never ceased to insist that true worship of God must begin from the heart. Isaiah repeats the indignant words of God to the Jews:

> "What care I for the number of your sacrifices? ...
> Wash yourselves clean!
> Put away your misdeeds from before my eyes;
>   cease doing evil; learn to do good.
> Make justice your aim: redress the wronged,
>   hear the orphan's plea, defend the widow" (Is 1:11, 16-17).

The Epistle of St. James recalls this Old Testament prophecy when it say: "Religion that is pure and undefiled before God and the Father is this: to care for orphans and widows in their affliction and to keep oneself unstained by the world" (Jm 1:27). The same theme is found in many other places in the Old Testament, e.g., 1 S 15:22; Ho 6:4-6; Jr 7; Am 4:4, 5:21-25; Mi 6:6-8. It is summed up in Psalm 50: "Do I [God] eat the flesh of strong bulls, or is the blood of goats my drink? Offer to God praise as your sacrifice and fulfill your vows to the most High" (v. 13-14). And this is confirmed by the words of Jesus to the Samaritan woman:

> "Believe me, woman, the hour is coming when you will worship the Father neither on this mountain nor in Jerusalem... The hour is coming, and is now here, when true worshippers will worship the Father in Spirit and truth, and indeed the Father seeks such people to worship him. God is Spirit, and those that worship him must worship in Spirit and truth" (Jn 4:21, 23-24).

It is wrong, however, to think in terms of "faith vs. cult" as some exegetes have done, or to disparage "cultic" religion. Neither the proph-

---

[78] CCC # 2174-2175, 2178.

ets nor Jesus opposed the expression of the internal worship of God to the cultic, external ceremonies which they themselves faithfully observed. As we see from his baptism by John (Mk 1:9-11), his praying in the Temple (Mk 11:15-19), his keeping of the Passover (Mk 14:12-31), and his participation in the synagogue services (Lk 4:14-30), Jesus and his apostles were pious Jews who faithfully observed the cultic law.

Moreover, in commanding the practice of Baptism (Mt 28:19) and the Eucharist (Lk 22:19; 1 Cor 11:24-25) Jesus formally instituted a new mode of external worship which was retained in the Gentile churches, when the ceremonial law ceased to be practiced.[79] In the development of these new rituals the Church found guidance in the principles that underlay the old ceremonial law of the Torah, rich in archetypal symbolism common to all the ancient religions but, in the case of the Jews, controlled by belief in one God. In these ceremonies also Christians could read the foreshadowing of the mysteries of the Incarnation and Trinity.[80]

Christian worship is of the Father, *through* the Son, and *in* the Holy Spirit and can be given *absolutely* only to them.[81] *Relatively* it is given to their images and symbols such as the Cross. Such worship of God by means of images is not the idolatry forbidden by the First Commandment, as long as it remains strictly relative.[82] For the Jews, however, even such relative worship of God through images was forbidden in order to shield them from the temptations to idolatry which surrounded them and into which in the days of the kings they actually fell.

> By adoring Astarte, the goddess of the Sidonians, and Milcom, the idol of the Ammonites, Solomon did evil in the sight of the Lord; he did not follow him unreservedly as his father David had done. Solomon then built a high place to Chemosh, the idol

---

[79] The Rites of Christian Initiation: Baptism and Confirmation, CCC # 1213-1321; and the Eucharist, # 1322-1419.

[80] CCC # 1093-1098.

[81] CCC # 2627.

[82] Gregory the Great, DS # 477; Nicaea II, DS # 601; CCC # 1159-1162.

of Moab, and to Molech, the idol of the Ammonites, on the hill opposite Jerusalem. He did the same for all his foreign wives, who burned incense and sacrificed to their gods (1 K 11:5-8; cf. also "The Letter of Jeremiah Against Idolatry" in Baruch 6).

The earthly presence of God incarnate in Jesus Christ has met this human longing for a *tangible* God that gave rise to idolatry, so that this temptation is no longer so dangerous to Christians. Hence, iconoclasm was condemned as heretical at the Councils of Nicaea II and Trent.[83] Icons and statutes of Jesus, Our Lady, and the saints are not only permitted but prescribed in Catholic churches.

The reverence given to the saints, however, is not "worship" (*latria*), but only "reverence" (*dulia*) and in the case of Mary "special reverence" (*hyperdulia*)[84] because of her special relation to Christ. This reverence toward the saints enhances, not detracts from, the worship we give God, since what we revere in them is the effect of God's grace. The saints are, as it were, icons of God, since in them shines forth in full splendor the "image of God" in which all humanity was created, and the glory of the Incarnate Word to whom they have been faithfully conformed.

Christians of the reformed churches often confuse *dulia* with *latria* and hence reject Catholic veneration of the saints and prayer to them; but it is not *latria* to pray to other creatures and to ask their intercession for us with God. In fact all community prayer consists in creatures praying for each other and calling on others to pray for them.[85] We read in the New Testament the request to the Church on earth, "First of all, then, I ask that supplications (*deéseis*), prayers, petitions, and thanksgiving be offered for every one" (1 Tm 2:1). Why then should it be wrong to ask the same of those members of the Church who are already with the Risen Lord?

In order that veneration should not be given to those who do not truly exemplify Christian holiness, the Church forbids the *public* ven-

---

[83] Nicaea II, DS # 600-603 and Trent, DS # 1823.

[84] Nicaea II, DS # 600-603.

[85] CCC # 946-962, 2634-2636, 2673-2682, 2683-2684.

eration of persons who have not been officially canonized as "saints," "holy ones."[86] The term "holy" (*qadosh*) is frequently used in the Old Testament, especially in the Holiness Code of Leviticus ("Keep your-self holy, because I am holy," Lv 11:44b). It refers especially to the setting aside of persons and things, places, times, and actions as *sacred*, that is, dedicated to God, in contrast to what is *profane* (from the Latin for "outside the shrine"), that is, for ordinary daily use but not as such sinful. For the Christian in a very real way all creation has again been made holy as God originally created it, sanctified by Christ ("Thus he declared all foods clean," Mk 7:19). However, the distinction of sacred from profane remains valid in that a special holiness belongs to some places, things, and persons which are centers, instruments, and sources through which God's grace is communicated to the world.

The internal acts of worship of intellect and will are first of all *devotion*, the prompt will to offer oneself to God in his service.[87] God's grace leads us to meditate on him and his "wondrous deeds" (Ps 66:3, 5) or contemplate him as "King of glory" (Ps 24:8-10). Its principal and proper effect is joy of mind, although secondarily it can cause sadness because of our sins and the world's sins and our consequent distance from God (Ps 42).

The second act of worship is *prayer*, which St. John Damascene[88] called "a raising of the mind to God" and "a reverent request of some fitting benefit from God." It is thus an act of the practical reason moved by the will. Jesus in his humanity prayed (cf. e.g., Lk 6:12; 9:18; 9:28; 11:1; 22:23; 22:41; 23:46; Jn 17); so do the angels, the saints, and all living persons. Wycliff and Quesnell thought that sinners and those not predestined cannot pray, but this opinion was condemned by the Church.[89] St. Thomas Aquinas thought those in purgatory cannot pray but only be prayed for, but other theologians disagree, and the Magisterium has not repudiated the practice of praying not only for but

---

[86] CCC # 828-829.

[87] St. Thomas Aquinas, *S.T.*, II-II, q. 82 who points out (a. 3) that contemplation causes devotion and (a. 4) gladness (*laetitia*) is its proper effect.

[88] *De fide orth.*, l. 3, c. 24; CCC # 2559-2565.

[89] DS # 1175-6 for Wycliff; DS # 2450 and 2459 for Quesnell.

to the "poor souls."[90] Certainly those who are in hell will not pray; if they had prayed sincerely they would never have ended there.

We can pray for anyone who is not damned (we do know not who, except the fallen angels, are damned) and we can pray for anything good, yet should pray principally for spiritual goods. We can never pray for a moral evil, but we can pray that someone suffer a proportionate physical evil as a remedial punishment or purifying trial.

Jesus himself has taught us to pray the Lord's Prayer, the model of all prayer (Mt 6:9-13; Lk 11:2-4).[91] Prayer can be mental or vocal, and vocal prayer requires at least an implicit and virtual attention. It also can be solitary ("Go to your inner room, close the door, and pray to your Father in secret," Mt 6:5-8) or in a small group.[92]

> "Again, amen, I say to you, if two of you agree on earth about anything for which they are to pray, it will be granted to them by my heavenly Father. For where two or three are gathered together in my name, there am I in the midst of them" (Mt 18:19-20).

Prayer can also be public and liturgical.[93] St. Paul says, "It is my wish, then, that in every place the men should pray, lifting up holy hands, without anger or argument" (1 Tm 2:8; cf. 1 Cor 11). The Church gives great care to its liturgy, as it did in reforming the liturgy at the Second Vatican Council, because "the law of prayer is the law of faith" (*lex orandi est lex credendi*).[94] Prayer properly includes the raising of one's mind and heart to God, petition for one's own and others' needs,

---

[90] *S.T.*, II-II, q. 83, 11 ad 3. CCC # 958 says "Our prayer for them [the "dead" for whom the Church offers her prayers] is capable not only of helping them, but of making their intercession for us effective." Since the blessed souls in heaven are not usually referred to as "dead," it would seem this text by "their intercession" means the intercession of the dead in purgatory and thus supports the common view that "the holy souls in purgatory" do intercede for us.

[91] CCC # 2759-2865 is an extended commentary on the Lord's Prayer.

[92] CCC # 2628-2649.

[93] CCC # 1076-1112.

[94] CCC 1074-1075. According to the article "Lex orandi, lex credendi," in *Catholicisme* 7:529-30 this phrase (in a slightly different form) is first recorded in Prosper of Aquitain's (attributed to Celestine I) *Indiculus de gratia Dei* (PL 51:209; DS 246).

praise of God, expression of confidence in him, and thanksgiving (1 Tm 2:1).

For all adults prayer is absolutely necessary for their salvation (Mt 7:7; 26:41; Lk 11:9; Jn 16:24; Jm 4:2-3). Origen, Tertullian, and St. Augustine wrote classic works on prayer,[95] the scholastics analyzed it, the great mystics recounted their experiences with it. Furthermore, we are commanded not only by the divine law to pray (Si 18:22; Lk 18:1; Col 4:2; Eph 6:17-18; 1 Th 5:17) but also by the natural law as is evident from the world-wide practice in all religions of some form of prayer.[96] In the Parable of the Persistent Widow, Jesus told us "to pray always without becoming weary" (Lk 18:1).[97]

Christians also pray to each other in that we ask each other for prayers, just as we pray to the saints, but with greater confidence in the saints because their inalienable union to God in perfect charity assures that their prayers are worthy and effective. The Council of Trent did not say we are bound to pray to saints, but only said it is good and useful according to the liturgical practice of the Church.[98]

Prayer never fails to merit before God, to satisfy for our sins, and to win a generous answer from God (Mt 7:8; Lk 11:9, 13; Jn 14:13-14; 16:24; 1 Jn 5:14; Ps 50:15), if it is made in sincere faith (Jm 1:6; Mt 21:22; Mk 11:24; Rm 10:13; Heb 4:16) and asks for what is necessary for salvation for oneself (Mt 7:11; Lk 11:13; 1 Jn 5:14, 16; Is 1:15). Prayer for the salvation of others is also powerful ("The fervent prayer of a righteous person is very powerful," Jm 5:16), but by their free will those for whom we pray can resist conversion.[99] To be effective prayer

---

[95] Tertullian, *De Oratione Liber: Tract on Prayer*; Origen, *On Prayer*, pp. 81-170; Augustine, *Faith, Hope, and Charity (Enchiridion)*. For a synthesis of Augustine's thought on the subject, see Thomas A. Hand, O.S.A., *St. Augustine on Prayer*.

[96] See S.D. Grill, "Prayer," *The Encyclopedia of Religion*, vol. 11, pp. 489-494 who notes that "prayer" has different meanings in different religions. For example, prayer in a non-theistic religion like Buddhism cannot be identical with prayer in the theistic religions.

[97] CCC # 2613 calls this (Lk 18:1-8) along with the Parable of the Importunate Friend (Lk 11:5-13), and the Parable of the Pharisee and the Tax Collector (Lk 18:9-14), "The three principal parables on prayer."

[98] DS # 1821.

[99] St. Thomas Aquinas writes, "It sometimes happens that prayer made for another is not effective, even though made devoutly and perseveringly and although it is for another's

must be persevering (Lk 11:5; 18:1; Mt 15:22) and presupposes that the one who prays is well-disposed to receive God's answer according to God's wisdom and will. As already mentioned, even those in the state of sin are heard by God if their prayer is sincere.

It accords with human nature that we should also give external expression to our internal prayer, and this instructs and encourages others to pray themselves. These external acts, in addition to liturgical and others forms of public prayer, are specifically: (1) adoration, (2) feasts, (3) sacrifice, (4) oaths, (5) vows, (6) blessings, (7) praises.

Adoration is an external act by which we express our submission to God by bowing, kneeling, prostrating, or simply folding or raising our hands (Gn 18:2, 43:26; Jos 5:15; 2 K 1:16, 19:18; Est 13:14; Jb 31:27; Mt 4:9; Rv 19:10; 22:8).[100]

Feasts are a second kind of act of worship which consists in commemorations and celebrations of God's great acts on our behalf, often preceded by preparatory fasts for the forgiveness of our sins. As the Third Commandment formerly required on the Sabbath, we now on Sundays and on "holy days of obligation" attend the Eucharistic assembly and abstain from servile work to praise and thank God. This obligation is serious, since without such a communal celebration the Christian community becomes weakened and our own fidelity is imperiled.[101]

> We should not stay away from our assembly, as is the custom of some, but encourage one another, and this all the more as you see the day drawing near (Heb 10:25).

"The day drawing near" indicates that we can hardly expect to share in the eternal liturgy before the Trinity in heaven, if we absent

---

salvation, because of an impediment on the part of the one for whom the prayer is said, as Jeremiah [15:1] says, 'The Lord said to me: Even if Moses and Samuel stood before me, my heart would not turn toward this people.' Nevertheless, such prayer will be meritorious for the one who prays from charity, according to the Psalm [Ps 35:13], 'My prayer is turned back into my bosom' on which the Gloss comments, 'Although it does not profit others, yet I am not deprived of my reward.'"

[100] CCC # 2628.

[101] CCC # 2043, 2168-2195.

ourselves from the liturgy on earth. Some young people say, "I don't get anything out of Mass." The Eucharist is not just "getting." It is first of all *giving* (offering) of ourselves to God and to our Christian community. We must not just be passive onlookers, but active participants. This communal worship is so essential to the very existence of a local Church that the obligation to take part is so serious that according to the *Catechism of the Catholic Church* failure to fulfill it without a reasonable excuse is a grave sin, although many Catholics today seem ignorant of its gravity.[102]

A third kind of act of worship and, indeed, the most perfect of all is *sacrifice*, that is, the offering of oneself or one's possessions to God in recognition that all we have is his gift. For the Christian the act of sacrifice can only be fulfilled by participation in the one perfect sacrifice which Christ offers to the Father.[103] "Sacrifice" can be taken in a broad sense: "Do not neglect to do good and to share what you have; God is pleased by sacrifices of that kind" (Heb 13:15-16). In a stricter sense it refers to an internal self-offering: "Let yourselves be built into a spiritual house to be a holy priesthood to offer spiritual sacrifices acceptable to God through Jesus Christ" (1 P 2:5, 9). In the most specific sense it refers to an external and public liturgical act: the Temple sacrifices of the Old Law and the Eucharistic Sacrifice of the New.[104] The natural law prescribes such an external recognition of the Creator as is evidenced by the rituals of most of the world religions.[105]

A standard definition of a sacrifice is "an offering of an external, sensible and permanent thing through some change or destruction of it by a priest to testify to God his dominion and our subjection." Nevertheless, note that "some change" such as the simple act of setting the offering aside or lifting it up suffices for a true sacrifice and therefore its destruction is not essential, although in the sacrifices of the Old Law this was a common feature. Therefore, in defining the offering of the

---

[102] CCC # 2181. "Those who deliberately fail in this obligation commit a grave sin."

[103] CCC # 613-614.

[104] CCC # 2099-2100.

[105] On sacrifice in primitive religions see Emile Durkheim, *The Elementary Forms of the Religious Life*, pp. 366-392. Aquinas argues, *S.T.*, II-II, q. 85, a. 1, that to offer sacrifice to God pertains to the natural law.

Eucharist as a sacrifice it is not necessary to discover in it any act of destruction (its consumption is not a destruction), but simply the transforming words of consecration, "This is my Body, This is my Blood."[106]

In the sacrifices of the Old Law the first fruits of agriculture, cereals, wine, oil, incense, birds, goats, sheep, and bulls were offered (cf. Lv 1-7).[107] The holocaust or whole burnt offering was offered on many occasions which required special solemnity. The sacrifices that were only partly burned and partly eaten included certain special rites such as that of Passover, the peace offerings (thanksgiving, votive, and free will offerings) which emphasized the fellowship between God and the offerers, and the atonement sacrifices which symbolized the restoration of friendship with God after some offense. Such sacrifices were offered by the patriarchs and the early kings, but then were entrusted solely to the priesthood.[108]

In the New Testament the Epistle to the Hebrews (9-10) develops a theology which explains how Jesus is the High Priest of the New Covenant and how his death on the Cross is the sacrifice replacing all the sacrifices of the Old Covenant. The same thought is expressed elsewhere: "Christ loved us and handed himself over for us as a sacrificial offering to God for a fragrant aroma" (Eph 5:2). It is implicit in Jesus' own institution of the Eucharist at the time of the Passover:

> "This is my body that is for you. Do this in remembrance of me. This cup is the new covenant in my blood. Do this, as often as you drink it, in remembrance of me." For as often as you eat this bread and drink this cup, you proclaim the death of the Lord until he comes (1 Cor 11:24b-26; cf. Mt 26:26-29; Mk 14:22-25; Lk 22:15-20).

---

[106] CCC # 1353 says, "In the *institution narrative* the power of the words and the action of Christ, and the power of the Holy Spirit, make sacramentally present under the species of bread and wine Christ's body and blood, his sacrifice offered on the cross once for all."

[107] See Roland de Vaux, O.P., *Ancient Israel*, pp. 415-456, on Old Testament sacrifices.

[108] In the time of Jesus, some Jews, such as Philo of Alexandria, gave elaborate symbolic interpretations of the religious and moral meaning of these rites. For example, Philo (F.H. Colson and G.H. Whitaker, translators, Loeb Library, vol. 8, *On the Virtues*, c. 26), explains the command against eating meat and milk at the same meal as a way of teaching non-violence.

Christians can also make other offerings, such as the money offering for the work of the Church at Mass, or the stipends offered for the support of the priests who offer a Mass as a prayer of petition for some answer from God, etc., as the widow's little offering for the Temple treasury commended by Jesus (Lk 21:1-4) or the collection for the poor made by St. Paul (1 Cor 16:1-4).[109] That there is a serious obligation to support the ministers of the Church is clear from the profession of faith imposed on the Waldensians and the condemnation of the views of Wycliff.[110]

A fourth kind of worship is to honor God by swearing an *oath* calling upon him as a witness that what one says is true. By swearing sincerely one acknowledges that God is all-knowing and that he will punish violations of the truth, i.e., the sin of perjury. When an oath includes a promise it must be must be fulfilled as a duty of religion as well as of truthfulness (Nb 30:3; Mt 5:33) and the obligation is to be strictly interpreted, although the gravity of the obligation depends on the nature of the promise.[111] The patriarchs of the Old Testament often swore by the Divine Name. Thus Abraham took an oath that he would live in peace with Abimelech (Gn 21:23) and required his servant to swear (Gn 24:3). Jacob asked Esau to swear (Gn 25:32) and Joseph also (47:31). God even swears by himself (Gn 22:16; Dt 32:40; Is 45:23)! The law, following the example of the patriarchs, also sometimes requires the taking of oaths (e.g., Ex 22:10; Dt 10:20).

Oaths, of course, are often in fact lies, "Their mouths speak untruth; their right hands are raised in lying oaths" (Ps 144:8, 10; Si 23:9-13; Jr 4:2), or deceitful promises. Unfortunately, in Jesus' time, some of the rabbis had developed (like laxist Catholic moralists later did) a sophistical casuistry (Mk 7:11-13) by which they excused certain dishonest oaths.[112] No doubt it was to correct such sophistry that Jesus in

---

[109] On the notion of a "stipend" see p. 352 above.

[110] Waldensians, DS # 797; Wycliff, DS # 1168.

[111] CCC # 2101-2102.

[112] CCC # 915, 2103. CCC # 2153-2154 says, "Following St. Paul, the tradition of the Church has understood Jesus' words as not excluding oaths made for grave and right reasons (for example in court). 'An oath, that is the invocation of the divine name as a witness to truth, cannot be taken unless in truth, in judgment, and in justice' (CIC can. 1199 # 1)."

the Sermon on the Mount referred to the Old Testament exhortations to fulfill one's promises (Ex 20:7; Lv 19:12; Dt 5:11), and then plainly declared:

> "I say to you, do not swear at all; not by heaven, for it is God's throne; nor by Jerusalem, for it is the city of the great King. Do not swear by your head, for you cannot make a single hair white or black. Let your 'Yes' mean 'Yes,' and your 'No' mean 'No.' Anything more is from the evil one" (Mt 5:34-37).[113]

This is echoed by the Epistle of St. James (5:12):

> But above all, my brothers, do not swear, either by heaven or by earth or by any other oath, but let your "Yes" mean "Yes" and your "No" mean "No," that you may not incur condemnation.

Because of these "plain" texts, many Christian sects have refused to take oaths. The best known example in the U.S.A. has been that of the Quakers who are permitted by our courts merely to "affirm" their testimony. The Waldensians, Lollards, Beguines, Begards, and the Fraticelli in the Middle Ages, and the Hussites, Anabaptists, and Mennonites of the Reformation period had preceded the Quakers in this refusal.

The Catholic Church, however, at the Fourth Lateran Council and the Council of Constance[114] defined that under proper conditions the taking of oaths is morally licit and may even be obligatory. The *Code of Canon Law*, canons 1191-1204, makes oaths mandatory in certain cases, and they are defended in the *Catechism of the Catholic Church*.[115]

Although some current exegetes still think that the words of Jesus and James quoted above show that Jesus really did forbid all oaths and even vows, this was not the understanding of his teaching in the early

---

[113] On the history of the interpretation of this text see Luz, *Matthew*, pp. 318-322.

[114] Fourth Lateran, DS # 795; Constance, DS # 1193.

[115] CCC # 2153.

Church. St. Paul frequently used oaths when he felt a need to impress his hearers with his seriousness (Rm 1:9; 2 Cor 1:23; Gal 1:20; Ph 1:8; cf. 1 Tm 5:11-12).

Hence, the Church, "interpreting Scripture by Scripture," has always understood this saying of the Lord not as forbidding the swearing of oaths as such but of false oaths. What Jesus meant was that one must speak the truth and keep one's promises even if one has made no vow or oath, since all excuses for lying or for false promises, such as some Pharisees had invented, were from the devil, "the father of lies" (Jn 8:44).

But if Christians always speak the truth, why should they ever take an oath? The reason is given by the writer of Hebrews when he explains why God swore "by himself" to Abraham to bless and multiply his descendants:

> Human beings swear by someone greater than themselves; for them an oath serves as a guarantee and puts an end to all argument. So when God wanted to give the heirs of his promise an even clearer demonstration of the immutability of his purpose, he intervened with an oath (Heb 6:16-17).

Thus the reason we are sometimes obliged to take an oath is not because without it we would lie, but because the cynical public will not believe us unless we swear that we are serious and willing to subject ourselves to punishment for perjury. Thus the need to take oaths reflects the sinful condition of humanity where lying and lack of trust is so common that it forces even honest people to take oaths in order to be taken seriously. Therefore, we should obey Jesus and always tell the truth for its own sake, yet we do not disobey him when we take an oath so as to be believed in a sinful world. Because St. Paul realized this, he did not hesitate to enforce his words with oaths when he saw his message might not otherwise be taken seriously even by the new Christians to whom he wrote.

A fifth way to worship God is to take a *vow* by which one promises God to do something possible and better than its opposite (Dt 22:21; Nb 30:3; Ec 5:3). While an oath may also contain a promise, it primarily calls God to witness to the swearer's sincerity; while a vow is more like a sacrifice, since by it the one who vows offers herself or himself to God to serve him in a special way.

A genuine vow is usually a public act but requires internal intention, deliberation, and freedom. To vow is to acknowledge God's supreme dominion since it promises God to serve him more completely. It is often undertaken either in thanksgiving for a past favor or in petition for a future favor, and hence is a matter of counsel rather than precept. It should not be an attempt to bargain with God but a sincere effort to cooperate with his will.

The Old Testament regulated the Nazarite vow (Nb 6) and provides many examples of other vows, such as the vow of Hannah in petition for a son (1 S 1:11) and David's vow to house the Ark of the Covenant (Ps 132:2). It also commanded:

> "When you make a vow to God, delay not its fulfillment. For God has no pleasure in fools; fulfill what you have vowed. You had better not make a vow than make it and not fulfill it" (Si 5:3-5; cf. Lv 27:2; Dt 23:22-24; Ps 22:26; 50:14; 56:13; 61:9; 65:2; 66:13; 76:12; Jb 22:27; Jon 2:10; Ml 1:14).

Yet the Old Testament recognizes that vows are often rashly taken, such as that of the hero Jephthah who swore:

> "Whoever comes out of the doors of my house to meet me when I return in triumph from [the war with] the Ammonites shall belong to the Lord. I shall offer him up in sacrifice" (Jg 11:31).[116]

But it was his own daughter who first came out to greet him. We also read how:

---

[116] In *Jephthah and His Vow,* David Marcus lines up the arguments for and against the opinion of the Church Fathers that Jephthah's daughter was not sacrificed but consecrated to virginity. Marcus inclines to the traditional view, but believes that the author of Judges deliberately leaves the outcome of the story ambiguous in order to emphasize the folly of making such a vow rather than on the other question whether a rash vow once made should actually be fulfilled. The rabbis generally held that it should not. He cites other biblical examples where a rash promise is deplored (Gn 24:14; 31:32; Jg 1:12, 17:2, 21:8; 1 S 14:24, 17:25).

> Saul swore a very rash oath that day, putting the people under this ban: "Cursed be the man who takes food before evening, before I am able to avenge myself on my enemies" (1 S 14:24).

Saul's oath fell on his own son Jonathan, although Jonathan defied the curse. Again, King Herod swore a foolish oath to the daughter of Herodias which forced him against his will to order the death of John the Baptist (Mk 6:23-26).

To show that the New Testament no more forbids vows than it does oaths, we again have the example of St. Paul who not only himself took the Nazarite vow (Ac 18:18) but approved of others doing so (Ac 21:23-26) to reassure the Jewish Christians.[117] Moreover, the sacraments of Baptism, of Marriage, and of Holy Orders, instituted by Christ himself through the Holy Spirit,[118] each involves a vow, for all Christians must offer their whole lives to God in Baptism, while the married are united to each other in Christ by the matrimonial vows and the hierarchical ministers to the Church by a vow to serve her and God in spiritual offices.

The Church has given special attention to two kinds of public vows, those of matrimony and those of consecrated life. The vow of matrimony forms a freely chosen *covenant* between the partners by which in an exclusive and permanent commitment they surrender their persons to each other to express in the manner intended by the Creator that fruitful love for which he distinguished human beings as male and female (Gn 1-2).[119]

Thus marriage pertains to the order of creation and the natural law, but Christ has elevated it for the baptized to a sacrament symbolizing his faithful love for his Church (Eph 5:21-33). As such it fulfills in a special way for earthly existence the baptismal covenant of the members of the Church with Christ which alone will remain forever in the Kingdom.[120]

---

[117] For exegesis of Acts 21:23-26 see Luke Timothy Johnson, *Acts*, pp. 373-380.

[118] Council of Trent, DS # 1600-1601; CCC # 1114, 1210.

[119] CCC # 1601-1666.

[120] GS # 48-50; FC # 11-16; CCC # 1615-1627.

The vow of consecrated life is a prophetic, eschatological expression of the baptismal covenant by which members of the Church witness to the coming of the Kingdom by anticipating it in a search for Christian perfection through the practice of the counsels of poverty, chastity, and obedience according to the rule and constitutions of some religious community.[121]

> He [Jesus] answered, "Some are incapable of marriage... because they have renounced marriage for the sake of the kingdom of heaven. Whoever can accept this ought to accept it" (Mt 19:12).
>
> Jesus said to him [the rich young man], "If you wish to be perfect, go, sell what you have and give to the poor, and you will have treasure in heaven. Then come, follow me" (Mt 19:21).

The reason for highlighting these three particular counsels is that by poverty all external possessions are sacrificed, by chastity the body is consecrated, and by obedience the soul (the will) is dedicated totally to the service of God,[122] in imitation of Jesus who was poor, celibate, and wholly obedient to his mission from the Father. "As it is written of me in the scroll, Behold, I come to do your will, O God" (Heb 10:7; quoting Ps 40:8-9).

Moralists generally agree that when in doubt about whether one has made a valid vow, or about what it obliges one to do, if it is solidly

---

[121] LG # 43-47; PC; CCC # 914-933, 944-945, 1618-1620. St. Thomas Aquinas discusses the three vows of religion in *S.T.*, II-II, q. 186, and the treatise *On the Perfection of the Spiritual Life*. Mt 19:12 literally speaks of "eunuchs" and Benedict Viviano, O.P., NJBC, p. 662, explains, "Three kinds [of eunuchs] are listed: [1] physically malformed, [2] castrated through the cruelty of men, for use as harem guards and courtiers (disapproved in Deut 23:1); [3] those who voluntarily refrain from marriage (*enouchizein* is here used metaphorically) in order to devote themselves more fully to the urgent demands of the kingdom (so too 8:22; 1 Cor 7:17, 25-35). The Jewish background of this strong teaching is found in Isaiah 56:3-5 and Qumran..." On Mt 19:21 Viviano comments (p. 662), "*If you would be perfect*: This is Matthew's major addition to the story. *Teleios* (perfect) can mean 'complete, mature,' or observant of all God's laws (cf. 5:48). The phrase in later times led to a distinction between the commandments (addressed to all believers) and counsels of perfection (addressed to a few). In Mt 5:48 the invitation to perfection is addressed to all. The distinction comes in the degrees of obligation; all are held to keep the commands (with forgiveness for repentant sinners), but not all are held to be celibate (19:12) or to sell all."

[122] CCC # 1973-1974.

probable that one is *not* obliged, it need not be fulfilled. Moreover, the obligation ceases when the work is no longer good or better than not doing it, or when the purpose of the vow or a condition on which the vow depends ceases. A legitimate superior of the one who has made a vow can nullify or dispense from its fulfillment.

A sixth and seventh way of worshiping God by external acts is by *blessings* and by *praises*. In taking an oath we invoke the Holy Name of God in witness of our testimony. In blessing God's creatures we call on God in acknowledgment that these creatures are his gifts to us which remind us of him and for which we are grateful. We also call on him to bring his creatures to their perfection so that they may fulfill the purposes for which the Creator made them.[123]

> Bless the Lord, all you works of the Lord
> > praise and exalt him above all forever (Dn 3:57; cf. 3:57-90).

In the Old Testament there are also the negative correlative of blessings, namely, *curses* in which God is called upon to punish evildoers and destroy their works. For example, in Deuteronomy we read the Liturgy of the Twelve Curses:

> The Levites shall proclaim aloud to all the men of Israel: "Cursed be the man who makes a carved or molten idol" ... And all the people shall answer, "Amen!" etc. (Dt 27:14-26; cf. 28:15-19).[124]

---

[123] CCC # 1167-1673 on sacramentals, which require the blessing of things, places, and persons. CCC # 1669 notes that the baptized can all give blessings, although certain blessings are proper to priests. CCC # 1078-1112 shows how the Holy Trinity is the source of all blessing.

[124] According to Joseph Blenkinsopp, NJBC, p. 106, "The twelve paragraphs are not strictly curses (the threatened evil is not specified) but apodictic legal formulations," the number of which may tally with the twelve tribes. "The anathema functioned to put the offender outside the community by making it impossible for him to participate in cult without cursing himself." He thinks their formulation suggests "a time when pentateuchal law was well on its way to final consolidation" since four of the offenses occur only in Lv 17:2-6 and not in Dt itself. Ian Cairns, *Word and Presence*, pp. 236-238 also thinks this Dodecalogue is a composition of the Deuteronomist using fragments of older materials.

Several of the Psalms (called the Imprecatory Psalms, 69:23-29; 70:3-5; 109:6-20; 129:5-8; 137:7-9) are filled with furious curses. Although these shock Christians today and were omitted from the liturgical Psalter after Vatican II, it is not right to reject them simply as "revenge"; rather they are intended as an expression of confidence in the justice of God who will not permit evil to go unpunished or the good unrewarded.

Yet in the New Testament Jesus said, "Love your enemies, do good to those who hate you, bless those who curse you, pray for those who mistreat you" (Lk 6:27-28) and St. Paul said, "Bless those who persecute you; bless and do not curse them" (Rm 12:14). Nevertheless, Jesus "cursed" the fig tree outside Jerusalem as symbolic of the doom which awaited the religious leaders in the city who refused to believe him (Mk 11:14, 20-26) and pronounced on them the Seven Woes (Mt 23:13-36) as he also proclaimed woe to the towns of Chorazin and Bethsaida (Lk 10:13-16). These "woes" are in fact prophetic curses. Moreover, Jesus and the apostles frequently curse the demons in exorcism (e.g., Mk 5:1-20; Lk 9:37-43, 10:17).

St. Paul also declared, "If anyone does not love the Lord, let him be accursed" (1 Cor 16:22) and twice exclaimed, "If anyone preaches to you a gospel other than the one you have received, let him be accursed!" (Gal 1:8-9). In exasperation (and no doubt with a touch of humor) at those who demanded the Gentile converts be circumcised, Paul cried out, "Would that those who are upsetting you might also castrate themselves!" (Gal 5:12). Again Paul excommunicated the incestuous Corinthian, "You are to deliver this man to Satan for the destruction of his flesh, so that his spirit may be saved on the day of the Lord" (1 Cor 5:5).

This last text shows us how and how not to curse. To pray that God will enact just punishment in order to reform the stubborn offender can be an act of love for the offender,[125] and then cursing can be

---

[125] *S.T.*, II-II, q. 25, a. 6 says, "We ought to hate in sinners that they are sinners, and love them as human persons capable of blessedness. This is to love them truly from charity because of God."

justified;[126] but when it is an act of hate of the offender whom we desire to destroy, it is evil. The danger is, of course, that our hate will be more sincere than our love and forgiveness. Hence the Epistle of St. James laments the fact that:

> No human being can tame the tongue, it is a restless evil, full of deadly poison. With it we bless the Lord and Father, and with it we curse human beings who are made in the likeness of God. From the same mouth come blessing and cursing. This need not be so, my brothers. Does a spring gush forth from the same opening both pure and brackish water? Can a fig tree, my brothers, produce olives, or a grapevine figs? Neither can salt water yield fresh (Jm 3: 8:12).

In praising and blessing God himself we recall his gifts to us, but our thoughts also turn from his creatures simply to him and his eternal glory.[127]

> Blessed are you, O Lord, the God of our fathers,
>   praiseworthy and exalted above all forever;
> And blessed is your holy and glorious name,
>   praiseworthy and exalted above for all ages
>   (Dn 3:52; cf. 3:52-56).

> I will bless the Lord at all times;
>   praise shall be always in my mouth (Ps 34:1)

> Let the word of Christ dwell in you richly, as in all wisdom you teach and admonish one another, singing psalms, hymns, and spiritual songs with gratitude in your hearts to God (Col 3:16).

Christians, to express their adoption as children of God in Christ, can also use the Name of God in begging for something from another

---

[126] If this excommunicated man is the same as the one mentioned in 2 Cor 2:5-11 St. Paul seems to have quickly relented and urged the Corinthian church to reconcile him, but most modern commentators believe they are different persons. See Victor Furnish, *II Corinthians*, pp. 164-166.

[127] CCC # 2644-2645.

person (Rm 12:1, Mk 5:7) or commanding them to do something (Mt 26:63; Mk 1:25) and such a form of praise is called an *adjuration*, as when Peter heals the crippled beggar, "In the name of Jesus Christ the Nazorean, rise and walk!" (Ac 3:6b). Above all we should use that Name in praising God. Thus God's Holy Name may be invoked by oaths, blessings, and praises, but the Second Commandment declares:

> You shall not take the name of the Lord, your God, in vain. For the Lord will not leave unpunished him who takes his name in vain (Ex 20:7; Dt 5:11).

"In vain" means to use the name of God without due reverence to God, as when oaths are used as a mere expression of anger or contempt, or dishonestly, or without real purpose.

Those who swear thoughtlessly, merely out of boorishness, do not really intend to take an oath, and the sin is probably venial, yet it expresses a lack of realization of the presence of God. Respect for the Holy Name led the Jews to avoid even pronouncing the Name (YHWH, the Tetragrammaton or Four Letters) revealed to Moses at the burning bush (Ex 3:13-15). However, this same respect prompted medieval Christians to practice the devotion to the Name of Jesus preached by Bl. John of Vercelli, O.P., and St. Bernardine of Siena, O.F.M. This devotion is still promoted in the U.S.A. by the Holy Name Society and by the recitation of the "Divine Praises" after the liturgical service of Eucharistic Benediction.[128]

We have now considered various acts of the virtue of religion. "Religion," however, is not always healthy; it can be mere "religiosity." To worship God in ways which for one reason or another imply a wrong notion of what God really is like is superstition. Such *superstitious* practices are generally venially sinful if they are simply based on ignorance or unreasonable fear, but they can be mortal sins if they deliberately foster a false idea of God or ask of him what is evil. The worst sin of this sort is *idolatry* forbidden by the First Commandment, and con-

---

[128] On the history of this devotion see M. Kelley, "Holy Name, Devotion to the," NCE, 7:76-77.

stantly denounced both by the prophets and the wisdom literature (e.g., Ezk 8-9; Ba 6; Dn 14; Ws 13-14).[129]

Also seriously sinful are practices aimed at obtaining magical or diabolic powers, or at discovering the future known only to God, such as *divination*, repeatedly condemned in the Bible even with the death penalty (Lv 20:6, 27; Dt 18:10-12; Is 28:15; Gal 4:10-11). Today such superstitious and pseudo-scientific practices as astrology and even devil-worship are again popular, although they are not always intended seriously.[130]

More widespread is irreligion or *religious indifference* practiced by people who try to ignore the ultimate questions of life, or who treat religion in a contemptuous or trivializing way, or even deny the reality of God. Some *tempt God* by failing to show due respect for his superior wisdom by making unconditional demands on him to show his power (Dt 6:16; Ex 17:7; Ps 78:18, 19, 56; Mt 4:7; 27:40).[131]

Among the sins against the virtue of religion are also included *perjury, sacrilege and simony. Perjury*, already discussed above, is taking an oath in God's Name to attest a lie (Lv 19:12; Zc 5:3, 4; Pr 6:16-19; Si 23:11; Mt 5:33).[132] It is a very serious sin, but thoughtless "swearing" in words but without any real intention of invoking God is often venial (Si 23:9-15). *Sacrilege* is an act of disrespect or violence to sacred persons, places, or things (Lv 10:1; 1 S 2:17; Dn 5:2; Jn 2:14). *Simony* is the buying and selling of sacred things (Pr 3:15; 1 Cor 4:1; Mt 10:8), named after Simon the Magician who tried to buy the miraculous powers of the Apostles (Ac 8:9-25).[133]

Is it simony for the clergy to ask for their necessary support from those whom they serve and to whom they administer the sacraments? Were not the apostles told by Jesus, "Without cost you have received, without cost you are to give" (Mt 10:8b)? True, but Jesus had also told them that they were to depend for their support on the generosity of

---

[129] CCC # 2084-2100.

[130] CCC # 2110-2117.

[131] CCC # 2118-2119.

[132] Innocent XI, DS # 2124, condemned laxist opinions justifying perjury.

[133] CCC # 2120-2121.

those to whom they ministered, for "the laborer deserves his keep" (Mt 10:10). St. Paul, accused by his enemies of seeking his own profit from preaching the Gospel, made an impassioned plea for the right of a preacher to receive his living in return for his ministry (1 Cor 9:18), but rather than give any handle to such accusations did in fact support himself by manual labor (1 Cor 4:12). The early Church did not insist that all follow Paul's example, and concluded it was not simony for ministers of the Gospel to accept a moderate living from those to whom they ministered. Rather than being simoniacal payment for the Gospel or the sacraments which must be given freely, this support is given in order that they might be able to provide this ministry:

> Presbyters who preside well deserve double honor, especially those who toil in preaching and teaching. For the scripture says, "You shall not muzzle an ox when it is threshing" [Dt 25:4] and, "A worker deserves his pay" [cf. Mt 10:10] (1 Tm 5:17-18; cf. 1 Cor 9:9-12).

Virtue of Obedience

After the virtue of religion, a second virtue that resembles justice in matters where the debt is strict but cannot be paid in full is *obedience*, which we have already considered as it is a counsel practiced under vow by those who live the consecrated life. But without a vow, this virtue is also needed by all Christians, as is evident from the Fourth Commandment, "Honor your father and your mother, that your days may be long in the land which the Lord your God gives you" (Ex 20:12; Dt 5:16; cf. Eph 5:12). The *Catechism of the Catholic Church* makes clear that this applies to "all those whom God, for our good, has vested with his authority."[134] In every community, authority and obedience are necessary not for the advantage of those in authority but for the common good in which authorities and subjects both share.

We can never fully repay the strict debt we owe our parents who gave us life and educated us. We owe our parents spiritual and material

---

[134] CCC # 2197.

help, especially in their old age; but first of all we owe them obedience
and honor because without these the family which is the basis of all
human society cannot be a functional community. This filial obedience
is often urged in the Old Testament (Dt 27:16; Pr 1:8; Si 7:29; Tob 4:3)
and in the New Testament as well (Mt 15:4-9; Eph 6:1-3; Col 3:20).
Especially strong are the eloquent essay on this topic by Ben Sirach (Si
3:1-18) and the words of Jesus to the Pharisees and scribes:

> "And why do you break the commandment of God for the sake
> of your tradition? For God said: 'Honor your father and your
> mother' [Ex 20:12], and 'Whoever curses father or mother shall
> die' [Ex 21:17]. But you say, 'Whoever says to father or mother,
> "Any support you might have had from me is dedicated to God,"
> need not honor his father.' You have nullified the word of God
> for the sake of your tradition" (Mt 15:3-7).

Jesus himself gave a loving example of obedience to Joseph and
Mary. As a boy of twelve, after being lost three days, he was found by
his anxious parents in the Temple. In response to their troubled questions, he revealed his life's mission: "Did you not know that I must be
in my Father's house?" (Lk 2:49), but then "went down with them and
came to Nazareth and was obedient to them" (Lk 2:51).[135] As a young
man at the marriage feast of Cana, after first replying to his mother's
concern about the lack of wine, "My time has not yet come," he then
yielded to her request and began his mission by working his first physical miracle (Jn 2:1-12). As his mission approached completion in
Gethsemane, he prayed, "My Father, if it is not possible that this cup
pass without my drinking it, your will be done!" (Mt 26:42). Finally, in
completing his mission on the Cross he was still mindful to say to his
mother, "'Woman behold your son.' Then to the disciple whom he
loved, he said, 'Behold your mother.' And from that hour the disciple

---

[135] According to Joseph A. Fitzmyer, *The Gospel According to St. Luke*, the Greek phrase
in Lk 2:49 which he and the NAB prefer to translate "in my Father's house" could also
mean "involved in my Father's affairs" or "among those people belonging to my
Father" (i.e., the Torah teachers to whom the boy Jesus was listening). See the reasons
Fitzmyer gives for each of the possible readings, pp. 443-444.

took her into his home" (Jn 19:26-27). Yet Jesus did not permit his filial love and obedience to stand in the way of his mission from his heavenly Father (cf. Mk 3:31-34; Mt 12:46-50; Lk 8:19-21; also Mt 8:21-22; Lk 9:59-62 and Mt 10:35-36; Lk 12:51-53 and Mt 10:37; Lk 14:26).

"Children obey your parents in everything, for this pleases the Lord" (Col 3:20). The *Catechism* explains this "everything" by saying, "Children should also obey the reasonable directions of their teachers and all to whom their parents have entrusted them. But if a child is convinced in conscience that it would be morally wrong to obey a particular order, he must not do so." It then says, "As they grow up, children should continue to respect their parents. They should anticipate their wishes, willingly seek their advice, and accept their just admonitions. Obedience toward parents ceases with the emancipation of the children; not so respect, which is always owed to them."[136]

Reciprocally parents have obligations to love and care for their children not as parental possessions but for the children's own sake as persons and gifts of God. Employers also have the duty to care for their employees (Si 33:31; Eph 6:9) and respect their freedom and dignity as persons. Parents have a special duty to see that their children receive the rites of initiation in the Church and a Christian education (Pr 23:13; Si 7:25; Eph 6:4; Col 3:21).

Married couples owe each other mutual love and care and the marital expression of their love (Mt 19:5; Eph 5:25; Tt 2:4; Col 3:18; 1 Tm 2:15). The husband as head of the family (in the sense already explained) has special responsibilities for the sustenance, protection, and Christian life of his family whose "priest" he is, while the wife has a special responsibility for the home environment (Col 3:18; Eph 5:33). For a husband to abuse his wife or children is an especially grave sin precisely because he is "head of the family" (Eph 5:21-32; 6:4, 9; Col 4:18-21; Tt 2:2) in whom they have put their trust. Similar respect is due others such as teachers and employers (1 Tm 6:1; 1 P 2:18) who have provided us assistance and guidance.

---

[136] CCC # 2217.

Virtue of Patriotism

A third virtue which deals with a strict debt of justice yet which, like
our debt to God and our parents, we cannot repay in full, is our debt to
our country — the virtue of *patriotism*. This virtue enables us to be fair
to our community and country and pay due obedience to its government officials and due respect to its civic symbols (Mt 22:15-22; Rm
13:1-7; 1 P 2:13-17). Respect for government authority and obedience
to its legitimate guidance is today often decried on the grounds that
blind obedience to such tyrants as Stalin and Hitler has led citizens to
cooperate passively in terrible crimes. The New Testament teaches
obedience to secular as well as ecclesiastical leaders, but only when
they do not exceed their lawful authority or violate natural or divine
law since, "We must obey God, rather than men" (Ac 5:29).

Authority is given by God to governments not for their own benefit, but to help those less experienced and prudent to do what is objectively right. As the Pauline writer says, "Remind them [the Christians
of Crete] to be under the control of magistrates and authorities, to be
obedient, to be open to every good enterprise" (Tt 3:1; cf. Rm 13:2, 7;
1 P 2:13).[137] It is also given sometimes to leaders in a community to
insure the unity of action of the community, even when the citizens
who obey are equal in prudence to those who rule them.[138] Both kinds
of authority are necessary in human life when they are used for the
common good and not merely for the good of a tyrant. Yet when we are
not sure that a lawful authority is exceeding his or her proper limits we
should obey, since otherwise authority would be of little benefit to us as
a guide. To disobey out of contempt for authority is an even more
serious sin, because it shows a rejection not merely of the person in
authority but of one's responsibility for the common good.

Those in authority must, in their turn, be obedient to God and the
law of the community and act only for the common good, promoting

---

[137] CCC # 2234-2246, 2254-2257.

[138] On the Thomistic arguments for the need of authority even in a community of equal,
virtuous adults, see Yves Simon, *A General Theory of Authority*.

honest morality and true education, justice, and material prosperity for all members of the community.[139] Nevertheless, an exaggerated nationalism which claims first place in power and prestige among the nations for one's country even at the cost of unjust war, or passively executes all orders of superiors however immoral, is not patriotism. According to the Fourth Gospel those leaders who conspired against Jesus were misled not only by their mistaken religious views but by their false patriotism:

> So the chief priests and the Pharisees convened the Sanhedrin and said, "What are we going to do? This man is performing many signs. If we leave him alone, all will believe in him, and the Romans will come and take away both our land and our nation." But one of them, Caiaphas, who was high priest that year, said to them, "You know nothing, nor do you consider that it is better for you that one man should die instead of the people so that the whole nation may not perish" (Jn 11:47-50).

Today, there is also an increasing emphasis on *ethnicity*, loyalty to one's own racial or cultural group within a nation or across national lines. This is an excellent expression of loyalty and solidarity to those with whom we have much in common and to those who have contributed especially to our own culture. We certainly ought to support legitimate efforts to obtain justice for our own group. But when group loyalty fosters envy and hatred of other groups or prejudice and discrimination against them, it is destructive and the source of violence.[140]

It is a very grave political error, fostered in the nineteenth century by romantic racialist theories, to believe either that to be united a nation must also be ethnically and culturally uniform, or that all those of one race or culture must be gathered into a single nation and territory. Ethnicity, although a value, must be subordinated to the common good of a nation-state, but this should be done not by an enforced uniformity of culture or language or the domination of one group over others, but

---

[139] CCC # 2235-2237, 2254.
[140] CCC # 1877-1896.

by a tolerant multiculturalism which is, nevertheless, loyal to the national common good. The difficulty of achieving such a community is enormous, given the need of people to identify with their own group and to perceive the outsider as the enemy, as is so apparent in the United States in the relations of black and white.

Christians should be convinced that the welfare of the global community is superior to that of any nation, and, analogously, the welfare of any nation is superior to that of the ethnic groups it contains; yet the world and the nations are enriched not harmed by cultural diversity. Our confidence that this is a real possibility should be strengthened by the example of the "catholicity" of the Catholic Church which (albeit with much difficulty and still only imperfectly) has been able to bring peoples of almost every culture into a remarkable unity of faith and today works constantly for international peace as manifested by the addresses of Pope Paul VI and Pope John Paul II to the United Nations in 1965, 1979 and 1995.

Thus ethnic or national zeal which exalts secular power over the authority of God and his Church is not true patriotism. The honor we owe secular authority must be subordinated to the supernatural reverence we give to the works of God's grace, to the Church and especially to the saints.

Virtue of Truthfulness

Some virtues which resemble justice regard debts which can be paid, but which we are not strictly bound in justice to repay. The first of these is *truthfulness*. The duty to tell the truth is not strictly obligatory in the sense that we do not have to reveal the truth to any but those who have a right to know it, *although we are strictly forbidden to tell anyone what is not true*. The Eighth Commandment is "You shall not bear false witness against your neighbor" (Ex 20:16)[141] and the Wisdom writings constantly reinforce this message, since a "lying tongue" and a "false witness" are among the seven things God especially hates (Pr 6:17, 19; cf. 4:24; 14:15; 19:5; 20:17; 26:24-25).

---

[141] CCC # 2464-2513.

He shall not dwell within my house who practices deceit.
He who speaks falsehood shall not stand before my eyes (Ps 101:7;
cf. 5:6-7).

The bread of deceit is sweet to a man
    but afterwards his mouth will be filled with
    gravel [i.e., lies are easy, but not the consequences] (Pr 20:17).

He gives a kiss on the lips [i.e., is a friend]
    who makes an honest reply (Pr 24:26).
A lie is a foul blot in a man,
    yet it is constantly on the lips of the unruly.
Better a thief than an inveterate liar,
    yet both will suffer disgrace (Si 20:23-24).

I know, says the Lord, his [Moab's] arrogance, liar in
    boast, liar in deed (Jr 48:30).

The New Testament strongly confirms this Old Testament condemnation of lying. Jesus lists "deceit" among the "evils which come from within and they defile" (Mk 7:22-23). Peter said to Ananias, "You have lied not to human beings, but to God" (Ac 5:4b) and Ananias, whose lie was aggravated by perjury, fell down dead.[142]

Stop lying to one another, since you have taken off the old self with its practices and have put on the new self, which is being renewed, for knowledge, in the image of its creator (Col 3:9).

The devil… was a murderer from the beginning and does not stand in truth, because there is no truth in him. When he tells a lie, he speaks in character, because he is a liar and the father of lies (Jn 8:44).

"Liars [and] perjurers" are listed in 1 Tm 1:9 along with the "lawless and unruly," "the unholy and profane." "Rid yourselves of all malice and all deceit, insincerity, envy, and all slander" (1 P 2:1). "Nothing unclean will enter [the heavenly Jerusalem], nor anyone who does abominable things or tells lies" (Rv 21:26b).

Truth is the most precious good, since, as we have seen, our whole

---

[142] See earlier discussion on p. 314, note 72.

life depends on knowing the goal to which we are called and how to get there. That ultimate goal is the vision of God who is Truth itself and can only be possessed as Truth through our spiritual intelligences. "A faithful God without deceit, how just and upright he is!" (Dt 32:4)). "O Lord... All your ways are mercy and truth" (Tb 3:2). "God who does not lie" (Tt 1:2). The common good of society consists first of all in the sharing of truth among its members. Without trust that our fellows will tell us the truth, we cannot live securely with them or enter into common action with them, nor obtain the truth they possess.

Therefore, the dissemination of lies as gossip and rumor, as propaganda, and as error (especially atheism and heresy) is the most dangerous of crimes against society. In the *Republic*,[143] Plato, perhaps more in irony than in earnest (for he loved truth), argued that the rulers of a state must tell "myths" about human inequality to keep their subjects content with the inequality necessary to a social organism. This idea has been taken all too seriously by modern tyrants who systematically feed their people with myths of national supremacy and glory, in what is called "misinformation" and "deniability." Eventually all that is built on lies will collapse. Others have argued that objective, scientific truth is the only moral imperative, forgetting that scientific truth in the modern sense is only one kind of truth and not the most fundamental.[144]

To speak truly is to communicate in a manner consistent with what one mentally thinks is true. Lying is to assert by word or act as true what I know (or think I know) to be false.[145] Note the term "assert" which implies a truth claim. Hence, when I tell a joke or relate a fictional story (as Jesus did in his parables) my manner of telling or the circumstances of my telling make clear that I am not *asserting* the historical

---

[143] IV, c. 1, 414-415.

[144] This error was a thesis in Jacques Monod's well known *Chance and Necessity*, 1967.

[145] CCC # 2482 uses St. Augustine's definition of "To lie is to speak or act against the truth in order to lead into error someone who has the right to know the truth." St. Thomas Aquinas, however, points out (*S.T.*, II-II, q. 110, a. 1 c.) that *formally* a lie consists in intentionally saying what one believes is not true, not in the intention to deceive, since one may know that one's lie may not actually be believed. Deception completes or "perfects" a lie but does not constitute it. Thus it would be an error to conclude from CCC # 2482 that it is permissible to say what one knows not to be true to someone just because that person has no right to know the truth. One may, however, give an answer to his question, which in the context is ambiguous as explained in the text.

truth of the story itself, although I may be "making a point" which I *am* asserting as true (as Jesus certainly did). We are morally bound to assert only the truth and to speak it to everyone who has a right to the information based on a true need to know.

Not everyone, however, has a need nor a right to know everything I may know, and therefore I have a right and sometimes a duty not to reveal to all what I know. This right not to reveal is either a right of *privacy* when I have good reasons for not wanting others to know something they have no need or right to know, or a duty of *confidentiality* when I have no right to reveal something whose revelation would infringe another's right of privacy or harm them unnecessarily in some other way.

What, then, are my obligations if someone tries to cause me by force or even by unjustified questions to reveal what I have no obligation to reveal or have a duty to conceal, thus infringing my right of privacy? What, for example, can I say if someone impolitely pries into my private affairs or violently threatens me with death if I do not reveal the whereabouts of a person they are trying to murder? I cannot lie to them, because lying, as St. Augustine argued,[146] is intrinsically and therefore always wrong, since it destroys the integrity of the liar to speak against his own mind and undermines society by destroying trust. But I can keep silent and may have the duty to do so.

But what if the form of the question or the situation makes my silence equivalent to revealing what I ought to conceal? Or if the questioner threatens violence if I do not answer? In such a situation one can give an answer that is not contrary to what one knows, but which at the same time does not reveal what one knows because it is ambiguous and might mean several things. Such an ambiguous reply leaves the wrongful questioner uncertain about what is meant and liable to self-deception by jumping to unwarranted conclusions. It is sometimes called a reply with a "mental reservation," but is better called simply an "ambiguous answer."

---

[146] St. Augustine of Hippo, *Against Lying (De Mendacio)*, pp. 176-178 (Pl 40:478-518; CSEL 41:413-66).

All human communication requires interpretation (*hermeneusis, exegesis*) and this interpretation cannot be made definitively without a knowledge of the circumstances of the communication. For example, I don't know whether you are joking or serious without knowing you well, the context of your words, and the manner of your speech. Hence the ambiguity of a remark depends on the situation and how the locution would have been taken by a reasonable person in that situation.

Thus Jesus said to his apostles:

> "You go up to the feast [in Jerusalem]. I am not going up to the feast, because my time has not been fulfilled." After he had said this, he stayed on in Galilee. But when his brothers had gone up to the feast, he himself also went up, not openly but as it were in secret (Jn 7:8-10).[147]

Jesus' disciples may have misinterpreted him (as they often did even what he spoke plainly), but in the circumstances his answer was ambiguous and could have meant, "At least not yet, nor openly." Such ambiguous answers are not justified when the questioner has a right to know plainly (the apostles had no right to know all Jesus' plans), but they are a necessary part of human life to protect our privacy and confidentiality. Yet we must not use this ambiguity of speech as an excuse for what is really lying.[148]

Hiding the truth is not always licit. Thus we must speak frankly (a) when we are required to confess the faith; (b) when we have the office to instruct someone, especially when we are paid to give information; (c) when questioned by a judge, superior, confessor or others who have the right to do so; (d) in making or fulfilling onerous con-

---

[147] Some manuscripts read "not yet" instead of "not going up to the festival" (Jn 7:8) as do Sinaiticus, Bezae, the Latin and OS, probably to avoid attributing deception to Jesus. Raymond E. Brown, *The Gospel According to John*, p. 308, solves the problem by saying that this is a "classic instance of the two levels of meaning in the Fourth Gospel [of which he gives other examples]. What Jesus really meant when he spoke of his 'time' is his 'hour,' the hour of his passion, death, and resurrection, and ascension to the Father; and this time is not to come at this festival of Tabernacles — it is reserved for a subsequent Passover."

[148] Innocent XI, DS # 2126, 2127.

tracts, etc. Innocent XI declared that when obtaining a promotion to office one must answer truthfully to state or church officials.[149]

The Old Testament relates some incidents in which righteous people seem to tell what are objectively lies for a good purpose. Abraham twice lies about Sarah being his sister (Gn 12:13; 20:2), as does Isaac (Gn 26:6-11); Rachel and Jacob play a trick on Isaac to get the blessing that belongs by right to his twin brother Esau (Gn 27); the Hebrew midwives lie to save the male children (Ex 1:17-21); Rahab lies to save the scouts (Jos 2:1-14; 6:25); Elisha lies to the Syrians (2 K 6:19). The Church Fathers tried valiantly to explain why these apparent lies were not such, as St. Augustine's famous excuse for Jacob's deception of Isaac to obtain the blessing that belonged to Esau: "It was not a lie, but a mystery"![150] Indeed it was prophetic, but on Jacob's part a lie.

How do we reconcile such narratives with the doctrine that since the Scriptures are the Word of God they cannot approve sin? It seems better to recognize that these stories have the literary character of folk tales in which part of the entertainment value is the clever, although unscrupulous, dodges by which a hero manages to make his way in a dangerous world. Jesus himself uses a similar literary device when he relates the Parable of the Unjust Steward and ironically concludes:

> "And the master commended that dishonest steward for acting prudently. For the children of this world are more prudent in dealing with their own generation than are the children of light" (Lk 16:8-9).

The inspired authors of the Bible, when they included such dishonest acts in their narratives without moral analysis or comment, expected the reader to understand the irony of such accounts, which show

---

[149] DS # 2128.

[150] "Furthermore, on attentive and faithful observation it becomes apparent that what Jacob did at his mother's bidding, in seeming to defend his father, is not a lie but a mystery. If we call it a lie, then all the parables and figures for signifying anything which are not to be taken literally, but in which one thing must be understood for another, will be called lies" (*Against Lying*, c. 10, 24, pp. 152ff.). He goes on to say that this was a prophetic action which truly signified the election of the Church in preference to Israel.

how God can bring good out of human frailties. In none of these stories is the point to instruct the reader in the art of lying, but rather to show that God protects those who trust in him even when their own understanding of ethics still leaves something to be desired. Although Rahab was a prostitute and a liar, nevertheless she had faith in God and compassion for the hunted men who took refuge in her house (Jos 2:1-24). Her lies were objectively, but probably not subjectively, wrong; her moral understanding was crude but sincere.

Essential to the virtue of honesty is also the ability to keep a secret — *confidentiality*. Secrets are either *natural* (when they are about matters people ordinarily expect to be kept private), or *promised* (when the receiver of the information has promised not to reveal what is told), or *professional* (when the receiver is a confessor, counselor, lawyer, etc. whose office binds them to maintain confidentiality).[151]

> A newsmonger reveals secrets;
> so have nothing to do with a babbler! (Pr 20:19).

> Discuss your case with your neighbor,
> but another man's secrets do not disclose;
> Lest hearing it, he reproach you,
> and your ill repute cease not (Pr 25:9-10).

> He who betrays a secret cannot be trusted,
> he will never find an intimate friend (Si 27:16).

> A king's secret it is prudent to keep,
> but the works of the Lord are to be declared and made known
> (Tb 12:7).

It is wrong to explore, manifest, or use secret information. A secret can be manifested (a) with at least reasonably presumed consent of the person involved; or (b) to someone who already knows; or (c) in order to prevent grave harm to the common good, or to the one who committed it, or to oneself. The same norms apply to information in letters and other documents.

In particular professionals such as lawyers and physicians and

---

[151] CCC # 2488-2492, 2508-2512.

counselors have the relative obligation of "professional secrecy" which can be breached only to prevent serious harm to a third party, to prevent suicide, etc. Priests, on the other hand, have the sacred and *absolute* obligation of secrecy about sins confessed in the Sacrament of Reconciliation which can never be violated for any reason whatsoever.[152]

Lies are often classified as officious (told for a good purpose but still lies), jocose (told for amusement but still deceptive), and pernicious (told to harm). They can also be by speech or by simulation in action, or motivated by hypocrisy, or even self-deprecation.

The Virtues of Gratitude and Leniency

A second virtue which enables us to pay debts that are truly obligatory but not in strict justice[153] is that of *gratitude* as it finds expression in words or deeds. To make a return for good done ourselves is an important duty, much praised in the Bible, as when Jesus commends the one leper out of the ten he had healed who returned to thank him (Lk 17:11-12), or when the penitent woman anoints Jesus' feet out of gratitude for his forgiveness (Lk 7:36-50). Many of the Psalms show us how to thank God (e.g., 9, 18, 21, 28, 30, etc.). Indeed, the greatest Christian act of worship is called the "Eucharist" or "Thanksgiving." Lack of gratitude is *ingratitude* (2 Tm 3:2), but there can also be an excessive expression of gratitude if we repay it too promptly or too lavishly as if paying a strict debt, thus offending the gift-giver by seeming to suggest that the gift-giver was only looking for a gift in return. Our gratitude should be appropriate: "Some gifts do one no good, and some should be paid back double" (Si 20:9).

As gratitude is a free repayment of something good done to us, so *leniency* is a virtue that enables us to refrain from demanding full recompense either in punishment or compensation for some injury done us. It moderates our natural tendency to demand full punishment for an offense, and is the opposite of the extremes of cruelty or permissive-

---

[152] CCC # 2490-2491.

[153] CCC only indicates these virtues indirectly in connection with other major virtues.

ness. "For your [God's] might is the source of justice; your mastery over all things makes you lenient to all" (Ws 12:16). "But the wisdom from above is first of all peaceable, gentle (*epieikés*, equitable, or lenient), compliant, full of mercy, and good fruits, without inconstancy or insincerity" (Jm 3:17).

While sometimes for the good of a person who injures us or refuses to pay his debts to us, we must demand justice, we should always consider the circumstances of the one who has done us wrong. Perhaps he is unable to pay back all he owes, and we demand only partial repayment, or none at all. Perhaps he deserves a heavy punishment, but we see that he is repentant and we lessen his sentence. In the Parable of the Unforgiving Servant (Mt 18:21-35), Jesus told of the master who was lenient to his wicked servant:

> "When he began the accounting, a debtor was brought before him who owed him a huge amount. Since he had no way of paying it back... [the master], moved with compassion, let him go and forgave him the loan" (Mt 18:24-25a, 27).

But the wicked servant then demanded that his fellow servants pay their debts to him in full. So, learning of this, the master, "handed him over to the torturers until he should pay back the whole debt" (Mt 18:34).

A third group of virtues that resemble justice although they do not place on us any debt at all, but simply render our actions an *appropriate* response to a situation are *liberality*, *affability*, and *friendliness*. *Liberality* tempers one's love of material things and helps us expend them well to promote the common good; "Let not your hand be open to receive and clenched when it is time to give" (Si 4:31; cf. Si 14:3-19; 31:1-11), as in the generosity of the widow who gave her last mite to the Temple (Lk 21:1-4,) or of Mary of Bethany who poured the expensive perfume on Jesus' feet to prepare his burial (Jn 12:1-6). Indeed, these two women were so generous, that their action also reflects the virtue of *magnificence* which we saw is a virtue related to fortitude. Jesus himself was quoted by St. Paul (in a saying which is not recorded in the Gospels themselves) that "It is more blessed to give than to receive" (Ac 21:35b). When the burden of collecting money for the poor and persecuted church in Jerusalem fell on Paul, he often urged liberality (Gal 2:6-10; Ac 11:27-30; 1 Cor 16:1-4; 2 Cor, chapters 8 and 9; Rm 15:25-29).

> Whoever sows sparingly will also reap sparingly, and whoever sows bountifully will reap bountifully. Each must do as already determined, without sadness or compulsion, for God loves a cheerful giver. Moreover God is able to make every grace abundant for you, so that in all things, always having all you need, you may have an abundance for every good work... The one who supplies seed to the sower and bread for food will supply and multiply your seed and increase the harvest of your righteousness (2 Cor 9:6-9a, 10).

Liberality often takes the form of *hospitality* which in the Old Testament, reflecting the culture of the Near East, was especially admired, as we see in the story of Abraham and Lot and the Three Angels (Gn 18:1-15; 19:1-11). In the New Testament it is one of the characteristic features of the early Church. "Contribute to the needs of the holy ones, exercise hospitality" (Rm 12:13). Heb 13:2 says, recalling Abraham and Lot, "Do not neglect hospitality, for through it some have unknowingly entertained angels" (cf. Mk 1:31; Lk 10:38-42, 19:1-10; Ac 16:40, 28:7; Rm 16:23; 1 Tm 5:10; Tt 1:8, 1 P 4:9).

The lack of liberality is *avarice*, stinginess, greed; its excess is *prodigality* (see Lk 15:13-14). Avarice is one of the seven capital sins because the love of money gives rise to all other kinds of sins of fraud, theft, and hard-heartedness toward the poor (Mk 12:40; Lk 17:19-30).[154]

Affability is a virtue which helps us give to others the respect and politeness we owe them out of respect for their human dignity (cf. Si 31:12-31; 32:1-13). Too much of this friendliness is *flattery*;[155] too little *moroseness*, rudeness, or aloofness. Jesus certainly exemplified this affability, so that in the Gospels we see the simple people flocking to him, to hear his words and feel his touch. Sirach says, "Be not surly in

---

[154] CCC # 1866, 2539, 2541, 2552.
[155] CCC # 2480.

your speech, nor lazy and slack in your deeds. Be not a lion at home, nor sly and suspicious at work" (Si 4:30-31). St. Paul commends this virtue to all Christians when he says:

> Put on then, as God's chosen ones, holy and beloved, heartfelt compassion, kindness, humility, gentleness, and patience, bearing with one another (Col 4:12-13).

Finally, *fairness* (a term often used for justice in general) is specifically a virtue assisting us to act according to the spirit (purpose) of the law rather than merely to its letter. As St. Paul said, "For the letter brings death, but the Spirit gives life" (2 Cor 3:6).[156] The Bible gives us the examples of the judgment of Solomon in a case where two women claimed the same baby and of Susanna where the young Daniel exposed her false accusers, to show that equity does not merely seek the formal *appearance* of justice, but seeks to be truly fair. The mechanical, purely formal application of written rules of justice can lead to grave injustices, as did some of the Pharisees' interpretations of the law (Mt 12:1-8).

This virtue of fairness in interpreting the law, however, should not be confused with the species of legal justice called *equity* (*epikeia*) which helps a judge make a fair decision in cases for which the law does not seem to have provided. Thus when Jesus healed on the Sabbath and said, "The Sabbath was made for man, and not man for the Sabbath" (Mk 2:27), he was using fairness, since he makes appeal to the purpose of the Sabbath law which was not only to promote divine worship but also to promote human health by a time of rest and recreation. St. Paul, on the other hand, was using equity when he permitted Christians to remarry in cases where the pagan spouse refused to remain in the marriage (the so-called "Pauline privilege," 1 Cor 7:12-14), because this was a situation about which Jesus had not spoken explicitly when he forbade the divorced to remarry ("I say, not the Lord," v. 12). Note, however, that equity should not be abused as a way of evading the law just because it is inconvenient.

---

[156] Of course this text has a richer meaning than the application given here.

The Gift of Piety

This list of nine kinds of virtue similar to justice, but not fully corresponding to its definition, is, no doubt, not exhaustive; but when St. Thomas Aquinas worked it out, he was reflecting his thorough knowledge of biblical ethics.[157] He relates the virtue of justice to the *Gift of Piety* of the Holy Spirit.[158] This Gift facilitates the reverence for God which pertains to the virtue of religion. But so also does the second Beatitude, "Blessed are the meek, for they will inherit the land" (Mt 5:5), because, says St.Thomas Aquinas,[159] meekness constrains the aggressive tendencies which cause us to rebel against authority and hence facilitates piety.

The Sacrament of Justice

A virtue not treated by Aristotle (although the Greek poets recognized it), but of great importance for Christians is *penance*, especially exercised in the Sacrament of Reconciliation.[160] As we owe honor to God for his benefits to us, so we owe (but cannot of ourselves fully repay), sorrow for the dishonor shown God, either through sins against the theological virtues or the virtue of religion or against our neighbor and

---

[157] Note that Aquinas, *S.T.*, II-II, q. 80, a. 1 ad 4, shows that many terms which indicate the virtue of justice and which might be considered its auxiliary virtues are in fact simply different aspects of justice in the strict sense.

[158] Aquinas, *S.T.*, I-II, q. 68, a. 4 ad 2, says that "piety" is a kind of justice that exhibits reverence to father and fatherland and hence is the name of a gift by which we show reverence to our heavenly Father. He also in *S.T.*, II-II, q. 121, a. 2 connects it with justice and assigns to it the Beatitude "Blessed are the meek," following St. Augustine's *Commentary on the Sermon on the Mount* I, c. 4, 11-12 and III, c. 11, 38 on the grounds that "meekness removes the impediments to justice." However, he also says that more properly piety relates to the Beatitudes "Blessed are those who hunger and thirst for justice" and "Blessed are the merciful." Note that the Latin *pietas* is not well translated by the English "piety" since it simply means "dutifulness" and is used by the Vulgate to translate Greek *eusébeia* (1 Tm 2:10, 3:16, 4:8, 6:6, 11; 2 Tm 3:5; 2 P 1:6) which above we have translated "religion." The Gift is mentioned in CCC # 1631. In CCC # 1674-1676, 1679, there is a discussion of "popular piety" in the sense of various sacramental practices.

[159] *S.T.*, II-II, q. 121, a. 2 c.

[160] CCC # 1420-1498.

ourselves. Our readiness of will to repair this dishonor as far as we can by acts of penance and of restitution is the *virtue of penance*[161] by which, as the common saying goes, "we make our peace with God." Thus through penance God's justice is acknowledged and gratitude is shown for his mercy. We need also to remember that insofar as we fail to purify ourselves through penance in this life, we must complete that purification after death in Purgatory, before we are prepared for heaven.[162]

The prophets of the Old Testament combine the promises of God with constant calls for repentance by the sinful people.

> Gird yourself and weep, O priests!
>   wail, O ministers of the altar!
> Come, spend the night in sackcloth,
>   O ministers of my God! ...
> Proclaim a fast,
>   call an assembly;
> Gather the elders,
>   all who dwell in the land
> Into the house of the Lord, your God,
>   and cry to the Lord! (Jl 2:13a, 14).

Christians realize that no act of reparation of ourselves is worthy to repair the injury we cause by sin. Only Christ's sufferings can do that. "But God proves his love for us in that while we were still sinners Christ died for us" (Rm 5:8). But acts of penance done in faith and love in union with Christ's sufferings are by grace truly reparative.[163] The Christian saints all exhibit this virtue in a high degree. Because of their great love for God and their sorrow that they have not always been true to this love and that others do not love him, they are eager to make up for the harm they and others have done.

Jesus, above all, showed this eagerness to do penance not for his

---

[161] *S.T.*, III, q. 85.

[162] CCC # 1030-1031; cf. Rv 21:27; Mt 5:25-26; Lk 12:32; 1 Cor 3:13-29; Mk 10:38; Lk 12:50.

[163] Council of Trent, DS # 1704-1707, 1712-1714.

own sins, but for ours, in his willingness to accept the Cross in order to show by his love of his Father's honor and our salvation how evil sin is and how great is the Father's mercy. Christians strive to practice this virtue by prayer, fasting, and almsgiving. The holy seasons of Advent and especially Lent are special times of grace and penance.

Summary of Norms

The positive norms of justice can be stated as follows:

1. Give to others their due by respecting their rights in obedience to the laws of God, church, and state; by sharing the common good with all according to their needs and deserts; and by exactly keeping your promises and paying your debts.
2. Show great honor to God by obedience to his commands, interior devotion, and external acts of worship such as sacrifice, prayer, intercession, praise, blessing, and celebration of God's benefits, and by fidelity to any vows you make and by truthful oaths when others require them of you.
3. Show great honor and obedience under God to parents and country; be discrete, honest, and open in communication, appropriately grateful for benefits, lenient in exacting repayment of debts or punishment of injuries; while striving to be liberal with one's possessions, affable in conversation, and fair in executing all laws.

The negative norms of justice can be stated thus:

4. Never fail to respect the rights of all by obedience to the laws of God and the just laws of church and state; nor fail to support the distribution of the common good to all members of society according to their needs and deserts, nor fail to keep your promises and pay your debts to the full as far as you are able.
5. Never give worship by prayer, adoration, or sacrifice to any being but the Holy Trinity; nor seek power by acts intended to tempt God or obtain diabolic help.
6. Never assert as true what you know to be false, nor fail to share the truth you possess with those who have a right to know it, nor reveal what you have no right to reveal.
7. Never cease to strive to live with others with appropriate expressions

of gratitude for benefits, leniency in exacting one's rights, liberality with regard to one's possessions, affability in manner, and fairness in all one's dealings with others.

Finally, it should be noted that the Ten Commandments all relate to justice and the basic rights already discussed. The first three deal with the virtue of religion, which helps us to worship the one true God (First Commandment); in the proper manner (Second Commandment); and at the right time (Third Commandment). The other seven deal with our duties to our neighbor: our basic right to society whose existence depends on respect for parents and social authorities (Fourth Commandment); our basic right to life (Fifth Commandment); our basic right to procreation (Sixth Commandment and Ninth Commandment); our secondary right to the private property needed to facilitate our basic right to earth's resources (Seventh Commandment and Tenth Commandment); and our basic right to truth (Eighth Commandment).

So stand fast with your loins girded in truth, clothed with justice as a breastplate, and your feet shod in readiness for the gospel of peace (Eph 6:14).

CHAPTER 9

LIVING IN LOVE

For this is the message we have heard from the beginning:
we should love one another (1 Jn:11).

A: FRIENDSHIP AND SEXUAL LOVE

Friendship

The English term "love" has to serve for many terms in the Scripture. It can stand for (1) our natural love for ourselves (Eph 5:29); (2) natural friendship between human beings (2 M 14:26); (3) God's love for his creatures (1 Jn 4:8); (4) God's good will toward sinners who do not return his love (Jr 31:3; Eph 2:4); (5) the graced love of friendship by which we love God for himself and our neighbor for God's sake, given us in baptism (Col 3:14; Rm 12:10); (6) the graced virtue given us by God by which we are able to live in and for him (1 Cor 13:13).[1]

Natural love can be either in the bodily sense appetites or in the spiritual will guided by reason, or both. True friendship (*philia*) is a love based on the good qualities the friends share in common. It includes two elements: (a) *benevolence* which seeks not just my own good but my friend's good, i.e., our common good; (b) *union*, the desire to be always *with* my friend.

> By the time David finished speaking with Saul, Jonathan had become as fond of David as if his life depended on him; he loved him as he loved himself (1 S 18:1).

---

[1] See C.S. Lewis, *The Four Loves* for the variety of meanings in the word.

One of his disciples, the one whom Jesus loved, was reclining at Jesus' side [at the Last Supper during which Jesus said,] "I give you a new commandment: love one another. As I have loved you, so you also should love one another. This is how all will know that you are my disciples, if you have love for one another" (Jn 13:23, 34-35).

Such loving friendship results in *identification* with one's friend (*extasis*, standing out of oneself), zeal for the friend's welfare (Ps 69:10; 1 K 19:14), *motivation* of all one's acts by this relationship to one's friend, and *vulnerability* (Sg 4:9) or sensitivity to all that affects one's friend. Thus a perfect union of the love of friendship requires that the friends are alike in mind and heart and that they want to share and actually do share one life together, so that their relation is not only mutual, but each thinks of the other as him or herself. That is why the parting of true friends is a kind of death. As Ruth said to her friend Naomi:

> Do not ask me to abandon or forsake you! for wherever you go I will go, wherever you lodge I will lodge, your people shall be my people, and your God my God. Wherever you will die I will die, and there be buried. May the Lord do so and so to me, if aught but death separates you from me! (Rt 1:16-17).

There are of course, as Aristotle pointed out,[2] lesser types of friendship. We have friends with whom we have in common only some kind of mutual *usefulness*, as the friendship of business partners, or fellow workers on some project. "Even by his neighbor the poor man is hated, but the friends of the rich are many" (Pr 14:20). We also have friends on the basis of mutual *pleasure*, as a tennis or bridge partner. Most of the people we call "friends" are probably of these kinds. Friendship in the full sense of the term described above is something special (see Si 6:5-17). "Let your acquaintances be many, but one in a thousand your confidant" (Si 6:6).

---

[2] *Nicomachean Ethics*, Bk. VIII, c. 4, 11156b 32 sq. See the famous treatise on friendship in Bks. VIII and IX of this work which cover every aspect of the subject.

And there are, of course, those who are "friends in name only" (Si 37:1), accusatory friends like Job's, treacherous "friends," like Judas was to Jesus (cf. Ps 41:10), and evil "friends" who get us into trouble. "Happy are they who do not follow the counsel of the wicked, nor go in the way of sinners, nor sit in the company with scoffers" (Ps 1:1). Yet as Aristotle says, "The man who is to be happy will therefore need virtuous friends."[3]

Sexual Love

The word "love" commonly suggests first of all sexual love, the love of man and woman. "Let him kiss me with kisses of his mouth! More delightful is your love than wine" (Sg 1:1). We have earlier discussed the problems the sexual drive produces for the virtue of moderation, and how Christian asceticism makes it possible to live chastely either in the single or the married state.[4] We have also discussed the questions of a kind of justice which arise in the relations of the family — justice to the spouse and to the children — and seen how this sort of justice is regulated by the Sixth and Ninth Commandments.[5] The fundamental question now arises about sexuality precisely as it is a relation of love.[6]

In the Scriptures and Christian tradition it was a commonplace that God created human beings sexual for the sake of *procreation*, although of course it was always recognized that the family brought many other values to human living. This view was based especially on the original blessing of Genesis 1:28, "Be fertile and multiply." In recent times, however, this tradition of emphasis on sex for procreation has come into conflict with the personalistic emphasis on romantic love.[7] Do not people fall in love for the sake of this intimate relation-

---

[3] *Ibid.*, Bk. IX, c. 9, 1170b 19.

[4] See pp. 212 ff. above.

[5] See pp. 354 ff. above.

[6] CCC # 355, 369-373, 383, 1601-1666, 2331-2400, 2514-2533.

[7] See Denis de Rougemont, *Love in the Western World*. De Rougemont attributed the rise of chivalric love in medieval Europe in part to influences from Islamic culture and to Manicheism.

ship even when they have no thought of children? To say, therefore, that procreation is "the primary end of marriage" and this intimate personal relationship is only one of the "secondary ends" seems to many in our culture quite unrealistic and impersonal.[8]

In rural societies children had always been regarded as a blessing because they were of economic advantage, but in today's urban, technological society children are an economic handicap. Thus the invention of new, more effective techniques of contraception favored the shift to this understanding of human sexuality. This shift has also been greatly favored by the rise of Freudian and other forms of modern depth psychology which show the profound influence of sexual drives on the development of the whole human personality and the risks of sexual repression.

This trend of thinking in favor of understanding sex primarily in terms of a love-relationship began to be felt well before Vatican II, and some exegetes even tried to show that while the Priestly tradition of Genesis 1 stresses procreation, the older Yahwist tradition of Genesis 2 seems to stress not the blessing of fertility on Adam and Eve but Adam's need in his loneliness for a companion like himself.[9]

> The Lord God said: "It is not good for the man to be alone. I will make a suitable partner for him." . . . When he brought her to the man, the man said, "This one, at last, is bone of my bones and flesh of my flesh. This one shall be called 'woman,' for out of 'her man' this one has been taken." This is why a man leaves his father and mother and clings to his wife, and the two of them become one body. The man and his wife were both naked, yet they felt no shame (Gn 2:18, 22b-25).

---

[8] See John T. Noonan, Jr., *Contraception*, an excellent study but biased by its attempt to show that the Church, by abandoning the view that procreation is the primary end of marriage, can and should change its teaching against contraception. In fact, although Vatican II, and Paul VI in *Humanae Vitae*, attempted to correct the mistaken view that the love of the partners is a mere means to procreation, the Council continued to teach that "Marriage and conjugal love are by their nature ordained toward the begetting and educating of children. Children are really the supreme gift of marriage and contribute very substantially to the welfare of their parents" (GS n. 50) and *Humanae Vitae* bases its condemnation of contraception on the principle of the "inseparability of the unitive and procreative meanings" of the marital act.

[9] See pp. 214 ff. above.

It is also pointed out that the Song of Songs taken in its obvious sense is a sensuous celebration of sexual love without any reference to procreation.[10]

Two Meanings of Marriage

Such theological debates led the Council in *Gaudium et Spes*[11] to use a more personalistic way of speaking of marriage without reference to "primary and secondary ends." Yet this same document in # 50 clearly emphasized the procreative purpose of marriage as explanatory of its special character:

> Marriage and conjugal love are by their nature ordained toward the begetting and educating of children. Children are really the supreme gift of marriage and contribute very substantially to the welfare of their parents... Marriage to be sure is not instituted solely for procreation. Rather, in its very nature as an unbreakable compact between persons, and the welfare of the children, both demand that mutual love of the spouses, too, be embodied in a rightly ordered manner, that it grow and ripen. Therefore, marriage persists as a whole manner and communion of life, and maintains its value and indissolubility, even when offspring are lacking — despite, rather often, the very intense desire of the couple.

During the Council, Paul VI had reserved to papal authority the decision on whether some of the new modes of regulating birth were contraceptive or not, and when he decided this question in the encyclical *Humanae Vitae* (1968)[12] he adopted a new terminology, speaking

---

[10] One of the latest interpretations of the Song is Luis Stadlemann, S.J., *Love and Politics: A New Commentary on The Song of Songs*, who thinks its purpose was to restore the rule of the Davidic Dynasty after the Exile by reconciling a Davidic king ("Solomon") with the native population of the Holy Land ("The Shulamite"). For a discussion of the various interpretations see the Anchor Bible commentary by M.H. Pope, *Song of Songs*. For the traditional allegorical interpretation see A. Robert and R. Tournay, in collaboration with A. Feuillet, *Le Cantique des Cantiques*.

[11] GS # 47-52 on marriage; on the population question # 87.

[12] AAS 60 (1968):490ff., translation in Claudia Carlen, *The Papal Encyclicals*, 5 vols., p. 227ff.

not of the "ends of marriage" but of the two "meanings" (*significationes*) of the marital act, its "unitive" and "procreative" meanings.[13] Yet, without giving preference to either of these meanings, he declared them to be inseparable even in individual acts. He concluded therefore that while for a sufficient reason the technical use of the woman's cycle of fertility and infertility to regulate birth is objectively moral, any technique intended to render naturally fertile acts sterile is contraceptive and therefore always immoral.

Two Inseparable Meanings

Some authors today attempt to find some contradiction between the teaching of *Gaudium et Spes* and *Humanae Vitae,* and declare that in fact today the Church has had to abandon the tradition that procreation is the specifying aspect of human sexual love. Consequently, they find the teaching of *Humanae Vitae* on contraception to be incoherent because its personalism cannot be reconciled with its "physicalistic" or "biologistic" arguments.[14]

Since the traditional teaching on the whole area of sexual morality hinged on the notion that God created us sexual that we might procreate,[15] for these authors this substitution of "meanings" for "ends" and the failure of *Humanae Vitae* to explicitly subordinate the unitive to the procreative meaning, justifies a radical revision of the whole moral theology of sexuality.[16] Hence some now accept all forms of

---

[13] *Humanae Vitae* # 12.

[14] For a discussion and refutation of these criticisms of the encyclical, see Janet E. Smith, *Humanae Vitae: A Generation Later.*

[15] See Noonan, *Contraception*, note 8 above, which traces the history of this teaching in detail.

[16] For the history of the controversy which centered in the views of Father Charles E. Curran see Larry Witham, *Curran vs. Catholic University: A Study of Authority and Freedom in Conflict.* Also *Vatican Authority and American Catholic Dissent: The Curran Case and Its Consequences,* edited by William W. May. For Curran's own case see his *Faithful Dissent* and for his ethical system see Richard Grecco, *A Theology of Compromise: A Study of Method in the Ethics of Charles E. Curran.* Further reflections are collected in *Dissent in the Church,* edited by Charles E. Curran and Richard A. McCormick, S.J.

contraception, and even "responsible" extra-marital and homosexual sexual activity, since these seem at least in some circumstances for some people to be the only realistic ways of expressing genuine personal love.

If we look more carefully at this issue, we must note that for Christian theology love is the supreme value and goal (end) not only of the sexual relationship but of *all* personal relationships, whether sexual or otherwise.

> Beloved, let us love one another, because love is of God; everyone who loves is begotten by God and knows God. Whoever is without love does not know God, for God is love (1 Jn 4:7-8).
>
> "'You shall love the Lord, your God, with all your heart, with all your soul, and with all your mind.' This is the greatest and the first commandment. The second is like it: 'You shall love your neighbor as yourself.' The whole law and the prophets depend on these two commandments" (Mt 22:37-40).

Consequently, we must say that the primary end of sexuality is love between the partners, as it is between them and their children and vice versa, and as it is in every good human relationship. The question, however, is what *specifies* sexual love as such; what makes it different from parental or filial or fraternal or friendly love?

Some would answer by saying that what characterizes sexual love is that it is the most *intimate* type of love, involving as it does the totality of the persons in its bodily expression through intercourse. Nevertheless, although it is true that in sexual love human intimacy is realized in a special way, this is the case only because of the differentiation of the human race into two complementary sexes. If humanity was unisex, there would still be a need for intimate human friendship and it would still have to have some form of bodily expression, but this would not be by the sexual, genital act as it now exists.

Thus what specifies sexual love is that humanity was created male and female with a drive to sexual union precisely in view of the *family* community through which only the expansion, continuity, and education of the human species can be attained. It was in this sense that

Catholic tradition spoke of procreation as the "primary end" of marriage, not as denying that it was first of all a relationship of love. Certainly, *Gaudium et Spes* and *Humanae Vitae* did not reject the truth of this tradition. The use of the term "meanings" for "ends" simply removes any merely utilitarian connotation that language about "ends and means" sometimes has.

The "meaning" or "signification" of an act is its purposefulness or teleology. When the Scripture says, "While he [Jesus] was in Jerusalem, many began to believe in his name, when they saw the signs he was doing" (Jn 2:23), it is to be understood that Jesus' acts were "signs" because they pointed to the fulfillment of his purpose, his mission of salvation.

Since procreation specifies this kind of love, the two meanings of union and procreation are inseparable. In human nature our "animality" which we have in common with other animals is inseparable from our "rationality" which makes us specifically different from other animals, because in us our rationality modifies every aspect of our animality. Similarly, the relation to the family qualifies every aspect of the friendship between a married couple, and its natural and consummative expression in the marital act.

This specificity is what *Humanae Vitae* formulated as "the principle of the inseparability of the unitive and procreative meanings of the marital act."[17] Contraceptive acts are those which have been deliberately deprived of their procreative meaning with the result that the unitive meaning is also erased, since the act no longer expresses total self-giving. Thus the contraceptive act is not and cannot be a true marital act but a defective substitute for it, just as a homosexual act is not and cannot be a true marital act.

---

[17] "The Church... in urging men to the observance of the precepts of the natural law, which it interprets by its constant doctrine, teaches as absolutely required that *in any use whatever of marriage* there must be no impairment of the natural capacity to procreate human life. This particular doctrine, often expounded by the Magisterium of the Church, is based on the inseparable connection, established by God, which man on his own initiative may not break, between the unitive and the procreative significance which are both inherent in the marriage act... (E)xcluded is any action, which either before, at the moment of, or after sexual intercourse, is specifically intended to prevent procreation — whether as an end or as a means." HV # 11, 12, 14 (Flannery translation).

Yet, since not all marital acts are naturally fertile, a permanently sterile couple or a couple who for good reasons perform only naturally sterile marital acts do nothing to erase the procreative meaning of these acts. In spite of their accidental sterility, these acts are still endowed with a procreative meaning in the plan of the Creator who willed them as part of his design for human sexuality in and for the family. If it is asked why God in the case of the human species has given the woman a cycle of fertility and infertility, the answer is not difficult to find. It is to bind the male to her continuously in a permanent marriage needed to provide for the long period of education required for human childhood, while limiting her fecundity.[18]

Sexual love, therefore, has a profound significance as the basic *school of love* through which, because of the strength of the sexual drive, its intense bodily intimacy, and its fruitfulness, human beings learn to love other humans generously, and through this to be able to return God's generous love. Hence, in the New Testament this natural "sacrament" or sign of the Creator's love for us, has been made a sacrament of Christ (Mk 10:1-16)[19] which signifies Christ's faithful love for the Church (Eph 5:21-32). In the light of this sacramental significance all that we have said earlier about sexuality, its control by asceticism and the obligations in justice it imposes, should be reviewed and synthesized.

Celibacy and Love

The disciples were incredulous when they heard Jesus' teaching against divorce and remarriage (Mt 19:1-12). He replied:

---

[18] For evolutionary attempts to explain the specifically human reproductive pattern see Irene Elia, *The Female Animal*, pp. 253-256.

[19] Note that the pericope on marriage Mk 10:1-12; Mt 19:3-9; is followed immediately by Jesus' blessing of children. Hugh Andersen, *The Gospel of Mark*, p. 239, points out that Mk 10:1-16 has a resemblance to the moral catechetical tradition reflected in the household codes (*haustafeln*) found in some of the Pauline epistles (Col 3:18-4:1; Eph 5:22-6:9; 1 P 2:13-3:7; Tt 2:1-10; 1 Tm 2:8-15, 6:1-2), but Robert H. Gundry, *Mark: A Commentary on His Apology for the Cross* raises some problems about this, pp. 440, 534-535.

"Some are incapable of marriage because they were born so,
some, because they were made so by others; some, because they
have renounced marriage for the sake of the kingdom of heaven.
Whoever can accept this ought to accept it" (Mt 19:12).

On another occasion Jesus promised:

"Amen, I say to you, there is no one who has given up house or
wife or brothers or parents or children for the sake of the kingdom of God who will not receive back an overabundant return in
this present age and eternal life in the age to come" (Lk 18:29-
30; cf. 14:26).

St. Paul praised celibacy since "the time is running out" (1 Cor
7:29) and, therefore:

An unmarried man is anxious about the things of the Lord, how
he may please the Lord. But a married man is anxious about the
things of the world, how he may please his wife, and he is divided.... I am telling you this for your own benefit, not to impose a restraint on you, but for the sake of propriety and adherence to the Lord without distraction (1 Cor 7:33-34a, 35).

In the early Church there were always men and women ascetics,
virgins, penitents, widows and widowers who followed this advice not
to marry, and by the fourth century dedicated celibacy became
institutionalized in the Church in the consecrated life of the three vows
of chastity, poverty, and obedience in both Eastern and Western
Churches.[20]

---

[20] CCC # 1579-1580, 914-16, 944-945, 1618-1620. Christian Cochini, S.J., *Origines
apostoliques du célibat sacerdotal*, and Roman Cholij, *Clerical Celibacy in East and
West*, have argued that the general canonical practice of the early Church both East and
West was to ordain married men as bishops, priests, and deacons but only on the
condition they and their wives agree to abstain from marital relations after ordination.
Roger Gryson, *Les origines du célibat ecclésiastique du premier au 5e siècle* thinks the
practice was more varied. Certainly the oft repeated statements that required clerical
celibacy originated in the Middle Ages in the Latin Church is erroneous. Pope Siricius
in a letter of 385 deplored abuses against a rule that required all clerics to abstain from
marital relations, DS # 185.

From at least the fourth century, in many places married men who were to be ordained priests were required to adopt celibate chastity. In the Eastern Churches after the seventh century Council of Trullo (which was never accepted by Rome as ecumenical), priests were permitted to remain married (but not to marry or marry a second time) after ordination. Yet in these Churches bishops are chosen only from celibates. In the Latin Church priestly celibacy has remained mandatory and when abuses have risen the obligation has been vigorously reasserted, although exceptions, as recently for clergy reconciled from Protestantism, have occasionally been permitted.

Two reasons are given for mandatory celibacy: (1) Priests ought not to appear less ascetically dedicated than non-ordained religious; (2) the offering of the Eucharistic Sacrifice fittingly requires that the presiding celebrant symbolize the Risen Christ. Jesus said to the Sadducees:

> "Are you not misled because you know not the scriptures or the power of God? When they rise from the dead, they neither marry nor are given in marriage, but they are like the angels in heaven" (Mk 12:24-25).

Thus celibacy "for the sake of the kingdom" (Mt 19:12b) symbolizes eternal, resurrected life, for which all Christians hope, but which they may be tempted by the cares of earthly, domestic life to forget.

Hence, it was that in the Old Law, although priests married, they were required to be ritually pure before offering the sacrifices, which meant abstaining from sex from the day before (Lv 15:16). "To their God they shall be sacred, and not profane his name; since they offer up the oblations of the Lord, the food of their God, they must be holy" (Lv 21:6).[21] Warriors in a "holy war" were also required to abstain from sex before battle (1 S 21:1-8; 2 S 11:11). New Testament priests who offer the Eucharistic Bread constantly and are leaders in the spiritual war

---

[21] It is to this law that Pope Siricius (DS # 185) refers and then argues that — since Jesus came not to abolish but to fulfill the Old Law (Mt 5:17), and that in the New Testament this fulfillment is found in the more perfect chastity of the Church as the spouse of Christ — the clergy ought to be perpetually celibate.

against sin, appropriately abstain throughout their ministry. By doing so they exhibit a love of God and their people patterned after that of Jesus and Paul.

The fact that some priests have been unfaithful to the celibacy they voluntarily accepted, and that in our sex-obsessed culture, not many men have the courage to accept this challenge of celibate priesthood is not surprising. The Church in its long history has seen the number of priests fall and rise many times and has experienced many scandals.[22] Jesus himself exclaimed, "The harvest is abundant but the laborers are few!" (Lk 10:2a), but he did not soften his demand, "Go sell what you have, and give to the poor and you will have treasures in heaven; then come, follow me" (Mk 10:21b). Rather he prayed, "Ask the master of the harvest to send laborers for his harvest" (Lk 10:2b). Is it really too much to ask of one called to the priesthood? To Peter who said to Jesus, "We have given up our possessions and followed you," Jesus answered:

> "Amen, I say to you, there is no one who has given up house or *wife* or brothers or parents or children for the sake of the kingdom of God who will not receive back an overabundant return in this present age and eternal life in the age to come" (Lk 18:28-30, my italics).[23]

When the laity claim that they have a right to the Eucharist which is denied them by the scarcity of men who will agree to be celibate

---

[22] See A.W.R. Sipe, *A Secret World*.

[23] The parallels in Mk 10:29 and Mt 19:29 omit "wife." Did Lk add this because of his regular attention to women's concerns? Or, on the contrary, as Elisabeth Schüssler-Fiorenza argues, *In Memory of Her*, pp. 145-146, because Luke claims, contrary to fact, that the wandering charismatics were only men and hence makes no mention of leaving a "husband" to follow Jesus? R.H. Gundry, *Mark*, pp. 558, 567 (and his *Matthew*, pp. 200, 435) thinks her explanation is undermined by Lk 14:6 "If anyone comes to me without hating his father and mother, *wife* and children, brothers and sisters and even his own life, he cannot be my disciple." He believes (p. 567) the Lucan version to be original (p. 567) and explains (p. 588) that the omission in the Petrine Mk (and in the dependent Mt) is due to avoidance of the problem raised by the tradition (1 Cor 9:5) that Peter was accompanied on his journeys by a woman. I.H. Marshall, *The Gospel of Luke: A Commentary on the Greek Text*, p. 688, also defends the authenticity of "wife" against E. Klostermann.

priests,[24] they should remember that it is their responsibility to encourage young men, especially their own sons, to have the heroism and dedication to respond to Jesus' call.

Married people share in this celibate asceticism of religious and priests in their own practice of married chastity and fidelity, which often requires of them some temporary abstinence for various reasons, including responsible parenthood. So do single persons who are preparing for a truly loving and unselfish marriage, since the best preparation for marriage is the self-control of pre-marital chastity which will make possible an unselfish love in the vicissitudes of married life. As for those who do not choose to marry, or ought not to marry, as those of confirmed homosexual orientation, the chaste single life can give freedom for service to others in Christian love.[25]

B: AGAPE

The Nature of Christian Love

The true unselfish, generous, creative love of man and wife even at the natural level, but above all when elevated by grace in the Christian Sacrament of Matrimony, helps us to understand the love between God and creatures both at the natural and the supernatural levels. This kind

---

[24] Edward Schillebeeckx, O.P., *Ministry: Leadership in the Community of Jesus Christ*, has argued that since, he claims, the laity have a "right to the Eucharist," where there is a shortage of priests, celibacy should be made optional, and local churches may validly ordain married members of their congregations as their priests. The Sacred Congregation for the Doctrine of the Faith insisted that he correct this work, which he tried to do in *The Church with a Human Face: A New and Expanded Theology of Ministry*, but he did not satisfy the Congregation. See its "Letter to Fr. Schillebeeckx regarding his book *Ministry*," *Origins* 14 (Jan. 24, 1985):523 and "Note on the Response of Fr. Schillebeeckx," *Origins* 14 (April 4, 1985):683. A noted biblical scholar, Pierre Grelot, *Église et ministères*, refuted Schillebeeckx's scriptural argument. See also the critiques by Albert Vanhoye, S.J., and Henri Crouzel, S.J., "The Ministry in the Church: Reflections on a Recent Publication," *The Clergy Review*, 5, 68 (May, 1983):156-174; and Walter Kasper, "Ministry in the Church: Taking Issue with Edward Schillebeeckx," *Communio*, Summer, 1983, 185-195.

[25] CCC # 2348-2350; homosexuality, # 2359.

of love has all the characteristics of a true natural friendship, but infinitely surpasses them, because it is God's own love shared with us. To repeat more fully the familiar text, already quoted:

> One of them [a scholar of the law] tested him by asking, "Teacher, which commandment in the law is the greatest?" He said to him, "You shall love the Lord, your God, with all your heart, with all your soul, and with all your mind [Dt 6:5]. This is the greatest and the first commandment. The second is like it: You shall love your neighbor as yourself [Lv 19:18; cf. Jm 2:8]. The whole law and the prophets depend on these two commandments" (Mt 22: 35-40).[26]

And in the Sermon on the Mount Jesus went even further, not only quoting the law but adding his own interpretation to it:

> "You have heard that it was said, 'You shall love your neighbor and hate your enemy.' But I say to you, love your enemies, and pray for those who persecute you, that you may be children of your heavenly Father, for he makes his sun rise on the bad and the good, and causes rain to fall on the just and the unjust" (Mt 5:43-45).

St. Paul, therefore, could say:

> Owe nothing to anyone, except to love one another; for the one who loves another has fulfilled the law. The commandments, "You shall not commit adultery; you shall not kill; you shall not steal; you shall not covet," and whatever other commandment there may be are summed up in this saying, "You shall love your neighbor as yourself." Love does no evil to the neighbor; hence, love is the fulfillment of the law (Rm 13:8-10).

---

[26] The phrase "a scholar of the law" is textually doubtful, but may be borrowed from the parallel passage of Luke 10:25. On the Great Commandment of Love see Ceslaus Spicq, O.P., *Agape in the New Testament*, 3 vols.; Gene Outka, *Agape: An Ethical Analysis*; Rudolf Schnackenburg, *The Moral Teaching of the New Testament*, pp. 15-167; Victor P. Furnish, *The Love Commandment in the New Testament*; John Piper, *"Love Your Enemies": Jesus' Love Command in the Synoptic Gospels and in the Early Christian Paranesis*.

and again:

> For the whole law is fulfilled in one statement, namely,
> "You shall love your neighbor as your self" (Gal 5:14).

Finally, in the great 13th Chapter of 1 Corinthians after praising love St. Paul concluded, "Faith, hope, and love remain, these three; but the greatest of these is love" (13:13). St. John could also say:

> In this way the love of God was revealed to us: God sent his only Son into the world so that we might have life through him. In this is love: not that we have loved God, but that he loved us and sent his Son as expiation for our sins. Beloved, if God so loved us, we also must love one another. No one has ever seen God. Yet, if we love one another, God remains in us, and his love is brought to perfection in us (1 Jn 4:9-12).[27]

Thus the culmination of Christian moral life is to be found in the love of God and neighbor founded in faith and motivated by hope. It is essential, however, to understand that the love spoken of in these texts is not just any kind of "love," a word which in English has to do duty for many different kinds of relationships which the Greek New Testament distinguishes. When God is said to be Love Itself the term in Greek is not *eros* nor *philia* but *agape*, a word distinctively Christian in its use, which is translated by the Latin term *caritas*, "charity," itself from the Greek *charis*, "favor" or "grace." Unfortunately, today "charity" in English is commonly used in the restricted sense of "giving to charity," i.e., almsgiving, and thus is even less helpful than the broad term "love."[28]

---

[27] Raymond E. Brown, *Gospel According to St. John*, Vol. 1, Jn 4:9-12.

[28] CCC of course speaks frequently of "love" and of "charity" in various senses: as Christ's love (# 2011); as a theological virtue (#1813) intimately related to hope (#1818, 1841); and also as a fruit of the Spirit (# 736); as the Great Commandment including all the commandments and virtues and unifying them (# 1822-1829, 1844-1845, 2055, 2069, 2086, 2093-2094, 2196-2197) and the opposite of sin (# 1885); as the soul of prayer (# 2658); as the great social commandment (# 1889); which unifies the Church (# 815) and animates its apostolate (# 864) and the consecrated life (# 914-930). It distinguishes it from "love" as a fundamental psychological drive (# 1765) and from conjugal love (# 1604-1605, 1643).

Agape is first of all, as the quotation from 1 John above indicates, "Not that we have loved God but that he has loved us."[29] But God has no need of his creatures, since he created them freely for their sake, not his own; so his love for us is not *eros*. Nor is it simply *philia*, "friendship," because the gap between God and creature is too great for them to meet on the same plane of shared life.[30] God's love for us — God himself — can only be *agape*, a love of pure generosity which is entirely for our sake, not for God's benefit, but which lifts us up to God's level. It is only because he has raised us up in a covenant relationship to him that we can truly have a friendship (*philia*) with him, and every desire (*eros*) of ours can be fulfilled in him.

Moreover, God's love for us through grace fills us with the same kind of generous love toward God, whom we then can love for himself alone, and it spills over into our love for our neighbor, even our enemies, whom we can love as God loves them, because for all their sins they are still his children.

Hence, this Great Commandment of Love is not two but one commandment, since through it in loving God we also love our neighbor for God's sake, because God loves them with the same love that God loves us.[31] Moreover, this kind of love of God includes the will to observe all the other commandments of God out of love for God and because we know that in his love for us, he would never demand anything of us except what is for the common good in which we and our neighbor share alike.

Therefore, those today who understand the word "love" in this command to refer to the pursuit of sensual pleasure or to mere sentimental good fellowship (the '60's slogan "Make Love not War" was often understood as meaning "Free Sex vs. the Draft"!), or who sup-

---

[29] Anders Nygren, *Agape and Eros*, and the critique of such views by another Protestant author, Gene H. Outka, *Agape: An Ethical Analysis*.

[30] "When one party [to a friendship] is removed to a great distance, as God is, the possibility of friendship ceases." *Nicomachean Ethics*, Bk. VIII, c. 7, 1159a 4.

[31] St. Thomas Aquinas, *S.T.*, II-II, q. 44, a. 2-3, explains why there are two precepts — love of God and of neighbor — and yet how these are one, since there is "one precept by which we are led to love God as [our] end; but another by which we are led to love [our] neighbor because of God as [our] end."

pose that Jesus tried to replace the commandments of morality, of chastity, truthfulness, honesty, and justice with a permissive hedonism have ignored the totality of his teaching.

The Bible never tires of trying to describe this divine love of friendship between God and created persons. "What we have seen and heard we proclaim now to you, so that you too may have fellowship with us; for our fellowship is with the Father and with his Son, Jesus Christ" (1 Jn 1:3).[32]

Some theologians, notably Peter Lombard, have held that this love is the Holy Spirit himself. Although it is certainly the fruit of the Spirit's indwelling, it is also a supernatural transformation of our soul and our whole person by which we have the virtue or capacity to respond to God's love and to share in it, as was declared by the Council of Trent.[33]

The Supremacy of Love

Why is love the most perfect of virtues? Natural friendship is not a virtue, although it is the "crown of all virtues" because founded on good character; but *agape* is the foundation of all the other virtues, and must therefore be itself a virtue. The theological virtues are the highest of all the virtues because their object is God himself. Christian love cannot exist without faith, since we cannot love a God we do not know, nor could it exist without hope, since we cannot love someone who is utterly beyond our reach. Yet faith is obscure and will be replaced by vision when we actually possess God. Hope exists only as long as we do not yet possess God. But love is the same in heaven as on earth and will last eternally in the possession of God (Col 3:14; 1 Cor 13:13). It is the flowering of faith and the fulfillment of hope.

---

[32] Not to burden the text with too long a list, cf. the following: Ps 103-105, 136; Is 41:13-20; Jdt 16:13-16; Mt 11:25-27; Jn 14:15-31; 15:10-17; 1 Jn 1:1-4; 3:1-2; 1 Cor 1:9; 6:17; Rm 8:14-17; Eph 2:15-23; 2 P 1:3-4; etc. The Church Fathers dwell often on this theme of friendship with God: St. John Chrysostom, PG, *In Ps.* 55:417; Athanasius, PG 27:534; Augustine, *In Jn.*, tr. 85, 35:1848 sq; Cyril of Alexandria, *In Jn.*, 15:4, PG 74:559-564; Bernard of Clairvaux, *Serm. in Cant.*, 1, n. 8; 68, n. 1, 3, PL 183:788.

[33] DS # 1528-1531 and 1561.

Without love there is no perfect virtue, since it is the form and completion of all the virtues (1 Tm 1:5; Rm 13:10). While prudence forms the moral virtues by ordering them to their end, love also forms the other two theological virtues, as well as prudence and the moral virtues, activating them toward their fulfillment and causing them to share in the very life of God, for "God is love" (1 Jn 4:16), i.e., the One whose very existence and life is to know and to love and only to know and love, and who creates all other true love.

Christian love is an infused virtue given by God in the degree God wishes (Eph 4:7) and its *subject is the will*. When we exercise it in acts of love and in acts of the other virtues motivated by love, it grows (Pr 4:18; Eph 4:15-16; Ph 1:9)[34] and this increase of love has no limit[35] but accelerates like a sort of "spiritual gravity," ever faster and faster.[36] The principle cause of this increase, however, is not our cooperation, but God's grace (Mk 9:40).[37]

Growth in Love

The three phases of growth in the spiritual life and of Christian perfection are simply this intensification of the love of God, under the influence of the Holy Spirit, working through his sevenfold gifts (Is 11:2; Rv 4:5; 5:6), and are traditionally called "the purgative, illuminative, and unitive ways."[38]

In the first phase, the love of God and neighbor is purified of selfishness.

> "Amen, amen, I say to you, unless a grain of wheat falls to the ground and dies, it remains a grain of wheat; but if it dies, it produces much fruit" (Jn 12:24).

---

[34] Trent, DS # 1535, 1574, 1582.

[35] Council of Vienne, DS # 891 against the Begards.

[36] See Reginald Garrigou-Lagrange, O.P., *The Three Ages of the Interior Life*, vol. 1, pp. 130-133.

[37] Trent, DS # 1535, 1545-1550, 1582.

[38] On the history of this and other divisions of the spiritual journey, see Pierre Pourat, "Commençants," *Dictionnaire de Spiritualité*, 21:1143-1156 and J. Lemaitre, "Contemplation III," *ibid.*, 22:1762-1871.

In the second phase this "pruned" love produces the fruits of good works.

> "I am the vine, and my Father is the vine grower. He takes away every branch in me that does not bear fruit, and everyone that does he prunes so that it bears more fruit" (Jn 15:1-3).

In the third and final phase it unites the soul intimately to God and *deifies* it.

> "Whoever loves me will keep my word, and my Father will love him, and we will come to him and make our dwelling with him" (Jn 14:23).

Love does not decrease directly of itself, since its principal cause is God who would never cause it to lessen (Rm 8:38; 1 Jn 3:9), nor even by venial sins, i.e., sins inappropriate to but not contradictory to the love of God (Pr 24:16). But it does decrease indirectly. The author of Revelation wrote to the Church of Ephesus, "You have lost the love you had at first" (Rv 2:4). Jesus warned, "Because of the increase of evil-doing, the love of many will grow cold" (Mt 24:12). This chilling of love happens when our acts of love become infrequent, thus preparing the way for mortal sins which completely kill love, because mortal sin is contradictory to love. "Whoever does not love a brother he has seen cannot love God whom he has not seen" (1 Jn 4:20). Thus charity is never taken from us by God, but we can lose it by our free will through mortal sin.[39] "When a virtuous man turns away from virtue to commit iniquity, and dies, it is because of the iniquity he committed that he must die" (Ezk 18:26; 33:12-13).

> If they, having escaped the defilements of the world through knowledge of our Lord Jesus Christ, again become entangled and overcome by them, their last condition is worse than their first. For it would have been better for them not to have known the way of righteousness than after knowing it to turn back from

---

[39] Trent, DS # 1540, 1542-3 against some Calvinists.

the holy commandment handed down to them. What is expressed
in the true proverb has happened to them, "The dog returns to its
own vomit" [Pr 26:11], and "A bathed sow returns to wallowing
in the mire" (2 P 2:20-22; cf. also Gal 5:4; 1 Cor 9:27; Rm 6:23,
8:15-17, 11:20-22; 2 Tm 1:6-7; Rv 2:4-5, etc.).

As we have already seen, the *formal object* or proximate motive
of love toward God is God's absolute goodness. The formal object of
love toward neighbor is the same goodness of God as this can be shared
with creatures.

> We love because he [God] first loved us. If anyone says, "I love
> God," but hates his brother, he is a liar; for whoever does not
> love a brother whom he has seen cannot love God whom he has
> not seen. This is the commandment we have from him, whoever
> loves God must also love his brother (1 Jn 4:19-21; cf. 3:11-24).

The *material object* of love is God as the goal of our life transcending
all that our nature can demand and the sharing of this same goal with all
created persons, the manifestation of God's perfection to all rational
creatures, along with the means by which this goal can be attained.
Therefore by the theological virtue of love we love: (a) God (Jn 14:28)
with desire, zeal, and delight (Jn 14:15, 21; 1 Jn 2:4, 3:18, 5:3; Mt
16:24, 22:37-38, 25:31-45; 1 Cor 10:31); (b) ourselves for God (Mt
6:19-20, 33; 1 Cor 9:27; 2 Cor 6:16-18; Rm 6:13, 19); (c) our neighbors, and even our enemies, not as sinners but as children of God. "If
your enemy be hungry, give him food to eat, if he be thirsty, give him
to drink; for live coals you will heap on his head, and the Lord will
vindicate you" (Pr 26:21-22; Mt 5:43-48; 6:12; Lv 19:17-18; Ex 23:4-
5; Rm 12:20-21).

Our duty to love our enemies strictly obliges us to love them as
human persons capable of salvation, and it is a counsel to love them
even as individuals (Pr 25:21). We must show the general signs of
respect to our enemies as to all other persons, except perhaps temporarily for a sufficient reason other than our enmity. For example, it
might be necessary to refuse to shake hands with Adolf Hitler when

---

[40] *Christian Instruction* (*De Doctrina Christiana*), cc. 27-30 (28-33), pp. 47-52.

this would seem to show approval of his behavior. But we must always forgive our enemies in our heart (Mt 5:23-24; 6:15; 18:35), even Adolf Hitler, and as far as possible seek their salvation.

The egotistic and selfish sin against love by *excess* is self-love or "narcissism." "Those who regularly give alms shall enjoy a full life; but those who are habitually guilty of sin are their own worst enemies" (Tb 12:10; cf. Ph 2:21; 2 Cor 10:14; 2 Tm 3:1-9; Jude vv. 5-16). Those people sin against love by *defect* who seek only material goods, neglect the means to salvation, or seek what is evil. "But God said to him [the complacent rich man], 'You fool, this night your life will be demanded of you, and the things you have prepared, to whom will they belong?'" (the Parable of the Rich Fool, Lk 12:16-21).

The Order of Love

St. Augustine raised the interesting question, later pursued by many other theologians, as to the proper "order of love" (*ordo amoris*), that is, "Should we love all equally or some more than others?"[40] The answer given by St. Thomas Aquinas[41] can be summarized as follows:

(1) Jesus said, "Whoever loves father or mother more than me is not worthy of me" (Mt 10:37; Lk 14:25; cf. Dt 6:5; Mt 22:37; Lk 14:26). Therefore, God is to be loved above all objectively and *appreciatively*; that is, we should acknowledge that God is more worthy of love than all creatures, even when we do not feel this supreme love most *intensively*. Hence, we should be willing to die rather than to reject God's love by sinning.

(2) After God we should love ourselves as regards the salvation of our souls.[42] "You shall love your neighbor as yourself" (Mt 22:39; Lv 19:18), but we should love our neighbor's soul more than our own bodies (Jn 10:11; 15:12; 1 Jn 3:16). It is permissible to love our own temporal life and goods more than those of our neighbors, but we must love the bodily good of our neighbor more than our own external goods. As St. Augustine says:

---

[41] *S.T.*, II-II, q. 27.
[42] Innocent XI, DS # 2163.

It is impossible for one who loves God not to love himself. For he alone has a proper love of himself who aims diligently at the attainment of the chief and true good; and if this is nothing else but God, as has been shown, what is to prevent one who loves God from loving himself? And then among men should there be no bond of mutual love? Yea, verily; so that we can think of no surer step towards the love of God than the love of man to man... Now you love yourself suitably when you love God better than yourself. What, then, you aim at in yourself you must aim at in your neighbor, namely that he may love God with a perfect affection. For you do not love him as yourself, unless you try to draw him to that good which you are yourself pursuing. For this is the one good which has room for all to pursue it along with you.[43]

(3) We should love virtuous persons appreciatively more than those of lesser virtue, but we ought to love both appreciatively and intensively persons to whom we are more closely related by kinship or friendship than those who are more distant.[44]

But if a widow has children or grandchildren, let these first learn to perform their religious duty to their own family and to make recompense to their parents, for this is pleasing to God... And whoever does not provide for relatives and especially family members has denied the faith and is worse than an unbeliever (1 Tm 5:4, 8; cf. Gal 6:10).

Thus we rightly prefer our own family, our own friends, our superiors and benefactors, our own country to others, because God has given them to us as our first responsibility. "Every living thing loves its own kind, every man a man like himself" (Si 13:14). By fulfilling that responsibility we should grow stronger in love so as to extend that love to ever wider circles. Those who "love humanity" and slight those close to them love little.

---

[43] *The Catholic and Manichaean Ways of Life*, FC, 1965, Chapters 19-28, PL 32:1309-1378.

[44] 1 Tm 5:3-16 on widows is discussed in detail by Phillip H. Towner, *The Goal of Our Instruction*, pp. 180-190. He concludes that this passage is a single unit and does not concern an "office" of widow, but the care by the Church of certain poor but worthy women without relatives to support them.

In the Parable of the Rich Man and Lazarus (Lk 16:19-31) we note that the beggar was "lying at his door." On the other hand the Parable of the Good Samaritan (Lk 10:29-37) reminds us that "our neighbor" may well be someone who comes into close relation with us through providence, and not by conventional relationships. Once the Samaritan had seen the man lying in the road, he could no longer ignore him.

The sin of *racism* does not arise only from a perception of the defects of groups other than our own. There is no denying that all groups have typical faults that make them liable to stereotyping and caricature by other groups. Rather, racism chiefly arises from a lack of love for others, even our enemies, just because they are human beings having most things, and especially the most fundamental things, in common with ourselves and our own group. Racism is best overcome by learning to love all human persons for the same reason that we ought to love ourselves, namely, that God loves us all as his children, whatever our defects.[45] "Here there is not Greek or Jew, circumcision or uncircumcision, barbarian, Scythian, slave, free; but Christ is all in all" (Col 2:11; cf. Gal 3:27-28).[46] Particularly sinful is anti-Semitism, the utterly wrong and ungrateful hatred of Jews on the false grounds that the Jews of today (or the vast majority of the Jews of the past) are responsible for

---

[45] CCC # 27, 1700-1715, 1929-1948.

[46] The phrase of Gal 3:28, "not male and female" is often cited by feminist theologians as the clearest text in the Bible asserting sexual equality. But note that Paul is not speaking of natural equality, but equality "in Christ Jesus," i.e., as to the graces conferred in baptism (Gal 3:27). "That Paul did not intend to abolish the gender roles between men and women is apparent from the discussion in 1 Cor 11:2-16." Frank J. Matera, *Galatians*, p. 143. See also Gal 5:6; 6:15; 1 Cor 7:19, and Eph 2:25. Perhaps it was to avoid any misunderstanding on this point that the parallel passage in Col 3:11 omits "neither male or female" and that some "early manuscripts (P 46, A) read 'For all of you belong to Christ (*este Christou*).' Others (S*), 'For you are all in Christ (*este en Christou*).' Both variants are probably attempting to make the present reading clearer by eliminating *heis* ('one') which might give the impression that the differences mentioned above no longer exist in fact... All the baptized form a single person in Christ: they are a new creation. See Gal 6:15" (Matera, p. 143). Thus the text has nothing to do with social or ecclesiastical roles, but with Church membership as a means of salvation; see also M. Boucher, "Some Unexplored Parallels to 1 Cor 11, 11-12 and Gal 3, 28: The New Testament and the Role of Woman," CBQ 31 (1969):50-58 and Ben Witherington, "Rite and Rights for Women — Galatians 3:28," NTS 27 (1980-81):593-604.

the death of Jesus, himself a Jew. Those Jewish religious leaders of two thousand years ago who did bear this responsibility, did so precisely because of the same fanaticism that leads people today to be anti-semites, a guilt we all share if we condone their bigotry.[47]

Moreover, in accordance with the order of love, Christians ought to have a special fraternal or filial love of Jews, because in Christ Jesus we have ourselves become adopted sons and daughters of the Covenant. As St. Paul tells us, we are only "wild olive branches" that have been "grafted into the rich root of the olive tree" and if we are holy it is only because our Jewish roots are holy. Paul warns us: "consider that you do not support the root; the root supports you" (Rm 11:13-24).

I have already pointed out the sinfulness of sexism, contempt for another because of their gender.[48] The same is true of contempt for those having physical or mental disabilities, including the disability to achieve heterosexual orientation.[49] Christian love is always compassionate and seeks to assure every human being of the love of God and the community for each person. But it is not sentimentality or denial of human defects physical, mental, or moral. Rather, it seeks healing for the sufferer or if this is impossible, support in carrying the Cross.

C: WORKS OF LOVE

The Inner Working of Love

St. Paul says, "For in Christ Jesus, neither circumcision nor uncircumcision counts for anything, but only faith working through love" (Gal 5:6). The "working" or *proper act* of the virtue of love is, of course, to love, which means to seek the true good of the one loved and to desire to live with that one in community. The internal fruits of

---

[47] See John Pawlikowski, *What Are They Saying About Christian-Jewish Relations?*
[48] See pp. 358 ff. above.
[49] See pp. 275 ff. above.

loving are *joy*, *peace*, and *mercy*,[50] its external fruits are good works for the sake of others. As St. Paul says:

> Love is patient, love is kind. It is not jealous, it is not pompous, it is not inflated, it is not rude, it does not seek its own interests, it is not quick-tempered, it does not brood over injury, it does not rejoice over wrongdoing but rejoices over the truth. It bears all things, believes all things, hopes all things, endures all things. Love never fails (1 Cor 13:4-8).

We have seen that the physical passion of love tends to end in physical *joy* in union with the beloved.[51] Hence spiritual love tends to a deeper and more total joy of the whole person in spiritual union. While physical joy is brief; spiritual joy can last forever.

> Set me as a seal on your heart
> as a seal on your arm;
> For stern as death is love,
> relentless as the nether world is devotion;
> its flames are blazing fire.
> Deep waters cannot quench love,
> nor floods sweep it away.
> Were one to offer all he owns to purchase love,
> he would be roundly mocked (Sg 8:6-7).

The Bible is full of praise of *peace* as the effect of love fulfilled. The Sabbath peace of the Old Testament foreshadows the eternal peace of heaven. It was an old greeting, as when Amasai, leader of David's Thirty Champions was moved by the prophetic Spirit to reply to David, when David in hiding asked for a password, "We are yours, O David; we are with you, O son of Jesse, Peace, peace to you; and peace to him who helps you; your God it is who helps you" (1 Ch 12:19). Jesus commanded his missionaries, "As you enter a house, wish it peace. If the house is worthy, let your peace come upon it; if not, let your peace return to you" (Mt 10:12-13). At the Last Supper he spoke the words

---

[50] CCC # 1829.

[51] See pp. 194 ff.

the priest repeats before distributing the Eucharist, "Peace I leave with you; my peace I give to you. Not as the world gives do I give it to you" (Jn 14:27), and after rising from death he greets the Twelve, "Peace be with you" (Jn 20:19, 21, 26). The mystics tell us that in the unitive way of the spiritual life, in spite of many trials and sufferings, they abide in profound peace at the depths of their souls.[52] St. Augustine defines peace as "the tranquility of order"[53] because love sets the whole universe in order and produces inner harmony in the soul and outer harmony between all members of a society.

Mercy flows from love, because when we truly love someone for their own sake, we forget their injuries to us and think only of what will be good for them. "May mercy, peace, and love be yours in abundance" (Jude v. 2). God's mercy (*hesed*) is a constant theme of the Old Testament (e.g., Ex 20:6; Dt 13:18; Tb 3:2; Ps 118:2; 136:1; Ws 9:1; Si 5:6; Is 16:5; Jr 31:20, etc.). And of all the traits of Jesus none is so evident to the whole world as his mercy, his compassionate willingness to suffer even the curse of the Cross for each one of us however wicked we may be. In doing so, he revealed to us what we find so hard to believe, that God is above all a merciful God.

> Blessed be the God and Father of our Lord Jesus Christ, who in his great mercy gave us a new birth to a living hope through the resurrection of Jesus Christ from the dead, an inheritance that is imperishable, undefiled, and unfading, kept in heaven for you who by the power of God are safeguarded through faith, to a salvation that is ready to be revealed in the final time (1 P 1:3-5).

---

[52] St. Teresa of Avila, speaking of God's gift to her of the transforming union says, "The person already referred to [she is evidently speaking of herself] found herself better in every way; however numerous were her trials and business worries, the essential part of her soul seemed never to move from that dwelling-place. So in a sense she felt that her soul was divided; and when she was going through great trials, shortly after God granted her this favor, she complained of her soul, just as Martha complained of Mary. Sometimes she would say that it was doing nothing but enjoying itself in that quietness, while she herself was left with all her trials and occupations so that she could not keep it company." *Interior Castles*, Seventh Mansion, Chapter 1, quoted in Juan Arintero, O.P., *The Mystical Evolution in the Development and Vitality of the Church*, vol. 2, p. 240. See Arintero's whole treatment of the Unitive Way, pp. 170-237.

[53] *De Civitate Dei*, XIX, c. 13, n. 1.

According to Aquinas[54] the Gift of the Holy Spirit which corresponds to charity is the supreme Gift of Wisdom (1 Cor 2:6-16) and the Seventh Beatitude, "Blessed are the peacemakers, for they will be called children of God" (Mt 5:9). This is so because love is the supreme virtue in the will, and wisdom in the intellect. Without perfect love we cannot be perfectly united to God, and only if we are perfectly united to God can we share in the divine wisdom. Reciprocally, only when we know God as he really is through true wisdom can we love him perfectly. Thus love and wisdom go hand in hand, and we have seen that to make peace is a great work of love. "Live in peace, and the God of love and peace will be with you" (2 Cor 13:11b). Since wisdom orders all things by truth and love by goodness, wisdom and love bring final peace, the eternal Sabbath, to the soul. Only those who dwell in such peace of soul can bring peace to others in a disordered world. Hence, before receiving the Eucharist we give to each other a kiss (or some other sign) of peace and mutual forgiveness. "Greet one another with a holy kiss. All the churches of Christ greet you" (Rm 16:16; cf. 1 Cor 16:20; 2 Cor 13:12).

The Corporal Works of Mercy

The *external* works of love are both physical and spiritual. Traditionally seven "Corporal Works of Mercy"[55] or "charity" in the modern sense (Mt 25:35-36) are enumerated: (1) feeding the hungry (Mt 25:35a); (2) giving drink to the thirsty (Mt 25:35b; Mt 10:42); (3) clothing the naked (Mt 25:38b); (4) extending hospitality to the homeless (Mt 25:38a); (5) caring for the sick (Mt 25:36b; Lk 16:19-31); (6) redeeming captives (Mt 25:36c); and (7) burying the dead (Tb 2:3-10; 12:12-13). These works cannot substitute for social justice, but they go beyond what is strictly demanded by justice to care even for the undeserving and unworthy, and add to justice "the personal touch." Such works are constantly urged both in the Old and New Testaments, as is vigorously summed up in the question of the Epistle of St. James (2:15-17):

---

[54] *S.T.*, II-II, q. 45.
[55] CCC # 2447-2449.

If a brother or sister has nothing to wear and has no food for the day, and one of you says to them, "Go in peace, keep warm, and eat well," but you do not give them the necessities of the body, what good is it? So also faith of itself, if it does not have works, is dead (cf. Dt 15:11; Is 58; Ezk 18:7; Pr 31:20; Si 29:1-20; Mt 6:1-4; 25:31-46; Lk 3:10-11; 16:19-31; 1 Tm 6:17-19; 1 Jn 3:17-18).

In giving alms to others who are in *extreme* necessity, we are not obliged to give them from what we ourselves extremely need, except when the common good demands it; but we have a grave obligation to give them what is superfluous for us, even at great (but not extreme) inconvenience to ourselves. When others are in grave necessity, we also are obliged to give them from our superfluities and even from our necessities if the inconvenience to us is only light.[56] For needs that are only *common*, we have the obligation to make some contributions to charity (Pr 14:21; Si 14:13-18; Rm 12:20; Jm 1:27). We should, however, be prudent in giving so as to do the most good we can with our resources rather than merely to be thought generous or to get rid of beggars (Si 12:4-5; 2 Th 3:10), and we should give cheerfully not grudgingly (2 Cor 9:7), generously (Tb 4:8-9), promptly (Pr 3:28), secretly (Mt 6:1-4), justly, and in right order (Si 12:1-7), so as to help the most deserving and all as far as our resources permit, thus fulfilling distributive justice.

The Spiritual Works of Love

Often it is forgotten that the "Spiritual Works of Charity" are even more needed than the corporal works. These are also traditionally listed as seven: (1) to pray for all (Mt 5:44); (2) to forgive (Mt 18:21-35); (3) to console the sad (2 Cor 1:4); (4) to bear the burdens of others (Gal 6:2); (5) to teach the ignorant (1 Tm 4:11-16); (6) to counsel the perplexed (1 Cor 8:1-13); (7) to correct the sinner (1 Cor 11:17-22).[57]

---

[56] Innocent XI, DS # 2112.

[57] For these last two works my biblical references are not to commands but to examples: 1 Cor 7:8-13 is an example of good counseling and 1 Cor 11:17-22 is an example of good correction.

This last spiritual work, the correction of the erring, is either "judicial" when it is by a superior, or "fraternal" when done by one's equal. Fraternal correction is a notable feature of the Christian community and is frequently recommended and regulated in the Bible as a serious responsibility of love (e.g., Lv 19:17; Si 19:13-16; Mt 18:15-20; Lk 17:3; 1 Th 5:14; 2 Th 3:15).

> Better is an open rebuke, than a love that remains hidden (Pr 27:5).
>
> He who loves correction loves knowledge, but he who hates reproof is stupid (Pr 12:2).
>
> Brothers, even if a person is caught in some transgression, you who are spiritual should correct that one in a gentle spirit, looking to yourself, so that you also may not be tempted (Gal 6:1).

To make such a fraternal correction one must have certitude of the fault, a real necessity for the correction, a suitable opportunity to speak with the person, and a real possibility of the correction having a good effect.

D: SINS AGAINST LOVE

Hatred and Sins Against Joy

While all sins are contrary to love, certain ones oppose it directly. Of these, obviously, hatred of God and our neighbor comes first.[58] Explicit hatred of God is the worst of all sins. Jesus said of those of the religious leaders who out of "envy" (*phthónos*, perhaps simply "ill will," Mk 15:10) rejected the love of God which he offered them:

> "Whoever hates me also hates my Father. If I had not done works among them that no one else ever did, they would not have sin; but as it is, they have seen and hated both me and my Father. But in order that the word written in their law might be fulfilled, 'They hated me without cause'" (Jn 15:23-25).

---

[58] CCC # 1765, 2262, 2303.

Hatred of our neighbor as a person is implicitly a hatred of the Creator, although it is right to hate the neighbor's sin as God hates it. This is the meaning of the Psalmist's, "Do I not hate, O Lord, those who hate you? Those who rise up against you do I not loathe?" (Ps 139:21; cf. Ws 14:9). The seriousness of the sin of hatred against our neighbor is to be judged by the seriousness of the harm it leads us to wish against the neighbor. We cannot truly hate ourselves, but we can righteously hate what is evil in us (our false self) and we can wrongly hate what is truly good for us. Whenever we sin we do injury to ourselves, as if we hated ourselves out of too much love for ourselves.

Besides hatred which is directly opposed to love, we can sin against the fruits of love. Thus the monastic tradition spoke of two capital sins opposed to the joy which flows from love. One is *acedia*, or sadness and boredom with spiritual goods, such as we sometimes feel with prayer.[59] "Because my heart was embittered and my soul was pierced, I was stupid and understood not; I was like a brute beast in your presence" (Ps 73:21-22). This sin comes from a revulsion from invisible, spiritual realities toward visible, worldly pleasures and distractions.

The remedy for such depression is perseverance in good works while waiting patiently for God's consolation. "Therefore, my beloved brothers, be firm, steadfast, fully devoted to the work of the Lord, knowing that in the Lord your labor is not in vain" (1 Cor 15:58).

The other capital sin that arises from lack of loving joy is *envy*, or sadness over the good happiness or achievements of our neighbor.[60] "And the patriarchs, envious of Joseph, sold him into slavery in Egypt, but God was with him and rescued him from all his afflictions" (Ac 7:9-10). "Envy and anger shorten one's life, worry brings us to a premature old age" (Si 30:24).[61] Its source is a lack of humility. The humble are not envious, because it does not trouble them that others have more than they do; they are content to make the best of what they have. It was the pride of Jesus' opponents that infuriated them at the love the people

---

[59] CCC # 1866, 2094, 2733. For Cassian on *acedia* see p. 169, n. 39.

[60] CCC # 1866, 2538-2540, 2533-2534, 2538-2540.

[61] See also Jb 11:20; Ws 2:24; Mk 7:22; Rm 1:29; Gal 5:21; Ph 1:15-17; Tt 3:3, Jm 4:2.

showed him. "For he [Pilate] knew that it was out of envy that the chief priests had handed him over" (Mk 15:10). Paul complains that:

> Some preach Christ from envy and rivalry, others from good will. The latter act out of love, aware that I am here for the defense of the gospel; the former proclaim Christ out of selfish ambition, not from pure motives, thinking they will cause me trouble in my imprisonment (Ph 1:15-17).

Against that fruit of love which is peace, is the sin of *discord* or disagreement arising from hatred (Si 27:14; 1 Cor 3:3; 2 Tm 2:24; Jude vv. 5-16).[62] One of the "six things the Lord hates" is "he who sows discord among brothers" (Pr 6:16-19; cf. Si 28:8-9). St. Paul wrote anxiously to the Corinthians about his third visit to them:

> For I fear that when I come I may find you not such as I wish, and that you may find me not as you wish, that there may be rivalry, jealousy, fury, selfishness, slander, gossip, conceit and disorder (2 Cor 12:20).

To the church of Rome he also wrote:

> I urge you, brothers, to watch out for those who create dissensions and obstacles in opposition to the teaching that you have learned; avoid them (Rm 16:17).

In private matters, discord produces angry *quarreling* in words, as Paul heard was going on in the church of Corinth: "For it has been reported to me about you, my brothers, by Chloe's people, that there are rivalries among you" (1 Cor 1:11). It even produces *strife* in deeds: "For where jealousy and selfish ambition exist, there is disorder and every foul practice" (Jm 3:16).

In public matters discord foments *rebellion*: exemplified by the

---

[62] CCC # 360, 1852, 1939, 2213, 2303.

"two revolutionaries" (Mt 27:38) crucified with Jesus;[63] and breeds *war*:[64] symbolized in the Book of Revelation by the rider on the red horse who "was given power to take peace away from the earth, so that people would slaughter one another. And he was given a huge sword" (Rv 6:4). In the Christian community discord leads to *schism*,[65] like that which Paul feared would eventuate in Corinth:

> First of all, I hear that when you meet as church there are divisions among you, and to a degree I believe it; there have to be factions among you in order that those who are approved among you may become known (1 Cor 11:18-19).

The evil consequences of all these sins against the joy and the peace that flow from true love, I have already discussed as various types of sins against justice and the virtues related to it.

Scandal

The final fruit of love is *beneficence*, seeking the good of others. Opposed to beneficence is "active" *scandal* — "giving scandal," placing a "stumbling block" in another's path (Mt 18:6-7; Rm 14; 1 Cor 8:7-13) — that is, behavior which leads others into sin either directly by tempting them, or indirectly by giving them a bad example.[66] When someone intends to cause another to sin just to make him or her a sinner, the scandal is "diabolic," as when Satan tempted Jesus (Mt 4:1-11). More commonly, the intention of scandal is simply to get someone to sin to one's own advantage, as when the high priests paid Judas to betray Jesus so they could be rid of Jesus' criticisms (Lk 22:1-6); or implicitly

---

[63] Traditionally these two condemned men are called "thieves" or "robbers," but the word in Mt 27:38 and Mk 15:27 is *lestai*, a term applied also to Barabbas (Jn 18:40). NAB rev. notes on this last verse that Barabbas was "a guerrilla warrior fighting for nationalistic aims, though the term can also denote a robber."

[64] CCC # 2307-2309, 2312-2317, 2327-2328.

[65] CCC # 817, 2089.

[66] CCC # 2284-2287, 2326.

when one does something that one knows may tempt another, as one who invites an alcoholic to a bar. If we actively give scandal, we have an obligation to try to repair it and to undo the damage we have caused.

"Passive" scandal is the "taking of scandal" by yielding to the temptation it occasions, either because of one's weakness and ignorance ("scandal of the weak"), as when an alcoholic takes a drink because someone else does; or because one maliciously interprets another's innocent action as evil ("pharisaic scandal"). Thus the Pharisees interpreted Jesus' dining with sinners as an approval of and share in their sin (Mt 11:16-19).

Love of our neighbor should lead us to avoid giving scandal not only by refraining from evil actions but even from what has the appearance of evil. Nevertheless, we should never omit fulfilling serious obligations just to avoid scandal to the weak, although we may sometimes omit the observance of merely positive laws, works of counsel or indifferent actions for this reason. Nor should we omit obligations or good works just to avoid pharisaic scandal, but we should omit indifferent actions that are offensive.

Thus Jesus never refused to eat with sinners or to heal people on the Sabbath in spite of the fact that this gave scandal to the Pharisees (Mk 2:13-17; Lk 5:27-32; 15:1-7; 19:1-10, etc.), but at other times he was always careful to observe the law to the letter (Mt 5:17-20). St. Paul also instructed his followers not to eat meat offered to idols when this might give offense to some member of their community or tempt them to do what they thought was wrong, although in fact there was no sin in eating such food (1 Cor 8). But Paul rebuked St.Peter when Peter gave a poor example in refusing to eat with non-Jews just to avoid giving scandal to the Jewish Christians (Gal 2:11-14).[67]

---

[67] On the exegesis of Gal 2:11-14, a very controversial text, see Hans-Dieter Betz, *Galatians*, pp. 105-112; Frank J. Matera, *Galatians*, pp. 84-91; and James D.G. Dunn "The incident at Antioch (Gal 2:11-18)," JSNT, 18 (1983):3-57. Peter was probably trying to deal with a difficult pastoral situation in a way not very different than Paul himself did on other occasions (Ac 21:15-26; 1 Cor 14), but Paul in this instance saw Peter's action as setting a dangerous precedent against which he had to protest.

Love and Law

Love seems antithetical to law, since love transcends any law, yet there is a law of love and it is the supreme law (Dt 6:5; Mt 22:34-40; Lk 10:25-28) which is the law of the Holy Spirit dwelling in the heart of the Christian in grace. "For the law of the spirit of life in Christ Jesus has freed you from the law of sin and death" (Rm 8:2).[68] Love is the law that orders all that we are and have to God in response to his love for us (1 Cor 13).[69] If we truly love God, our wills are united to God's, and therefore, what his wisdom teaches us through the natural and revealed laws of morality is what we want to do and are able to do by the power of his love which he shares with us through grace. Love, says St. Paul, "bears all things, believes all things, hopes all things, endures all things. Love never fails" (1 Cor 13:7-8). All that God wants of us is to love him and serve our neighbor. For as God the Father said to Catherine of Siena, "The only thing you can do for me is to serve your neighbor."[70] "So faith, hope, and love remain, these three, but the greatest of these is love" (1 Cor 13:13).

The Sacrament of Love

As the supreme command is the love of God and neighbor, and the supreme virtue which gives form and life to all the other virtues is Christian love, so the supreme sacrament to which all the others tend is the Eucharist. The Eucharist is at once the sacrament of love and the supreme act of Christian worship, which unifies and animates the Christian community.[71] It is the source and school of all the virtues, since in it we meet Christ and are empowered to live in him.

---

[68] See James D.G. Dunn, *Romans 1-8*, pp. 416-418, who translates this "the law of the Spirit of Life" and rejects the assumption of many exegetes that for St. Paul "Law" (Torah) is always opposed to "Spirit" (Gospel).

[69] See also Lk 6:27-28; Jn 13:34-35; 15:12-13; 1 Jn 3:16; 1 Cor 13; Rm 13:8-10; Eph 5:1.

[70] *Dialogue*, c. 6.

[71] CCC # 1322-1419.

Each time that we participate in the Eucharistic Liturgy, we learn the virtues of humility, penance, and reconciliation as we join in the *Kyrie Eleison* or other penitential prayer. Our faith is then instructed, through hearing the Word of God in the Scriptures and the preaching, and confessed in the Creed.

Our hope is aroused as we hear God's promises, and bring to him the offering of our lives purified by the asceticism and strengthened by the courage with which we wage our spiritual warfare daily. All that we are is joined to Christ, true God and true Man, as with him in the Holy Spirit we offer ourselves and all creation to God in the supreme sacrificial act of religion, the Eucharistic Prayer.

In this mysterious act of sacrifice we are joined with Christ so that our lives and prayers are transformed in his grace and become truly righteous, truly just in him. And finally in Holy Communion we are united to Christ in the wedding banquet of love and to all our brothers and sisters in Christ and the Holy Spirit.

Then, in the blessing and dismissal (*Ite Missa est*) we are sent out to witness the Gospel in humble, loving service, so that our lives may be a continuous Eucharist. We are to be like the first church in Jerusalem after Pentecost whose members "devoted themselves to the teaching of the apostles and to the communal life, to the breaking of the bread and to the prayers" (Ac 2:42).

Summary of Norms

The positive norms of love are:

1. "You shall love the Lord your God with all your heart, with all your soul, with all your mind, and with all your strength" and "You shall love your neighbor as yourself" (Mk 12:29, quoting Dt 6:4-5 and Lv 19:18).
2. You shall cultivate the inner joy, peace, and mercy that flow from love and carry out the exterior spiritual and corporeal works of mercy to your neighbor according to your state in life and the order of love under the direction of the wisdom of the Holy Spirit.

The negative norms of love are:

3. Never hate God or will the harm of any of God's creatures or cease to seek the good of them all as far as it is possible for you.
4. Never stifle the joy of love by acedia or envy, nor the peace of love by discord in words, or such deeds as quarreling, strife, unjust rebellion or war, nor place a stumbling block in another's way.

E: SUMMARY OF MORAL THEOLOGY

The saints have all told us that God has most perfectly revealed himself in Christ on the Cross. If we want to know how to live our lives, therefore, we must look at the crucifix.[72]

There we see that the whole life of Jesus was motivated by love, love for his Father who had given him his mission and love for his neighbors, which for him as the New Adam included all humanity of all ages, even his enemies. Jesus, as a human like us except for sin, was guided along this troubled path by his Father with a wisdom surpassing all human understanding. We, his disciples, walk the same way by *faith* and by the true *prudence* that comes from grace.

This faith, which guides every step of our journey, is the light of the Holy Spirit, sent by the Father to anoint Jesus the Messiah, and to call us to follow him as his disciples. Hence no action of ours can lead us toward God that is not guided by faith in Christ. This wisdom of Jesus is seen most clearly of all in what to the world (as St. Paul says: 1 Cor 1:18-25) seems like utter folly, namely, so living his life that it would finish on the Cross in absolute witness of the truth of God. All human intelligence, knowledge, science, and progress serve our lives only insofar as they square with the Cross and the truth of faith which the Cross witnesses and seals. To walk by any other light is to plunge into the abyss of eternal death.

The law of Christ, the New Law, the Gospel, therefore, is more than a set of rules. It is Jesus' own teaching brought alive in our hearts by the Holy Spirit and confirmed by him through the teaching of the

---

[72] See Garrigou-Lagrange, *The Three Ages of the Interior Life*, vol. 2, pp.481-487, on devotion to the Passion of Christ and to the Mater Dolorosa.

shepherds of the Church commissioned by him to keep us on the straight and narrow path. Theologians seek to formulate and systematize this teaching to help us further, but their human systems are trustworthy only when conformed to the teaching of our God-commissioned pastors. The holy, orthodox faith alone can find a way through the thicket of error and confusion produced by human pride, one-sided, subjective thinking, human stupidity and the cunning lies of the Accuser.

This Law of Christ and of the Holy Spirit is final and for all ages, as is Christ himself, but in our understanding and its complete fulfillment it reveals itself in the changing vicissitudes of history. To be true to its unchanging truth we must recover it and reformulate it in our own times and circumstances and preach it anew, listening to the voice of the Holy Spirit in every age and culture.

At the turning point of history, Jesus on the Cross came to the terrible brink of despair, "My God, my God why have you forsaken me?" (Mk 15:34, cf. Ps 22:18) and descended to the dead. Yet the Gospel which he witnessed even in his death and commitment to the Father is the Good News of *hope*. He died only to rise again and ascend to the Father, thus promising to us that no matter how dark the world becomes for us, God's promises made through the prophets, God's kingdom, will certainly come to fulfillment. This is not merely "hope" in the sense of an uncertainty, or mere probability; it is absolute hope grounded on the almighty power and trustworthiness of God. Because we hope for this kingdom of truth and justice, peace and love, we do not put our trust in the passing things of this world distorted by sin, nor in ourselves, but in a transformed and glorified world to come.

Consequently, the Christian life for all Christians, not just for ascetics, is an ascetical life, requiring the renunciation of many pleasures near at hand in view of far distant, promised joy. It is a life of *moderation* of our yearnings for pleasure in sex, food, drink, comfort, companionship; a sober and simple life that frees us for more enduring and profound happiness. Therefore, Jesus died on the Cross for us a virgin, poor, naked, humiliated, free of every attachment except his love for God and for sinful, indulgent humankind.

This same moderation and detachment from whatever is worldly is found also in inner *self-control* with regard to all pleasures, *meekness* with regard to anger, *clemency* with regard to disciplining others, *studiousness* with regard to seeking the truths that are important, and *humility* with regard to our roles in the community. This moderation expresses itself outwardly in society by *modesty* in dress, *decorum* in behavior, and an appropriate *playfulness* in recreation. The friendliness, simplicity, gentleness, attention, and humility of Jesus in his dealings with all, whatever their station in life or merits, thinking only of their needs, manifests these lesser human virtues in all their beauty. It is this moderation in the use of this passing world that gives beauty to human character, and beckons us on in hope toward God's everlasting glory.

The life of hope also demands the asceticism of *courage*, in the constant struggle to be true to God against the current of the world which flows against us. This courage is greatest not in fighting, for Jesus was a man of peace not violence, but in endurance in witness to truth and out of a love for one's enemies which refuses to strike back. This is the true spiritual warfare which Jesus waged and won against the legions of Lucifer. The hope for victory is that God's kingdom will "come on earth as it is in heaven." Such courage is supremely shown in Jesus' martyrdom on the Cross, and in Mary's compassion at his side. Only in dying with Jesus do Christians come to life. In lesser ways Jesus manifested this same spirit of hope in his *magnanimity*, undertaking to conquer the Devil himself and in his *magnificence*, expending even the last drop of his precious blood for us. But it is even more perfectly shown in his *patience* with our sins, and his *perseverance* throughout his whole life on his way to the Cross.

The life of love, to which wisdom and prudence lead us and for which moderation and courage free and strengthen us, is first of all a life of *justice* or righteousness, a dutiful concern not merely for our own rights but for those of God and neighbor. How can there be a kingdom of God, unless in the human community justice and peace reign and no one is neglected, not even the poorest, the most wretched, the worst? The freedom which grace brings is not just the personal liberation given by moderation and courage, but the liberation of all the world's oppressed. For this there must be *commutative* justice between persons, and social justice in which each member of the community contributes his or her part (*legal justice*) and receives his or her fair share (*distributive justice*) of the common good.

Jesus manifested such justice in his careful observance of the law of his people, the Jews, and the universal law of God's creation, in his constant concern for all he met, especially the most neglected, and in the righteous anger with which he exposed every injustice, civil and religious.

This spirit of justice and duty Jesus showed especially in *religion*, by his constant service of God in the Temple and in prayer and praise, and by his supreme sacrifice; also in his *piety* and *obedience* toward his parents, and his care of his mother from the Cross, as well as his love for his own Jewish people and his respect for the religious and civil authorities who killed him. Most of all he showed total obedience to the mission he had received from his Father and for which he died on the Cross.

That mission was to the Truth and it was Jesus' *truthfulness* that sentenced him to death. Yet in all his zeal for God and his outrage at injustice, he sought the conversion of the offenders, not their destruction, by his *leniency*. To all who did him the least service, as to the Samaritan woman who gave him a cup of water, he showed great *gratitude* and repaid it with concern for their salvation. His *liberality* was shown in this constant service of the unworthy, whom he met not with contempt but with *affability* and *friendliness*, candid in declaring the moral law, yet seeking the spirit of the law, not merely its letter, with *equity* in view of human weakness.

Yet Jesus never stopped at justice, because for him justice was only an expression of a more profound *love* or charity, which flowed from his eternal union with his Father in the Holy Spirit who is Love, and spread out to every creature, seeking for them the conversion of their hearts, the forgiveness of their sins, and their union in the eternal community of the Trinity, the Kingdom of God, which is already present in hope here on earth in the community of the Church. Jesus, the New Adam, gave birth to the Church, the New Eve and bride of Christ, from his wounded heart on the Cross — the Church which someday, when faith yields to vision and hope is fulfilled, will be perfectly united to him forever. In this community centered in Christ we begin to experience the paradise of his love to which his Wisdom has guided us: the *joy* that flows from the indwelling Trinity, the *peace* that comes from harmony with our fellow Christians, God's *mercy* and our mutual reconciliation.

Thus in Mary, the mother of Jesus, standing beside his Cross we see in feminine, motherly, and heroic form the response of the Church, of all Jesus' disciples, the perfect response to her Son's perfect manhood. In the perfect sacrificial love of Jesus and Mary, Mother of the Church, New Adam and New Eve, we behold the total image of God's design for humanity through which God has revealed himself to us.

Hence it is on the Cross that Jesus manifests to us what it is to be a Christian, a member of Christ's Body, the Church, but a pilgrim Church still journeying toward the promised land and eternal wedding feast. This journey is begun and continued only in the power of the grace of the Holy Spirit. The food which nourishes and strengthens us on the way is the Eucharist, the central sacrament of the Church, in which Jesus remains present with us in faith and hope to keep alive our love for him and for each other, in mercy, peace, and joy. In the Eucharist we find Jesus, and in Jesus we find our true selves as God is forming us to be forever.

The title of this book was chosen because the phrase "living the truth in love" (Eph 4:15, *letheuontes en agape*) indicates that Christian morality is conformity to our true humanity, God's own image transformed by grace and expressed through love. It is "the truth that dwells in us and will be with us forever" (2 Jn v. 2). "Nothing," St. John writes, "gives me greater joy than to hear that my children are walking in the truth" (3 Jn v. 4). The phrase can also be translated "*speaking* the truth in love" and this declares that we must bear witness to the truth by our lives which alone can make our preaching the Gospel effective.

> *Moral theology, therefore, is nothing more than a meditation on Jesus present in the Eucharist, a remembrance of the Cross and the Resurrection to be relived by us in our own times. To follow Jesus as his witnessing Church to the Father in the power of his Spirit is "living the truth in love."*

ABBREVIATIONS OF FREQUENTLY CITED WORKS

AAS *Acta Apostolicae Sedis*

Abbott , Walter M., S.J., ed., Rev. Msgr. Joseph Gallagher, translation editor, *The Documents of Vatican II* (Baltimore: Geoffrey Chapman, 1966)

    DH "Declaration on Religious Freedom" (*Dignitatis Humanae*), 1965

    DV "Dogmatic Constitution on Divine Revelation," (*Dei Verbum*), 1965

    GS "Pastoral Constitution on the Church in the Modern World," (*Gaudium et Spes*), 1965

    LG "Dogmatic Constitution on the Church" (*Lumen Gentium*), 1964

    NA "Declaration on the Relationship of the Church to Non-Christian Religions" (*Nostra Aetate*), 1965

    OT "Decree on Priestly Formation," (*Optatam Totius*), 1965

    SC "Constitution on the Sacred Liturgy" (*Sacrosanctum Concilium*), 1963

ABD *The Anchor Bible Dictionary*, David Noel Freedman, ed., 6 vols. (New York: Doubleday, 1992)

ACW *Ancient Christian Writers* (New York: Paulist Press)

ANF *The Ante-Nicene Fathers*, translations of the writings of the Fathers down to A.D. 325, Alexander Roberts and James Donaldson, eds. (Edinburgh: T & T Clark, reprint Grand Rapids: Eerdmans, 1989, 1990)

AP *The Apostolic Fathers, The Fathers of the Church*, vol.1, translated by F.X. Glimm, J.M.-F. Marique, S.J., G.G. Walsh, S.J. (New York: Cima Publishing Co., 1947)

CA *Centesimus Annus*, John Paul II, *Origins* 20 (May 16, 1991): 1-24

CBQ *Catholic Biblical Quarterly*

CCC   *The Catechism of the Catholic Church* (Rome: Libreria
        Editrice Vaticana, 1994)
CCL   *Code of Canon Law, The*. Latin-English edition, translation
        prepared under the auspices of the Canon Law Society of
        America (Washington, DC: Canon Law Society of America,
        1983)
CDF   *Congregation for the Doctrine of the Faith*
DACL   *Dictionnarie d'archeologie chrétienne et de liturgie*, Fernand
        and Henri Leclercq, eds. 15 vols. in 29 (Paris: Letouzey et
        Ane, 1907-53)
DS   Denzinger, Henricus and Adolphus Schönmetzer, *Enchiridion
        Symbolorum Definitionum et Declarationum de Rebus Fidei et
        Morum*. 36th ed. Rome: Herder, 1976. Partial English transla-
        tions in *The Sources of Catholic Dogma*, trans. by Roy J.
        Deferrari (St. Louis: Herder, 1957) and *The Church Teaches*,
        trans. by John F. Clarkson and others (St. Louis: B. Herder
        Book Co., 1955); see also Tanner.
DSAM   *Dictionnaire de spiritualité, ascetique et mystique: doctrine et
        histoire*, Marcel Viller, S.J., F. Cavellera, and J. de Guibert,
        S.J., eds. (Paris: G. Beauchesne, 1937-)
DTC   *Dictionnaire de Théologie Catholique, A.* Vacant, E.
        Mangenot, E. Amann, eds., 15 vols. (Paris: Letouzey et Ane,
        1930-1950)
EDNT   *Exegetical Dictionary of the New Testament*, Horst Balz and
        Gerhard Schneider, eds. (Grand Rapids: Eerdmans, 1993)
EP   *Encyclopedia of Philosophy, The*, Paul Edwards, ed. 6 vols. in
        3. (Macmillan/Free Press, Reprint ed., 1972)
FC   *Fathers of the Church* (Washington, DC: The Catholic
        University of America Press)
JBL   *Journal of Biblical Literature*
JSNT   *Journal for the Study of the New Testament*
JSOT   *Journal for the Study of the Old Testament*
NAB   *New American Bible*, rev. Psalms and New Testament (1991)
NCE   *New Catholic Encyclopedia*, 15 vols. (New York: McGraw-
        Hill, 1967)
NJB   *New Jerusalem Bible* (Garden City, NY: Doubleday, 1985)
NJBC   *The New Jerome Biblical Commentary*, Raymond E. Brown,
        S.S., Joseph A. Fitzmyer, S.J., and Roland E. Murphy, O.
        Carm., eds. (Englewood Cliffs, NJ: Prentice-Hall, 1990)

NPF   *A Select Library of Nicene and Post-Nicene Fathers of the Christian Church*, Philip Schaff and Henry Wace, eds., 14 vols. (New York: Christian Literature, 1890-1900)

PG   *Patrologia Graeca* (Migne)

PL   *Patrologia Latina* (Migne)

RSV   *Revised Standard Version of the Bible*

Tanner, Norman P., *Decrees of the Ecumenical Councils From Nicaea I to Vatican II*, 2 vols. (Washington, DC: Georgetown University Press/ London: Sheed and Ward, 1990)

TDNT   *Theological Dictionary of the New Testament*, Gerhard Kittel, ed.; Geoffrey W. Bromley, tr. and ed., 10 vols. (Grand Rapids: Eerdmans, 1964-1976)

TDOT   Botterweck, Joannes and Helmer Rindgren, *Theological Dictionary of the Old Testament*, John T. Willie, tr. (Grand Rapids: Eerdmans, 1974-1990)

TH   *The Thomist*

TS   *Theological Studies*

BIBLIOGRAPHY

Achtemeier, Paul J., *"Omne Verbum Sonat*: The New Testament and the Oral Environment of Late Western Antiquity," JBL, 109 (1990), 3-27.

Adler, Mortimer J., *Art and Prudence*, reprint of 1937 ed. (New York: Arno Press, 1978).

Adnés, Pierre, "Mariage spirituel," DTS, tom. 10, 387-408.

Aland, Kurt, *Did the Early Church Baptize Infants?*, trans. and introduced by G.R. Beasley-Murray, Library of History and Doctrine (Philadelphia: Westminster Press, 1963).

Ali, A. Yusuf, Trans. and Commentary, *The Holy Qur'an* (Published by American Trust Publications for The Muslim Student Association of the U.S. and Canada, 2nd ed. June, 1977).

Althaus, Paul, *The Theology of Martin Luther*, trans. by R.C. Schultz (Philadelphia: Fortress Press, 1966).

Ambrose of Milan, St., *De paradiso*, PL 14:265-314; *Hexameron, Paradise, and Cain and Abel*, trans. by J.J. Savage, FC, vol. 42 (Washington, DC: Fathers of the Church, Inc., 1961).

_____, *De Jacobo*, PL 14:569-596; *Jacob and the Happy Life*, pp. 117-186, in *Seven Exegetical Works*, trans. by M.P. McHugh, F.C., vol. 65 (Washington, DC: The Catholic University of America and Consortium Press, 1972).

_____, *In Lucam*, PL 15:1527-1850.

_____, *De Officiis* 16:25-184; *Duties of the Clergy (De Officiis Ministerorum)*, trans. by J.J. Savage, Schaff, NPF, 2nd series, vol. 10, pp. 1-89.

Andersen, Hugh, *The Gospel of Mark*, New Century Bible (Greenwood, SC: 1976).

Andersen, F.I. and D.N. Freedman, *Hosea*, Anchor Bible (Garden City, NY: Doubleday, 1980).

Anderson, Gary, "Celibacy or Consummation in the Garden? Reflections on Early Jewish and Christian Interpretations of the Garden of Eden," *Harvard Theological Review* 82 (2, 1989), 124-148.

Anderson, Gerald, ed., *Witnessing to the Kingdom* (Maryknoll, NY: Orbis Books, 1982).

Apostolic Constitutions, PG 1:555-1156; critical ed. F.X. Funk, *Didascalia et Constitutiones Apostolorum*, 2 vols. (Paderborn, 1905).

Apostolic Fathers, The, 2 vols., trans. by Kirsopp Lake, Loeb Classical Library (Cambridge, MA: Harvard University Press/ London: W. Heinemann, 1985); also *The Didache, the Epistle of Barnabas, the Epistles and the Martyrdom of St. Polycarp, the Fragments of Papias, and the Epistle to Diognetus*, trans. by James A. Kleist, S.J., ACW, vol. 6 (Westminster, MD: Newman Press, 1948); and *The Apostolic Fathers*, trans. by F.X. Glimm, J.M.-F. Marique, S.J., G.G. Walsh, S.J., FC, vol. 1 (New York: Cima Publishing Co., 1947).

Appel, Gersion, *A Philosophy of Mizvot: The Religious-Ethical Concepts of Judaism, Their Roots in Biblical Law and the Oral Tradition* (New York: KTAV Publishing House, 1975).

Ariès, Philippe, *Centuries of Childhood: A Social History of the Family*, trans. by R. Baldick (New York: Knopf, 1962).

Ariès, Philippe and Georges Dubay, general eds., *A History of Private Life*, trans. by Arthur Goldhammer (Cambridge, MA: Belknap Press of Harvard University, 1987), vol 1., *From Pagan Rome to Byzantium*, Paul Veyne, ed.

Arintero, John (Juan) G., O.P., *The Mystical Evolution in the Development and Vitality of the Church*, trans. by Jordan Aumann, O.P. (St. Louis: B. Herder Book Co., 1951).

Aristotle, *The Basic Works of Aristotle*, ed. Richard McKeon (New York: Random House, 1941).

_____, *The Nicomachean Ethics*, with English trans. by H. Rackham, Loeb Classical Library (London: W. Heinemann, 1926).

Aron, Robert, in collaboration with Georgette Elgey, trans. by Humphrey Hare, *The Vichy Regime, 1940-44* (London: Putnam, 1958).

Ashley, Benedict M. (Winston), O.P., *The Theory of Natural Slavery According to Aristotle and St.Thomas* (Notre Dame, IN, 1941; Ann Arbor, MI: Edward Brothers Lithoprinters).

_____, *Theologies of the Body: Humanist and Christian* (St. Louis: Pope John Center, 1985).

_____, "Scriptural Grounding of Concrete Moral Norms," in *Persona Verità e Morale*, Atti del congresso Internazionale di Teologia Morale (Rome, 7-12 Aprile; Rome: Città Nuova Editrice, 1987), pp. 637-651 and TH, 52 (1988), pp. 1-22.

_____, "Compassion and Sexual Orientation" in Jeannine Grammick and Pat Furey, eds., *The Vatican and Homosexuality: Reactions to the "Letter to the Bishops of the Catholic Church on the Pastoral Care of Homosexual Persons"* (New York: Crossroad, 1988), pp. 105-111.

_____, "Contemporary Understandings of Personhood," *The Twenty-Fifth Anniversary of Vatican II: A Look Back and A Look Forward*, Proceedings of the Ninth Bishops' Workshop, Dallas, Texas,

Russell E. Smith, ed. (Braintree, MA: The Pope John Center, 1990), pp. 35-48.

_____, "Gender and the Priesthood of Christ: A Theological Reflection," TH 57, 3 (July 1993), 343-379.

_____, *Thomas Aquinas: Selected Spiritual Writings*, co-authored with Matthew Rzeczowski, O.P. (Hyde Park, NY: New City Press, 1994).

_____, "What is the End of the Human Person: The Vision of God and Integral Human Fulfillment," in *Moral Truth and Moral Tradition: Essays in Honour of Peter Geach and Elizabeth Anscombe*, ed. by Luke Gormally (Dublin and Portland, OR: Four Courts Press, 1994), pp. 68-96.

_____, *Justice in the Church: Gender and Participation* (Washington, DC: Catholic University of America Press, 1996).

Ashley, Benedict M., O.P. and Albert S. Moraczewski, O.P., "Is the Biological Subject of Human Rights Present from Conception" in Peter J. Cataldo and Albert S. Moraczewski, O.P., eds., *The Fetal Tissue Issue: Medical and Ethical Aspects* (Braintree, MA: Pope John Center, 1994), pp. 33-59.

Ashley, Benedict, O.P. and Kevin D. O'Rourke, O.P., *Healthcare Ethics: A Theological Analysis* (St. Louis: Catholic Health Association of the United States, 3rd ed., 1989).

Athanasius, St., *The Life of St. Antony*, trans. by R.T. Meyer, ACW, vol. 10 (Westminster, MD: Newman, 1950); PL 26: 835-975.

Attridge, H.W., *Hebrews*, Hermeneia Commentaries (Philadelphia: Fortress Press, 1989).

Audet, Jean-Paul, *La Didaché: Instructions des Apôtres*, Études Bibliques (Paris: J. Gabalda, 1958).

Augustine of Hippo, St., *The Lord's Sermon on the Mount with Seventeen Related Sermons*, trans. by D.J. Kavanaugh, FC, vol. 11 (Washington, DC: Catholic University of America Press), pp. 19-200; PL 34:1229-1308.

_____, *Tractates to the Gospel of St. John*, trans. by J.W. Rettig, FC, 3 vols. PL 35:1379-1976.

_____, *Quaestiones Evangeliorum*; PL 35:1321-1364.

_____, *De utilitate jejunii*; PL 40:70-714.

_____, *De libero arbitrio*; PL 42:577-602.

_____, *Confessions*, trans. with an introduction and notes by Henry Chadwick (New York: Oxford University Press, 1991).

_____, *De Civitate Dei*, Loeb Library, Latin, English trans. W.M. Greene, G.E. McCracken, D.S. Wisen, P. Levine, E.M. Sanford and W.M. Green, 7 vols. (Cambridge, MA: Harvard University Press/ London: W. Heinemann, 1957-72).

_____, *Treatises on Various Subjects*, trans. by M.S. Muldowney, S.S.J., et al., FC, vol. 16 (New York: Fathers of the Church, Inc., 1952). "Lying" (*De Mendacio*), trans. by Sr. Mary Sarah Muldowney, S.S.J., pp. 47-112; PL 40: 487-518, and "Against Lying," trans. by Harold B. Jafee (*Contra Mendacium*), pp. 113-182; PL 40; 517-548.

_____, *The Way of Life of the Catholic Church in The Catholic and Manichean Ways of Life (De moribus ecclesiae catholicae et De Moribus Manichaeorum)*, trans. by Donald A. Gallagher and Idella J. Gallagher (Washington, DC: Catholic University of America Press, 1966).

_____, *Faith, Hope, and Charity (Enchiridion)*, trans. by Louis A. Arand, S.S., ACW (Westminster, MD: Newman Bookshop, 1947), pp. 114-120; PL 40:231-291.

_____, *The Rule of St Augustine: Masculine and Feminine Versions*, with introduction and commentary by Tarsicius J. Van Bavel, O.S.A, trans. by R. Canning, O.S.A. (London: Darton, Longman and Todd, 1984).

Ayo, Nicholas, C.S.C., *The Lord's Prayer: A Survey Theological and Literary* (Notre Dame, IN: University of Notre Dame Press, 1990).

Baasland, Ernst, "Der Jakobusbrief als Neutestamentliche Weisheitschrift," *Studia Theologica* 36:2 (1982), 119-139.

Baelz, P.R., *Ethics and Belief* (London: Sheldon Press, 1977).

Bahnsen, Greg L., *Theonomy in Christian Ethics*, 2nd ed. (Nutley, NJ: Craig, 1983).

Baier, Kurt, "Ethics: Deontological Theories," and "Ethics: Teleological Theories," in *Encyclopedia of Bioethics*, ed. by Warren T. Reich (New York: Free Press, 1978), pp. 412-421.

Bailey, Derrick S., *Homosexuality and the Western Christian Tradition* (Hamden, CT: Shoe String Press, 1975).

Balentine, Samuel E., *Prayer in the Hebrew Bible: The Drama of Divine-Human Dialogue, Overtures to Biblical Theology* (Philadelphia: Fortress Press, 1993).

Ballacchino, Salvatore M., *The Household Order Texts: Colossians 3:18-4:1; 1 Peter 2:17-3:9; 1 Timothy 2:8-15 (5:1-2) and Titus 2:1-10, Present State of the Question and Assessment* (unpublished diss., Washington, DC: John Paul II Institute for Studies in Marriage and Family, 1992).

Balthasar, Hans Urs von, "A Theology of the Evangelical Counsels," *Cross Currents* (Spring, 1966), 213-337; (Summer, 1966), 326-338.

_____, "Nine Propositions on Christians Ethics" in Ratzinger, Schürmann, Balthasar, *Principles of Christian Morality* (San Francisco: Ignatius Press, 1986), pp. 77-104.

Barbeau, Clayton, *The Head of the Family* (Chicago: Regnery, 1961).

Bargant, Dianne, *What Are They Saying About Wisdom Literature?* (Ramsey, NJ: Paulist Press, 1984).

Barish, Jonas A., *The Anti-theatrical Prejudice* (Berkeley: University of California Press, 1981).

Barr, James, *Holy Scripture: Canon, Authority, Criticism* (Philadelphia: Westminster Press, 1983).

_____, "Ancient Biblical Laws and Modern Human Rights," in *Justice and Holy: Essays in Honor of Walter Harrelson*, ed. by Douglas A. Knight and Peter J. Paris (Atlanta: Scholars Press, 1989).

Barr, Sydney O., *The Christian New Morality: A Biblical Study of Situation Ethics* (New York: Oxford University Press, 1969).

Barth, Karl, *Ethics*, trans. by G.W. Bromley (New York: Seabury Press, 1981).

Barth, Markus, *The Epistle to the Ephesians*, 2 vols., Anchor Bible 34, 34A (Garden City, NY: Doubleday, 1974).

Barton, John, "Approaches to Ethics in the Old Testament," in John Rogerson, ed., *Beginning Old Testament Study* (Philadelphia: Westminster Press, 1982), pp. 113-130.

Basil of Caesarea (the Great), St., *The Morals* in *The Ascetic Works of St. Basil*, trans. by Sr. M. Monica Wagner, C.S.C., FC, vol. 9 (New York: Fathers of the Church, Inc., 1950), pp. 71-206.

Bayer, Edward J., *Rape Within Marriage: A Moral Analysis* (Lanham, MD: University Press of America, 1985).

Baylor, Michael G., *Action and Person: Conscience in Late Scholasticism and the Young Luther* (Leiden: E.J. Brill, 1977).

Beach, W. and H.R. Niebuhr, *Christian Ethics: Sources of the Living Tradition* (New York: Ronald Press, 1955).

Beauchamp, Tom L. and James F. Childress, *Principles of Biomedical Ethics*, 3rd ed. (New York: Oxford University Press, 1989).

Becker, Joachim, *Messianic Expectations in the Old Testament*, trans. by David E. Green (Philadelphia: Fortress Press, 1977).

Bell, Rudolph, epilogue by W.N. Davis, *Holy Anorexia* (Chicago: University of Chicago Press, 1987).

Benedict of Nursia, St., *The Rule of St. Benedict*, with introduction and notes by A.C. Mersel and N.L. de Mastro (Garden City, NY: Doubleday/ Image Books, 1975).

_____, *The Rule of St. Benedict*, in Latin and English with notes by Timothy Fry et al., translators and eds. (Collegeville, MN: Liturgical Press, 1981).

Bennett, Gerald, Christine Vourakis and Donna S. Woolf, eds., *Substance Abuse: Pharmacologic, Developmental, and Clinical Perspectives* (New York: Wiley, 1983).

Benson, Leonard G., *Fatherhood: A Sociological Perspective* (New York: Random House, 1968).

Bentham, Jeremy, "Principles of Penal Law", part 2, c. xi, pp. 441-450 and Appendix "On Death Punishment," pp. 525-532, in *Works of Jeremy*

Bentham, vol. 1., ed. by John Bowring (New York: Russell and Russell, 1962).

Berger, Peter, *The Sacred Canopy: Element of a Sociological Theory of Religion* (New York: Doubleday Anchor Books, 1969).

Bernard of Clairvaux, St., *The Steps of Humility*, trans. with introduction and notes, as a study of his epistemology by George Bosworth Burch (Cambridge: Harvard University Press, 1940).

Bernard, A., "Usure: La Formation de la Doctrine Ecclésiastique sur l'usure," DTS 15 (2), 2316-2335.

Best, Ernest, *1 and 2 Thessalonians*, Harper's New Testament Commentaries (New York: Harper's, 1972).

Betz, Hans-Dieter, "Paul," ABD, 5: 186-201.

_____, *Galatians*, Hermeneia Commentaries (Philadelphia: Fortress Press, 1979).

_____, "Cosmogony and Ethics in the Sermon on the Mount," in *Cosmogony and the Ethical Order: New Studies in Comparative Ethics*, ed. by Robin W. Lovin and Frank E. Reynolds (Chicago: University of Chicago Press, 1985), pp. 158-176.

Birch, Bruce C., "Biblical Hermeneutics in Recent Discussion: Old Testament" and with Daniel J. Harrington, S.J., "Biblical Hermeneutics in Recent Discussion: New Testament" *Religious Studies Review* 10, 1 (Jan. 1984), 1-10.

_____, *Let Justice Roll Down: The Old Testament, Ethics, and Christian Life* (Louisville, KY: Westminster/John Knox Press, 1991).

Birch, Bruce C. and Rasmussen, Larry L., *Bible and Ethics in the Christian Life* (Minneapolis: Augsburg Publishing, 1976).

Birch, Bruce C. et al., eds., *Liberating Life: Contemporary Approaches to Ecological Theology* (New York, 1990), pp. 9-26.

Blackwell, Richard, *Galileo, Bellarmine, and the Bible: Including a Translation of Foscarini's Letter on the Motion of the Earth* (Notre Dame, IN: University of Notre Dame Press, 1991).

Blanchard, Robert J. and D. Caroline Blanchard, eds., *Advances in the Study of Aggression*, 2 vols. (New York: Academic Press, 1984).

Blank, Josef, "Does the New Testament Provide Principles for Modern Moral Theology," in *Concilium* 25 (1967), 9-22 (New York: Paulist Press, 1967).

Blenkinsopp, Joseph, *Wisdom and Law in the Old Testament* (Oxford: Oxford University Press, 1983).

_____, *Prophecy and Canon: A Contribution to the Study of Jewish Origins* (Notre Dame, IN: University of Notre Dame Press, 1977).

_____, *Ezra-Nehemiah*, Old Testament Library (Philadelphia: Westminster Press, 1988).

Blomfield, Morton W., *The Seven Deadly Sins: An Introduction to the History of a Religious Concept, with Special Reference to Medieval English Literature* (Ann Arbor: Michigan State University, 1952, reprint 1967).

Boadt, Lawrence, C.S.P., *Jeremiah 26-52, Habakkuk, Zephaniah, Nahum*, Old Testament Message (Wilmington, DE: Michael Glazier, 1982).

Böckle, Franz and Jacques Pohier, *The Death Penalty and Torture*, in *Concilium* (New York: Seabury Press, 1979).

Bohr, David, *Catholic Moral Tradition: In Christ, A New Creation* (Huntington, IN: Our Sunday Visitor Press, 1990).

Bok, Sissela, *Lying: Moral Choice in Public and Private Life* (New York: Vintage, 1979).

_____, *Secrets: On the Ethics of Concealment and Revelation* (New York: Vintage, 1984).

Bokser, B.M., "Messianism, the Exodus Pattern, and Early Rabbinic Judaism," James H. Charlesworth, et al., *The Messiah*, pp. 239-269.

Boling, R.G., *Judges*, Anchor Bible 6A (Garden City, NY: Doubleday, 1975).

Boling, R.G. and G.E. Wright, *Joshua*, Anchor Bible 6 (Garden City, NY: Doubleday, 1982).

Bonaventure, St., *Journey of the Mind to God*, in *The Works of St. Bonaventure*, trans. by José de Vinck (Paterson, NJ: St. Anthony Guild Press, 1960), vol. 1, pp. 1-58.

Boswell, John, *Christianity, Social Tolerance, and Homosexuality: Gay People in Western Europe from the Beginning of the Christian Era to the Fourteenth Century* (Chicago: University of Chicago Press, 1980).

Boucher, M., "Some Unexplored Parallels to 1 Cor 11, 1-12 and Gal 3, 28: The New Testament and the Role of Women," CBQ 31 (1969), 50-58.

Bourgeault, S.J., Guy, *Decalogue et morale chrétienne: Anxiété patristique sur l'utilisation et l'interprétation chrétienne du decalogue de c.60 a c. 220* (Paris: Desclée, 1971).

Bourke, Vernon J., *History of Ethics*, 2 vols. (Garden City, NY: Doubleday/ Image Books, 1970).

Boyle, Joseph M., Jr., R.D. Lawler, and W.E. May, *Catholic Sexual Ethics* (Huntingdon, IN: Our Sunday Visitor Press, 1985).

Boyle, Patrick J., *Parvitas Materiae in Sexto in Contemporary Catholic Thought* (Washington: University Press of America, 1986).

Braaten, Carl E., *Eschatology and Ethics: Essays on the Theology and Ethics of the Kingdom of God* (Minneapolis: Augsburg Publishing House, 1974).

Bright, John, *Jeremiah*, Anchor Bible 21 (Garden City, NY: Doubleday, 1964).

Brint, Steven, *In an Age of Experts: The Changing Role of Professionalism in Politics and Public Life* (Princeton: Princeton University Press, 1994).

Bronstein, Phyllis and Carolyn Pape Cowan, eds., *Fatherhood Today: Men's Changing Role in the Family* (New York: John Wiley, 1988).

Brown, Peter, *Society and the Holy in Late Antiquity* (Berkeley: University of California Press, 1982).

————, *Augustine's Sexuality*, Center for Hermeneutical Studies in Hellenistic Modern Culture, 46th colloquy, 22 May, 1983 (Berkeley: Theological Union and University of California, 1983).

————, *The Body and Society: Men, Women, and Sexual Renunciation in Early Christianity* (New York: Columbia University Press, 1988).

Brown, Raymond E., S.S., *The Gospel According to John*, 2 vols., Anchor Bible 29, introduction, trans. and notes (Garden City, NY: Doubleday, 1966).

————, *The Critical Meaning of the Bible: How a Modern Reading of the Bible Challenges Christians, the Church, and the Churches* (New York: Paulist Press, 1981).

————, *The Epistles of John*, Anchor Bible 30 (Garden City, NY: Doubleday, 1982).

————, *The Birth of the Messiah*, 2 vols., Anchor Bible Reference Library (Garden City, NY: Doubleday, rev. ed., 1993).

————, *The Death of the Messiah*, 2 vols., Anchor Bible Reference Library (Garden City, NY: Doubleday, 1993).

————, "God's Future Plan for His People: (1) Messiah" NJBC, pp. 1310-1312.

Brown, Raymond E., S.S., and Sandra Schneider, I.H.M., "Hermeneutics," NJBC, pp. 1146-1165.

Brownmiller, Susan, *Against Our Will: Men, Women and Rape* (New York: Simon and Schuster, 1975).

Bruce, F.F., *The Epistle to the Galatians*, New International Greek New Testament Commentary (Grand Rapids: Eerdmans, 1982).

————, *The Epistles to the Colossians, to Philemon, and to the Ephesians*, New International Commentaries on the New Testament (Grand Rapids: Eerdmans, 1984).

Brueggemann, Walter, *First and Second Samuel* (Louisville: John Knox, 1990).

Brundage, James A., *Law, Sex and Christian Society in Medieval Europe* (Chicago: University of Chicago Press, 1987).

Brunner, Emil, *The Divine Imperative: A Study in Christian Ethics* (Philadelphia: Westminster Press, 1947).

Buchanan, George Wesley, "Jesus and Other Monks of New Testament Times," *Religion in Life* 48 (1979), 136-142.

Budd, P.J., *Numbers* (Waco, TX: Word Bible Commentary, 1984).

Buijs, Joseph, ed., *Maimonides: A Collection of Critical Essays* (Notre Dame, IN: University of Notre Dame Press, 1988).

Bullough, Vern L., *Homosexuality: A History* (New York: New American Library, 1979).

Bultmann, Rudolf, *Theology of the New Testament* (New York: Charles Scribner's Sons, 1951-55). Trans. of 1st edition; a German 4th edition was published Tübingen: Mohr, 1961.

Butler, Ignatius W., *The Moral Problems of the Theater* (Washington, DC: Catholic University of America Press, 1958).

Bynum, Caroline Walker, *Holy Feast and Holy Fast: The Religious Significance of Food to Medieval Women* (Berkeley: University of California Press, 1987).

Cabrol, F., "Jeunes," DACL 7 (2) 2481-2501.

Caffara, Carlo, *Living in Christ* (San Francisco: Ignatius Press, 1987).

Caird, G.B., *A Commentary on the Revelation of St. John the Divine* (New York: Harper and Row, 1966).

Cairns, Ian, *Word and Presence: A Commentary on the Book of Deuteronomy*, International Theological Commentary (Grand Rapids: Eerdmans, 1992).

Callahan, Joan ed., *Ethical Issues in Professional Life* (New York: Oxford University Press, 1988).

Caludot, Michel Dortel, "Vie Consacrée," Part II, DTS, fasc. 104, pp. 663-703.

Calvin, John, *Institutes of the Christian Religion*, 2 vols., The Library of Christian Classics, ed. by John T. McNeill, trans. by Ford Lewis Battles (Philadelphia: Westminster Press, 1960).

Camenisch, Paul F., *Grounding Professional Ethics in a Pluralistic Society* (New York: Haven Press, 1983).

Campbell, Dennis M., *Doctors, Lawyers, Ministers: Christian Ethics in Professional Practice* (Nashville: Abingdon, 1982).

Carlen, Claudia, *The Papal Encyclicals*, 5 vols. (1981: reprint, Ann Arbor, MI: Ann Arbor Press: Pierian Press, 1990).

Carman, John Braistead, *The Theology of Ramanuja* (New Haven: Yale University Press, 1964).

Carmichael, Calum M., *The Laws of Deuteronomy* (Ithaca, NY: Cornell University Press, 1974).

Carmigniac, Jean, "Le Notre Pere: Notes Exegetique, *Maison Dieu* 85 (1966), 7-35.

Carré, A.M., O.P., *Hope or Despair*, trans. by René Hague (New York: P.J. Kenedy and Sons, 1955).

Carter, Warren, *What are They Saying about Matthew's Sermon on the Mount?* (New York: Paulist Press, 1994).

Cassian, St. John, *Institutes and Conferences*, Schaff, NPF, 2nd series, vol. XI, pp. 201-546; PL 49:53-476; PL 49:477-1328.

Cassuto, U., *A Commentary on the Book of Genesis*, 2 vols., trans. by Israel Abrahams (Jerusalem: The Magnes Press, Hebrew University, 1961).

Cath, Stanley M., Alan Gurwitt, Linda Gunsberg, eds., *Fathers and Their Families* (Hillsdale: NJ: Analytic Press, 1989).

Catherine of Siena, St., *Dialogue*, Classics of Western Spirituality, ed. and trans. by Susanne Noffke, O.P., (New York: Paulist Press, 1980).

Cessario, Romanus, O.P., *The Moral Virtues and Theological Ethics* (Notre Dame, IN: University of Notre Dame Press, 1991).

Charlesworth, James H., *The Messiah: Developments in Earliest Judaism and Christianity*, First Princeton Symposium on Judaism and Christian Origins, 1987 (Minneapolis: Fortress Press, 1992), pp. 239-269.

Childs, Brevard S., *The Book of Exodus* (Philadelphia: Westminster Press, 1974).

_____, *Introduction to the Old Testament as Scripture* (Philadelphia: Fortress Press, 1979).

_____. *Old Testament in a Canonical Context* (Philadelphia: Fortress Press, 1985).

_____, *Biblical Theology of the Old and New Testaments: Theological Reflections on the Christian Bible* (Minneapolis: Fortress Press, 1993).

Cholij, Roman, *Clerical Celibacy in East and West* (Leominster, Herefordshire, England: Fowler Wright Books, 1989).

Clark, Francis, S.J., "A New Appraisal of Late Medieval Theology," *Gregorianum* 46 (1965), 733-765.

Clark, Stephen B., *Man and Woman in Christ: An Examination of Man and Woman in the Light of the Scriptures and the Social Sciences* (Ann Arbor, MI: Servant Books, 1980).

Clement of Alexandria, *Stromata*, PG 8:685-1382 and 8:9-602, partial trans. in ANF, vol. 2.

Clement of Rome, *The Epistles of St. Clement of Rome and St. Ignatius of Antioch*, trans. and annotated by James A. Kleist, S.J., ACW, vol. 1 (Westminster, MD: Newman Bookshop, 1946); see also *Apostolic Fathers*.

Clements, R.E., *Old Testament Theology: A Fresh Approach* (Atlanta, GA: John Knox, 1979).

Clifford, Richard J., "The Hebrew Scriptures and the Theology of Creation," TS 46 (1985), 507-523.

Cochini, Christian, S.J., *Origines apostoliques du célibat sacerdotal* (Paris: P. Lethielleux, Le Sycomore, 1980); reviewed by H. Crouzel, S.J., *Nouvelle Revue Theologigue*, 1971, pp. 649-653 and Charles Martin, S.J., *Nouvelle Revue Theologique*, 105 (1983), 437-438.

Cochrane, Arthur C., "Natural Law in Calvin" in *Church and State Relations in Ecumenical Perspective*, Elwin A. Smith, ed. (Pittsburgh: Duquesne University Press, 1966), pp. 176-217.

Cohen, Jeremy, *"Be Fertile and Increase, Fill the Earth and Master It"*: *The Ancient and Medieval Career of a Biblical Text* (Ithaca, NY: Cornell University Press, 1989).

Cohn, Haim H., "The Penology of the Talmud," *Jewish Law in Ancient and Modern Israel* (New York: KTAV Publishing House, 1971), pp. 61-82.

Coleman, Gerald D., S.S., *Human Sexuality: An All-Embracing Gift* (Staten Island, NY: Alba House, 1992).

Colish, Marcia L., "Cosmetic Theology: The Transformation of a Stoic Theme," in *Assays: Critical Approaches to Medieval and Renaissance Texts*, vol. 1, ed. by Peggy A. Knapp and Michael Stugrin (Pittsburgh: University of Pittsburgh Press, 1981), pp. 3-14.

_____, *The Stoic Tradition from Antiquity to the Early Middle Ages*, vol. 2, *Stoicism in Christian Latin Thought through the Sixth Century* (Leiden: E.J. Brill, 1985).

Collange, Jean-Francois, *De Jésus à Paul, Le champ éthique* (Geneva: Labor et Fides, 1980).

Collins, Adela Yarbro, *The Apocalypse*, New Testament Message (Wilmington, DE: Michael Glazier, 1979).

Collins, John J., *The Apocalyptic Imagination: An Introduction to the Jewish Matrix of Christianity* (New York: Crossroad, 1984).

Collins, Raymond, "Scripture and the Christian Ethic," *Proceedings of the Catholic Theological Society of America* 29 (1974), 215-41.

_____, *Divorce in the New Testament* (Collegeville, MN: Liturgical Press, 1992).

_____, *Christian Morality: Biblical Foundations* (Notre Dame, IN: University of Notre Dame Press, 1986).

Commissio Theologica Internationalis, *La conscience que Jesus avait de lui-meme et de sa mission.* Quatre propositions avec commentaire. *Gregorianum* 67 (1986), pp. 413-427.

Compagnioni, Francesco, "Capital Punishment and Torture in the Tradition of the Catholic Church," Franz Böckle and Jacques Pohier, eds., *The Death Penalty and Torture*, in *Concilium* (New York: Seabury-Crossroad, 1979), pp. 39-53.

_____, *La specificita della morale cristiana* (Bologna: Edizioni Dehoniane, 1972).

Congar, Yves M.-J., O.P., *A History of Theology*, trans. and ed. by Hunter Guthrie, S.J. from article "Théologie," DTS XV, pp. 221-288.

_____, *I Believe in the Holy Spirit*, trans. by David Smith, 3 vols. (New York: Seabury Press, 1983).

Congregation for the Doctrine of the Faith, "Declaration on Certain Problems of Sexual Ethics" (*Personae Humanae*), Dec. 29, 1975, Flannery, pp. 486-499.

_____, "Sterilization in Catholic Hospitals," 12 March 1975, Flannery, pp. 454-455.

_____, "Declaration on the Question of the 'Admission of Women to the

Ministerial Priesthood" (*Inter Insigniores*), Oct. 15, 1976, AAS 69 (1977); *Origins* 6, 33 (Feb. 3, 1977), 518-531.

————, "Declaration on Euthanasia," May 5, 1980, Flannery, pp. 441-453.

————, "Letter to Fr. Schillebeeckx Regarding his Book Ministry," *Origins* 14 (Jan. 24, 1985), 523 and "Note on the Response of Fr. Schillebeeckx," *Origins* 14 (April 4, 1985), 683.

————, "Instruction on Certain Aspects of 'The Theology of Liberation'" (*Libertatis nuntius*) (Boston: St. Paul Editions, 1984) and "Instruction on Christian Freedom and Liberation (Boston: St. Paul Editions, 1986).

————, "Letter to the Bishops of the Catholic Church on the Pastoral Care of Homosexual Persons," 1986, in Jeannine Grammick and Pat Furey, eds., *The Vatican and Homosexuality* (New York: Crossroad, 1988), pp. 1-12.

————, "Instruction on Respect for Human Life in its Origin and on the Dignity of Procreation" (*Donum Vitae*) (Rome: Vatican Polyglot Press, 1987).

————, "Instruction on the Ecclesial Vocation of the Theologian," May 24, 1990, *Origins*, 20 (July 5, 1990), 117-26.

Congregation for Religious and Secular Institutes, "*Instructio de vita contemplativa et de monialium clausura,*" Nov. 10, 1969, AAS, 61 (1969), 674-690; "The Contemplative Dimension of Religious Life," Feb. 12, 1981, *Origins*, 10 (35), 550-560.

Conn, Walter E., "Post-Conventional Morality: An Exposition and Critique of Kohlberg's Analysis of Moral Development in the Adolescent and Adult," *Lumen Vitae* 32 (1975), 213-230.

Connery, John R., S.J., "Morality of Consequences: A Critical Appraisal," TS 3 (1973), 396-414.

————, "The Notion of Sin in Light of the Theory of the Fundamental Option," *Louvain Studies* 9 (1983), 363-382.

————, "The Non-Infallible Moral Teaching of the Church," TH 51 (1987), 1-16.

Conrad, Edgar W., *Reading Isaiah*, Overtures in Biblical Theology (Minneapolis: Fortress Press, 1991).

Conzelmann, Hans, *An Outline of the Theology of the New Testament* (New York: Harper and Row, 1969).

————, *1 Corinthians*, Hermeneia Biblical Commentaries (Philadelphia: Fortress Press, 1975).

Copelston, Frederick, S.J., *Religion and the One: Philosophies East and West* (New York: Crossroad, 1982).

Countryman, L. William. *Dirt, Greed and Sex: Sexual Ethics in the New Testament and Their Implications for Today* (Philadelphia: Fortress Press, 1988).

Coyne, G.V., M. Heller, and J. Zycinski, *The Galileo Affair, a Meeting of Faith and Science: Proceedings of the Cracow Conference*, 24-27 May 1984 (Vatican City: Specola Vaticana, 1985).

Craghan, J., *Esther, Judith, Tobit, Jonah, Ruth*, Old Testament Message (Wilmington, DE: Michael Glazier, 1982).

Cranfield, C.E.B., *A Critical Exegetical Commentary on the Epistle to the Romans*, 2 vols., International Critical Commentary (Edinburgh, 1975-1979).

Cranx, F. Edward, *The Development of Luther's Thought on Justice, Law, and Society* (Cambridge, MA: Harvard University Press, 1959).

Crenshaw, J.L., *Ecclesiastes*, Old Testament Library (Philadelphia: Fortress Press, 1987).

Crossan, John Dominic, *The Historical Jesus: The Life of a Mediterranean Jewish Peasant* (San Francisco: Harpers, 1991).

Crossin, John W., *What Are They Saying About Virtue?* (New York: Paulist Press, 1985).

Crouzel, Henri, S.J., *L'Église Primitive Face au Divorce, Theologie Historique*, n. 13 (Paris: Beauchesne, 1970).

————, *Origen*, trans. by A.S. Worrall (San Francisco: Harper and Row, 1989).

Crow, Michael Bertram, *The Changing Profile of the Natural Law* (The Hague: Martinus Nijhoff, 1977).

Cruz, Hieronymus, *Christological Motives and Motivated Actions in Pauline Paranesis* (Frankfort-am-Main/NewYork: P. Lang, 1990).

Curran, Charles E., *Ongoing Revision* (Notre Dame, IN: University of Notre Dame Press, 1975).

————, *Directions in Fundamental Moral Theology* (Notre Dame, IN: University of Notre Dame Press, 1985).

————, *Free and Faithful Dissent* (Kansas City, MO: Sheed and Ward, 1987).

————, *Toward an American Catholic Moral Theology* (Notre Dame, IN: University of Notre Dame Press, 1987). See especially, "The Historical Development of Moral Theology," and "Moral Theology in the United States: An Analysis of the Last Twenty Years," pp. 3-19 and 20-51.

————, *The Living Tradition of Catholic Moral Theology* (Notre Dame, IN: University of Notre Dame Press, 1992).

Curran, Charles E. with Richard A. McCormick, S.J., eds., *Readings in Moral Theology* (New York: Paulist Press):
    No. 1. *Moral Norms and Catholic Tradition*, 1979.
    No. 2. *The Distinctiveness of Christian Ethics*, 1980.
    No. 3. *The Magisterium and Morality*, 1982.
    No. 4. *The Use of Scripture in Moral Theology*, 1984.
    No. 5. *Official Catholic Social Teaching*, 1986.
    No. 6. *Dissent in the Church*, 1986.

D'Arcy, M.C., S.J., *The Mind and Heart of Love* (New York: Meridian Books, 1956).

d'Entrèves, A.P., *Natural Law: An Historical Survey* (New York: Harper, 1951, 1965).

Daly, Robert J., S.J., ed., *Christian Biblical Ethics: From Biblical Revelation to Contemporary Praxis* (New York: Paulist Press, 1984) with response of John Dedek, "Scripture and the Christian Ethic: A Response," *Proceedings of the Catholic Theological Society of America* 29 (1974), 243-246.

Danby, Herbert, *The Mishnah*, trans. with introduction and notes (Oxford: Oxford University Press, 1933).

Dancy, J.C., *The Shorter Books of the Apocrypha* (Cambridge: Cambridge University Press, 1972).

Danielou, Jean, *The Development of Christian Doctrine Before the Council of Nicaea:* vol. 1, *The Theology of Jewish Christianity* (London: Darton, Longman & Todd, 1964), and vol. 2, *Gospel Message and Hellenistic Culture* (Philadelphia: Westminster Press, 1973).

Davies, Eryl W., *Prophecy and Ethics: Isaiah and the Ethical Tradition of Israel*, JSOT Supplement Series 16 (Sheffield: JSOT Press, 1981).

Davies, Philip R. and Richard T. White, *A Tribute to Geza Vermes: Essays on Jewish and Christian Literature and History*, JSOT Supplement Series 100. (Sheffield: Sheffield Academic Press, 1990).

Davies, W.D., *The Setting of the Sermon on the Mount* (Cambridge: Cambridge University Press, 1966).

De Koninck, Charles, *De la primauté du bien commun contre les personalistes* (Laval: University of Laval, 1943) and "In Defense of St. Thomas," *Laval Théologique et Philosophique*, 1 (2, 1945), 1-103.

Debner, Claudia Bialke, ed., *Chemical Dependency: Opposing Viewpoints* (St. Paul, MN: Greenhaven Press, 1985).

Dedek, John, "Scripture and the Christian Ethic: A Response [to Raymond Collins]," *Proceedings of the Catholic Theological Society of America* 29 (1974), 243-246.

Deeken, Alfons, *Process and Permanence in Ethics: Max Scheler's Moral Philosophy* (New York: Paulist Press, 1974).

Deidun, Thomas J., *New Covenant Morality in Paul* (Rome: Biblical Institute Press, 1981).

Delhaye, Phillipe, "La théologie morale d'hier et d'aujourdh'ui," *Revue Sciences Religieuse*, 27 (1953), 112-130.

_____, *Permanence du Droit Naturel* (Brussels: Editions Nauwelaerts, 1960).

_____, *Le Decalogue et sa place dans la moral chrétiennne* (Brussels: La Pensée Catholique, 1963).

Deman, Thomas, O.P., *Socrate et Jésus* (Paris: L'Artisan Du Livre, 1944).

_____, *Aux origins de la théologie morale* (Montreal: Institute d'Études Médiévales, 1951).

_____, "Intrinsically Evil Acts: An Historical Study of the Mind of St. Thomas," TH 43 (1979), 385-419.

Deming, Will, "Mark 9.42-10, 12, Matthew 5.27-32, and B.NID. 13b: A First Century Discussion of Male Sexuality," NTS, 36:1 (Jan. 1990), 130-141.

Dent, N.J., *The Moral Psychology of the Virtues* (Cambridge: Cambridge University Press, 1984).

Derrett, J.D.M., *Law in the New Testament* (London: Darton, Longman and Todd, 1970).

Dewar, Lindsay, *An Outline of New Testament Ethics* (Philadelphia: Westminster Press, 1949).

Di Lella, A.A., *The Book of Daniel*, Anchor Bible 23 (Garden City, NY: Doubleday, 1978).

Dibelius, Martin, *James*, rev. by H. Greeven, Hermeneia Commentaries (Philadelphia: Fortress Press, 1975).

Dickie, Robert B. and Leroy S. Rouner, eds., *Corporations and the Common Good* (Notre Dame, IN: University of Notre Dame Press, 1986).

Didache, Apostolic Fathers, Loeb Classical Library, trans. by Kirsopp Lake, vol. 1, pp. 303-334 (see also Audet's edition).

Dodd, C.H., *The Bible and the Greeks* (London: Hodder, 1935).

_____, *Gospel and Law* (New York: Columbia University Press, 1951).

_____, "Natural Law in the New Testament" (1946), *New Testament Studies* (Manchester: Manchester University Press, 1967), pp. 129-142.

Dogan, Mattei and Dominique Pellasy, *How to Conquer Nations: Strategies in Comparative Politics* (Chatham, NJ: Chatham House Publishers, 1984).

Doms, Herbert, *The Meaning of Marriage*, trans. by G. Sayer (New York: Sheed and Ward, 1939).

Donfried, K.P., "The Allegory of the Ten Virgins as a Summary of Matthean Theology," JBL 93 (1974), 415-28.

Doorly, William J., *Obsession with Justice: the Story of the Deuteronomists* (New York: Paulist Press, 1994).

_____, *Prophet of Justice: Understanding the Book of Amos* (New York: Paulist Press, 1992).

Douglas, Mary, *Purity and Danger: An Analysis of the Concepts of Pollution and Taboo*, 1966, reprint (London/Boston/ Henley: Routledge & Kegan Paul, 1979).

Drucker, Peter, "Management as a Social Function and a Liberal Art," in his *The New Realities in Government and Politics, in Economics and Business, in Society and World View* (New York: Harper and Row, 1990).

Drury, John, *Tradition and Design in Luke's Gospel* (Atlanta: John Knox, 1976).

Duffy, Stephen, "Our Hearts of Darkness: Original Sin Revisited," TS 49 (December 1988), 597-622.

Dulles, Avery, S.J., *A History of Apologetics*, Theological Resources (New York: Corpus Books, 1971).

_____, *Models of Revelation* (Garden City, NY: Doubleday, 1983).

_____, *Models of the Church*, expanded ed. (Garden City, NY: Doubleday/ Image Books, 1987).

_____, *The Craft of Theology: From Symbol to System* (New York: Crossroad, 1992), especially "The Magisterium and Theological Dissent," pp. 105-118.

Dunn, James D.G., "The Incident at Antioch (Gal 2:11-18)," JSNT 18 (1983), 3-57.

_____, *Romans 1-8*, Word Biblical Commentary, Vol. 38 (Dallas: Word Books, 1988).

_____, *Jesus, Paul and the Law: Studies in Mark and Galatians* (Louisville, KY: Westminster/Knox, 1990).

Dupont, Jacques, O.S.B., *Les Béatitudes*, rev. ed. (Paris: J. Gabalda, 1973), vol. I: Literary Problems, II: Happy the Poor, III: Comparison of Luke and Matthew's Versions.

_____, "Le Notre Père:Notes exégétiques," 85 (1966), 7-35. *Nouvelles Études sur les Actes des Apôtre*, Lectio Divina 118 (Paris: Éditions du Cerf, 1984).

Durkheim, Emile, *The Elementary Forms of Religious Life*, trans. by J.W. Swain (New York: Collier Books, 1961).

Duska, Ronald, and M. Whelan, *Moral Development: A Guide to Piaget and Kohlberg* (New York: Paulist Press, 1975).

Dwyer, John C., *Foundations of Christian Ethics* (New York: Paulist Press, 1987).

Earle, Ralph and Gregory Crow, with Kevin Osborn, *Lonely All the Time: Recognizing, Understanding, and Overcoming Sex Addictions: For Addicts and Co-Dependents* (New York: Pocket Books, 1989).

Edwards, George, *Jesus and the Politics of Violence* (New York: Harper and Row, 1972).

Eige, Francis A., ed., *The Professions in Ethical Context: Vocations to Justice and Love* (Villanova, PA: Villanova University Press, 1986).

Elia, Irene, *The Female Animal*, Introduction by Ashley Montagu (New York: Henry Holt, 1988).

Epiphanius, St., *Expositio Fidei*, PG 42:773-832 (last section of the *Panarion*).

Etienne, J., "Théologie Moral et renouveau biblique," *Ephemerides Theologicae Lovanienses*, 40 (1964), 232-241.

Eusebius of Caesarea, *Church History*, II, c. 23, trans. in Schaff, NPF, vol. 1, first series, PG 20:45-906.

Evagrius Ponticus, *Traité Pratique ou Le Moine*, SC 170-171, ed. Antoine and Claire Guillaumont (Paris: Éditions du Cerf, 1971): Introduction, "Théorie de huit pensées principales," vol. 170, pp. 63-91, and *The Praktikos: Chapters on Prayer*, trans. with introduction and notes by John E. Bamberget (Spencer, MA: Cistercian Publications, 1972).

Evans, Craig A., "Life-of-Jesus Research and the Eclipse of Mythology," TS 54 (March 1993), 3-36.

Farrer, Austin, *A Rebirth of Images: The Making of St. John's Apocalypse* (Albany, NY: State University of New York Press, 1986).

Ferguson, John, "The Cardinal Virtues," *Moral Values in the Ancient World* (London: Methuen, 1958), pp. 24-52.

Feuillet, André, *Jesus and His Mother According to the Lucan Infancy Narrative and According to St. John*, trans. by L. Maluf (Still River, MA: St. Bede's Publications, 1974).

Fichtner, J., "Orge," TDNT 5:392-409.

Finnis, John, *Natural Law and Natural Rights* (Oxford: Clarendon Press, 1980).

_____, *Fundamentals of Ethics* (Washington, DC: Georgetown University Press, 1985).

_____, *Moral Absolutes: Tradition, Revision, and Truth* (Washington, DC: Catholic University of America Press, 1991).

Fiorenza, Elisabeth Schüssler, "You are not to be called Father," *Cross-Currents* (Fall 1979), 356-58.

_____, *In Memory of Her: A Feminist Theological Reconstruction of Christian Origins* (New York: Crossroad, 1984); see reviews in JBL 104 (1985), 72 and *Journal of Religion* 65 (1985), 83-88.

_____, "Toward a Feminist Biblical Hermeneutics: Biblical Interpretation and Liberation Theology," in C.E. Curran and R.A. McCormick, eds., *The Use of Scripture in Moral Theology: Readings in Moral Theology*, No. 4 (New York: Paulist Press, 1984).

Fitzmyer, Joseph A., S.J., *The Gospel According to Luke*, 2 vols., Anchor Bible, 28, 28A (Garden City, NY: Doubleday, 1981, 1985).

_____, *To Advance the Gospel: New Testament Studies* (New York: Crossroad, 1981), especially "The Matthean Divorce Texts and Some New Palestinian Evidence," pp. 79-111.

_____, *Scripture and Christology: A Statement of the Biblical Commission with a Commentary* (New York: Paulist Press, 1986).

_____, *Luke the Theologian: Aspects of His Teaching* (New York: Paulist Press, 1989).

_____, "Romans" in NJBC, pp. 830-868.

_____, "Pauline Theology," NJBC, pp. 1382-1416.

_____, *Romans: A New Translation with Introduction and Commentary*, Anchor Bible (Garden City, NY: Doubleday, 1993).

Flannery, Austin, O.P., ed., *Vatican Collection*, vol. 2, *Vatican Council II: More Postconciliar Documents* (Northport, NY: Costello Publishing Co., 1982).

Fletcher, Joseph, "Four Indicators of Humanhood: The Enquiry Matures," *Hastings Center Report* 4, pp. 4-7, with replies in *Correspondence* 5 (4), pp. 43-45.

_____, "Humanist Ethics: The Groundwork," in *Humanist Ethics: Dialogues on Basics*, ed. Morris B. Storer (Buffalo, NY: Prometheus Books, 1980), pp. 253-60.

Fohrer, George, "The Righteous Man in Job 31," James L. Crenshaw, and J.T. Willis, eds., *Essays in Old Testament Ethics* (New York: KTAV Publishing House, 1974), pp. 1-22.

Ford, John C., S.J., and Gerald Kelly, S.J., *Contemporary Moral Theology*, vol. 1, *Questions in Fundamental Moral Theology* (Westminster, MD: Newman Press, 1964).

Fox, Marvin, *Interpreting Maimonides: Studies in Methodology, Metaphysics and Moral Philosophy* (Chicago: University of Chicago Press, 1990), "Maimonides and Aquinas on Natural Law," pp. 124-151.

Francis of Assisi, St., *St. Francis of Assisi: Writings and Early Biographies (Omnibus of Sources)*, trans. and ed. by Marion Habig, O.F.M. (Chicago: Franciscan Herald Press, 1972).

Francis de Sales, St., *Treatise on the Love of God*, trans. by Vincent Kern (Westminster, MD: Newman Press, 1962).

Frank, Karl Suso, "Vie Consacrée," I, 4, "Le consecration des vierges," DTS, fasc. 104, cols. 655-661.

Franks, Isaac, "Maimonides and Aquinas on Man's Knowledge of God: A Twentieth-Century Perspective" in Joseph A. Buijs, ed. *Maimonides: A Collection of Critical Essays* (Notre Dame, IN: University of Notre Dame Press, 1988), pp. 284-305.

Freeman, R. Edward, ed., *Business Ethics: The State of the Art*. The Ruffine Series in Business Ethics (New York: Oxford University Press, 1991).

Frei, Hans, *Eclipse of Biblical Narrative* (New Haven: Yale University Press, 1974).

Freyne, Seán, "The Bible and Christian Morality," in J.P. Mackey, ed., *Morals, Law, and Authority* (Dayton, OH: Pflaum, 1969), pp. 1-38.

Friedman, Richard Eliott, "Torah (Pentateuch)," ABD, vol. 6: 605-622.

Friesen, Gary, with J. Robin Maxson, *Decision Making and the Will of God: A Biblical Alternative to the Traditional View* (Portland, OR: Multnomah, 1980).

Frijda, Nico H., *The Emotions* (Cambridge: Cambridge University Press, 1986).

Fuchs, Joseph, S.J., *Human Values and Christian Morality* (Dublin: Gill and Macmillan, 1970).

_____, "The Absoluteness of Moral Terms," *Gregorianum* 52 (1971), 415-458.

_____, *Christian Ethics in a Secular Arena* (Washington, DC: Georgetown University Press, 1984).

_____, "Christian Morality: Biblical Orientation and Human Evaluation," *Gregorianum* 67 (1986), 745-63.

Fuerst, W.J., *The Five Scrolls*, Cambridge Biblical Commentary (Cambridge: Cambridge University Press, 1975).

Fulton, R.B., *Adam Smith Speaks to Our Times: A Study of His Ethical Ideas* (Boston: Christopher Publishing House, 1963).

Funk, Robert W., *The Five Gospels: The Search for the Authentic Words of Jesus* (New York: Macmillan, 1993).

Funk, Robert W. with Mahlon H. Smith, *The Gospel of Mark* (Polebridge Press, 1990), reviewed by C.C. Carlson, CBQ 52 (1990), 557-558.

Furnish, Victor Paul, *Theology and Ethics in Paul* (Nashville: Abingdon Press, 1968).

_____, *The Love Command in the New Testament* (Nashville: Abingdon Press, 1972).

_____, *II Corinthians*, Anchor Bible 32a (Garden City, NY: Doubleday, 1984), pp. 164-166.

_____, *The Moral Teaching of Paul: Selected Issues*, 2nd ed. (Nashville: Abingdon Press, 1985).

Gallagher, John A., C.S.P., *The Basis for Christian Ethics* (New York: Paulist Press, 1985).

Gallagher, Raphael, C.S.S.R., "The New Words: Fundamental Option," *Furrow* 34 (March 1983), 162-3.

_____, *Time Past, Time Future: A Historical Study of Catholic Moral Theology* (New York: Paulist Press, 1990).

Galot, Jean, *The Mystery of Christian Hope*, trans. by M.A. Bouchard (Staten Island, NY: Alba House, 1977).

Gandhi, Mahatma, *Non-Violence in Peace and War, 1942-1949*, with new introduction by Paul F. Power, 2 vols. (New York: Garland Publishers, 1972).

Gannon, Thomas M., S.J., *The Catholic Challenge to the American Economy: Reflections on the U.S. Bishops' Pastoral Letter on Catholic Social Teaching and the U.S. Economy* with the complete text of the Bishops' Letter (New York: Macmillan, 1987).

Garden, Clinton E., *Biblical Faith and Social Ethics* (New York: Harper, 1960).

Garrigou-Lagrange, Reginald, O.P., *The Three Ages of the Interior Life*, 2 vols.

trans. by Sister M. Timothea Doyle, O.P. (St. Louis: B. Herder Book
Co., 1947-48).

Gay, Peter, *The Enlightenment*, 2 vols. (New York: Alfred Knopf, 1967).

Geach, Peter, *The Virtues*. The Stanton Lectures 1973-1974 (Cambridge:
Cambridge University Press, 1977).

Geisler, Norman L., *Christian Ethics: Options and Issues* (Grand Rapids:
Baker, 1989).

Gelin, Albert, *The Key Concepts of the Old Testament* (New York: Sheed and
Ward, 1955).

Genovesi, Vincent, S.J., *Expectant Creativity: The Action of Hope in Christian
Ethics* (Lanham, MD: University of America Press, 1982).

Gerhardsson, Birger, *The Ethos of the Bible* (Philadelphia: Fortress Press,
1981).

Getty, M.A., *Philippians and Philemon*, New Testament Message (Wilmington,
DE: Michael Glazier, 1980).

Gilleman, Gérard, S.J., *The Primacy of Charity* (Westminster, MD: Newman
Press, 1959).

Gillon, L.-B., O.P., "L'imitation du Christ et la moral de saint Thomas,"
Angelicum, 36, (1959), pp. 263-286.

_____, *Christ and Moral Theology* (Staten Island, NY: Alba House, 1967).

Glasson, F.T., "Philippians 2:6-11," *New Testament Studies* 21 (1974-75), 133-
39.

Gleason, Robert W., S.J., *Grace* (New York: Sheed and Ward, 1962).

Glendon, Mary Ann, *Rights Talk: The Impoverishment of Political Discourse*
(New York: The Free Press/ Macmillan, 1991).

Goethals, Gregor T., "TV's Iconic Imagery in a Secular Society," *New
Theology Review*, 6 (Feb. 1993), 40-53 excerpted from *The
Electronic Golden Calf: Images, Religion, and the Making of
Meaning* (Cambridge, MA: Cowley Publications, 1990).

Goldberg, Stephen, *The Inevitability of Patriarchy* (New York: William
Morrow and Co., 1974).

Goldman, Alan H., *The Moral Foundations of Professional Ethics* (Totowa,
NJ: Rowman and Littlefield, 1980).

Goldstein, J., *I and II Maccabees*, Anchor Bible 41 and 41A (Garden City, NY:
Doubleday, 1976, 1983).

Gonbola, Patricia A., and Edward H. Thompson, Jr., "Single-Parent Families,"
Handbook of Marriage and the Family, edited by Marvin B.
Sussman and Suzanne K. Steinmetz (New York: Plenum Press,
1987), pp. 397-418.

Gorman, Frank H., Jr., *The Ideology of Ritual: Space, Time and Status in the
Priestly Theology*, JSOT, Supplement Series 91 (Sheffield: JSOT
Press, 1990).

_____, "When Law Becomes Gospel: Matthew's Transformed Torah," *Listening*, 24, 3 (Fall 1989), 227-241.

Görres, Ida Frederike, *Is Celibacy Outdated?*, trans. by Barbara Waldstein-Wartenberg in collaboration with the author (Westminster, MD: Newman Press, 1965).

Gowan, Donald E., *Eschatology in the Old Testament* (Philadelphia: Fortress Press, 1986).

Grammick, Jeannine and Pat Furey, eds., *The Vatican and Homosexuality: Reactions to the "Letter to the Bishops of the Catholic Church on the Pastoral Care of Homosexual Persons"* (New York: Crossroad, 1988), pp. 105-111. The Letter is translated on pp. 1-12.

Grant, Robert M., "The Decalogue in Early Christianity," HTR 40 (1947), 1-17.

Gray, John, *I and II Kings*, rev. ed., Old Testament Library (Philadelphia: Westminster Press, 1970).

Grecco, Richard, *A Theology of Compromise: A Study of Method in the Ethics of Charles E. Curran* (New York: P. Lang, 1991).

Greeley, Andrew, and William McManus, *Catholic Contributions: Sociology and Polity* (Chicago: Thomas More Press, 1987).

Gregorios, P., *Cosmic Man: The Divine Presence* (Geneva, 1980).

Gregory the Great, St., *XL Homiliarum in Evangelia*, PL 76:1075-1312.

_____, *Epistles*, PL 77:441-1328.

_____, *Homilies on Ezekiel* (Lib. 1, 11: CCL 142, 170-172) from *The Liturgy of the Hours According to the Roman Rite* (New York: Catholic Book Publishing Co., 1975), IV, p. 1366.

_____, *Morals on the Book of Job*, trans. John Henry Parker, 4 vols. (Oxford, 1844-50).

Gregory of Nyssa, St., *The Great Catechism*, NPF Second Series, vol. 5, c. 8, pp. 482-484.

_____, *On Virginity* 46.369B-376B, translated in *From Glory to Glory: Texts from Gregory of Nyssa's Mystical Writings*, selected with an introduction by Jean Danielou; trans. and edited by Herbert Musurillo (Crestwood, NY: St. Vladimir's Seminary Press, 1979).

Grelot, Pierre, *Sens Chrétien de l'Ancien Testament* (Paris: Desclee, 2nd ed., 1962).

_____, *Les Poèmes du Serviteur*, Lectio Divina (Paris: Éditions du Cerf, 1981).

_____, *Église et ministères: pour un dialogue critique avec Edward Schillebeeckx* (Paris: Éditions du Cerf, 1983).

Gremillion, Joseph, *The Gospel of Peace and Justice: Catholic Social Teaching Since Pope John XXIII* (Maryknoll, NY: Orbis Books, 1976).

Gribomont, Jean, "Monachisme," DTS, tom. 10, cols. 1524-1617.

Griffin, Ricky W., *Management*, 3rd ed. (Boston: Houghton Mifflin, 1990).

Grill, S.D., "Prayer," *Encyclopedia of Religion*, 11: 489-494.

Grisez, Germain G., with the help of Joseph M. Boyle, Jr., Basil Cole, O.P., John M. Finnis, John A. Geinzer, Jeannette Grisez, Robert G. Kennedy, Patrick Lee, William E. May, and Russell Shaw, *The Way of the Lord Jesus*: vol. 1, *Christian Moral Principles*, vol. 2, *Living a Christian Life* (Quincy, IL: Franciscan Press, 1993; Chicago: Franciscan Herald Press, 1983). See B. M. Ashley's review discussion, "Christian Moral Principles," in TH 48, 3 (1984), 450-460 and "What is the End of the Human Person: The Vision of God and Integral Human Fulfillment."

Grisez, Germain and Russell Shaw, *Beyond the New Morality* (Notre Dame, IN: University of Notre Dame Press, 3rd ed., 1988; 1st ed., 1974).

————, *Fulfillment in Christ* (Notre Dame, IN: University of Notre Dame Press, 1991). Short version of *Christian Principles*, vol. 1.

Groeschel, Benedict J., O.F.M. Cap., *The Courage to be Chaste* (Mahwah, NJ: Paulist Press, 1985).

Gryson, Roger, *Les origines du célibat ecclésiastiques du premier au septième siècle* (Brussels: Editions J. Duclot, 1970).

Guardini, Romano, *The Virtues: On Forms of Moral Life* (Chicago: Regnery, 1967).

Gula, Richard M., S.S., *What Are They Saying About Moral Norms?* (New York: Paulist Press, 1981).

Gundry, R.H., *The Use of the Old Testament in St. Matthew's Gospel* (Leiden: E.J. Brill, 1967).

————, *Matthew* (Grand Rapids: Eerdmans, 1982).

————, *Mark: A Commentary on His Apology for the Cross* (Grand Rapids: Eerdmans, 1993).

Gustafson, James M., "The Place of Scripture in Christian Ethics: A Methodological Study," *Interpretation* 24 (1970), 430-455.

————, *Can Ethics Be Christian?* (Chicago: University of Chicago Press, 1975).

————, *Protestant and Roman Catholic Ethics: Prospects for Rapprochement* (Chicago: University of Chicago Press, 1978).

————, *Ethics from a Theocentric Perspective*, 2 vols. (Chicago: University of Chicago Press, 1981).

Gutiérrez, Gustavo, *A Theology of Liberation: History, Politics and Salvation*, trans. and ed. by Sr. Caridad Inda and John Eagleson (Maryknoll, NY: Orbis Books, 1973).

Haag, Ernest van den and John P. Conrad, *The Death Penalty: A Debate: Pro Ernest van den Haag and Con John P. Conrad* (New York: Plenum Press, 1983).

Habel, N., *The Book of Job*, Old Testament Library (Philadelphia: Fortress Press, 1985).

Hacker, Paul, *The Ego in Faith: Martin Luther and the Origin of Anthropocentric Religion* (Chicago: Franciscan Herald Press, 1970).

Hadas, Moses, ed. and trans., *The Third and Fourth Books of Maccabees* (New York: Harper and Bros., 1953).

Hall, David R., *The Seven Pillories of Wisdom* (Mercer, GA: Mercer University Press, 1990).

Hallet, Garth, S.J., "The 'Incommensurability' of Values," *Heythrop Journal*, 28 (1987), 373-387.

Hamel, Edouard, S.J., "L'Usage de l'Écriture Sainte au théologie morale," *Gregorianum* 47 (1966), 56-63.

Hamel, Ronald P. and Kenneth R. Himes, O.F.M., *Introduction to Christian Ethics: A Reader* (New York: Paulist Press, 1989).

Hand, Thomas A., O.S.A., *St. Augustine on Prayer* (Westminster, MD: Newman Press, 1963).

Hanigan, James P., *What They are Saying About Sexual Morality* (New York: Paulist Press, 1982).

————, *Martin Luther King, Jr. and the Foundations of Nonviolence* (Lanham, MD: University Press of America, 1984).

————, *As I Have Loved You: The Challenge of Christian Ethics* (New York: Paulist Press, 1986).

Hanson, A.T., *The Pastoral Epistles*, New Century Bible (Grand Rapids: Eerdmans, 1982).

Hanson, Paul D., *The People Called: The Growth of Community in the Bible* (San Francisco: Harper and Row, 1986).

Harakas, Stanley Samuel, *Toward a Transfigured Life: The Theoria of Eastern Orthodox Ethics* (Minneapolis: Light and Life Publishing Co., 1983).

Häring, Bernard, C.SS.R., *The Law of Christ*, 3 vols. (New York: Seabury Press, 1978-1981, originally 1961).

————, *Free and Faithful in Christ: Moral Theology for Clergy and Laity*, 3 vols. (New York: Seabury Press, 1978-81 [1992]).

Häring, Bernard, with Louis Vereecke, "La theologie morale de S. Thomas d'Aquin a S. Alphonse de Liguori," *Nouvelle Revue Théologique* 7 (1955), 673-692.

Harner, Philip, *Understanding the Lord's Prayer* (Philadelphia: Fortress Press, 1975).

Harrelson, Walter, *The Ten Commandments and Human Rights* (Philadelphia: Fortress Press, 1981).

Harrington, Daniel, S.J., *Light of All Nations: Essays on the Church in New Testament Research*, Good News Studies 3 (Wilmington, DE: Michael Glazier, 1982).

————, "Biblical Hermeneutics in Recent Discussion: New Testament" with

Bruce C. Birch, "Biblical Hermeneutics in Recent Discussion: Old Testament" *Religious Studies Review* 10, 1 (Jan. 1984), 1-10.

Harrington, Wilfrid J., O.P., *Understanding the Apocalypse* (Washington/ Cleveland: Corpus, 1969).

Hartshorne, Charles, *The Divine Relativity* (New Haven: Yale University Press, 1964).

Harvey, A.E., *Strenuous Commands: The Ethic of Jesus* (Philadelphia: Trinity Press International/ London: SCM Press, 1990).

Harvey, John F., O.S.F.S., and Jeffrey Keefe, *The Homosexual Person: New Thinking in Pastoral Care* (San Francisco: Ignatius Press, 1987).

Hatterer, Lawrence J., M.D., *The Pleasure Addicts: The Addictive Process — Food, Sex, Drugs, Alcohol, Work and More* (South Brunswick and New York: A.S. Barnes, 1980).

Hauerwas, Stanley, *Character and the Christian Life: A Study in Theological Ethics* (San Antonio: Trinity University Press, 1979).

_____, *Unleashing the Scriptures: Freeing the Bible from Captivity in America* (Nashville: Abingdon Press, 1993).

Hauke, Manfred, *Women in the Priesthood? A Systematic Analysis in the Light of the Order of Creation and Redemption*, trans. by David Kipp (San Francisco: Ignatius Press, 1988).

Hausher, I.I., "L'origine de la théorie orientales des huits péchés capitaux," *Orientalia Christiana* 86 (1933), 164-175.

Hegermann, H., "Sophia," EDNT, vol. 3, pp. 258-261.

Heine, Susanne, *Women in Early Christianity: A Reappraisal* (Minneapolis: Augsburg Publishing House, 1987).

Hellwig, Monika, *What Are They Saying About Death and Christian Hope?* (New York: Paulist Press, 1978).

Hendriks, N., *Le moyen mauvais pour obtenir une fin bonne: Essai sur la troisième condition de principe de l'acte à double effet* (Rome: Herder, 1981).

Henry, A.M., O.P., ed., *Man and His Happiness*, Volume III, Theology Library (Chicago: Fides Publishers, 1952).

Henry, Carl F.H., *Christian Personal Ethics* (Grand Rapids: Eerdmans, 1957).

Herron, Thomas J., *The Dating of the First Epistle of Clement to the Corinthians: The Theological Basis of the Majoral View* (Rome: Gregorian University, 1988).

Hildebrand, Dietrich von, *In Defense of Purity* (New York: Longmans Green, 1931).

_____, *Jesus and Ethics* (Philadelphia: Westminster Press, 1968).

Hillers, D.H., *Lamentations*, Anchor Bible 7A (Garden City, NY: Doubleday, 1972).

Hilton, Rabbi Michael with Fr. Gordian Marshall, O.P., *The Gospels and*

Rabbinic Judaism: A Study Guide (Hoboken, NJ: KTAV Publishing House/ New York: Anti-Defamation League B'nai Brith, 1988).

Himes, Kenneth, O.F.M. "Scripture and Ethics: A Review Essay," *Biblical Theology Bulletin* 15, 2 (1985), 65-73.

Hinningsen, Gustav and John Tedeschi, eds. in association with Charles Amiel, *The Inquisition in Early Modern Europe: Studies on Sources and Methods* (Dekalb, IL: Northern Illinois University Press, 1986).

Hippolytus, St., *The Apostolic Tradition of Hippolytus*, trans. with introduction and notes by Burton Scott Easton (New York: Archon Books, 1962).

Hollander, H.W., and M. De Jonge, *The Testaments of the Twelve Patriarchs: A Commentary*, with trans. (Leiden: E.J. Brill, 1985).

Hixson, Richard F., *Privacy in Public Policy: Human Rights in Conflict* (New York: Oxford University Press, 1987).

Hoose, Bernard, *Proportionalism: The American Debate and its European Roots* (Washington, DC: Georgetown University Press, 1987).

Houlden, James Leslie, *Ethics and the New Testament* (New York: Oxford University Press, 1982 [1973]).

Howell, David B., *Matthew's Inclusive Story: A Study in the Narrative Rhetoric of the First Gospel*, JSNT, Supplement Series 42 (Sheffield: Sheffield Academic Press, 1990).

Hoyt, Robert, ed., *The Birth Control Debate: Interim History from the Pages of the National Catholic Reporter* (Kansas City, MO: National Catholic Reporter, 1969).

Hughes, Gerald J., "Infallibility in Morals," TS, 34 (1973), 415-28.

Hutchinson, D.H., *The Virtues of Aristotle* (London: Routledge and Kegan Paul/ Methuen, 1986).

Idziak, Janine Marie, *Divine Command Morality: Historical and Contemporary Readings*, Texts and Studies in Religion (New York/Toronto: Edwin Mellen, 1980).

Ignatius of Antioch, St., *The Epistles of St. Clement of Rome and St. Ignatius of Antioch*, trans. and annotated by James A. Kleist, S.J., ACW, vol. 1 (Westminster, MD: Newman Bookshop, 1946); see also *Apostolic Fathers*.

Innocent III, Pope, *On the Misery of the Human Condition* (*De miseria humanae conditionis*), Donald R. Howard, ed, trans. by M.M. Dietz (Indianapolis: Bobbs-Merrill, 1969).

International Theological Commmission, "The Consciousness of Christ Concerning Himself and His Mission," in *International Theological Commission: Texts and Documents, 1969-1985* (San Francisco: Ignatius Press, 1989), pp. 267-304.

International Theological Commission, *Theology, Christology, Anthropology, April, 1983* (Washington, DC: United States Catholic Conference, Publication 893, 1983).

Jacquard, Albert, *In Praise of Difference: Genetics and Human Affairs*, trans. by Margaret M. Moriarty (New York: Columbia University Press, 1984).

Jacquemet, J., "Jésus-Ouvrier," *Catholicisme* 6:810-812.

Jakobvitz, Sir Immanuel, *Jewish Medical Ethics: A Comparative and Historical Study of the Jewish Religious Attitude to Medicine and Its Practice* (New York: Bloch Publishing Co., 1975).

Janssens, Louis, "Ontic Evil and Moral Evil," *Louvain Studies* 4 (Fall, 1972-73), 115-156. Reprinted in Curran and McCormick, *Readings in Moral Theology*, No. 1: *Moral Norms and Catholic Tradition*, pp. 72-73.

Japhet, Sara, *I and II Chronicles*, The Old Testament Library (Louisville: Westminster/John Knox, 1993).

Jarrett, Bede, O.P., *S. Antonino and Medieval Economics* (St. Louis: Herder, 1914).

Jensen, Joseph, "Isaiah 1-23", NJBC, pp. 229-244.

Jeremias, Joachim, *Infant Baptism in the First Four Centuries*, trans. by D. Cairns, Library of History and Doctrine (Philadelphia: Westminster Press, 1962).

————, "The Lord's Prayer in Modern Research," *The Expository Times* 71 (Oct. 1959-Sept. 1960), 141-146.

Jerome,St., *Epistola 66.1 to Pammachius*, PL 22: 325 ff.

————, *Contra Jovinianum*, PL 23: 211-338.

Jervis, L. Ann, " 'But I Want You to Know...': Paul's Midrashic Intertextual Response to the Corinthian Worshippers (1 Cor 11:2-16)," *Journal of Biblical Literature* 112, 2 (Summer 1993), 231-246.

Jewett, Robert, *Paul's Anthropological Terms: A Study of Their Use in Conflict Settings* (Leiden: E.J. Brill, 1971).

John of the Cross, St., *The Ascent of Mt. Carmel, Complete Works*, ed. and trans. by E. Allison Peers (Westminster, MD: Newman Press, 1954), vol. 1, pp. 9-314.

John Paul II, Pope, *Love and Responsibility* (New York: Farrar, Straus, Giroux, 1981).

————, Encyclical, "Rich in Mercy" (*Dives in Misericordia*), 30 November 1980 (AAS 72), 1215-1228.

————, Catechesis, *Original Unity of Man and Woman: Catechesis on the Book of Genesis*, Preface by Donald W. Wuerl (Boston: St. Paul Editions, 1981).

————, Encyclical "On the Dignity of Work" (*Laborem Exercens*), 14 September 1981 (AAS 73), pp. 577-647.

————, Encyclical, "The Christian Family in the Modern World" (*Familaris Consortio*), 22 November 1981 (AAS); Flannery, *Vatican II: More Postconciliar Documents*, n. 122, pp. 815-898.

_____, Encyclical, "The Mother of the Redeemer," *Redemptoris Mater*, March 25, 1987, n. 6 (Washington, DC: United States Catholic Conference, 1987).

_____, "Discourse to the International Congress of Moral Theology," April 10, 1986 in *Persona, Verità et Morale: Atti del Congresso Internazionale di Teologia Morale Rome*, 7-12 April, 1986 (Rome: Cittá Nuova Editrice, 1987), p. 12.

_____, Encyclical, "On The Dignity and Vocation of Woman," (*Mulieris Dignitatem*), August 15, 1988, *Origins* 18, 17 (6 Oct. 1988), 261-283.

_____, Apostolic Exhortation, "Guardian of the Redeemer," Aug. 15, 1989 (Boston: St. Paul Books and Media, 1989).

_____, Address, "The Interpretation of the Bible in the Church," April 23, 1993, *Catholic International* 4 (1993), 301-305 with commentary of J.A. Fitzmyer, S.J., *America*, 27 Nov. (1993), 112-115.

_____, Encyclical "The Splendor of Truth" (*Veritatis Splendor*), August 6, 1993, *Origins* 23 (14 October 1993), 298-236 (Vatican City: Libreria Vaticana, 1993).

_____, "Apostolic Letter on Ordination and Women" (*Ordinatio Pastoralis*), May 22, 1994, *Origins* 24, 4 (9 June 1994), 50-52.

Johnson, Elizabeth A., *She Who Is: The Mystery of God in Feminist Theological Discourse* (New York: Crossroad, 1993).

Johnson, J.T., *Just War Tradition and the Restraint of War: A Moral and Historical Inquiry* (Princeton, NJ: Princeton University Press, 1981).

Johnson, Luke Timothy, *Acts*, Sacra Pagina, Vol. 5 (Collegeville, MN: Michael Glazier/Liturgical Press, 1992).

Jones, David Clyde, *Biblical Christian Ethics* (Grand Rapids: Baker Books, 1994).

Jones, L. Gregory, *Transformed Judgment: Toward a Trinitarian Account of the Moral Life* (Notre Dame, IN: University of Notre Dame Press).

Jones, Helen C. and Paul W. Lovinger: with a Foreword by C. Everett Koop, *The Marijuana Question: And Science's Search for an Answer* (New York: Dodd, Mead, 1985).

Jones, Cheslyn, Geoffrey Wainwright, Edward Yarnold, *The Study of Spirituality* (New York: Oxford University Press, 1986).

Jonsen, Albert A. and Stephen Toulmin, *The Abuse of Casuistry: A History of Moral Reasoning* (Berkeley: University of California Press, 1988).

Jónson, Gunnlauger A., *The Image of God: Genesis 1:26-28 in a Century of Old Testament Research*, Conjectanea Biblica, Old Testament Series, n. 26 (Almqvist and Wiksell International, 1988).

Joranson, Philip N. and Ken Butigan, ed., *Cry of the Environment: Rebuilding the Christian Creation Tradition* (Santa Fe: Bear and Co., 1984).

Joyce, George Hayward, S.J., *Christian Marriage: An Historical and Doctrinal Study* (New York: Sheed and Ward, 1933).

Julianus Pomerius, *The Contemplative Life*, trans. and annotated by Sister M. Josephine Suelzer, ACW, vol. 4 (Westminster, MD: Newman Press, 1947).

Jung, Carl Gustav with M.L. Franz, J.L. Henderson, J. Jacobi, and A. Jaffé, *Man and His Symbols* (Garden City, NY: Doubleday, 1964).

Kaiser, Robert Blair, *The Politics of Sex and Religion: A Case History in the Development of Doctrine, 1962-1984* (Kansas City: Leaven Press, 1985).

Kaiser, Walter C., Jr., *Toward Old Testament Ethics* (Grand Rapids: Zondervan/Academie Books, 1983).

Karlen, Arno, "Homosexuality as a Mental Illness," *International Journal of Psychiatry*, 10 (March 1972), pp. 108-113.

Käsemann, Ernst, *Jesus Means Freedom* (Philadelphia: Fortress Press, 1970).

Kasper, Walter, Bishop, "Ministry in the Church: Taking Issue with Edward Schillebeeckx," *Communio*, Summer, 1983, 185-195.

_____, "Theological Foundation Human Rights," *The Jurist*, 50 (1990), 148-166.

Keane, Philip, S.S., *Christian Ethics and Imagination* (New York: Paulist Press, 1984).

Keck, Leander, "Ethics in the Gospel According to Matthew," *Iliff Review* 41 (1984), 39-56.

Kee, Howard Clark, *Knowing the Truth: A Sociological Approach to New Testament Interpretation* (Minneapolis: Fortress Press, 1989).

Keenan, James F., S.J., "The Casuistry of John Major, Nominalist Professor of Paris (1506-1531)," *Annual Society of Christian Ethics, 1993*, pp. 205-222.

Kelly, J.N.D., *The Epistles of Peter and of Jude* (London, 1969).

Kelsey, David H., *The Uses of Scripture in Recent Theology* (Philadelphia: Fortress Press, 1975).

Kieckhefer, Richard, *European Witch Trials: Their Foundations in Popular and Learned Culture, 1300-1500* (Berkeley: University of California Press, 1976).

Kiely, Bartholomew, "The Impracticality of Proportionalism," *Gregorianum* 66 (1985), 656-666.

Kilner, John F., "A Pauline Approach to Ethical Decision-Making," *Interpretation*, vol. 43 (1989), pp. 366-379.

Kimpel, Benjamin Franklin, *Moral Principles in the Bible: A Study of the Contribution of the Bible to a Moral Philosophy* (New York: Philosophical Library, 1956).

Kippley, John and Sheila, Foreword by Donald A. Prem, M.D., *The Art of*

Family Planning, 3rd ed. (Cincinnati: Couple to Couple League, International, 1985).

Kissinger, Warren S., *The Sermon on the Mount: A History of Interpretation and Bibliography* (Metuchen, NJ: Scarecrow Press and American Theological Library Association, 1975).

Klassen, William, "War in the New Testament," ABD VI:867-875.

Klopenborg, John S., *Q Parallels; Synopsis, Critical Notes and Concordance* (Sonoma, CA: Polebridge Press, 1988).

Kluxen, Wolfgang, "Maimonides and Latin Scholasticism" in Shlomo Pines and Yirmiyahu Yovel, *Maimonides and Philosophy*, pp. 224-232.

Knauer, Peter, S.J., "The Hermeneutic Function of the Principle of Double Effect," *Natural Law Forum* 12 (1967), 140-162.

Knight, Douglas A. "Cosmogony and Order in the Hebrew Tradition," in Lovin and Reynolds, *Cosmogony and Ethical Order*, pp. 133-157.

Knohl, Israel, *The Sanctuary of Silence: The Priestly Torah and the Holiness School* (Minneapolis: Augsburg Fortress, 1994).

Knowles, M.D., O.S.B, *Christian Monasticism* (New York: McGraw-Hill, 1969).

Knox, John, *The Ethics of Jesus in the Teaching of the Church* (Nashville: Abingdon Press, 1961).

Kobleski, Paul J., "The Letter to the Ephesians," NJBC, pp. 883-889.

Koester, Helmut, "*Nomos Physeos*: The Concept of Natural Law in Greek Thought," Jacob Neusner ed., *Religions in Antiquity: Essays in Memory of Erwin Ramsdell Goodenough* (Leiden: E.J. Brill, 1968), pp. 521-541.

Kohansky, Mendel, *The Disreputable Profession: The Actor in Society* (Westport, CT: Greenwood, 1984).

Kohlberg, Lawrence, "Moral Development," *International Encyclopedia of the Social Sciences* (1968) 10:483-494.

Komonchak, Joseph, "Ordinary Papal Magisterium and Religious Assent," in *Contraception, Authority and Dissent* (New York: Herder, 1969).

Kors, Alan C. and Edward Peters, eds., *Witchcraft in Europe 1100-1700: A Documentary History* (Philadelphia: University of Pennsylvania Press, 1972).

Kosnick, Anthony, et al., *Human Sexuality: New Directions in American Catholic Theology, a Study Commissioned by the Catholic Theological Society of America* (Garden City, NY: Doubleday, 1979).

Kraemer, Hendrik, *The Bible and Social Ethics* (Philadelphia: Fortress Press, 1965).

Kraemer, Ross S., Review of Elisabeth Schüssler Fiorenza, *In Memory of Her*, JBL 104 (1985), 722-25.

Kruschwitz, Robert B. and Robert C. Roberts, eds., *The Virtues: Contemporary*

Essays On Moral Character (Belmont, CA: Wadsworth Press, 1987).

Kümmel, W.G., "Luc en accusation dans la theologie contemporaine" in F. Neirynck, ed., *The Gospel of Luke*, pp. 3-19.

Küng, Hans and Jürgen Moltmann, eds., *The Ethics of World Religions and Human Rights* in *Concilium*, 1990/2 (Philadelphia: Trinity Press International/ London: SCM Press, 1990).

Labuschagne, L., *The Incomparability of Yahweh in the Old Testament* (Leiden: E.J. Brill, 1966).

Lagrange, M.-J., *La Morale de l'Évangile: Reflexions sur 'les morales de l'évangile' de M.A. Bayet* (Paris: Bernard Grasset, 1931).

Lamarche, P., *Zacharie IX-XII* (Paris: Études Bibliques, 1961).

Lamb, Michael E., ed., *The Father's Role: Cross-cultural Perspectives* (Hillsdale, NJ: L. Erlbaum Associates, 1987).

Lambden, Stephen N., "From Fig Leaves to Fingernails: Some Notes on the Garments of Adam and Eve in the Hebrew Bible and Select Early Post-Biblical Jewish Writers," in Paul Morris and Deborah Sawyer, *A Walk in the Garden: Biblical, Iconographical, and Literary Images of Eden*, JSOT, Supplement Series 136 (Sheffield: Sheffield Academic Press, 1992), pp. 74-90.

Larcher, C., O.P., *Le Livre de la Sagesse ou La Sagesse de Solomon*, 3 vols. Étude Bibliques, N.S. 3 (Paris: J. Gabalda, 1984).

Laurin, Robert B. ed., *Contemporary Old Testament Theologians* (Valley Forge, PA: Judson Press, 1970), especially the article of N.K. Gottwald, pp. 23-62.

Lawler, Michael G., *Symbol and Sacrament: A Contemporary Sacramental Theology* (New York: Paulist Press, 1987).

Le Guillou, M.G., O.P. "La morale de St. Thomas," *Supplement: Vie spirituel* 17 (1951), 171-184.

Lechowski, J., "Sin (in the Bible)," NCE, 13:226-241.

Lecler, Joseph, *Toleration and the Reformation*, trans. by T.L. Westow (New York: Association Press, 1960).

Leclercq, Jacques, *Christ and the Modern Conscience* (London: G. Chapman, 1962).

Lee, Bernard J., *Galilean Jewishness of Jesus: Retrieving the Jewish Origins of Christianity* (New York: Paulist Press, 1988).

Lee, Patrick, "Permanence of the Ten Commandments: St. Thomas and His Modern Commentators," TS 42 (Sept. 1981), 422-443.

Legrand, Lucien, *The Biblical Doctrine of Virginity* (New York: Sheed and Ward, 1963).

Lehmann, Paul, *Ethics in a Christian Context* (New York: Harper and Row, 1963).

Leith, John H., *John Calvin's Doctrine of the Christian Life*, Foreword by
     Albert C. Outler (Louisville, KY: Westminster/Knox 1989).

Lemeer, P.B.M., O.P., *De Desiderio Naturali ad Visionem Beatificam*,
     Angelicum diss. (Rome: Angelicum, 1948).

Lewis, C.S., *The Four Loves* (New York: Harcourt-Brace-Jovanovich, 1960).

Lewis, W.H., *The Splendid Century* (New York: William Sloan Associates,
     1954).

L'Hour, J., *La moral de l'alliance* (Paris: Gabalda, 1966).

Liebaert, Jacques, *Les enseignments moraux des péres apostoliques*
     (Gembloux: J. Duculot, 1970).

Lienhard, Marc, *Luther's Witness to Christ: Stages and Themes of the
     Reformer's Christology*, trans. by E.H. Robertson (Minneapolis:
     Augsburg, 1982).

Lifton, Robert Jay, *The Nazi Doctors* (New York: Free Press, 1986).

Lillie, William, *Studies in New Testament Ethics* (Edinburgh: Oliver and Boyd,
     1961).

Lindbeck, George, "Scripture, Consensus, and Community," *This World*, Fall
     1988, pp. 5-24.

Little, David and Sumner B. Twiss, *Comparative Religious Ethics: A New
     Method* (San Francisco: Harper and Row, 1978).

Lohfink, Norbert, *Theology of the Pentateuch: Themes of the Priestly Narrative
     and Deuteronomy*, trans. by Linda M. Mahoney (Minneapolis:
     Augsburg Fortress, 1994).

Lohmeyer, Ernst, *"Our Father": An Introduction to the Lord's Prayer* (New
     York: Harper and Row, 1965).

Lohse, E., *A Commentary on the Epistles to the Colossians and to Philemon*,
     Hermeneia Commentaries (Philadelphia: Fortress Press, 1971).

Lonergan, Bernard, S.J., "The Transition from a Classicist World-View to
     Historical-Mindedness," *A Second Collection*, edited by W.F.J.
     Ryan, S.J., and B.J. Tyrell, S.J. (Philadelphia: Westminster Press,
     1974), pp. 1-9.

_____, *Method in Theology* (New York: Herder and Herder, 1972).

Long, LeRoy Edward, Jr., "The Use of the Bible in Christian Ethics," *Interpre-
     tation* 19 (1965), 149-162.

Longenecker, Richard N., *Galatians*, Word Biblical Commentary (Dallas:
     Word Books, 1990).

Lonning, Per, *Creation — An Ecumenical Challenge*. Reflections issuing from
     a study by the Institute for Ecumenical Research, Strasbourg, France
     (Macon, GA: Mercer University Press, 1989).

Lottin, Odon, O.S.B., *Psychologie et Moral au XIIe et XIIIe siècles*, 6 vols.
     (Louvain: Abbaye du Mont Cesar, 1942-60).

_____, "Les dons du S. Esprit chez les theologiens depuis Pierre Lombard usqu'à S. Thomas d'Aquin," t. 4, Pt. 2, n. 2, 329-456.

Lovin, Robert W. and Frank E. Reynolds, *Cosmogony and Ethical Order: New Studies in Comparative Ethics* (Chicago: University of Chicago Press, 1982).

Lubac, Henri de, S.J., *Surnaturel: etudes historiques* (Paris: Aubier, 1946).

_____, *Exégèse mediéval: Les quatre sens de l'écriture* 2 (4) vols. (Paris: Aubier, 1960).

_____, *The Mystery of the Supernatural* (New York: Herder and Herder, 1967).

_____, *A Brief Catechesis on Nature and Grace* (San Francisco: Ignatius Press, 1980).

Luz, Ulrich, *Matthew 1-7: A Commentary*, trans. by Wilhelm C. Linss (Minneapolis: Augsburg, 1989).

Lynn, David B., *The Father: His Role in Child Development* (Monterey, CA: Brooks/Co. Publishing Co., 1974).

Lyonnet, S., "Sin." in *Theological Dictionary of the Bible*, ed. X. Léon-Dufour, rev. ed. (New York: Seabury Press, 1973), pp. 50-55.

Machan, Tibor R., ed., *The Libertarian Reader* (Totowa, NJ: Rowman and Littlefield, 1982).

MacIntyre, Alasdair, *After Virtue: A Study in Moral Theory* (Notre Dame, IN: University of Notre Dame Press, 1981).

_____, *Whose Justice? Whose Rationality?* (Notre Dame, IN: University of Notre Dame Press, 1987).

_____, *Three Rival Versions of Moral Inquiry*, Gifford Lectures, 1988 (Notre Dame, IN: University of Notre Dame Press, 1990).

Mackin, Theodore, S.J., *The Marital Sacrament* (New York: Paulist Press, 1989).

MacNamara, Vincent, *Faith and Ethics: Recent Roman Catholicism* (Washington, DC: Georgetown University Press, 1985).

_____, "The Use of the Bible in Moral Theology," *Month* 29 (March 1987), 104-107.

Maestro, Marcello T., *Cesare Beccaria and the Origins of Penal Reform*, Foreword by Norval Morris (Philadelphia: Temple University Press, 1973).

Mahoney, John, S.J., *The Making of Moral Theology: A Study of the Roman Catholic Tradition* (New York: Oxford University Press, 1986).

Maimonides, *The Guide for the Perplexed*, trans. by M. Friedlander (London: George Routledge and Sons/ New York: E.P. Dutton and Sons, 2nd rev. ed., 1947).

_____, *The Commandments*, trans. by Rabbi Dr. Charles B. Chavel

(London/NewYork: The Soncino Press, 1967): Vol. 1: *The Positive Commandments*, Vol. 2: *The Negative Commandments*.

Malherbe, Abraham J., *Social Aspects of Early Christianity*, 2nd ed. (Philadelphia: Fortress Press, 1983).

Malina, Bruce J., *The New Testament World: Insights from Cultural Anthropology* (Atlanta: John Knox Press, 1981).

Maly, Eugene H., "Celibacy," *The Bible Today*, 34 (Feb. 1968), 2392-2400.

_____, *Sin: Biblical Perspectives* (Dayton: Pflaum Press, 1973).

Manson, T.W., *Ethics and the Gospel* (New York: Charles Scribner's Sons, 1960).

Marcus, David, *Jephthah and His Vow* (Lubbock, TX: Texas Tech Press, 1986).

Maritain, Jacques, "The Purification of Means," and "The Doctrine of Satyagraha as Set Forth by M.K. Gandhi," *Freedom in the Modern World* (New York: Charles Scribner's Sons, 1936) pp. 139-192 and 215-223.

_____, *The Person and the Common Good* (New York: Charles Scribner's Sons, 1947).

_____, *Moral Philosophy: An Historical and Critical Survey of the Great Systems* (New York: Scribner, 1964).

Marshall, I.H., *The Gospel of Luke: A Commentary on the Greek Text*, New International Greek Text Commentary (Grand Rapids: Eerdmans, 1978).

_____, *The Acts of the Apostles*, Tyndale New Testament Commentaries (Grand Rapids: Eerdmans, 1980).

Marshall, Jay W., *Israel and the Book of the Covenant: An Anthropological Approach to Biblical Law*, Society of Biblical Literature, dissertation Series, n. 140 (Atlanta: 1993).

Marshall, Laurence Henry, *The Challenge of New Testament Ethics* (London: Macmillan, 1964).

Martimort, Aimé Georges, *The Signs of the New Covenant* (Collegeville, MN: Liturgical Press, Revised Second Edition, 1968).

Martin, Brice L., *Christ and the Law in Paul* (Leiden: E.J. Brill, 1989).

Martin, Charles, S.J., Review of Christian Cochini, S.J., *Origines apostoliques du celibat sacerdotal*, 1980, *Nouvelle Revue Theologique*, 105 (1983), 437-438.

_____, Review of R. Cholij, *Clerical Celibacy* in *Nouvelle Revue Theologique*, 105 (1983), 437-438.

Martin, Francis, *The Feminist Question: Feminist Theology in the Light of Christian Tradition* (Grand Rapids: Eerdmans, 1994).

Martin, George, ed., *Scripture and the Charismatic Renewal* (Ann Arbor, MI: Servant, 1979).

Martin, R.P., *2 Corinthians*, Word Bible Commentary (Waco, TX: Word
    Books, 1986).

Martin-Achard, Robert, "Théologie de l'"Ancien Testament et Confessions de
    Foi," *Revue de Théologie et Philosophie*, 117 (1985), 81-91.

Mason, R., *The Books of Haggai, Zechariah, and Malachi*, Cambridge Biblical
    Commentary (Cambridge University Press, 1977).

Matera, Frank J., *Galatians*, Sacra Pagina, vol. 9 (Collegeville, MN: Michael
    Glazier/Liturgical Press, 1992).

Maxwell, William D., *The Liturgical Portions of the Genevan Service Book
    Used by John Knox While a Minister of the English Congregation of
    the Marian Exiles at Geneva 1556-1559* (London: The Faith Press,
    1931, 1965).

May, Gerald G., *Addiction and Grace* (San Francisco: Harper and Row, 1988).

May, William E., *Becoming Human* (Dayton: Pflaum Publishing Co., 1975).

_____, *The Nature and Meaning of Chastity* (Chicago: Franciscan Herald
    Press, 1976).

_____, *Moral Absolutes: Catholic Tradition, Current Trends, and the
    Truth*, Marquette Lecture, 1989 (Milwaukee: Marquette University
    Press, 1989).

_____, *An Introduction to Moral Theology* (Huntington, IN: Our Sunday
    Visitor, 1991) includes, "Natural Law in the Thought of Germain
    Grisez, John Finnis, and Joseph Boyle," pp. 59-81.

_____, "Marriage and the Complementarity of Male and Female,"
    Anthropotes, 8 (1 June 1992), 41-60.

May, William E., with John F. Harvey, *On Understanding Human Sexuality*
    (Chicago: Franciscan Herald Press, 1976).

May, William W., ed., *Vatican Authority and American Catholic Dissent: The
    Curran Case and Its Consequences* (New York: Crossroad, 1987).

Mazza, Enrico, *Mystagogy* (New York: Pueblo Publishing Co., 1989).

McCarter, P.K., Jr., *I and II Samuel*, Anchor Bible (Garden City, NY:
    Doubleday, 1980-1984).

McCarthy, John J., M.D., Mary Catherine Martin, M.S.N., Ph.D. and Marjorie
    Gildehorn, M.A., *The Ovulation Method* (Washington, DC: The
    Human Life and Natural Family Planning Foundation, 1978).

McConville, J. G., *Law and Theology in Deuteronomy. Journal for the Study of
    the Old Testament*, Supplement Series 33 (Sheffield: JSOT Press,
    1984).

McCormick, Richard A., S.J., *Ambiguity in Moral Choice* (Milwaukee:
    Marquette University, 1973).

_____, *Notes on Moral Theology: 1965-1980* (Washington, DC: University
    Press of America, 1981).

_____, *Notes on Moral Theology: 1981-1984* (Washington, DC: University
    Press of America, 1984).

_____, "Moral Theology 1940-1989: An Overview," TS 50 (1989), 3-24.

McCormick, Richard A., S.J., and Paul Ramsey, eds., *Doing Evil to Achieve Good: Moral Choice in Conflict Situations* (Chicago: Loyola University Press, 1978).

McCreesh, T.P., O.P., "Wisdom as Wife: Proverbs 31:10-31," *Revue Biblique*, 92 (1985), 25-46.

McDonough, Enda, *Gift and Call: Towards a Christian Theology of Morality* (St. Meinrad, IN.: Abbey Press, 1975).

McDowell, Banks, *Ethical Conduct and the Professional's Dilemma: Choosing between Service and Success* (New York: Quorum Books, 1991).

McInerny, Ralph, "The Case for Natural Law," *Modern Age*, Spring 1982: 168-174.

_____, *Ethica Thomistica: The Moral Philosophy of Thomas Aquinas* (Washington, DC: Catholic University of America Press, 1982).

McKane, William, *Proverbs: A New Approach*, The Old Testament Library Commentaries (Philadelphia: Westminster Press, 1970).

McKee, L. and M. O'Brien, eds., *The Father Figure* (London/New York: Tavistock Publications, 1983).

McKenzie, John L., S.J., "Shepherd," pp. 902-904; "Virgin," p. 944, *Dictionary of the Bible* (Milwaukee: Bruce, 1965).

_____, *A Theology of the Old Testament* (Garden City, NY: Doubleday, 1974).

McMahon, Kevin Thomas, *Sexuality: Theological Voices* (Braintree, MA: Pope John Center, 1987).

McNeill, John T. and Helena M. Gamer, *Medieval Handbooks of Penance: A Translation of the Principle 'Libri Penitentiales'* (New York: Columbia University Press, 1938, 1990).

McSorley, Harry J., *Luther: Right or Wrong?* (New York: Newman Press, 1969).

Meade, David G. *Pseudonymity and Canon: An Investigation into the Relationship of Authorship and Authority in Jewish and Earliest Christian Tradition* (Grand Rapids: Eerdmans, 1986).

Mealand, David L., *Poverty and Expectation in the Gospels* (London: SPCK, 1980).

Meeks, Wayne A., "The Polyphonic Ethics of the Apostle Paul," *The Annual of the Society of Christian Ethics*, 1988, pp. 17-29.

_____, *The First Urban Christians: The Social World of the Apostle Paul* (New Haven: Yale University Press, 1983).

_____, *The Moral World of the First Christians* (Philadelphia: Westminster Press, 1986).

_____, *The Origins of Christian Morality: The First Two Centuries* (New Haven: Yale University Press, 1993).

_____, " 'To Walk Worthily of the Lord': Moral Formation in the Pauline

School Exemplified by the Letter to the Colossians," in *Hermes and Athena: Biblical Exegesis and Philosophical Theology*, edited by Eleonore Stump and Thomas P. Flint (Notre Dame, IN: University of Notre Dame Press, 1993), pp. 37-58, with comments "Moral Authority and Pseudonymity" by Eleonore Stump, and Meek's response, pp. 59-76.

Meer, Haye van der, *Women Priests in the Catholic Church: A Theological-Historical Investigation*, trans. by Arlene and Leonard Swidler (Philadelphia: Temple University Press, 1973).

Meier, John P., *A Marginal Jew: Rethinking the Historical Jesus*, 2 vols., The Anchor Bible Reference Library (Garden City, NY: Doubleday, 1991-1994).

Meilaender, Gilbert C., *Theory and Practice of Virtue* (Notre Dame, IN: University of Notre Dame Press, 1984).

Merkelbach, Benedict H., O.P., *Summa Theologiae Moralis ad mentem D. Thomae et ad normam juris novi*, 3rd rev. ed., 3 vols. (Paris: Desclée de Brouwer, 1938).

Messner, Johannes, *Social Ethics: Natural Law in the Western World* (St. Louis: Herder, 1965).

Metz, J.B. and J.P. Jossua, *Theology of Joy*, in *Concilium* (New York: Herder and Herder, 1974).

Meyer, Charles, *A Contemporary Theology of Grace* (Staten Island, NY: Alba House, 1971).

Meyer, Roger, *Psychopathology and Addictive Disorders* (New York: Guilford Press, 1986).

Michel, A., "Surnaturel," DTC, vol. 14, pt. 2: 2854-59.

Miguens, Manuel, O.F.M., "On Being a Christian and the Moral Life: Pauline Perspectives" in William E. May, *Principles of Catholic Moral Life* (Chicago: Franciscan Herald Press, 1981), pp. 89-110.

Miletic, Stephen F., *"One Flesh" (Eph 5:22-24; 5:31): Marriage and the New Creation*, Analecta Biblica (Rome: Biblical Institute Press, 1988).

Milgrom, Jacob, "Priestly 'P' Source," ABD, vol. 5: 454-461.

_____, *Numbers [Ba-midbar]*: The traditional Hebrew Text with the New JPS Translation/ commentary by Jacob Milgrom (Philadelphia: Jewish Publication Society, 1990).

Millard, A.R. and D.J. Wiseman, eds., *Essays on the Patriarchal Narratives* (Winona Lake, IN: Eisenbrauns/ Inter-Varsity Press, 1983).

Miller, John W., *Biblical Faith and Fathering: Why We Call God "Father"* (New York: Paulist Press, 1989).

Miller, J. Michael, C.S.B., *What Are They Saying About Papal Primacy?* (New York/Ramsey: Paulist Press, 1983).

Milner, Henry, *Sweden: Social Democracy in Practice* (New York: Oxford University Press, 1989).

Minear, Paul S., *Commands of Christ: Authority and Implications* (Nashville: Abingdon Press, 1972).

Miranda, José P., *Marx and the Bible* (Maryknoll, NY: Orbis Books, 1974).

Mitcherlich, Margarete, M.D., trans. by C. Tomlinson, *The Peaceable Sex: On Aggression in Women and Men* (New York: Fromm International Publishing Corp., 1987).

Moberly, Elizabeth R., M.D., *Homosexuality: A New Christian Ethic* (Greenwood, SC: Attic Press, n.d.).

_____, "Counseling the Homosexual," *The Expository Times*, June, 1985, pp. 261-266.

Moberly, R.W.L., *The Old Testament of the Old Testament* (Minneapolis: Fortress Press, 1992).

Molien, A., "Loi" and "Loi naturelle," in DTC, vol. 9, pt. 1, cols. 871-910.

Moll, Helmut, *The Church and Women: A Compendium* (San Francisco: Ignatius Press, 1988).

Moll, Willi, *Father and Fatherhood*, trans. by E. Reinecke and P.C. Bailey (Notre Dame, IN: Fides, 1966).

Moltmann, Elizabeth Wendel, *A Land Flowing with Milk and Honey: A Perspective on Feminist Theology* (New York: Crossroad, 1986), Chapter 2, "What is Patriarchy?" pp. 29-41.

Moltmann, Jürgen, *Theology of Hope: On the Ground and the Implications of Christian Eschatology*, trans. by J.W. Leitch (New York: Harper and Row, 1967).

_____, *Theology of Play*, trans. by Reinhard Ulrich (San Francisco: Harper and Row, 1972).

Montague, George T., S.M., *Maturing in Christ* (Milwaukee: Bruce Publishing Co., 1964).

_____, *Our Father, Our Mother* (Steubenville, OH: Franciscan University Press, 1990).

Monter, William, *Frontiers of Heresy: The Spanish Inquisition from the Basque Lands to Sicily* (New York: Cambridge University Press, 1990).

Moor, Douglas J., "The Law of Moses or the Law of Christ," *Continuity and Discontinuity: Perspectives on the Relationship between the Old and New Testaments*, ed. by John S. Feinberg (Wheaton, IL: Crossway, 1988), pp. 203-218.

Most, William G., *The Consciousness of Christ* (Front Royal, VA: Christendom College Press, 1980).

Mott, Stephen Charles, *Biblical Ethics and Social Change* (New York: Oxford University Press, 1982).

Moule, C.F.D., "Prologomena: The New Testament and Moral Decisions," *Expository Times*, 74, pp. 370-373.

Mouw, Richard J., *The God Who Commands* (Notre Dame, IN: University of Notre Dame Press, 1990).

Muilenburg, James, *The Way of Israel: Biblical Faith and Ethics* (Philadelphia: Fortress Press, 1982).

Mulhern, Philip F., O.P., *Dedicated Poverty: Its History and Theology* (Staten Island, NY: Alba House, 1973).

Mullady, Brian Thomas, O.P., *The Meaning of the Term "Moral" in St. Thomas Aquinas*, Studi Tomistici n. 27, Pontificia Accademia di S. Tommaso (Rome: Libreria Editrice Vaticana, 1986).

Murphy, Francis X., C.SS.R., *Moral Teaching in the Primitive Church* (Glen Rock, NJ: Paulist Press, 1968).

Murphy, Roland E., O. Carm., "Wisdom," ABD, pp. 920-931.

_____, "The Canticle of Canticles," NJBC, pp. 462-465.

Murphy-O'Connor, Jerome, O.P., *Becoming Human Together: The Pastoral Anthropology of St. Paul*, 2nd rev. ed. (Collegeville, MN: Liturgical Press, 1982).

_____, "Sin and Community in the New Testament." in *The Mystery of Sin and Forgiveness*, ed. Michael Taylor (Staten Island, NY: Alba House, 1971).

Murray, John Courtney, S.J., *We Hold These Truths* (New York: Sheed and Ward, 1960).

Myers, J., *1 Chronicles, 2 Chronicles*, and *Ezra-Nehemiah*, Anchor Bible, 12-14 (Garden City, NY: Doubleday, 1965).

National Conference of Catholic Bishops, "Principles to Guide Confessors in Questions of Homosexuality" (Washington, DC: NCCB, 1973).

Neirynck, F., ed., *L'Evangile de Luc/ The Gospel of Luke*, rev. and enlarged ed. (Leuven: Leuven University Press, 1989).

Nellas, Panagiotis, *Deification in Christ: Orthodox Perspective on the Nature of the Human Person*, trans. by Norman Russell, with a foreword by Bishop Kallistos of Diokleia (Crestwood, NY: St. Vladimir's Seminary Press, 1987).

Neuhaus, Richard John, gen. ed., *Biblical Interpretation in Crisis: The Ratzinger Conference on Bible and Church*, Encounter Series (Grand Rapids: Eerdmans, 1989).

Neusner, Jacob, *The Rabbinic Traditions About the Pharisees Before 70*: Part I, *The Masters* (Leiden: E.J. Brill, 1971).

_____, *Introduction to the Talmud* (New York: Harper and Row, 1984).

_____, *Torah Through the Ages: A Short History of Judaism* (London: SCM Press/Philadelphia: Trinity Press International, 1990).

Nicolas, J.-H., O.P., *Les profondeurs de la grace* (Paris: Beauchesne, 1968).

Nicolosi, Joseph, *Reparative Therapy of Male Homosexuality: A New Clinical Approach* (Northvale, NJ: Jason Aronson, Inc., 1991).

Niebuhr, H. Richard, *Christ and Culture* (New York: Harper and Row, 1951).

_____, *The Responsible Self* (New York: Harper and Row, 1963).

Niebuhr, Reinhold, *An Interpretation of Christian Ethics* (New York: Harper, 1935).

_____, *Man's Nature and His Communities* (New York: Charles Scribner's Sons, 1978).

Nielsen, E., *The Ten Commandments in New Perspective* (Naperville, IL: Allenson, 1968).

Nielsen, W., *The Theology of Calvin*, trans. by H. Knight (Philadelphia: Westminster Press, 1956).

Nineham, D.E., *The Gospel of St. Mark*, Pelican Gospel Commentaries (New York: Seabury Press, 1968).

Nitsch, Thomas O, Joseph M. Phillips, Jr., and Edward L. Fitzsimmons, *On the Condition of Labor and the Social Question One Hundred Years Later*, Commemorating the 100th Anniversary of *Rerum Novarum*, and the Fiftieth Anniversary of the Association of Social Economics (Lewiston/Queenston/Lampeter, Canada: The Edwin Mellen Press, 1994).

Noah, M., *The Deuternomistic History*, JSOT Supplement (Sheffield: 1981).

Noonan, John T., Jr., *The Scholastic Analysis of Usury* (Cambridge, MA: Harvard University Press, 1957).

_____, "An Almost Absolute Value in History," John T. Noonan, Jr., ed., *The Morality of Abortion: Legal and Historical Perspectives* (Cambridge, MA: Harvard University Press, 1970), pp. 1-59.

_____, *Bribes* (New York: Macmillan, 1984).

_____, *Contraception: A History of its Treatment by the Catholic Theologians and Canonists*. Enlarged Edition (Cambridge, MA: Belknap Press of Harvard University Press, 1986).

North, C.R., *The Suffering Servant in Deutero-Isaiah*, 2nd ed. (London, 1956).

North, Helen F., "Canons and Hierarchies of the Cardinal Virtues in Greek and Latin Literature," in *The Classical Tradition: Literary and Historical Studies in Honor of Henry Caplan* (Ithaca, NY: Cornell University Press, 1966), pp. 165-183.

Novatian, *The Trinity. The Spectacles. Jewish Foods. In Praise of Purity. Letters*, trans. by Russell J. DaSimone, FC, v. 67 (Washington: Catholic University of America Press, 1974).

Nygren, Anders, *Agape and Eros*, trans. by Philip S. Watson (New York: Harper and Row, 1969).

_____, "Love," *The Encyclopedia of the Lutheran Church*, ed. J. Bodensec (Minneapolis: Augsburg Publishing House, 1965), vol. 2, 1345-1347.

O'Brien, William, *The Conduct of Just and Limited War* (New York: Praeger, 1981).

O'Collins, Gerald, S.J., *Jesus Risen: An Historical, Fundamental, and Systematic Examination of Christ's Resurrection* (New York: Paulist Press, 1987).

_____, *Interpreting the Resurrection: Examining the Major Problems in the Stories of Jesus' Resurrection* (New York: Paulist Press, 1988).

O'Connell, Matthew, "Commandment in the Old Testament," TS 21 (1960), 351-403.

O'Connell, Timothy, *Changing Roman Catholic Moral Theology: A Study in Josef Fuchs* (Ann Arbor, MI: University Microfilms, 1974).

_____, *Principles for a Catholic Morality*, rev. ed. (San Francisco: Harper and Row/Crossroad, 1990).

O'Connor, James, *The Gift of Infallibility* (Boston: St. Paul Editions, 1986).

O'Day, Gail R., "The Ethical Shape of Pauline Spirituality," *Brethren Life and Thought*, 32 (Spring, 1987) 81-92.

O'Donnell, John, S.J., *Hans Urs von Balthasar* (Collegeville, MN: Liturgical Press/Michael Glazier, 1992).

O'Donohoe, James, "Toward a Theology of Sin," *Church*, Spring 1986, 48-54.

_____, "The Use of Virtue and Character in Applied Ethics," *Horizons* 17 (1990) 228-43.

O'Donovan, Oliver, *Resurrection and Moral Order: An Outline for Evangelical Ethics* (Grand Rapids: Eerdmans, 1986).

O'Toole, Robert F., S.J., *Who is a Christian? A Study in Pauline Ethics* (Collegeville, MN: Liturgical Press/ Michael Glazier, 1990).

Oberman, Heiko, *The Harvest of Medieval Theology: Gabriel Biel and Late Medieval Nominalism* (Cambridge: Cambridge University Press, 1963).

Ogletree, Thomas W., *The Use of the Bible in Christian Ethics: A Constructive Essay* (Philadelphia: Fortress Press, 1983).

Olivier, B., O.P., "Pour une théologie morale renouvelée," *Moral chrétienne et requêtes contemporaines* (Paris, 1954), pp. 219-255.

Olson, Carol, *The Book of the Goddess* (New York: Crossroad, 1983).

Olson, Denis T., *Deuteronomy and the Death of Moses: A Theological Reading* (Minneapolis: Augsburg Fortress Press, 1994).

Orford, Jim, *Excessive Appetites: A Psychological View of Addictions* (Chichester, NY: Wiley, 1985).

Origen, trans. by Rowan A. Greer, Classics of Western Spirituality (New York: Paulist Press, 1979), pp. 81-170; PG 11, 425-562.

Orsy, Ladislas M., S.J., "Magisterium: Assent and Dissent," TS 8 (1987) 473-497.

_____, *The Church Learning and Teaching: Magisterium, Assent, Dissent, Academic Freedom* (Wilmington, DE: Michael Glazier, 1987).

Osborn, Eric F., *Ethical Patterns in Early Christian Thought* (Cambridge: Cambridge University Press, 1976).

Otto, Rudolf, *The Idea of the Holy* (London: Oxford University Press, 2nd ed., 1950).

Ouelett, Marc, "The Foundations of Christian Ethics According to Hans Urs von Balthasar," *Communio* 17 (Fall, 1990), 379-401.

Outka, Gene, *Agape: An Ethical Analysis* (New Haven: Yale University Press, 1972).

Owens, Thomas J., "Scheler's 'Emotive' Ethics," *Cross Currents*, Spring, 1966, 144-152.

Oxford Dictionary of the Bible, The, ed. by F.L. Cross (London/New York: Oxford University Press, 1974).

Palladius, *Lausiac History* (Westminster, MD: Newman, 1965).

Parke-Baylor, G.H., *Yahweh: The Divine Name in the Bible* (Waterloo, Canada: Wilfrid Laurier University Press, 1975).

Paschius Radbertus, *De Fide, Spe, et Caritate*, Corpus Christianorum: Continuatio Mediaevalis, xcvii, ed. Bede Paulus, O.S.B. (Turnholt: Brepols, 1990).

Paul VI, Pope, Encyclical "On Priestly Celibacy" (*Sacerdotalis caelibatus*), 24 June 1967 (AAS, 59 (1967), pp. 657-697), Flannery, n. 95, pp. 285-317.

_____, Encyclical "On the Regulation of Births" (*Humanae Vitae*) AAS 60 (1968) 490 ff., Flannery, n. 102, pp. 397-416.

Pawlikowski, John, *What Are They Saying About Christian-Jewish Relations* (New York: Paulist Press, 1990).

Pazdan, Mary Margaret, O.P., *The Son of Man: A Metaphor for Jesus in the Fourth Gospel* (Collegeville: Michael Glazier/Liturgical Press, 1991).

Perkins, Pheme, *Love Commands in the New Testament* (New York: Paulist Press, 1982).

_____, "Paul and Ethics," *Interpretation* 38 (July 1984), 268-280.

_____, "New Testament Ethics: Questions and Contexts," *Religious Studies Review* 10 (Oct. 1984), 321-327.

Peter, Carl J., "Original Justice," and "Original Sin" in NCE 10, 774-801.

Peter Lombard, *Sententia in IV Libris*, 3rd ed., 2 vols. (Rome, Grottoferata: Collegio de St. Bonaventura ad Claras Aquas, 1916).

Peters, Edward, *Torture* (New York: Basil Blackwell, 1985).

Petit, Francois, "La decadence de la morale, jalons d'histoire." Supplement: *Vie Spirituel* 17 (1951), 556-564.

Phan, Peter C., *Social Thought: Message of the Fathers of the Church* (Collegeville, MN: Liturgical Press, 1984).

Philibert, Paul, O.P., "Lawrence Kohlberg's Use of Virtue in His Theory of Moral Development," *International Philosophical Quarterly* 15 (1975), 455-479.

Phillips, Kevin, *The Politics of Rich and Poor* (New York: Random House, 1990).

Philo Judaeus, *Works*, ed. with trans. by F.H. Colson, Loeb Library (Cambridge, MA: Harvard University Press, 1966).

Phipps, William, *Was Jesus Married?* (New York: Harper and Row, 1970).

Pieper, Josef, *Happiness and Contemplation*, trans. by Richard and Clara Winston (New York: Pantheon, 1958).

_____, *Leisure, the Basis of Culture*, trans. by Alexander Dru, with an introduction by T.S. Eliot (New York: New American Library, 1963).

_____, *The Four Cardinal Virtues* (Notre Dame, IN: University of Notre Dame Press, 1966).

_____, *About Love* (Chicago: Franciscan Herald Press, 1974).

_____, *On Hope*, trans. by Mary Francis McCarthy (San Francisco: Ignatius Press, 1986).

Pierce, C.A., *Conscience in the New Testament* (London: SCM Press, 1955).

Pinckaers, S., O.P., "La morale de St. Thomas: est-elle Chrétienne?" *Nova et Vetera* 1976:93-107.

_____, "La question des acts intrinsèquement mauvais et le 'proportionalisme,' *Revue Thomiste* 84 (Dec. 1984), 618-624.

_____, *TheSources of Christian Ethics*, trans. by Sister Mary Thomas Noble, O.P. (Washington, DC: Catholic University of America Press, 1995).

Pinckaers, Servais (Th.) and Pinto de Oliveira, Carlos Josaphat, eds., *Universalité et permanence des lois morales* (Fribourg Suisse: Editions Universitaires/Paris: Editions du Cerf, 1986).

Pines, Shlomo and Yirmiyahu Yovel, eds., *Maimonides and Philosophy*, Papers presented at the Sixth Jerusalem Philosophical Encounter, May 1985 (Dodrecht/Boston/Lancaster: Martin Nijhoff, 1986).

Pinto de Oliveira, Carlos-Josaphat, O.P., ed. *Novitas et Veritas Vitae: Aux Sources du Renouveau de La Morale Chretienne*, Études d'ethique chrétienne (Paris: Editions du Cerf, 1991).

Piper, John, *"Love Your Enemies," Jesus' Love Command in the Synoptic Gospels: A History of Tradition and Interpretation of Its Uses* (Cambridge: Cambridge University Press, 1979).

Pius XII, Pope, "Radio Message on Rightly Forming Conscience in Christian Youth," March 23, 1952, *Acta Apostolicae Sedis* 44 (1952) 27.

_____, Encyclical, *Sacra virginitas*, March 15, 1954, n. 32, Claudia Carlen, *The Papal Encyclicals, 1939-1958* (New York: McGrath Publishing Co., 1981), p. 244.

Placher, William C., *A History of Christian Theology: An Introduction* (Philadelphia: Westminster Press, 1983).

Plato, *Republic*, trans. and with Introduction by H.D.P. Lee (Harmondsworth, England: Penguin Classics).

Plaut, W. Gunter, *Book of Proverbs: A Commentary* (New York: Union of American Hebrew Congregations, 1961).

Plé, Albert, O.P., *Duty or Pleasure: A New Appraisal of Christian Ethics* (New York: Paragon House Publishers, 1987).

_____, *"De Ordine Caritatis*: Charity, Friendship and Justice in Aquinas' *Summa Theologiae*," TH 53 (1989) 124-54.

Plevnik, Joseph, S.J., *What Are They Saying About Paul?* (New York: Paulist Press, 1986).

Poddimatam, Felix M., O.F.M. Cap., *Fundamental Option and Mortal Sin* (Bangladore: Asian Trading Corporation, 1986).

Polycarp of Smyrna, St., *The Epistles and the Martyrdom of St. Polycarp, The Didache, the Epistle of Barnabas, the Fragments of Papias, and the Epistle to Diognetus*, trans. by James A. Kleist, S.J., ACW, vol. 6 (Westminster, MD: Newman Press, 1948); see also *Apostolic Fathers.*

Pontifical Biblical Commission (with a foreword of recommendation by Cardinal Joseph Ratzinger), "The Interpretation of the Bible in the Church," *Origins*, 23, n. 29 (Jan. 6, 1994), 499-524.

Pool, Robert, *Eve's Rib: The Biological Roots of Sex Differences* (New York: Crown Publishers, 1994).

Pope, Marvin, *The Song of Songs*, Anchor Bible 7C (Garden City, NY: Doubleday, 1977).

Portalié, Eugène, S.J., *A Guide to the Thought of St. Augustine* (Chicago: Regnery, 1960).

Porter, Jean, "Desire for God: Ground of the Moral Life in Aquinas," TS, 47 (March 1986) 48-68.

_____, *The Recovery of Virtue: The Relevance of Aquinas for Christian Ethics* (Louisville: Westminster/John Knox Press, 1990).

Potterie, Ignace de la, S.J., "'Mari d'une seule femme;' Le sens théologique d'une formule paulinienne" in *Paul de Tarse: Apôtre du Notre Temps* (Rome: Abbaye de S. Paul, 1979), 619-638.

Prickett, Stephen, *Words and the Word: Language, Poetics and Biblical Interpretation* (Cambridge: Cambridge University Press, 1986).

Primavesi, Ann, *From Apocalypse to Genesis: Ecology, Feminism and Christianity* (Tunbridge Wells, England, 1991). Answered by D. J. Hall, "The Integrity of Creation: Biblical and Theological Background of the Term" in *Reintegrating God's Creation* (Geneva, 1987).

Quay, Paul M., S.J., *The Christian Meaning of Human Sexuality* (Evanston, IL: A Credo House Book, 1985).

Quell, G. et al., "Harmantano" in *Theological Dictionary of the Bible*, ed. G. Kittel, trans. by G. Bromley (Grand Rapids: Eerdmans, 1969), vol. 1, pp. 267-316.

Quesnell, Quentin, "Made Themselves Eunuchs for the Kingdom of Heaven (Mt 19:12)," *Catholic Biblical Quarterly*, 30 (July, 1968), 335-358.

Quinn, Jerome D., "Celibacy and the Ministry in Scripture," *The Bible Today*, 46 (Feb. 1970), 3163-3175.

_____, *Letter to Titus*, with notes, translation commentary, and an introduction to the *Pastoral Epistles*, Anchor Bible (Garden City, NY: Doubleday, 1990).

Rad, Gerhard von, *Deuteronomy*, Old Testament Library (Philadelphia: Westminster Press, 1966).

_____, *Old Testament Theology*, trans. by D.M.G. Stalker, 2 vols. (New York: Harper, 1962-1965).

_____, *Wisdom in Israel* (Nashville, TN: Abingdon Press, 1972).

Rahner, Karl, S.J., "On the Question of a Formal Existential Ethics," *Theological Investigations* (Baltimore: Helicon Press, 1963), vol. 2, pp. 217-234;

_____, "Dogmatic Reflections on the Knowledge and Self-Consciousness of Christ," *ibid.*, vol. 5, pp. 193-215.

_____, "The 'Commandment' of Love in Relation to the other Commandments," *ibid.*, vol. 5, pp. 445-51.

_____, "Original Sin," *Encyclopedia of Theology*, edited by Rahner (New York: Seabury Press, 1975), pp. 1148-1155.

_____, *Foundations of Christian Faith*, trans. William V. Dych (New York: Seabury Press, 1978).

Rambaux, Claude, *Tertullien face aux morales des trois premiers siécles* (Paris: Societé d'Edition 'Les Belles Lettres,' 1979). Conclusion, pp. 408-410.

Ramsey, Ian, "Toward a Rehabilitation of Natural Law," in *Christian Ethics and Contemporary Philosophy* (London: SCM, 1966), pp. 382-396.

Ramsey, Paul, *Basic Christian Ethics* (New York: Charles Scribner's Sons, 1950).

_____, *Deeds and Rules in Christian Ethics* (New York: Charles Scribner's Sons, 1967).

Rasmussen, Albert Terrill, *Christian Ethics: Exerting Christian Influence* (Englewood Cliffs, NJ: Prentice-Hall, 1956).

Ratzinger, Cardinal Joseph, "Sources of Moral Theology: Keynote Address at a Workshop for 250 Bishops," and "Sources of Moral Theology: Closing Address," *The Priest* (September 1984), 10-18 and 19-30.

_____, "Bishops, Theologians and Morality," *Origins* 13, 40 (1984), 658-666.

_____, "Dissent and Proportionalism," *Origins* 13:0 (1984), 666-669.

_____, *Death and Eternal Life*, trans. by Michael Waldstein, ed. by Aidan Nichols, O.P., *Dogmatic Theology*, ed. by Johann Auer, no. 9 (Washington, DC: Catholic University of America Press, 1988).

_____, "Biblical Interpretation in Crisis: On the Question of the Foundations and Approaches of Exegesis Today," in Richard John Neuhaus, ed., *Biblical Interpretation in Crisis: The Ratzinger Conference on Bible and Church*, Encounter Series (Grand Rapids: Eerdmans, 1989), pp. 1-23.

_____, "Reconciling Gospel and Torah: The Catechism," *Origins*, 23 (Feb. 24, 1994) 621, 623-628, n. 2, 624-5.

Rawls, John, *A Theory of Justice* (Cambridge, MA: Harvard University, Belknap Press, 1971).

Rees, D.A., "The Ethics of Divine Commands," *Proceedings of the Aristotelian Society*, New series 57 (1956-57).

Reese, Thomas J., S.J., *Archbishop: Inside the Power Structure of the American Catholic Church* (San Francisco: Harper and Row, 1989).

_____, *A Flock of Shepherds: The National Conference of Catholic Bishops* (Kansas City, MO: Sheed and Ward, 1992).

Regan, G., *New Trends in Moral Theology* (New York: Newman Press, 1971).

Reicke, B., *Epistles of James, Peter, and Jude*, Anchor Bible 37 (Garden City, NY: Doubleday, 1964).

Reid, David P., *What Are They Saying About the Prophets?* (New York: Paulist Press, 1986).

Reitz, Miriam, *Adoption and the Family System: Strategies for Treatment* (New York: Guilford Press, 1992).

Richard of St. Victor, *Benjamin Minor*, PL 196:1-64.

Ricoeur, Paul, *The Conflict of Interpretations: Essays in Hermeneutics* (Evanston, IL: Northwestern University Press, 1974).

Riesner, Rainer, "Jesus as Preacher and Teacher," in H. Wansbrough, ed., *Jesus and the Oral Gospel Tradition*, pp. 185-210.

Robert, A. and R. Tournay, in collaboration with A. Feuillet, *Le Cantique des Cantiques*, Études Bibliques (Paris: Gabalda, 1963).

Roberts, J.M., "The Old Testament Contribution to Messianic Expectations" in James H. Charlesworth, et al., *The Messiah Developments in Earliest Judaism and Christianity* (Minneapolis: Fortress Press, 1992), pp. 39-51.

Rockmore, Tom, William J. Gavin, James G. Colbert, Jr., and Thomas J. Blakeley, *Marxism and Alternatives: Towards the Conceptual Interaction Among Soviet Philosophy, Neo-Thomism, Pragmatism, and Phenomenology*, Sovietica series (Boston/Dordrecht: D. Reidel Publishing Co., 1981).

Rodinson, Maxime, "A Critical Survey of Modern Studies on Muhammad," in Merlin L. Schwartz, ed., *Studies on Islam* (New York: Oxford University Press, 1981).

Rogers, C. "Moses: Meek or Miserable," *Journal of Evangelical Theological Studies* (1986), 257-63.

Rommen, Heinrich A., *The Natural Law* (St. Louis: B. Herder, 1947).

Rondet, Henri, S.J., *The Grace of Christ: A Brief History of the Theology of Grace* (Westminster, MD: Newman Press, 1966).

_____, *Original Sin* (Staten Island, NY: Alba House, 1972).

Ross, W. David, *The Right and the Good* (Oxford: Clarendon, 1930).

Rossi, Philip J., S.J., *Together Toward Hope: A Journey to Moral Theology* (Notre Dame, IN: University of Notre Dame Press, 1983).

Rougemont, Denis de, *Love in the Western World*, trans. by Montgomery Belgion (New York: Pantheon, 1956).

Rousseau, Jacques, *Lettres Morale* in *Oeuvres complètes*, 4 vols., B. Gagnebin and Marcel Raymond, eds. (Paris: Gallimard, 1969) vol. I, pp. 1091-1118.

_____, *Emile, ibid.*, I, pp. 245-868.

Royo, Antonio, O.P. and Jordan Aumann, O.P., *The Theology of Christian Perfection* (Dubuque, IA: Priory Press, 1962).

Rubin, Julius H., *Religious Melancholy and Protestant Experience in America* (New York: Oxford University Press, 1994).

Ruether, Rosemary Radford, "Feminism the End of Christianity? A Critique of Daphne Hampson's Theology and Feminism," *Scottish Journal of Theology* 43 (1990), 390-400.

Russell, Letty M., ed., *Feminist Interpretations of the Bible* (Philadelphia: Westminster Press, 1985).

Sacks, Robert D., *A Commentary on the Book of Genesis,* Ancient Near Eastern Texts and Studies, vol. 6 (Lewiston/Queenston/Lampeter, 1990).

Sage, Athanase A.A., *The Religious Life According to St. Augustine*, edited by John E. Rotelle, O.S.A. (Brooklyn: New City Press, 1990).

Sahar, Shulamith, *Childhood in the Middle Ages*, trans. by Chaya Galai (London/New York: Routledge, 1992).

Salm, C. Luke, ed., *Readings in Biblical Morality* (Englewood Cliffs, NJ: Prentice-Hall, 1967).

Sampley, Paul, *Pauline Partnership in Christ: Christian Community and Commitment in the Light of Roman Law* (Philadelphia: Fortress Press, 1980).

Sanders, E.P., "On the Question of Fulfilling the Law in Paul and Rabbinic Judaism," in *Donum Gentilicum: New Testament Studies in Honour of David Daube*, ed. by E. Bammel, C.K. Barrett, and W.D. Davies (Oxford: Clarendon Press, 1978), pp. 103-126.

_____, *Jesus and Judaism* (Philadelphia: Fortress/London: SCM Press, 1985).

_____, *Jewish Law from Jesus to Mishnah* (Philadelphia: Trinity Press International/London: SCM Press, 1990).

Sanders, Jack, *Ethics in the New Testament* (Philadelphia: Fortress Press, 1975).

Sanders, James A., *Torah and Canon* (Philadelphia: Fortress Press, 1972).

————, *Criticism* (Philadelphia: Fortress Press, 1984).

————, *Canon and Community: A Guide to Canonical Criticism* (Philadelphia: Fortress Press, 1984).

Santmire, Paul, "Retranslating 'Our Father': The Urgency and the Possibility," *Dialog* 16 (1977), 102-104.

Santurri, Edmund N. and William Werpehowski, eds., *The Love Commandments: Essays in Christian Ethics and Moral Philosophy* (Washington, DC: Georgetown University Press, 1992).

Sattler, H. Vernon, "An Agenda to Reject Celibacy," *Homiletic and Pastoral Review*, 91 (June, 1991), 72-77.

Schama, Simon, *Citizens: A Chronicle of the French Revolution* (New York: Alfred A. Knopf, 1989).

Scheffler, Samuel, ed., *Consequentialism and Its Critics* (Oxford: Oxford University Press, 1988).

Scheler, Max, *Formalism in Ethics and Non-Formal Ethics of Value: A New Attempt Toward the Foundation of an Ethical Personalism*, trans. by M.S. Frings and R.L. Funk (Evanston, IL: Northwestern University Press, 1973).

Schelke, Karl, *Theology of the New Testament*, 4 vols., vol. 3: *Morality* (Collegeville, MN: Liturgical Press, 1973).

Schemes, B.L., *The Psychology of Emotions* (Cambridge, England: Keith Oakley, 1992).

Schillebeeckx, Edward, O.P., *Celibacy* (New York: Sheed and Ward, 1967).

————, *Revelation and Theology*, 2 vols. (New York: Sheed and Ward, 1967).

————, *Jesus: An Experiment in Christology* (New York: Crossroad/ Seabury, 1979) with clarifications in *Interim Report on the Books Jesus and Christ* (New York: Crossroad, 1981).

————, *Ministry: Leadership in the Community of Jesus Christ* (New York: Crossroad, 1981).

————, *The Church with a Human Face: A New and Expanded Theology of Ministry* (New York: Crossroad, 1985).

Schmitt, Emile, *Le Mariage Chrétien dans l'Oeuvre de Saint Augustin: In théologie baptismale de la vie conjugale* (Paris: Etudes Augustiniennes, 1983).

Schnackenburg, Rudolf, *Christian Existence in the New Testament*, 2 vols. (Notre Dame, IN: University of Notre Dame Press, 1968 and 1969).

————, *The Moral Teaching of the New Testament* (New York: Seabury Press, 1973).

Schockenhoff, Eberhard, *Bonum hominis: Die anthropologischen und theologischen Grundlagen der Tugendethik des Thomas von Aquin* (Mainz: Matthias-Grünewald-Verlag, 1987).

Scholem, Gershom, *The Messianic Idea in Judaism* (New York: Schocken Books, 1971).

Scholz, Franz, "Problems on Norms Raised by Ethical Borderline Situations," in Charles E. Curran and Richard A. McCormick, S.J., eds., *Readings in Moral Theology*, No. 1, *Moral Norms and Catholic Tradition* (New York: Paulist Press, 1979), pp. 164-165.

Schrage, Wolfgang, *The Ethics of the New Testament*, trans. by David E. Green (Philadelphia: Fortress Press, 1988).

Schüller, Bruno, S.J., "What Ethical Principles Are Universally Valid?" *Theology Digest* 19 (March, 1971), 24, trans. of "Zur Problematik allgemeinen ethischer Grundsatze," *Theologie und Philosophie* 45 (1970).

_____, "The Double Effect in Catholic Thought," in Richard A. McCormick and Paul Ramsey, *Doing Evil to Achieve Good* (Chicago: University of Chicago Press, 1978), p. 191.

_____, "The Moral Dimension — Specificity of Christian Ethics," in William J. Kelly, ed., *Theology and Discovery: Essays in Honor of Karl Rahner, S.J.* (Milwaukee: Marquette University Press, 1980), pp. 307-327.

_____, *Wholly Human: Essays on the Theory and Language of Morality* (Washington, DC: Georgetown University Press, 1986).

Schultz, Siegfried, *Neutestamentliche Ethik* (Zurich: Theologischer Verlag, 1987).

Scroggs, Robin, *The New Testament and Homosexuality* (Philadelphia: Fortress Press, 1983); criticized by Peter von der Osten-Saken, "Paulininisches Evangelium und Homosexualität," *Berliner Theologisches Zeitschrift* 3:1 (1986), 28-49.

Sebeok, Thomas A. and Jean Umiker-Sebeok, eds., *Speaking Apes: A Critical Anthology of Two-Way Communication with Man* (New York: Plenum Press, 1980).

Selling, Joseph A., and Jans, eds., *The Splendor of Accuracy: An Examination of the Assertions Made by "Veritatis Splendor"* (Grand Rapids: Eerdmans, 1994).

Selwyn, E.G., *The First Epistle of St.Peter*, Greek Text with Intro. and Notes. 2nd ed. (London: Macmillan, 1947) Essay I, 313-362.

Senft, Christophe, *La première épître de Saint Paul aux Corinthiens* (Geneva: Labor et Fides, 1990).

Settles, Barbara H. "A Perspective on Tomorrow's Families," *Handbook of Marriage and the Family*, edited by Marvin B. Sussman and Suzanne K. Steinmetz (New York: Plenum Press, 1987), pp. 3-36.

Sex and Gender: A Theological and Scientific Inquiry, ed. by Mark M. Schwartz, A.S. Moracewski, O.P., and James A. Monteleone, M.D. (St. Louis: Pope John Center, 1983).

Sherman, Nancy, *The Fabric of Character: Aristotle's Theory of Virtue* (New York: Oxford University Press, 1989).

Shivanandan, *Natural Sex* (New York: Rawson Wade, 1979).

Sidgwick, Henry, *The Methods of Ethics* (1886, rev. ed. of 1931, reprint, Boston: Beacon Press, 1964).

Simon, Yves R., *A General Theory of Authority* (Notre Dame, IN: University of Notre Dame Press, 1962).

_____, *The Tradition of Natural Law* (New York: Fordham University Press, 1965).

Singer, Peter, *Animal Liberation: A New Ethics for our Treatment of Animals* (New York: Avon, 1977).

Sipe, A.W. Richard, *A Secret World: Sexuality and the Search for Celibacy*, with a Foreword by Robert Coles, M.D. (New York: Brunner/Mazel, 1990); reviewed by James J. Gill, S.J., 40 *Commonweal* 118 (Feb. 8, 1991), 108-110.

Sittler, Joseph, *The Structure of Christian Ethics* (Baton Rouge, LA: Louisiana State University Press, 1958).

Ska, Jean Louis, S.J., *"Our Fathers Have Told Us": Introduction to the Analysis of Hebrew Narrative* (Rome: Editrice Pontificio Instituto Biblico, 1990).

Skehan, Patrick W. and Alexander A. Di Lella, *The Wisdom of Ben Sira*, Anchor Bible 39, translation and notes by Skehan, introduction and commentary by Di Lella (New York: Doubleday, 1987).

Slomowski, Antoine, *L'état primitive de l"homme dans la tradition de l'église avant saint Augustin* (Paris: Gabalda, 1928).

Smart, James D., *The Past, Present, and Future of Biblical Theology* (Louisville, KY: Westminster/John Knox, 1979).

Smith, Ervine, *The Ethics of Martin Luther King, Jr.* with bibliographical essay by Janine Anderson Sawada, *Studies in American Religion*, vol. 2 (New York/Toronto: Edwin Mellen Press, 1981).

Smith, Janet E., *Humanae Vitae: A Generation Later* (Washington, DC: Catholic University of America Press, 1991).

Smith, Morton, *Palestinian Parties and Politics that Shaped the Old Testament* (London: SCM Press, 1987).

Söding, Thomas, *Das Trias Glaube, Hoffnung, Liebe bei Paulus: Exegetische Studie*, Stuttgarten Biblelstudien, n. 150 (Stuttgart: Verlag Katholisches Bibelwerk GmbH, 1992).

Soggin, J. Alberto, *Introduction to the Old Testament*, The Old Testament Library (Louisville, KY: Westminster/John Knox, 1989).

Sokolowski, Robert, *The God of Faith and Reason: Foundations of a Christian Theology* (Notre Dame, IN: University of Notre Dame Press, 1982).

Spanneut, Michel, *Le Stoicisme des pères de l'église de Clement de Rome a Clement d'Alexandrie* (Paris: Editions du Seuil, 1957).

_____, *Tertullien et les premiers moralists africains* (Gembloux/Paris: Éditions J. Duculot/Lethielleux, 1969).

_____, *Permanence du Stoïcisme de Zenon à Malraux* (Gembloux: J. Duculot, 1973).

Spero, Shubert, *Morality, Halakha, and the Jewish Tradition* (New York: KTAV, 1983).

Spicq, Ceslas, O.P., *The Mystery of Godliness*, trans. by J. Martin (Chicago: Fides, 1954).

_____, *The Trinity and Our Moral Life According to St. Paul*, trans. by Sister Marie Aquinas (Westminster, MD: Newman Press, 1963).

_____, *Théologie Morale du Nouveau Testament*, 2 vols. (Paris: Lecoffre, 1965).

_____, *Agape in the New Testament*, 3 vols. (St. Louis: Herder, 1963).

Spohn, William H., S.J., *What Are They Saying about Scripture and Ethics?* (New York: Paulist Press, 1985).

_____, "The Use of Scripture in Moral Theology," TS 47 (1986), 88-102.

Stack, H.L. and G. Stemberger, *Introduction to the Talmud and Midrash*, trans. by Markus Bockmuehl (Edinburgh: T & T Clark, 1991).

Stadlemann, Luis, S.J., *Love and Politics: A New Commentary on The Song of Songs* (New York/Mahwah, NJ: Paulist Press, 1990).

Stamm, Johann J. and Maurice E. Andrew, *The Ten Commandments in Recent Research*, Studies in Biblical Theology, second series (Naperville, IL: Allenson, 1962).

Steinbock, Richard A., ed., *The Psychology of Pain* (New York: Rosen Press, 1980).

Stendahl, Krister, "Biblical Theology: Contemporary." *Interpreter's Dictionary of the Bible* (Nashville: Abingdon, 1962), vol. 1, pp. 418-32.

Stephens, William N., *The Family in Cross-Cultural Perspective* (New York: Holt, Rinehart and Winston, 1963).

Stevens, Edward, *Making Moral Decisions* (New York: Paulist Press, rev. ed., 1981).

Stock, Michael, O.P., "Conscience and Super-Ego," TH, 1961, p. 544 ff.

Stoeckle, Bernard, "Flucht in das Humanum? Erwagungen zur Diskussion uber die Frage nach dem Proprium christlicher Ethik." *Internationale katholische Zeitschrift (Communio)* 6 (1977), 312-324.

Stott, J.R.W., *Christian Counter-Culture. The Message of the Sermon on the Mount* (Leicester, UK: Inter-Varsity, 1978).

Strecker, Georg, "Strukturen einer neutestamentliche Ethik," in *Zeitschrift für Theologie und Kirche* 75 (1978), 117-146.

Stuhlmacher, Peter, *Historical Criticism and Theological Interpretation of Scripture: Toward a Hermeneutic of Consent* (Philadelphia: Fortress Press, 1977).

Suggs, M.Jack, "The Christian Two Ways Tradition: Its Antiquity, Form, and

Function," in David Edward Aune, ed., *Studies in New Testament and Early Christian Literature: Essays in Honor of Allen P. Wikgren*, Supplement to New Testament Studies, vol. 33 (Leiden: E.J. Brill, 1972), pp. 60-74.

Sullivan, Francis, S.J., *Magisterium: Teaching Authority in the Catholic Church* (Ramsey, NJ: Paulist Press, 1984).

Sunday, Peggy Reeves, *Female Power and Male Dominance: On the Origins of Sexual Inequality* (Cambridge: Cambridge University Press, 1981).

Suso, Henry, O.P., *The Life of the Servant*, trans. by James M. Clark (London: James Clarke, 1952).

Sussman, Marvin B. and Suzanne K. Steinmetz, eds., *Handbook of Marriage and the Family* (New York: Plenum Press, 1987).

Swartly, William M., *Slavery, Sabbath, War and Women: Case Issues in Biblical Interpretation* (Scottdale, PA: Herald Press, 1983).

Swift, Louis J., *The Early Fathers on War and Military Service*, Message of the Fathers of the Church (Collegeville, MN: Liturgical Press, 1983).

Szasz, Thomas A., *Pain and Pleasure: A Study of Bodily Feelings* (London: Tavistock Publishing, 1957).

Tambasco, Anthony, *The Bible for Ethics* (Washington, DC: University Press of America, 1981).

Teale, A.E., *Kantian Ethics* (Westport, CT: Greenwood Press, 1975).

Tedeschi, John, *The Prosecution of Heresy: Collected Studies on the Inquisition in Early Modern Italy* (Binghamton, NY: Medieval and Renaissance Texts and Studies, 1991).

Tertullian, *De jejuniis*, PL 2:953-978.

————, *De spectaculis*, PL 1:627-662.

————, *De Oratione Liber: Tract on Prayer*. Latin text with critical notes, English trans. and notes by Ernest Evans (London: S.P.C.K, 1953); PL 1:1149-1196.

Theissen, Gerd, *The First Followers of Jesus: A Sociological Analysis of the Earliest Christianity* (London: SCM Press Ltd., 1978).

————, *The Gospels in Context: Social and Political History in the Synoptic Tradition*, trans. by Linda M. Maloney (Minneapolis: Fortress Press, 1991).

Thérèse of Lisieux, St., *Autobiography of a Saint*, trans. by Ronald Knox (London: William Collins, Son & Co., 1958).

————, (Manuscripts autobiographique, Lisieux, 170-172) from *The Liturgy of the Hours According to the Roman Rite* (New York: Catholic Book Publishing Co., 1975), IV, p. 1451.

Thielicke, Helmut, *Theological Ethics*, 3 vols., ed. William H. Lazareth (Philadelphia: Fortress Press, 1966).

Thiering, Barbara, "The Biblical Source of Qumran Asceticism," *Journal of Biblical Literature* 93 (3 Sept. 1974), 429-444.

Thils, Gustave, *Tendences actuelles en théologie moral* (Gembloux: Duculot, 1940).

Thiselton, Anthony C., *The Two Horizons: New Testament Hermeneutics with Special Reference to Heidegger, Bultmann, Gadamer, and Wittgenstein* (Grand Rapids: Eerdmans, 1980).

Thomas Aquinas, St., *Expositio et lectura super Epistolas Pauli Apostoli* (Turin/Rome: Marietti, 1953), commentaries on *Galatians, Ephesians, 1 Thessalonians* (Albany, NY: Magi Books 1966). Selections from Aquinas' commentary on 1 Corinthians trans. by M. Rzeczkowski in B.M. Ashley, *St. Thomas Aquinas: The Gifts of the Spirit* (Hyde Park, NY: New City Press, 1995).

_____, *De caritate, Quaestiones disputatae*, vol. 2 (Turin/ Rome: Marietti, 1954); *On Charity*, trans. by Lottie H. Kendzierski (Milwaukee: Marquette University Press, 1960).

_____, *De perfectione spiritualis vitae, Opuscula theologica*, vol. 2 (Turin/ Rome: Marietti, 1954).

_____, *De veritate, Quaestiones Disputatae*, vol. 1 (Turin/Rome: Marietti, 1953); trans. as *On Truth*, 3 vols. by Mulligan-McGlynn-Schmidt (Chicago: Regnery, 1952-1954).

_____, *Expositio super X libros Ethicorum Aristotelis ad Nicomachum* (Turin/Rome: Marietti, 1949).

_____, *Expositio super librum Beati Dionysii De divinis nominibus Expositio* (Turin/Rome: Marietti, 1950).

_____, *Scriptum super sententiis Magistri Petri Lombardi*, ed. M. F. Moos, 4 vols. (Paris: Lethielleux, 1947-1956).

_____, *Summa Theologiae*, bilingual ed., 60 vols. (New York: McGraw-Hill, 1964-1980).

Thompson, J.A., *The Book of Jeremiah*, New International Commentary on the Old Testament (Grand Rapids: Eerdmans, 1980).

Thomson, Judith Jarvis, "A Defense of Abortion," *Philosophy and Public Affairs*, Fall 1971, pp. 47-66.

Thurian, Max, *Marriage and Celibacy* (London: SCM Press, 1959).

Tinder, Glenn, "Can We Be Good Without God?" *The Atlantic Monthly*, Dec. 1989, pp. 69-85.

Toner, Jules, *The Experience of Love* (Washington/Cleveland: Corpus Books, 1968).

Torrance, Thomas F., *The Doctrine of Grace in the Apostolic Fathers* (Grand Rapids: Eerdmans, 1948).

Tournay, R.J., O.P., *Quand Dieu parle aux hommes le langage de l'amour*, Cahiers de la *Révue Biblique* 21 (Paris: Gabalda, 1982).

Tov, E., *The Book of Baruch*, Society of Biblical Literature Texts and Translations (Missoula, MT: 1975).

Towner, Philip H., *The Goal of Our Instruction: The Structure of Theology and Ethics in the Pastoral Epistles* (Sheffield: ISOT Press, 1989).

Towner, W. Sibley, *Daniel*, International Biblical Commentary (Atlanta: John Knox, 1985).

Tracy, David, *Blessed Rage for Order: The New Pluralism in Theology* (New York: Seabury Press, 1975).

_____, *The Analogical Imagination: Christian Theology and the Culture of Pluralism* (New York: Crossroad, 1981).

_____, *Plurality and Ambiguity: Hermeneutics, Religion, Hope* (San Francisco: Harper and Row, 1987).

Tribble, Phyllis, *God and the Rhetoric of Sexuality* (Philadelphia: Fortress Press, 1978).

Troeltsch, Ernst, *The Social Teaching of the Christian Churches*, 2 vols. (New York: Harper, 1960).

Tromp, Nicholas J., *Primitive Conceptions of Death and the Nether World in the Old Testament* (Rome: Pontifical Biblical Institute, 1969).

Tugwell, Simon, O.P., *Ways of Imperfection: An Exploration of Christian Spirituality* (Springfield, IL: Templegate, 1985).

_____, *The Beatitudes: Soundings in Christian Traditions* (London: Darton, Longman, and Todd, 1980).

Turner, Victor, *The Ritual Process: Structure and Anti-Structure*, reprint (Ithaca: Cornell University Press, 1979).

Ulpian, *Digesta* (*Corpus Juris Civilis*), I, tit. 1, leg. 1, quoted in S.T., I-II, q. 94, a. 2 c.

United States National Conference of Catholic Bishops, "To Live in Christ Jesus: A Pastoral Letter of the American Bishops on the Moral Life" (Washington, DC: United States Catholic Conference, 1976).

_____, "Renewing the Earth," Dec. 12, 1991, *Origins*, vol. 21, n. 27, p. 432.

United Nations Universal Declaration of Human Rights (New York: United Nations Publications, 1948).

Van Eijk, T.H.C., "Marriage and Virginity, Death and Immortality," in Jacques Fontaine and Charles Kannengiesser, eds., *Epektasis: Mélanges patristiques offerts au Cardinal Jean Daniélou* (Paris: Beauchesne, 1972), pp. 209-235.

Van Ort, Johannes, *Jerusalem and Babylon: A Study into Augustine's City of God and the Sources of His Doctrine of the Two Cities* (New York: E.J. Brill, 1991).

Van Riet, Georges, *Thomistic Epistemology*, 2 vols. (St. Louis/London: B. Herder Book Co., 1963).

Vanhoye, Albert, S.J., *L'Apôtre Paul: Personnalité, Style et Conception du Ministère* (Leuven: Leuven University Press, 1986).

Vanhoye, Albert, S.J. and Henri Crouzel, S.J., "The Ministry in the Church: Reflections on a Recent Publication," *The Clergy Review*, 5, 68 (May, 1983), 156-174.

Vann, Gerald, O.P., *Morals Maketh Man* (New York: Sheed and Ward, 1960).

Vaught, Carl G., *The Sermon on the Mount: A Theological Interpretation* (Albany, NY: State University of New York, 1986).

Vaux, Roland de, O.P., *Ancient Israel*, trans. by J. McHugh, (New York: McGraw-Hill, 1961).

Vecchio, Georgio del, *Philosophy of Law* (Washington, DC: Catholic University of America Press, 1953).

Vereecke, Louis, C.SS.R., "Preface à l'Histoire de la Theologie Morale Moderne," *Studia Moralia*, I, Academia Alfonsiana Institutum Theologiae Moralis (Rome: Editrice Ancora, 1963), 87-120.

_____, "Moral Theology, History of (700 to Vatican Council I)," NCE 9:1120-22.

Verhey, Allen, *The Great Reversal: Ethics and the New Testament* (Grand Rapids: Eerdmans, 1984).

Verkamp, Bernard, "Cultic Purity and the Law of Celibacy," *Review for Religious*, 30 (1971), 199-217.

Veyne, Paul, ed., *A History of Private Life*, Phillipe Ariès and Georges Duby, general eds., Vol. 1, *From Pagan Rome to Byzantium*, trans. by Arthur Goldhammer (Cambridge, MA: Belknap Press of Harvard University Press, 1987).

Virtue, William D., *Absence and Desire in Christian Married Love*, unpublished S.T.L. dissertation (Washington, DC: The Pontifical John Paul II Institute for Studies in Marriage and Family, 1990).

Viviano, Benedict T., O.P., *Study as Worship*, Studies in Judaism in Late Antiquity 26 (Leiden, 1978).

_____, *The Kingdom of God in History* (Wilmington, DE: Michael Glazier, 1988).

_____, "The Gospel According to St. Matthew," NJBC, pp. 630-674.

Vries, Piet Penning de, S.J., *Discernment of Spirits According to the Life and Teachings of St. Ignatius Loyola* (New York: Exposition Press, 1973).

Waddell, Helen, trans. and ed., *The Desert Fathers* (New York: Sheed and Ward, 1942).

Wadell, Paul J., C.P., *The Primacy of Love: An Introduction to the Ethics of St.Thomas Aquinas* (New York: Paulist Press, 1992).

Wainwright, Geoffrey, "Types of Spirituality" in Cheslyn Jones, Geoffrey Wainwright, Edward Yarnold, S.J., eds. *The Study of Spirituality* (New York: Oxford University Press, 1986), pp. 592-605.

Walgrave, Jan Hendrik, *Unfolding Revelation: The Nature of Doctrinal Development,* Theological Resources (Philadelphia: Westminster/London: Hutchinson, 1972).

Walker, Leonora E., *The Battered Woman* (New York: Harper and Row, 1980).

Wallace, James D., *Virtues and Vices* (Ithaca, NY: Cornell University Press, 1978).

Walsh, Mary Roth, ed. *The Psychology of Women: Ongoing Debates* (New Haven, CT: Yale University Press, 1987).

Walsh, Michael J., ed., *Commentary on the Catechism of the Catholic Church* (Collegeville, MN: Liturgical Press, 1994).

Wansborough, H., ed., *Jesus and the Oral Gospel Tradition,* JSNT, Supplement Series 64 (Sheffield: Sheffield Academic Press, 1991).

Ward, K., *Ethics and Christianity* (London: Allen and Unwin, 1970).

Ware, Kallistos, *The Orthodox Way* (Crestwood, NY: St. Vladimir's Seminary Press, 1979).

Watkin, Dom Aelred, *The Enemies of Love* (New York: Paulist Press, 1965).

Watts, J., *Isaiah 1-33, 34-66,* Word Biblical Commentary 24, 25 (Waco, TX: Word, 1985-1987).

Weinfeld, Moshe, *Deuteronomy 1-11,* The Anchor Bible, 5 (Garden City, NY: Doubleday, 1991).

_____, "The Decalogue: Its Significance, Uniqueness, and Place in Israel's Tradition," *Religion and Law: Biblical-Judaic and Islamic Perspectives,* ed. by Edwin B. Formage, et al. (Winona Lake, IL: Eisenbrauns, 1990), pp. 10ff.

Weiser, A., *The Psalms,* Old Testament Library (Philadelphia: Fortress Press, 1962).

Weiss, Raymond L., *Maimonides' Ethics: The Encounter of Philosophic and Religious Morality* (Chicago: University of Chicago Press, 1991).

Weissleder, Wolfgang, "Aristotle's Concept of Political Structure and the State," in Ronald Cohen and Elman R. Service, eds., *Origins of the State: The Anthropology of Political Evolution* (Philadelphia: Institute for the Study of Human Issues, 1978), pp. 187-203.

Weithman, Paul. J., *Justice, Charity and Property: The Centrality of Sin to the Political Thought of Thomas Aquinas,* Harvard University dissertation, 1988 (Ann Arbor, MI: University Microfilms International, 1988).

Wendland, Heinz-Dieter, *Ethik des Neues Testament* (Göttingen: Vandenhoeck and Ruprecht, 1978).

Wenham, C., *The Book of Leviticus,* New International Commentary on the Old Testament (Grand Rapids: Eerdmans, 1979).

Wenham, Gordan J., *Numbers: Introduction and Commentary* (Leicester, England/Downers Grove, IL: Inter-Varsity Press, 1981).

Westermann, Claus, *Isaiah 40-66*, Old Testament Library (Philadelphia: Fortress Press, 1969).

_____, *Elements of Old Testament Theology*, trans. by Donald W. Stott (Atlanta: John Knox, 1982).

_____, *Genesis 1-11*; *Genesis 12-36* and *Genesis 37-50* (Minneapolis: Augsburg Fortress, 1984-86).

_____, *The Parables of Jesus In the Light of the Old Testament* (Edinburgh: T & T Clark, 1990).

White, R.E., *Biblical Ethics: The Changing Continuity of Christian Ethics* (Atlanta: John Knox, 1979).

_____, *Christian Ethics: The Historical Development* (Atlanta: John Knox, 1981).

Whybray, R. H., *Isaiah 40-66*, New Century Bible (Grand Rapids: Eerdmans, 1981).

_____, *The Making of the Pentateuch: A Methodological Study*, JSOT, Supplement Series # 53. (University of Sheffield, England, 1987).

_____, *Wealth and Poverty in the Book of Proverbs* (Sheffield: JSOT Press, 1990).

Wiebe, Ben, *Messianic Ethics: Jesus' Proclamation of the Kingdom of God and the Church in Response* (Waterloo, Ont.: Herald Press, 1992).

Wiel, Constant Van De, *History of Canon Law*, Louvain Theological and Pastoral Monographs, n. 5 (Louvain: Peeters Press, 1991).

Wildberger, Hans, *Isaiah 1-12: A Commentary*, trans by T.H. Trapp (Minneapolis: Fortress Press, 1990).

Wilder, Amos N., *Kerygma, Eschatology, and Social Ethics* (Philadelphia: Fortress Press, 1966).

Wilkens, Michael J., *The Concept of Disciple in Matthew's Gospel* (Leiden: E.J. Brill, 1988).

Williams, Bruce, O.P., "Homosexuality: The New Vatican Statement," TS 48 (1987), 259-277.

Willis, John R., S.J., *The Teachings of the Church Fathers* (New York: Herder and Herder, 1966).

Wills, Gary, *Inventing America: Jefferson's Declaration of Independence* (Garden City, NY: Doubleday, 1981).

Wilson, R.R., *Genealogy and History in the Biblical World*, Near Eastern Researches 7 (New Haven, CT: Yale University Press, 1977).

Wilson, William Julius, *The Truly Disadvantaged: The Inner City, the Underclass, and Public Policy* (Chicago: University of Chicago Press, 1987).

Winandy, J., O.S.B., "Une curieux casus pendens: 1 Corinthians 11:10 et son interpration," NTS 38 (Oct. 1992), 621-629.

Winston, D., ed., *The Wisdom of Solomon*, Anchor Bible 43 (Garden City, NY: Doubleday, 1979).

Wire, Antoinette Clark, *The Corinthian Women Prophets: A Reconstruction Through Paul's Rhetoric* (Philadelphia: Fortress Press, 1990).

Wiseman, Donald J., *1 and 2 Kings*, Tyndale Old Testament Commentaries (Downers Grove, IL: Inter-Varsity Press, 1993).

Witham, Larry, *Curran vs. Catholic University: A Study of Authority and Freedom in Conflict* (Riverdale, MD: Eddington-Rand, 1991).

Witherington, Ben, III, "Rite and Rights for Women — Galatians 3.28," NTS 27 (1980-81), 593-604.

_____, *Women in the Ministry of Jesus: A Study of Jesus' Attitudes to Women and their Roles as Reflected in his Earthly Life* and *Women in the Earliest Churches*, Society for New Testament Studies Monograph Series, Nos. 51 and 59 (Cambridge: Cambridge University Press, 1984 and 1988).

_____, *Women and the Genesis of Christianity*, ed. Ann Witherington (Cambridge: Cambridge University Press, 1990).

Wogaman, J. Philip, *Christian Ethics: An Historical Introduction* (Louisville, KY: Westminster/John Knox, 1993).

Wojcicki, Edward, *A Crisis of Hope in the Modern World*, foreword by Henri J. Nouwen (Chicago: Thomas More Press, 1991).

Wolff, Hans Walter, *Anthropology of the Old Testament* (Philadelphia: Fortress Press, 1974).

_____, *Joel and Amos*, Hermeneia Commentaries (Philadelphia: Fortress Press, 1977).

_____, *Micah the Prophet* (Philadelphia: Fortress Press, 1981).

Womer, Jan L., trans. and ed., *Morality and Ethics in Early Christianity*, Sources of Early Christian Thought (Philadelphia: Fortress Press, 1987).

Woodcock, George, *Anarchism: A History of Libertarian Ideas and Movements* (Cleveland: Meridian Books, 1962).

Wright, Christopher J.H., *Living As the People of God: The Relevance of Old Testament Ethics* (Leicester, England: Inter-Varsity Press, 1983).

Wright, David P., "Unclean and Clean" (OT) ABD 6:729-741.

_____, "Holiness (OT)," ABD 3:237-249.

Yarbrough, O. Larry, *Not Like the Gentiles: Marriage Rules in the Letters of Paul* (Atlanta: Scholars Press, 1984).

Yoder, John Howard, *The Politics of Jesus* (Grand Rapids: Eerdmans, 1972).

Zedda, Silverio, S.J., *Relativo e Assoluto nella moral di San Paolo* (Brescia: Paideia Editrice, 1984).

Zimmerli, W., *Old Testament Theology in Outline* (Atlanta: John Knox, 1979).

_____, *Ezekiel 1 and 2*, Hermeneia Commentaries (Philadelphia: Fortress Press, 1979, 1993)

BIBLICAL INDEX

ECCLESIASTES (QOHELETH)

SONG OF SONGS

LUKE

1 CORINTHIANS

2 CORINTHIANS

GALATIANS

1 PETER

2 PETER

1 JOHN

SUBJECT INDEX